Featuring never-before-seen photos and artifacts from Dolly Parton's personal archive,

as well as an exclusive foldout listing of her sixty-plus years of performances, this beautifully photographed book shares the remarkable story—in Dolly's own words—of how she became one of the world's most dazzling and beloved performers. From a front porch in rural Tennessee to the world's largest stages, with stops in Nashville, Hollywood, Dollywood, and more along the way, *Star of the Show* reveals how Dolly turned a dream, a God-given talent, and a whole lot of grit and hard work into the unforgettable stage presence and undeniable star power that continues to endear her to fans around the world today.

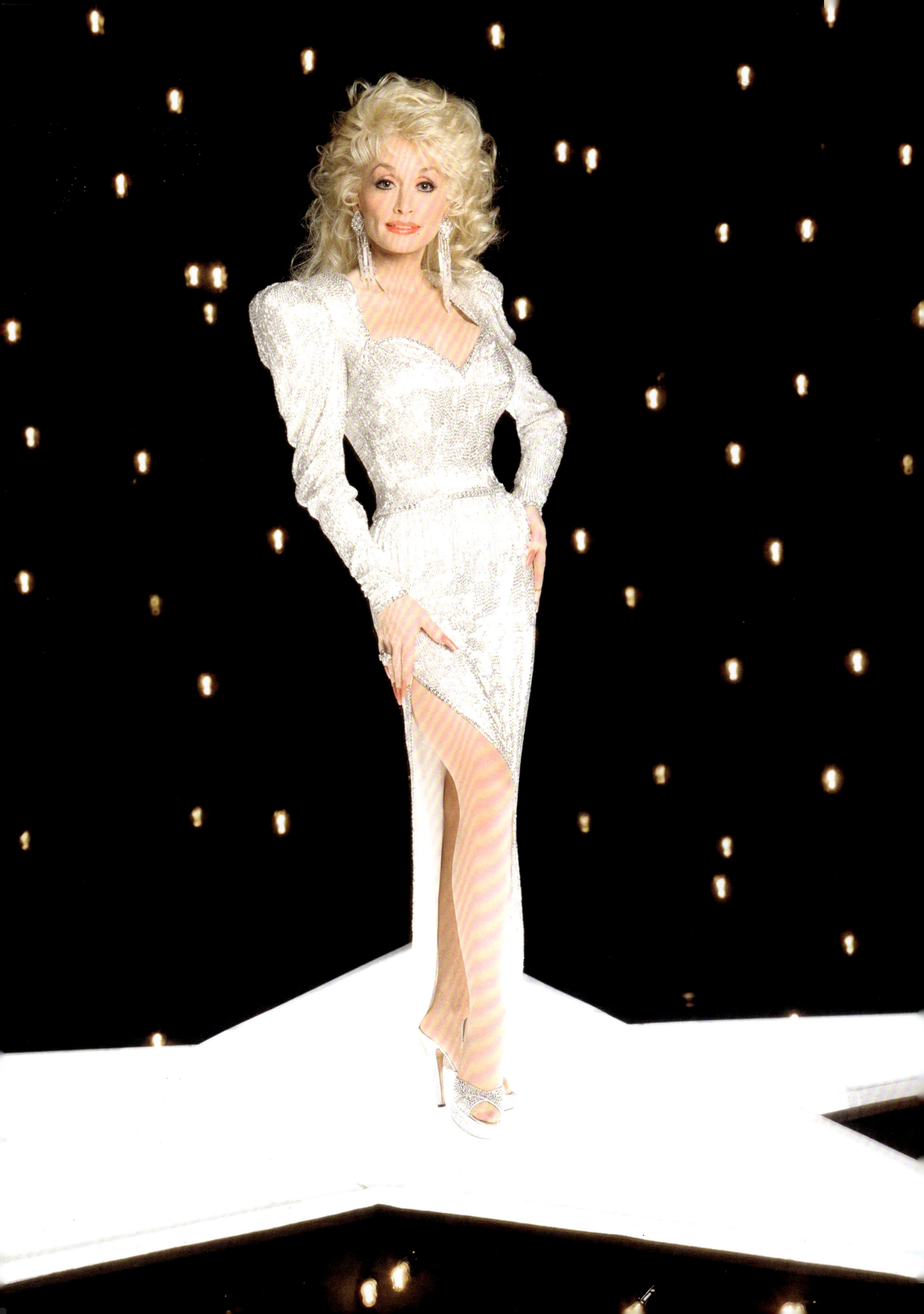

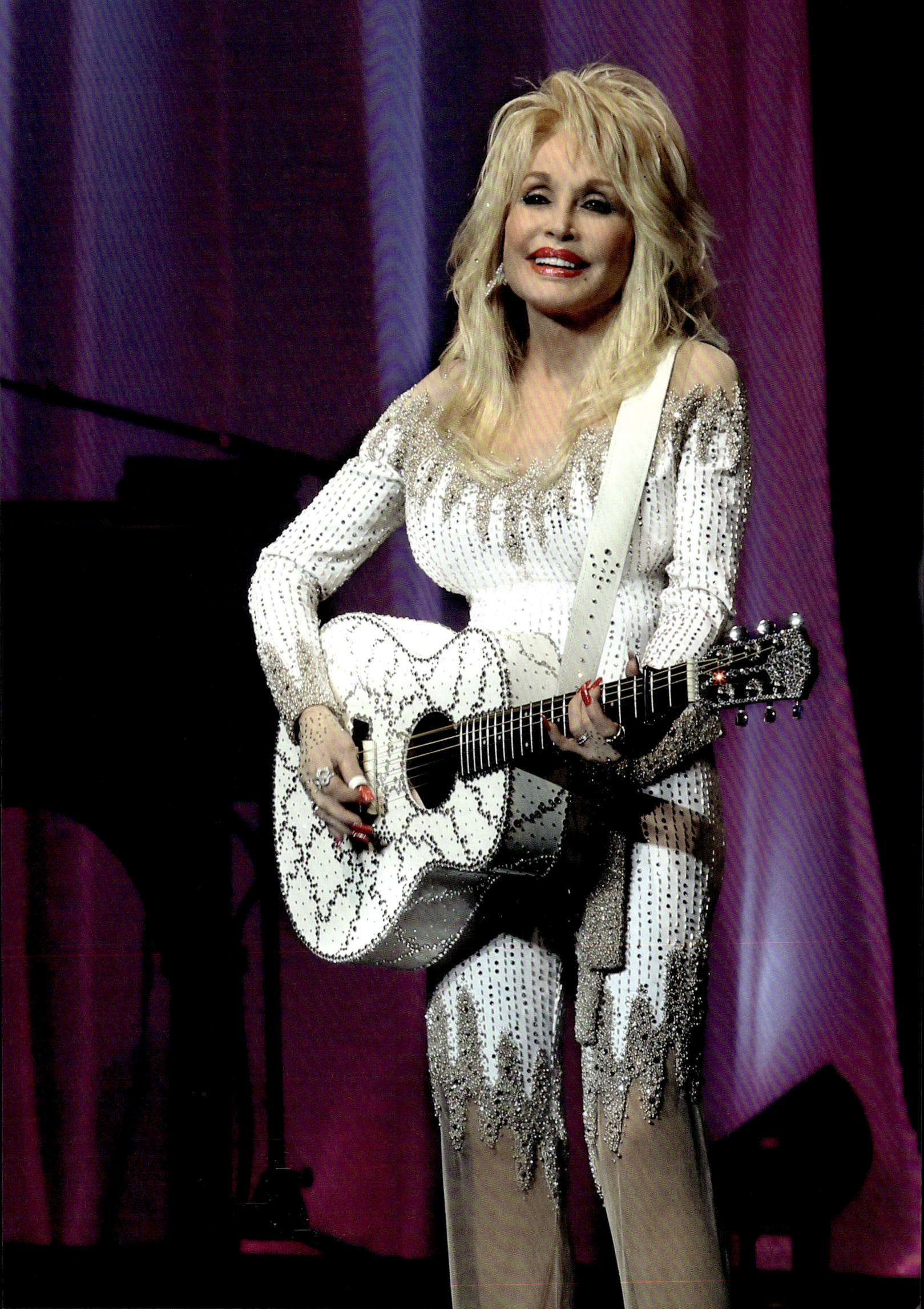

DOLLY PARTON
STAR OF THE SHOW

MY LIFE ON STAGE

By

DOLLY PARTON

with Tom Roland

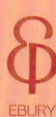

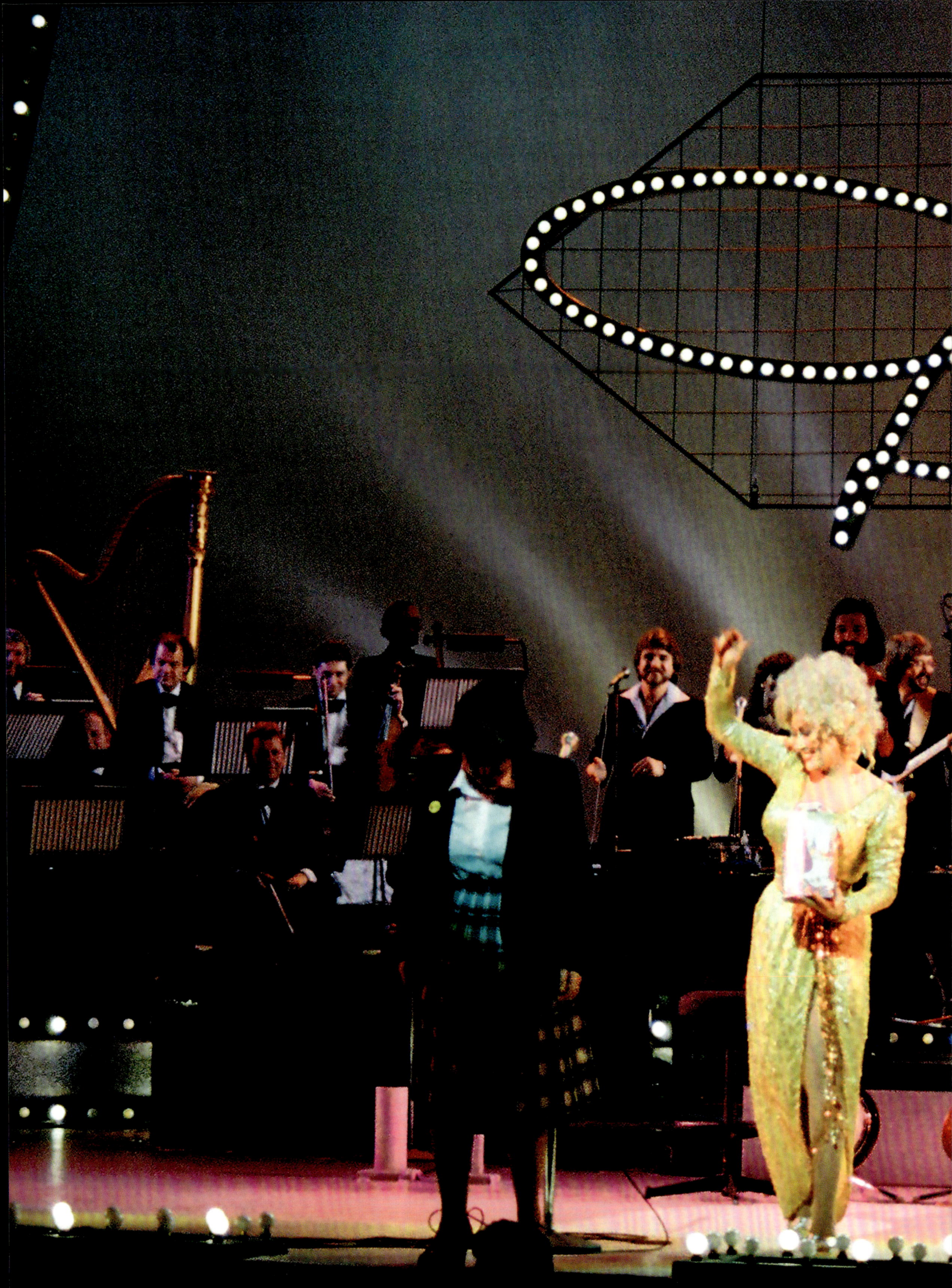

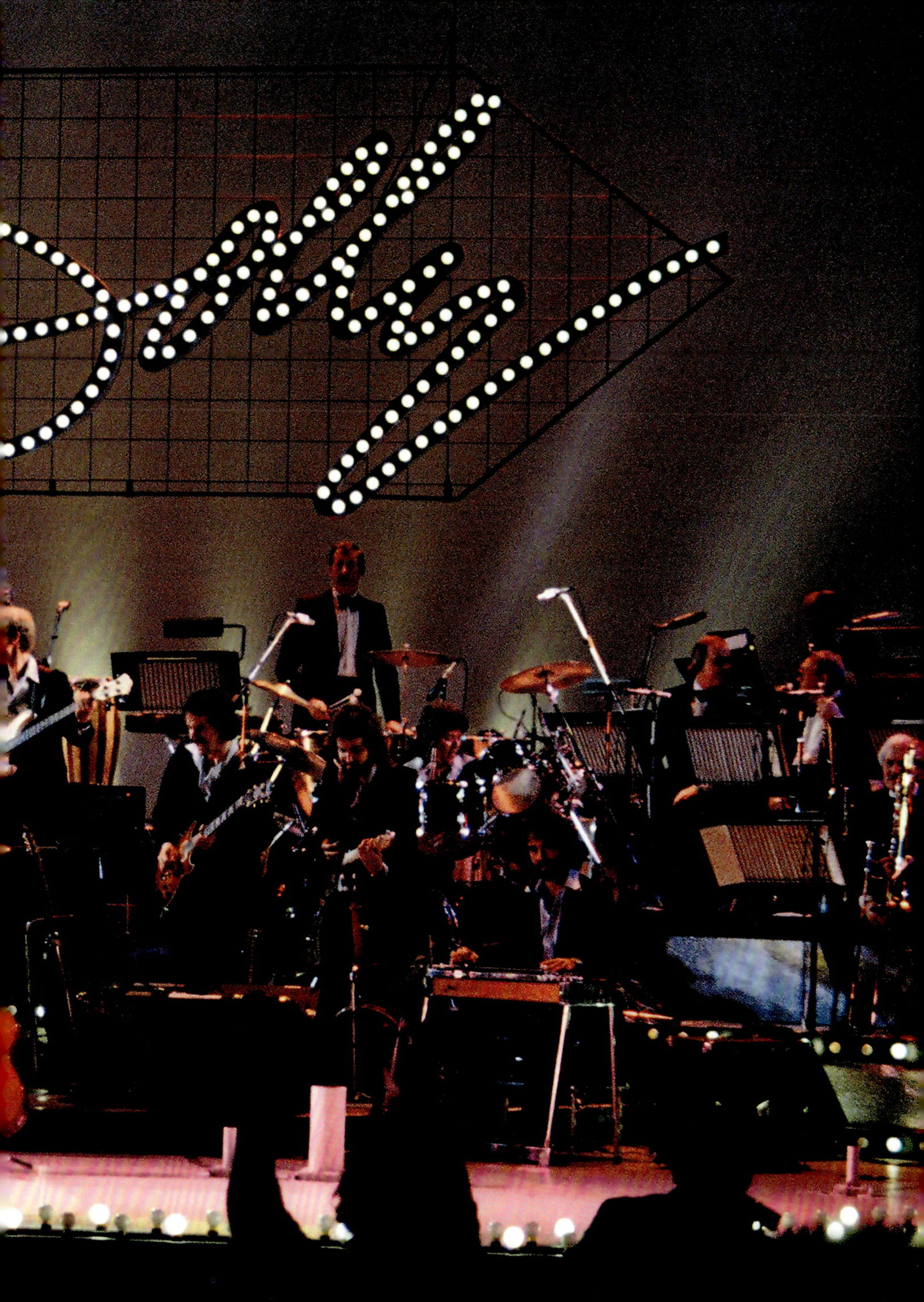

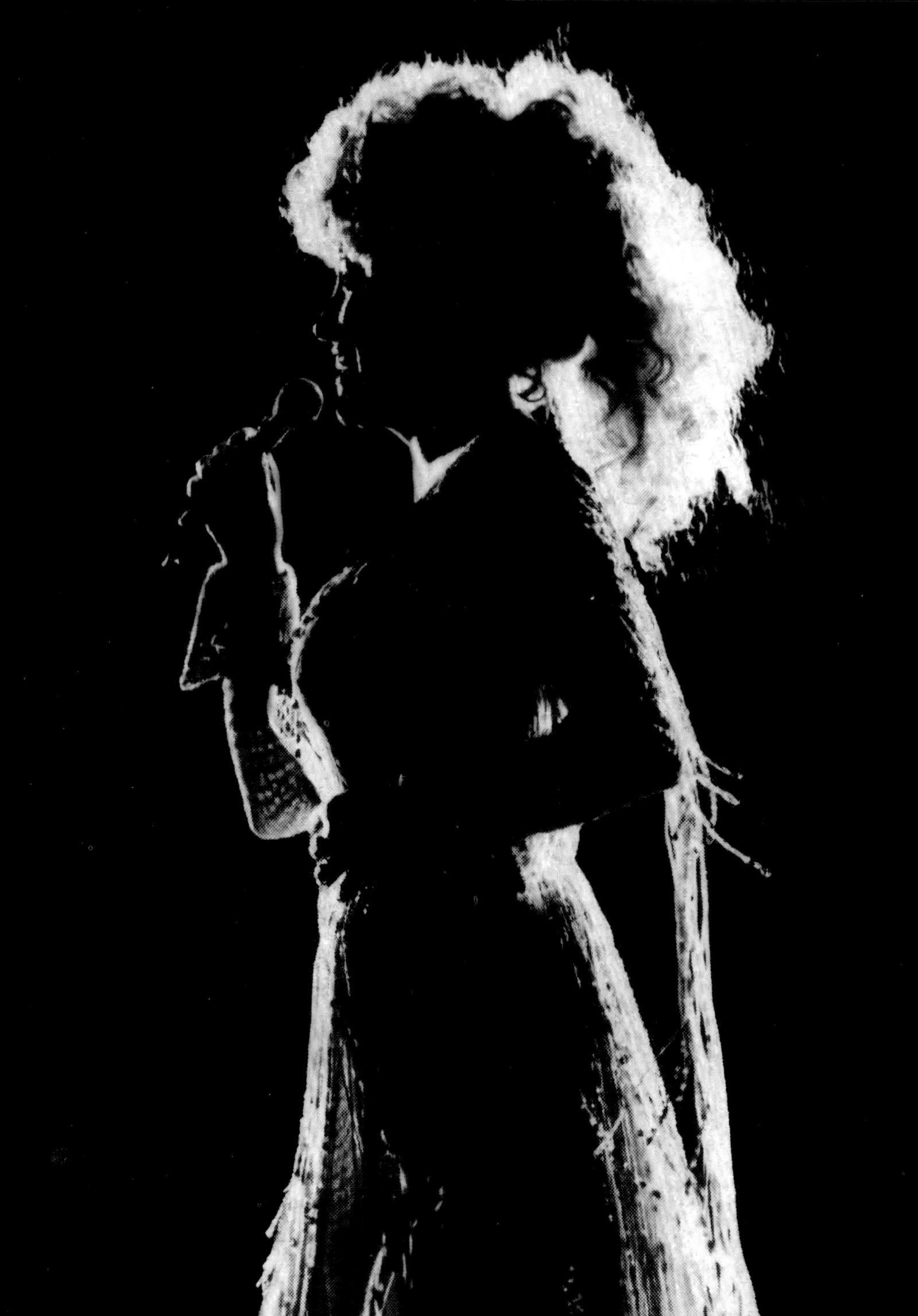

Contents

INTRODUCTION
13

"Start" of the Show
1946–1967
17

The Porter Years
1967–1974
41

Light of a Brand-New Day
1974–1980
81

Superstar of the Show
1980–1986
143

From Hollywood to Dollywood
1986–1998
177

Returning to My Roots
1998–2005
223

Better Days, Pure & Simple
2005–2016
253

New Stages
2016 & Beyond
299

STARRING DOLLY PARTON:
CONCERTS, APPEARANCES, AND PERFORMANCES, 1957–2025
296

DOLLY'S ALBUMS
326

ACKNOWLEDGMENTS
332

DOLLY'S VIDEOS
330

PHOTOGRAPHY CREDITS
333

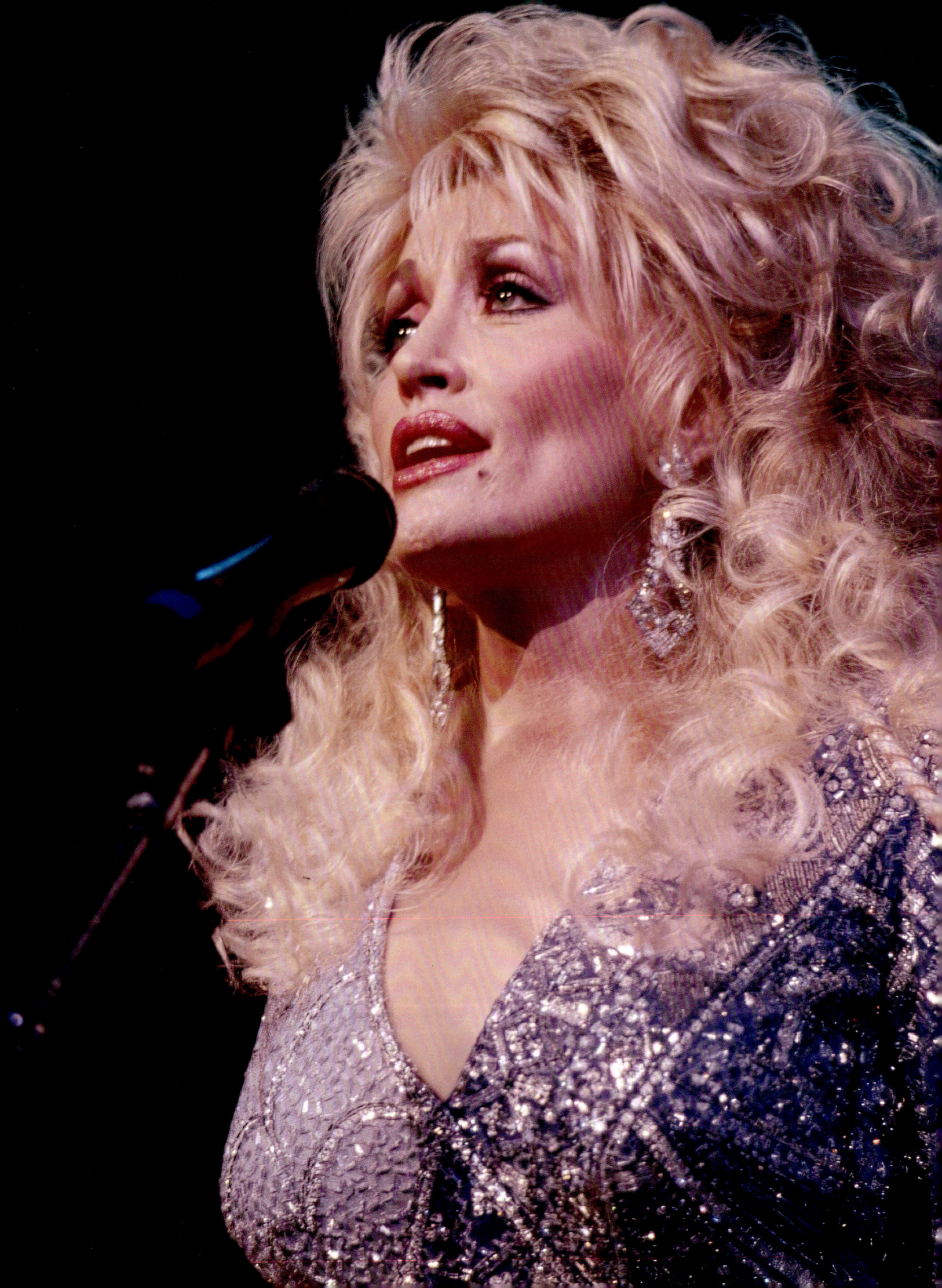

I DON'T PLAY SECOND FIDDLE
IN NOBODY'S BAND

AND I'M NO BACKUP SINGER
AND I WON'T BE A FAN

AND I'M NOBODY'S CO-STAR
I JUST PLAY LEADING ROLES . . .

AND I WON'T PLAY A PART
UNLESS IT'S STAR OF THE SHOW

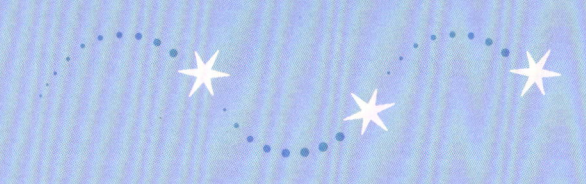

DOLLY PARTON, "STAR OF THE SHOW," 1979

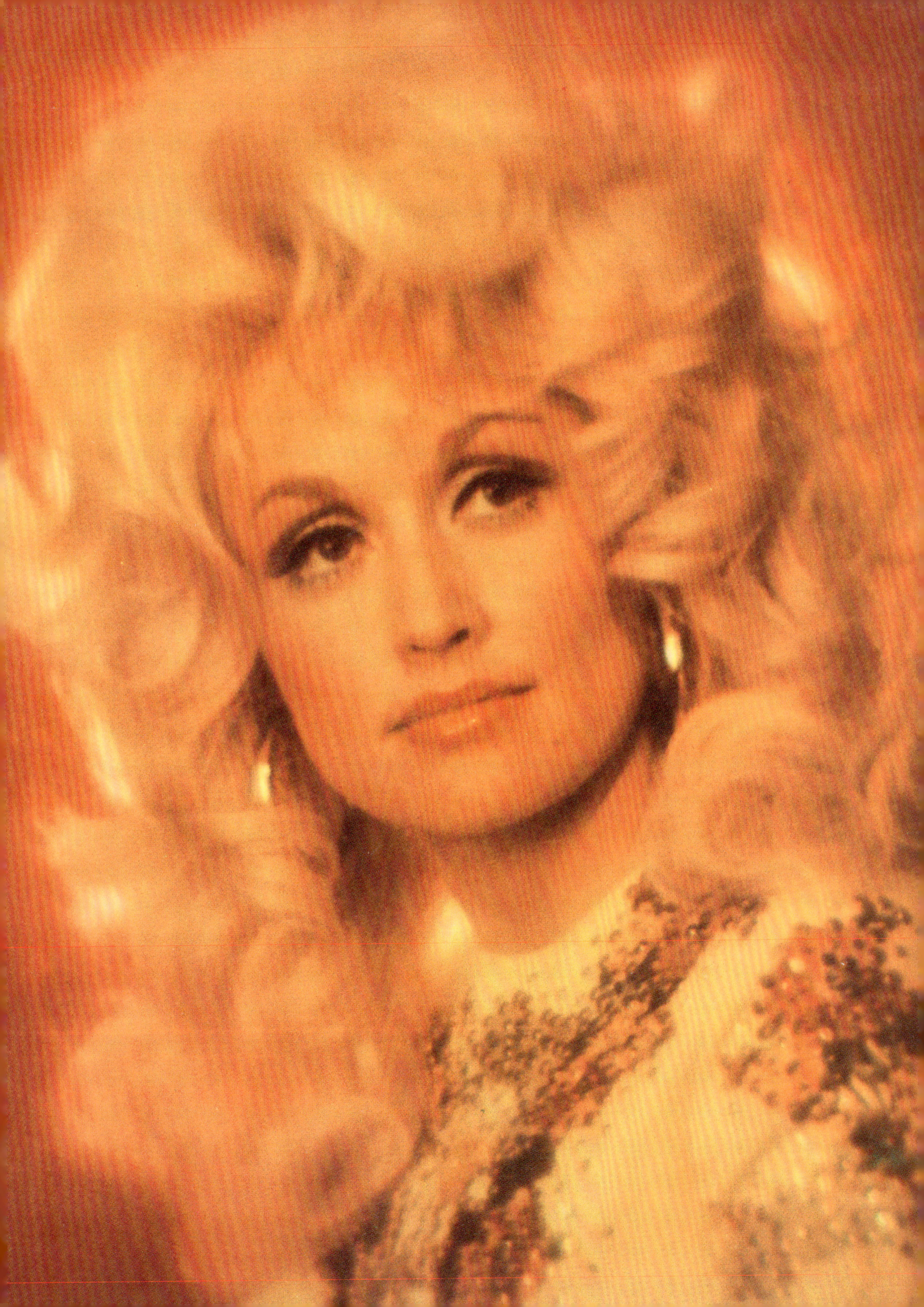

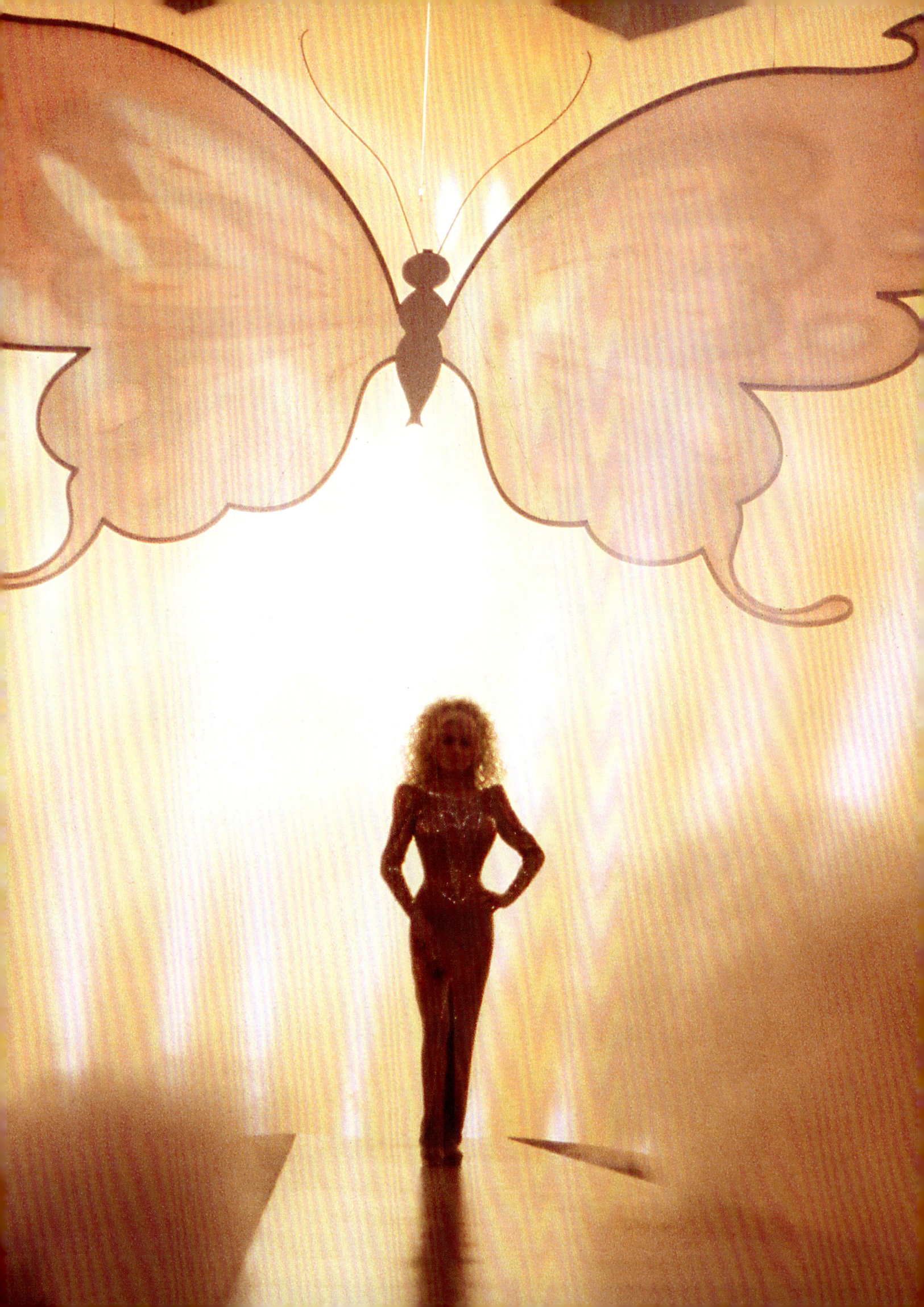

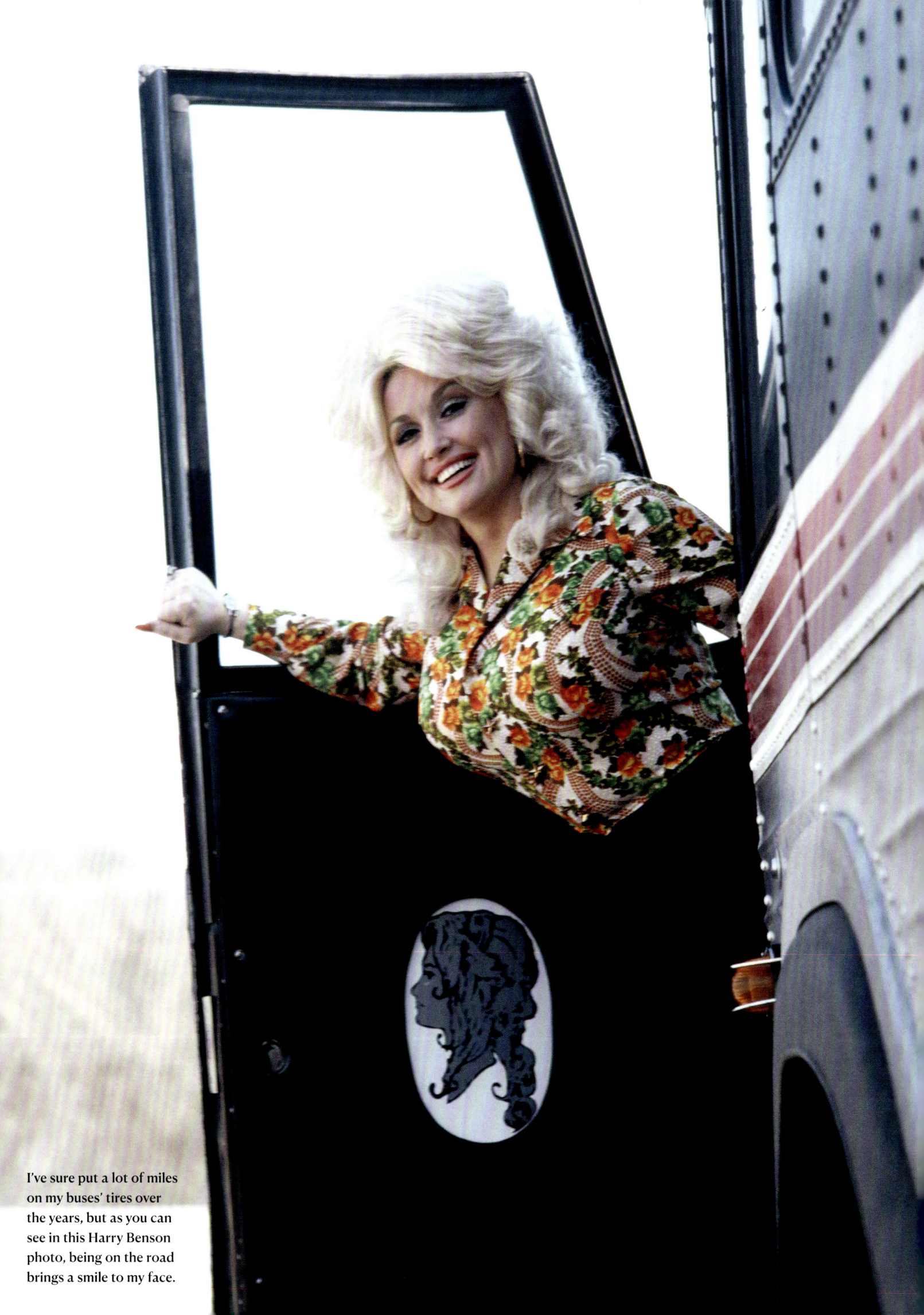

I've sure put a lot of miles on my buses' tires over the years, but as you can see in this Harry Benson photo, being on the road brings a smile to my face.

Introduction

So many miles, so many smiles.

So many years, so many tears.

So many memories that have made up my life on the road and on the stage.

All of my life, I have had a dream in my heart and a gleam in my eye, whether it be a sparkle concerning the dream or the actual spotlight itself. Either way, I'm comfortable with the light shining on me. It was my dream to be a star from the time I was old enough to wish upon one.

I wish I may, I wish I might, become the star I wish tonight.

One day, those wishes and dreams all came true and, of course, I owe it all to God and to you, the fans, and to all the people along the way who have polished and buffed my star to make sure that I could always keep shining.

Looking in from the outside, one tends to believe that the life of a star is always easy and beautiful. People have no earthly idea of the sacrifices that must be made along the way to make dreams and wishes come true. I have paid my dues. Believe me, I have.

I've sacrificed time with family and friends.

I gave up vacations for work without end.

24/7, 365.

But I was willing to make the sacrifice.

Empty or full, I've carried my pail.

You don't drink the water if you don't dig the well. Grindstones and rhinestones have made up my life, and you ask, was it worth the sacrifice?

Well, I reckon it was, because here I am, willing and ready to take you on a journey through my journals of dates and spaces, names and places, detailed information about how I came to be the star of the show.

Dolly

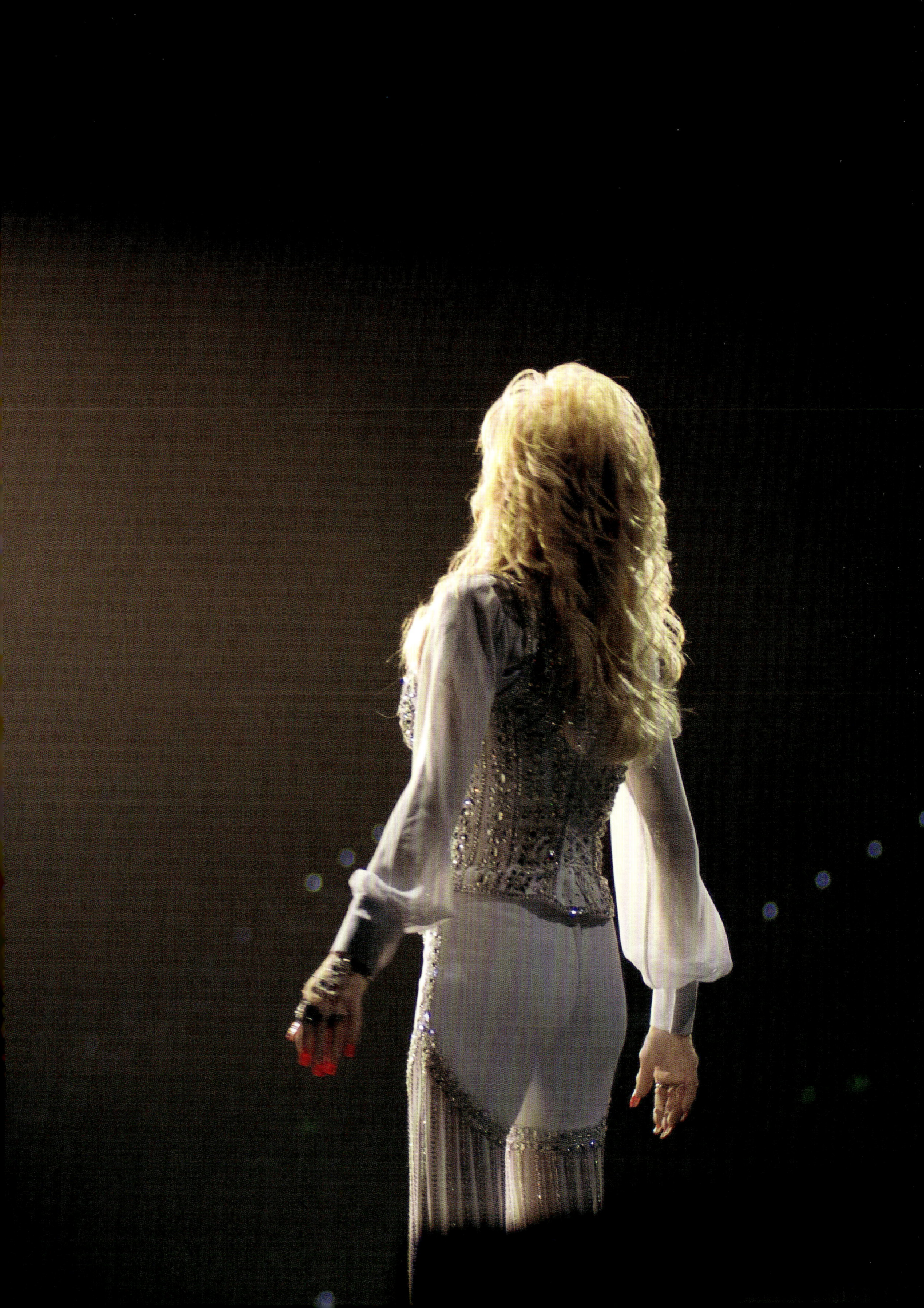

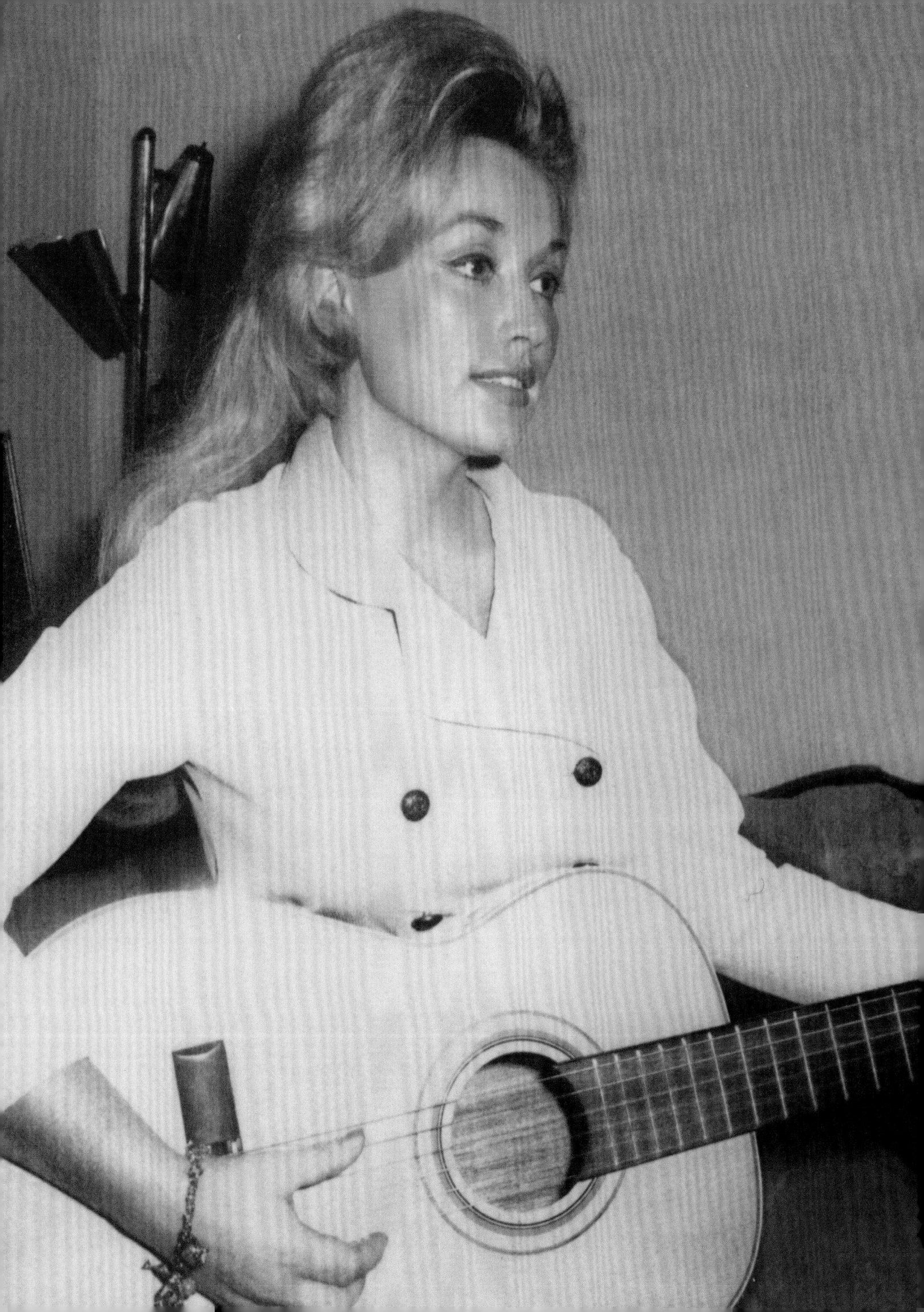

"Start" of the Show

1946-1967

1946 - 1967

Every journey has a starting point, and Dolly Parton's path to center stage began on the porch of her childhood Tennessee mountain home.

It started with a make-believe microphone and mic stand and took her to a series of live radio and TV shows, parades, concerts, a marching band, and the Grand Ole Opry.

It helped that some of her uncles were musicians and gave Dolly the kind of attention and support that keeps kids inspired and excited about their future career choices, though she was so determined that she didn't need a whole lot of encouragement. She was going down this road no matter what.

The star of the show got off to an early start, and she never took her foot off the gas until she got where she wanted to go.

—TOM ROLAND

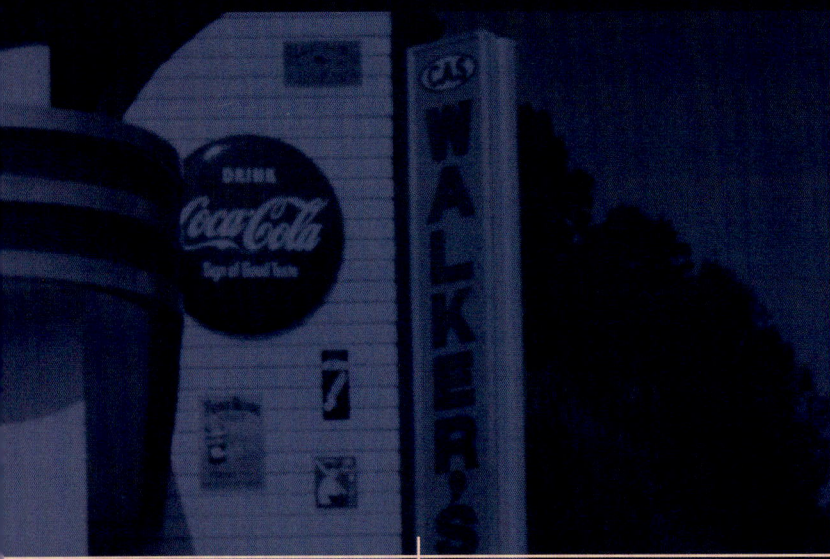

JULY 1956
Dolly begins performing as a regular singer on *The Cas Walker Farm and Home Hour* in Knoxville.

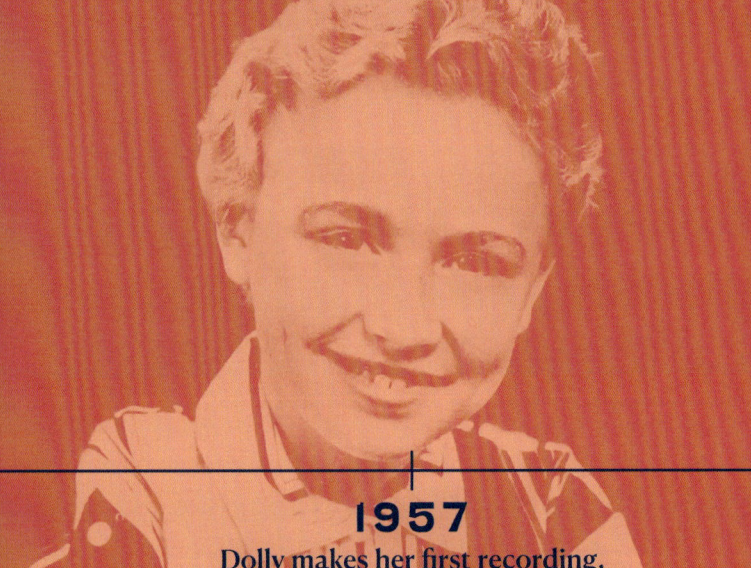

1957
Dolly makes her first recording, "Puppy Love," for Goldband Records. The single is released in 1959.

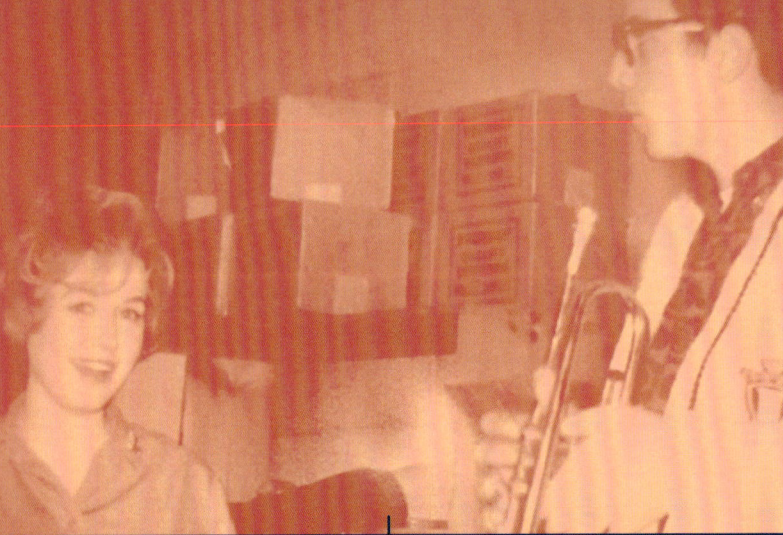

JUNE 1962
Dolly records "It's Sure Gonna Hurt." Credited to "Dolly Parton with the Merry Melody Singers," this is her first single on a major label.

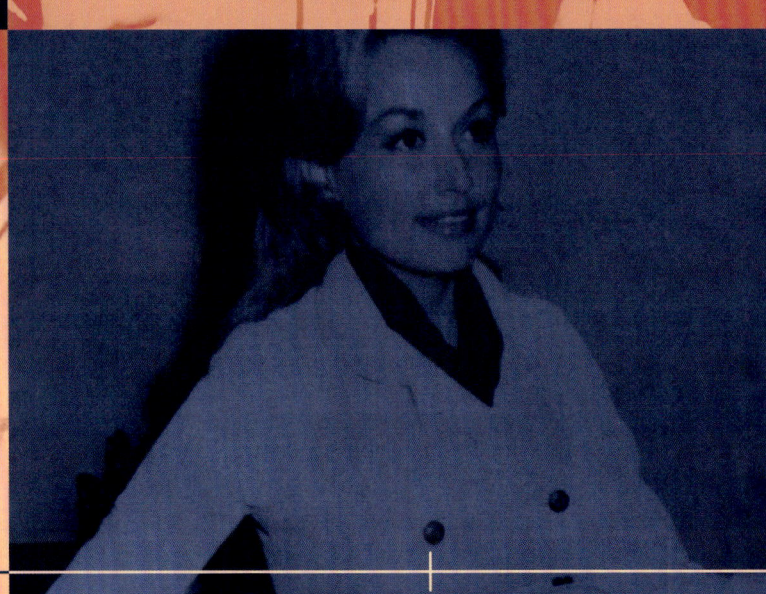

FEBRUARY 1965
Fred Foster signs Dolly and Bill Owens to Combine Music and Dolly to Monument Records.

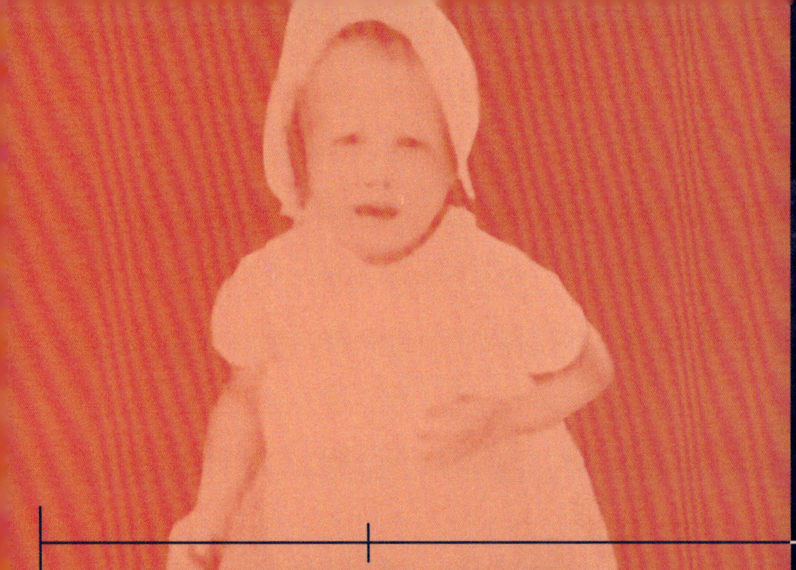

JANUARY 1946
Dolly Rebecca Parton is born on January 19 to Robert Lee Parton and Avie Lee Parton in Sevier County, Tennessee.

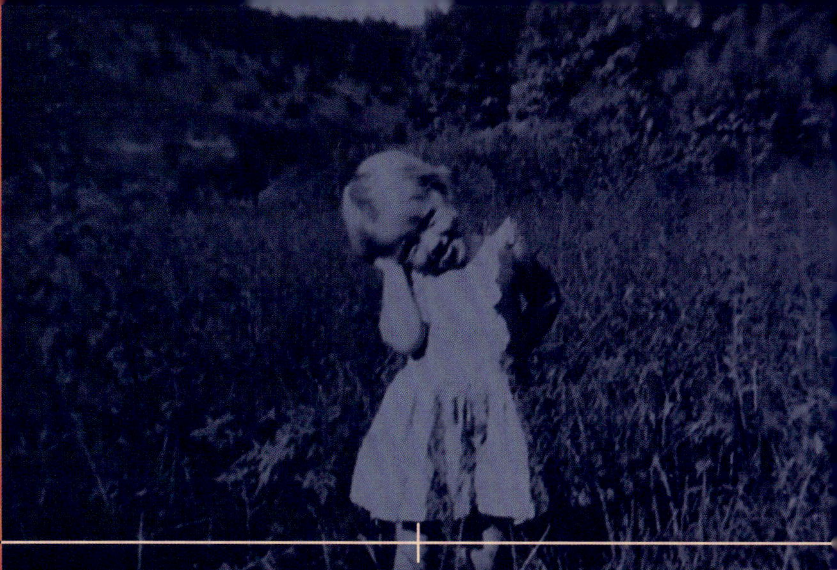

1951
Dolly writes her first song, "Little Tiny Tasseltop."

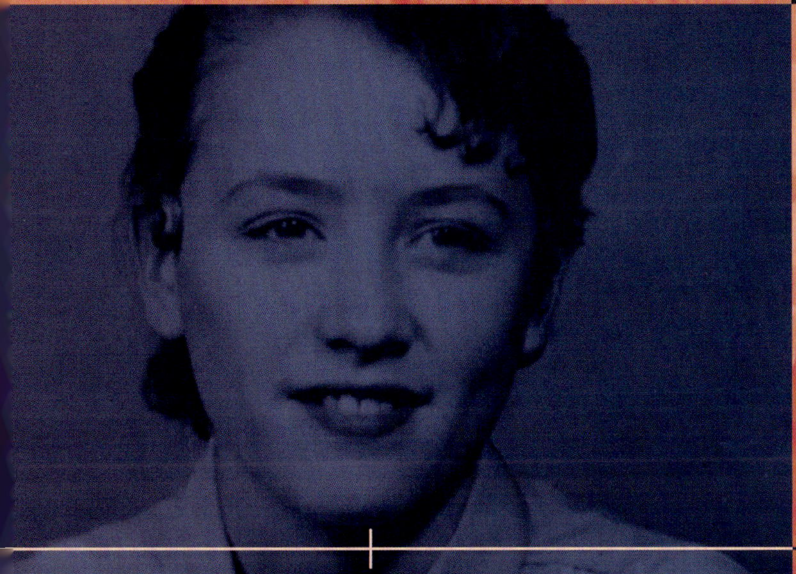

JULY 1959
Dolly gives her first performance at the Grand Ole Opry. Introduced by Johnny Cash, she performs George Jones's "You Gotta Be My Baby" and gets three encores.

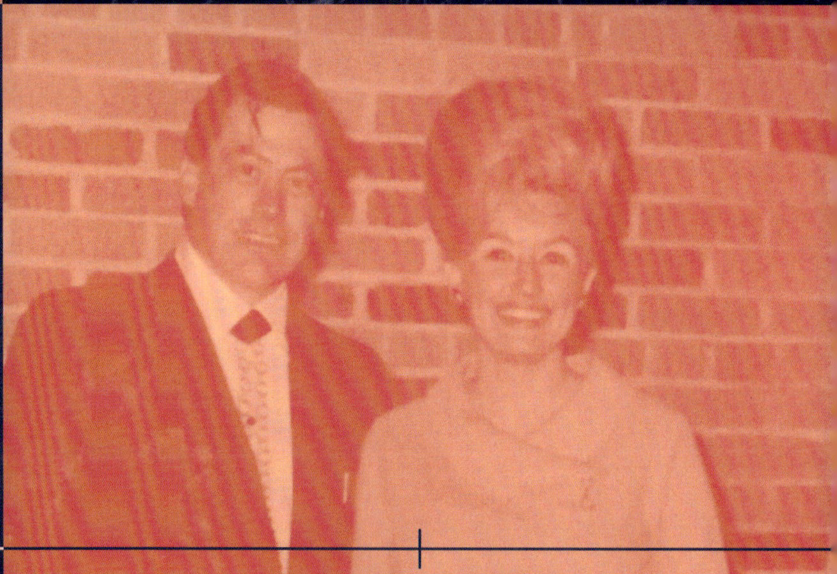

JUNE 1962
Dolly and her Uncle Bill Owens are signed to Tree Publishing and Mercury Records in Nashville.

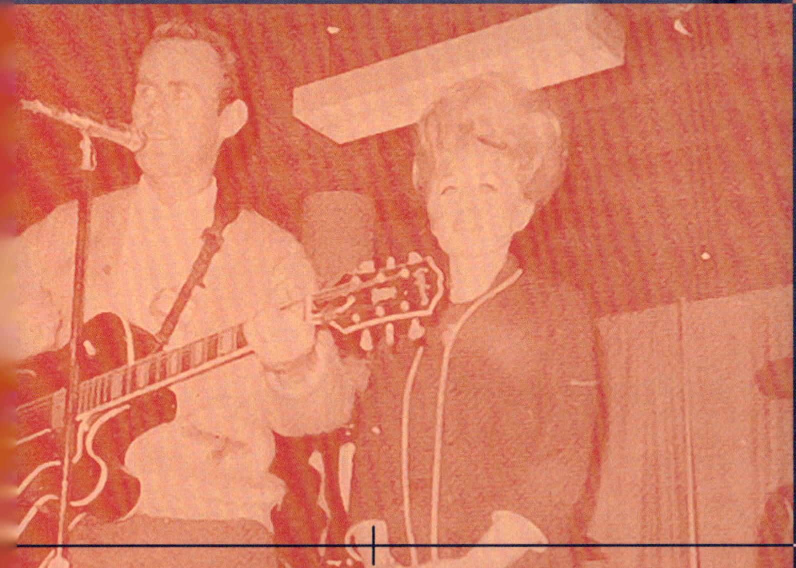

JANUARY 1966
Bill Phillips makes the Top Ten with recordings of two Parton–Owens songs, "Put It Off Until Tomorrow" and "The Company You Keep."

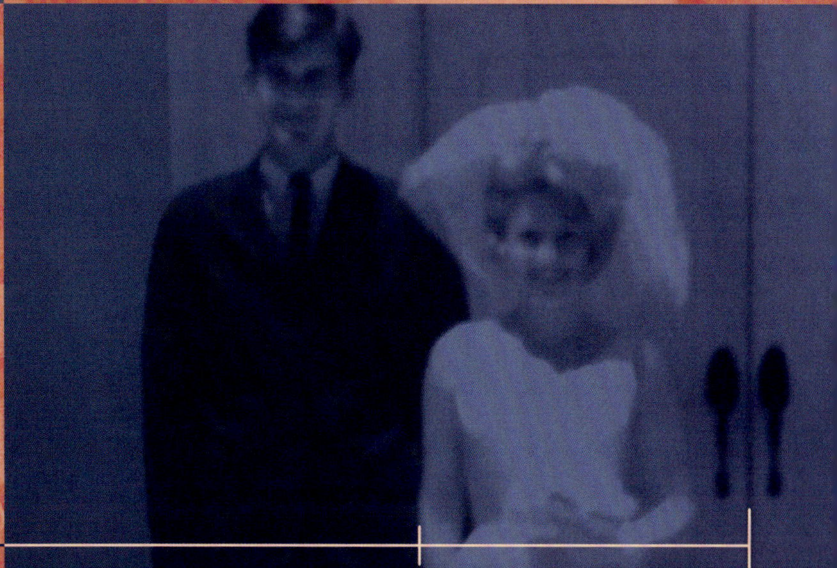

MAY 1966
Dolly and Carl Dean elope in Ringgold, Georgia (to keep her out of the Tennessee newspapers), with Dolly's mother as a witness. They keep their marriage secret.

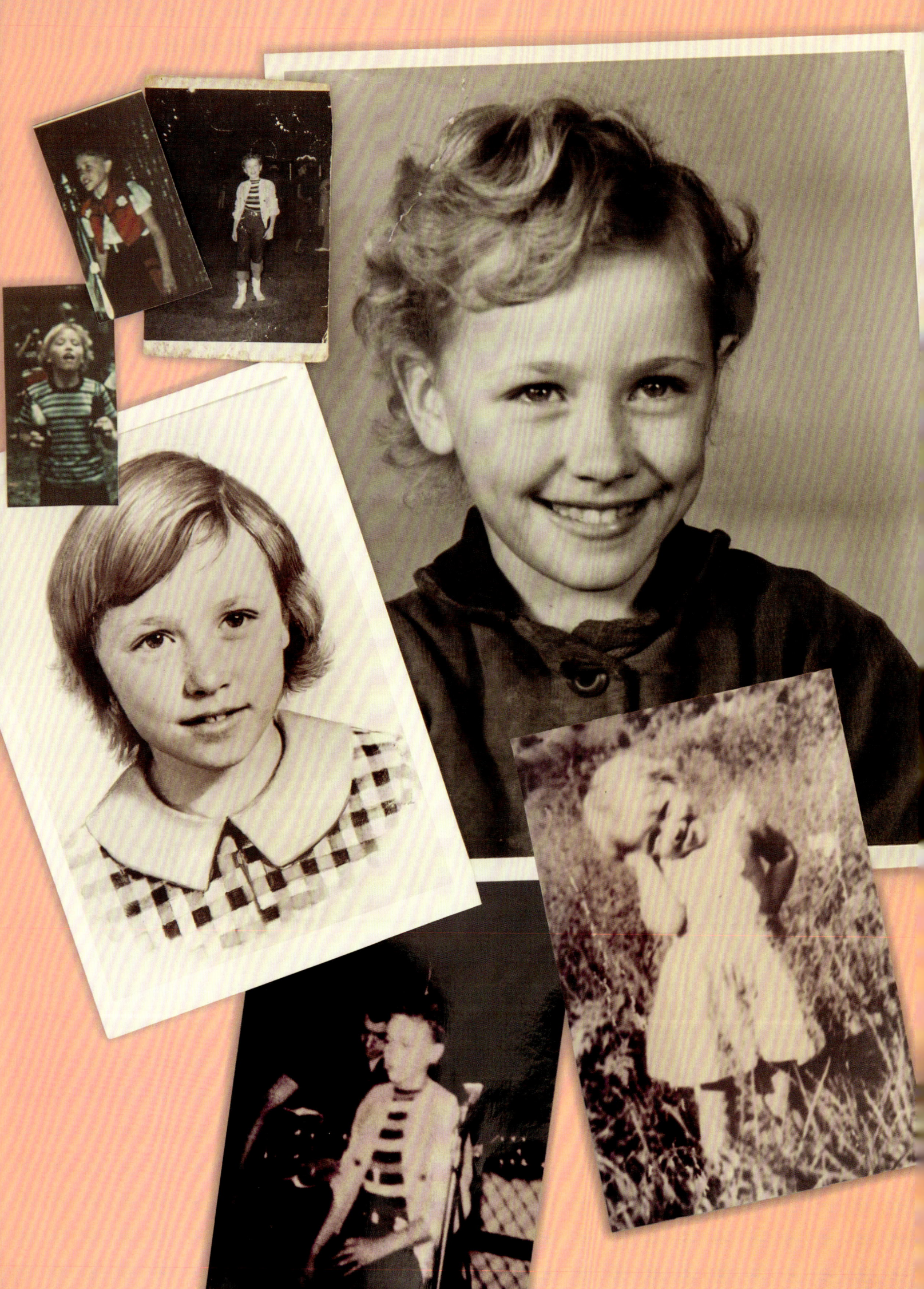

*I*f you'd visited my family's home in Locust Ridge, Tennessee, in the 1950s, the only stars you'd have seen were the ones lighting up the nighttime sky.

But I was determined that eventually the world would pay attention to the one in training on the ground. From my very earliest years, I wanted to be a star. Based on my surroundings, it wasn't the most obvious career path, but I was determined to take it. And frankly, music was the only thing I cared to do.

My very first memory was musical. In those years, my daddy was a sharecropper, and the woman who owned the land we lived on—we called her "Aunt Marth"—sang. It went, "Tip-toe, tip-toe, Little Dolly Parton . . . Tip-toe, tip-toe, ain't she fine. She's got a red dress; she's got nine. She's got a red dress, just like mine." As I've often said, I was amazed she knew a song with my name in it!

We didn't have a TV until I was about ten, and we didn't even have a car, so it wasn't like I could go to concerts. People like Elvis Presley, Fats Domino, and Chet Atkins played in East Tennessee—from Kingsport down to Knoxville and Maryville—but there were no Partons in the seats. We did have a battery-operated radio for a time, and we listened when we could to the Grand Ole Opry. But when the battery lost its juice, we lost the Opry too.

Since we didn't have much entertainment from outside, we had to make our own, and most of my brothers and sisters had some kind of musical talent. In fact, our whole extended family was very musical, and my earliest influences were my mama and my aunts and uncles and grandparents. Several of my relatives performed on local radio stations, and even in clubs.

I was a kid who needed a lot of attention. I had plenty of pent-up energy, too, so I had to funnel it somewhere. There was no way I could act up in a family as big as ours without getting in trouble! So I learned to focus on my music. I would write all these songs, and I'd come up with these licks on the guitar. And when somebody would come to our house, Mama would say, "Run and get your guitar and sing that song" for whoever had just arrived. So I got to sing, and I saw early on that that would get me lots of attention. Of course, that only made me want to perform even more. If a visitor thought I was good, then I wanted to keep at it. I wanted to write better songs and sing better songs.

In the Smoky Mountains, most of the songs you heard were gospel or country or bluegrass or maybe some blues. If you put all of it together, it was basically what you'd call "mountain music"—songs about hardworkin' people in the backwoods. Life, love, broken hearts, God, poverty, family, and moonshine—we sang about it all. And I was determined that I would sing those kinds of songs all over the world, not just at home.

Of course, if you want to be on a stage, you have to practice, and although I can't tell you the exact date of my first performance, I can tell you where it took place: it was on the front porch of our house. I ran a tobacco stick down between the cracks of the porch and put a tin can on top for a microphone. But I wasn't the only one singing on that porch. My sisters and brothers liked to perform too. We'd all sing at different times, but I think I spent a lot

"Start" of the Show

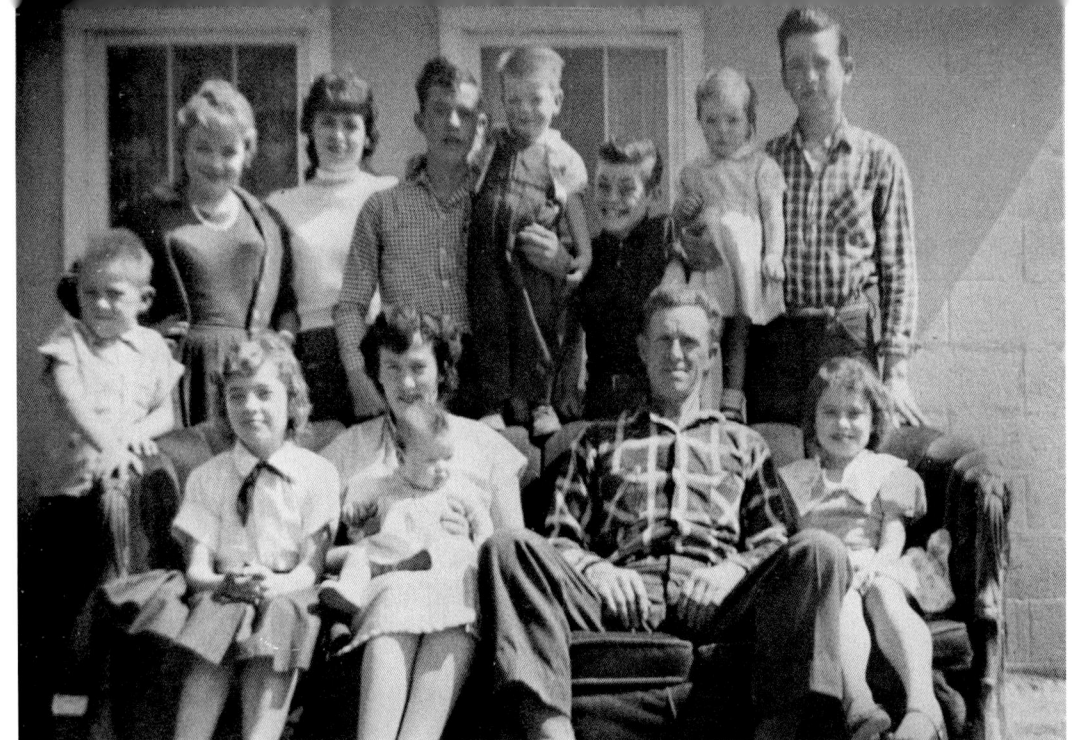

A 1960 family portrait on the very porch where I gave some of my first shows. Seated: Stella, Mama, Rachel (on Mama's lap), Daddy, and Cassie. *Back row:* Randy, me, Willadeene, Denver, Floyd, Bobby, Freida, David.

more time than them on that pretend stage because I was feeling things out to see if it was what I wanted to do. I sang my heart out on that porch, and I did it time after time, always dreaming of one day singing in front of a bunch of people, even though it was mostly the other kids and the animals that I was performing for back then.

Once I had my "show" down, I expanded it and roped a couple of my sisters into being my backup singers. We kind of felt like The Supremes, and I was convinced that the world was out there just waiting for me to get off the porch and come sing for them.

When I thought about my future, I always obsessed about being a singer, but I also had the idea that I could be a songwriter. So I worked on those skills at the same time. I wrote my first song, "Little Tiny Tasseltop," around the age of five:

> *Little tiny tasseltop*
> *You're the only friend I got*
> *I love you an awful lot*
> *Hope you always stay*

If you think anything about my career is corny, you can blame it on "Little Tiny Tasseltop," since it was about a corncob doll my mama made for me. But looking back, I think it kind of shows that I had a natural talent for writing songs. The melody was catchy, it had a structure, and the last line is practically a greeting card. I'm my own toughest critic, but that's not bad for a little kid!

Star of the Show

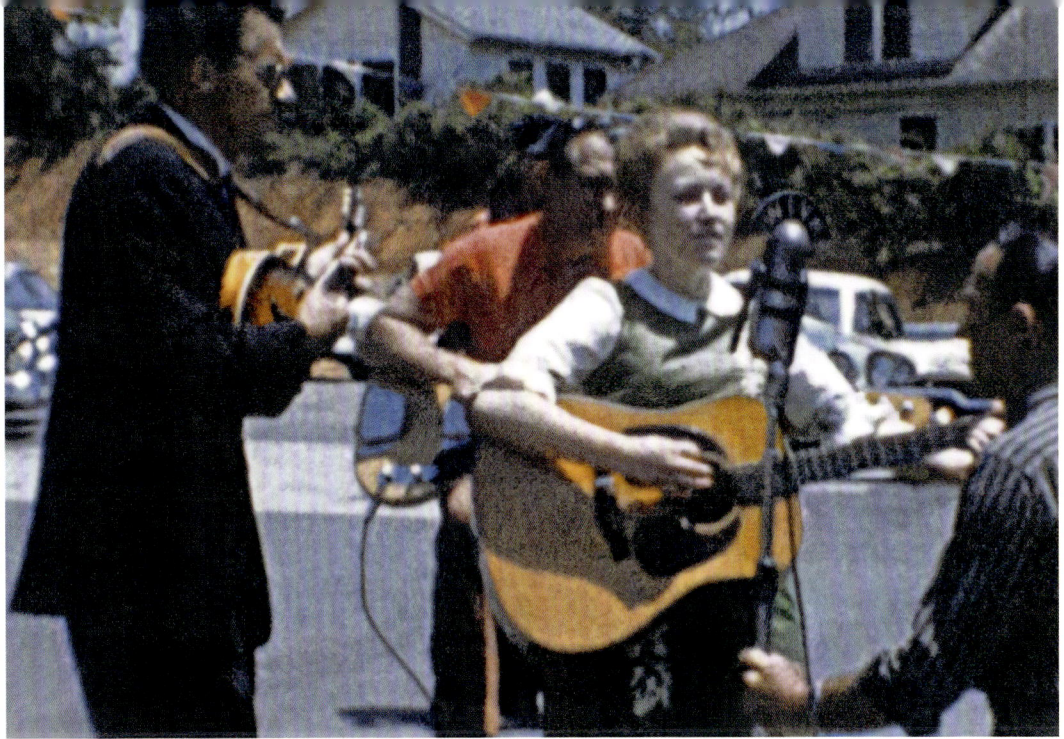

I love putting on a show wherever I can. This one was broadcast live on Knoxville radio station WIVK from a parking lot in Fountain City, Tennessee.

I was constantly making up songs and writing them down, planning for that day when I could go out into the world and sing them. I was proud of the world I grew up in, and I wanted to take my stories about life in the mountains of Tennessee to the rest of the world.

I suppose I saw myself as a musical evangelist in training. I wasn't necessarily planning to do gospel tent shows with wild altar calls, but I did want to take songs about my people to other parts of America that I hadn't even seen yet.

I came by that viewpoint naturally. My grandfather was a hellfire-and-brimstone Pentecostal preacher. His version of spirituality wasn't necessarily for me, though I'm still very much a believer and always have been, of course. I just see my relationship with God a little differently.

But I was also, whether I realized it or not, part of a tradition. Many artists develop the foundations of their sound in the church, particularly in country and in rhythm and blues. You can hear it in music by Aretha Franklin, Willie Nelson, Sam Cooke, Johnny Cash, and Hank Williams—they all drew on their gospel upbringing. So it shouldn't come as a big surprise that the church had a hand in my musical education too.

One church played an especially big role. It was an abandoned chapel with broken windows and a beat-up piano that didn't hardly play at all. But I was fascinated by those black-and-white keys, and I'd sing by the piano and even took some of the strings from inside it to create my own makeshift dulcimer. In that church, I talked to God directly and realized I didn't feel I needed a preacher to communicate for me. I also told Him about my dreams of being a star. I guess He heard me.

"Start" of the Show

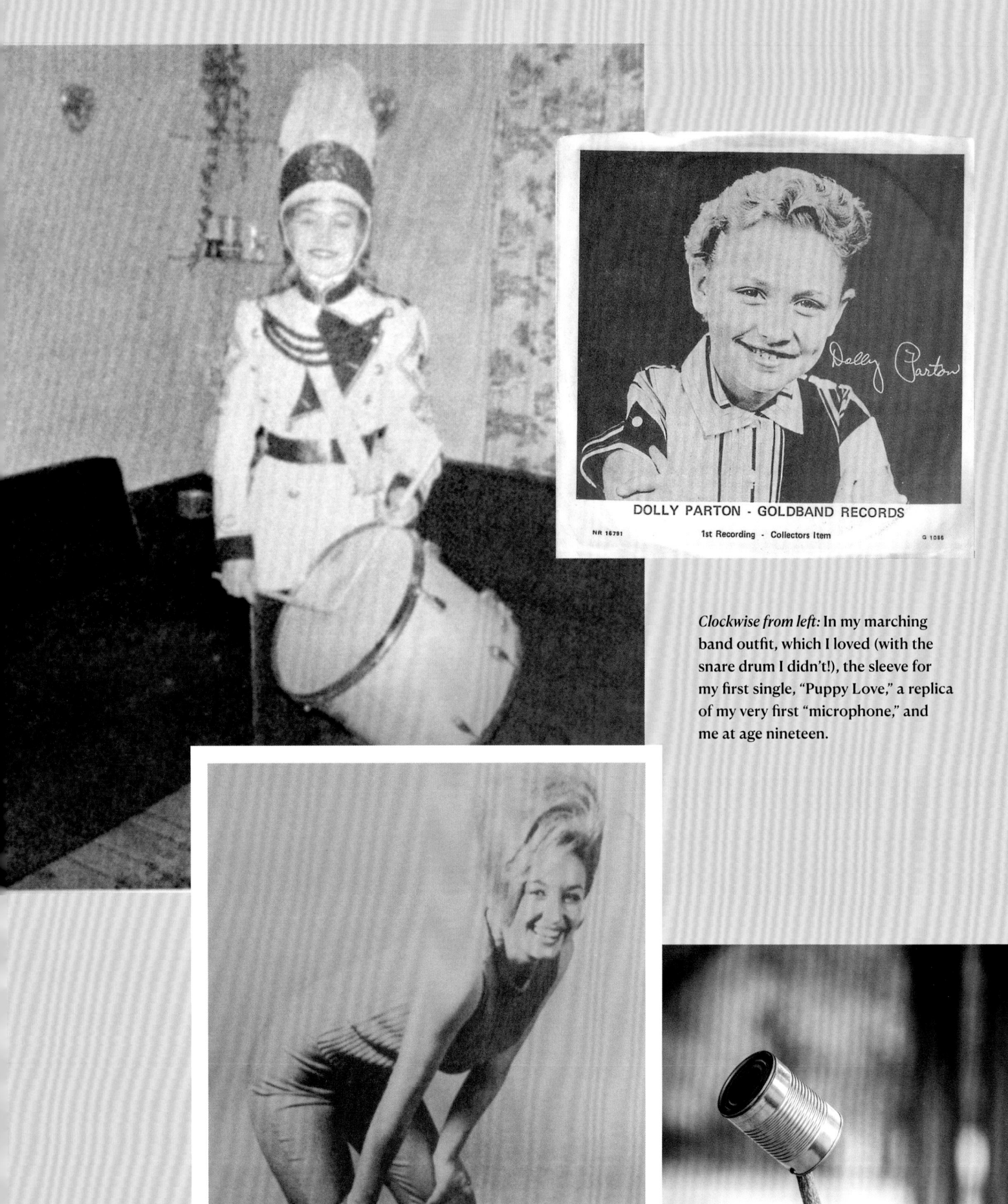

Clockwise from left: In my marching band outfit, which I loved (with the snare drum I didn't!), the sleeve for my first single, "Puppy Love," a replica of my very first "microphone," and me at age nineteen.

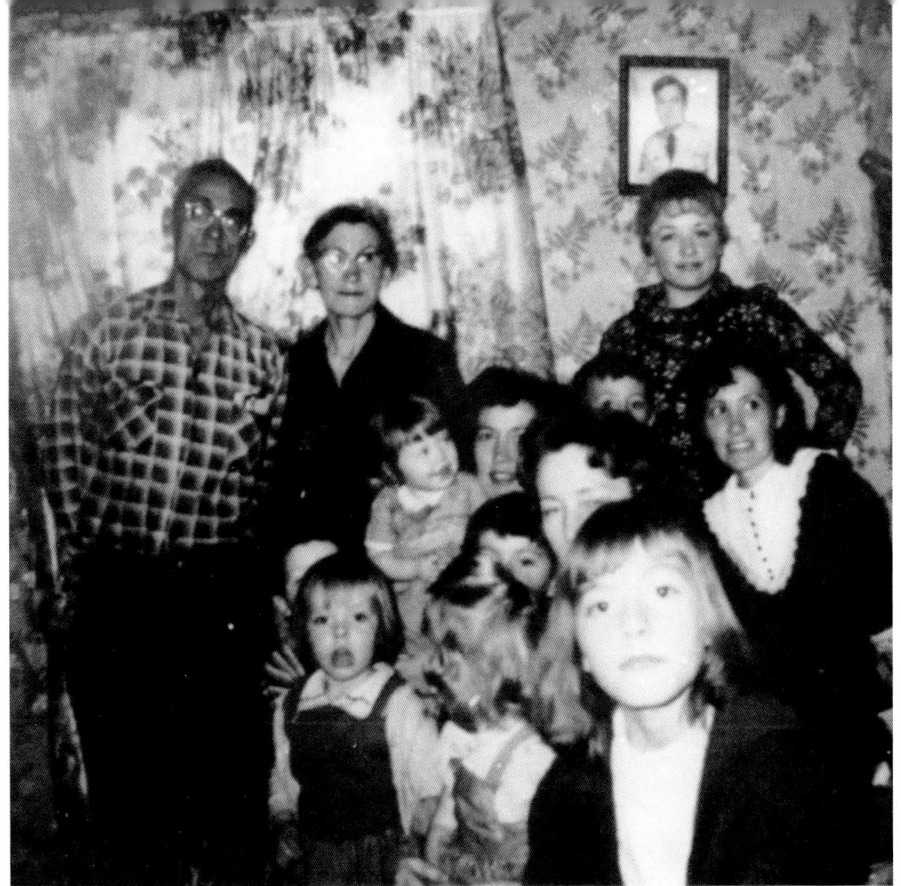

My fifteenth birthday celebration—my grandparents
(left) and me (right) in the back.

Not all the church experiences were good, however. I remember when a few of my sisters and I started singing on the sanctuary circuit. Daddy would take us to different churches around East Tennessee, and he'd wait in the parking lot while we sang for the congregation. At one stop, the worshippers got all worked up, and they kept reaching toward the stage. We were wondering, *Are we really that good?*

Well, not quite. When we glanced behind us, we saw that the minister had three snakes in his hands, and he seemed to be teasing them, agitating them, daring them to bite. I'd seen people speak in tongues in church before, but I'd never seen them worship with forked tongues! Thankfully, Daddy decided this was a day that he was going to come into the church and hear us sing. When he saw the preacher dangling poisonous serpents and moving in our direction, he ran up, grabbed us, and whisked us out the door. Fortunately, I've never had another show quite like that!

Daddy wasn't the only one looking out for us. I was fortunate to have three uncles who played different roles that helped get me ready to become an artist: Uncle Louis, Uncle Henry, and Uncle Bill Owens. Uncle Louis and Uncle Bill were both musicians, and when I was eight years old, Uncle Louis gave me my first guitar, a smaller model made by Martin. I called it my "baby Martin," and it really was kind of like my baby. I gave it lots of attention and grew up as an artist while holding it close to me.

"Start" of the Show

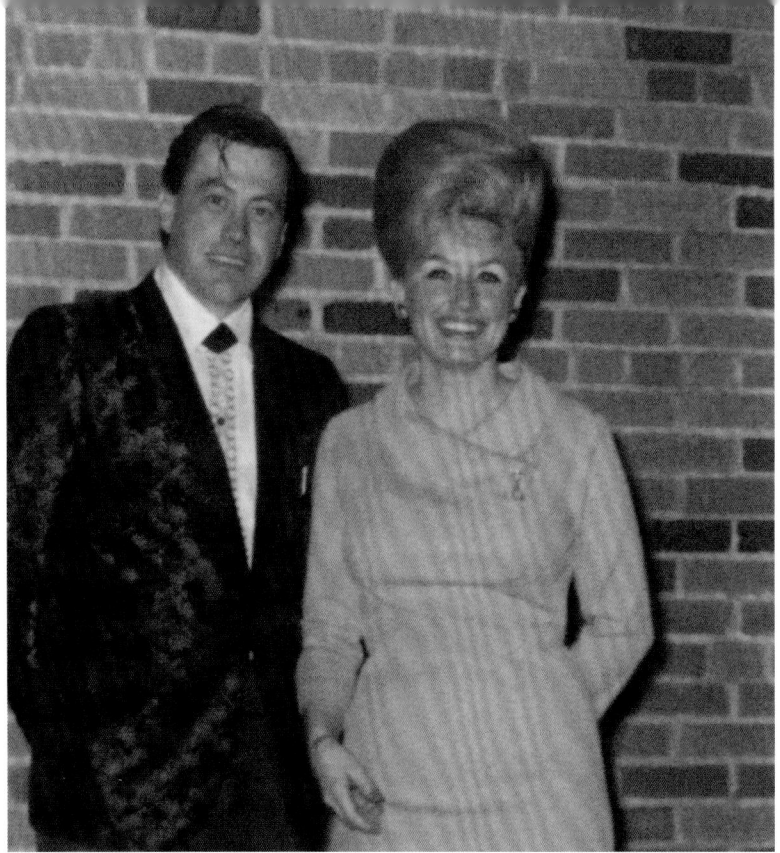

Me and Uncle Bill, my first manager
(and a great guitar teacher!).

Uncle Bill taught me chords on the guitar and showed me some of the important stuff, like the right way to make chords with the left hand, pick with the right hand, and tune it. Every time he showed me a new chord, I learned it right away—and I figured out how to combine it with other chords or notes to create new music. I spent so much time with my guitar that I got little calluses on my fingers, and they would hurt and blister. Most of the kids would give up before they learned to play like that. I never gave up. I never gave up for anything. Uncle Bill said, "You know, you're going to have to get them calluses, because that's going to have to harden so you can make better chords and you can play more things." I was devoted to that little guitar, and I thought, *Well, it's going to serve me, and I'm going to serve it.*

One of my great-grandmas—we called her Mammy—played the dulcimer, and she also played the banjo. As a little-bitty kid, I remember seeing some of the older people playing that old dulcimer, and the autoharp was a big deal too. Mother Maybelle Carter, from the Carter Family, played the autoharp and also played the guitar, and when I started playing the guitar, I wanted to be Mother Maybelle Carter, so that's when those finger blisters and calluses had to start growing. If I wanted to play "Wildwood Flower" like she did, I was going to have to bear down on those chords on that guitar.

Uncle Bill also greased the skids to get me my first regular performing job. He introduced me to Cas Walker, a Knoxville character who had a radio show, *The Cas Walker Farm and Home Hour,* that had run on Knoxville radio stations since the 1920s. Cas was known as the "millionaire grocer" because he had made a lot of money with his grocery chain, Cas Walker's Supermarket. He was firm about what he offered his customers—he was determined to have the lowest food prices in East Tennessee—but he also told them, "If you don't like Cas Walker prices, don't come in here." He'd say the same thing on his radio show: "If you don't like what you hear, go somewhere else!"

Cas reminded me of my own people. He was so country and so corny and so down-to-earth. He had no education. And they tell me that he had actually started his business taking groceries in a wheelbarrow back and forth to people's houses, and then eventually he'd set up a little roadside fruit-and-vegetable stand. That's where it started, and before he knew it, he had stores all over Tennessee, East Tennessee, and different parts of Kentucky, and I think even some in Virginia.

Cas was just a simple man who had a good business mind, but he was very controversial, and at the time, he kind of got really called out a lot for it. He would get on the air and just talk about anything and everything, not knowing that he shouldn't. He didn't care either. I learned what to say and what not to say from him, but I also learned the business end of things from him. I'd watch how he would maneuver, and I'd watch how he would treat the artists and people. He treated us all with respect.

He helped build careers in the process. Carl Smith was the first artist he launched to stardom. Carl had a string of country hits beginning just a few years before I joined the *Farm and Home Hour,* and he became a member of the Grand Ole Opry and eventually the Country Music Hall of Fame. Cas helped develop The Everly Brothers, too, and he disowned them when they switched from country music to rock 'n' roll! He also had Carl Butler and his wife, Pearl, on his show at the time I was introduced to him. Carl and Pearl had a no. 1 single of their own just a few years later with "Don't Let Me Cross Over."

When Uncle Bill introduced me to Cas, I'd already heard his voice on the radio, seen his face on the tube, and read his name on grocery signs. I blurted out, "I'd like to work for you!" And I meant it. I was only ten years old, but I was already tired of working on the farm for my daddy!

Cas liked hearing that. He told me later that the reason he hired me was because I said I wanted to *work*. To start, he put me on his radio show. It operated out of a small studio on Gay Street with room for an audience of about sixty people. Uncle Bill went with me that first time I sang on the radio, and I was nervous as heck—as you might expect. When my name was called, it seemed like the longest trip to get to the microphone, and for the first few seconds, I was a little timid. But the people in the seats were paying attention, everything was working okay, and by the end, I was full-throated Dolly Parton. The audience clapped so long and so loud that I had to do an encore. It was not what I'd expected. I'd only prepared one song, but Uncle Bill yelled, "Sing it again!" So I did.

"Start" of the Show

SAXY AND I KNOW IT

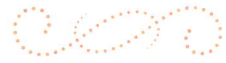

I've never defined myself as a musician, but I have learned how to play several instruments over the years as I've tried to bring my songs to life in the way I hear them in my head.

I never learned to read music. I can play chords, but I never know for sure if I'm playing a C major or an F-sharp minor, and—to be honest—I don't really care. Some people believe there are rules around how music works and how you're supposed to make it, but if you follow the rules you might wrap chains around your creativity and limit it. Plus, with my long nails, I had to find a way to improvise if I wanted to keep writing and working on songs!

My first instrument was a guitar—I had a few rigged-up homemade instruments that made great writing tools, but as I've mentioned, my Uncle Louis gave me my first real guitar, my baby Martin. Uncle Bill would teach me a new chord, and I'd spend hours working with it, trying to play it in conjunction with some of the other chords he'd taught me, then I'd try to write a song around it.

When I was in high school, since they didn't have a place for guitars in the marching band, I took up the snare drum. I never got particularly good at it, but there were so many people in the band—and the sound in a stadium or gymnasium isn't great anyway—that any echo or imprecision I caused wasn't noticed!

The dulcimer and autoharp are mountain instruments—many people associate them with musicians like The Carter Family. The Dobro, the fiddle, and the banjo are all bluegrass instruments, so they were all interesting to me too. I'd figure out how to make a noise with them, then figure out how to make the sounds fit into the songs I wrote.

I never played piano much, but I learned the basics just enough to write songs on it and play a song or two on stage, which added a little something extra to my concerts. When it comes to harmonica, I think you have to have a good set of lungs for that—and some people say I have that. It's the same with the saxophone. I slapped some rhinestones on it and played a haphazard version of the Boots Randolph song "Yakety Sax," which some people know better as the theme to *The Benny Hill Show*.

I'm a performer and an entertainer, and even though I'm not that great on any of the instruments I play, I can make a show of it. Ain't that what entertainment is all about?!

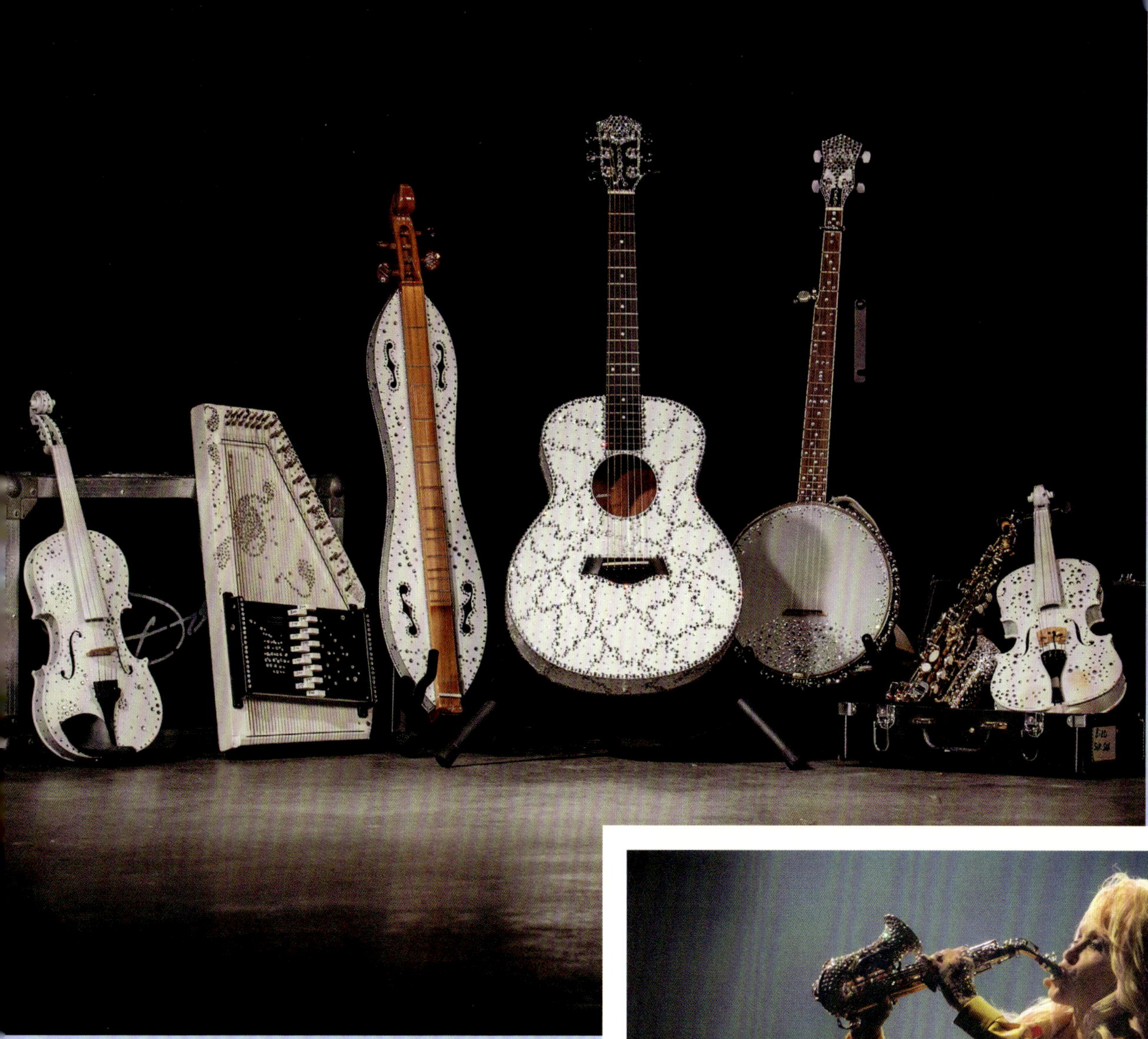

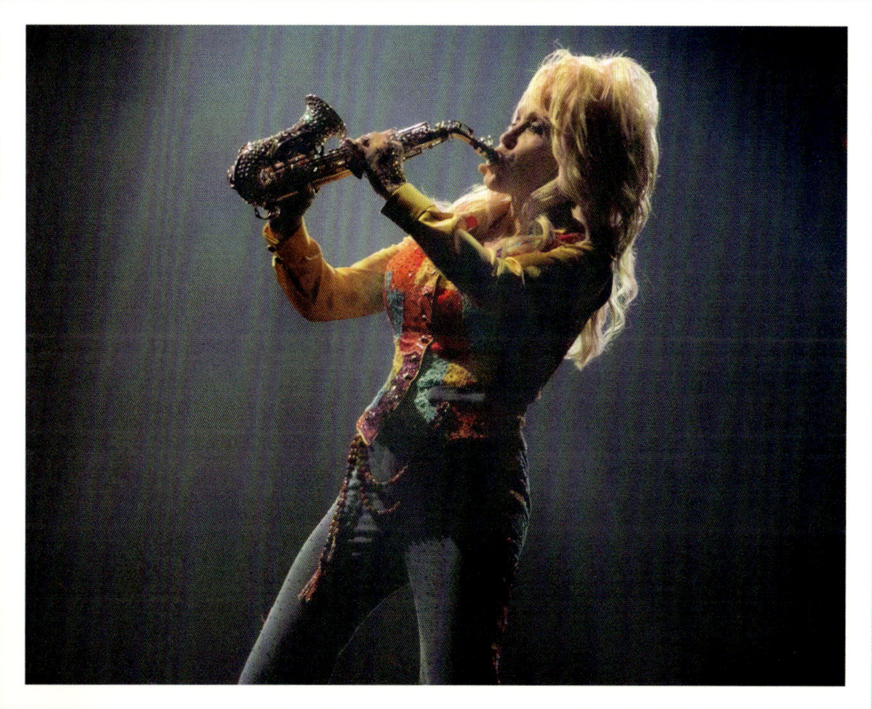

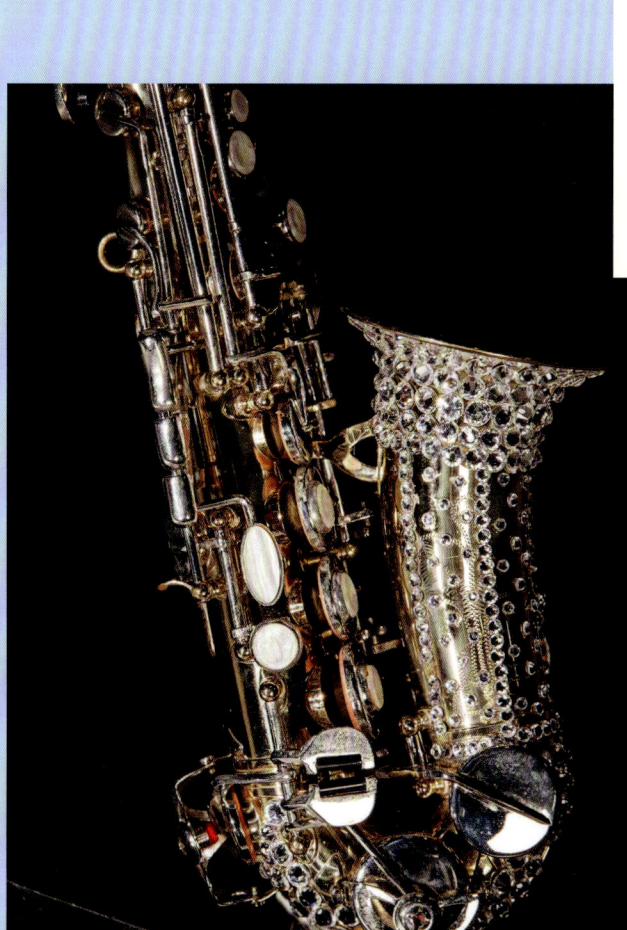

Top: Some of the tools of my trade—two fiddles framing an autoharp, dulcimer, acoustic guitar, banjo, and alto saxophone.
Center: That's me doing my best Boots Randolph imitation!
Bottom: I don't know if rhinestones improve the sound and tone, but they sure add some sparkle to my saxophone!

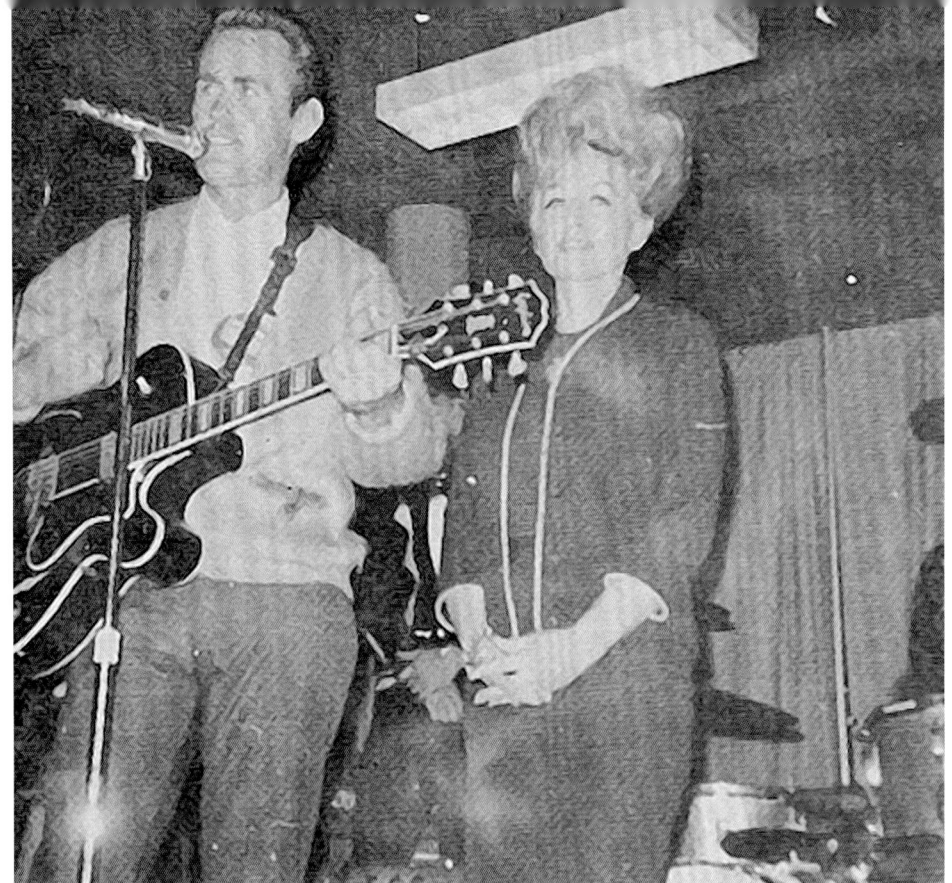

Uncle Bill and I wrote a song called "Put It Off Until Tomorrow," and I sang background on Bill Phillips's hit version.

I became a regular member of the radio show cast, mostly appearing during the summer and on holidays since I still had to go to school. I would stay in Knoxville with my Aunt Estelle and Uncle Dot Watson—Estelle was my mama's oldest sister.

Cas also put me in his traveling road show, playing in different small towns in the region. One of them was the Pines Theater on Court Street in my hometown, Sevierville. I received five dollars a show, which was a lot of money to a ten-year-old. Bigger money came when I entered one of Cas Walker's greasy pole competitions. He put a one-hundred-dollar bill at the top of the pole, then covered the pole with grease, and anyone who could climb up the pole and grab the money got to keep it. I went out and got soaked, and then I rolled around in the dirt so it would cling to my jeans and give me some traction. When I had my chance, I started up the pole—and darn it if I didn't make it all the way to the top! A lot of people complained, saying it was rigged, but Cas asked, "How the hell do you rig a greasy pole?" and no one argued! With the winnings, I went out and bought our family's first TV, which brought us into the modern world but also meant my parents could finally see me on *The Cas Walker Show*.

I learned so much about performing in those early days, and one thing I figured out right away was that you work on holidays. When I was eleven, Maryville hosted a Fourth of July parade as part of a weeklong Hillbilly Homecoming, and entertainment before the fireworks included Cas Walker's Entertainers: Carl Butler, Uncle Bill, and me, among about a half dozen other local artists.

Star of the Show

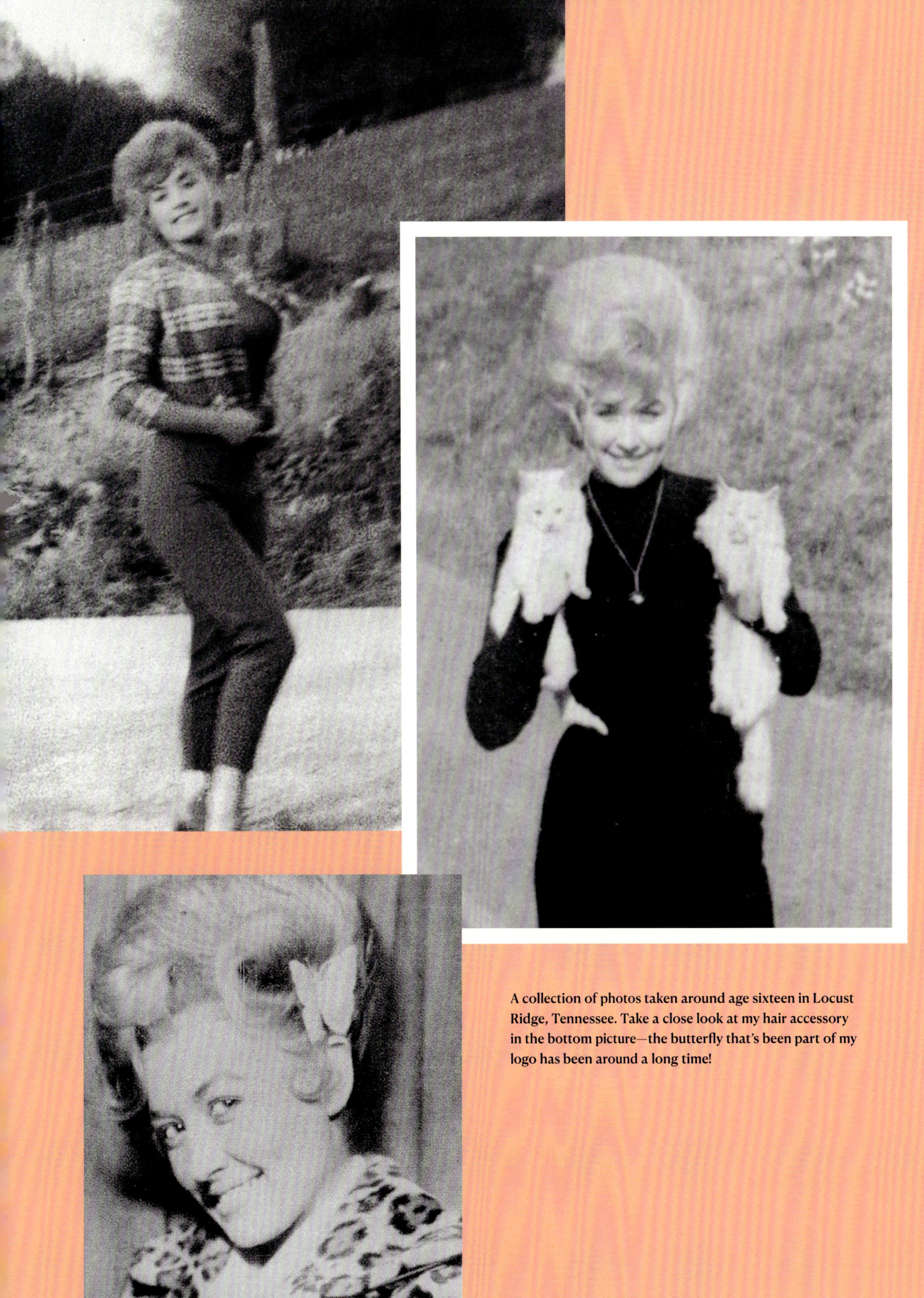

A collection of photos taken around age sixteen in Locust Ridge, Tennessee. Take a close look at my hair accessory in the bottom picture—the butterfly that's been part of my logo has been around a long time!

MICROPHONES
Through the Years

When you've been singing and recording and performing for nearly seven decades, a lot's going to change. And that includes technology and equipment. I wouldn't be the star of the show if you couldn't hear me, and without microphones, cables, amplifiers, speakers, and a crew to set them up and make them all work, in the studio and on stage, you wouldn't!

Here's a collection of mics that I have used on the road and in the studio and—to the best of my recollection—when I used them. They're quality products, and they all worked! Many of them still do—and they sound great. We've sure come a long way since my tin can and tobacco stick on our porch!

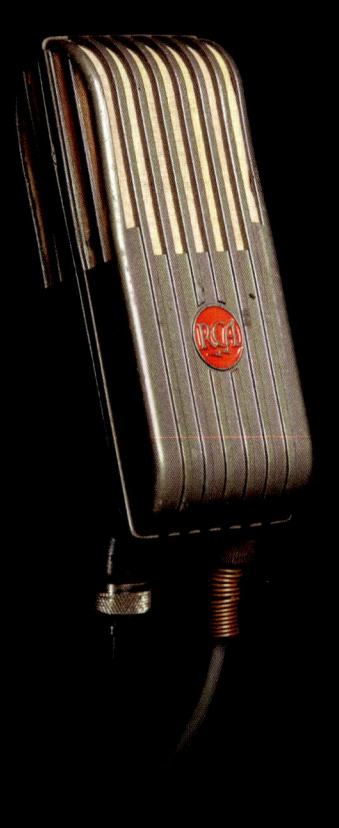

RCA SK50
Cas Walker radio shows, 1940s

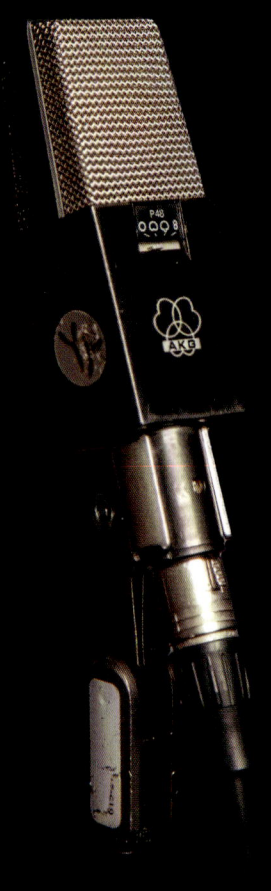

AKG C414
Numerous recordings, 1970s

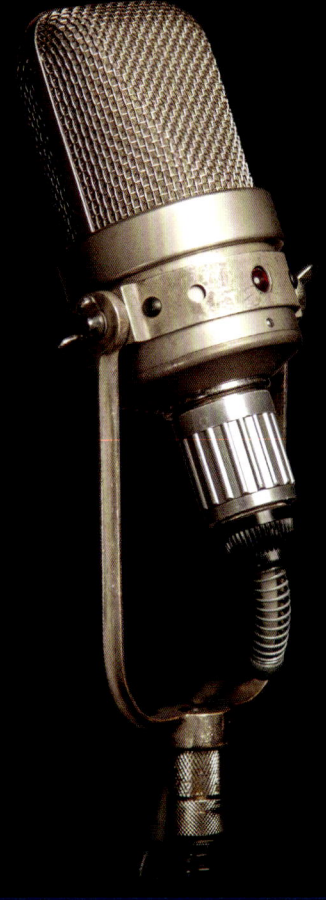

NEUMANN M49
"You Can't Make Old Friends" recording, 2013

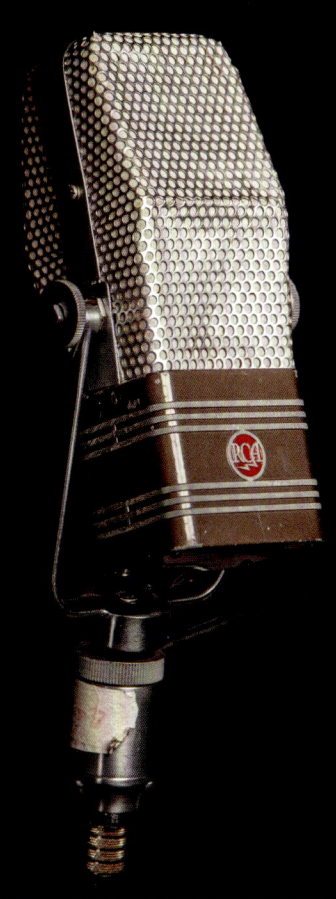

RCA 44
Grand Ole Opry, 1959

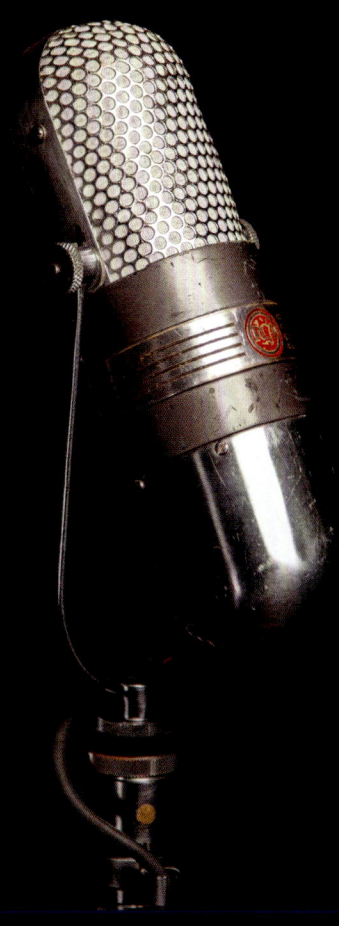

RCA 77D
Goldband recordings, 1959

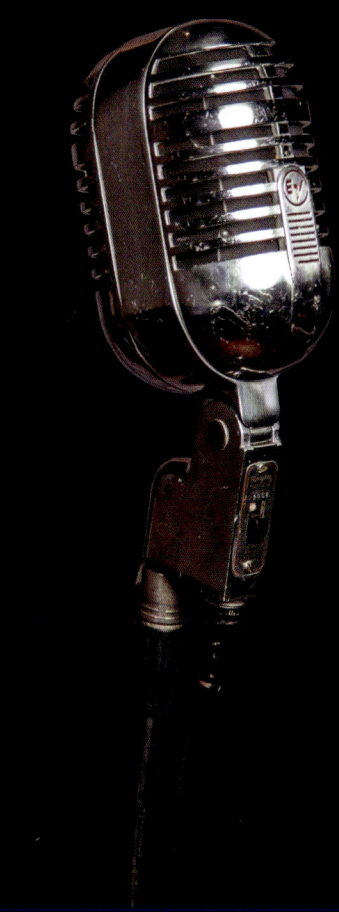

**ELECTROVOICE
CARDYNE II MODEL 731**
Live shows, early 1960s

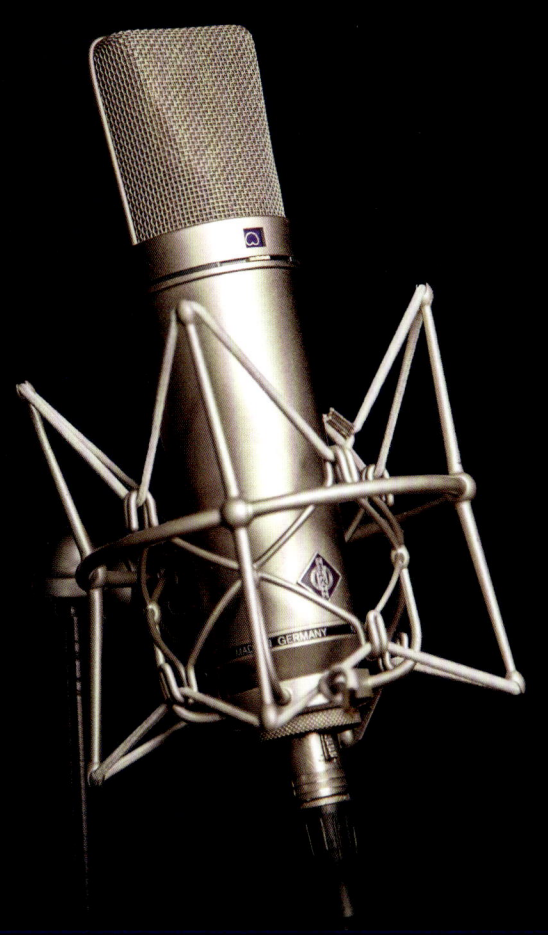

NEUMANN U87
"Jolene," "I Will Always Love You" recordings, 1973

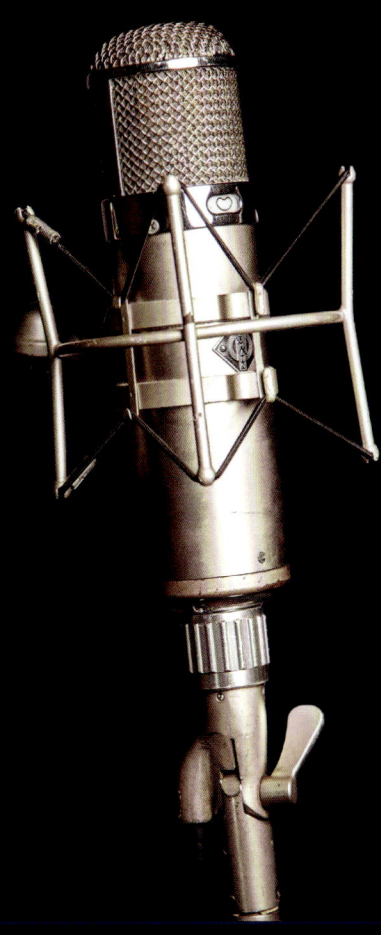

NEUMANN U47
Specific years unknown

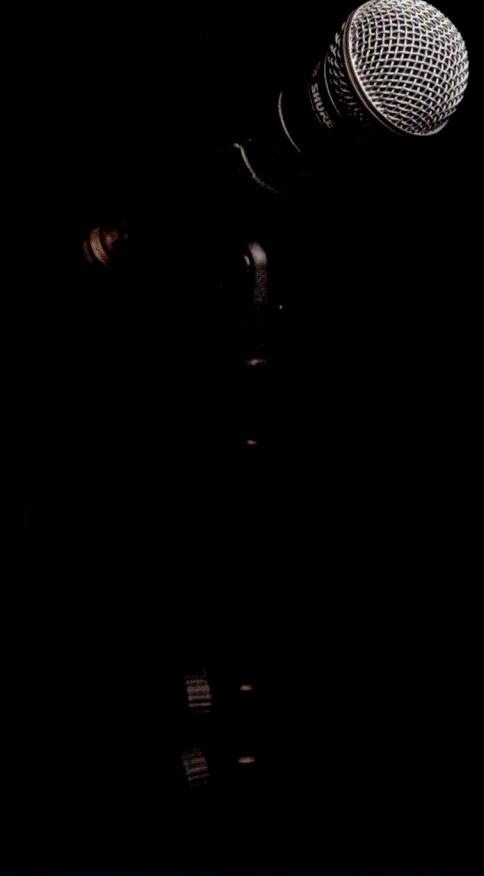

SHURE SM58
Live mic used since 1967 at the Opry

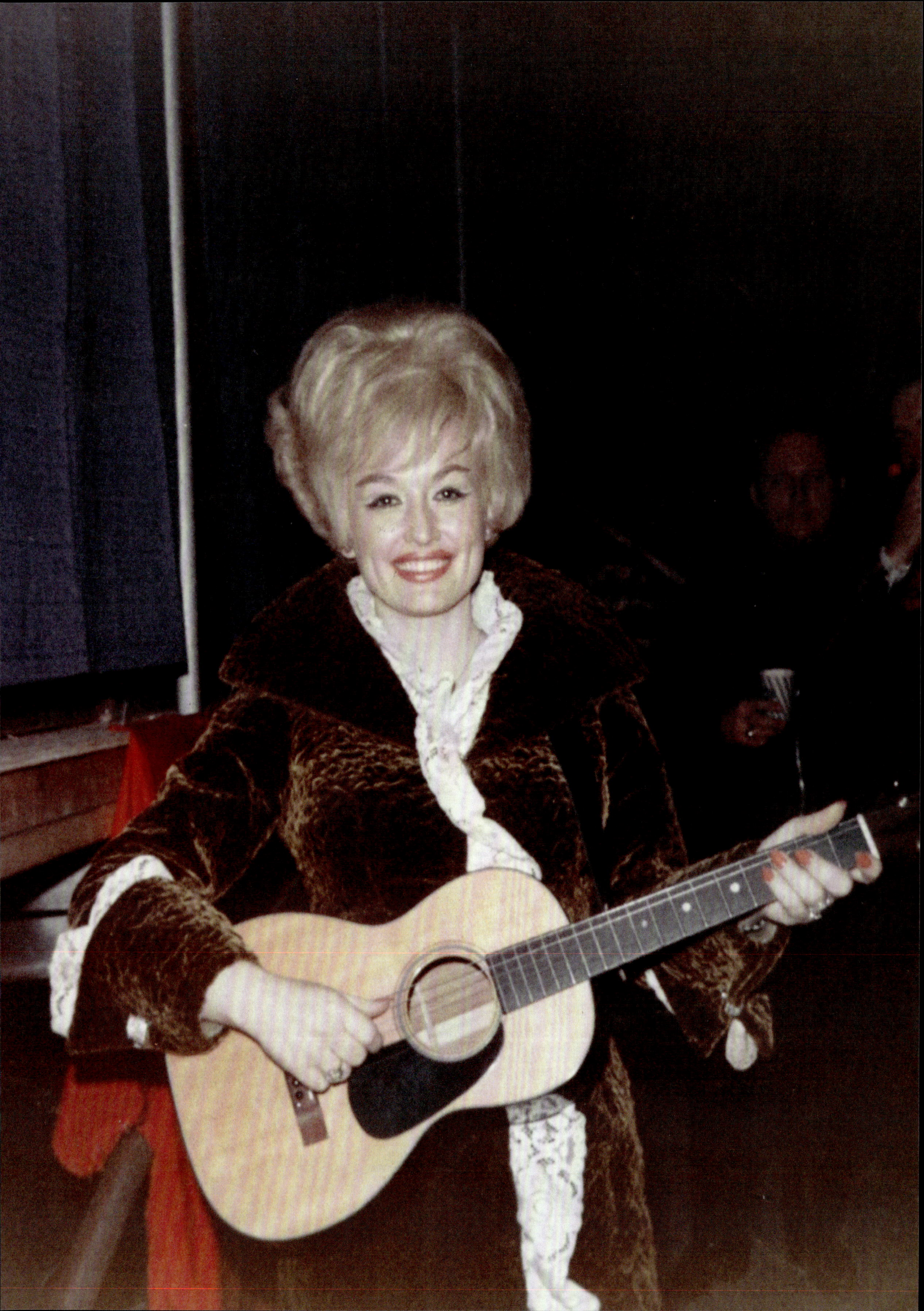

I also realized that if I was going to be a country star, touring would involve a bus. I *hated* the school bus, but I knew I had to get over that. And fortunately, my first long bus ride involved music. My Uncle Henry, one of Mama's brothers, was in the military, stationed in Lake Charles. My Uncle Bill was staying down there with him. Next door was a studio, and they became friends with the owner. They had some conversations, and they told me that if I could get to Lake Charles, I could make my first record at the Goldband recording studio. It took some wrangling, but I got my grandma Rena to go with me, and we took off on the 800-mile bus trip to Cajun country. It was exciting—I'd never been outside the state of Tennessee!—but we ran into trouble when we got to Birmingham, Alabama. We got off the bus to use the restroom, but when we returned to the buses, we got confused and couldn't figure out which one was ours. We ended up missing our connection, and my grandma got very distraught. I took it upon myself to figure it out, and the people at the bus station helped us determine when the next bus to Lake Charles would be available. It seemed like forever before we were able to get out of Birmingham, but I can look back now and realize that navigating that hurdle at the bus station gave me confidence years later when things on the road weren't working the way I expected.

The single I recorded, "Puppy Love," didn't do much, but it was a start. And it got some airplay in Tennessee when Grandma and I got back to the Smoky Mountains.

As everything started to take off, Uncle Bill decided we should try to get me on the Grand Ole Opry. Nashville was five or six hours away on the old highway—the interstate didn't exist yet. He'd drive me there, and we'd find our way to the Ryman Auditorium, a converted church with no air-conditioning where the Opry was held every Saturday night.

Today, security is tight around the Opry, but in the 1950s, it was rather loose. Artists swapped stories and partied outside the back entrance, and when a lot of them had time to kill, they'd cross the alley and hang out at what's now Tootsies Orchid Lounge. Uncle Bill was a maneuverer. He was able to charm his way into the inner circle of some artists and their managers, and he would invariably try to convince them that I should be on the stage.

It was a long time before it happened, and there were many nights when Uncle Bill and I slept in the car in Nashville because we couldn't afford a hotel room. But eventually, we struck gold. Carl and Pearl Butler, the duo who I worked with on Cas Walker's show, had a hand in it. They were at the Opry that night, and they helped persuade Jimmy C. Newman—the *C* stood for "Cajun"—to give up one of his two songs so I could make my debut. I never forgot that Jimmy did that. It was so selfless of him to let a young girl who didn't have that much going for her in Nashville sing in his place.

That night at the Opry, Johnny Cash introduced me. I remember seeing him perform even before that, when Uncle Bill and I used to travel back and forth. Johnny was like Elvis—he stirred up everything in me. He was just so sexy, and he moved around in all these weird ways. I found out later that was probably just because of what he might've been on or coming off of at the time, but still—his whole persona was just charismatic and downright magical. Having Johnny Cash introduce me was a *really* big deal. His deep, rich voice gave

"Start" of the Show

the name "Dolly Parton" some extra authority, and for a short spell, I was captivated by the situation. Every time Uncle Bill and I had visited the Opry, I'd look at that world-famous microphone stand and the wooden floor and the rows of pews of the Ryman and dream that someday it might be me in that spot. Now I was right where I'd dreamed, and I almost froze. It felt surreal.

I held back a little at the beginning, but when someone took a flash photo from the audience, I snapped into the role, and all the training on Knoxville radio—and on the front porch in Locust Ridge—paid off. I was determined to give the people their money's worth for that one song, and by the end, I just let loose. Before it was all over, I got three encores.

Somewhere along the line, Uncle Bill and I signed on as songwriters with Tree Publishing, the Nashville company that had the rights to Elvis's "Heartbreak Hotel." The contract paid fifty dollars a week and created an extra incentive to keep writing even while I was still at Sevier County High School and on Cas Walker's show. Not that I needed any incentive to write. It's something I still do almost every day.

I also joined the school marching band, which was kind of a hoot. As I've mentioned, it didn't have parts for marching guitar players, and I didn't play trumpet or clarinet or tuba or even flute. But my friend Judy Ogle wanted to be in the band, and she wanted *me* to be in the band with her, so I joined the band playing snare drum. Trust me, I'm no drummer. I'm a lot better with a guitar.

The band director was so good about it. He knew I was a songwriter. He'd heard me sing, he'd seen me on some of the local TV shows, and he knew I wasn't going to take that drum seriously because I'm not a drummer. But I wanted to wear a uniform.

We lived way back in the country, and Daddy didn't want me running about after hours and all that, so I wasn't allowed to march at all the ball games. But I got to go to a few games, and I got to wear that uniform. And I remember when I did get to go, I got this horrible bruise on my leg from banging that snare drum while we marched.

Ultimately, I wasn't much of a student because I was much more focused on studying country music and my career path. I turned eighteen in January 1964, and when graduation day came on the last Friday in May, I collected my diploma and then took a bus the next morning to Nashville. I always make jokes that I left home with my matching luggage: four paper bags from the same grocery store and my guitar. But I did!

Most of my fans know I met my future husband, Carl Dean, that first day in Music City. One odd little side note, however, is that it was also a holiday. Not Dolly Parton Day though—it was Decoration Day, which was the name then used for Memorial Day. Of course, by now, everyone knows the story of how Carl and I met outside the Wishy Washy, and the rest was history.

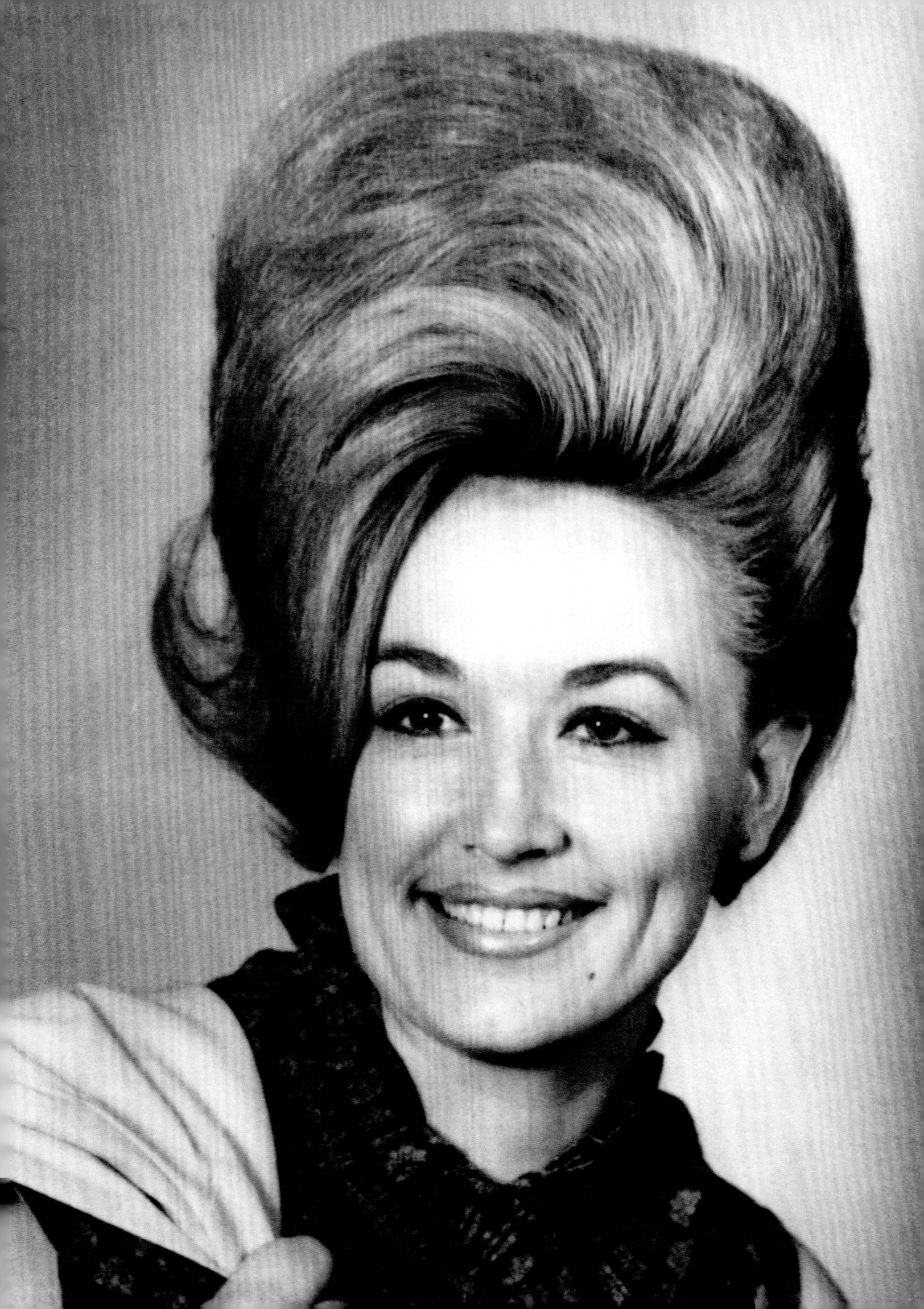

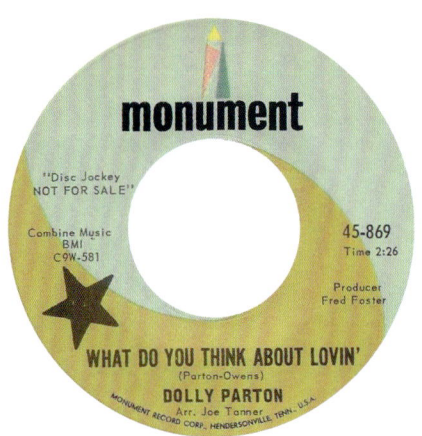 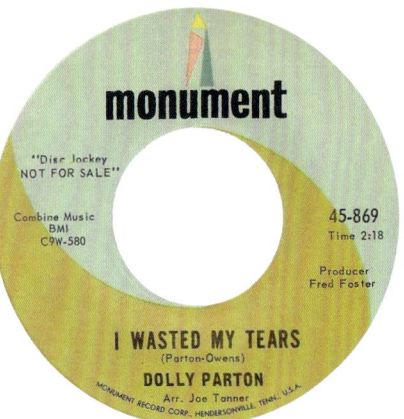 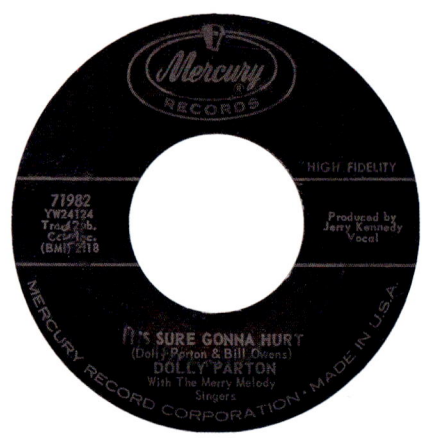

I was so happy to have my first chart records as a
solo artist with Monument Records in the mid-1960s.
I also recorded a song for Mercury when I was visiting
Nashville regularly with Uncle Bill.

Eventually, I signed a contract as an artist with Monument Records, and I performed regularly on a couple of Nashville-based morning TV programs: *The Eddie Hill Show* and *The Ralph Emery Show*. I didn't have a car yet, so Ralph would pick me up at my apartment on the way to the studio, and he'd drive me home when the cameras stopped rolling.

I signed with a booking agency called One Niters, Inc. It was run by Brenda Lee's manager, Dub Allbritten, though there weren't that many shows for a while. During one Christmas season, I played a Toys for Tots concert at the Nashville Fairgrounds with Ray Stevens and Chet Atkins. And I went back to Knoxville in the fall of 1966 for a couple of shows on back-to-back nights, one of which was a radio concert at the Civic Coliseum downtown with a whole bunch of stars, including Johnny Cash and June Carter.

There were some interesting shows in 1967. I performed at Disneyland during a country music night that featured Glen Campbell. And there was another show that was kind of a hodgepodge of entertainment genres. I shared the bill with the R & B group The Drifters and with Emmett Kelly, the famous sad-faced circus clown.

Most of the time, I had to work with a house band instead of my own, but those experiences were really good for me. As a young artist, I liked seeing how other people handled situations, good and bad. For instance, if the band was terrible and I hadn't had a chance to rehearse, I was always good at singing a cappella. I would just sing some old mountain song like Mama used to!

I write a lot of those kinds of songs today. In fact, one of the things that I'm most loved for in my career is when I do a song on stage called "Little Sparrow." It's just me singing it a cappella, but it reminds me of some of the old melodies, like "Come All You Fair and Tender Ladies" and "Barbara Allen." If you're a true artist and you're determined to get out there and look and sound good, you can always make a moment into a show.

Little did I know that my touring life was about to go into overdrive overnight.

Star of the Show

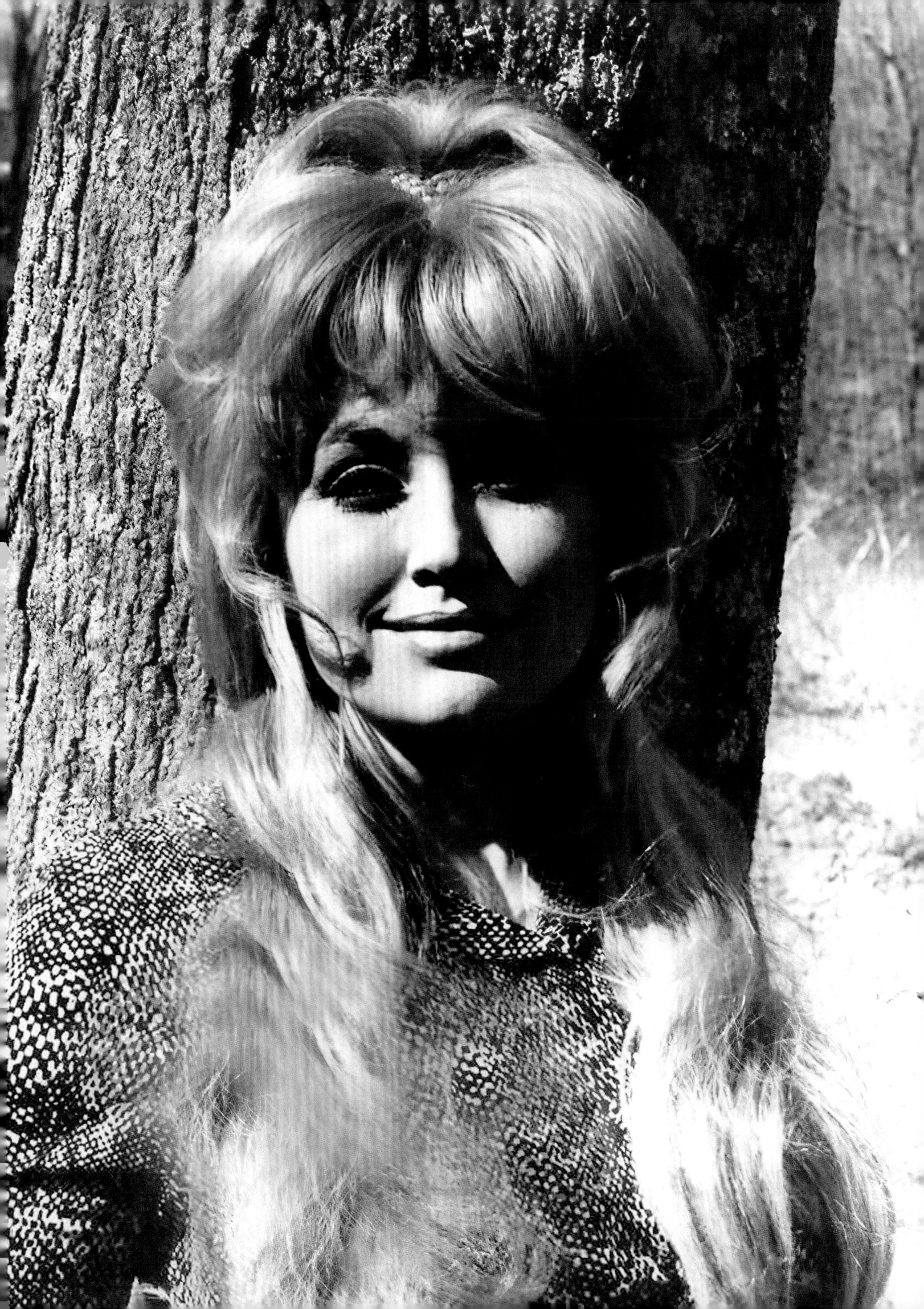

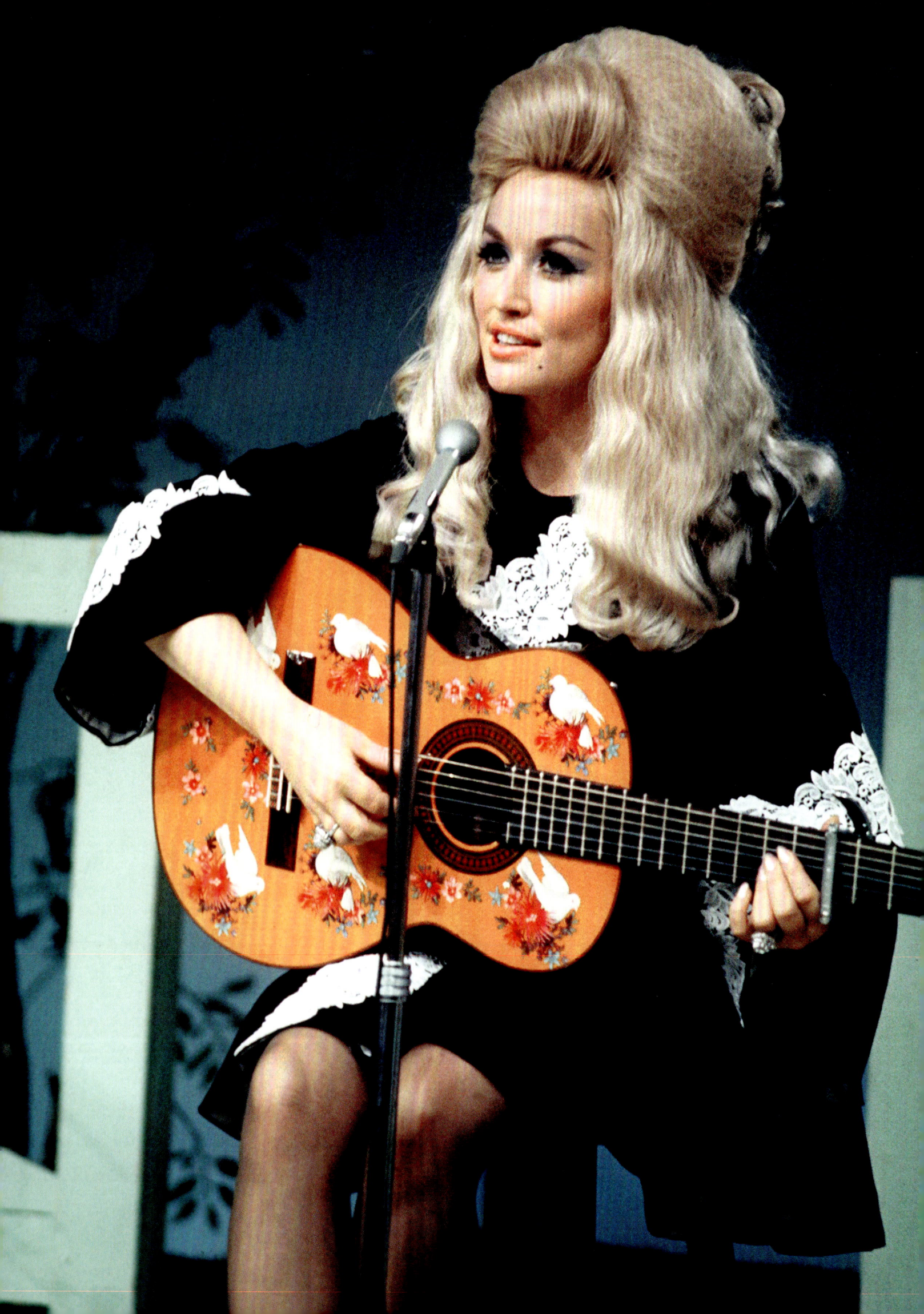

The Porter Years

1967–1974

1967–1974

The odds that any given artist is going to make it upon arriving in Nashville are really slim. Nobody makes it without a little help.

Dolly beat the really slim odds in part because of a really slim artist. Other people took an interest in her before Porter Wagoner did, but no one—aside from Dolly herself—played a bigger role in helping her ascent from a struggling new singer to a rising star. She became a duet partner and key attraction in Porter's concert lineup and on his syndicated TV series, *The Porter Wagoner Show*.

Most of the time, Porter believed in Dolly just as much as she did. But there were also moments when they argued intensely because their visions for her career were so different. Their disagreements increased as Dolly's popularity grew.

Dolly would, no doubt, have made it sooner or later, but the exposure Porter gave her likely speeded up her ascent. Their seven years together went from rosy to rocky, but their union was an important factor in propelling Dolly from an unknown talent to star of the show.

—TOM ROLAND

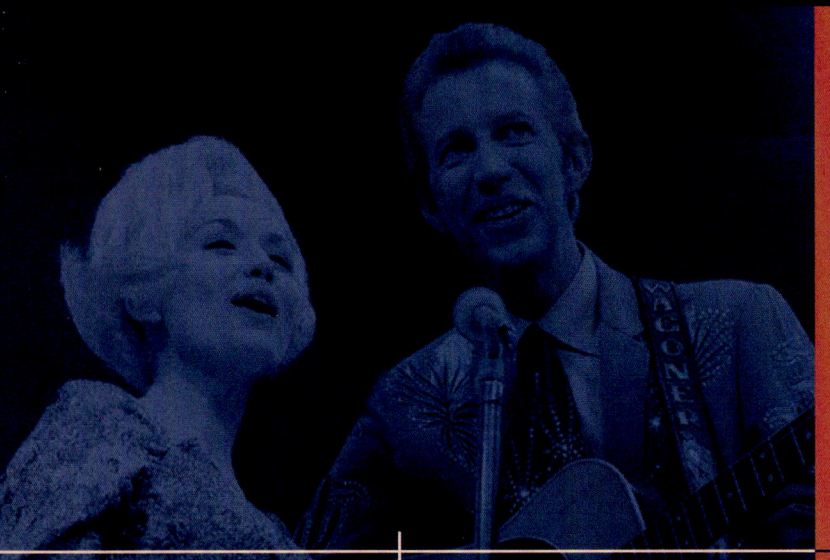

SEPTEMBER 1967
Dolly first appears on *The Porter Wagoner Show*.

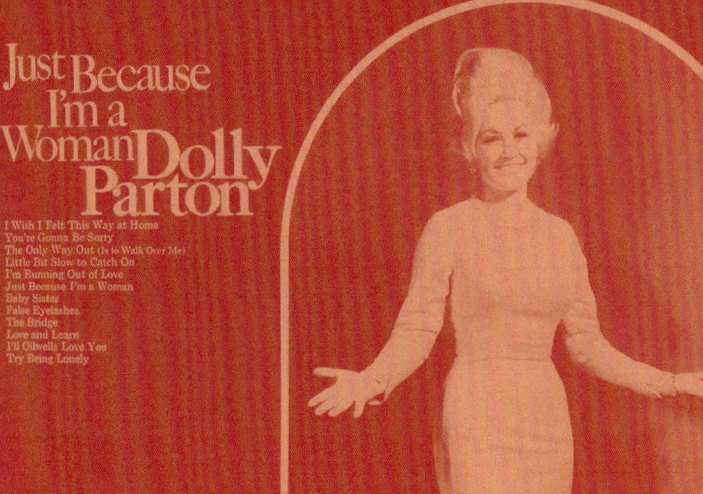

MAY 1968
Dolly's first solo single for RCA, "Just Because I'm a Woman," is released. This is also the title of her first solo album for the label.

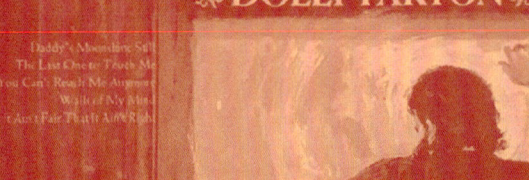

APRIL 1971
Dolly's solo single "Joshua" becomes her first no. 1 hit.

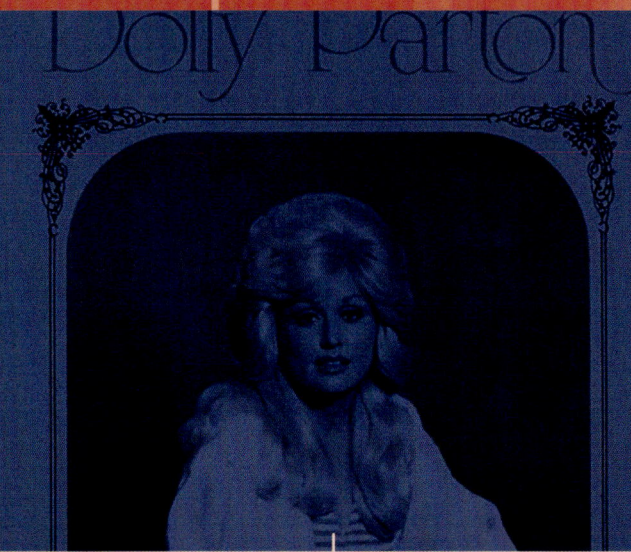

OCTOBER 1973
"Jolene" is released. A few months later, it reaches no. 1 on the country charts and no. 60 on the pop charts.

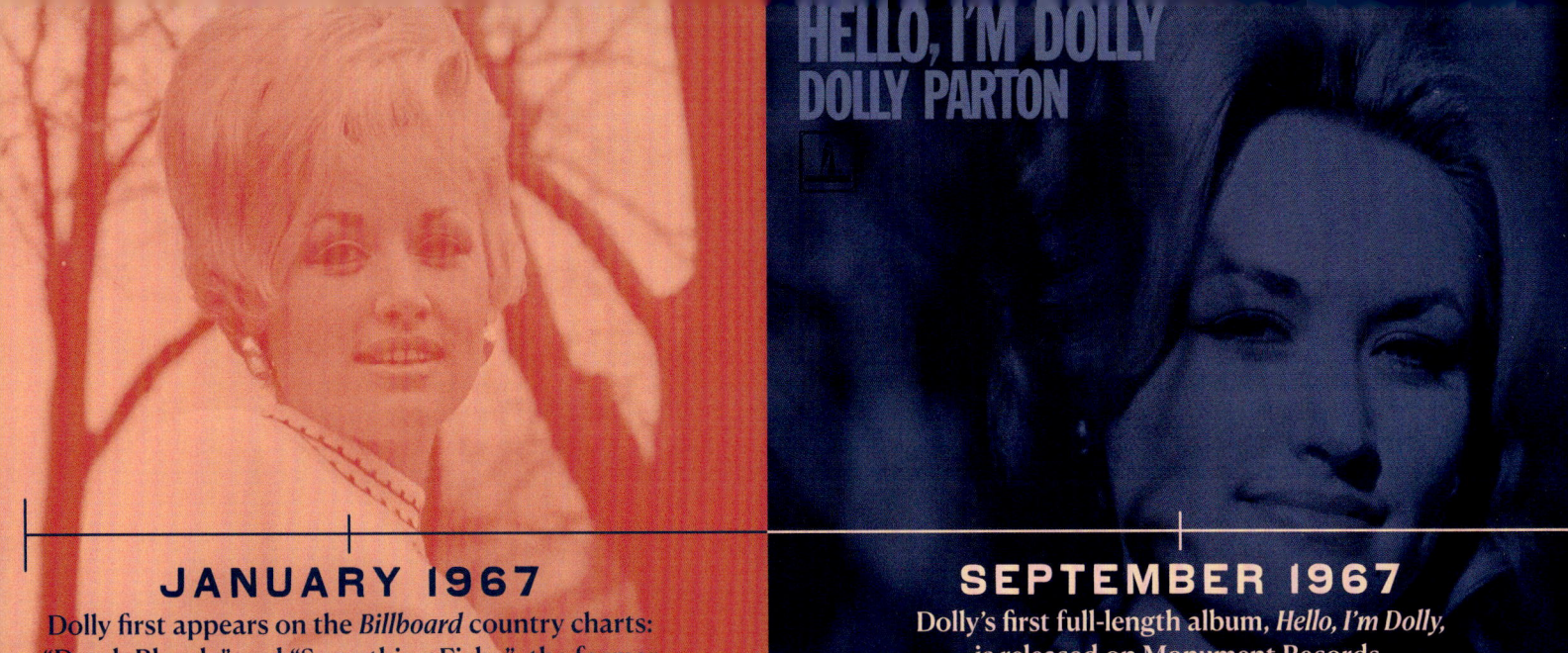

JANUARY 1967
Dolly first appears on the *Billboard* country charts: "Dumb Blonde" and "Something Fishy"; the former peaked at no. 24 and the latter at no. 17 on the Hot Country Songs chart later in the year.

SEPTEMBER 1967
Dolly's first full-length album, *Hello, I'm Dolly*, is released on Monument Records.

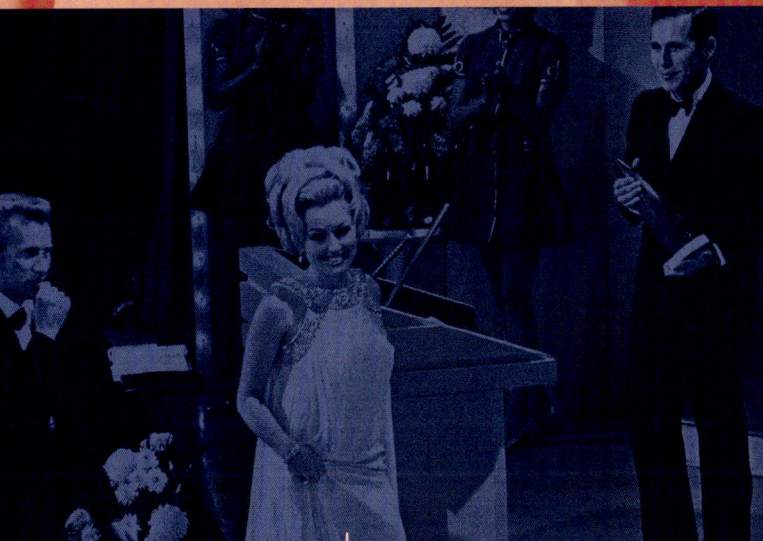

OCTOBER 1968
Dolly and Porter win the Country Music Association award for Vocal Group of the Year, as well as the Music City News award for Duet of the Year.

JANUARY 1969
Dolly is inducted as a member of the Grand Ole Opry.

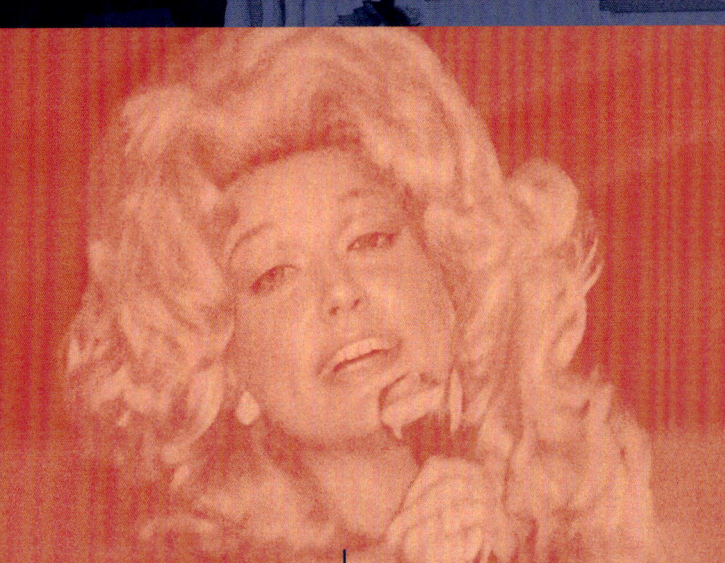

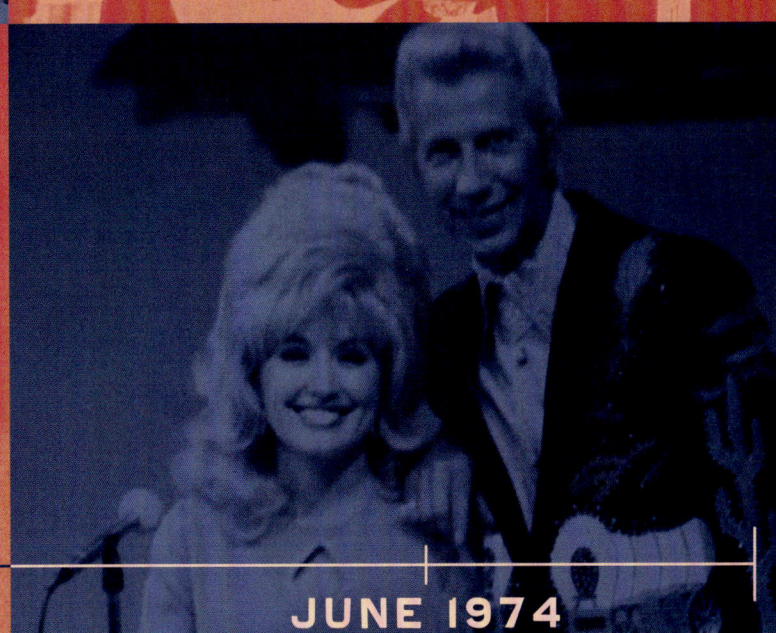

MARCH 1974
Dolly's no. 1 single, "I Will Always Love You," is released. Her next three singles, including "Love Is Like a Butterfly," also reach no. 1 on the country charts.

JUNE 1974
Dolly departs the Porter Wagoner television and road show.

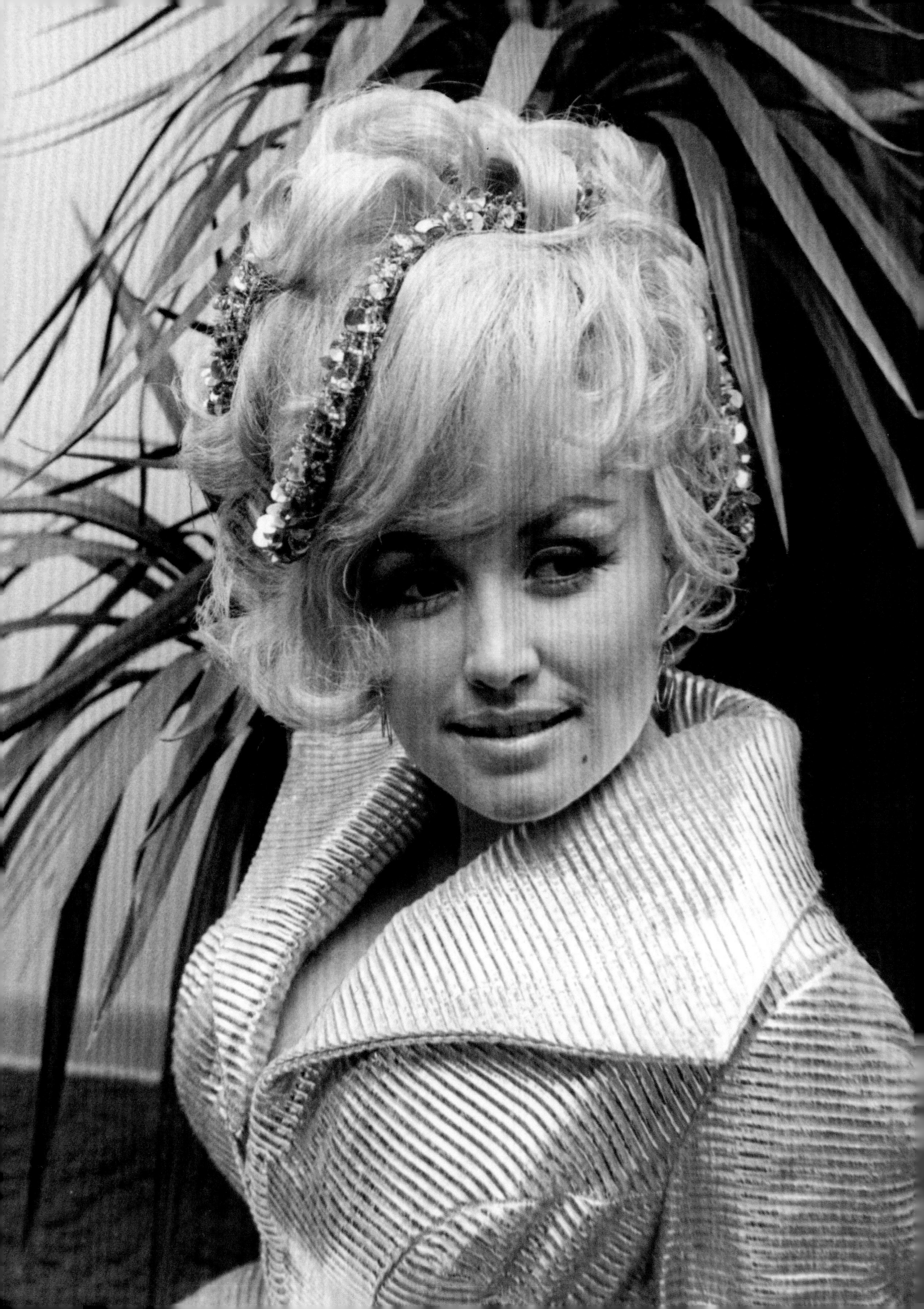

I will always love Porter Wagoner.

Sometimes it wasn't *easy,* but for about seven years, we were the right combination, and I owe him eternally for believing in me. Working as Porter's female duet partner—or "girl singer," as women were referred to in the business then—taught me a lot about showbiz, about how to treat people, about how to connect with fans from the concert stage, and about putting your nose to the grindstone even if you're a household name. To be honest, it also taught me a few things that I did *not* want to do when I got total control of my own career. But my time with Porter gave my solo career a big boost, and I will always appreciate the doors he opened for me as his girl singer.

It wasn't a job I sought out. Heck, I didn't even know it was available. When I first got the call about meeting with Porter, I assumed it was about some songs I had written and sent to Porter and his duet partner, Norma Jean. I thought that they were probably going to record one, and I was very excited about that. I had no idea that Porter was going to ask me to become part of the show.

When I went in to talk to him, I took my guitar and sang my song "Everything's Beautiful (in Its Own Way)." While I played, Porter sat there like a statue, not giving me a clue about what he was thinking. When I finished, he said, "That's a beautiful, beautiful, beautiful song." I said, "Well, have you heard any of the songs I've been sending for you and Norma Jean?" And he said, "Well, Norma Jean's not going to be with us anymore, and that's what I wanted to talk to you about. She's going to be leaving the show, moving back to Oklahoma City, and I was wondering if you would like to be the girl singer on the show." And I said, "Well, I might have to think about that." Then after thinking for about two seconds, I said, "Yes!"

He offered me $60,000 a year—but that was like $1 million to me! And I immediately thought about all the things I could do for me and my family. *That was a lot of money back then.* But the job was going to require a lot of time. Porter and I would end up doing more than one hundred shows a year, and when we returned to Nashville, there'd be plenty of days when I'd need to be on the set for tapings of *The Porter Wagoner Show* or in the recording studio.

Working with one of country music's biggest stars also meant that I'd have more exposure than I'd been getting as a solo act, and it provided another way for me to get my songs recorded. I did end up writing many of our duets, and Porter also recorded solo versions of some of the songs I wrote during our seven years together.

I found out later that he'd auditioned Tammy Wynette before he called me, but he didn't think they were a good fit musically. She ended up becoming one of my best friends in the business and formed her own partnership, both professionally and personally, with George Jones. Looking at the big picture, I think it worked out for everyone.

Of course, Porter had a few conditions. For one, he insisted that I dress conservatively since he had a family show, even if some of the humor was a little bawdy. I was okay with that. Then, after talking about clothing, he asked if I knew Minnie Hems. I thought he was

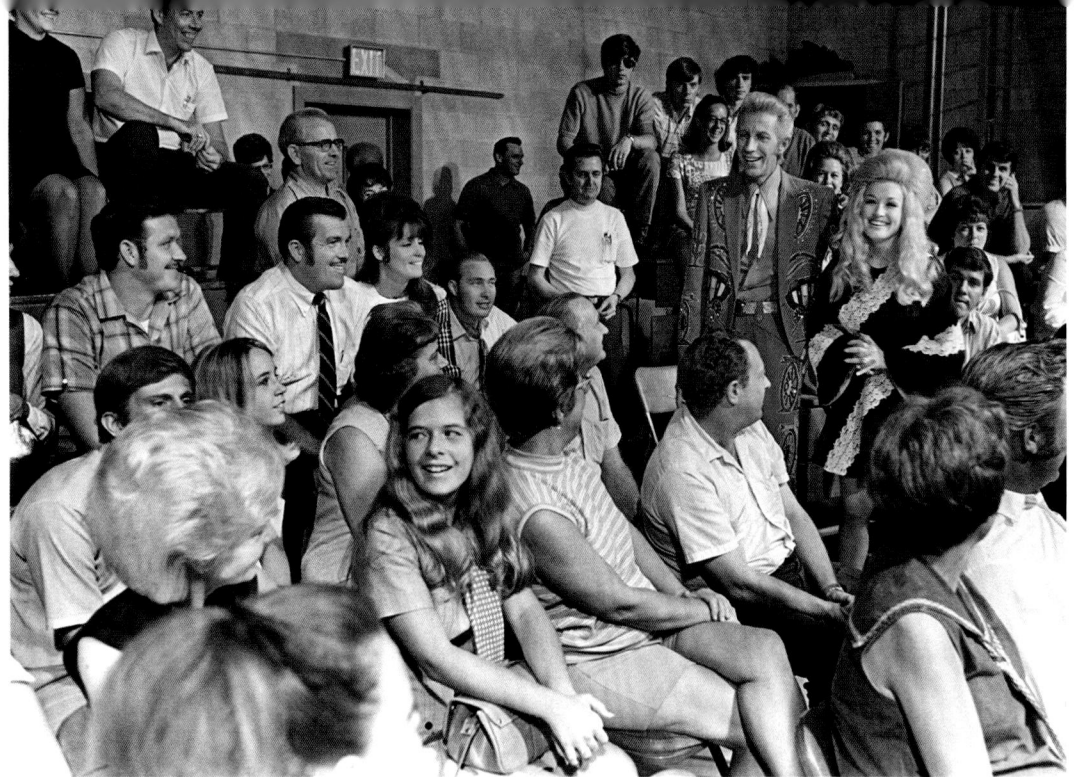

Porter and I often greeted the audience in between segments when we shot *The Porter Wagoner Show* at the WSM-TV studio in Nashville.

talking about a costume designer—I had this image of a lady sewing rhinestones on the Wagonmasters' stage outfits—so I told him no, I didn't know Minnie Hems. He looked at me funny, and I finally figured out that he was asking if I knew *many hymns*! He wanted me to do gospel music in the set! We got a good laugh out of that, especially after I started reeling off titles like "When the Roll Is Called Up Yonder," "Amazing Grace," "Are You Washed in the Blood?," and "Old-Time Religion."

Good thing we got past that little flub because Porter was serious about gospel songs. I ended up doing "How Great Thou Art" as a showstopper on a regular basis.

It was trial by fire when we hit the road, especially because the world was so different in 1967. If a couple of artists formed a duo now, radio stations would make a big deal about it on their morning shows, and it'd be all over social media and the internet. People would know where and when every show would be, and everyone who attended would be posting concert videos so people everywhere could see and hear the spectacle—and comment on it!

Well, when I hit the road with Porter, I found that almost nobody knew I was coming. Newspapers didn't pay a whole lot of attention to country music in those days, so hardly any of them had reported that Norma Jean had left. Some country radio stations might have known about the change, but even if disc jockeys were talking about it, not all the fans caught the news. There weren't any country television networks then either—no CMT or TNN—and there were no music videos. So most fans didn't even know what I looked like yet.

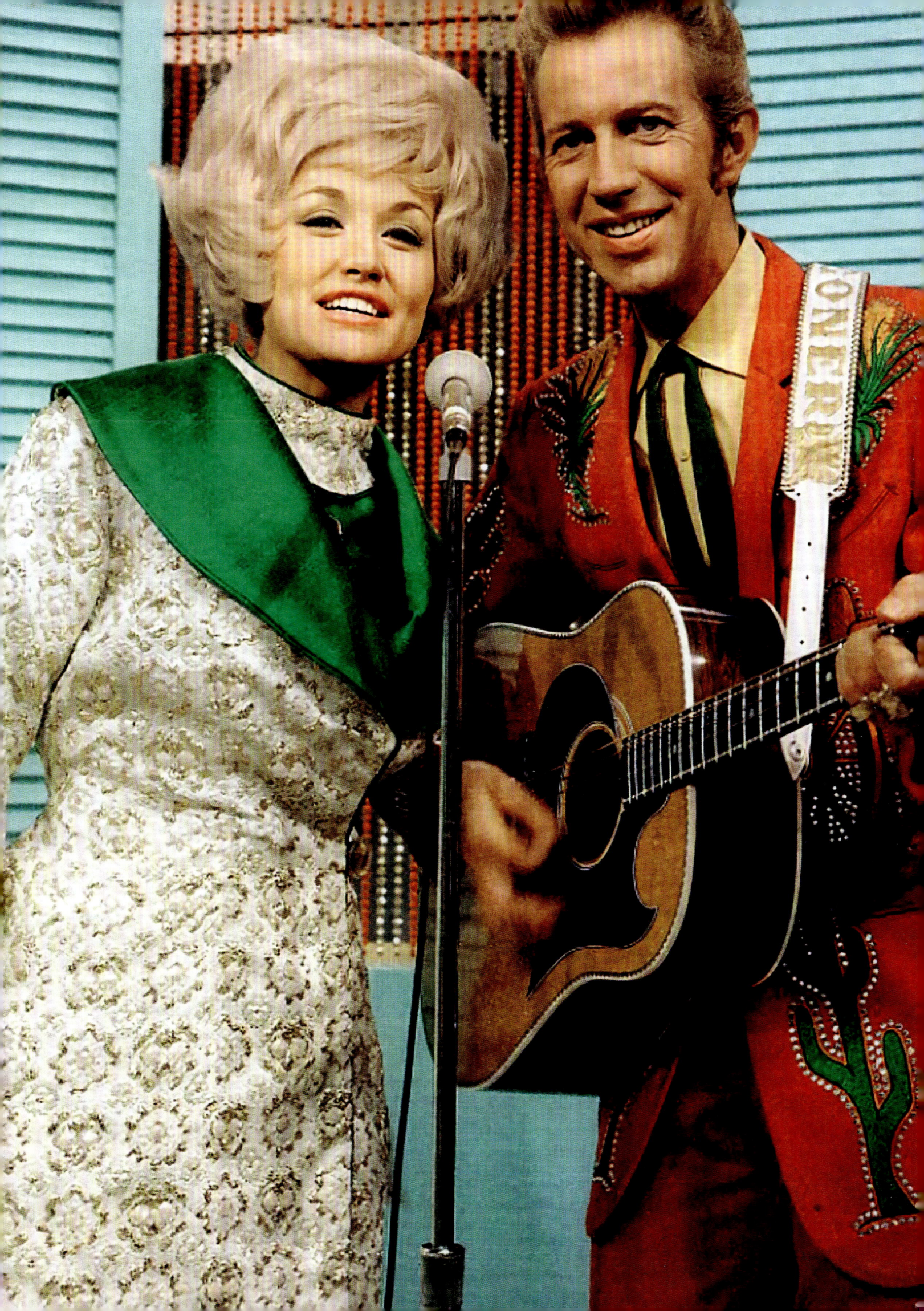

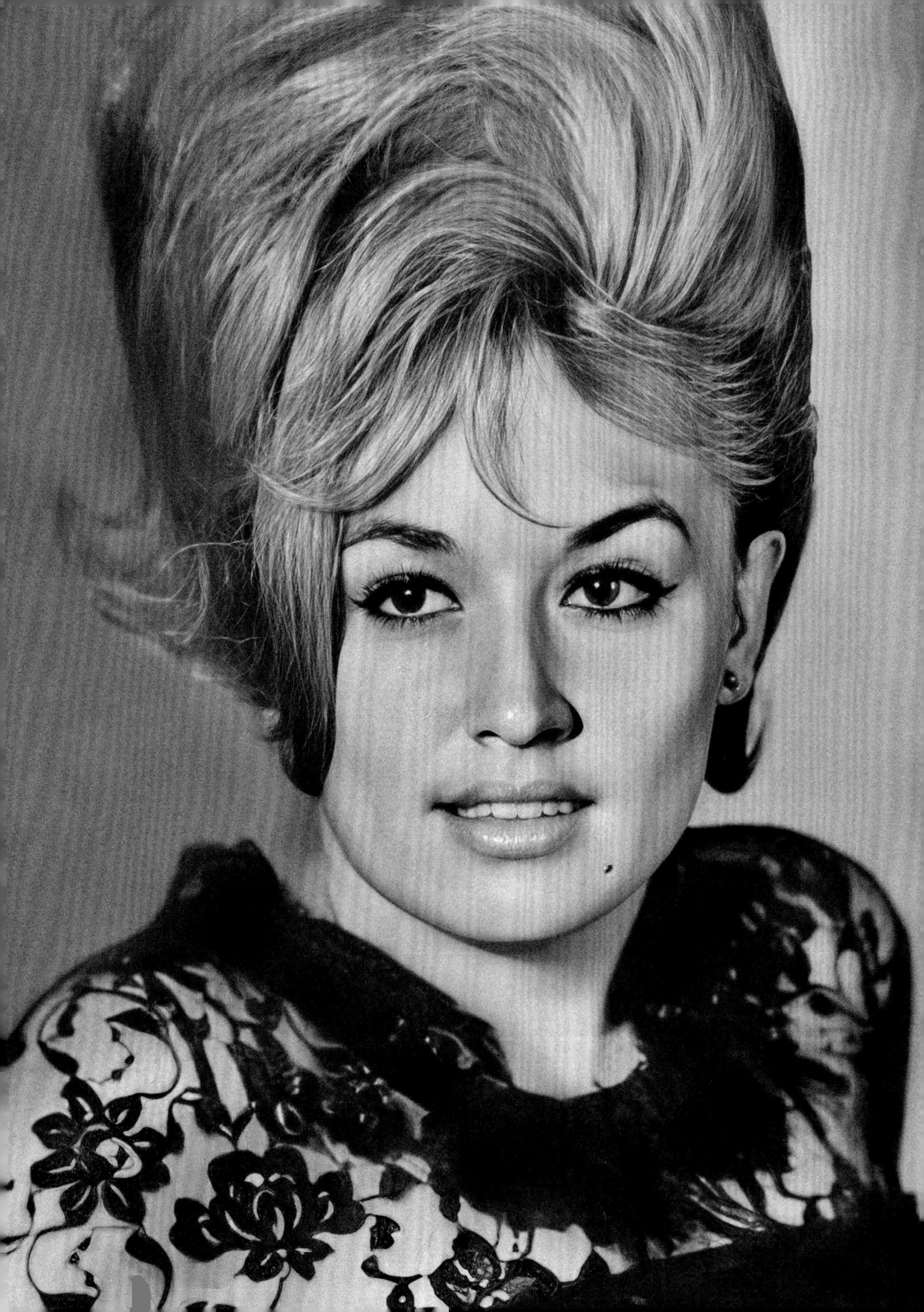

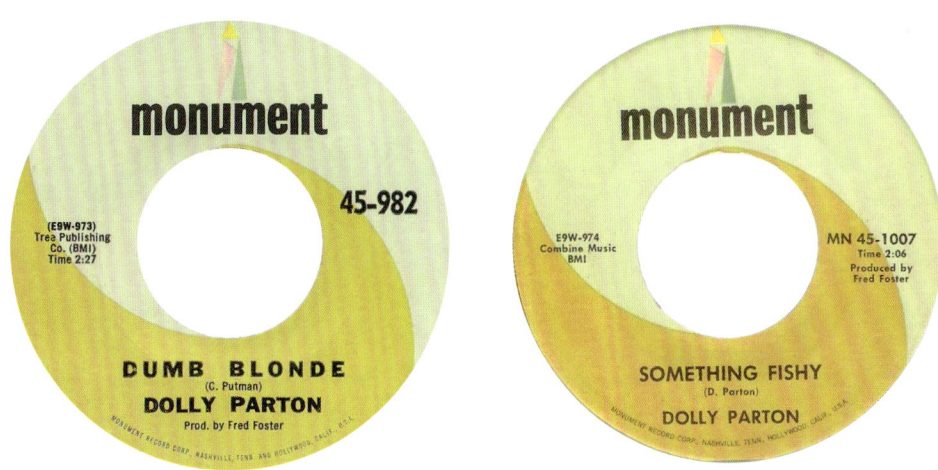

My first two charted singles. "Dumb Blonde" went to no. 24, and "Something Fishy" peaked at no. 17 on the *Billboard* Hot Country Singles chart.

While I was *not* being featured with Porter in visual media, Norma Jean was! She was still singing with him on episodes of *The Porter Wagoner Show,* and *Road to Nashville,* a concert movie that was playing at drive-in theaters, had her singing with the Wagonmasters. Plus, newspaper ads in some of the first cities on the tour still listed Norma Jean as part of the show.

It created one of the most uncomfortable times of my whole career. Norma Jean was a big star, a wonderful gal, and we've stayed friends to this day. I admired and loved her, and it wasn't easy to take the place of somebody I'd been watching for years back home on *The Porter Wagoner Show*.

I'm sure a lot of people thought Porter was pulling a bait and switch on them with this goodbye–Norma Jean thing when I walked out on stage. I might have been singing a Top 20 song with "Something Fishy," but they probably thought there was something fishy with me!

At least that's what the reaction seemed like. The first show was in Virginia, and I expected that I would be a surprise to a lot of fans. Sure enough, I got booed. It was a terrible, terrible feeling. And I thought, *Whoa! Well, this will never do. I'm going to have to do something to get these people to change their minds.*

I understood it, too, because even *I* was disappointed that I was taking Norma Jean's place. I wanted a place of my own in country music. I didn't want to replace Norma Jean. It was a big opportunity, but it wasn't fun. I had an uneasy feeling when audience members yelled, "Where's Norma Jean?"

Not that I stayed down for long. I decided I was going to win these people over, whether they liked it or not! I had to fill about twenty minutes in the show, and I had two songs—"Something Fishy" and "Dumb Blonde"—that had made the Top 40 on the country charts. A lot of people hadn't connected the name Dolly Parton with those songs, but the concerts helped make that possible. Porter always gave his stamp of approval when he talked about

The Porter Years

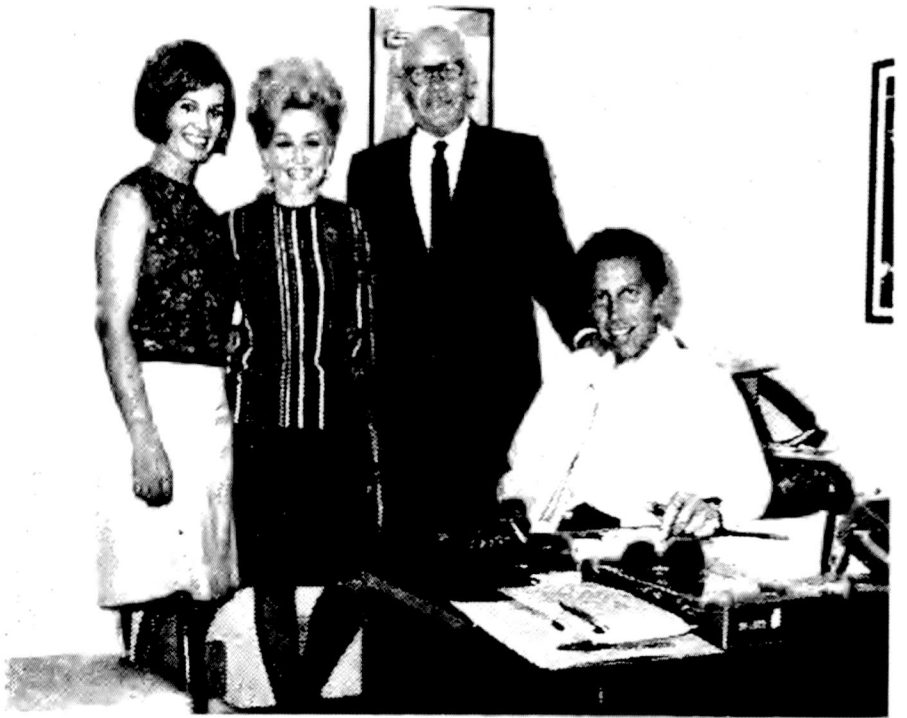

Hello & Goodbye

The Porter Wagoner TV Show in Nashville has a new female star, Dolly Parton (second from left). Dolly replaces Norma Jean (left), who is leaving the show to get married (see Cash Box, Sept. 9, p. 46). Shown here with Dolly and Norma are W. E. Moeller (third from left) of the Moeller Talent Agency, Porter's booking agent, and Porter himself (seated).

Cash Box—September 16, 1967

Norma Jean shocked a lot of people when she left Porter Wagoner's show—including me! Here we are pictured during the official press announcement.

me from the stage, and when the audiences heard us singing together, you could sense the resistance wearing off.

In the meantime, other parts of the new relationship started taking hold. Porter went to the top brass at RCA, Steve Sholes and Chet Atkins, and insisted they buy out my contract with Monument Records and put me on their label, which would allow Porter to release duet albums with me. He also demanded that they give me a solo recording contract, and he promised that he'd pay RCA every dime the label lost if the deal didn't work out. Luckily for me—and for him—it did.

A lot of the decision-makers in Nashville were convinced that women couldn't sell records and that they weren't cut out to headline concerts. Kitty Wells was the only female artist in those early days who had top billing. And yet when *Billboard* ran a story about me replacing Norma Jean, the article right next to that piece had Steve Sholes bragging that RCA had more "good-selling country girl singers" than any other label in town. That included Dottie West, Connie Smith, Skeeter Davis, Norma Jean, Liz Anderson, and Lynn Anderson. Within a few weeks of that story running, they had me too.

Around the same time, Sevierville held the first Dolly Parton Day back home. Porter's producer, Bob Ferguson, officially announced the recording deal on stage. The mayor presented me with a key to the city, and the Gatlinburg Chamber of Commerce gave me a special certificate.

Star of the Show

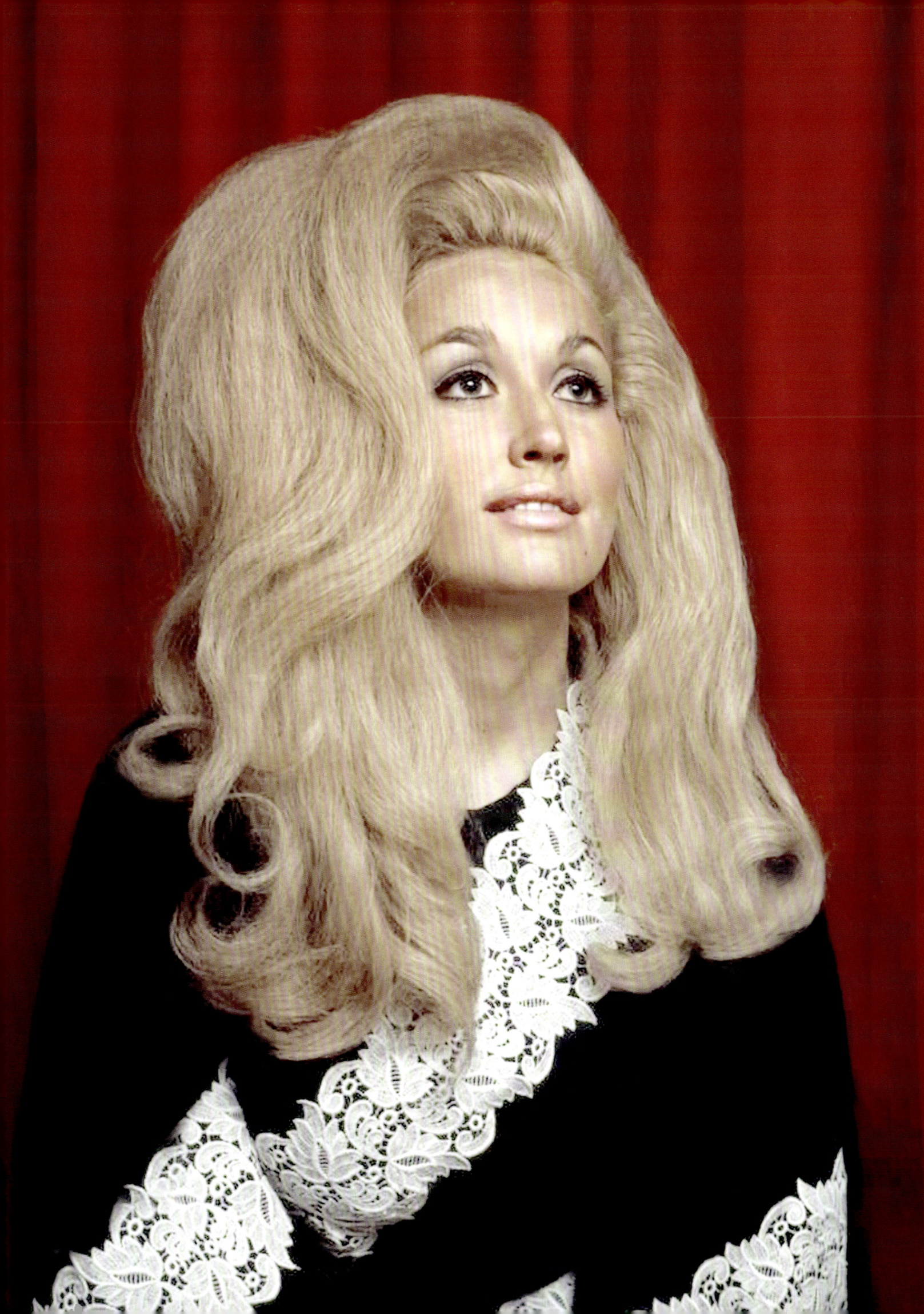

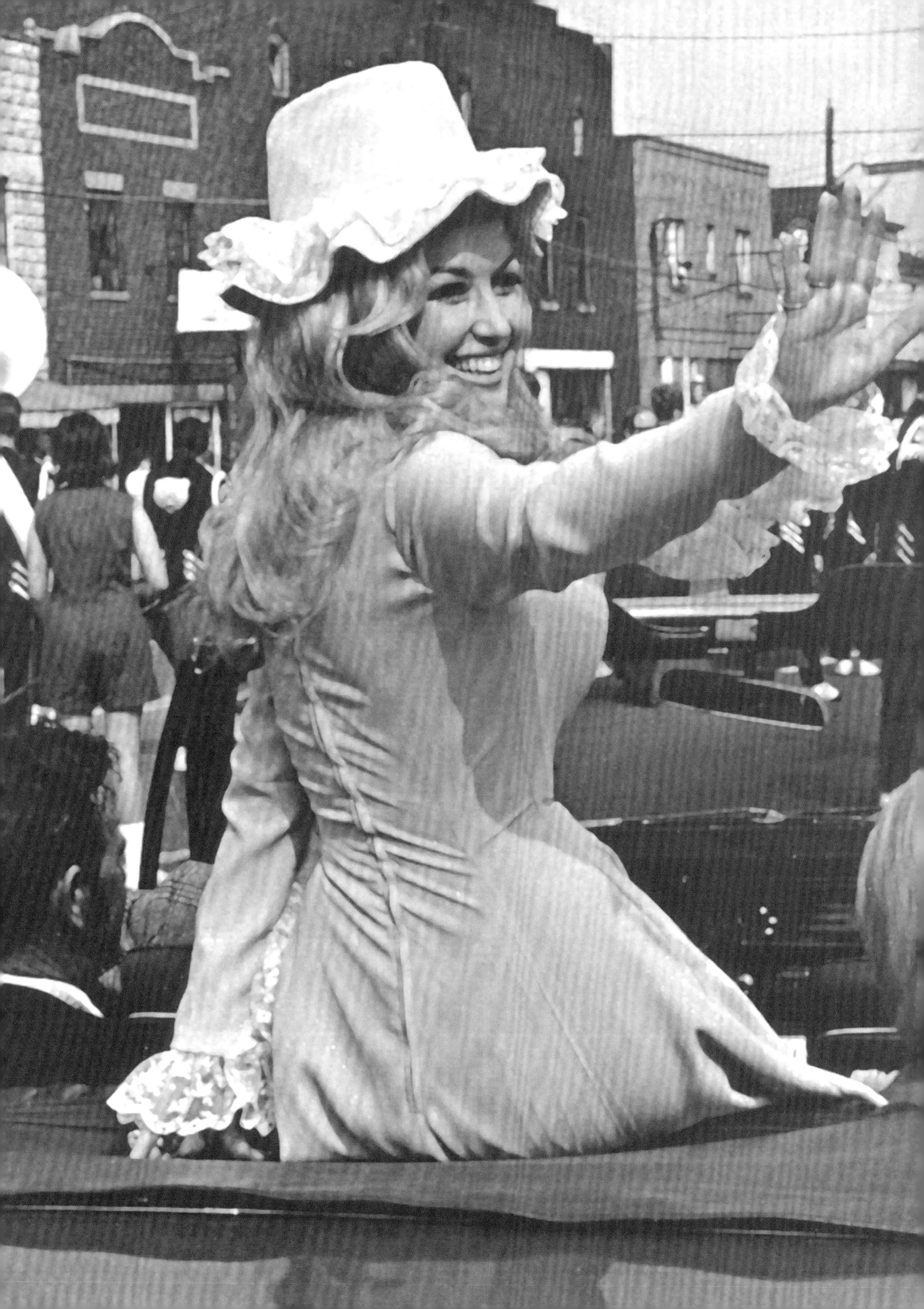

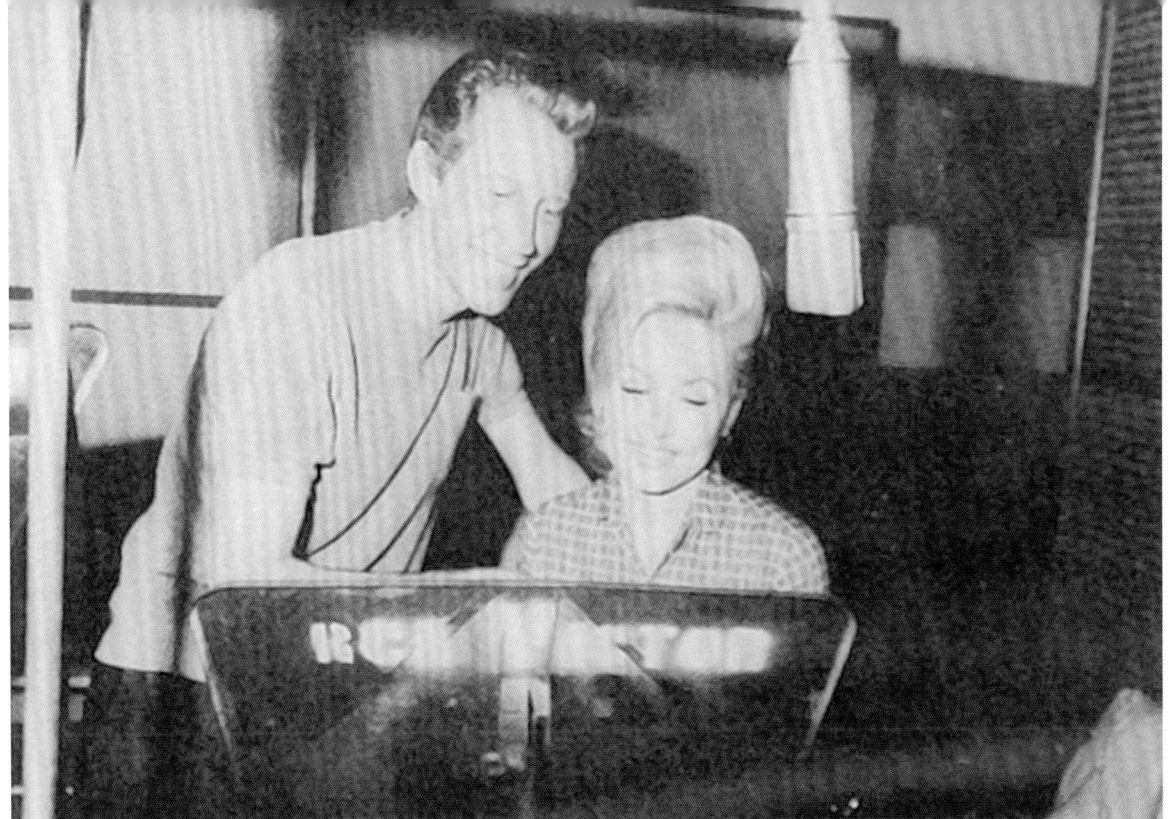

Porter and me reviewing notes and charts during our
first recording session at historic RCA Studio B.

It was a roller coaster of emotions. My parents didn't see me sing in public very often, but they were there that day. So were some of my old classmates, including a few who were part of the group when I had played the drum in the marching band.

Dolly Parton Day became a fairly regular occurrence for several years, and it helped to establish something that became a mission for my career. I always wanted to be helpful and useful and important and to be loved and respected by my people. I also wanted to represent our family name and our people in a great way. I knew there were great needs in the county, such as band uniforms and scholarship funds. It was Uncle Louis who helped me start my very first fund for the Sevier County High School.

We didn't stay in town too long on that first Dolly Parton Day. Porter's bus took the whole Wagonmasters troupe back to Nashville so we could perform that same night on the Grand Ole Opry. It was the first time I'd been on the show since I debuted in 1959.

A few days later, Porter and I had our first duet recording session at RCA Studio B, the same studio where Elvis Presley recorded many of his hits. I was running late, and when I got there, I pulled up to the alley and didn't even head to the parking lot. I just parked my big ol' car outside the back door, and I was so flustered that the front bumper hit the building itself. The gash in the bricks is still there today. The Country Music Hall of Fame and Museum provides tours of the studio, and the guides make a point of telling visitors all about my little fender bender.

The Porter Years

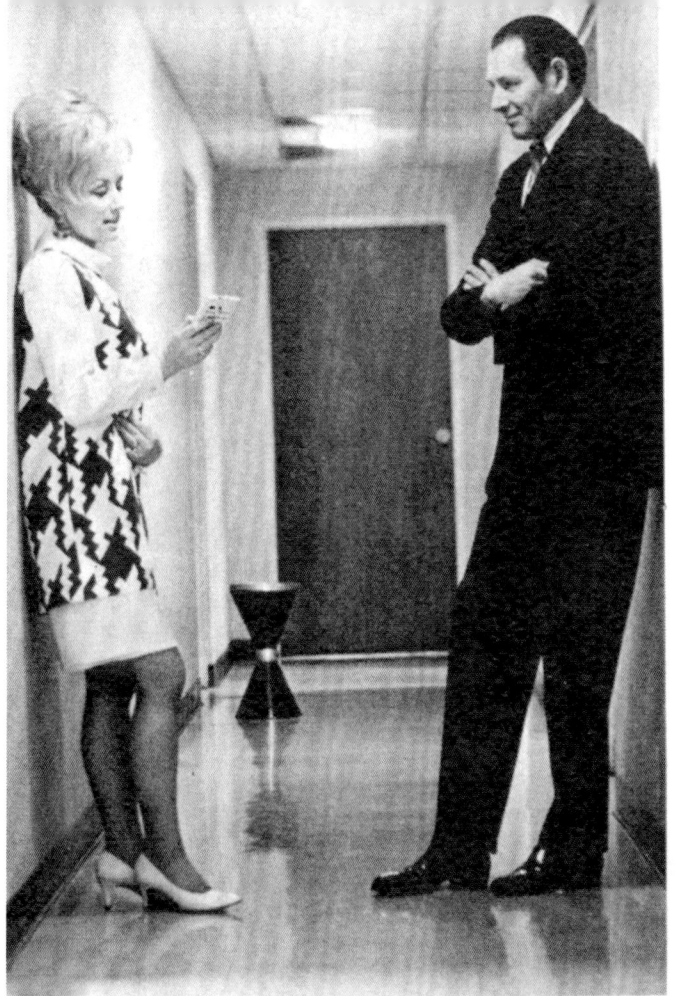

Working in the studio in the 1960s. You were expected to be professional—I knew to show up dressed as nicely as I would for most any office-type role or job.

The day after that first studio booking, Porter and I recorded again, and one of the songs from that session, "The Last Thing on My Mind," became our first duet single. We sang it at the Grand Ole Opry when we performed there for the first time as a duo during Thanksgiving weekend, and it entered the national charts by the end of the year. As more concert dates rolled out, we suddenly had a hit that was *our song* that we could play each night. By the beginning of 1968, the "Where's Norma Jean?" hecklers were long gone.

In the meantime, my first appearance on *The Porter Wagoner Show* ran that fall. The way syndicated shows worked in that era was the program would be recorded in a Nashville TV studio, the distribution company would send several tapes to affiliates, and after the affiliates ran them in their market, they would mail them ahead to another station to air the following weekend. So an episode that was broadcast in one city in October might not run in another city until November or even December.

In that first installment, Porter wore a chartreuse rhinestone suit with shiny sparkles outlining crosses, a cactus, and some other plants. He called me "one of the finest little gals that I've ever met." I sang "Dumb Blonde" in my matching chartreuse dress (but no rhinestones!), and at the end of the show, I started singing again, only to have Porter come over and cut

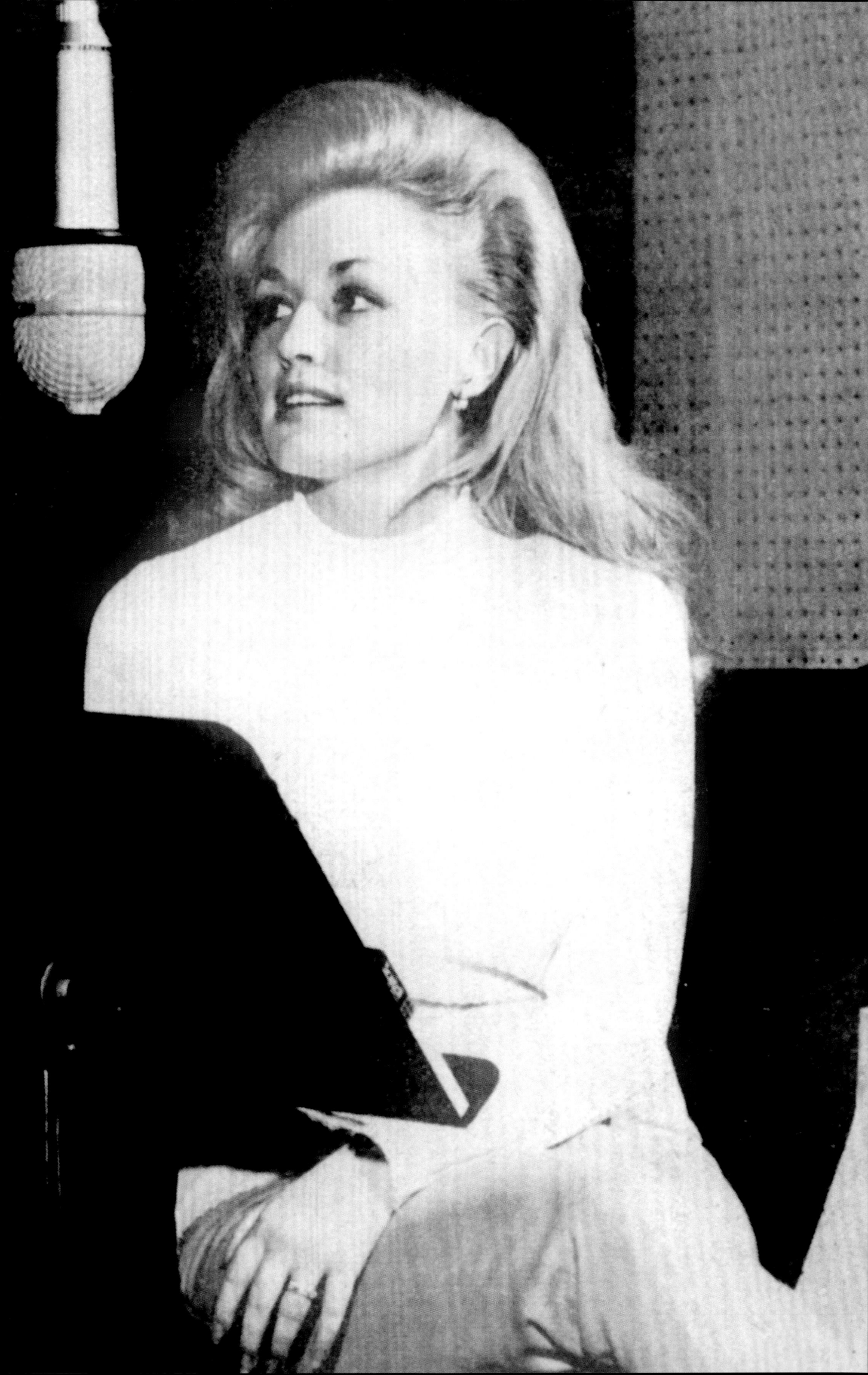

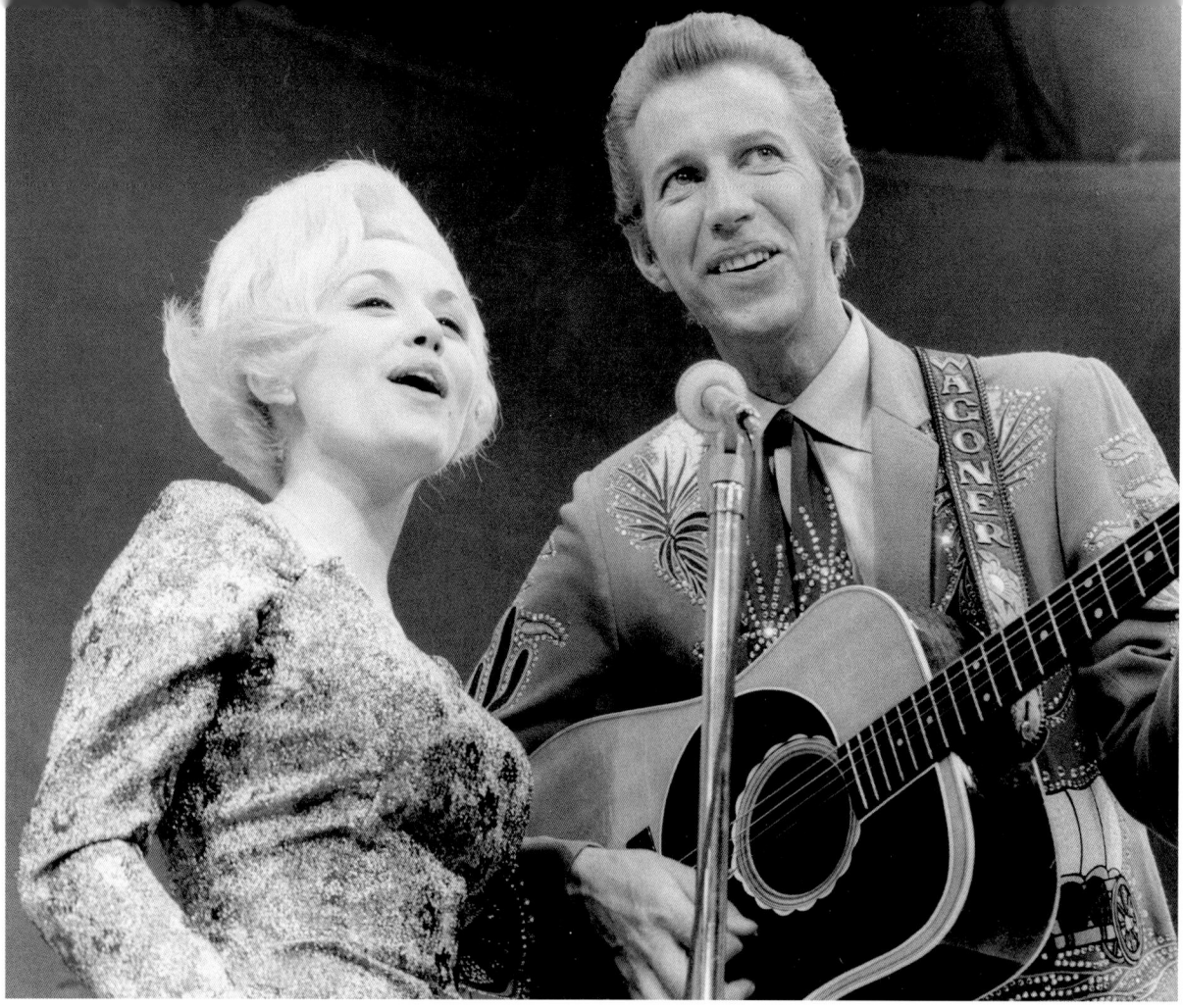

Porter went to bat for me when I became his duet partner, and we became quite the team on stage.

me off. And that's the way it went out to the affiliates. It looked like he was hogging the microphone, but the truth is, those old shows were not well organized. Each show ran thirty minutes, which meant you had a time limit. But there were no clocks in the studio. Sometimes you'd think you were going to get another song in, and you'd have to say good night in the middle of it. So Porter was not being rude when he took over the microphone in the middle of my song. That would not happen today because TV shows and specials are much better planned and laid out.

When we hit the road, Porter's show, like many country concerts in that era, operated a lot like a miniature version of the Grand Ole Opry, using the same sort of variety concept that had fueled vaudeville at the time the Opry first went on the air. The music was punctuated with bits of comedy, and Porter was one of the best at delivering those lines. The band was often the butt of his jokes, particularly bass player Speck Rhodes, whose stage getup included gaudy plaid suits and blacked-out front teeth. Porter sometimes introduced Speck as "what they throwed off the Tallahatchie Bridge," goofing on the Bobbie Gentry song "Ode to Billie Joe." But Porter made fun of himself too. Sometimes he told the audience he hadn't gotten much sleep in the hotel because the maid kept knocking. "Finally, about noon," he'd say with perfect timing, "I got up and let her out!"

Star of the Show

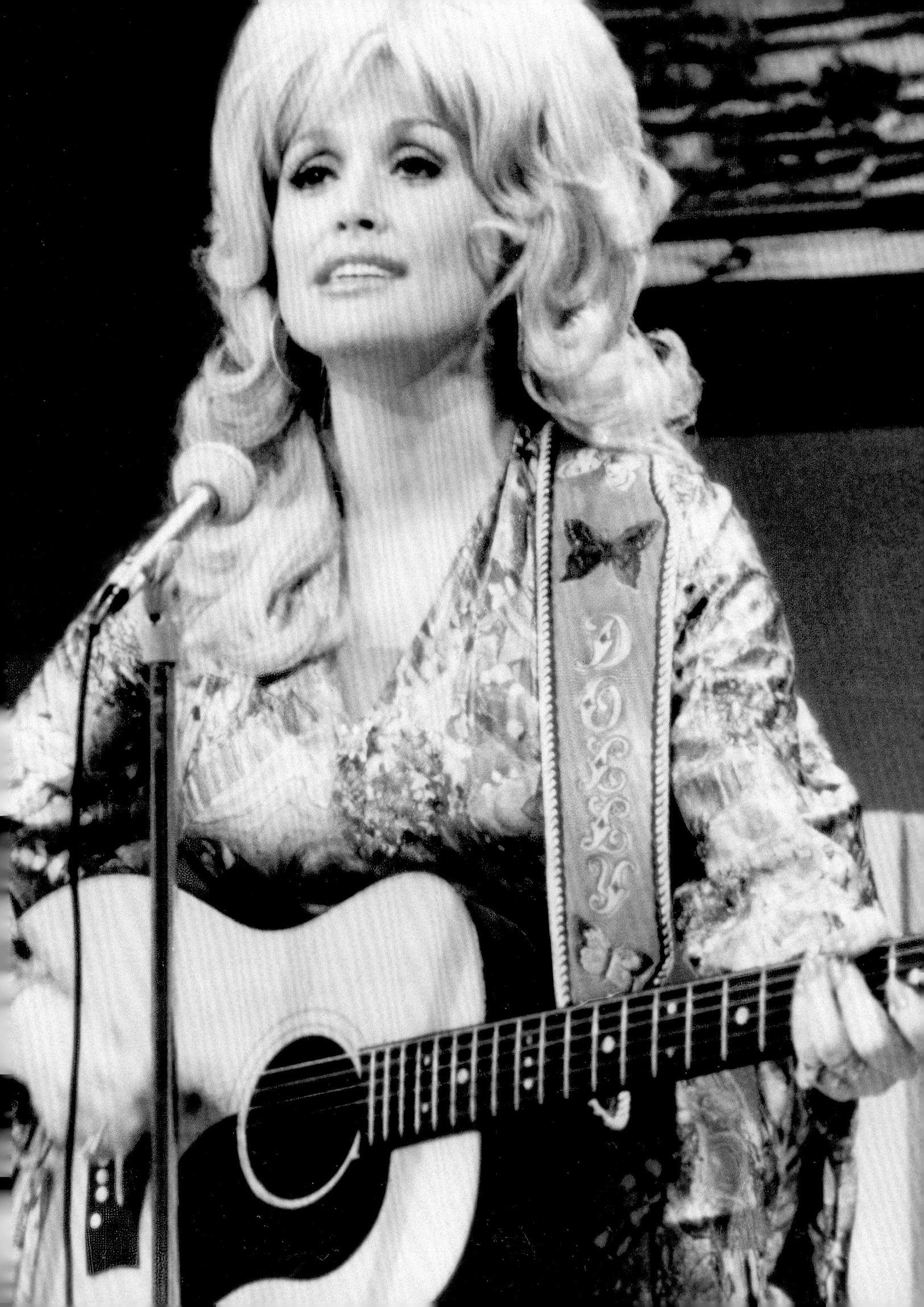

Spotlight

THE GRAND OLE OPRY

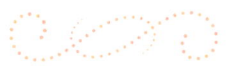

When I was growing up, I wanted to be a star more than anything else. As part of that, I also wanted to be part of the Grand Ole Opry.

We had an old battery radio, so it was special when we got a chance to hear even part of a broadcast. Hank Williams, Eddy Arnold, Red Foley, Bill Monroe—I heard them all on the Opry and tried to imagine what the Ryman Auditorium, where they performed, was like. *Grand* was the right word for how it played out in my imagination!

I had been with Porter's show for a little over a year when I became a member, but joining the Opry wasn't about Porter or my connection to him. This was about me and the Grand Ole Opry. I was proud to be there, especially knowing how much my daddy loved the Grand Ole Opry. He loved Roy Acuff and Kitty Wells and Ernest Tubb and Hank Snow—all those talented people.

The Opry started as a live WSM-AM show in 1925, and the Ryman Auditorium hosted the show beginning in the 1940s. When the show moved to the new Grand Ole Opry House in 1974, workers marked and cut a circle of wood from the spot on the Ryman stage where the lead singer's microphone stand was usually located and moved it to the new Opry House stage. That way, every time someone steps up to the microphone in the new venue, they're still standing on the same planks of wood where Johnny Cash, Patsy Cline, Marty Robbins, Loretta Lynn, Lefty Frizzell, the Carter Family, and Elvis Presley sang their hits. That's always been special for me.

I couldn't be at the Ryman the last night the Opry was held there. Porter and I were booked in Fresno, California. But the next day, we were back in Nashville for the first night at the new Opry House. I wore a green jumpsuit, and at the end of the first show, I stepped onto that special circle of wood and sang "Jolene," then Porter and I wrapped with "The Right Combination."

There've been lots of memorable shows at the Opry House since then. And when I celebrated fifty years as an Opry member, NBC shot a whole special there with a bunch of my friends—Emmylou Harris, Hank Williams Jr., Lady A, Toby Keith, and Dierks Bentley, to name just a few—all performed some of my songs.

Being a member of the Grand Ole Opry will always be one of the biggest honors of my career. It really has meant a great deal to me.

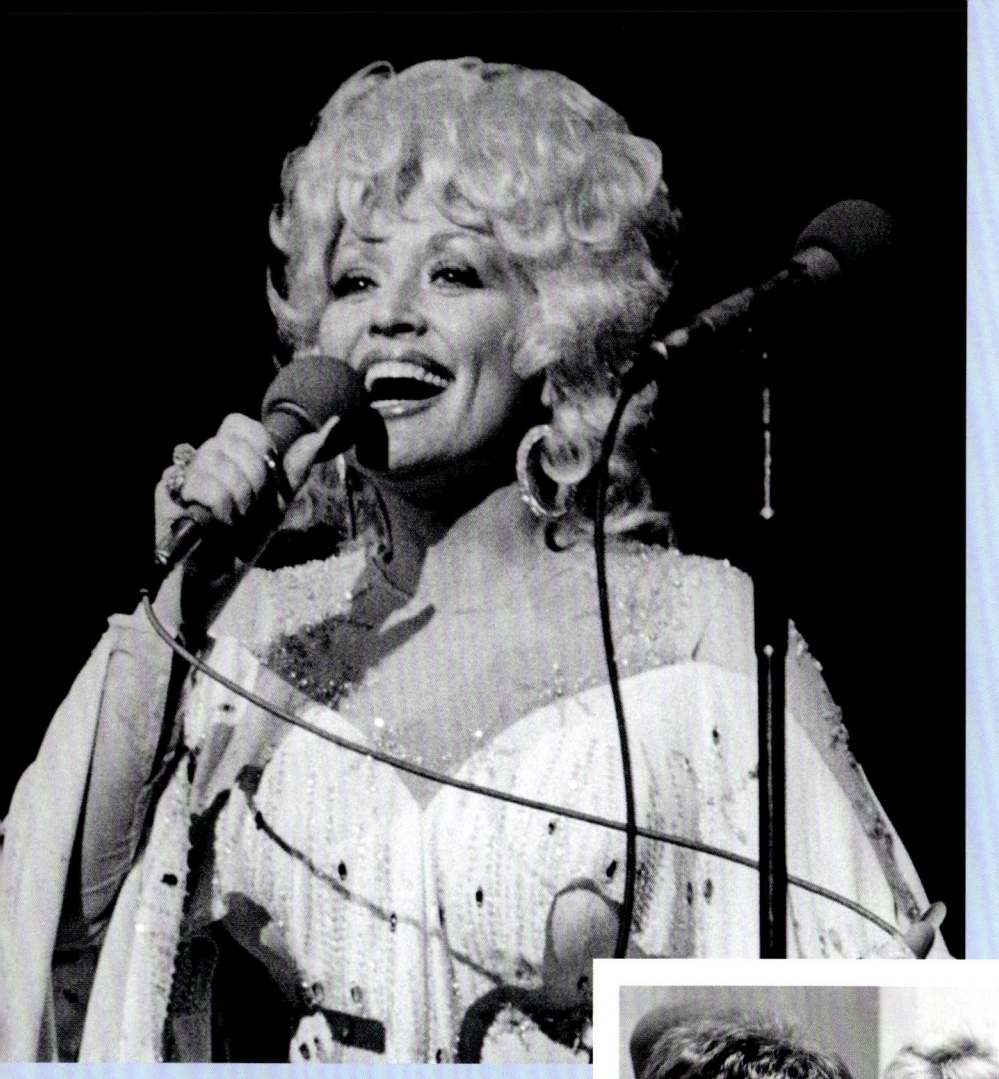

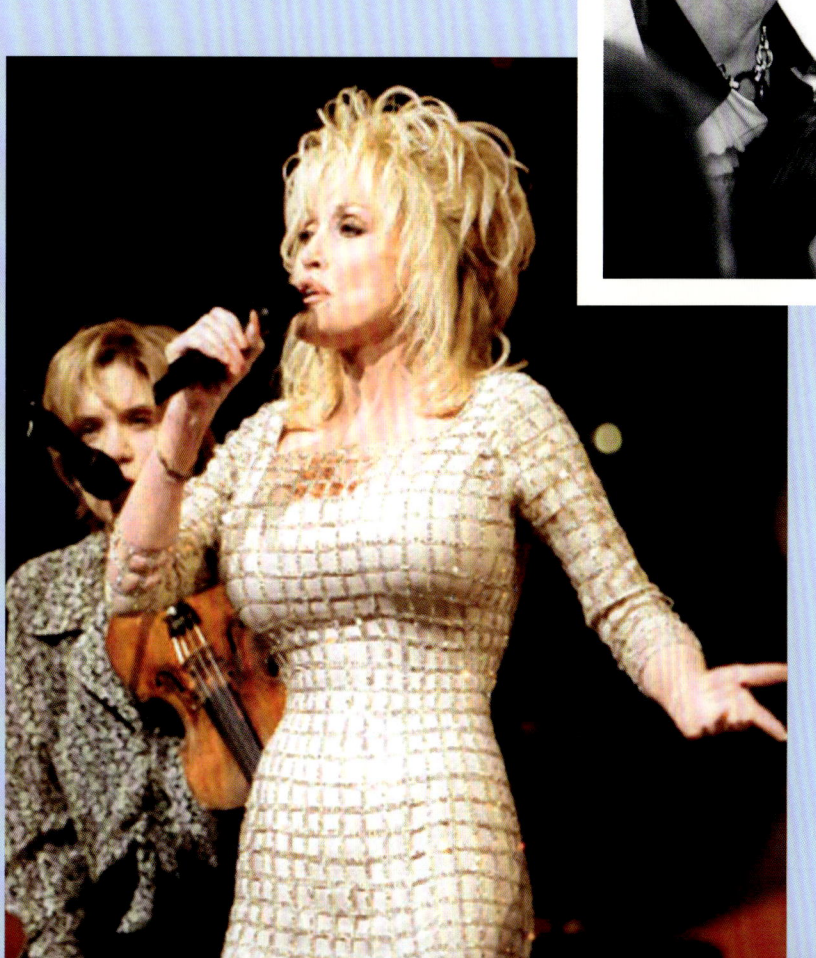

WSM Radio, the Grand Ole Opry, the Opryland Theme Park, and even the Opryland Hotel (now the Gaylord Opryland Resort) have provided me with more opportunities than I can count to share my music with people. Paul and Linda McCartney's family met Porter and me at Opryland after our last show together. Alison Krauss played fiddle for me during a show at the Grand Ole Opry House.

OPRY QUESTIONAIRE

Please fill out and return to WSM in the enclosed self-addressed, stamped envelope. Thank you.

STAGE NAME: Dolly Parton
REAL NAME: Dolly Parton (Dean) (Married Name)
PRESENT ADDRESS: 814 Reeves Rd.
PHONE NUMBER: 833-0470
PLACE OF BIRTH: Sevier Co. Tenn.
DATE OF BIRTH: 1-19-46
BROTHERS & SISTERS: 6 bro. 5 Sisters
WHERE EDUCATED: Sevier Co. High School and different elementary Schools in Sevier Co.
HOBBIES AS A CHILD: Writing Songs - playing piano and guitar
RELATIVES IN SHOW BUSINESS: Bill Owens
FATHER'S NAME AND OCCUPATION: Robert Lee Parton - Construction Worker
MOTHER'S NAME AND OCCUPATION: Avie Lee Parton - Housewife & (Mother)!!
WHAT DID YOU WANT TO BE WHEN YOU GREW UP? A singer and writer and a Member of the Opry
WHAT INCIDENT, IF ANY, STARTED YOU IN MUSIC? A Musical background in family
FIRST JOB IN MUSIC: Cas Walker Show in Knoxville
FIRST JOB IN RADIO: Cas Walker show in Knoxville
TO WHOM OR WHAT DO YOU OWE MUCH OF YOUR SUCCESS: Bill Owens (uncle)
ESTIMATED MILES YOU TRAVEL PER YEAR: app. 100,000 miles
YOUR BIGGEST SELLING RECORD: Just Because I'm a Woman (Jeannies Afraid of the da..)
YOUR SECOND BIGGEST SELLING RECORD: Put it Off until Tomorrow
LARGEST AUDIENCE TO WHICH YOU HAVE PLAYED: 50,000
DATE YOU JOINED THE OPRY: 1-4-69
WIFE (OR HUSBAND'S) NAME: Carl T. Dean
WHEN MARRIED: 5-30-66
WHERE: Ringold Ga.
CHILDREN'S NAMES AND BIRTHDATES: none

WHAT INSTRUMENTS DO YOU PLAY? Guitar, Piano
HOW DID YOU LEARN TO PLAY? From uncle Bill Owens
WHAT DO YOU DO ON YOUR FREE DAYS? Work!! in pub. Co - fish - Golf & write
AWARDS AND HONORS YOU'VE RECEIVED: CMA award with Porter Wagoner best duet - BMI award on Put it Off until tomorrow - Most Promising Singer from several places -
HAVE YOU SERVED IN THE MILITARY? IF SO, WHAT BRANCH, WHERE AND WHEN? No

HOW DO YOU TRAVEL? With the Porter Wagoner Show on a custom built bus
SONGS YOU'VE WRITTEN: App. 300 songs with not enough room to write titles
TV SHOWS ON WHICH YOU HAVE APPEARED: Johnny Carson - Kraft Music Hall - Bill Anderson - Wilburn Bro - Porter Wagoner show as a regular
RADIO SHOWS ON WHICH YOU HAVE APPEARED: (Ralph Emery) and hundreds of other small radio shows Nothing important except Ralph Emery
OVERSEAS APPEARANCES: None

YOUR RECORD LABEL: RCA
YOUR BOOKING AGENT: Top Billing
MOVIE APPEARANCES: none

HEIGHT: 5'1"
COLOR OF EYES: Green
COLOR OF HAIR: Blonde
ANYTHING YOU'D LIKE TO ADD:

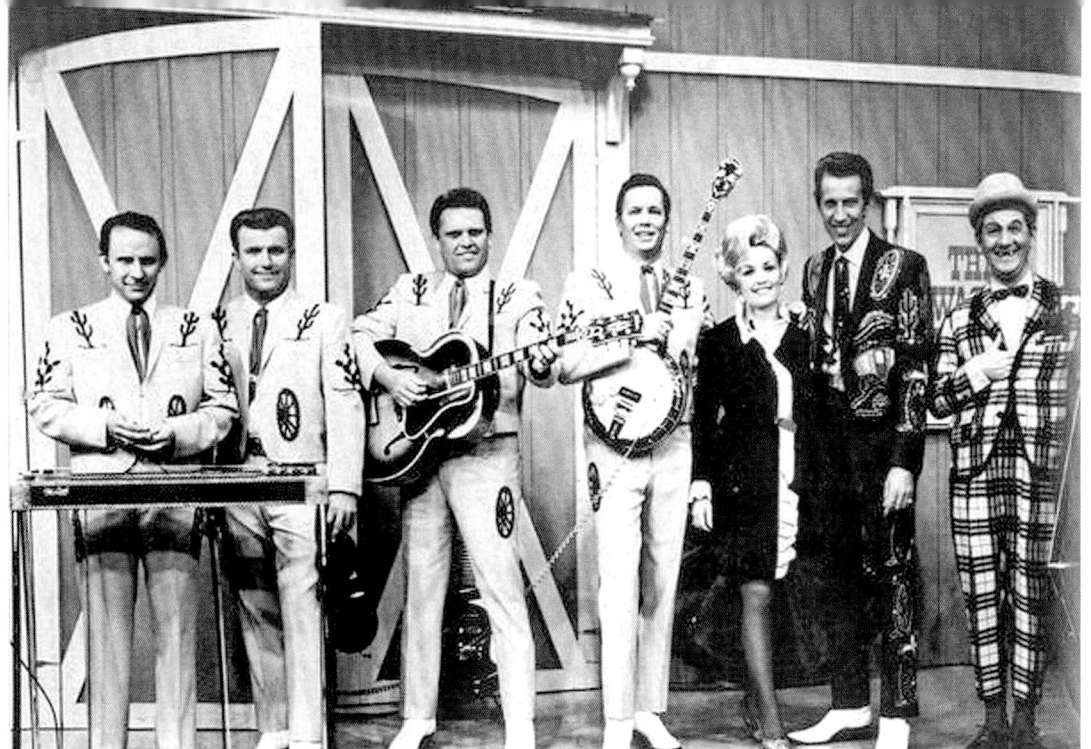

With The Wagonmasters during a break in the action. *From left:* Don Warden, Mack Magaha, George McCormick, Buck Trent, me, Porter, and Speck Rhodes.

Like the Opry, the road shows often had big lineups of artists. When we played Austin that first year, Porter and I shared the stage with David Houston, Tammy Wynette, Don Gibson, and Charley Pride. In San Antonio, we wrapped the show after Jimmy C. Newman, Tom T. Hall, Hank Thompson and the Brazos Valley Boys, Bobby Bare, and Dave Dudley. In Greensboro, North Carolina, we played alongside Ferlin Husky, Jack Greene, Jeannie Seely, and Billy "Crash" Craddock. There were so many of us on some of the shows that the promoters had trouble keeping all the artists straight. In the first ads for that Greensboro concert, they reversed the names under the photos of me and Jeannie.

Touring was like a jumbled family road show back then because the lineups kept changing daily. The artists you saw on Friday in Roanoke might be completely different from the lineup the next night in Philadelphia. The artists and the bands all knew one another, and since the bills were different in every city, you got to know just about every other artist and touring musician in the course of just a year or two. That first year, we met up with Johnny Cash, Sonny James, Waylon Jennings, Bill Monroe, Ray Price, Bill Anderson, Conway Twitty, Lefty Frizzell, Hank Williams Jr., Mother Maybelle and the Carter Family, Ernest Tubb, and a bunch more. A lot of times, we'd see them again a week or two later at the Opry.

Instead of having a driver, the Wagonmasters took turns driving the bus. Thinking back now, that was kind of dangerous, since it was difficult sometimes to get sleep on the road. But some of them were very reliable, particularly Don Warden, who played steel guitar with the band. He was also Porter's manager. Don would go backstage after the show and collect the money for Porter's show, so he was the money man. He was small in stature, but very smart. He was a big man when it came to his intelligence, his heart, and his knowledge of the business.

The Porter Years

That first year, the touring felt overwhelming. We were sharing holidays with fans, seeing significant places, and feeling like we were on the cusp of history-making events. We spent New Year's Eve in Shreveport, received honorary citizenship honors in Louisiana, saw the New York skyline from across the Hudson River when we did a concert in Jersey City, played the world-famous Shrine Auditorium in Los Angeles, and attended Nashville's Grammy Awards. At a horse track we played in Pensacola, Florida, Hank Locklin, whose big hit was "Please Help Me, I'm Falling," fell off a pony when he went for a ride in the afternoon. He broke his arm and had to perform that night without his guitar.

Porter had learned from all the other great artists he'd worked with early in his career—people like Red Sovine and many others who had come before him. I'd always done the same thing, and I still do—there's lots to be learned from people who've gone before you. I picked up a whole lot from Porter about performing on stage. I learned how to talk to an audience. I learned how to play against the other artists on the stage and how to play to the musicians—and how to have fun with that without it being distracting.

I learned a little about what not to do, too, in the same way that I learned that kind of thing from Cas Walker's show. But there was a lot that I learned from Porter that I appreciate to this day, and every now and then I'll do something on stage and think, *Well, that's just like Porter would do.*

As stimulating as that first year was, the road started to become a bit of a blur. The shows were great and the fans were enthusiastic, but every venue was different, and you often relied on one or two key people for assistance once you got there. The next day, you went on to a new cast of characters and another concert hall with a layout that was completely different from the day before. It could be confusing, and the hours were unpredictable—sometimes you got to town in the morning, sometimes you arrived in the afternoon. And if you spent a night in a hotel, you would occasionally need to check the phone book in the drawer of the nightstand the next morning to see what city you were in.

I had my own bedroom on Porter's expensive tour bus. Don Warden made sure I had a place to be alone, away from those hairy-legged Wagonmasters. And I made use of all the downtime by writing songs on napkins, hotel stationery—just about any scrap of paper I could get my hands on. I often wrote sitting on the bed in that little room.

In the fall of 1968, Porter and I both received our first nominations from the Country Music Association (CMA), and we ended up winning Vocal Group of the Year. In fact, we won CMA trophies as a duo in three of the next four years.

I was also a finalist in 1968 for Female Vocalist of the Year. I didn't win, but it was kind of a preview of what was to come. Porter was very proud that I received that nomination. He was genuinely happy for me, and it confirmed that he'd made a good choice for the "girl singer" in his show.

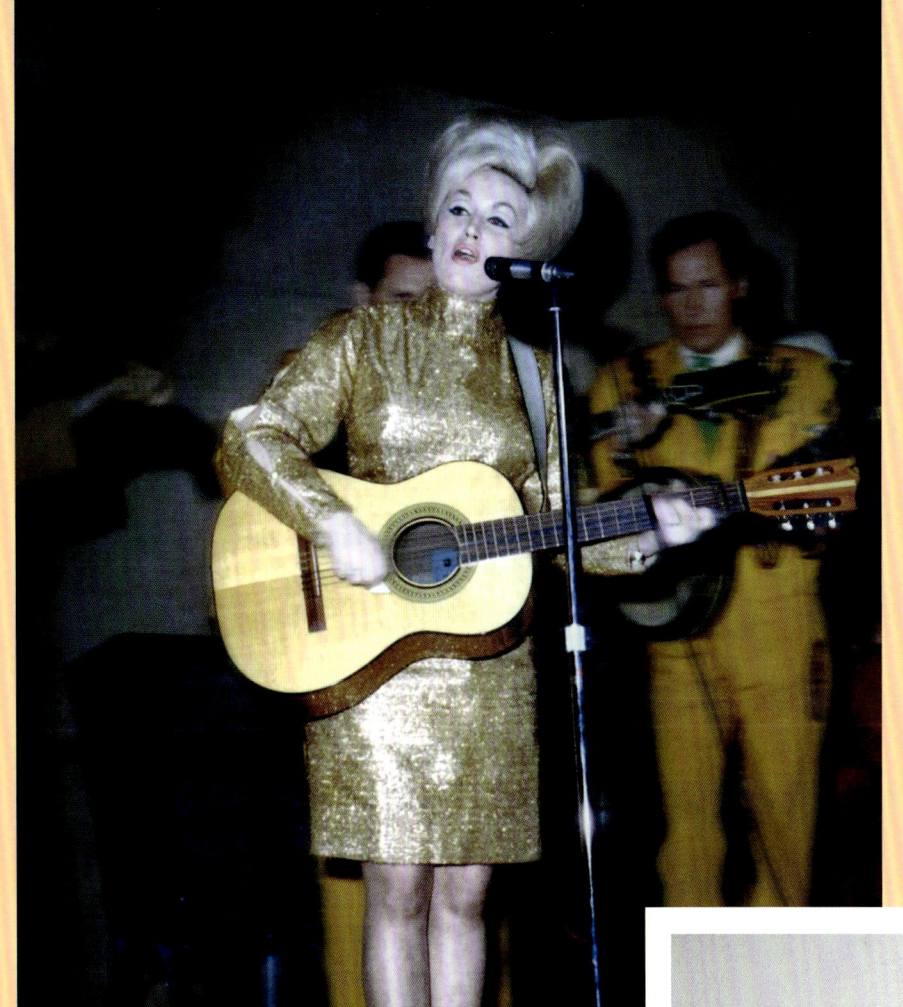

Elvis Presley had his gold lamé suit, and this dress—worn during a show in Asheville, North Carolina—is sort of akin to that. The poster is from a concert in Lubbock, Texas, and the other pictures could have been taken just about anywhere. It seems like I *was* just about anywhere in those days!

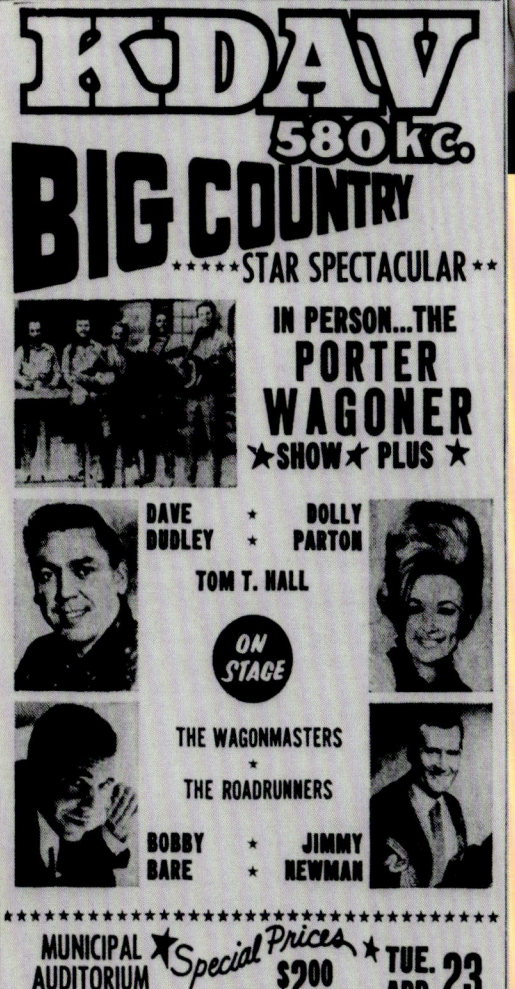

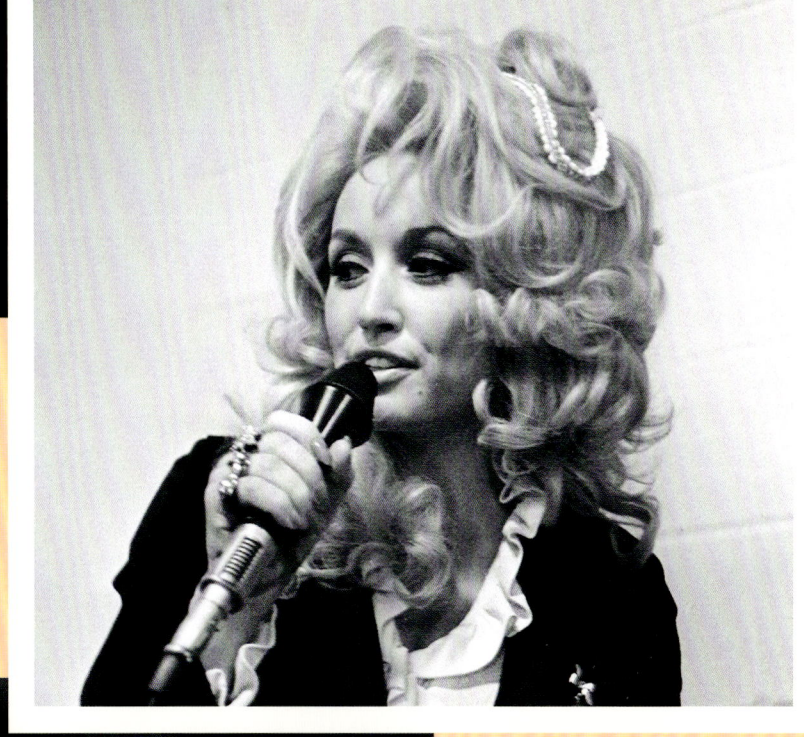

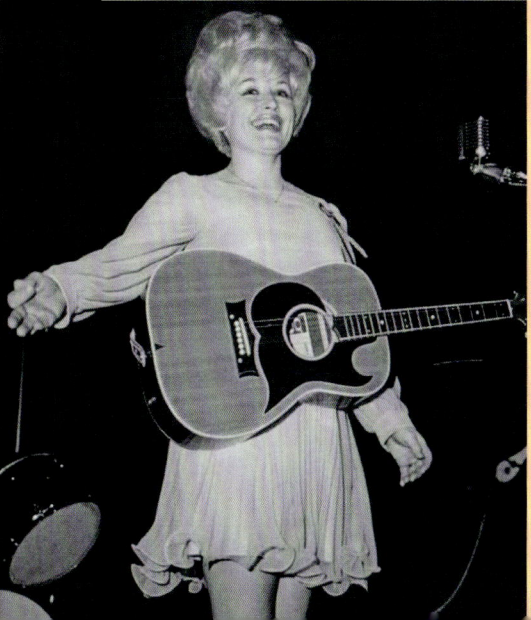

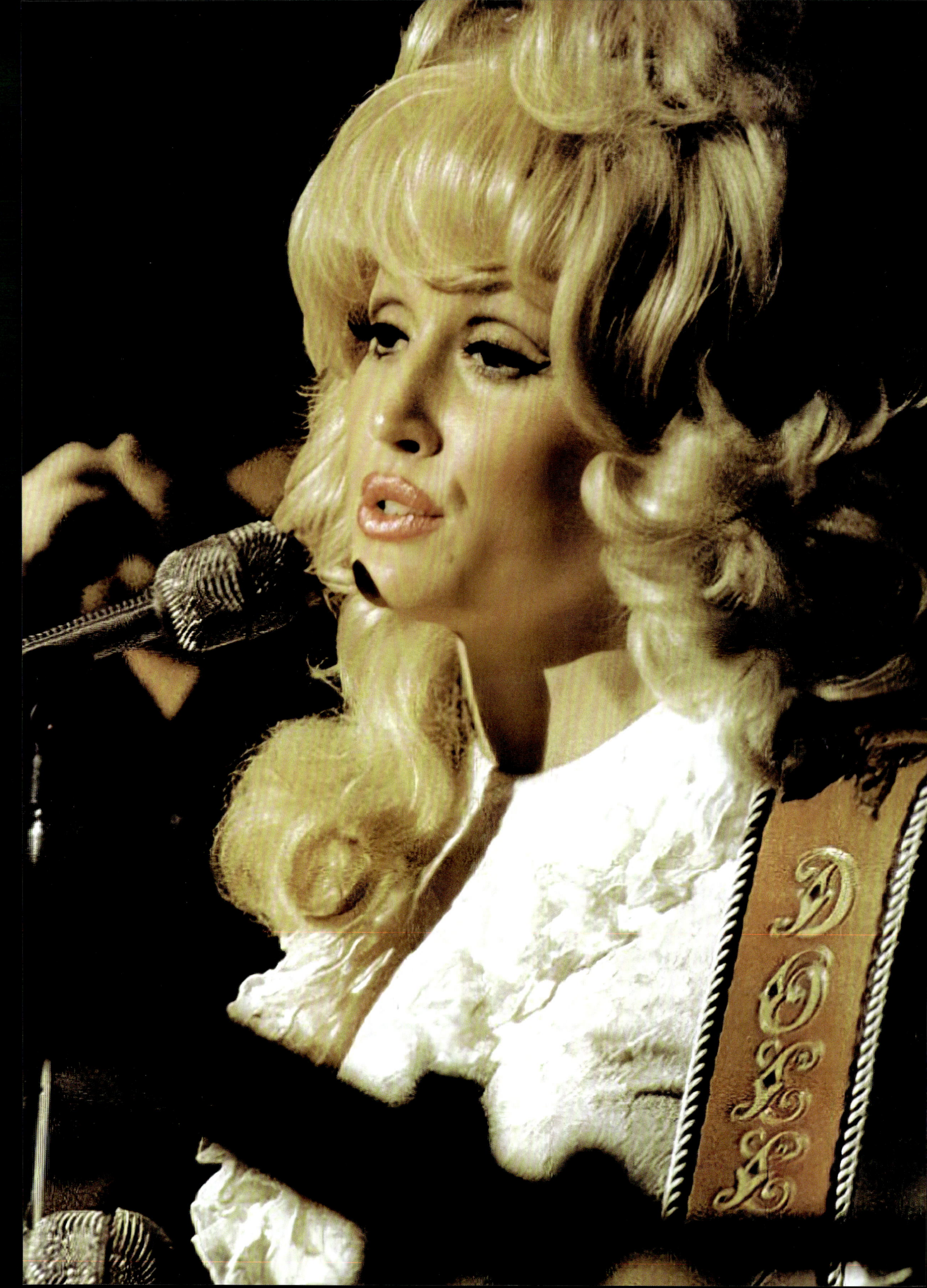

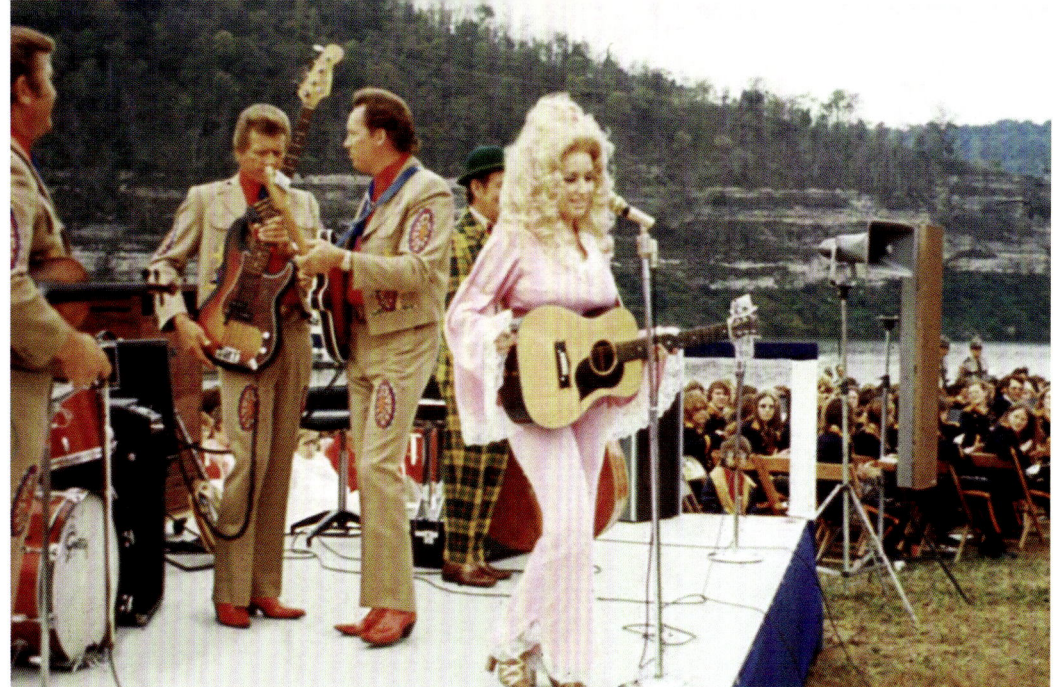

With The Wagonmasters at the public dedication of the Cordell Hull Dam in Carthage, Tennessee. From left behind me are Mack Magaha, George McCormick, Buck Trent, and Speck Rhodes. It was humid that day—my hair was even bigger than it normally would be!

Both of us released solo singles amid the duets, and our recording careers helped draw more people to our concerts and gave us more hits to play during our sets. Porter earned Top 5 singles in 1968 and 1969, and he got a Top 10 in 1972. I scored a Top 5 single in 1970 with a remake of the Jimmie Rodgers song "Mule Skinner Blues (Blue Yodel No. 8)" and got my first no. 1 in 1971 with "Joshua."

Because we were popping out music that played on their car radios, the fans got to hear a whole string of songs they knew when they saw us in person.

The concerts had a built-in flow. Typically, the Wagonmasters opened for about ten minutes, I did a solo set that ran twenty minutes, Porter came out and did thirty-five minutes of solo material, and then we closed with forty-five minutes' worth of duets—it was kind of like the TV show, without the guests. But with all those different setups—a group, a solo female, a solo male, and a duet—the concerts didn't need any guests since the sound kept changing throughout the show.

It was a bit of a country music formula that lots of folks were doing at that time. In addition to Porter and me, some of the other "package shows" included George Jones and Tammy Wynette, Conway Twitty and Loretta Lynn, Don Gibson and Dottie West, Johnny Cash and June Carter, Kitty Wells and Johnny Wright, Glen Campbell and Bobbie Gentry, and Jack Greene and Jeannie Seely.

Porter and I got an additional boost when the Grand Ole Opry added me to the cast. I had always wanted to be a member. Back home and in country music, the epitome of success was to be on the Grand Ole Opry. To become a member was a big deal.

The Porter Years

I thought back to how I'd performed on my porch at my Tennessee mountain home, imagining that one day I was going to be on the Grand Ole Opry. By becoming an official member, I would forever be associated with the Opry. It was a dream come true. And it still is.

Porter made a lot of money as our stars rose, and he shared some of the wealth. The Wagonmasters all got bonus checks now and again, and Porter showered me with gifts. He gave me necklaces, rings, and a Cadillac, and those presents got a lot of attention in the media.

But my paycheck never changed through all of that. I kept asking for a raise and never got one. He would buy me all these things and say, "Consider that your raise." I said, "I don't want the gifts. I want to buy my own gifts. I want the money."

Fans would sometimes ask if we were married, and I'd usually tell them, "Yes, but not to each other!"

I did love Porter in my own way, and since it seemed we were always together and Carl didn't appear often in public, my husband was almost like a ghost to the fans. Their fascination with Porter and me was bound to keep tongues wagging, and it did.

Adding to that, we probably came off like a married couple on stage. Porter laughed, I laughed, we sang love songs in harmony, and even when we weren't exactly in unison, we still came off well together. One of the keys to harmony singing is coordinated phrasing. Listen to the Eagles and you hear the singers all start every line and end every note at precisely the same time. Porter had figured out over the years that words that end in *s* are the hardest to get in sync, so on phrases that wrapped with that sound—like "camp meetin's went for weeks" and "the aisles were always filled at altar calls" in "Daddy Was an Old Time Preacher Man"—Porter sang the final *s* and I did not. So even if we didn't line up perfectly, people heard only one *s,* making it less obvious that we weren't ending our words at the same exact time.

Our working relationship was complicated by the difference in our ages—both our physical ages and our professional ones. Porter hailed from a different generation, and he had already been having hits for more than a dozen years when we had that first meeting at his office in 1967. The hit-making period of most recording careers lasts only three to five years, so Porter had beat the odds even before I came along. When we started having hits, it extended his time at the top, and he wanted to make it last as long as possible. My career was just taking off, and I was busting at the seams to see where I could take it.

When he hired me, Porter had told me that I'd get a solo every week on the TV show and could choose my own songs. Sometimes he didn't like my choice and would tell me, "No, you're not doing that one." Of course, that never went over well, and sometimes I would do it anyway, and then we'd have an argument. Like with "The Bridge"—it was a song that ended in a suicide. I loved the drama and the emotion in it, but Porter thought it was morbid. Instead of singing the song he wanted, when it was my turn, I just did "The Bridge" by myself.

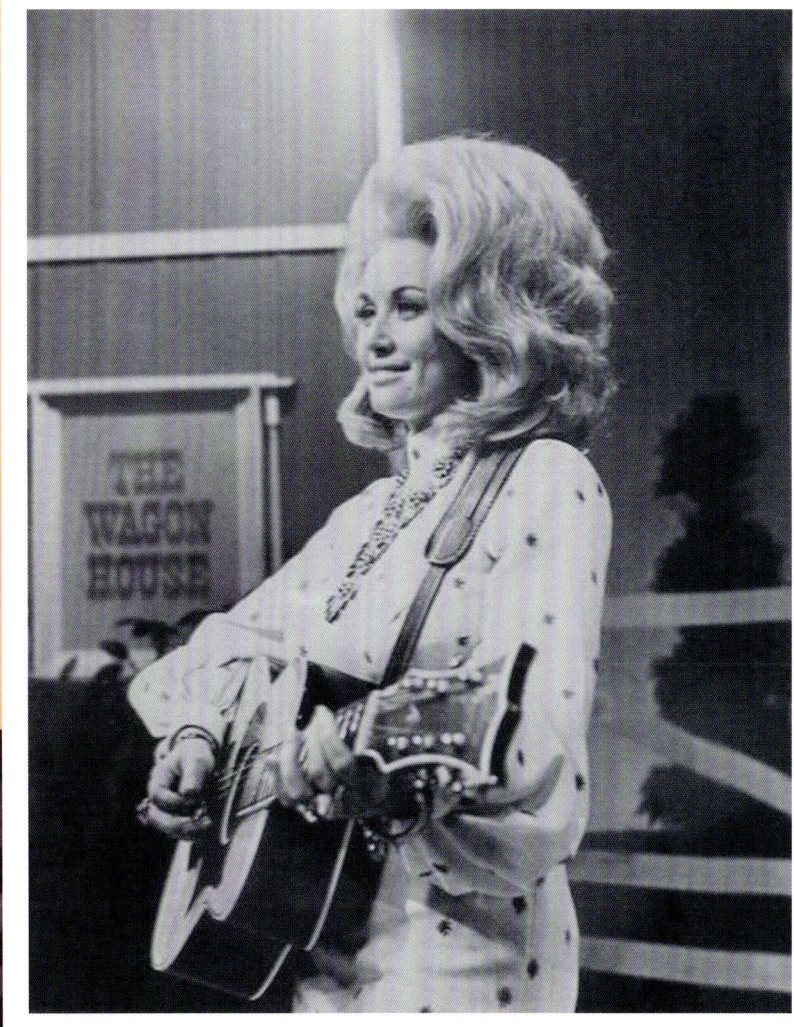

We appeared on all kinds of stages during the Porter years in all kinds of situations. We played to the camera on *The Porter Wagoner Show,* performed for intimate crowds in small theaters, and shared stages with a big list of co-stars in package shows.

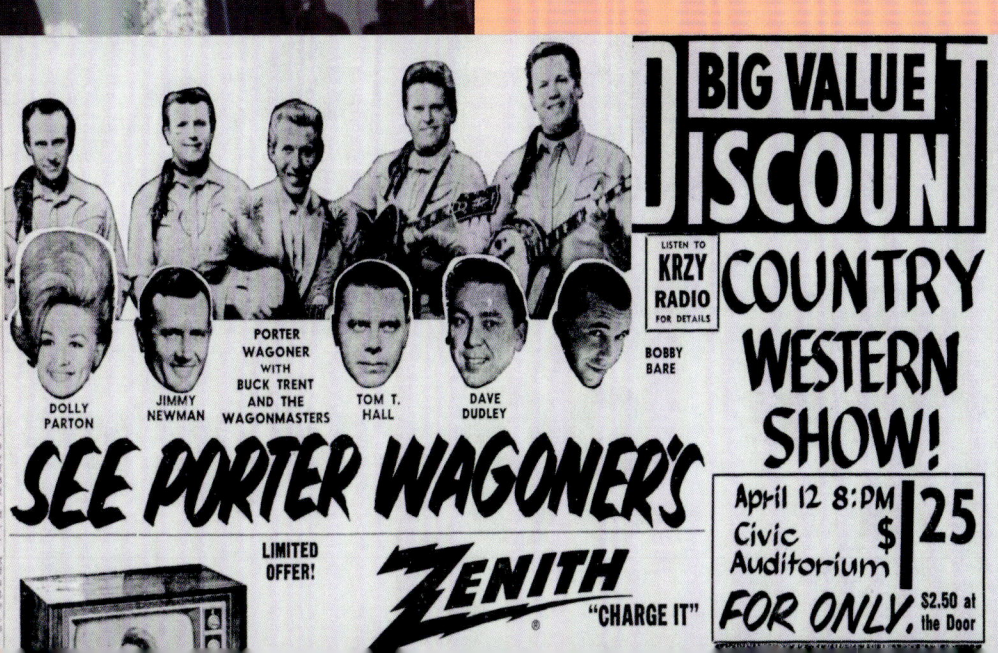

THE JOKE'S ON ME

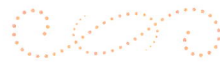

They say that laughing at yourself is healthy, not to mention a sign of resilience.

It's especially important if you're in the public eye. If you're able to joke about your weaknesses or flaws or the things that make you stand out, then it's really hard for critics or mean people to drag you down or get to you in any way.

That's partly why I've always said that if I hadn't been born a woman, I'd have been a drag queen. I'm not making fun of drag queens—they're great—but I have no problem laughing at some of the outrageous clothing I've worn on stage. I've always told my audiences how much I appreciate them spending their hard-earned money to buy a Dolly Parton concert ticket, 'cause it costs a lot to look this cheap!

I came by my sense of humor pretty naturally. Country folks like to rib each other. More often than not, it's meant as a sign of affection, as it always was in our home growing up. But it was also a coping mechanism. Other kids at school made fun of the way I dressed and my ambitions of becoming a country singer, and I learned that if I poked fun at myself first, it caught them off guard and disabled their ability to do so.

Plus, people have a natural tendency to react the opposite of how you present yourself. If you're always bragging about how great you are, they can't wait to knock you off your pedestal. But if you take a swipe at yourself, they know you don't think you're better than anyone, and they're more likely to want to help build you up.

Comedy also has a deep history in country music. The early Grand Ole Opry shows had plenty of jokesters, such as Lonzo and Oscar, Rod Brasfield, Homer and Jethro, Stringbean, the Duke of Paducah, and Sarie and Sally. And, of course, there was the Queen of Country Comedy, Minnie Pearl. When Minnie told jokes, they were usually harmless stories about fictitious people. If she did mention a real person by name, they were either in on the joke or she knew they wouldn't be offended.

But most of the time, once she yelled "Howdeeee!," the jokes that followed were about her—she poked fun at her stockings, her dresses, her looks, or her lack of a boyfriend.

Many of the musical artists back then—including Grandpa Jones, Bill Carlisle, Uncle Dave Macon, and Porter Wagoner—told wisecracks on themselves too. It was pretty easy to follow in that tradition.

I was one of twelve kids in a poor family. So sometimes I referred to my parents as "horny hillbillies." And, of course, I heard plenty of dumb-blonde jokes. I wasn't offended by them. After all, as I've often said, I knew full well I wasn't dumb—and that I wasn't a blonde!

It was always easy to get a snicker by talking about my biggest . . . assets. I know it, and I admit it. I often told audiences that I knew they'd brought binoculars so they could get a good look, and that "I can assure you they're real"—after all, those wigs were made from real hair!

Trust me, I've been the punch line to a whole bunch of jokes. I don't mind that there's such a thing as a "Dolly Parton joke." I made up most of 'em myself!

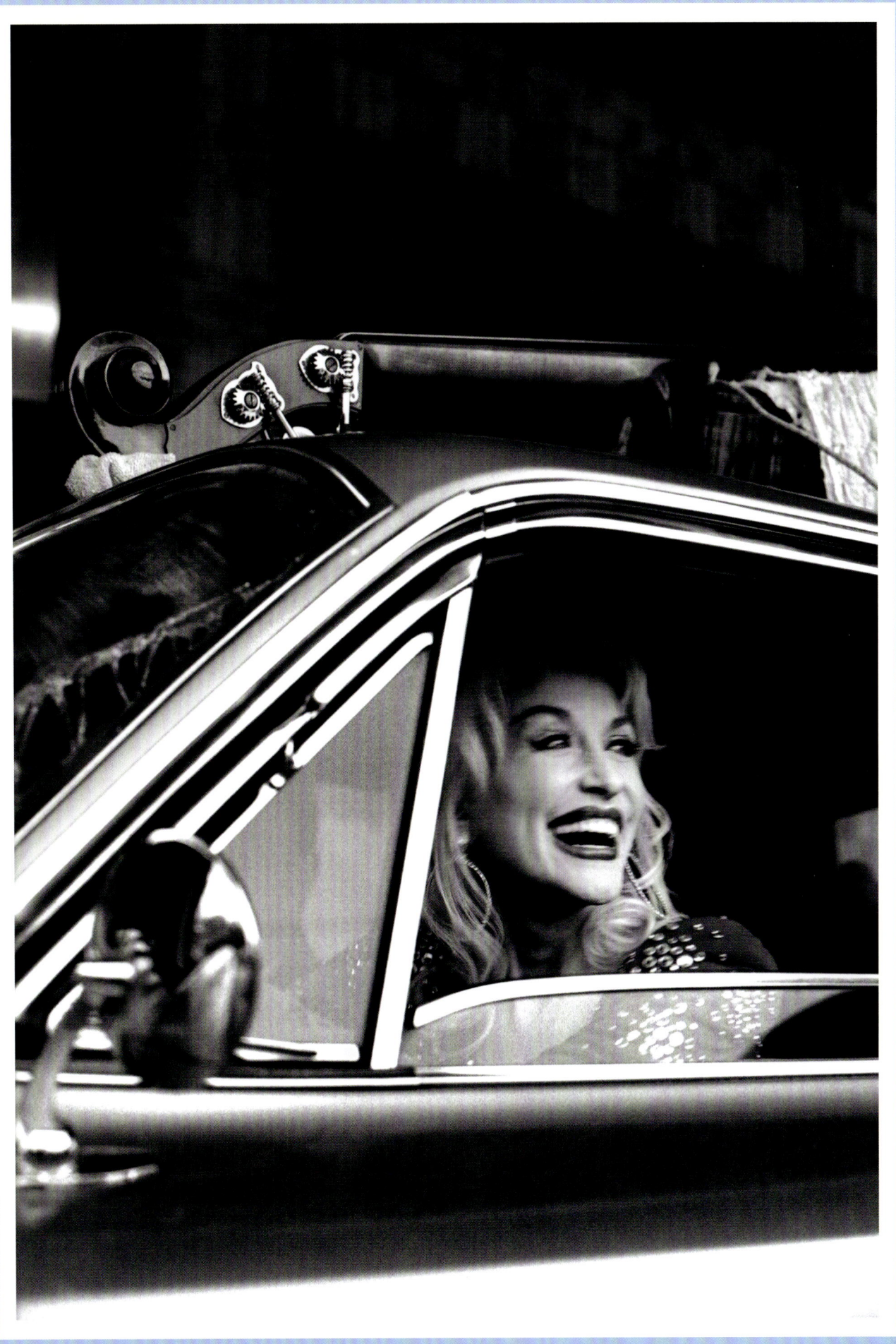

I've often said I was born with a happy heart—and that's still true. Life's too short not to smile and have fun!

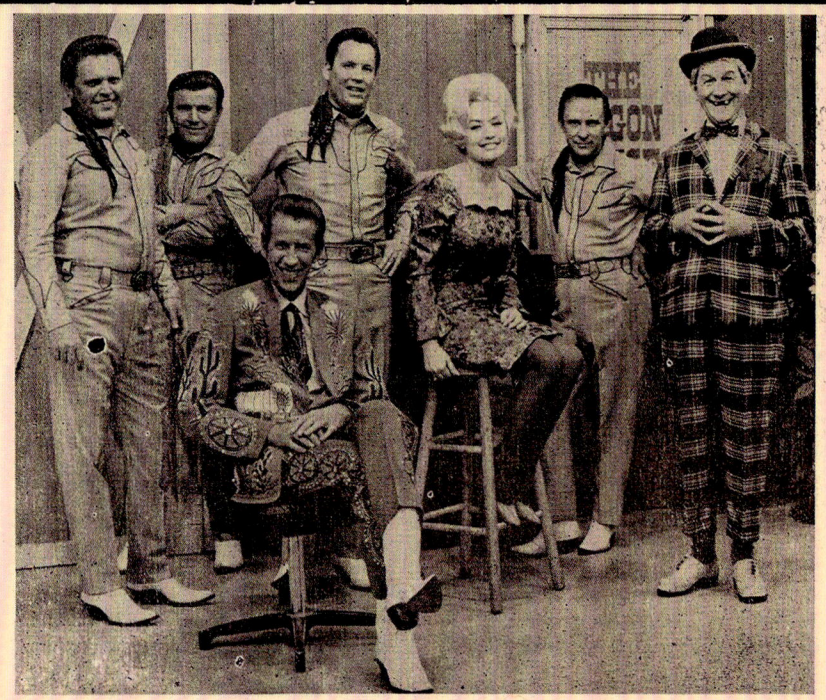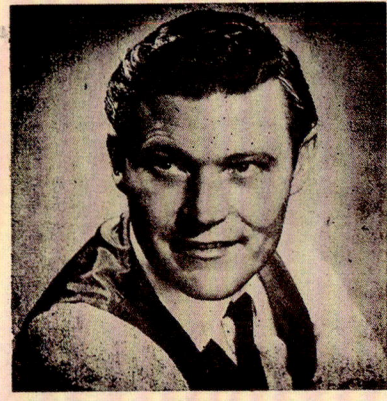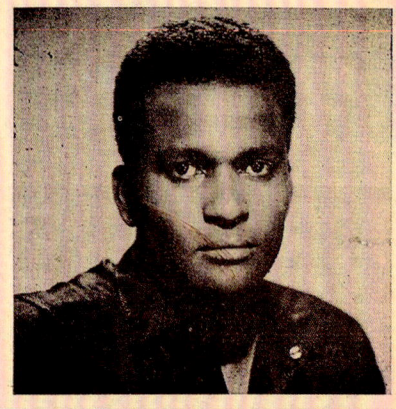

Little things like that caused us to start having a lot of problems. I was making my way as an artist, and he was already an established one. It was his show, but I was trying to grow in the business and grow as an artist myself. But trying to grow within somebody else's show when he takes everything as a threat or gets mad if you're getting more attention than him—what ends up growing is tension. You have to know your own place, so to speak, and my place was anywhere I felt I needed to be. I thought, *You ain't my director. God is.*

Still, I was doing what I had always wanted to do—singing country music across America on stages big and small. There were plenty of city auditoriums and state fairs in the South and the Midwest, the Opry appearances, and the weekly performances on *The Porter Wagoner Show*. We landed on other TV programs, too, including *The Mike Douglas Show, Hee Haw,* and *The David Frost Show,* and we were on the CMA Awards. And there was a historic appearance at Madison Square Garden in New York City where we shared the bill with Sonny James, Conway Twitty, Loretta Lynn, Faron Young, and a few others. That concert was such a major event that ads for it appeared in the morning newspaper in Nashville, nine hundred miles away. I had a feeling of pride about that. I remember thinking, *Here we are, hillbillies in the city. But proud hillbillies in the city.*

One of the biggest highlights of my whole life came while I was traveling with the band. We'd gone out to Washington State and to Oregon—farther than we usually did. And I got the flu. I was so sick in my little room on the bus, and I missed a couple of shows. We were in Eugene, Oregon, and I thought, *I have got to try to get out on stage tonight.* I was going crazy in that tiny room. I was so sick that it took me all day to get dressed and to get my makeup on, but I mustered up enough strength and courage to do it.

I told Porter that I wanted to go on that night, and so I went out and did my little show first. I told the audience, "Look, I don't know if I'm even going to make it through this show," but their inspiration and their love gave me strength. I was giving it everything I had, and when I did "Coat of Many Colors," I got a standing ovation. I just broke down and cried my eyes out, you know, being so sensitive, being so sick, and being so weak. I was weaker than water when I went back to the bus that night, and I wrote a song called "Eugene, Oregon." It's one of my favorite songs.

My working relationship with Porter got harder when the media started covering us differently. We were still known officially as Porter Wagoner and Dolly Parton—his name came first. But there were times when the reporters wrote stories about us where they put the focus on me and made Porter secondary. In one case, a reviewer overlooked Porter almost entirely until the last three paragraphs.

Porter was not real happy about it. It was, after all, *The Porter Wagoner Show*. He'd often remind me, "This ain't the Dolly Parton show." And he was right. But it wasn't like I was writing those stories. I never even met the reporters. But it made for some very uncomfortable times between us—and for me.

STAGE LOOKS
Through the Years

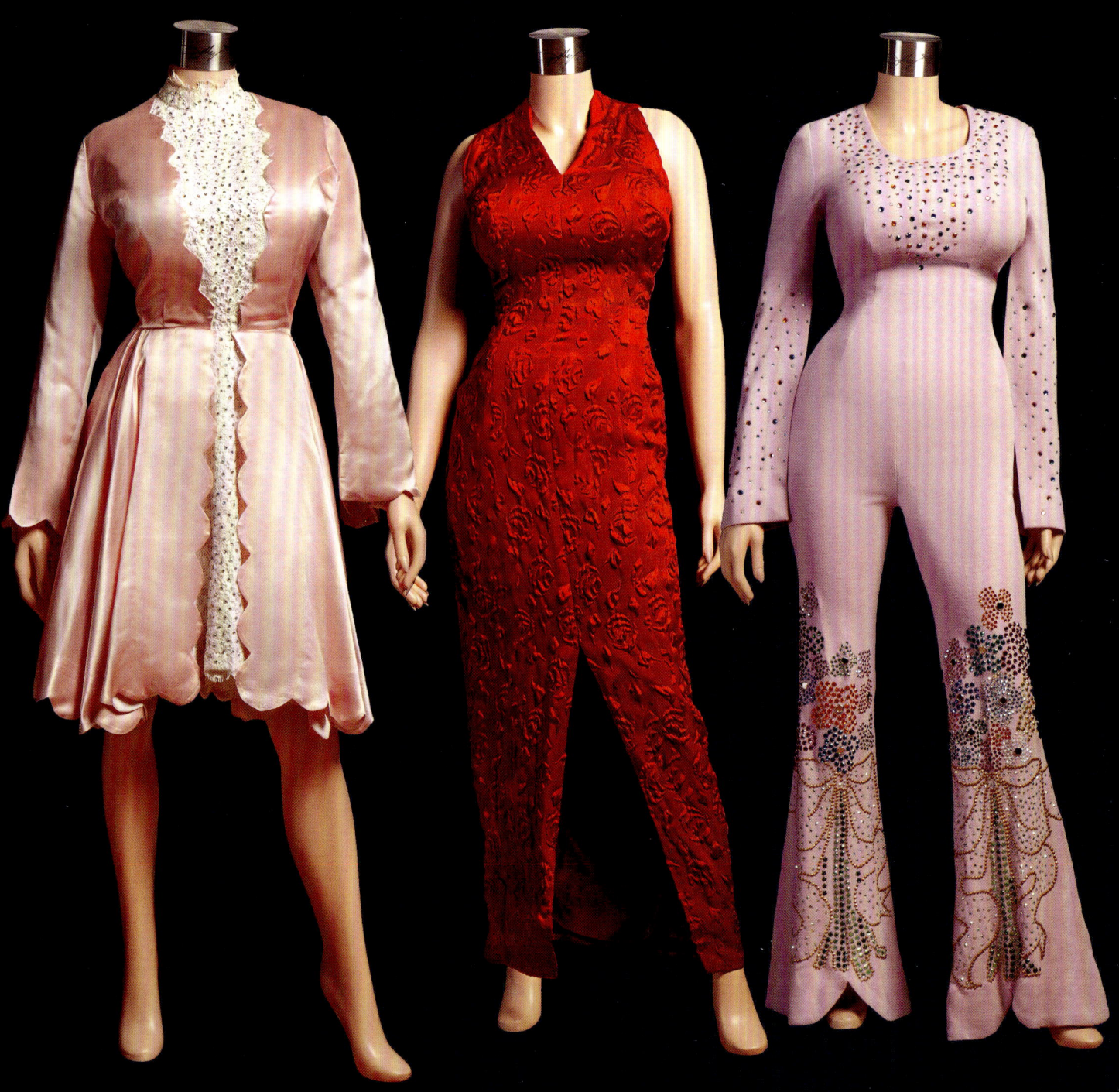

I wore this pink satin Lucy Adams dress to record my very first live album at my alma mater, Sevier County High School.

I wore this gown to perform at the 1972 CMA Awards with some of my favorite gals!

I got to host my very last episode on *The Porter Wagoner Show* in this lavender "Lucy Suit"... I even brought my Traveling Family Band!

The Wagonmasters were never a problem. Speck Rhodes may have played a comedian on stage, but behind the scenes, he was very, very intelligent and very well spoken. He was amazing as a person, and he would also give me a lot of good advice and talk to me about things or compliment me in ways that I needed.

And Don Warden was the mediator. He always tried to keep the peace and tried to keep things going. When I'd be upset—real upset—he'd say, "Oh, I wouldn't get too down about that. Porter will be fine tomorrow. Everything will be all right."

Our original deal was for five years, but when Porter asked, I agreed to stay with the show longer. I could not travel on that bus with Porter anymore, though, so I bought a little camper and hired my Uncle Henry to drive my best friend, Judy, and me back and forth. It was not as dependable as a bus, but we made it there, and sometimes Judy would share the driving with Henry. Judy was ex-military, and more than capable of taking the wheel. She was a good driver. And I was, too, when needed.

I'm glad I hung on with Porter for a few more years because during my last two or three years, I met a fan at one of the concerts who inspired one of my biggest hits. I remember looking down at this beautiful little girl. Her eyes were just so green, and her hair was red, kind of like Judy's hair has always been. And she said, "Could you sign this to Jolene?" And I said, "I love that name." Going to the bus, I just kept saying "Jolene, Jolene, Jolene" so I'd remember the name until I could write it down. "Jolene, Jolene, Jolene"—that eventually became the first chorus of "Jolene." Of course, I knew exactly who to give that name to in a song!

Around the same time I wrote "I Will Always Love You" as a way of saying goodbye to Porter. I would indeed always love him and everything that he did for me, though I knew I needed to go out on my own. It was tricky since I'd signed a contract and we weren't anywhere near the expiration date. But after I recorded that song, we occasionally talked about how important it was for me to break away. While we were proud of our success—we had released at least two Top 10 duets every year for a decade, a dozen total—we agreed we'd both sell more records if we focused on our solo careers. Finally, when we were playing Tulsa in 1974, Porter agreed that I could leave his show. Three days later, he called a small press conference at Fireside Studios in Nashville—our joint venture—to announce we were splitting. He was going to continue producing my records, but I was heading off on my own.

My emotions were really mixed as we wound it down. We still had several months of shows to do, and endings often bring a lot of sadness, especially when they're drawn out. But I was making plans for a new band and for the next phase in my career, and that was exciting.

The Porter Years

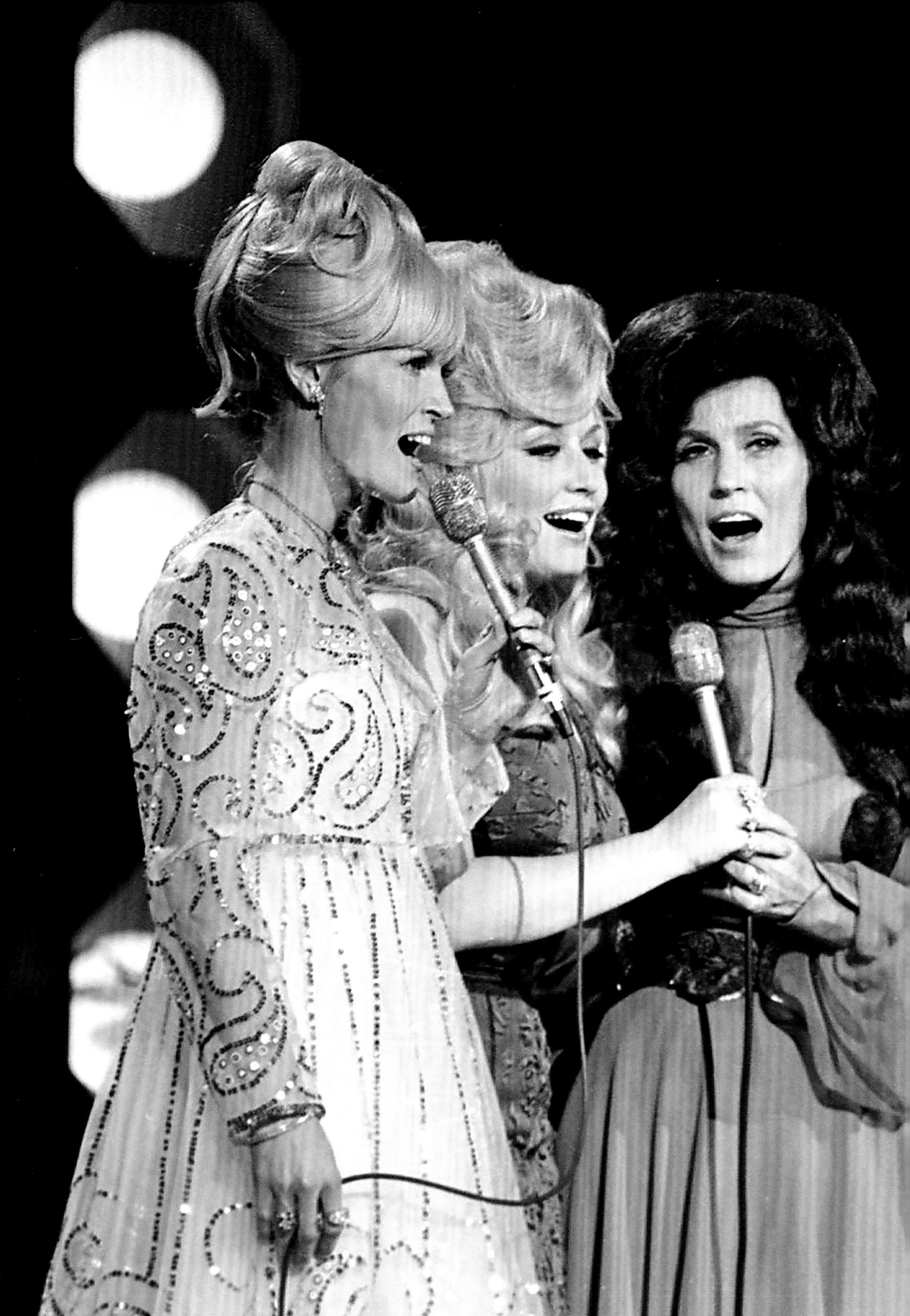

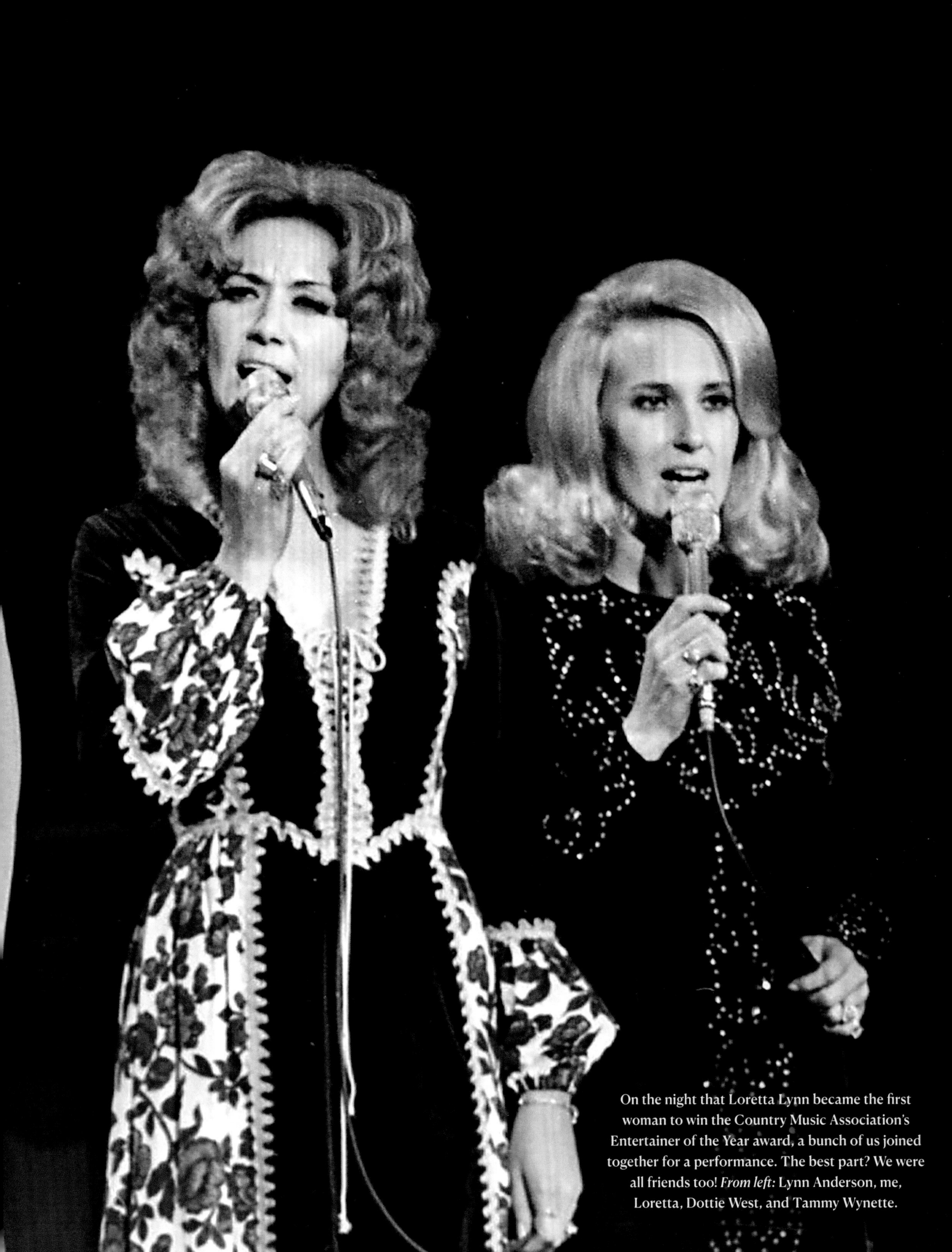

On the night that Loretta Lynn became the first woman to win the Country Music Association's Entertainer of the Year award, a bunch of us joined together for a performance. The best part? We were all friends too! *From left:* Lynn Anderson, me, Loretta, Dottie West, and Tammy Wynette.

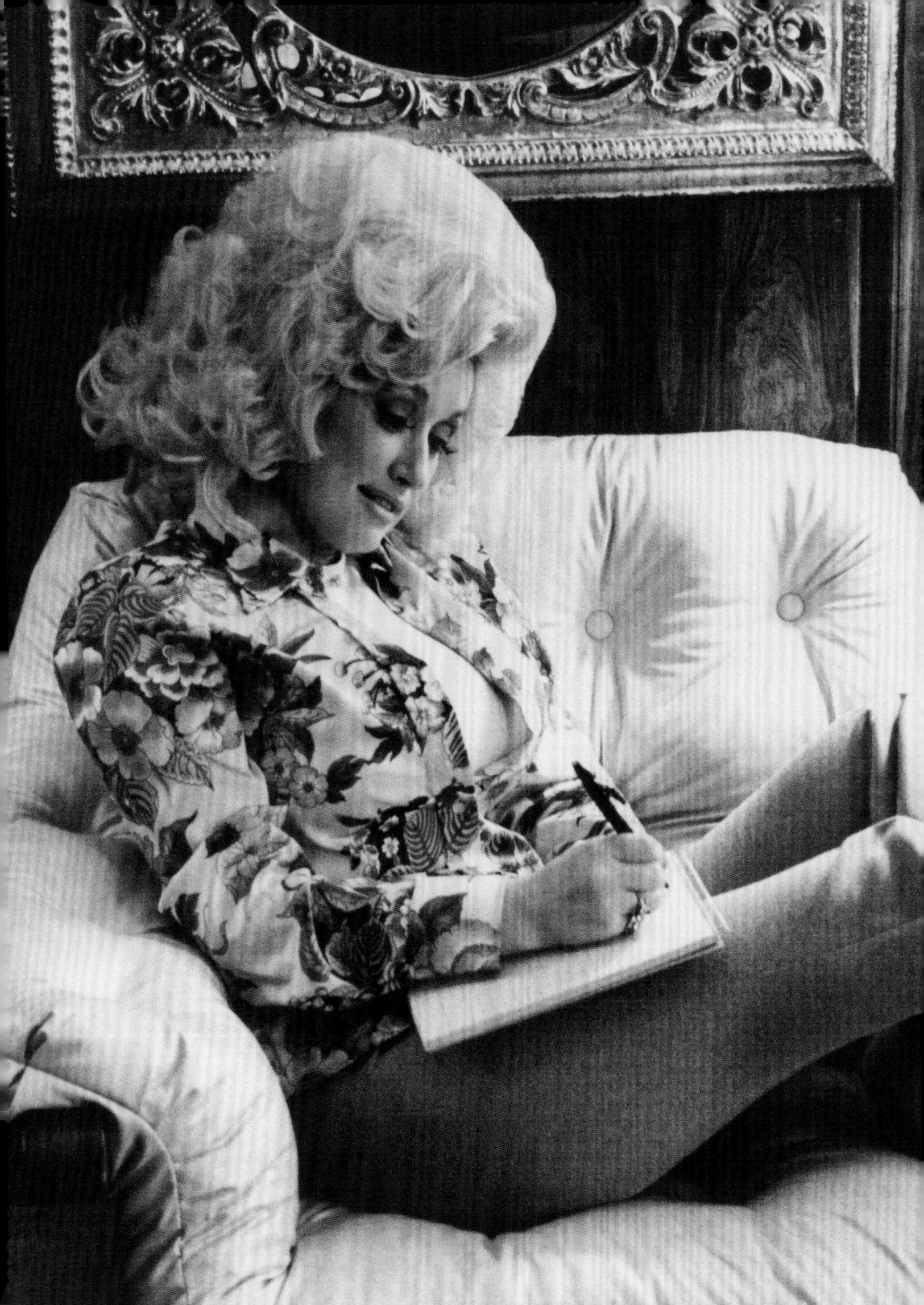

Among the shows we did at that time was an appearance on the Opry when it moved from the Ryman Auditorium in downtown Nashville to the new Grand Ole Opry House. It was a big moment in country music history—Richard Nixon played piano during the first show in March 1974—and I was there, though it was a blur. On top of the emotions I was experiencing in my own career, we were touring on the West Coast. I had to fly into Nashville after a Friday concert to perform in that first show at the Opry House on Saturday, then fly back out to the West Coast for a Sunday booking. That's a lot of travel to do for a few songs, but I needed to be there. And why wouldn't I want to be there? It was historic. It was like an Opry House–warming party: the show had found a new home, and the president of the United States was coming to Nashville and taking part in the Opry for the first time ever. No matter who's in office, it's always been a big deal when the president wants to acknowledge us in Nashville.

A short time later, I started playing solo shows again, beginning with a couple of benefits in Atlanta and Nashville.

Then, in June, Porter and I gave our last out-of-town concert, in Davenport, Iowa. One minute I'd be sad, contemplating the chapter that I was closing. But then I'd get excited, thinking about all the possibilities the future held.

Porter was particularly eye-catching that night. He wore a sky-blue suit and lavender boots with all his trademark rhinestones sparkling.

The concert was a little strange. We expected it to be emotional, but the Wagonmasters started laughing. And laughing. And laughing. I didn't know what they were laughing about—they were always cutting up—but I'm sure their emotions were just on edge. They were not happy that we were breaking up. That was going to take a big chunk out of the show, and I'm sure that it put them in doubt about what might be on the horizon.

But they didn't stop laughing on stage until Porter gave a little speech. The whole audience knew this was the end of our run, and Porter wanted to make it clear that there were no hard feelings. He said it was his idea for me to set out on my own, and he wanted everyone to hear the full story "right from the horse's mouth." And then he gave a little whinny, and people laughed.

I did finally break down before it was all over, but there was still one more concert to do. We had booked a show at a fiddling championship at the Opryland theme park at the tail end of Fan Fair, a big festival in Nashville that the Country Music Association sponsored for country fans. Bluegrass musician Sam Bush finished seventh in the contest, and Paul McCartney, who was on vacation and staying at a farm owned by songwriter Curly Putman, who wrote "Dumb Blonde," brought his family to the concert.

The Porter Years

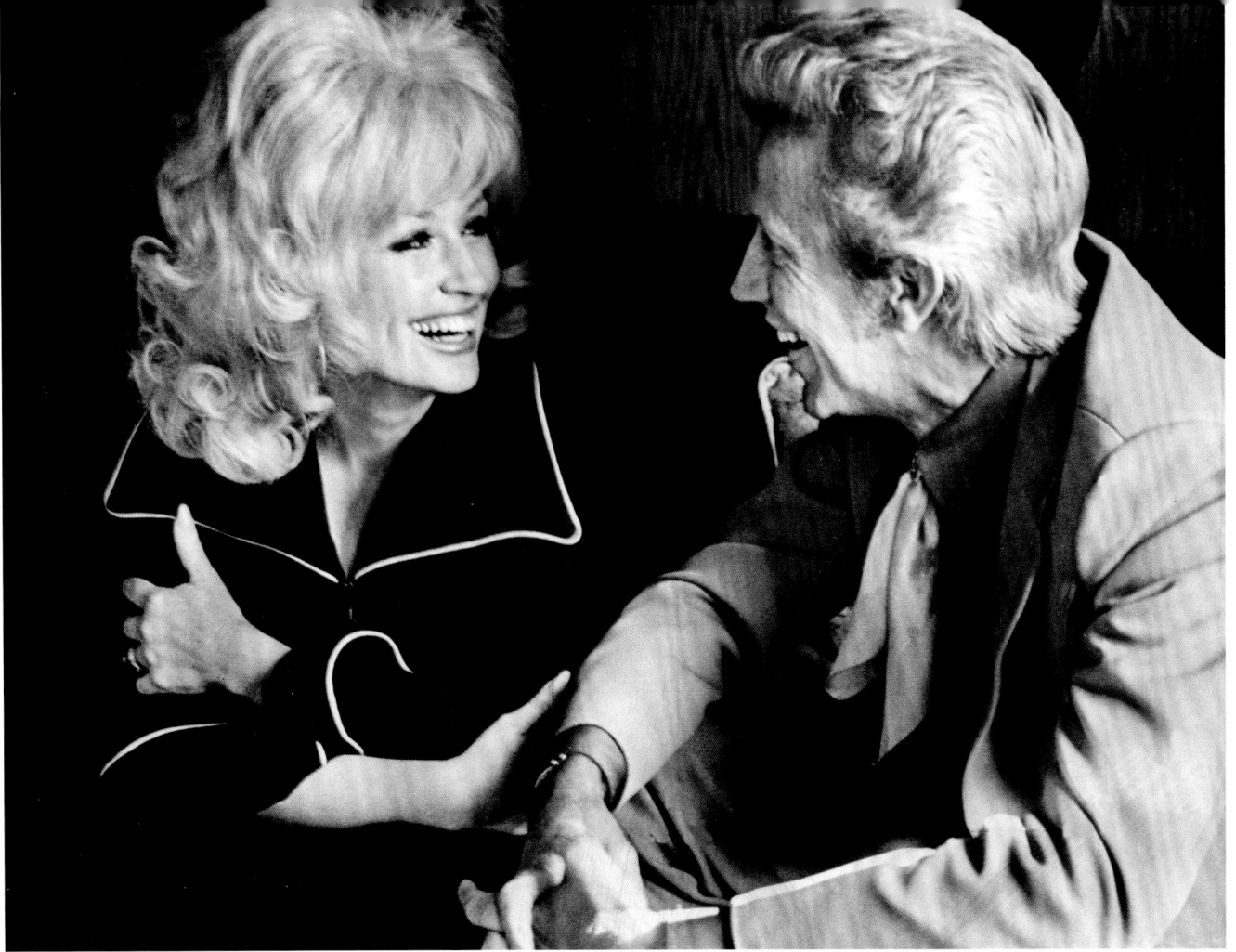

Porter had a grab bag full of corny jokes.
Even though we had our ups and downs, he could
always make me laugh.

I didn't know they were there while I was performing, but it wouldn't have mattered. I would have given the same show either way. But it was a great surprise when I saw them afterward. They were very sweet when they came backstage, and I was very excited. Paul McCartney was at Opryland for our last concert! I remember thinking it was a big deal for country music, a big deal for Nashville, and certainly a big deal for us. And I know it was!

It was a nice way for Porter and me to end our seven-year musical relationship, though it took years for us to completely bury the hatchet. He sued me a few years later, and after we put that to bed, we reunited at the Opry House in the '80s for my ABC TV series *Dolly!*

Still, the song I'll always associate with Porter was the one that went no. 1 just a week before that final performance during Fan Fair, "I Will Always Love You." I really will always love Porter.

Star of the Show

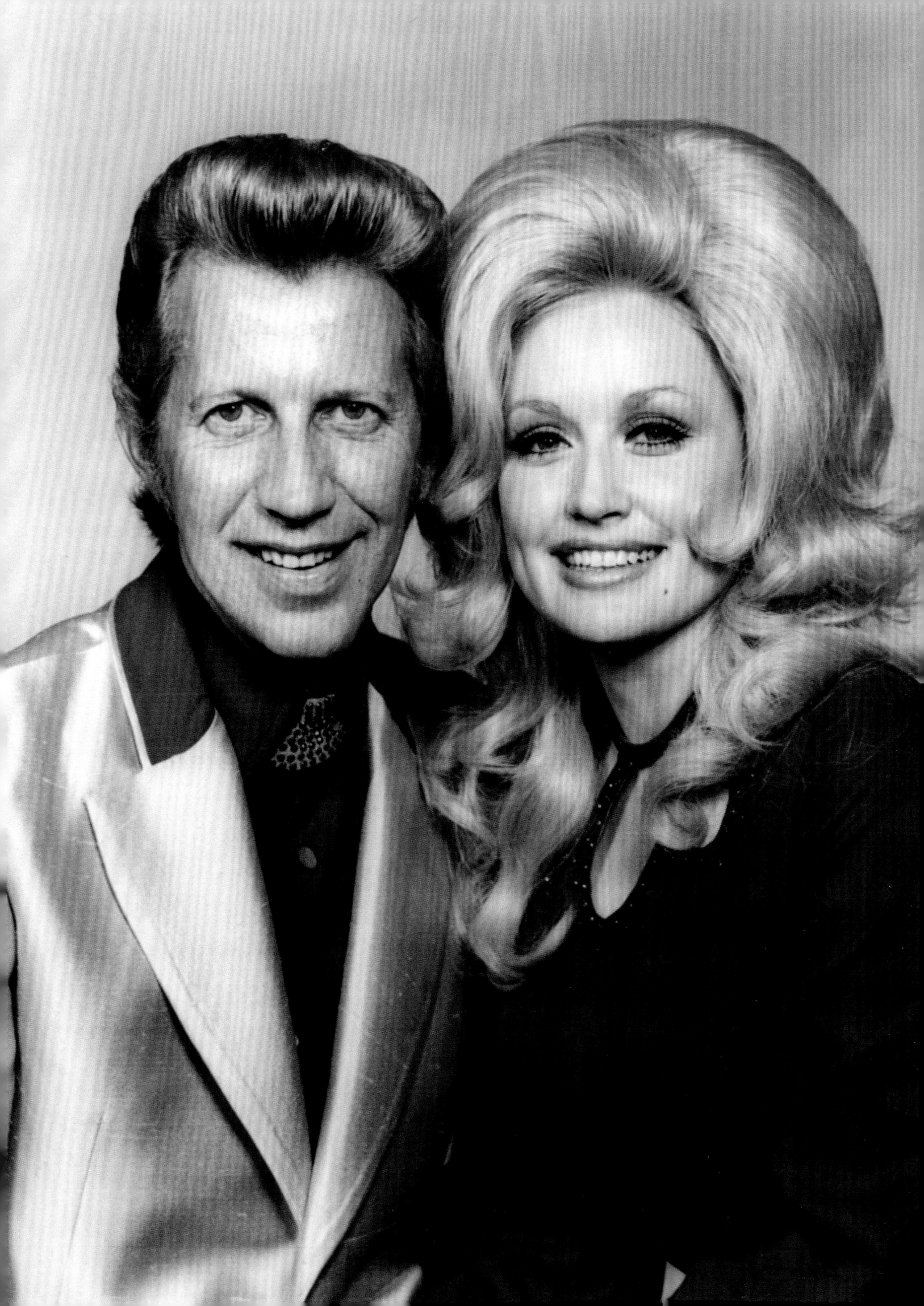

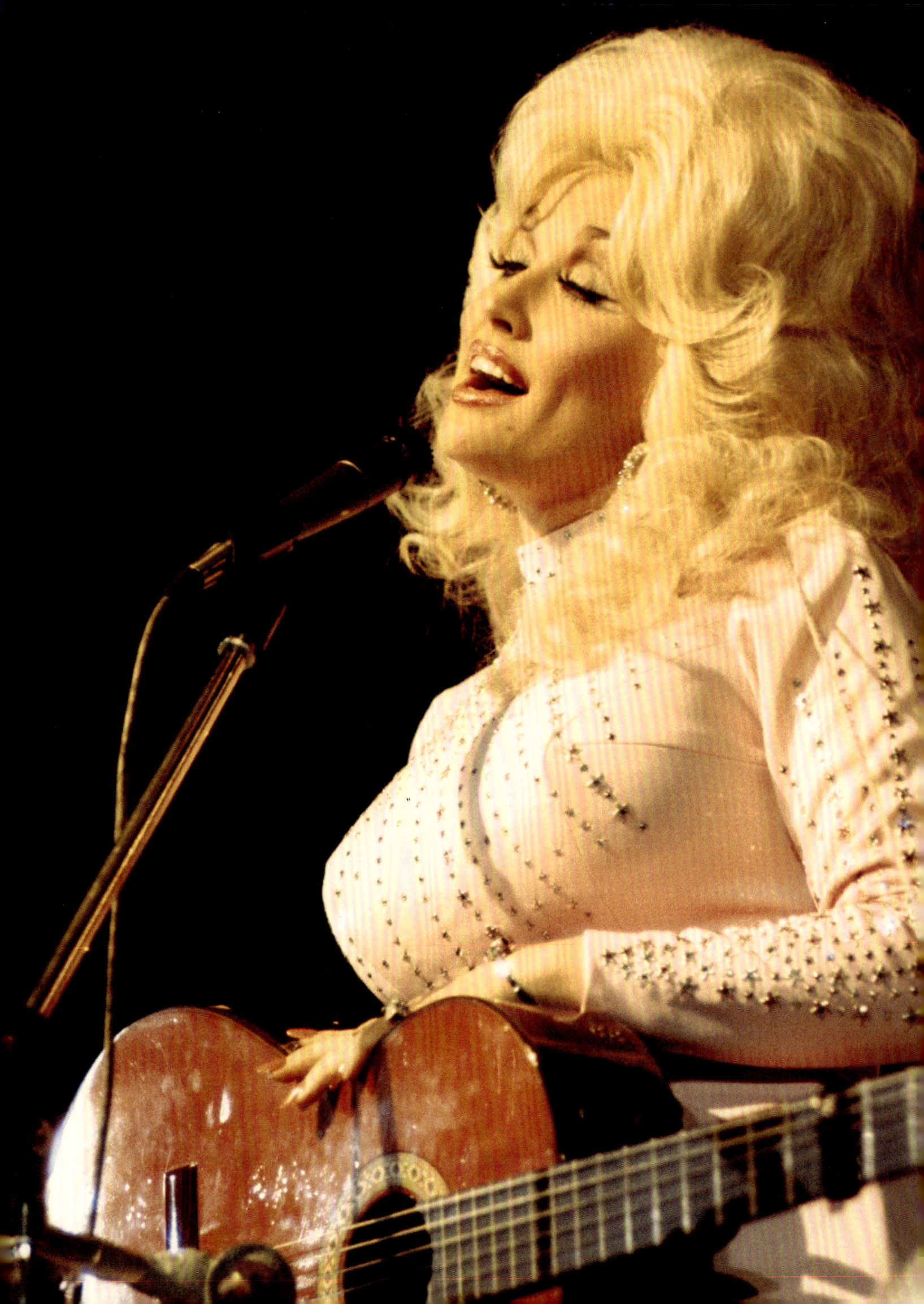

Light of a Brand-New Day

1974-1980

1974 - 1980

When Dolly parted ways with Porter Wagoner, he told the world that he felt she'd been held back at awards shows, and in the public eye, by her role as his duet partner. As if to prove him right, the Country Music Association honored her as a solo artist for the first time in 1975, crowning her Female Vocalist of the Year for the first of two straight years. In 1978, the CMA named her Entertainer of the Year.

But her newfound freedom was a challenge. The risk was hers, the responsibility of running an organization was hers, and her first supporting group, the Traveling Family Band, had her siblings and other relatives all relying on her.

The skills she picked up on *The Porter Wagoner Show* paid off in 1976 when she got her own syndicated TV show, *Dolly*, which opened the door to even wider success. By the end of the next year, she'd begun her career as a crossover artist, starting with "Here You Come Again." That led to bigger venues and new fans all over the world.

—TOM ROLAND

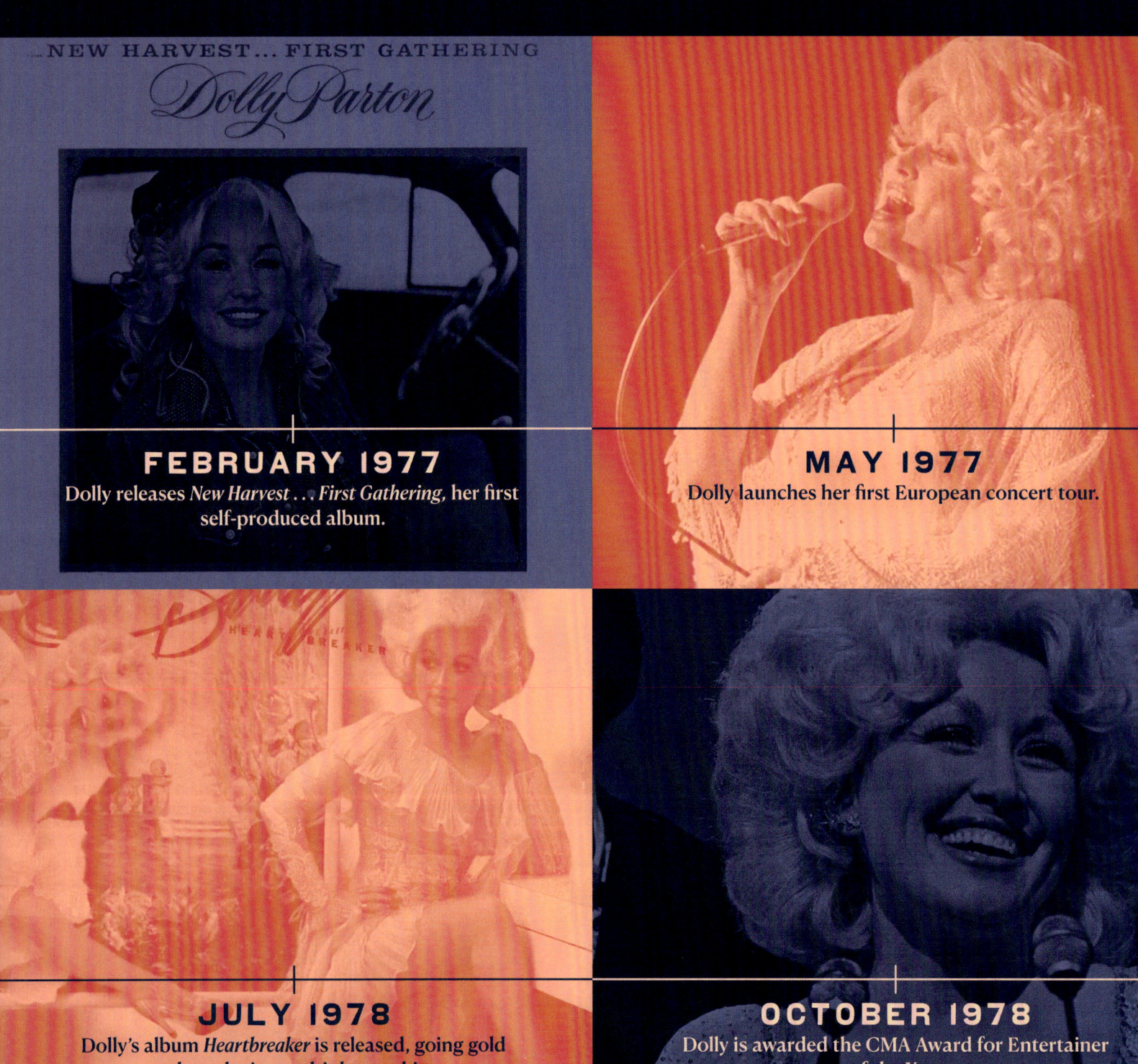

FEBRUARY 1977
Dolly releases *New Harvest... First Gathering*, her first self-produced album.

MAY 1977
Dolly launches her first European concert tour.

JULY 1978
Dolly's album *Heartbreaker* is released, going gold and producing multiple no. 1 hits.

OCTOBER 1978
Dolly is awarded the CMA Award for Entertainer of the Year.

OCTOBER 1975
Dolly wins the CMA Female Vocalist of the Year award for the first time.

SEPTEMBER 1976
Dolly's syndicated television show, *Dolly*, premieres. It is the most expensive show produced out of Nashville at the time.

OCTOBER 1977
"Here You Come Again" is released. It reaches no. 1 on the country charts in December and goes platinum in April 1978, and becomes Dolly's first pop crossover hit.

FEBRUARY 1978
For the album *Here You Come Again*, Dolly wins her first Grammy for Best Country Vocal Performance by a Female.

MAY 1979
Dolly's album *Great Balls of Fire* is released, goes gold, and produces another multi-week no. 1 hit, "You're the Only One."

MAY 1979
Dolly launches her Great Balls of Fire Tour and visits Asia and Australia for the first time.

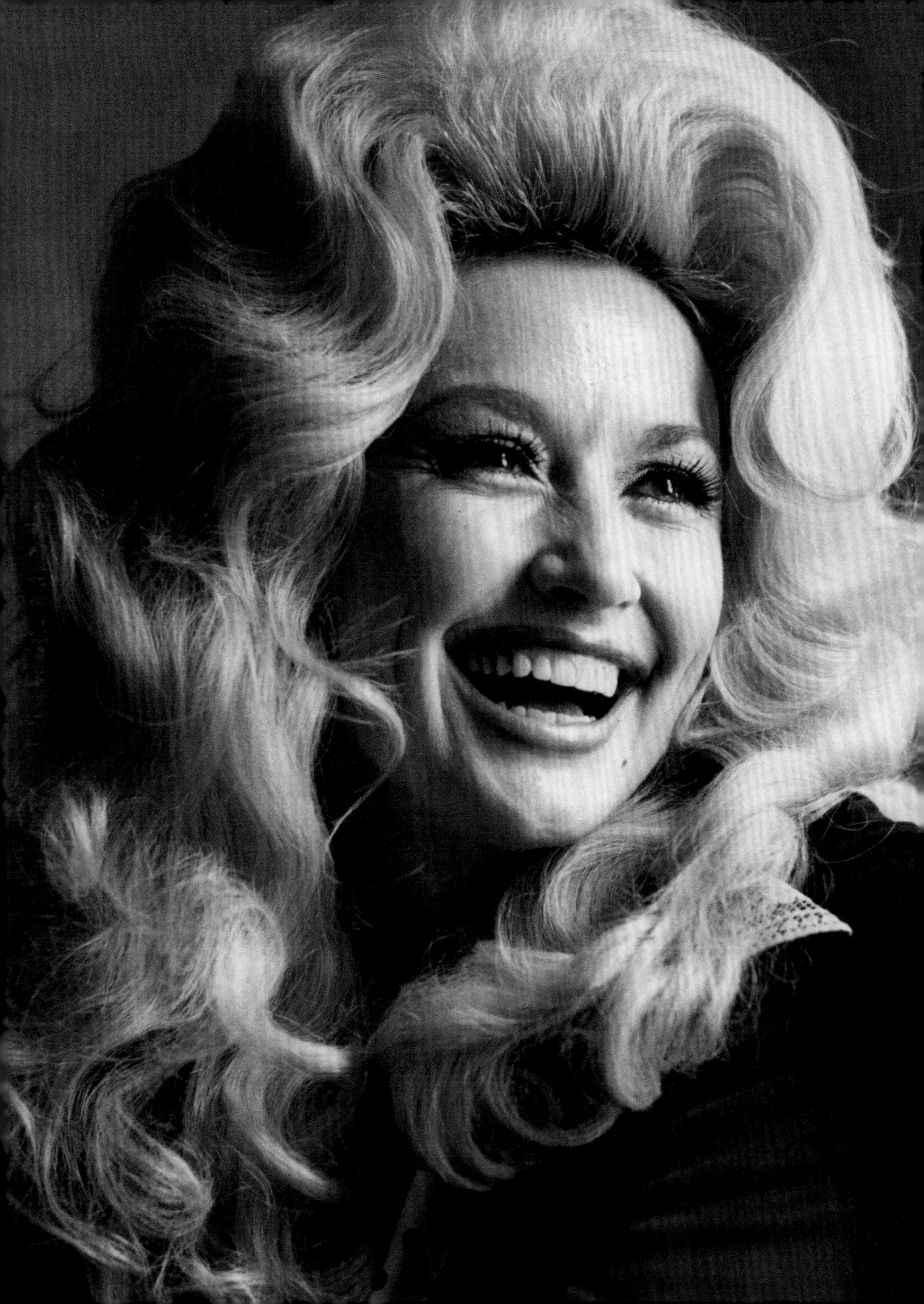

I didn't have a clean break when I stopped being the "girl singer" on *The Porter Wagoner Show*. My contract with him didn't end until about a month after our last performance together, and under our agreement, Porter still produced my solo records—at least in the short run.

Taking the stage alone after so long was strange, to say the least. Heading out on my own was exactly what I wanted, but since I was still linked to Porter, I got heckled now and again. But instead of yelling "Where's Norma Jean?"—like they did back when I joined his troupe—they'd ask, "Where's Porter?"

As if I knew—heck, I was happy to be away from him.

I don't think most fans meant to be mean, but since I'd been part of Porter's entourage for seven years, people thought of us as an inseparable pair. We were getting a professional divorce, and I'm sure they thought it was funny to yell that stuff. But it didn't help as I dealt with the emotions I was feeling.

It was exciting and scary at the same time. A lot of people don't realize all you go through in your life—the things that you sacrifice, the gut-wrenching decisions that you have to make, and the feelings that you have about all of it. But I live by my gut, so I had to make those decisions, and I paid for them. During that whole time, I was under a lot of emotional stress. I was happy to be heading out on my own, but I couldn't be happy that somebody had gotten hurt in the process. Real happiness didn't come until later, when I felt that things had leveled out. But I knew I'd done the right thing. That I never doubted.

As I started out on my first solo dates, I was finally the opening act, leading into headliners like Jerry Reed, George Jones and Tammy Wynette, or Merle Haggard. I played a good number of shows with Merle in those days, and we developed a mutual admiration. If I see someone who reminds me of someone I already know and love, I just kind of bring them in, and he reminded me of one of my brothers, so I automatically cared about him. I knew about his history and his hard times growing up, about his being in jail. And I'm one of those people who thinks I can always save everybody, whether I can or not. I have that thing in me, a servant's heart, that makes me want to try to help someone if I can. I see the best in everyone.

When Merle and I would travel to all these places, we were like two kids, in a way—kind of like I would be with a brother. We'd make up stupid games, or we'd see a town on a mileage sign and create some story about how that town got its name. As a side benefit of our friendship, Merle even recorded one of my songs, "Kentucky Gambler."

But I was also fortunate to have my actual brothers and sisters at my side. I had always thought that if I struck gold as a country singer, I would take my family with me. So now that I was on my own, I got them to join me on tour. They became the Traveling Family Band, and they went with me across America for the next two years. It was kind of like we were taking our little front porch concerts on the road!

Light of a Brand-New Day

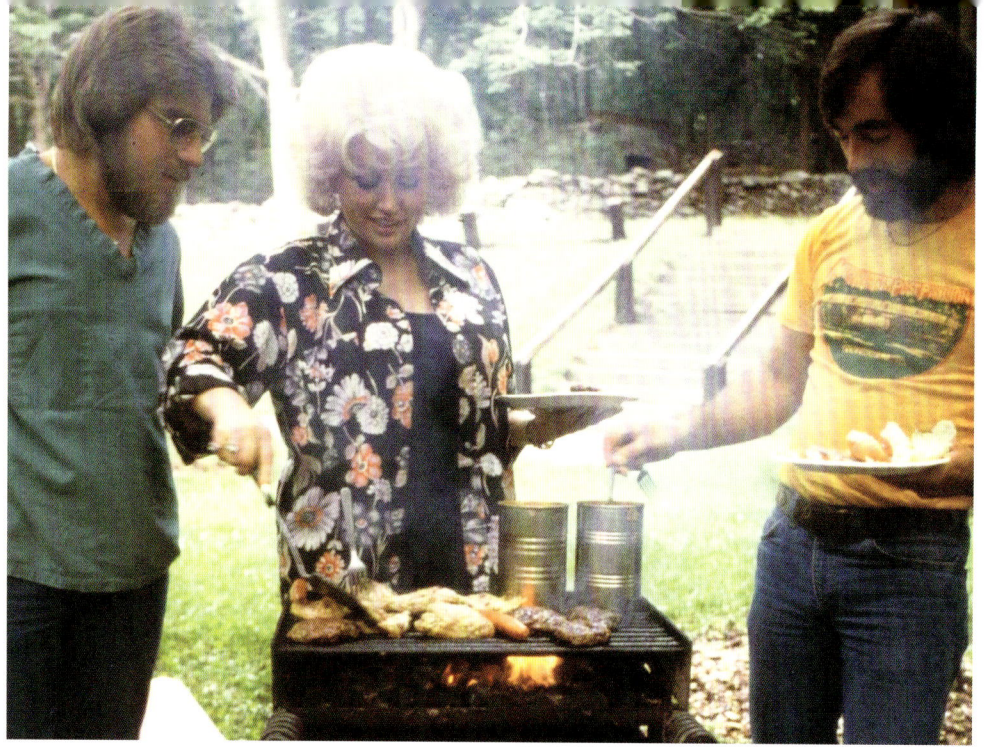

During my early solo tours, we would often look for roadside parks and outdoor spots near venues where we could cook out and chill. Here, I'm grilling with Richard Dennison and Joe McGuffee.

It was high pressure. I had always wanted to be an artist, but it also meant that I was suddenly the head of my own company. I had never been particularly bossy with my brothers and sisters, but now I was supposed to be their employer. As a company owner, I had to worry about expenses and other things that I'd never much considered before. Porter had always been responsible for that stuff.

At the beginning of my solo touring career, concert fees weren't all that large. It wasn't unusual to gross only $2,500 a night, and once you started deducting all the costs, there wasn't much left. I had paid for the bus, I had paid for the band, and I had paid for the costumes—mine and theirs—so there were lots of expenses. And I was spending on new outfits, wigs, makeup—not to mention fingernails and nail polish.

That meant we would take pretty much whatever concert offers we were getting. Thank God Carl had a good job, because a lot of times I'd have to borrow money to afford all of those things. And I had to do that for many, many years before I started making any real money.

We got our first bus that summer, just in time to ride up to Lima, Ohio, for the Allen County Fair. We played two shows that day, an afternoon concert and a night performance, and as excited as we were, there was nothing glamorous about it. That's not a complaint. When you play the fair circuit, you're an attraction, just like the Ferris wheel, the cotton candy, or the midway. Particularly at that time, at that fair, the stage was small, and it wasn't that much higher than the ground where some of the fans were seated.

PORTLAND CIVIC AUDITORIUM
8:00 P.M.
FRI. FEB. 27

All Seats Reserved $4.50, $5.50, $6.50, $7.00 Tickets Now On Sale Civic Aud. Box Office, 222 SW Clay St. Portland 97201, Meier & Frank - Lipman's - Stevens & Sons, Salem & Lloyd Center, Lincoln Savings & Loan
Mail Orders include self addressed stamped envelope and mail to Civic Aud. Box Office

---

KWJJ & JACK ROBERTS PRESENT
THE DOLLY PARTON FARON YOUNG SHOW

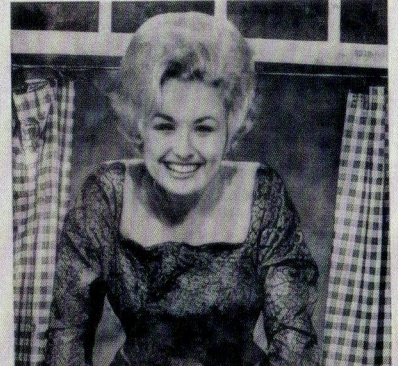

DOLLY PARTON
& FAMILY TRAVELIN' BAND

FARON YOUNG
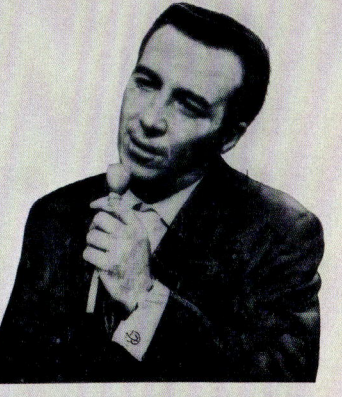
& HIS COUNTRY DEPUTIES

Produced By Jack Roberts   17522 Bothell Way NE Bothell, Wa. 98011 206 485-6511

Hatch Show Print—Nashville

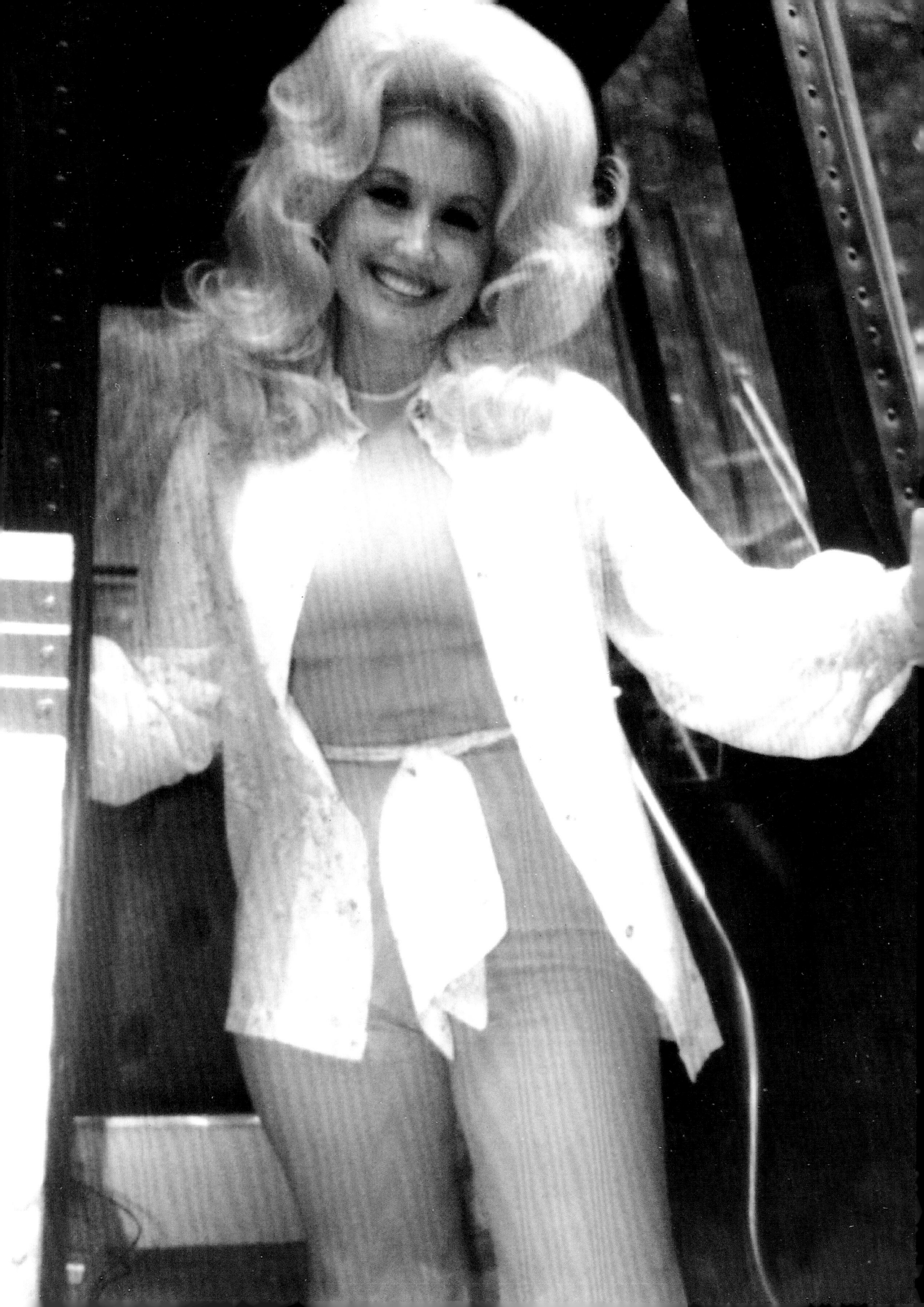

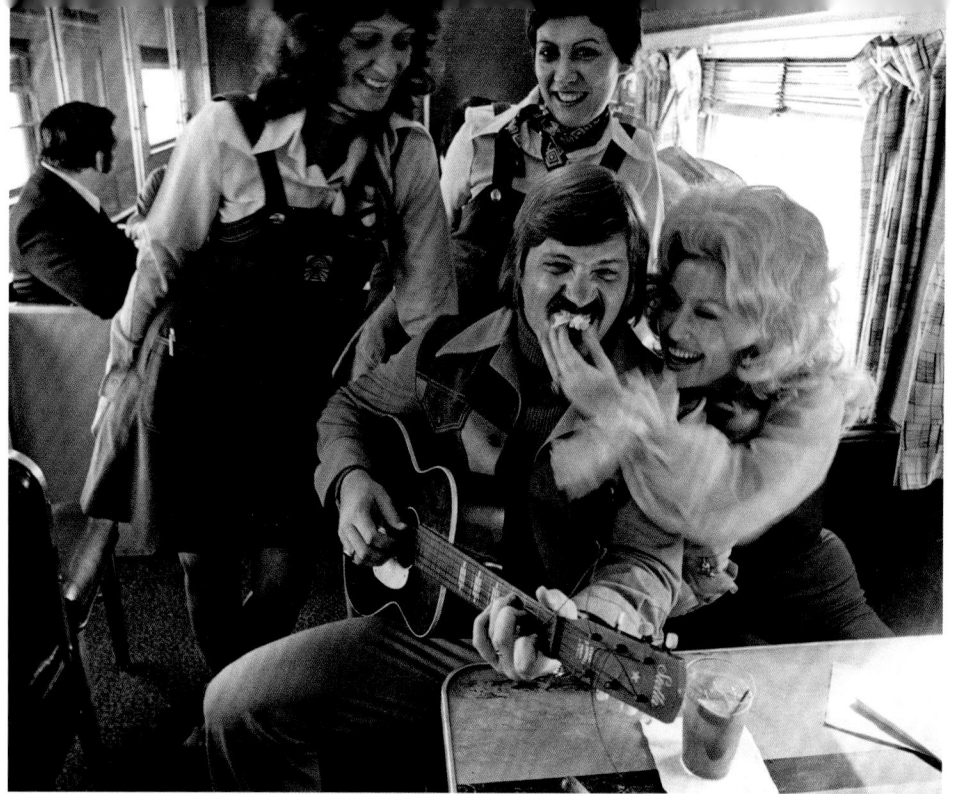

Clowning around on tour. I swear I'm putting food in
his mouth, not taking out his false teeth!

But the fairs were still fun. The band loved going out on the midway and eating all that food, and they could get away with it because people didn't know what they looked like. I couldn't go out. If I had, I might have never gotten back, and the way that concerts ran in those days, I might have interviews to do on the bus during the afternoon with local reporters. But I always had the band bring a load of stuff back to me from the midway. One way or another, I was going to have that Italian sausage with all the onions and peppers on it. And they'd bring those funnel cakes that we're now famous for at Dollywood too. I loved that fair food—in its own way, it's better than anything you can get at the finest restaurant in town.

As I continued touring on my own, I scrapped the Porter Wagoner duets from my set lists. Playing those songs would only increase the "Where's Porter?" questions, and I thought it might also look like I was still leaning on him. The truth is, a few of my solo songs—particularly "Coat of Many Colors," "Jolene," and "I Will Always Love You"—had already surpassed the impact of those records, so I made them the central part of my concerts. I always included a gospel section, too, and I filled out a portion of the show with songs by other women in the business. I'd do "Stand by Your Man," "It Wasn't God Who Made Honky Tonk Angels," "Rose Garden," and "Funny Face."

Having the Parton clan around helped keep my feet on the ground. I had always said that if I made it, I wouldn't abandon my hometown. I felt like I was bringing the mountains with me. And the Traveling Family Band made that part of the job a little easier, especially for the Appalachian songs. When I played "My Tennessee Mountain Home," "Coat of Many Colors," or "Applejack," my siblings knew what I was singing about. They had all

Light of a Brand-New Day

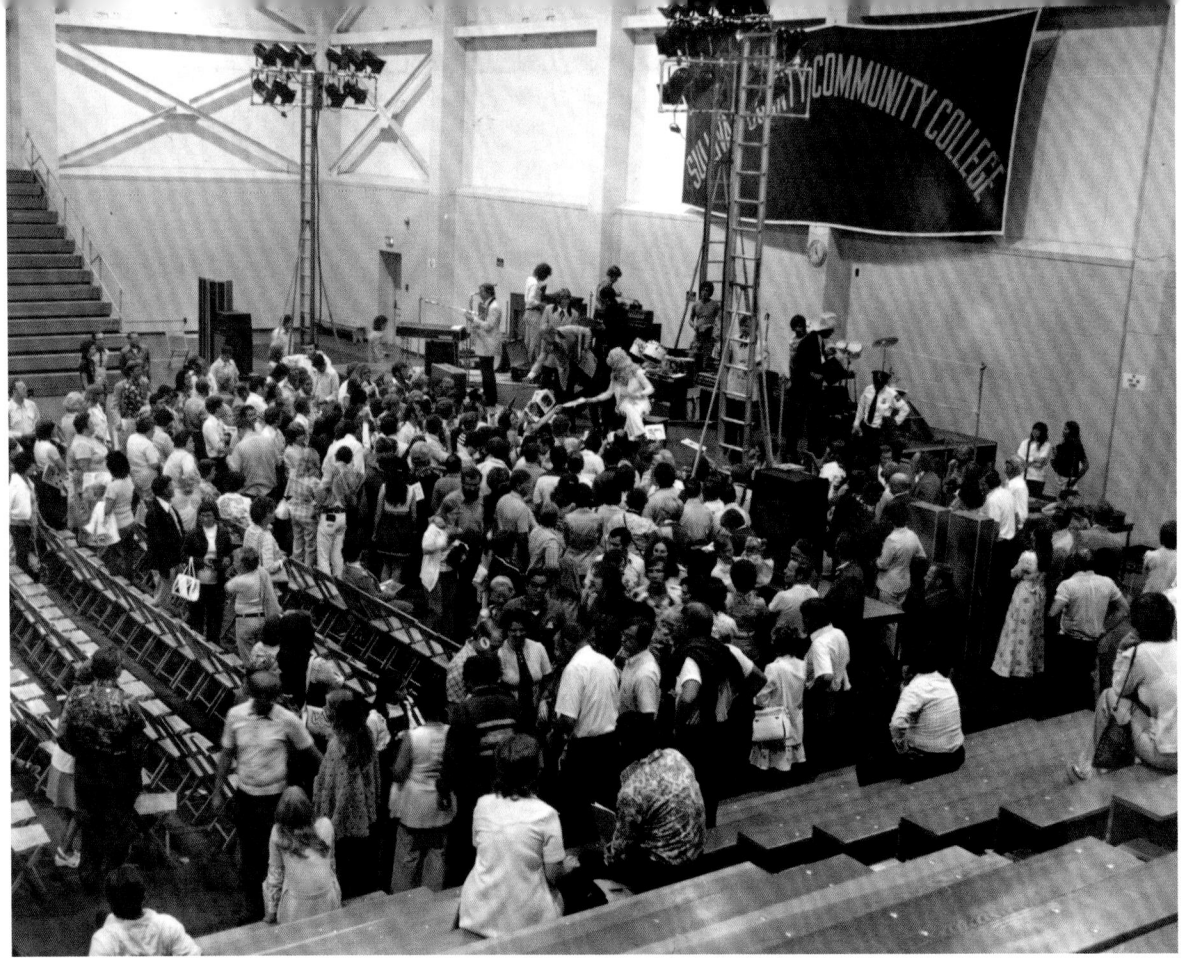

The fans are the whole reason to go on tour, so I made a point of meeting them near the front of the stage after concerts. I'd sign autographs for anyone who wanted them, until either the place emptied out or Don Warden said we had to go.

experienced the same things that birthed those songs, and those performances further established just who I was as an artist and as a person.

Uncle Louis helped too. He was really great with the merchandise, and he took along Richie Owens—his son, my first cousin—who now does so much work with the family and has produced some of my records. Sometimes you can make more money on merchandise than on the shows, so Uncle Louis sold not only my merchandise but also other people's merchandise, whether it be hats or T-shirts or coffee cups or whatever. He was always good at that.

Traveling as much as we did, we would periodically find places to stop that felt like home. Occasionally, we'd throw a mini picnic in a park. One time, we stopped in Sinking Spring, Ohio, about eighty miles east of Cincinnati. Dayne Puckett, who sometimes sold merch at the concerts, had grown up there, and his mom, Setty Puckett, made supper for everybody. It meant so much to have a home-cooked meal in a real house—rather than a hotel—and to feel a deeper connection with a member of our road family.

It's not always easy working with family, though, and I soon realized that I'm a better boss with other people. I wasn't very strict about the rules of the road, and sometimes it was

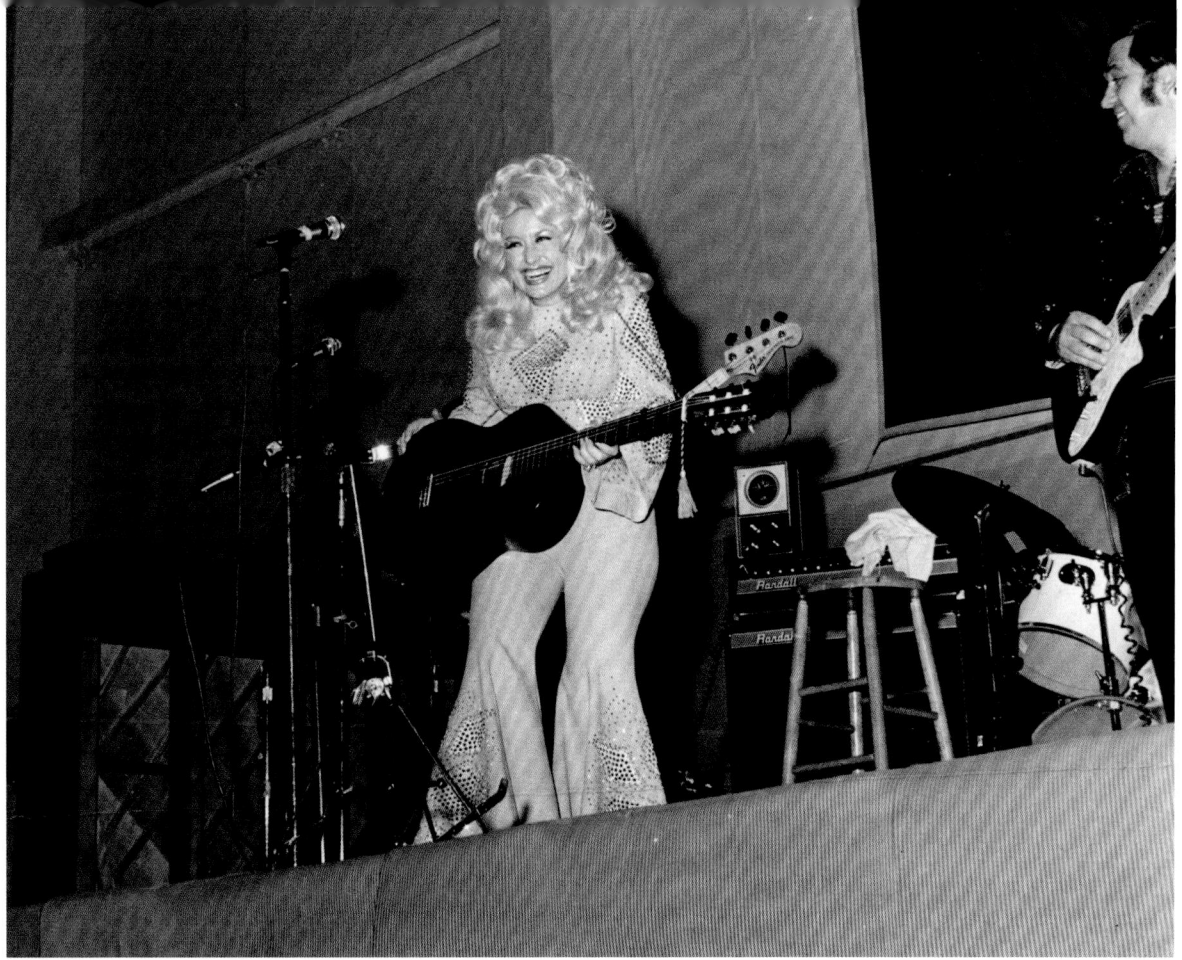

Notice all those microphones set up for whatever instrument I might play during the course of the night. Concert production has come a long way since the '70s!

like herding cats out there. That occasionally put some pressure on me as I learned to be an employer. The road was an adventure, and the temptation was always there for people to go off exploring. I didn't want to nag when I felt someone was starting to get out of line, but I also felt some responsibility. They were supporting me, and I thought I should be a little bit protective.

Fortunately, Don Warden laid down the law a little better than I did. He told everyone that if they missed call time for the bus, they'd be left behind and would be responsible for getting to the next gig on their own. The whole crew knew he was serious.

After playing steel guitar with the Wagonmasters for almost two decades, Don came with me when I broke away from Porter, though the two of them stayed friends throughout the years. Don managed me in those early days, taking care of the day-to-day finances and operations. He knew all the ins and outs of touring, was in charge of buying the bus and renovating it, and even knew how to fix it—or, at the very least, could identify what the likely problem was when the bus broke down.

Don was a quiet man, and although you'd never know it, he was an ex-military guy—tough as a pine nut. He didn't take crap from anybody. I remember one time he slung a promoter

Light of a Brand-New Day

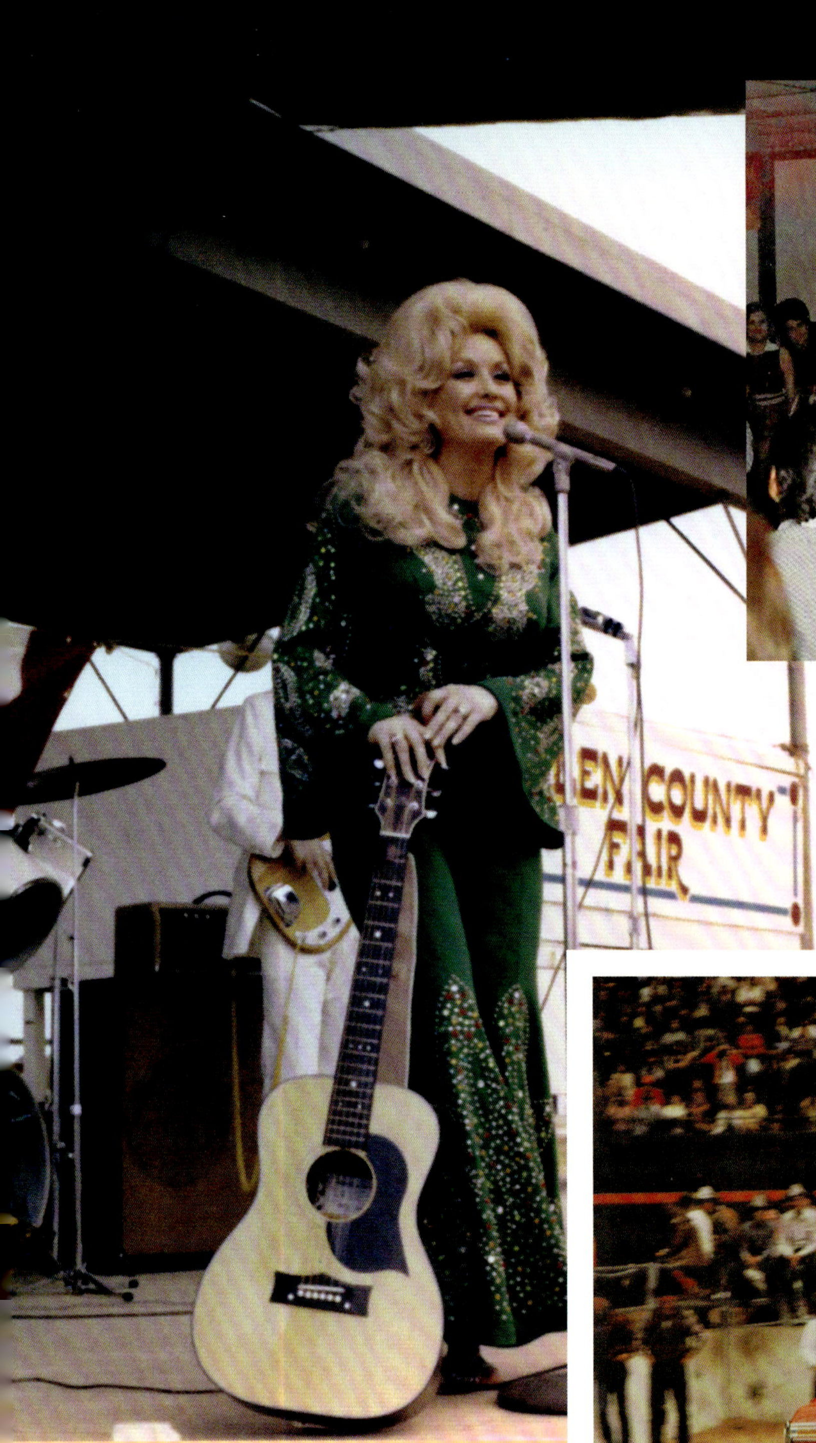

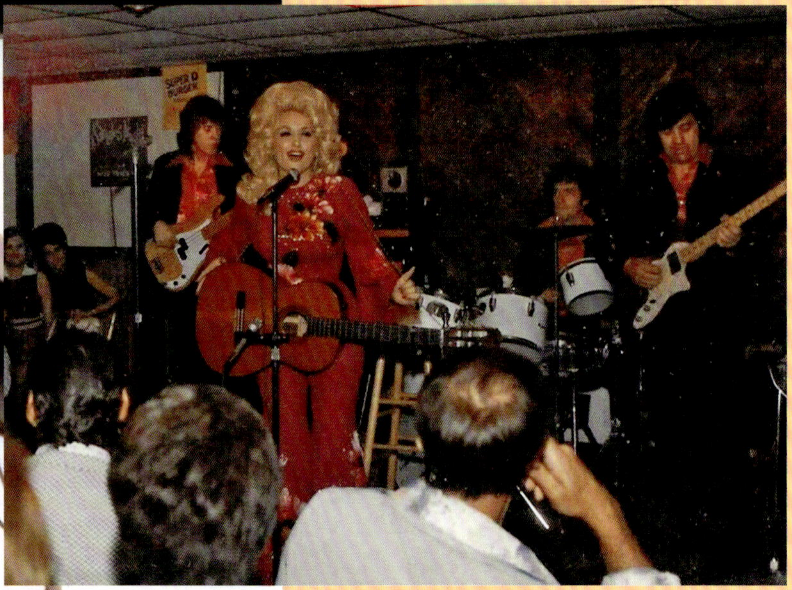

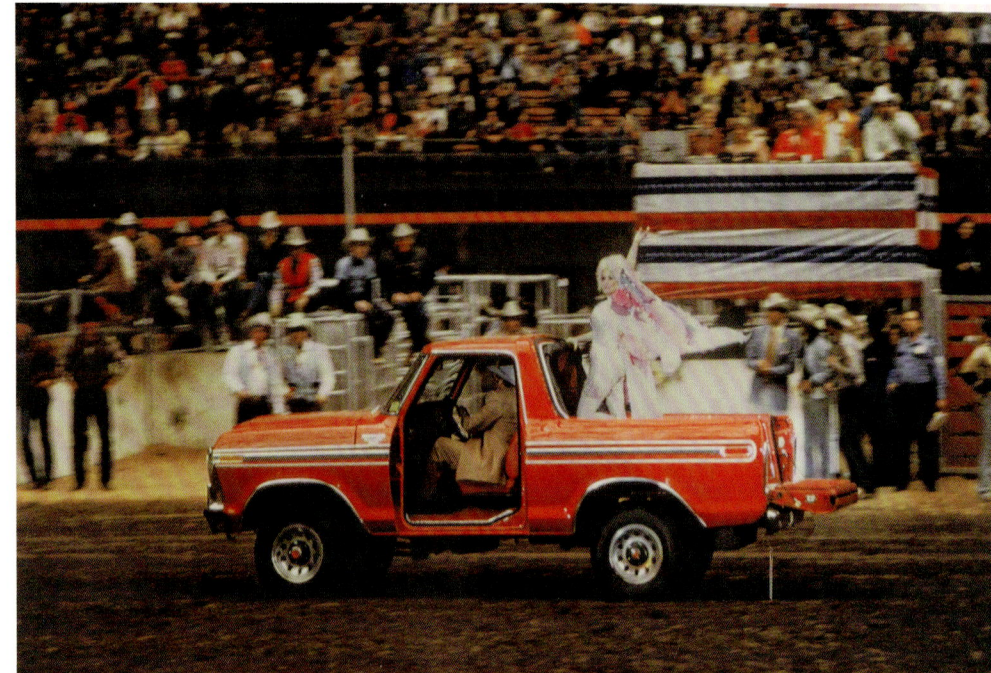

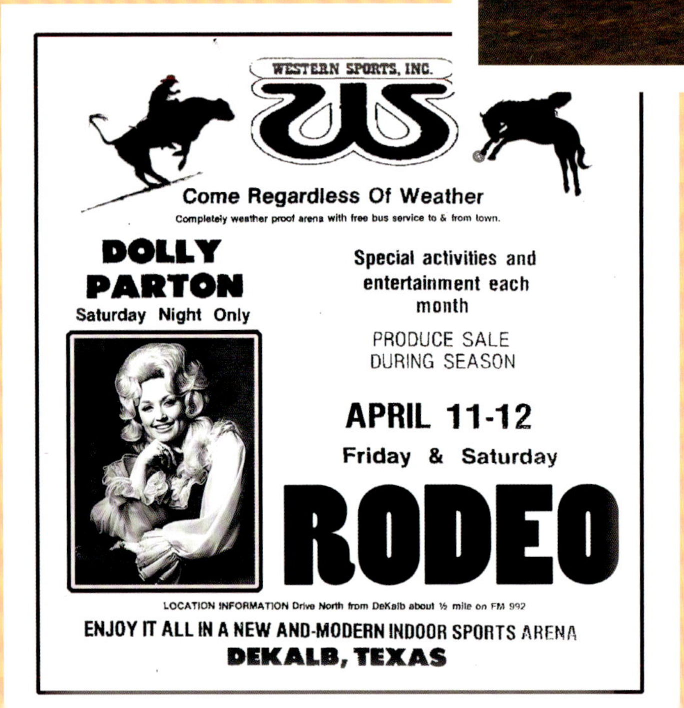

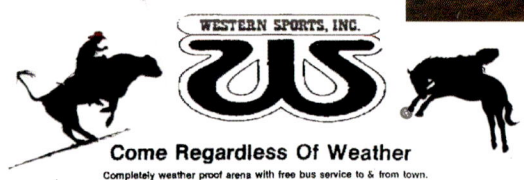

The upper left photo is from a show in Lima, Ohio, on the weekend that we traveled for the first time in my own tour bus. In the photo next to it, my brother Randy is on the left, Bill Uhrig on the right, and Dwight Puckett is on the drums. Below that, bull riders sat high in the saddle at rodeos, but I rode in on a pickup truck!

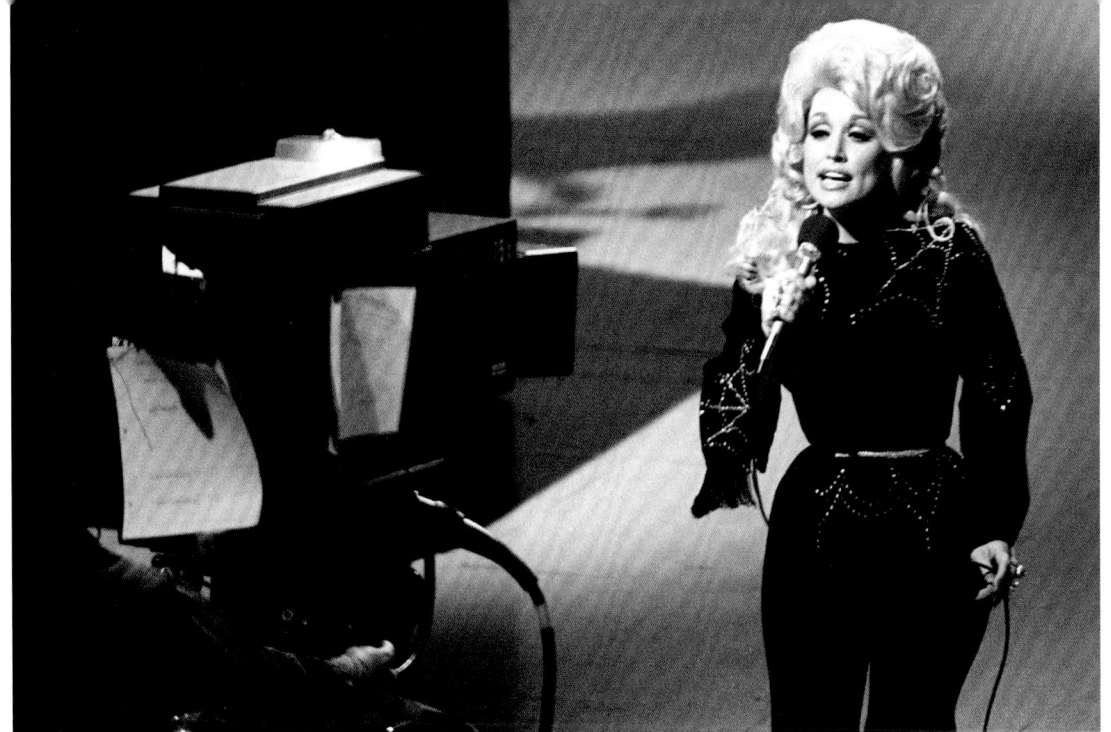

I may be singing to a cold metal camera, but the whole time I was keeping in mind the people all over America watching TV and trying to connect on an emotional level.

up against the wall to get the money owed us for a show. He was like, "That's our money. You go get it." I don't know what the guy thought Don might do, but I know we got paid that night!

One of the ways I expanded my horizons as a solo artist came when I flew to London for the International Festival of Country Music. It was my first overseas performance, and I was one of a dozen artists, including Dottie West, Skeeter Davis, Marty Robbins, and Jeanne Pruett, playing Wembley Arena. I was looking forward to going to a foreign country, and kind of glad that I was going to be with some fellow singers and musicians. I knew we were going to be looked after by the producers and booking agents, which meant we didn't have to worry about doing a whole lot of things ourselves, like being personally responsible for getting in and out of hotels—that sort of thing. Traveling in a group like that can be helpful.

Playing all those beautiful old buildings and seeing England was like going back in time. It was another world. Being in some of those buildings that matched what I had envisioned in my mind but never thought I would see in person had me thinking of all the fairy tales I had read over the years. It felt like I was living in one.

After London, I made my Scandinavian debut at the Scandinavium in Gothenburg. Sweden is forty-four hundred miles from Nashville, and it takes sixteen hours to fly there—not including the time it takes to get your tickets processed and to get the luggage loaded at the start and then unloaded at the end. That's some travel!

Light of a Brand-New Day

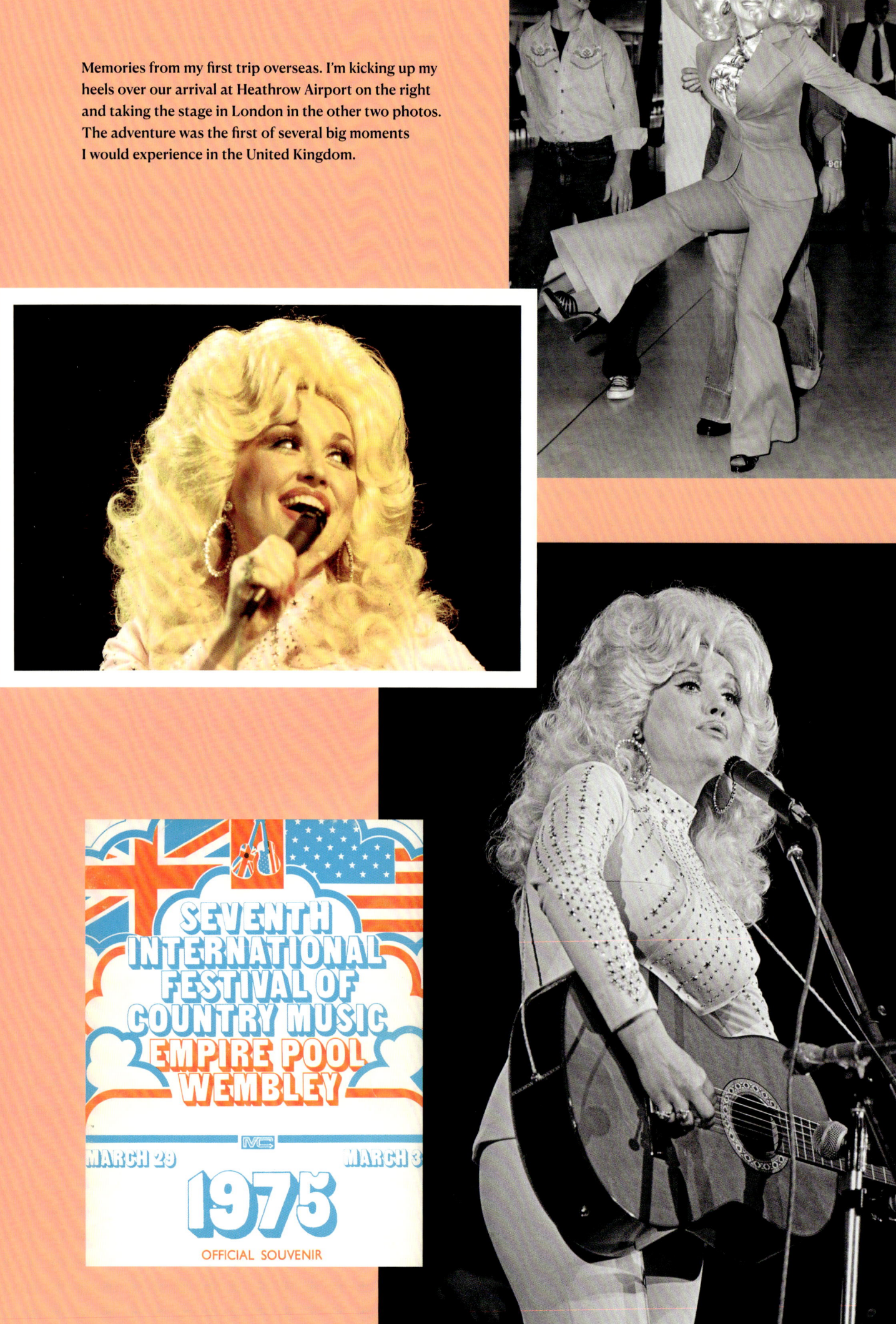

Memories from my first trip overseas. I'm kicking up my heels over our arrival at Heathrow Airport on the right and taking the stage in London in the other two photos. The adventure was the first of several big moments I would experience in the United Kingdom.

But I was determined to work. I had dreamed my whole life of becoming the star of the show, and now that I had the opportunity, I was going for it. The harder I worked, the bigger my audience would grow and the faster I could pay off the debts that I still owed Porter from the agreement I signed to split our business. So I think I took just about anything that came my way: I played gymnasiums, theme parks, campgrounds, concert halls—even a prison rodeo in Huntsville, Texas!

That's right—Texas used to have inmates compete at a rodeo to raise money for the prison system, and people bought tickets to the event, which included a concert. There were twenty thousand in attendance when I sang in Huntsville in 1975.

One of the elements I added to the set around then was a little 78 rpm bit. It was sometimes fun to play records at the wrong speed. If you put a 45 rpm single on the turntable but ran it at 78 rpm, the song went faster and made the singer sound like one of those old Chipmunks records. So I worked up a thing with my singers for "Do I Ever Cross Your Mind," a gospel-sounding song I'd written. We sang it a cappella at the right speed, then did it at a quicker, higher-pitched pace. Sometimes I even laughed in that Chipmunks pitch. It was kind of goofy, but it was fun and created a special moment for the fans during the concert.

On top of the concert performances, television producers started paying attention. I sang "Love Is Like a Butterfly" on Jerry Lewis's MDA Labor Day Telethon, wearing a red outfit with rhinestones, backed by the Traveling Family Band. I did "Butterfly" in pink chiffon on the CMA Awards, with a full string section and female harmony singers backing me up off camera. Before the year was over, the band supported me again when I sang "Jolene" on *The Midnight Special* in a black jumpsuit with disco-ball sparkles. Shortly afterward, I got a deal to host my own syndicated TV show for the first time. I was building on the lessons I had learned working with Porter. Not everyone is comfortable in front of a camera, but I was. I was also doing something that hadn't been done before: becoming the first female country singer to host her own regular national show.

We were trying to get pop names and actors to make the show as big as it could be. We knew we'd have the country people—and we did—but I was happy that so many other artists were willing to be guests because they were really, really hot at the time. KC and the Sunshine Band came on my show when the group first started and KC was just a boy. And we had Marilyn McCoo and Billy Davis Jr., Pure Prairie League, and The Hues Corporation, the group that did "Rock the Boat."

The first time I met Kenny Rogers, actually, was when he appeared on the show. We had this goofy opening number where he was hidden in a box, knocking on the walls from the inside while I sang "Knock Three Times." It was corny, but it fit both of us perfectly, and you could tell through the rest of the show just how comfortable we were together. Our friendship started there and lasted for decades.

Light of a Brand-New Day

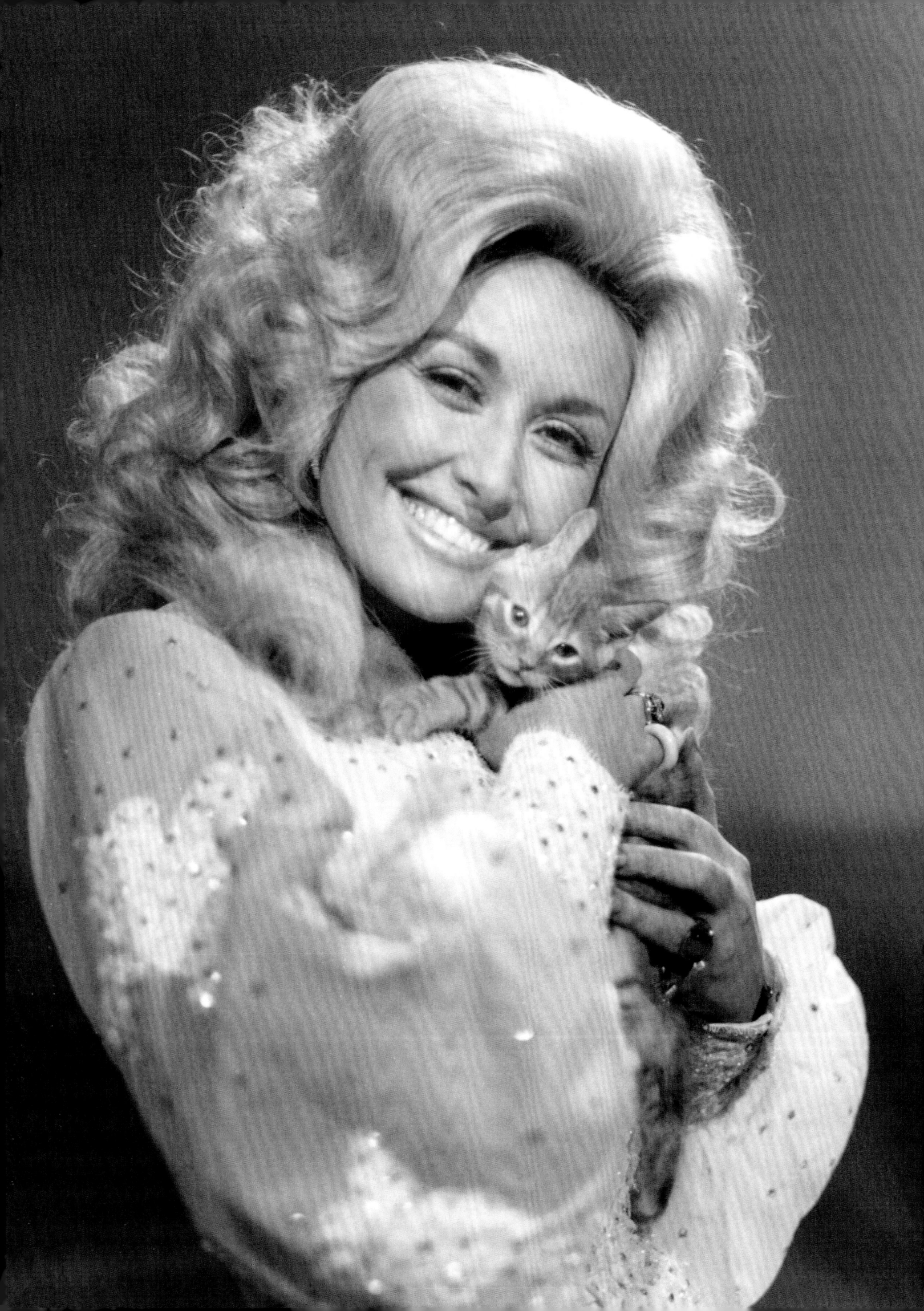

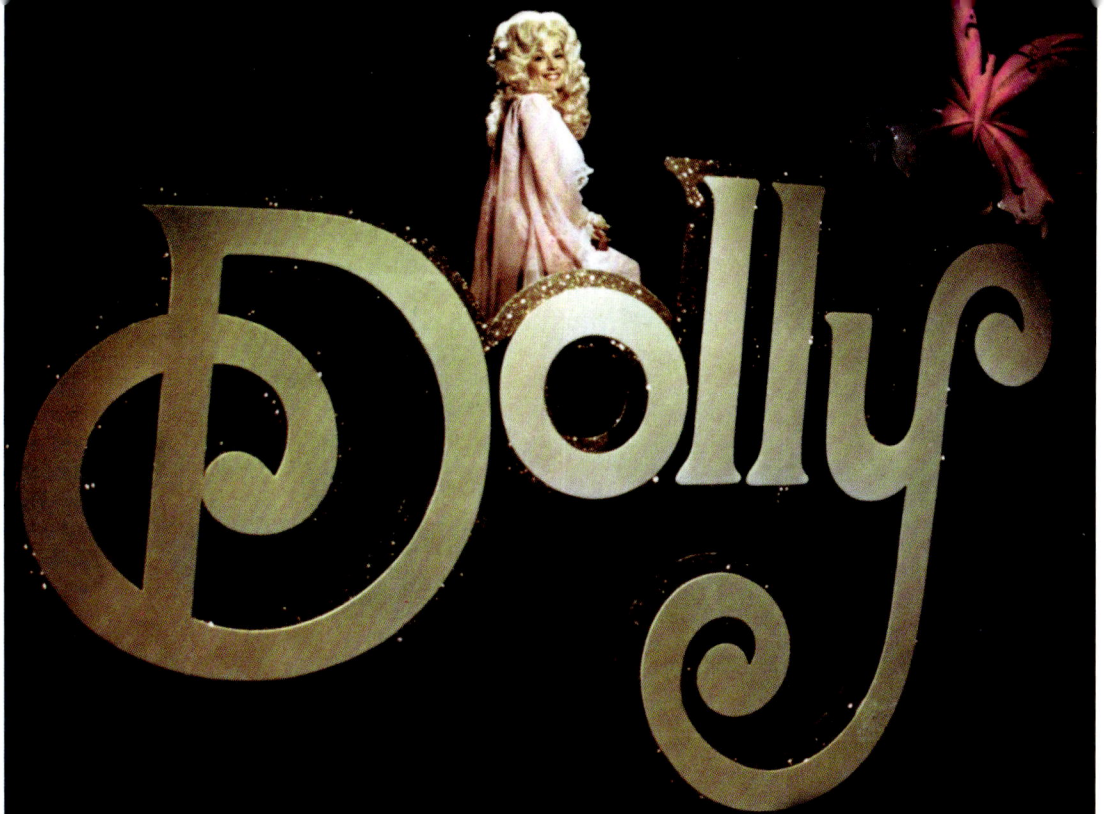

> I hope every show brings people some good music, a little bit of laughter, and a good-sized dose of inspiration.

The *Dolly* show was also the first time that Linda Ronstadt and Emmylou Harris sang with me on a public stage. We did "Silver Threads and Golden Needles," and the results were amazing. It's harder to line up tight harmonies for three people than it is for two, and yet the Trio—as we would later call our little side group—was perfect.

Around that time, I parted ways with the Traveling Family Band. It wasn't easy. They were my brothers and sisters, and I wanted what was best for them. But I was ready to expand my sound and felt like it would require musicians who were a little more versatile. The press has at times written about that moment as if I was being cruel, but the truth is, most bands break up at some point, and it was kind of our time for that. My family knew what was happening with my music, and some of them were ready for their own next adventures. In the end, we didn't have any issues. But it does go to show that you have to make some hard decisions when you're the head of a company.

At the time, I didn't feel like I had reached my full potential. As much as I'd played every available show, a lot of my concert bookings in small venues were frustrating. The sound systems were often bad, and so was the lighting. I wanted to make my concerts—and my whole career—bigger and better. I'd become friends with Mac Davis, and when I talked with him about my situation, he suggested I meet his manager, Sandy Gallin, in Los Angeles. So I did.

I thought we were going out to a restaurant, and I, of course, was totally overdone in all my gaudy getup. I was staying at the Beverly Hilton Hotel, and when I walked down, Sandy

Light of a Brand-New Day

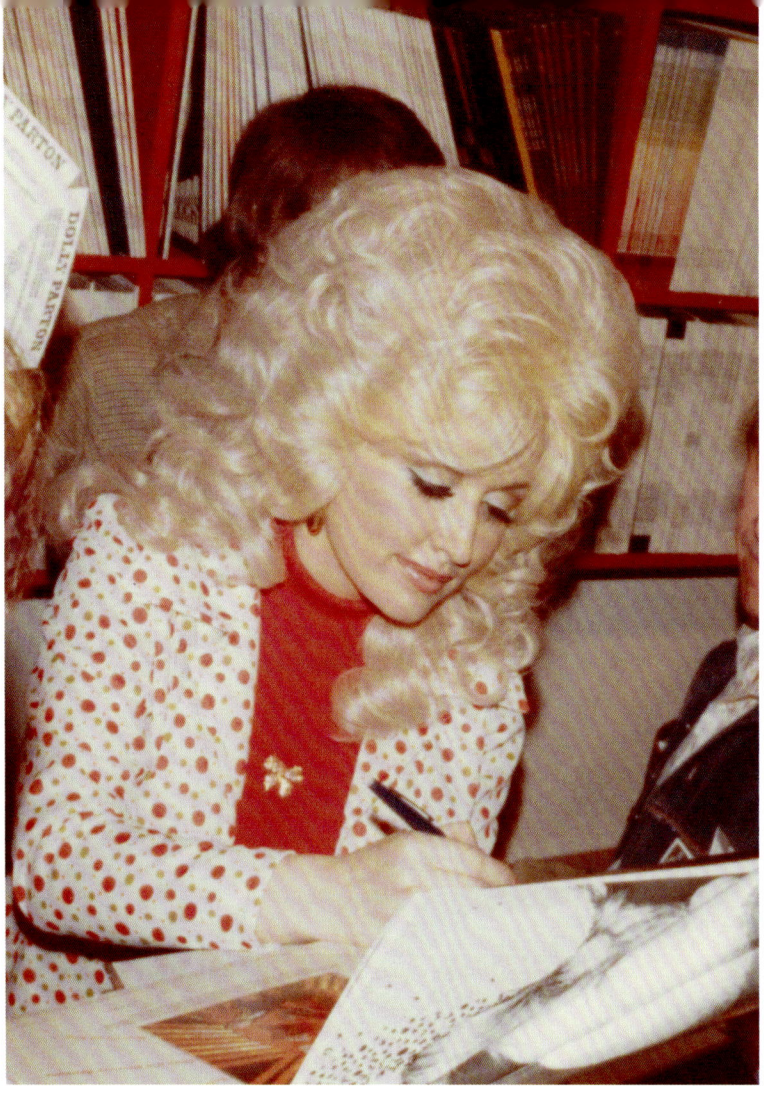

My sister Cassie ran my fan club for many years. Here I am signing autographs at Fan Fair—now called CMA Fest—in the 1970s.

pulled up in a convertible, which wasn't going to be good for my wig. I said, "First of all, you've got to put the top up on that car." And he said, "Second of all, where the hell do you think we're going?"

As it turned out, we were going to his house. He said, "Well, I can't talk to you with all them clothes." So he went and got me one of his shirts and some corduroy pants. Because he was short, with my high heels, the pants fit. But anyway, we talked all night long, until it was like three o'clock in the morning.

We hit it off, and he thought—just as I did—that I could be a bigger star.

I thought the best way to do that would be to make my brand of country wider. I would keep my East Tennessee songs in the set—and my country hits too—but I wanted to explore other forms of music. I thought it would get the attention of people who didn't necessarily listen to country music, and maybe grow my fan base. But I needed a band that could adapt to all those different sounds.

Star of the Show

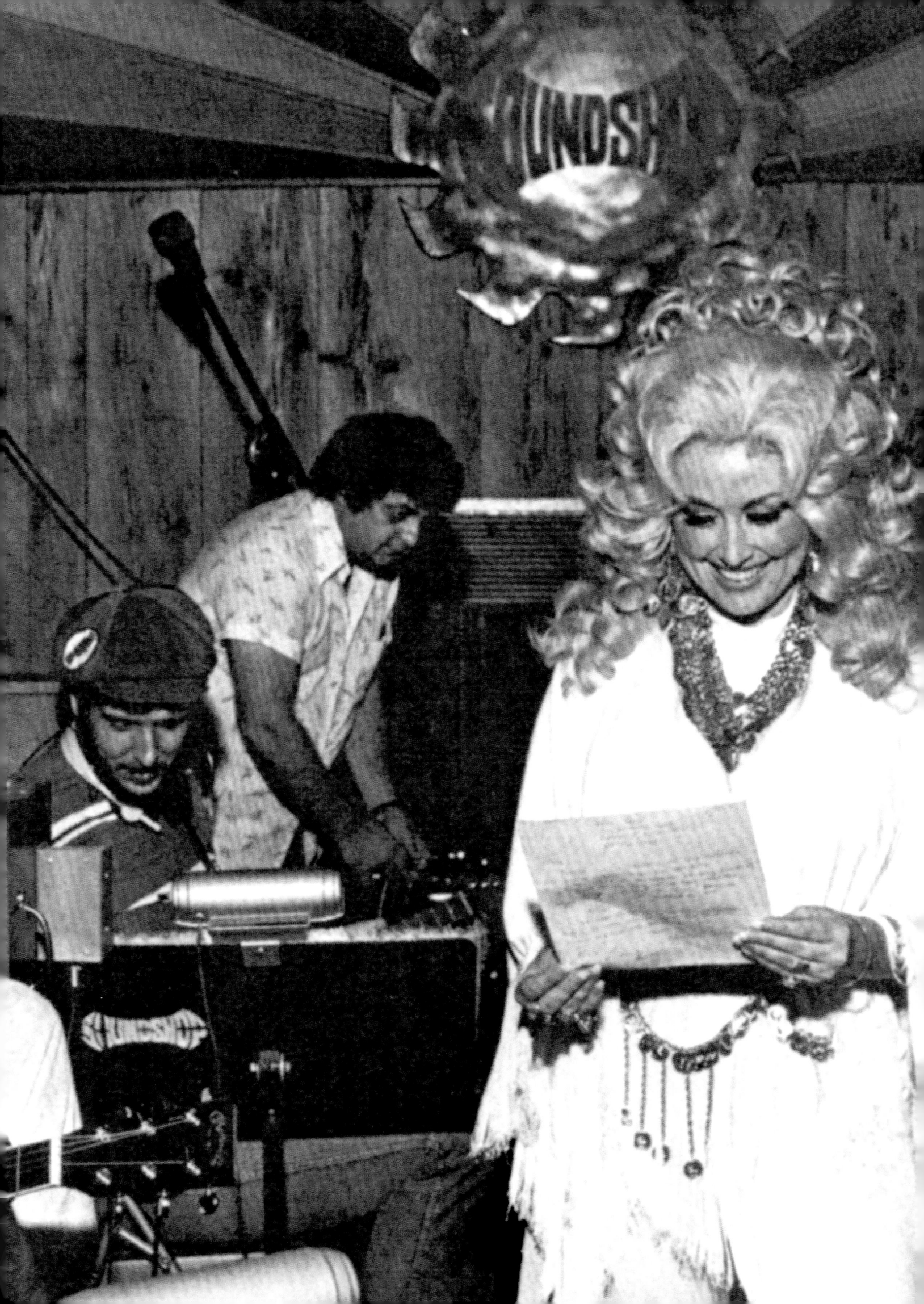

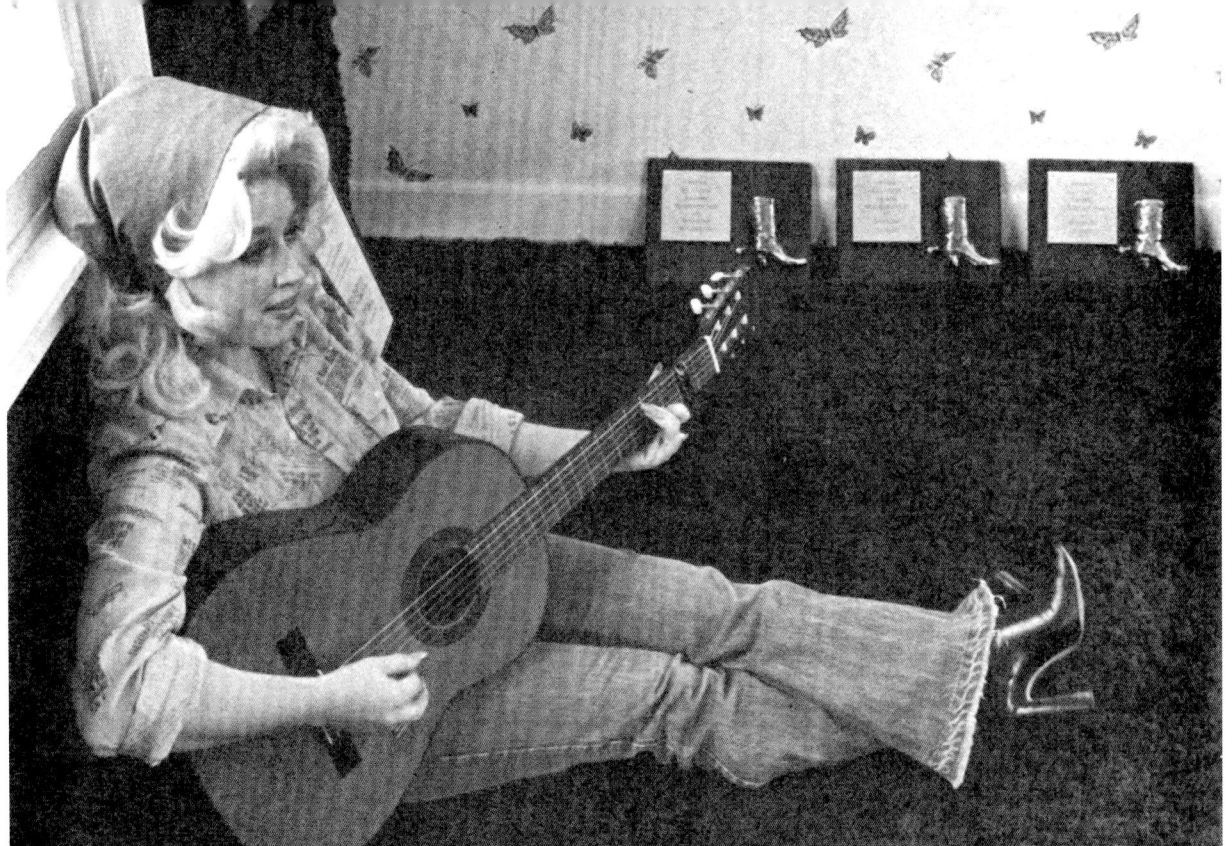

Every song in the set list started out as a few words and some simple chords. I still try to write music every chance I get.

With some help from Gregg Perry, who was in my very first band and is still with me, and Richard Dennison, I assembled a band that was part-Nashville, part-California, and versatile. We called the band Gypsy Fever since I traveled a lot and so did they!

After finishing my last album produced with Porter—*All I Can Do*—in 1976, I started assembling my next one, which I would produce with the help of Gregg Perry. With *New Harvest . . . First Gathering*, I felt I could start making my kind of country music. In addition to the obvious country songs, I included a little gospel and a little R & B, which probably surprised some people. But when I was home in Nashville with my husband, Carl—particularly in the early years of our marriage—we listened a lot to WVOL, a Nashville R & B station. The songs were mostly about working-class issues, love, and heartbreak, with some obvious gospel roots—just like a lot of country music.

So on *New Harvest . . . First Gathering,* I covered "My Girl," by the Temptations, which I renamed "My Love," and I redid Jackie Wilson's "(Your Love Has Lifted Me) Higher and Higher," which became the opening song for many of my shows. It brought a lot of energy to the concerts, which I thought was important if we were going to attract people beyond the country fans who were already coming out to see me.

Light of a Brand-New Day

THE GOSPEL ACCORDING TO DOLLY

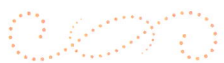

Words in the Bible can mean a lot of different things to people. I guess that's why so many folks say you shouldn't talk about religion. But my granddaddy was a preacher. I grew up around religion, so I can't help but talk about God. Deep down I believe we are all connected to Him, and to one another because of Him. I always have. And I have no shame about that. But I'll never tell you what you should believe because we each have our own journey with faith and with God.

My daddy used to take us Parton girls to sing for congregations all around East Tennessee, so the church played a big role in my introduction to music. Since then, I've made it a point to make a joyful noise to the Lord, and I've done so throughout my career.

In my early years, I would sing "How Great Thou Art" in concert. My grandfather inspired one of the hits I wrote during the Porter Wagoner years, "Daddy Was an Old-Time Preacher Man." There's also a gospel component to songs like "The Seeker," "Everything's Beautiful (in Its Own Way)," "God Won't Get You," "He's Alive," "Hello God," "Do I Ever Cross Your Mind," "Light of a Clear Blue Morning," and others.

I am proud that the Gospel Music Association elected me to the Gospel Music Hall of Fame in 2009, not only for my music but I feel for my faith too. My faith is part of every decision I make, everything I do.

In fact, a prayer is part of my preshow ritual. After I get my makeup on and I'm all dressed and ready to go on stage, I always stop . . . and I always pray.

I pray for God to protect me, to protect everybody, to let me be a blessing and to let me do something to glorify Him in the coming moments—basically, to let us do well and leave the audience happy, satisfied, and pleased with the performance. After I've said that prayer, I just kind of pace for a few minutes in my soul like a racehorse, until the lights hit me. Then I'm off to the races.

I know God is with me, and that He'll help me have the right words for the night, sing all the notes, smile, and "shine."

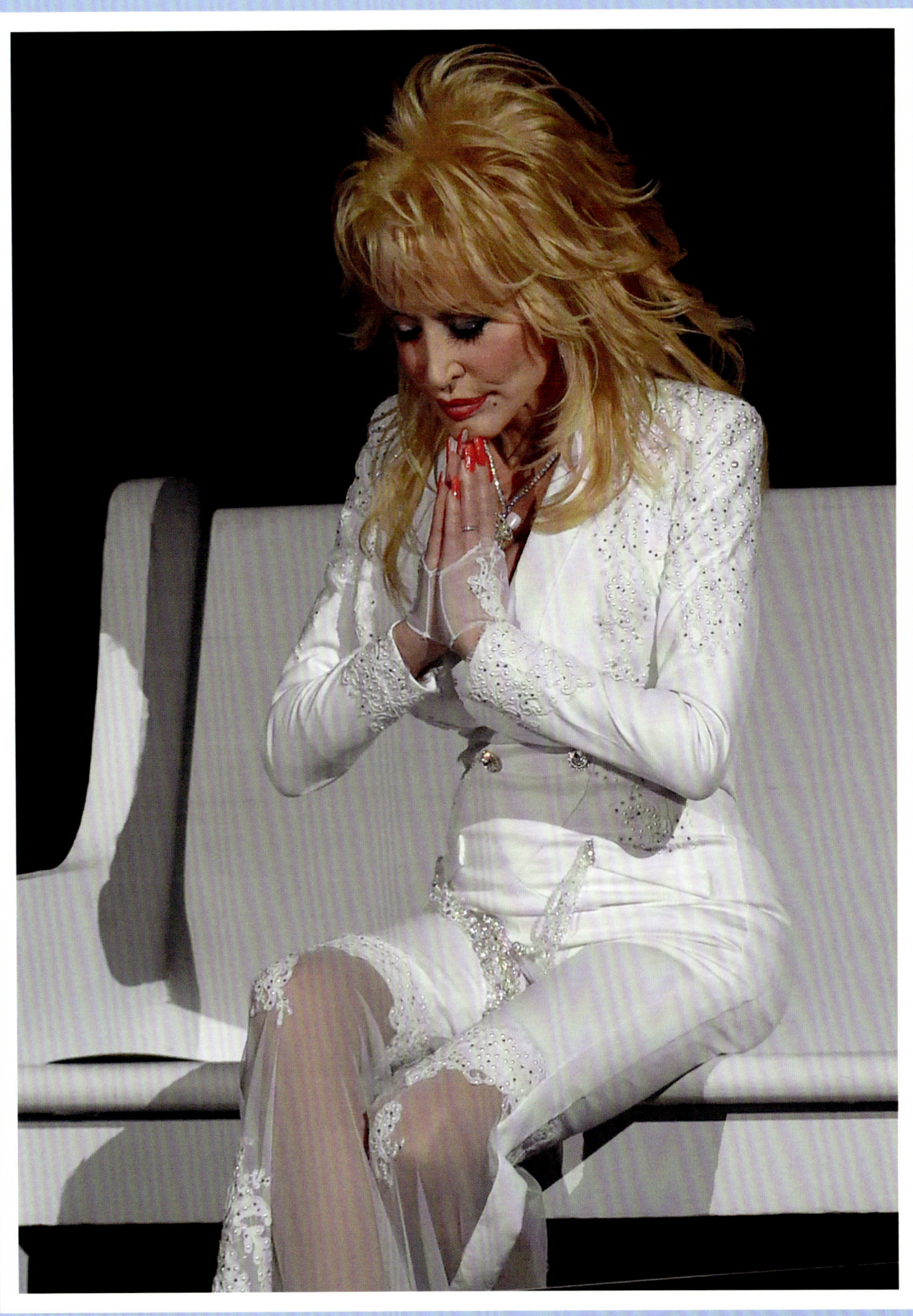

I've always integrated inspirational music into my live shows. This one is from a 2015 concert at the Ryman Auditorium in Nashville, the same stage where I made my Grand Ole Opry debut.

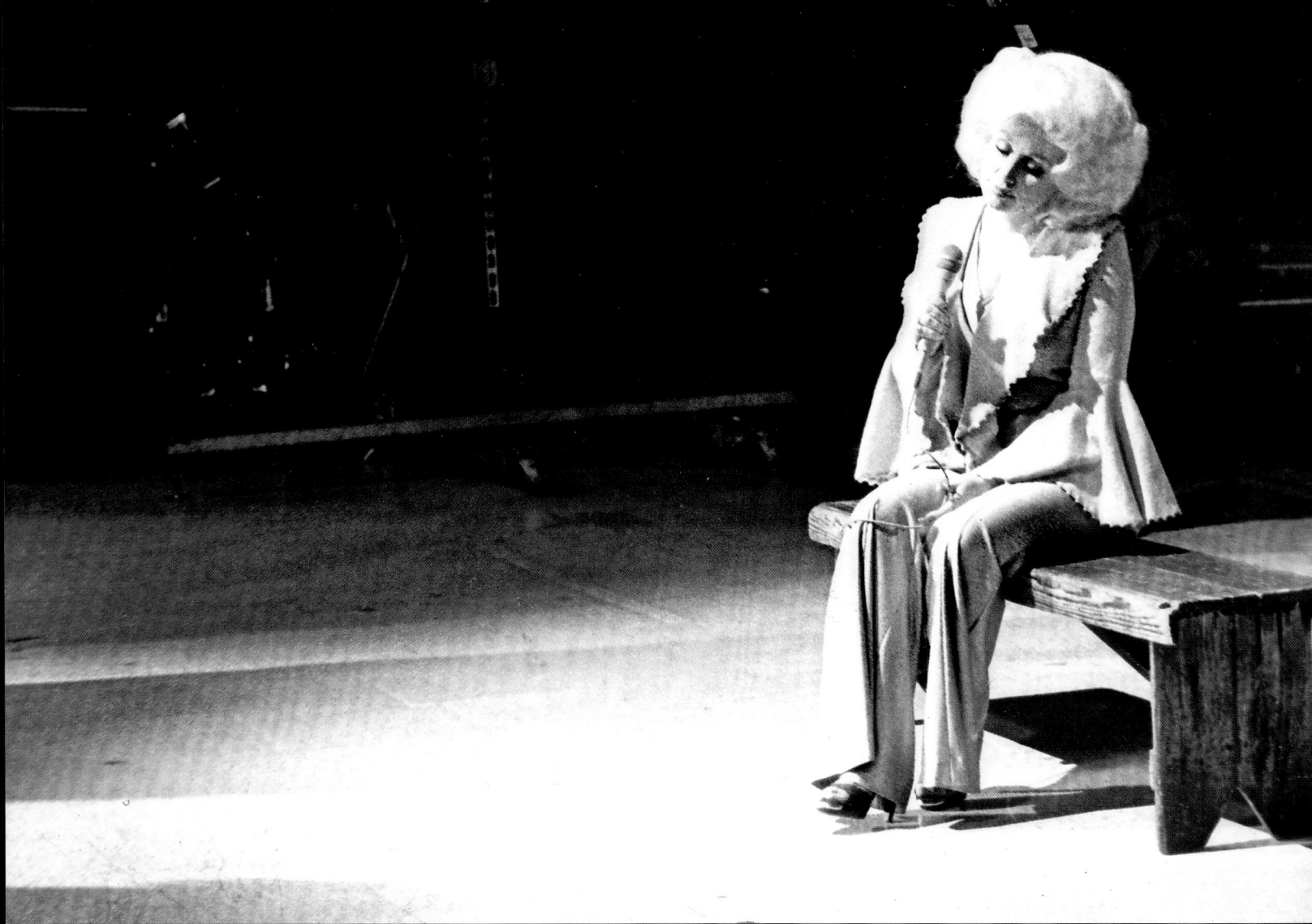

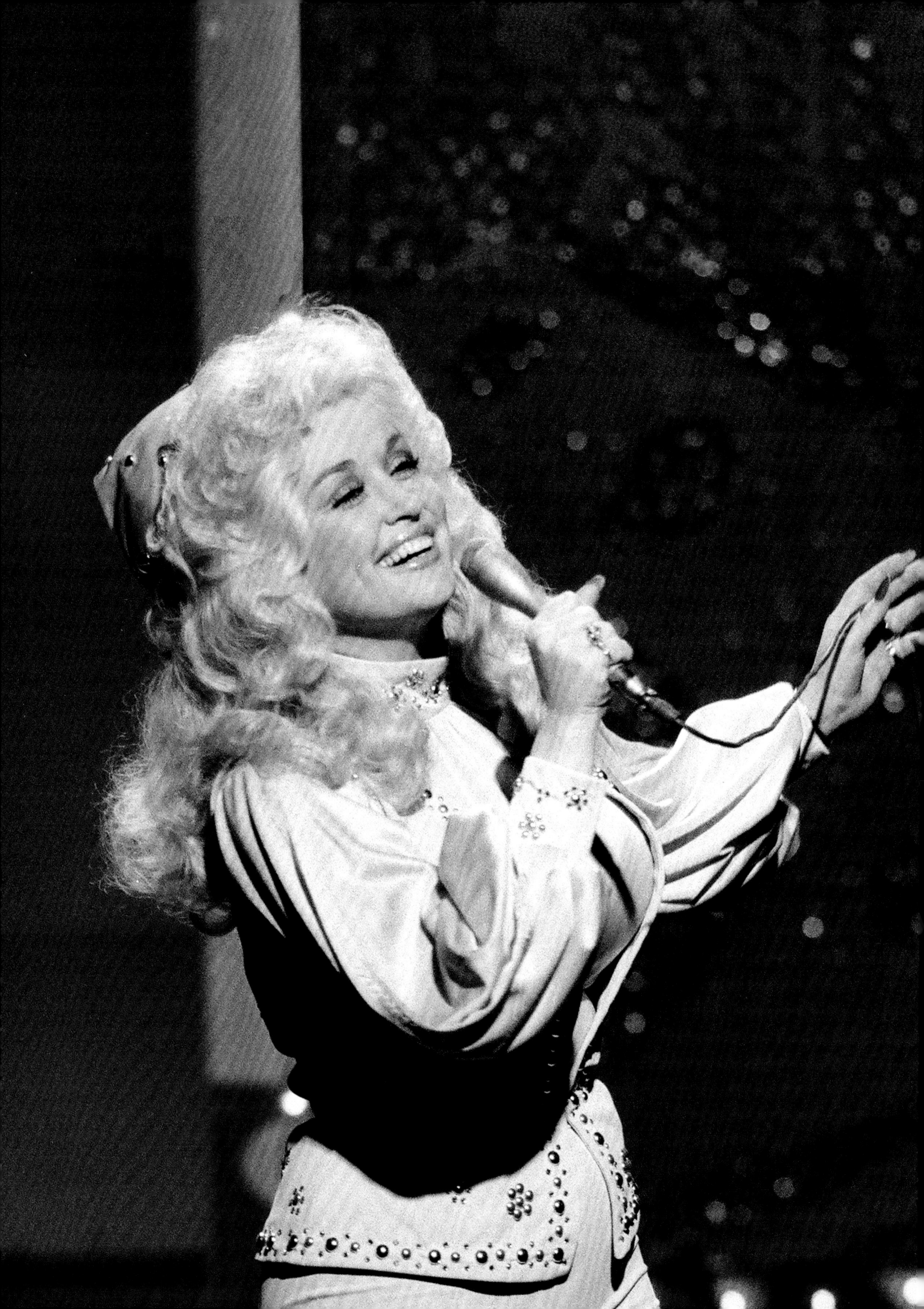

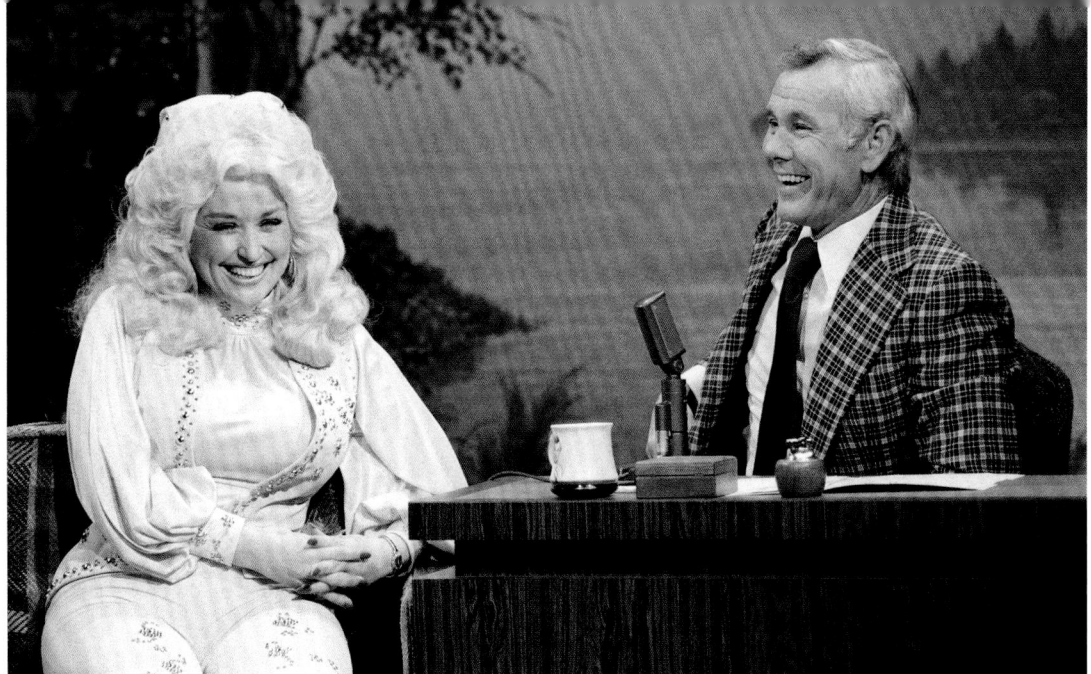

Johnny Carson was considered a starmaker in the 1970s. If you got invited to appear on *The Tonight Show*, there was little doubt good things were happening in your career.

Around the same time, Gypsy Fever debuted in a show at Donk's Theatre, an old movie house in Mathews County, Virginia. It was one of the last shows we did before stepping up to a new level of concert halls, and when Gregg went to use the venue's piano, he played just one note on it and broke a string. Fortunately, he had an electric piano with him, and we were able to pull off the show. But that name—Donk's—was odd enough that it became something we referred to in the future when we talked about paying our dues. Not that we were complaining then. We worked with what was available and were happy to play for folks wherever we could. But the more you played places with those kinds of shortcomings, the more you appreciated it when you got to perform in places that were better equipped.

Sandy kept finding ways to get me more attention—beginning with an appearance on *The Tonight Show* with Johnny Carson, where I sang "Higher and Higher" and "Me and Little Andy," sort of announcing to the general public that the new Dolly Parton would be harder and harder to stuff into a small musical box. *The Tonight Show* was momentous. It came the same day I turned thirty-one—nice birthday present, right? And it gave me some credibility since it was a big, well-known TV program that was seen by millions. Not many country artists got to perform on it—it was a big deal.

Johnny Carson and I had this sweet connection. He seemed to always want to do right by me. I felt that he was very protective of me. He was a Midwestern boy—born in Iowa and raised in Nebraska—and he respected the fact that I was a country girl. No matter how I looked on the outside, I felt that he saw the real me, and I thought he was on my side. And I thought he kind of sensed in those early days that I was a little bit of a fish out of water in that setting. He wanted to make sure that I was okay. I always loved that about him, and I'm still grateful for it.

Light of a Brand-New Day

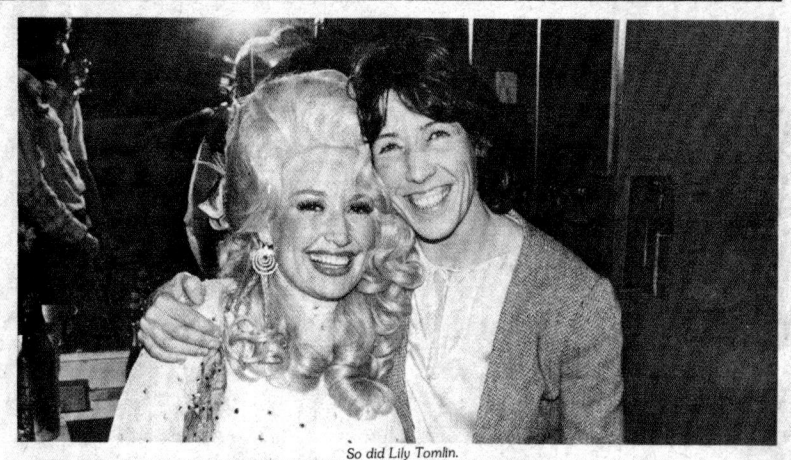

Takes New York By Storm

So did Lily Tomlin.

As part of her push to "reach more people", Dolly Parton came, saw and conquered New York recently with six sold out shows at the Bottom Line. After her Friday midnight show, RCA Records tossed an ultra-lavish party for Dolly atop the World

> The turnout for my three nights at the Bottom Line in New York City—and for a party at the World Trade Center's Windows on the World restaurant—was incredible. I met my future *9 to 5* costar Lily Tomlin and so many other people too!

Right after that, I hit the road with Willie Nelson for a handful of arena shows in Texas and New Mexico. Willie's crowd was often a little rowdier than my audience, and in San Angelo, Texas, the venue didn't sell alcohol, but it allowed ticketholders to bring in their own beer. Some folks in the audience apparently brought a lot with them. A fight broke out, and before it was all over, a bunch of fans with floor seats folded up their chairs and used them as a barrier to attack the stage. It was one of the few shows in that time period when I didn't go out after the concert to sign autographs. It was just too unsafe.

Willie's audience and mine, believe it or not, are very similar though. They're country people, after all—*T* for Texas, *T* for Tennessee! They could get rowdy with Willie and his band 'cause they were usually smoking and drinking. But the bottom line is they were out there to have fun. And so were we.

Willie always did a lot of really slow ballads too. So when he would sing something like "Blue Eyes Crying in the Rain," the audience would get quiet as a mouse. Same thing with me. They would be rambunctious if I was singing "Two Doors Down" or "Great Balls of Fire," but they would listen closely when I would do "Coat of Many Colors" and songs like that.

After Willie, a run of spring tour dates included more than a half dozen where we opened for Mac Davis, and I shot a TV special, *Sounds Like Home,* with Mac in Los Angeles. And having Sandy as my new manager was paying dividends. Not only did he start getting me onto all sorts of TV specials and variety shows, but he also helped me land appearances on things like a few episodes of *Hollywood Squares,* where I was seated alongside Harvey Korman, Leslie Uggams, Joan Rivers, and Paul Lynde.

But in May, a couple of major concert bookings made a big splash beyond the country world. First, I played three nights at the Bottom Line in New York City. It was a small club

Star of the Show

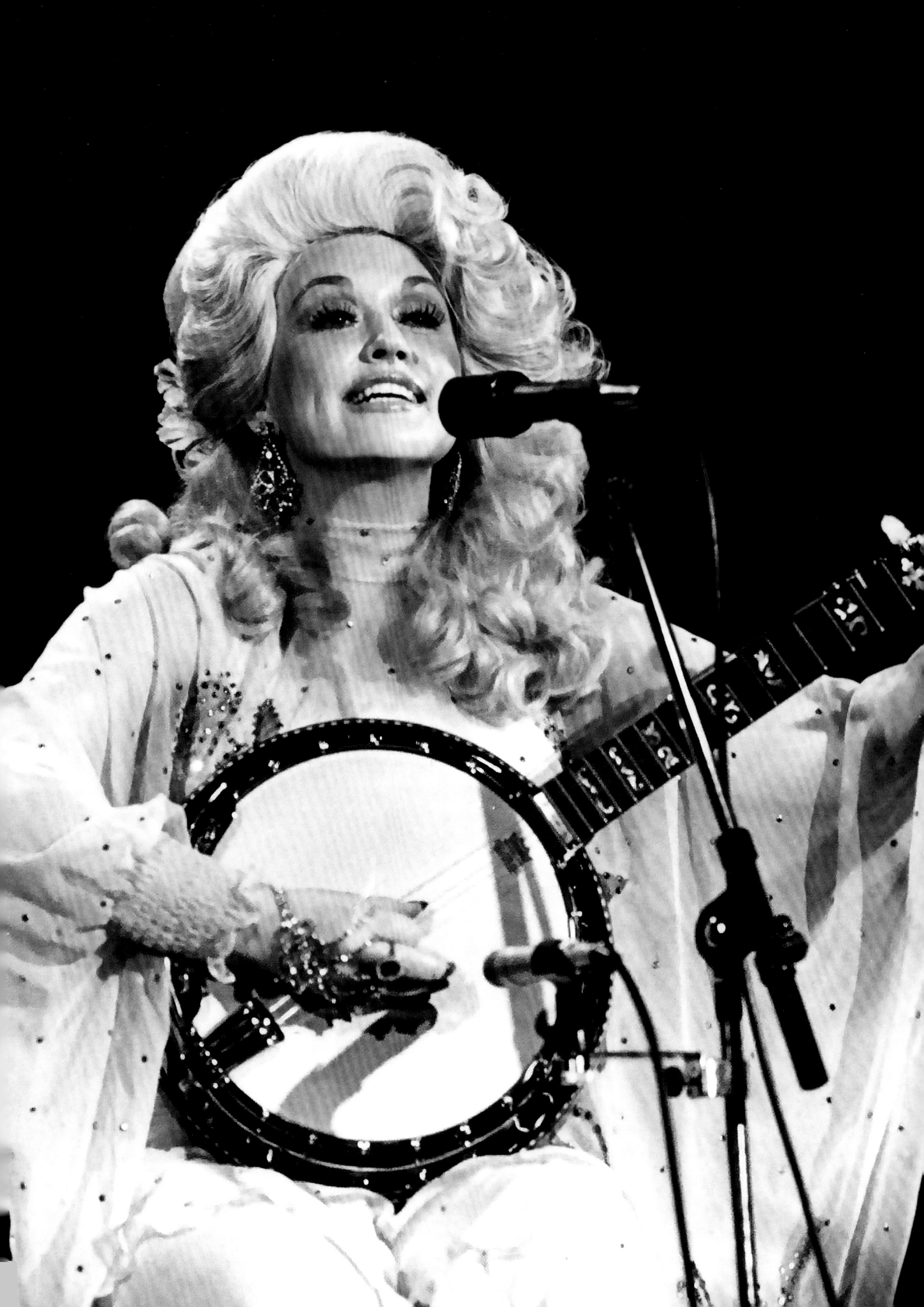

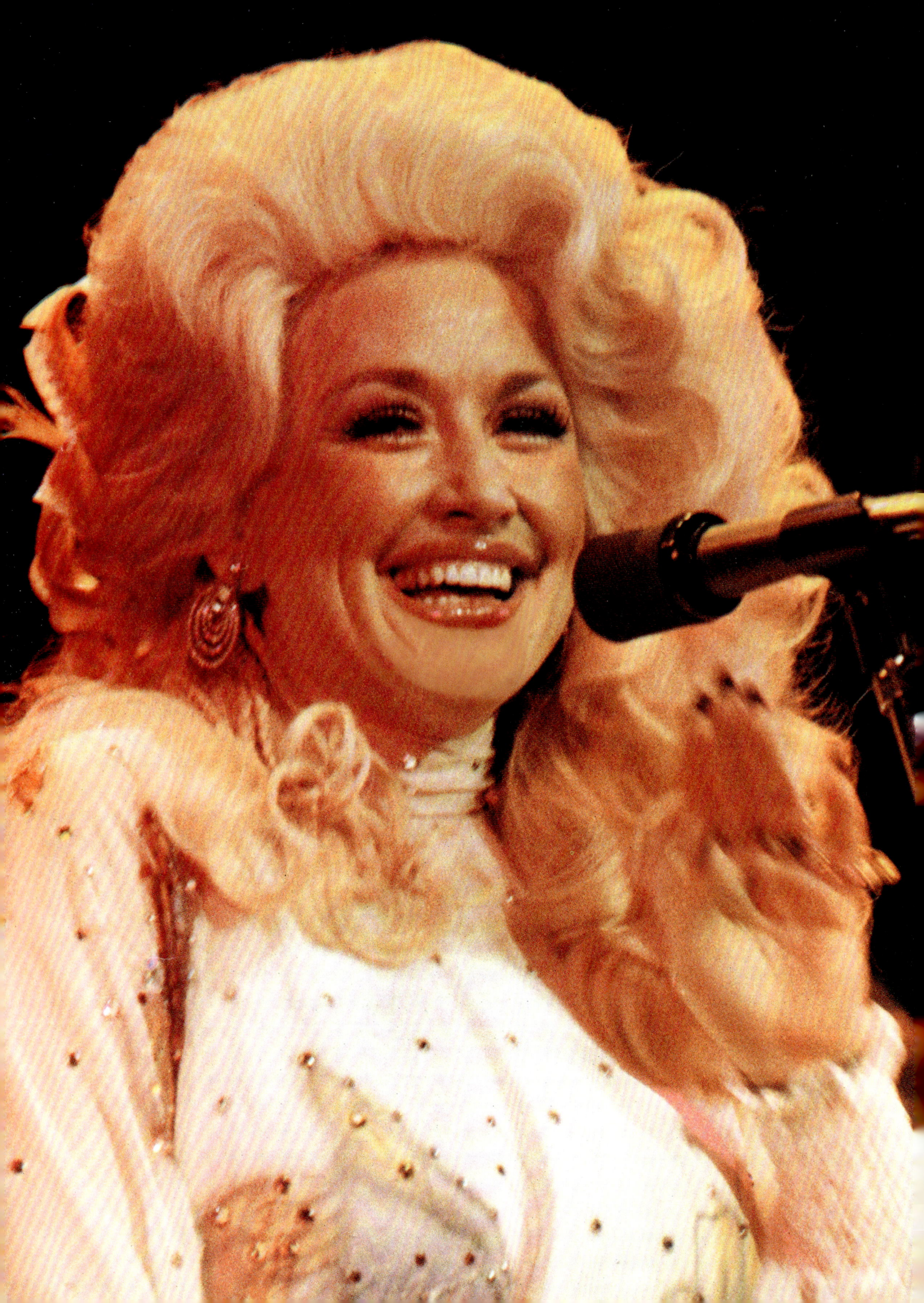

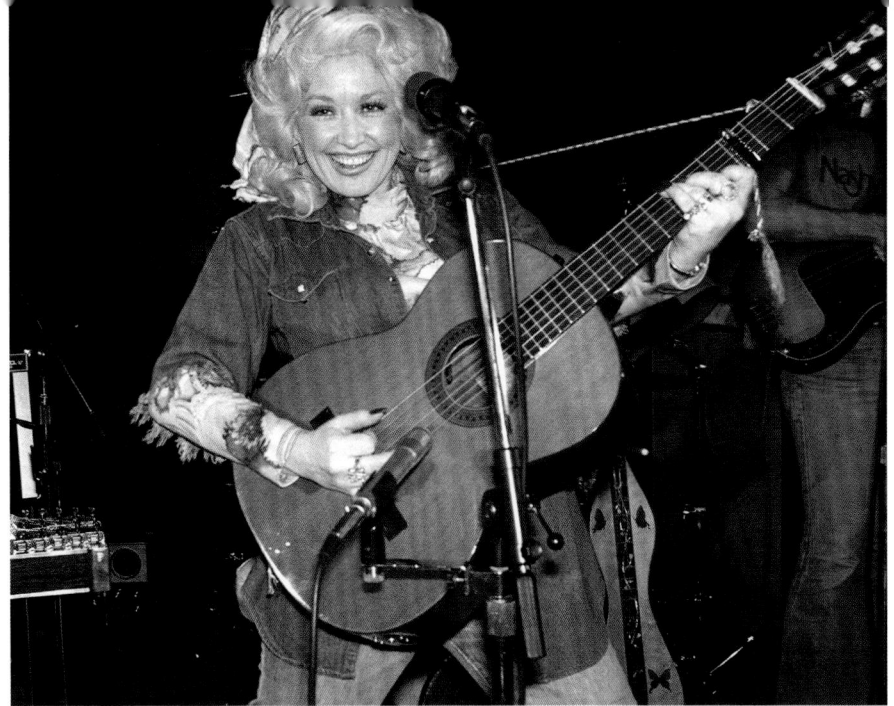

Let it be known that the nail on that middle finger
was playing a hot lick, not making a rude statement!

with only four hundred seats in Greenwich Village, which has always been one of the most creative neighborhoods in Manhattan. Between the shows, a party was thrown at Windows on the World, way up at the top of the World Trade Center, and many of the stars who had seen me came out: Mick Jagger, Olivia Newton-John, Andy Warhol, Candice Bergen, John Belushi, Nona Hendryx, Robert Duvall, Lily Tomlin, Phoebe Snow, *Monty Python*'s Eric Idle—all this was for me?! It was quite the surprise, but it turned out there was sort of an underground thing happening. People were talking about the new girl in town—she writes and she's different and she sings and she's over the top. Music executives had long said that country artists weren't welcome in New York, but the turnout at that party proved that country music wasn't just for cowboys and farmers. I'd always believed all sorts of people enjoyed what country music is about, and that proved it.

Having all those stars in the audience at the Bottom Line probably sounds like it would've been a high-pressure show. And it was—but not because of them. When the room went dark and the spotlight was shining in my eyes, I couldn't see them very well. It felt like any other show. Whatever pressure I experienced was because I was focused on giving the best show I could. I was mindful of where I was—in front of a New York City audience.

Those shows at the Bottom Line ended up being a highlight of my career. The concerts were well received, and they solidified my long love affair with the Big Apple. It also didn't hurt to have photos in circulation of me getting a hug from Mick Jagger!

Little did I know that while I was feeling like the belle of the ball at the Bottom Line, my team had another monumental moment cooked up for me. I was scheduled to do a full-fledged tour of the United Kingdom for the first time, so Gypsy Fever came with me across the Atlantic. What my team didn't tell me—until I was on the plane and there was no turning back—was that I would also be performing for the queen, as Britain was celebrating her Silver Jubilee.

Light of a Brand-New Day

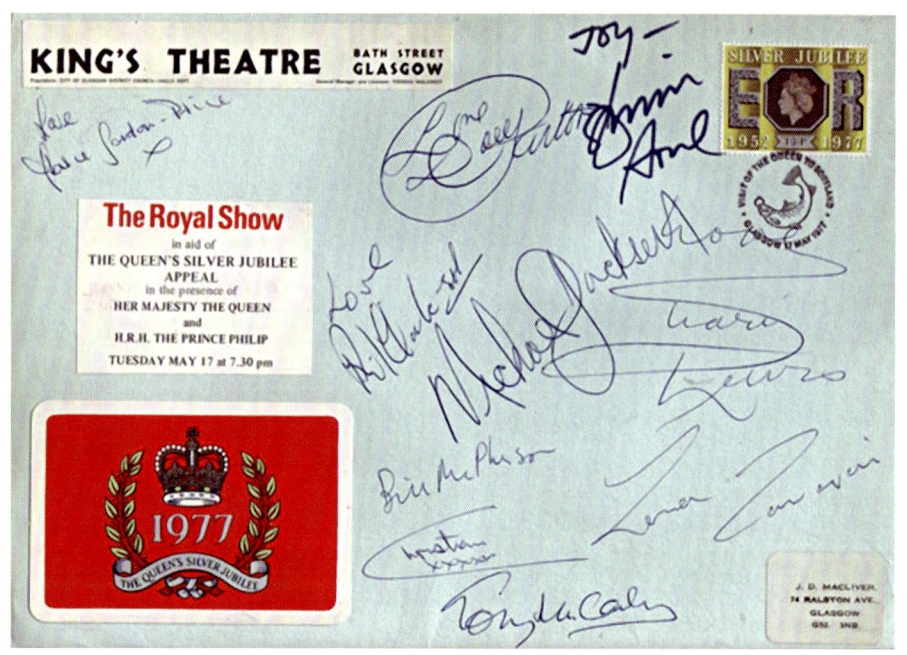

Above: Many of the guests who appeared at the queen's Silver Jubilee in Glasgow, Scotland—including Michael Jackson and me—autographed an invitation to the show.
Left: The moment I met Queen Elizabeth, I couldn't help but feel like, underneath it all, we were two women with a lot in common.
Below: My arrival at Heathrow to perform at the Jubilee.

Queen Elizabeth (left) chats with Dolly Parton (right) following a gala performance Tuesday at King's Theater in Glasgow, Scotland. Other performers included Shari Lewis (second from left) and actor David Soul (second from right).

Dolly Parton in Scotland: Meeting of Two Queens

GLASGOW, Scotland (AP)— Country singer Dolly Parton was a star of the royal variety gala show staged here for Queen Elizabeth II.

Dolly was greeted by both the Queen and her husband, Prince Philip, Duke of Edinburgh, in the performers' lineup after the three-hour entertainment Tuesday night at the King's Theater.

The royal couple are in Scotland on an 11-day visit, first of a series of silver jubilee tours of Britain marking the queen's 25 years on the throne.

DOLLY FLEW to Britain for the show, as did David Soul, the actor in the television cop series "Starsky and Hutch."

Soul turned singer and found himself a heartthrob among Glasgow teen-agers who packed his performances last month.

Dolly Parton's success in a festival of country and western music in London, and Soul's hit in Glasgow ensured their invitations to perform with topflight British entertainers before the royal family.

Dolly flew to London on Wednesday to tape an interview for the British Broadcasting Corp.

Proceeds from the Glasgow gala, organized by former Lord Provost (Mayor) of Glasgow Peter McCann, went to charity.

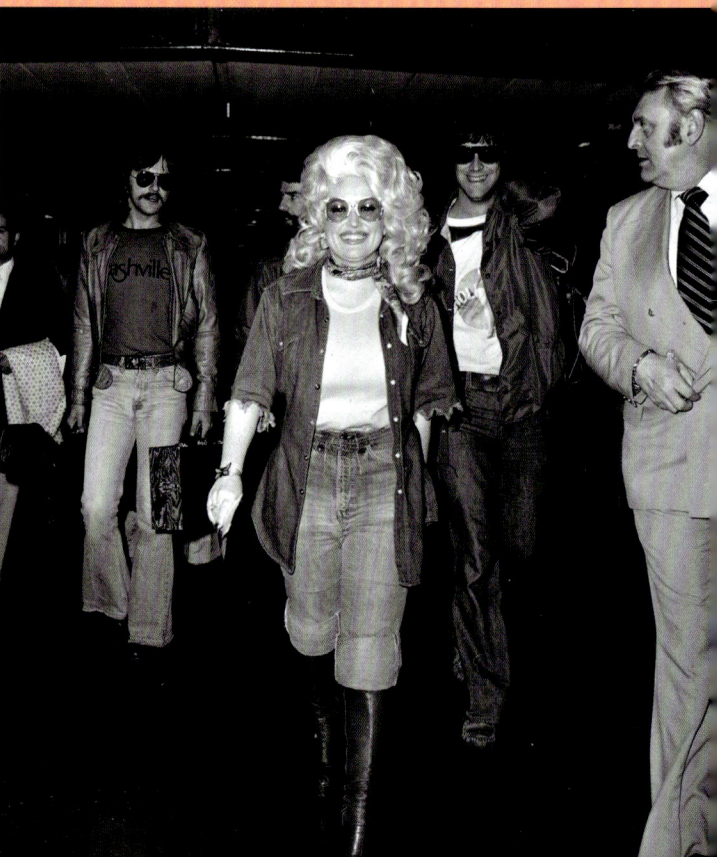

I had always been fascinated by royalty when I was growing up. There we were, having to share beds in a little shack in the mountains of Tennessee, and the idea that people were living in opulence, wearing crowns, and having butlers wait on their every command was almost incomprehensible. I was so excited when I found out I was going to sing for the queen that I jumped around on the plane and couldn't stop talking.

It would be a three-hour show at the King's Theatre in Glasgow, Scotland, the day after we touched down at Heathrow Airport in London, so I had barely twenty-four hours to get prepared after hearing my big surprise during the flight. I'm not that formal, so all the protocol made me nervous. Would I curtsy properly? Would I slip up and call her "Liz" instead of "Your Majesty"? Would I be able to blurt out anything at all?

The queen worked her way through a reception line that also included The Jacksons, Petula Clark, and David Soul before she got to me. She was beautiful—and, truth be told, I wanted so badly to just reach out and touch her crown! I didn't, of course, and I got through all the protocol okay. She was about four inches taller than I am, but I wore bigger heels, so we kind of saw eye to eye. She and I had a really nice moment together. We looked into each other's eyes, and I felt like she knew me and I knew her. And it was just a real warm feeling. In my heart, I couldn't help but feel she was a special person.

I was really pleased with the show and my performance. I sang "Jolene" and "The Seeker," and when I stole a glance at the queen, I could see she was clapping ever so "discreetly," as one media outlet later described it. That made me happy.

The Silver Jubilee was taped for a TV special that aired ten nights later while I was performing in Liverpool for the first time. I knew it was the place where The Beatles had originally formed, and it was near the end of my British tour. My husband, Carl, was a huge fan of rock music, so being in the same city where John Lennon and Paul McCartney met for the first time made me wish Carl could've been part of the trip. It made me miss him even more.

I had a little special time off to be with Carl when I got back to the States, but the summer is always the best time to tour, so at the end of June, I hit the road again. This time, the schedule was heavy with Mac Davis dates. We played seven different cities together, though only two of those stops were one-nighters. The other bookings were all six- or seven-day visits to small theaters in the Northeast, including a run in Toronto. And Carl was able to get away for a little bit during that summer and come join me on the road.

One of the bookings was in Valley Forge, Pennsylvania. It was during that engagement that I wrote "Two Doors Down" on Holiday Inn stationery while the band was literally "two doors down . . . laughin' and drinkin' and havin' a party." You never know where or when a song idea's going to come to you!

When you're working these kinds of shows, staying in one place for a week, the band has a good, good time. They get a chance to get out and see all the things that are going on locally, find all the good restaurants, and do all the points of interest. It can be kind of like having a little paid vacation.

Light of a Brand-New Day

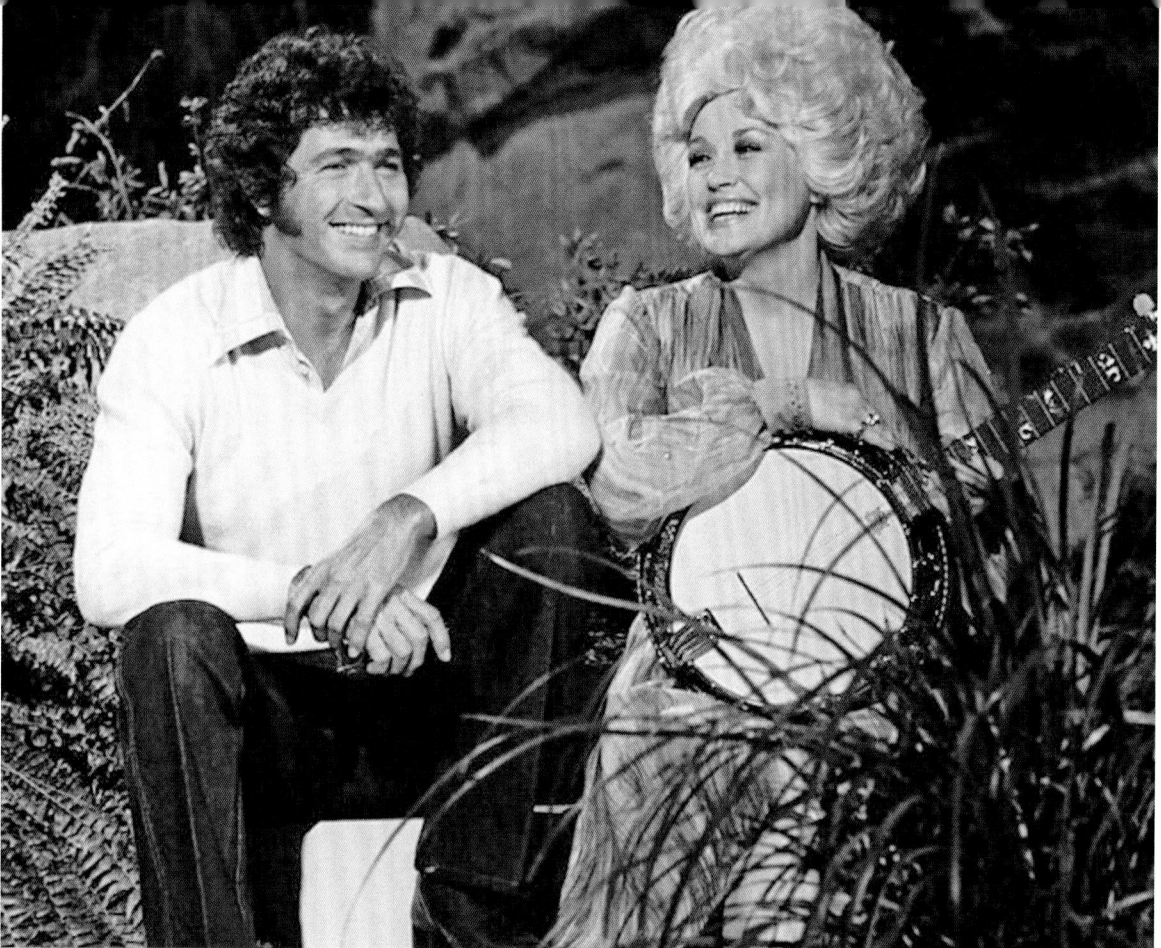

Mac Davis and I chat before my solo number
on the special *Mac Davis: Sounds Like Home.*

Mac and I would get together and write songs because we didn't get out and traipse about. He would get out more than I did, but we would sit in the room, talk about stuff, and write songs.

Mac and I had a lot in common. We were both singer-songwriters who had hosted our own TV shows, and we were kind of on the same trajectory in the movies. He made his big-screen debut a couple years later in the movie *North Dallas Forty*; I, of course, debuted in *9 to 5* after that.

He was cute and really sensitive, and it made all the girls love him—including me! But he was also a regular guy, and men admired him just as much as women. Mac never acted like a celebrity—even though he was one—and few people had more impact on my life. He was, to paraphrase one of his own song titles, one hell of a man.

In August of that year, I played a run of state and county fairs, including two—the Allentown Fair in Pennsylvania and the Wisconsin State Fair just outside of Milwaukee—with Kenny Rogers, who had just had his first no. 1 country hit, "Lucille," that spring. While we were in Wisconsin, we heard that Elvis Presley had died. I think the Gatlin Brothers were on the bill, because I've always recalled that Larry Gatlin gave me the news about Elvis.

Star of the Show

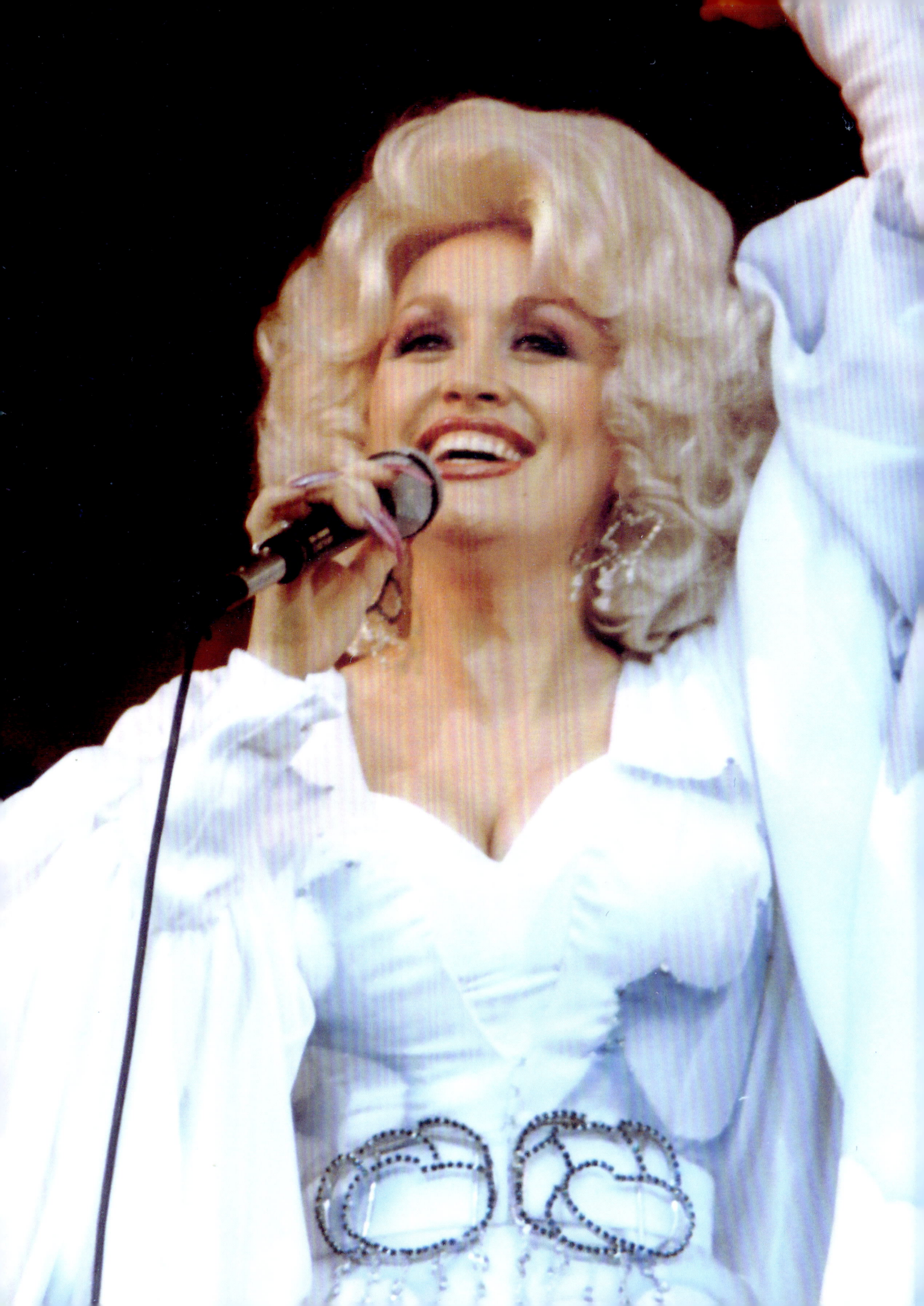

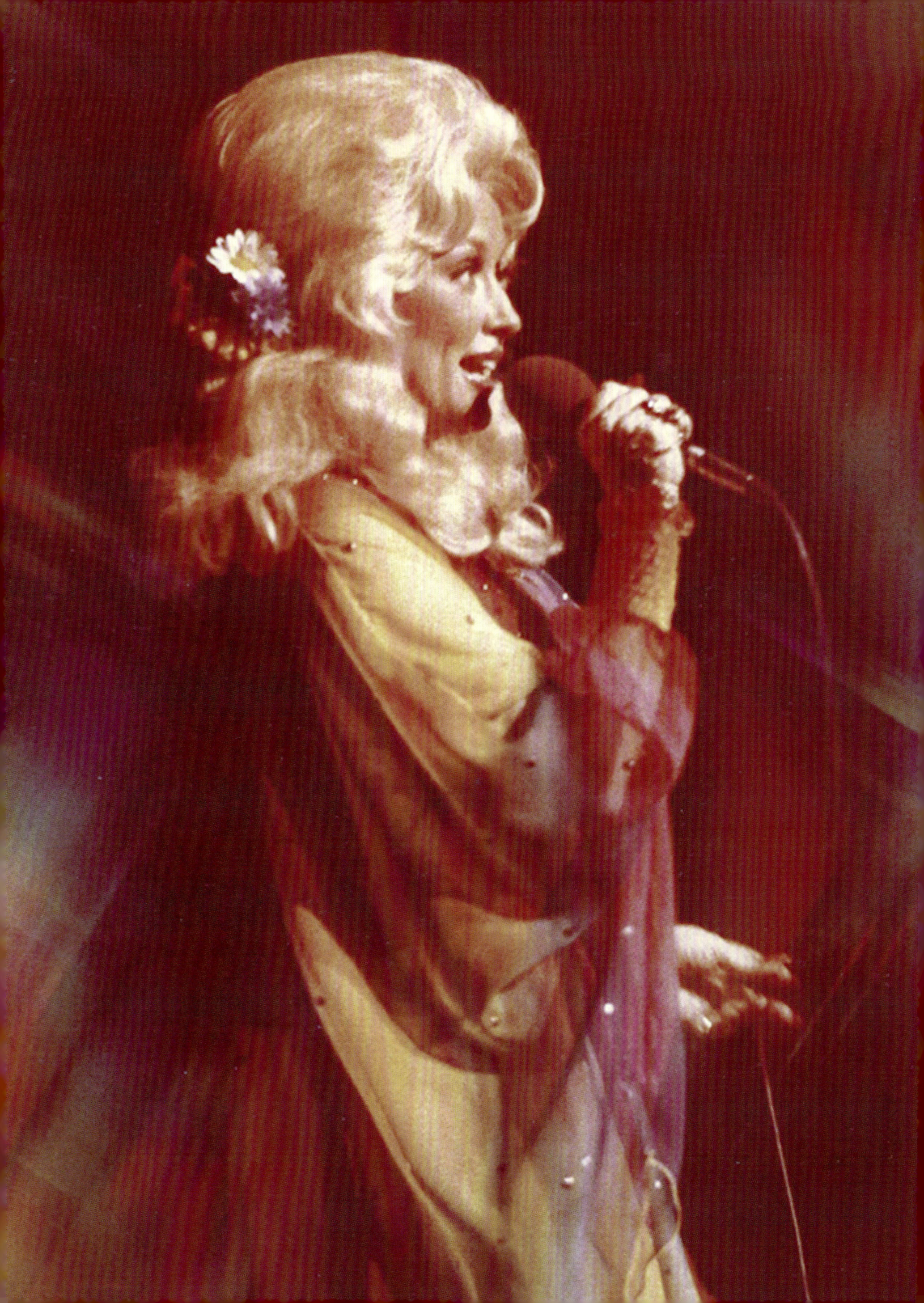

It was a terrible shock. Elvis had wanted to record "I Will Always Love You," but when his manager demanded half of the publishing rights to it, I turned him down. I'd always hoped that somehow Elvis would end up recording one of my songs—he was the biggest music star on the planet when I was in the early stages of my journey, of course—but there was no way now that that would happen.

I knew several people who worked with Elvis, and I hurt bad for them. I even cried, but I wasn't crying on stage about it. It was one of those times when the show must go on. But I do remember feeling so bad about his death—like everyone, I was just so shocked. It was like getting hit in the gut with a wrecking ball, as Miley Cyrus would say.

Because Elvis and I had some common business acquaintances, I felt that I had a small window into his world, and I honestly always felt a little sad for him. He couldn't go anywhere in public without being recognized and without people making fools of themselves because of all the stuff he stirred up inside them. I know what it's like to be recognized in public—it's kind of funny to watch somebody's eyes get really big and to see their jaw drop—but I think I've always been able to be more accessible and approachable than Elvis. I hope I have, anyway! He created a fantasy with his songs and a mystery with his decision to avoid doing much media. So many of my songs are about my life, or about real people I knew, that people kind of know me through my music. I think I've been able to experience fame in a way that Elvis never did.

As if I needed to be reminded to stay grounded (I didn't, but . . .), less than a week later, I performed at the Indiana State Fair between the first and second half of the Steiner Championship Rodeo. The cows and the horses made quite an impression. Even though they weren't around for my performance, you could, uh, smell their "influence." So much for bein' a star!

I made a surprise appearance the next month on the Grand Ole Opry and happened to be there the night that a young woman from Oklahoma made her debut. Reba McEntire sang "Sweet Dreams" in a way that I think would have made Patsy Cline happy. I was impressed with her—and I still am! Over the years, she's become one of my closest friends in the business.

I kept working right up until a week before Christmas that year, and I ended it with a new closing song for my live show, "Here You Come Again." That song really did change so many things. Sandy got me together with Charles Koppelman, who was known for his ability to find hit songs for people. And Charles brought Gary Klein, who produced the song, to the table. It wasn't just a country hit—it crossed over, went to no. 3 on the *Billboard* pop chart, became my first gold single, and led to my first Grammy, for the *Here You Come Again* album.

Another sign that everything was working well came early in 1978 when I joined Glen Campbell and Roy Clark as cohost of the three-hour NBC show *50 Years of Country Music*.

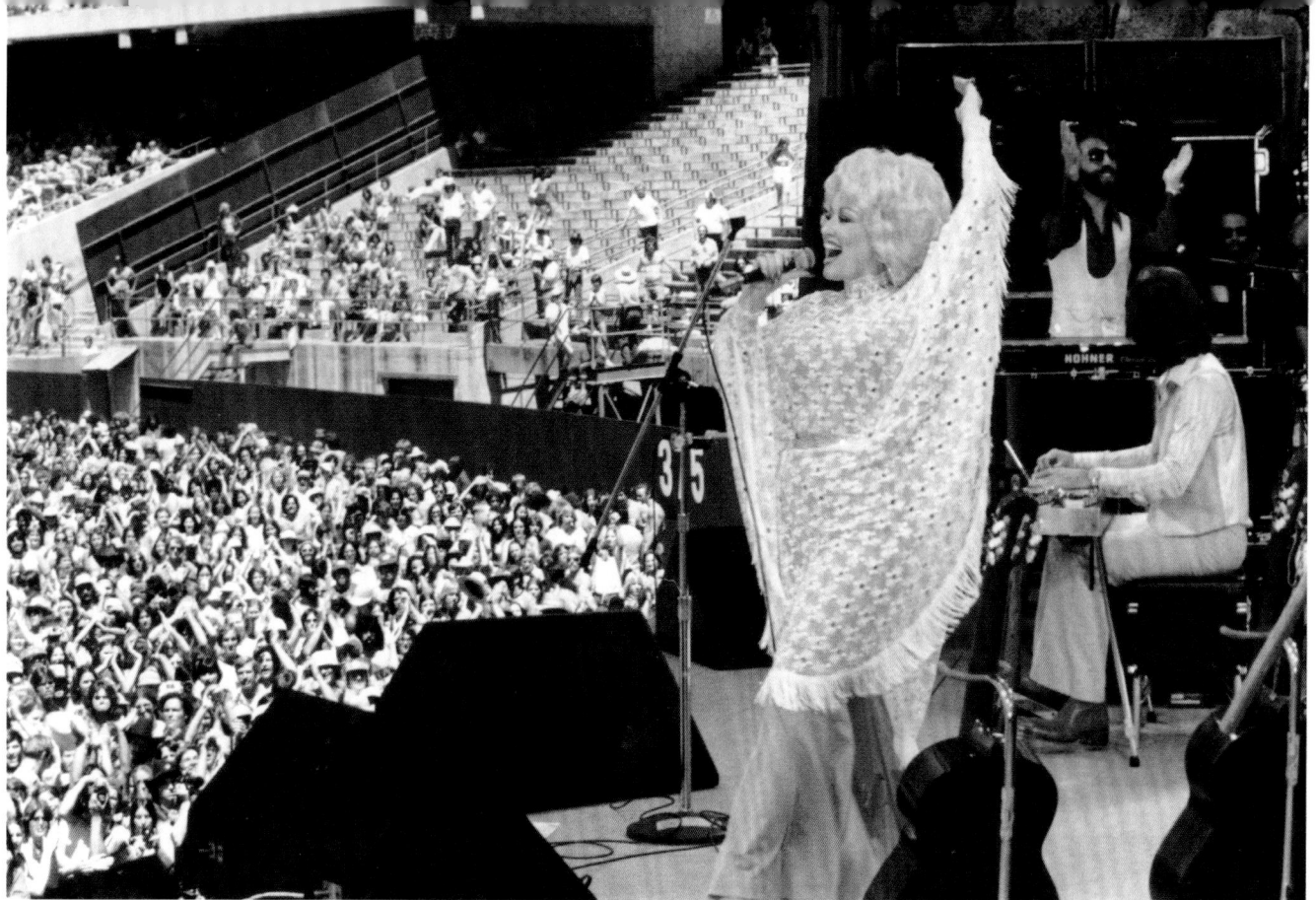

After "Here You Come Again" was released, the changes were instant—I played larger venues for bigger, more diverse crowds. I was happy to see all those people, and to see them responding!

I got to sing "Here You Come Again." I'm guessing that established country fans all knew me as the voice on "The Seeker" and "Jolene" and "I Will Always Love You," but some of the new fans I was making may not have known those songs. I also performed "Mule Skinner Blues" with Bill Monroe and did a Hank Williams medley with Glen and Roy. So I got to be part of country's current sound but also got to help bring its past to life in front of a national TV audience. It was a great opportunity.

A few months later, I sang "Two Doors Down" on ABC's *Cher... Special*. That was a nice moment. I'd always watched Cher's TV shows and admired her fashion, not to mention her bravery in leaving a duo when she knew it had run its course! I got to do a segment with her, too, and I even got an Emmy nomination for Best Supporting Actress in a Variety or Musical Special!

Just a few weeks later, the Here You Come Again Tour launched in Charleston, West Virginia. During that tour, I got to play for forty-six thousand people—a larger live audience than I'd ever had before—as part of the Day on the Green in Oakland, California. Now, I'm not gonna pretend that all forty-six thousand people were there to see me, and in fact, that was a big reason to do that show. The Beach Boys were the headliner, and the bill also included Norton Buffalo, Elvin Bishop, and Linda Ronstadt.

Star of the Show

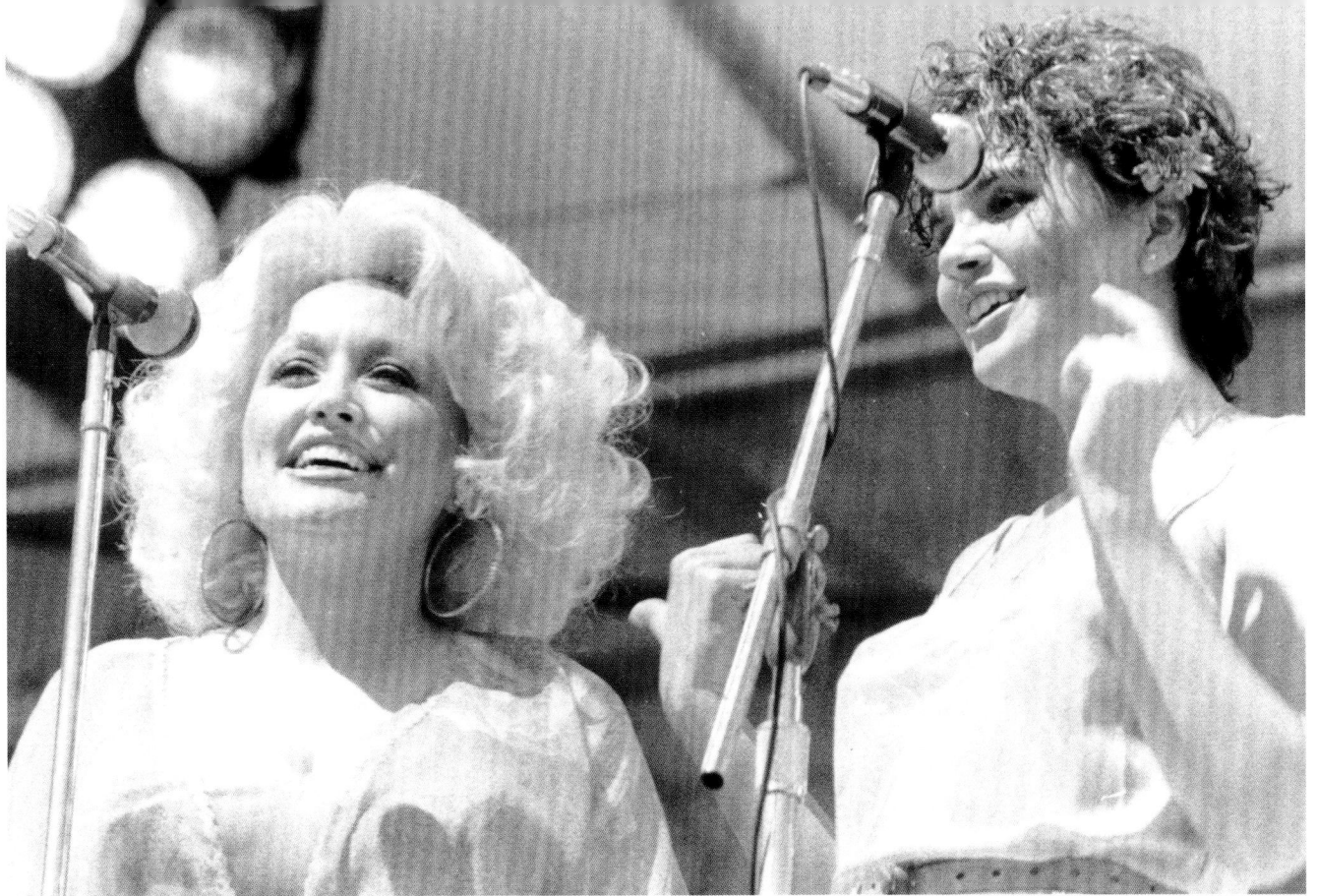

Me and Linda Ronstadt and 46,000 other people
at A Day on the Green in Oakland, California.
What a day it was!

Linda and Emmylou Harris and I had already been talking for nearly a year about recording a Trio album, and that's why Linda and I were both in Oakland that day. Bill Graham, a legendary concert promoter, had this idea to bring the three of us together in concert for the first time. Unfortunately, Emmylou was already booked and couldn't make it, but it was still great for me and Linda.

I thought this crowd was not going to like me. They were there to have fun and hoot and holler and smoke and drink in the summer sun. I was convinced they were not going to want to hear me singing my pitiful little country songs. But it turned out, they did.

I went on stage when it was still afternoon, and even though it was early, and it wasn't a typical country crowd, I got a standing ovation. Well, most of them were standing already, but the ones who were sitting down got up! And that was just the *start* of the show. I played mostly my own songs, and then I hit 'em at the end with "Here You Come Again" and got another standing ovation. And I sang with Linda that day. She was hot as a pistol at that time. I felt—just as I did when "Here You Come Again" exploded—like I'd kind of made it by being on that bill.

Light of a Brand-New Day

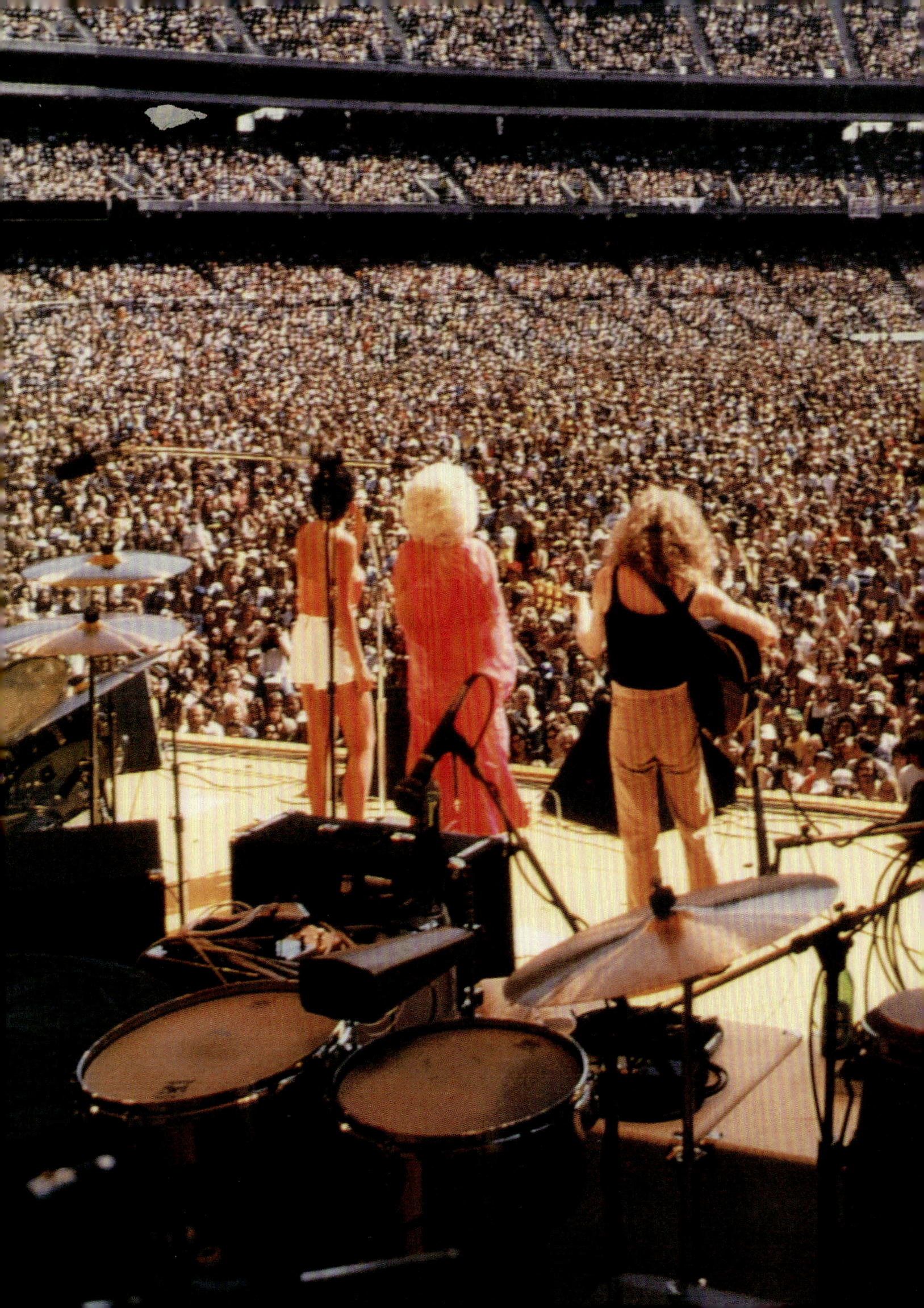

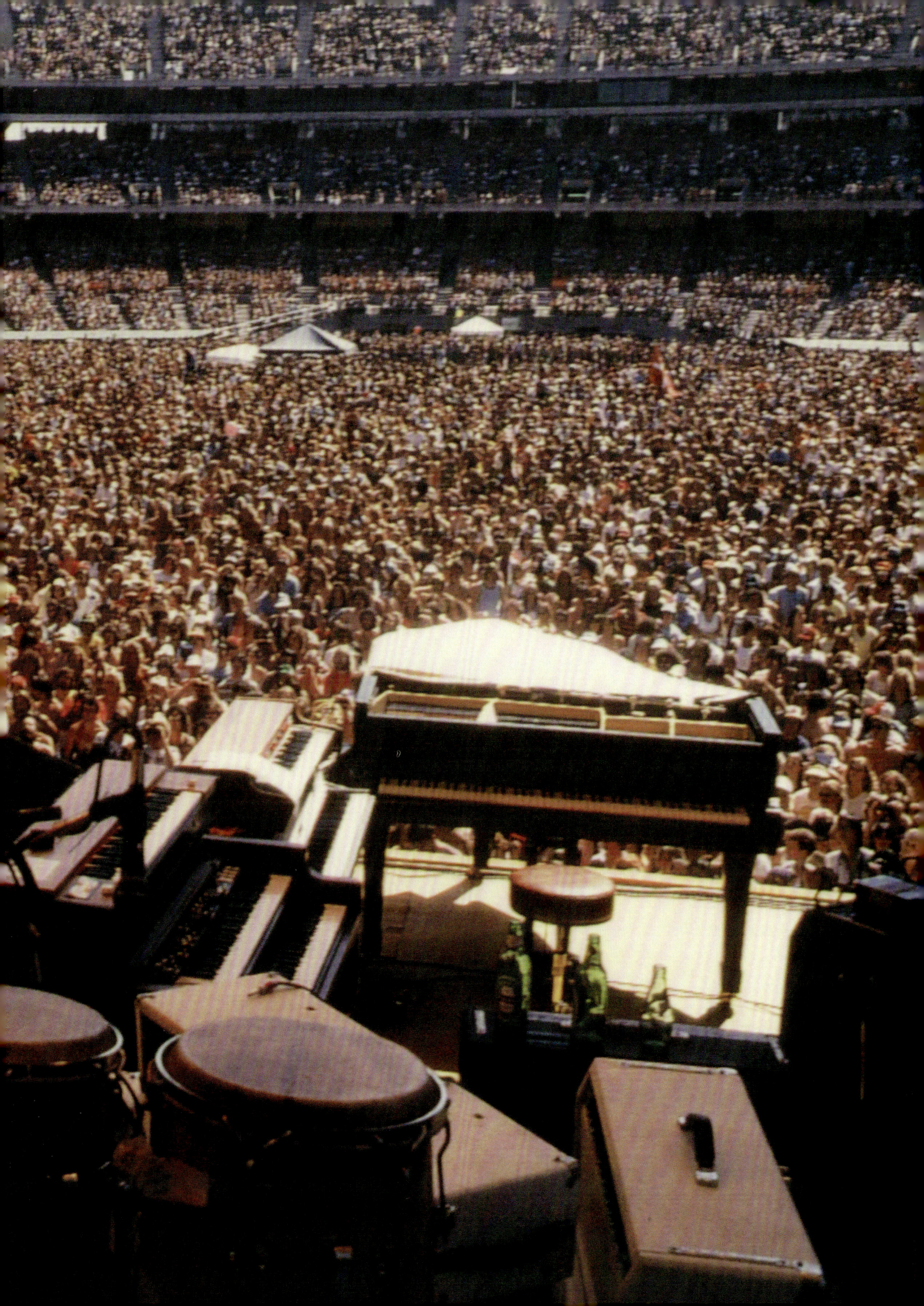

STAGE LOOKS
Through the Years

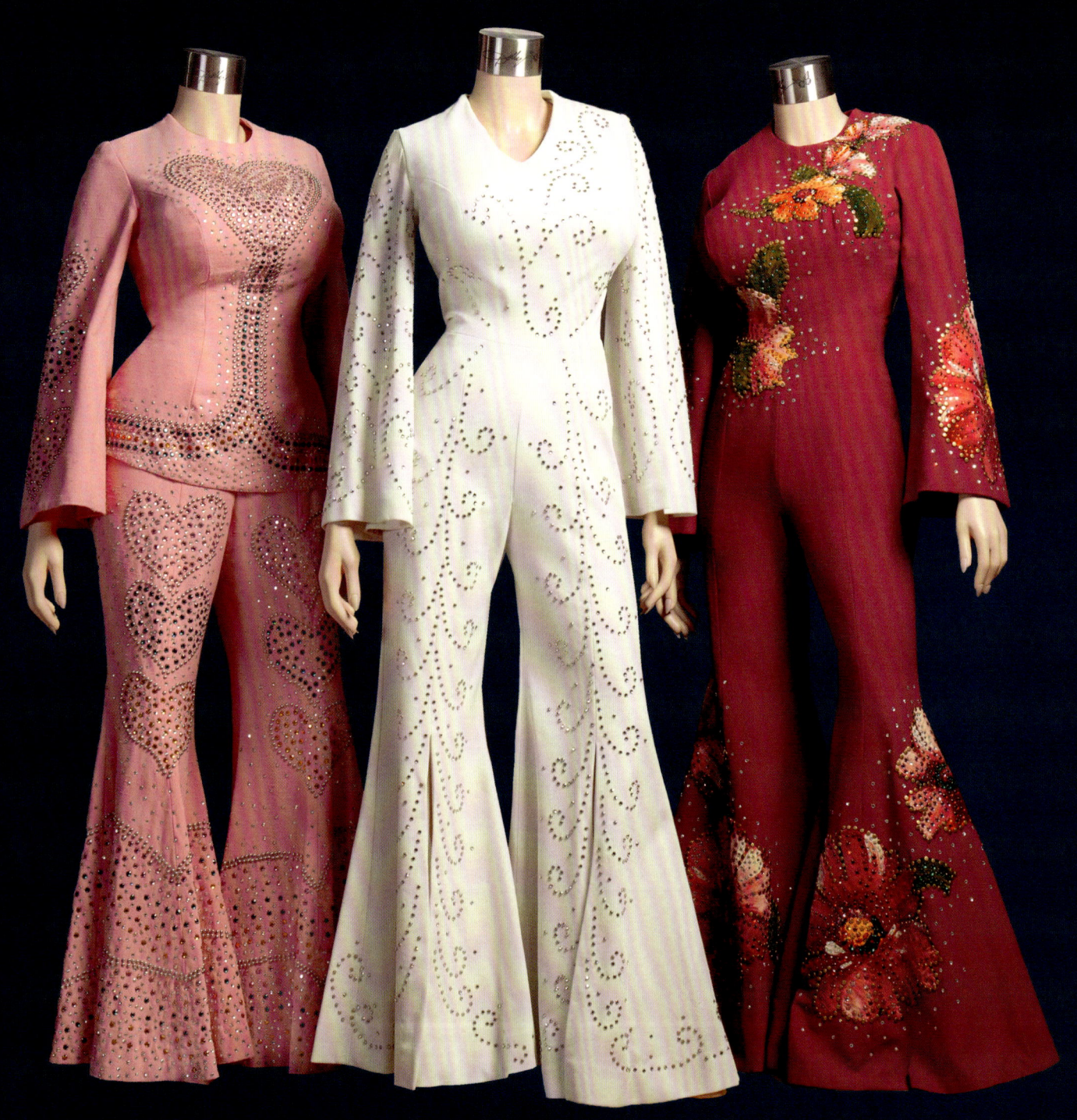

I wore this candy-heart-inspired Lucy suit to perform on the Grand Ole Opry's fiftieth anniversary special.

Lucy Adams made me this white jumpsuit for my very first solo show in Atlanta, Georgia, after leaving Porter.

You might recognize this Lucy suit from my 1976 variety show, when I performed "Do I Ever Cross Your Mind" on 78 rpm!

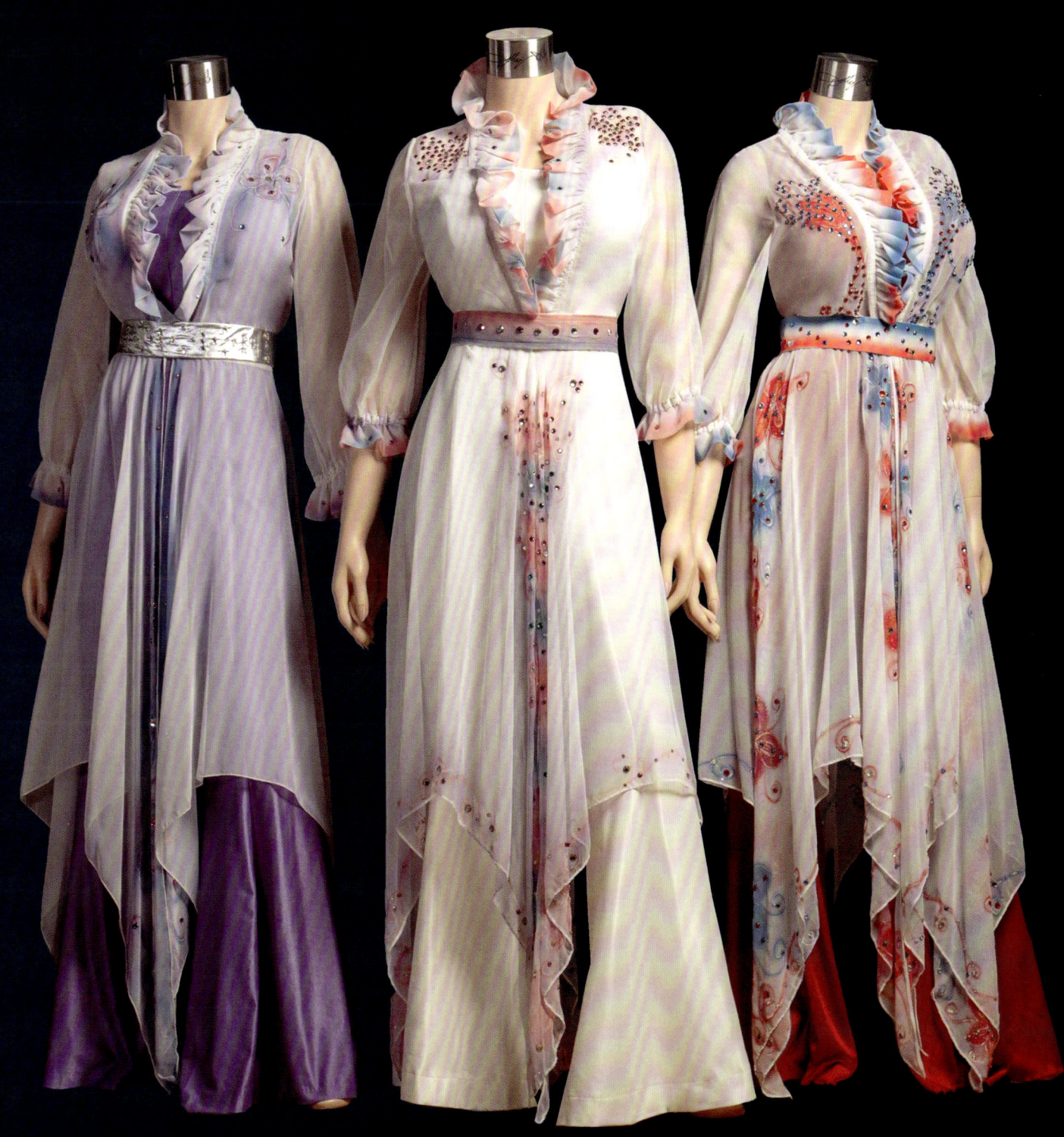

I had Lucy Adams make me an overlay-and-jumpsuit combo in almost every color of the rainbow to wear on tour!

I performed on the steps of New York's City Hall wearing this look.

This look is special to me because I wore it to perform at the Kentucky State Fair in 1978.

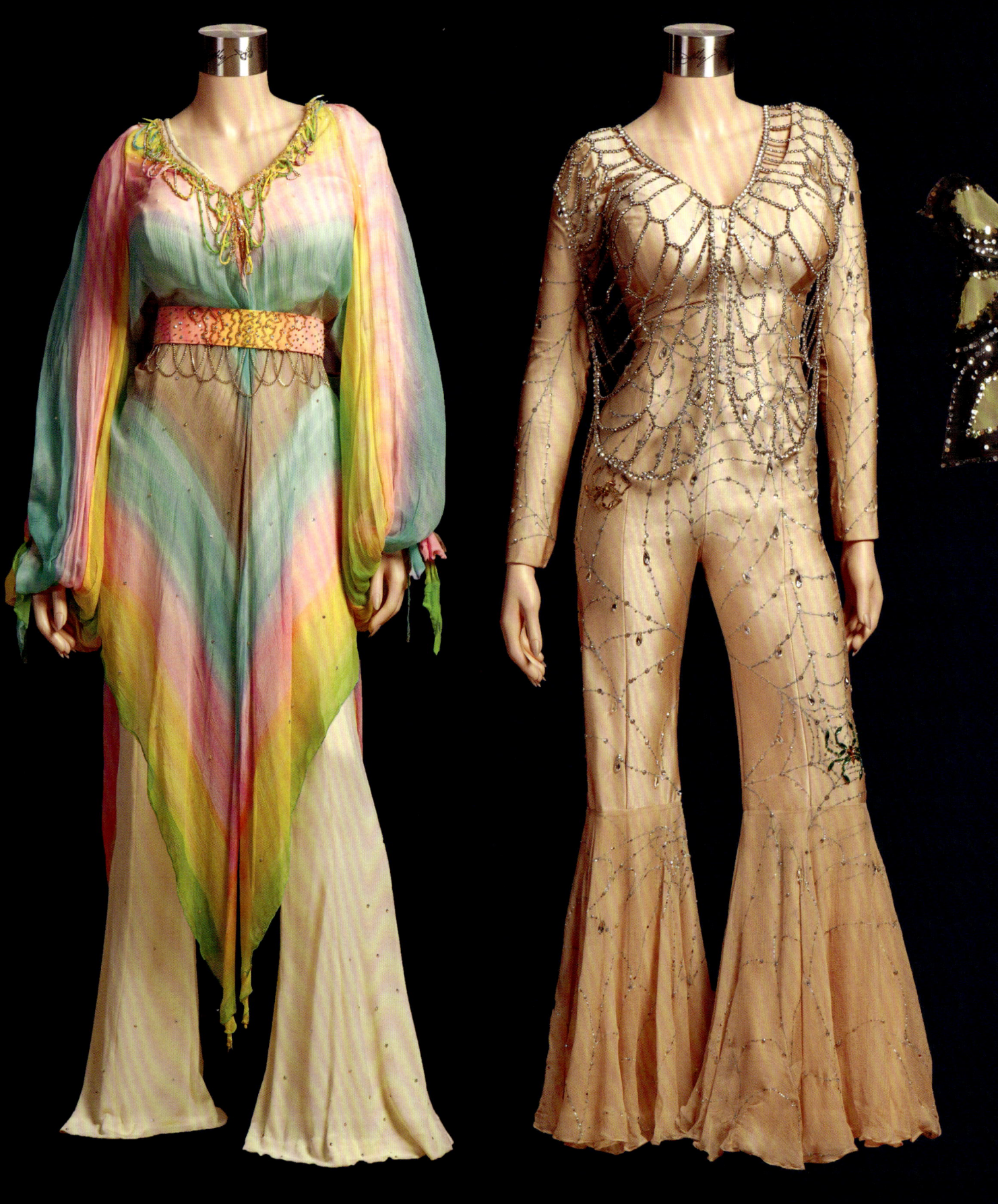

I felt like a girl of many colors wearing this while performing in London in 1978!

I wore this spiderweb jumpsuit to perform with Emmylou Harris and Linda Ronstadt at my 1979 show in Los Angeles.

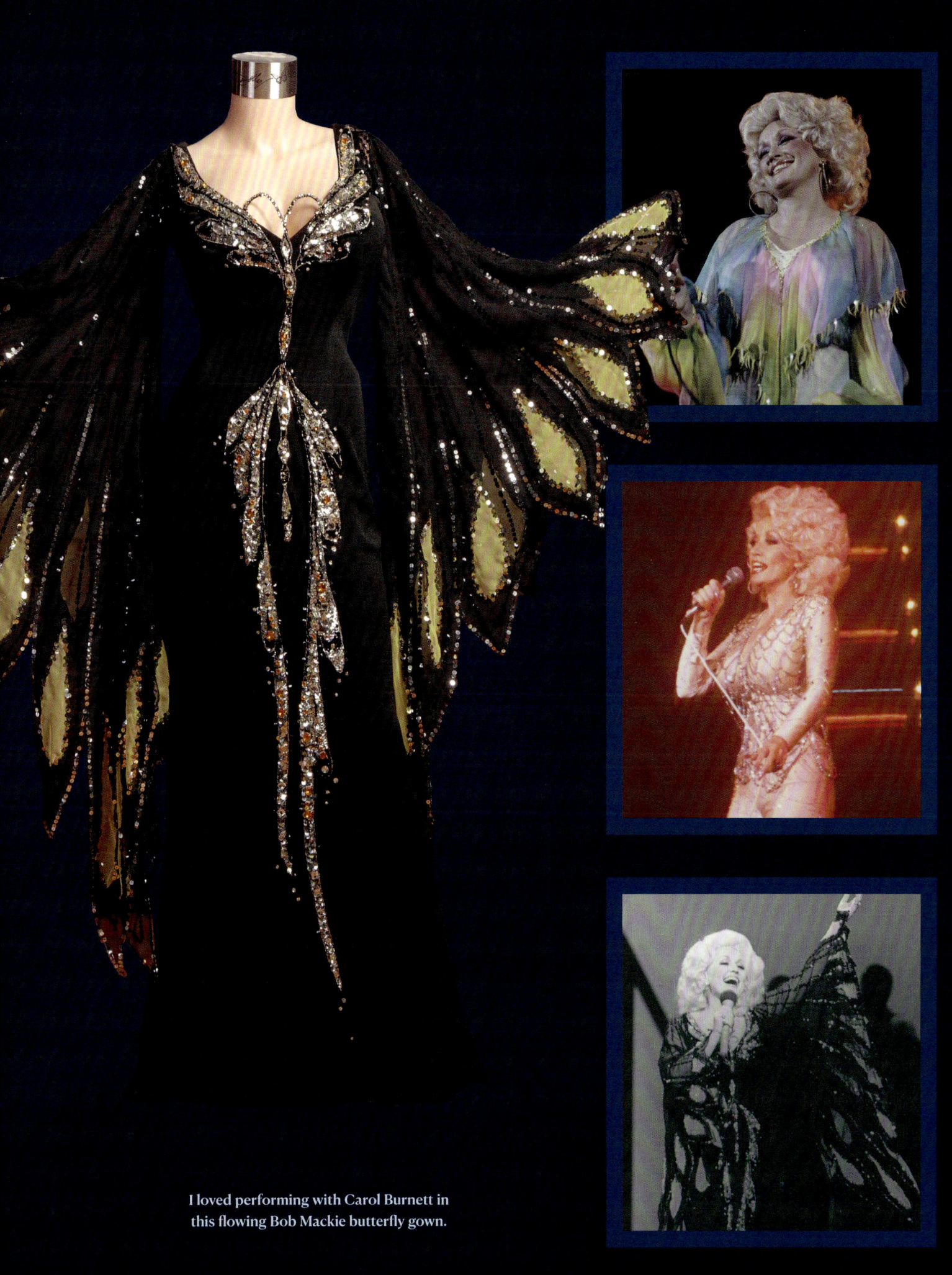

I loved performing with Carol Burnett in this flowing Bob Mackie butterfly gown.

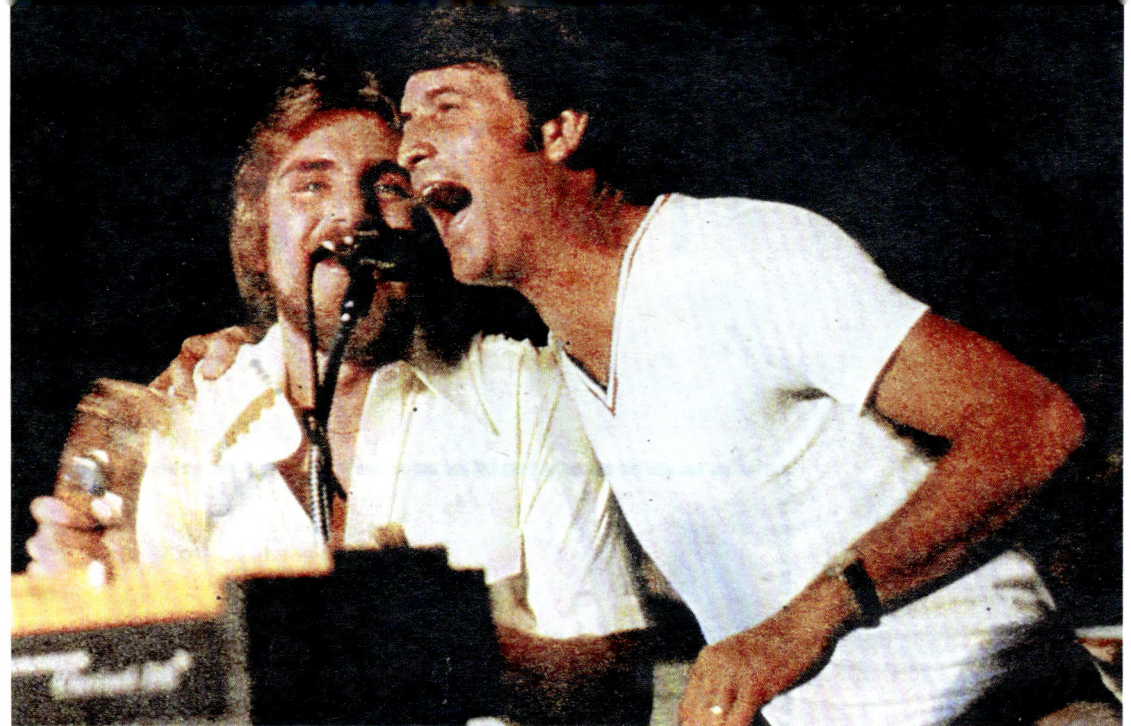

Surprise! Carl joins Richard Dennison during the Kentucky State Fair as part of the backing vocal group on "Higher and Higher." Looks like he's singing louder and louder!

It was a great summer. Eddie Rabbitt, Andrew Gold, and Narvel Felts all opened for me at different times, and Eddie and I were known to sometimes include a duet of the old Everly Brothers hit "Let It Be Me" during our shows.

I also got surprised at the Kentucky State Fair. Carl loved the song "Higher and Higher," and I opened my show with that for a while. One day when we started "(Your Love Has Lifted Me) Higher and Higher," I thought, *What in the world?* The singers sounded awful! I thought, *Who's hitting those bad-ass notes?* I turned around, and it was Carl!

Even when he joined me on the road, Carl rarely came to my shows because he was afraid if I messed up, he'd be like a daddy watching his kid—he'd want to help me but wouldn't know how or what to do. But he loved fairs—he loved the food and he especially loved going to the stockyards and seeing all the animals. He had come up to Louisville for the fair. It wasn't a far drive for him from Nashville—and he'd pulled one over on me.

I thought, *Well, I'm gonna fix his goose.* So I leaned down to speak to security when we finished the song and said, "Did you see that guy in the white T-shirt that was up on stage singing with the group? I don't know who that is. You need to go hold him until somebody finds out because that could be dangerous for all of us." I was hoping they would take him to jail, you know, and we'd have to go get him out after the show. But when security was leading him off, Don Warden came and said, "No, no, no! That's Dolly's husband!"

That was the first and only time Carl was ever on a stage, and the fact that he was so into it still cracks me up to this day. The other singers were sounding so good that he thought he was too! I'll never forget that show. And I'll never forget him.

Star of the Show

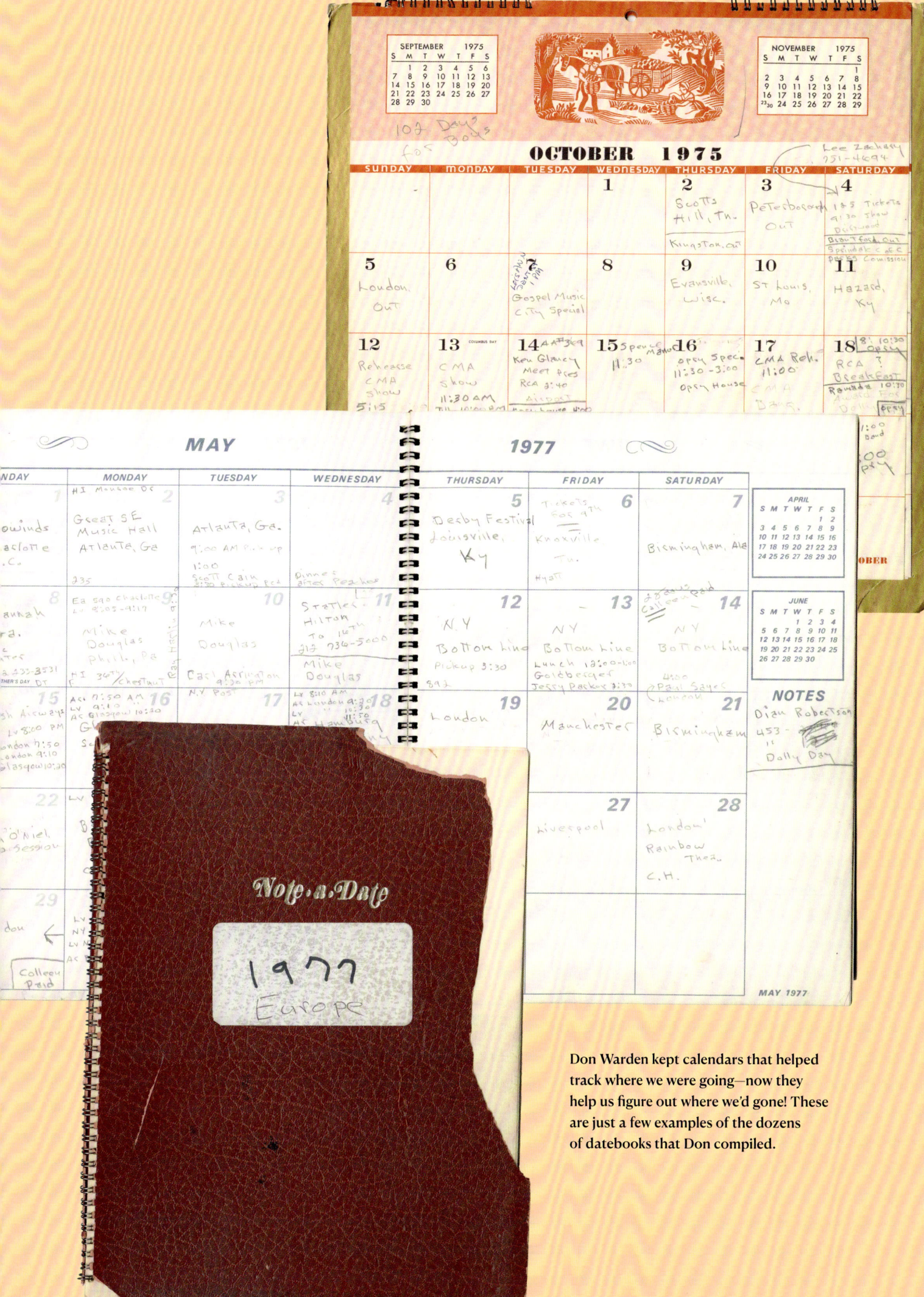

Don Warden kept calendars that helped track where we were going—now they help us figure out where we'd gone! These are just a few examples of the dozens of datebooks that Don compiled.

ROAD MEMORIES
Through the Years

Over the years, I've been blessed to be surrounded by a lot of talented and wonderful people on stage and on the road. You're meeting a lot of them in the pages of this book! As I think back on all those memories—and all those miles—I can't help but think of them and the times we shared. So here are a few of them . . . with some stories of their own from this journey we've all taken together!

GREGG PERRY
Musical Director (1976–83; *Dolly: An Original Musical*)

"With Gypsy Fever, she wanted a band that could not only keep up with her material on stage, but could also go into the studio. Studio work and live work are often two very different animals. On tour, you have a set number of songs, and you do those same songs over and over, often mimicking the record because that's what the fans want to hear. You do that every night until you put together another show. That takes a musician with a certain mindset. In the studio, you're hearing things for the first time, and the job is to be creative with it and to come up with the things that make a record. It's two very, very different approaches to playing music, but she assembled a band that could do both."

CHERYL RIDDLE
Wig Stylist (1985–present)

"I think God's got a little special eye He keeps on her. We were at Dollywood and there was a parade scheduled for that afternoon. It's just dark, gloomy, and pouring down rain. She was asked, 'Should we cancel the parade?' And she was like, 'No, let's do it!' And I swear she came out ready for the parade, and the clouds parted. That kind of thing has happened *numerous* times, maybe because she has a lot of faith."

DANNY NOZELL
Manager (2005 to present)

"My mission is to preserve her legacy, to expand her legacy, and to continue to reach younger generations, to educate them on someone who is a real role model worth looking up to, who has built everything in a true rags-to-riches story. She's someone who believes in God and has been blessed. She gives so much, and she gets more in return. It's that thing—the more you give, the more you receive."

JENNIFER O'BRIEN
Background Vocalist (1989 to present)

"She's not only the star of the show—she's the star of every room she enters. We can walk into a department store, and I'll see everybody freeze. It's enough to make the hair on your arm stand up, and it happens almost everywhere she goes. I've never known anyone with the energy she has. I've never known anyone with the creative depth—she wakes up every morning with twenty new dreams. And twenty-year-olds can't keep up with her. She's just like the Energizer Bunny."

JIMMY MATTINGLY
Fiddler (1989–present)

"I've seen her in the studio singing a gospel-type song, and when she gets in the zone singing, you just have to let her go. She's somewhere else, and you're going to get some magic out of it if you do. It's incredible. When she's singing and performing, it's part of her soul. Her DNA comes out in her music."

KENT WELLS
Producer (2003–present); Band Leader & Musical Director (2003–present); Guitarist (1989–present)

"When she got inducted at the Rock & Roll Hall of Fame, I was fortunate to be there with her, and that was really special. I'm just a country boy from Arkansas, and the whole hallway is just full of rock stars. It's Bruce Springsteen sitting there on a road case two feet away from me, just shooting the bull with Ed Sheeran and Annie Lennox. I mean, it was insane. Needless to say, I was awestruck. All I can remember is, here are all these rock stars, and we're rehearsing on stage, and then she comes into the room and the whole room gets quiet and everybody just rushes over to her, like little kids with Santa Claus. It was like they were greeting the queen."

MICHAEL DAVIS
Keyboards; Audio Engineer (1989–present)

"The demographic of the people who come to see Dolly has always been wide. There are little girls with their parents, teenagers, older folks, gay couples, six-foot-five Dolly impersonators. And they all kind of fit together. In a place like the Greek Theatre—or something about that size—you actually can see everybody, not just the first few rows, and I remember looking up at the Greek Theatre one night—we were playing '9 to 5'—and up at the very top was this backlit couple jitterbug dancing to the song. I have this memory in my head to this day of looking up and seeing those two people dancing and thinking, 'What a magic time this is, for them as well as us.'"

BRYAN SEAVER
Head of Security (2007–present)

"Dolly is a farmer. Just like Pap-Paw would get up early in the morning and farm tobacco, Dolly wakes up in the morning and starts farming songs. That's her job. And she gets up and she does it. She grows one song and grows another song; grows a third song and fourth song. And then she takes a break and decides whether she can go to sleep for the for the rest of the night. It's very much a farmer's way of life. She's just farming ethereal music, rather than corn and tobacco."

RICHARD DENNISON
Background Vocalist (1975–present); Creative Director/Velvet Apple Music (1974–present)

"You've got to be qualified if you're going to go on the road, but you've also got to be able to hang and go with the flow. It's not always going to be your way, and you just have to adjust to the different personalities you're living with and working with. You've got to have that type of personality, and everybody's not cut out for it. But certainly, Dolly was made for it. It's not easy, but if it's your passion, you absolutely love it."

RICHIE OWENS
Producer; Family Historian; Band Member
1998–1999; 2002–2010)

"Dolly is brilliant at sequencing her songs for a set. She knows how to weave in the new stuff at the right time and tell the story and make it attach to the other songs so that everything segues forward. She's great about keeping that roller coaster going up and going down to create an emotional ride, which is what you want. By the time you get to the end of it, she's got you just completely built up for that last big moment that'll take your breath away. She's hitting you with '9 to 5' into ending with 'I Will Always Love You,' but throughout, you're doing 'Jolene,' 'Coat of Many Colors,' and all the other great stuff she includes throughout the whole show. You can't go without having the greatest hits. But she pulls the right stuff from those records, like a more ambient version of 'Little Sparrow' or the song 'Appalachian Memories,' which sets her up great for talking about 'Coat of Many Colors' or her 'Tennessee Mountain Home.' She weaves a beautiful story."

STEVE SUMMERS
Creative Director (2006–present); Dollywood Performer/Entertainment Manager (1991–2005)

"Dolly is a worker. And when people say they work for Dolly Parton, that's no joke. You're going to work because *she* works, and none of us can outwork her. It isn't possible. I've been trying for years! You also cannot outthink her, because as soon as you think you've figured out Einstein's theory, she already knows it. She goes, 'I was wondering when you'd get that.' That's just how she is. Dolly and I went through our share of trial and error—I got a lot wrong at the beginning—but she used those as training tools instead of chastising moments. It was never, 'What the hell have you done?' It was always, 'Hey, I don't know that this is great, but what if we did *this*?' She's a real teacher. People don't do that, for the most part. But she did. And still does."

TOM RUTLEDGE
Guitarist (1975–77; 1981–1983; 1987–1988; 2013–present); GM/Velvet Apple Music; Vocal Producer (2013–present)

"One night on the bus late, everybody had gone to bed except me and the driver, and she was sitting there in the galley, where she'd obviously been in deep thought. She started saying, 'I'm not sure people in Nashville see what I could be, what I'm going to be.' She said, 'I believe I'm going to be in Broadway plays. I'm going to be on *The Tonight Show*. I'm going to make pop records and have hits, and I'm going to be in the movies. These are things that I can do, but nobody sees me that way.' I remember thinking, 'Boy, those are big goals.' But within a few years of that conversation, she'd done all that. I told a young artist this story one time. I said, 'Don't let other people steal your dream. Just because what you want seems impossible, that doesn't mean it's going to be impossible, because there's always a first person that does something that's never happened before.' I'm proud that I still work for one of those people."

VICKI HAMPTON
Background Vocalist (1991–present)

"I remember being on a private plane with her, flying back to Nashville after a recording session in L.A., and her saying something like, 'Vicki, I'm thinking I want to hire you as one of my singers.' She already had three singers; she didn't need a fourth. But there was something that she sensed in me that made her invite me to come along. That was a poignant moment in my life, to hear her say, 'I want you to bring your gift to be a part of mine.' She may have said something sensitive about me and my heart and the extension of my talent, but I think she just sensed something inward. It was just something about my essence that drew her to me and me to her."

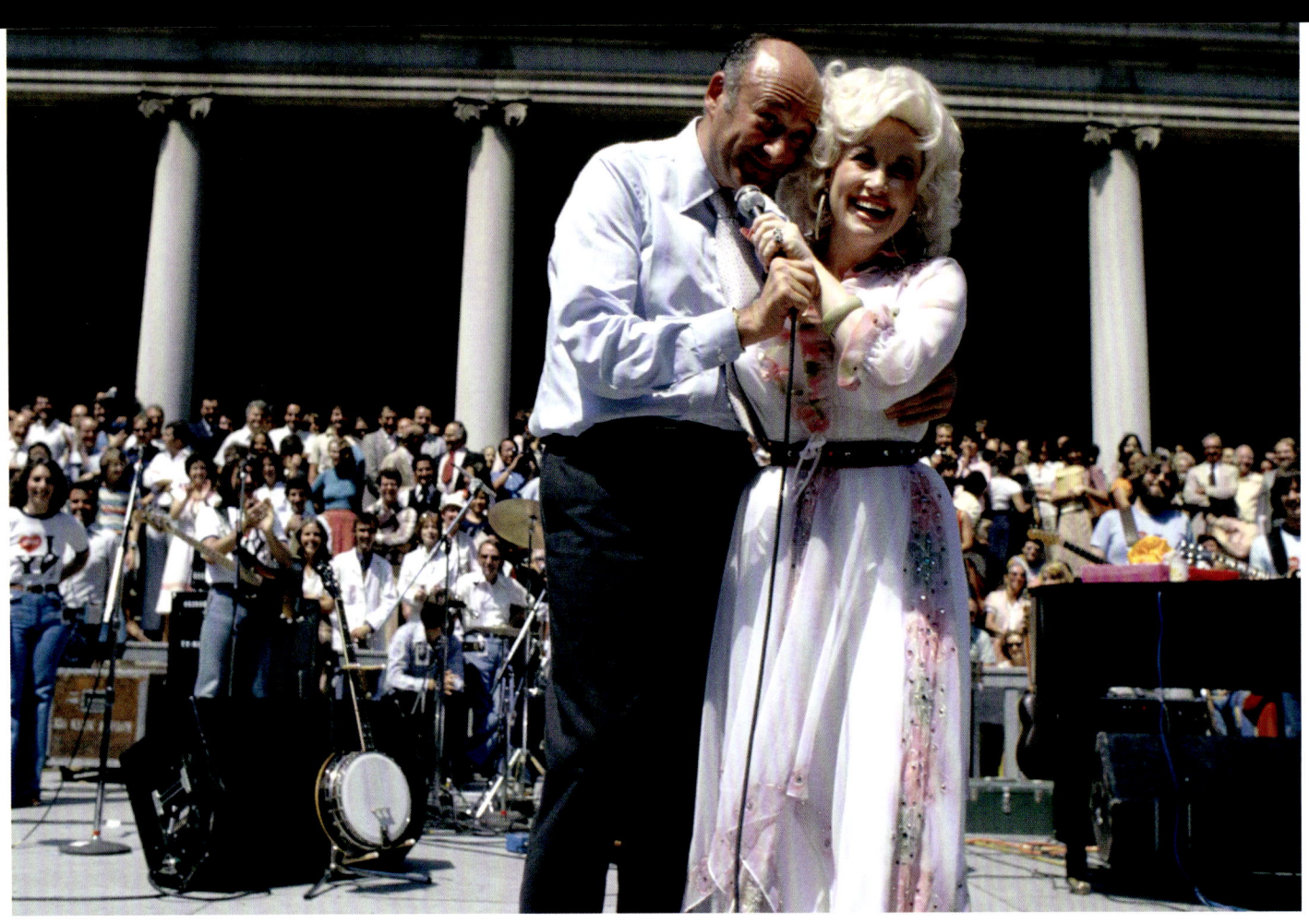

New York City Mayor Ed Koch joins me to address the crowd during a lunchtime concert on the steps of City Hall in 1978.

That August I went back to New York City. I headlined at the Palladium, but to bring attention to the show, I gave a free lunchtime concert on the steps of City Hall. Ed Koch was mayor at the time, he loved the cameras, and there were plenty there for the event. He presented me a key to the city and gave me a big ol' kiss, and I ended up playing banjo at City Hall for more than thirty-five thousand fans. There was even a Dolly Parton look-alike who showed up at the foot of the stage. Dolly "tribute artists" make their way into a lot of my concerts, and I love that!

The Palladium show was full of energy, and afterward I headed over to Studio 54, the famous disco that was frequented by the likes of Andy Warhol, Bianca Jagger, Halston, and Liza Minnelli and was the inspiration for the Chic song "Le Freak." The club threw a hillbilly-themed party and brought in several farm animals—a horse, a goat, a turkey, and two geese—plus some cornstalks and apple pie for a roped-off section they renamed Barnyard 54. Aretha Franklin and boxer Joe Frazier came out, and "Tennessee Waltz" was played in my honor. Eddie Rabbitt, who was born in Brooklyn, went with me to the party. When we decided to leave, he surprised me with an Eddie Rabbitt mask, and we left the club with me in disguise.

Star of the Show

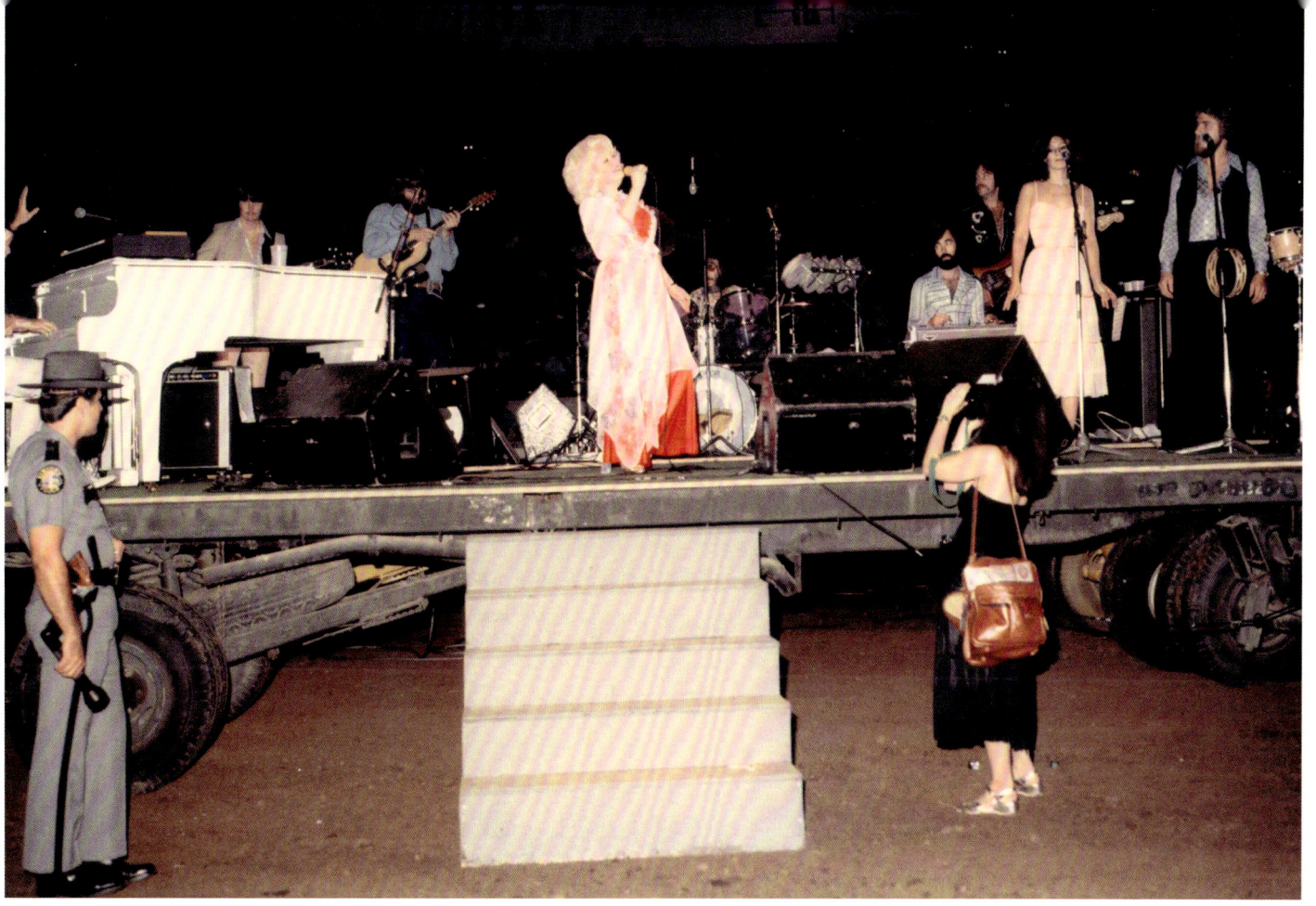

Touring in the 1970s was less structured than it is today. I'm seen here performing for thousands of people on a flatbed truck, which doubled as our stage. In those days, we'd play anywhere the fans wanted to see us!

In October, I sang my new single, "Heartbreaker," at the CMA Awards, which became another of my best—and worst—TV moments. CMA voters often pick the Entertainer of the Year winner based on live performances, and when Ronnie Milsap opened the envelope, Johnny Cash whispered the answer to him, and he said, "Dolly Parton." I accepted the honor amid a mini personal crisis. Just a few minutes before the award was announced, I felt a rrrrrrrip in my dress. It busted out right up the middle over my abdomen. Kenny Rogers's then-wife lent me a black fur coat, which I held in front of me, and then I laughed through the acceptance speech: "I guess it's like my daddy said, 'You shouldn't try to put fifty pounds of mud in a five-pound sack.'" If they were gonna give me that award, I was certainly going to get up on stage to accept it, no matter what!

A few weeks later, I took off for Europe—eight shows in Norway, Sweden, Denmark, and Germany, and six more in England. I was back in the United States in time for Thanksgiving and spent the holidays at home.

We kind of treated 1979 the same way we did 1978. In January, I shot a TV special—this one was with Carol Burnett at the Grand Ole Opry House. We sang and danced and laughed—some of it was country but a lot of it wasn't. It was just two gals who became fast friends and got to share it with the world. I think it came across to viewers at home.

Light of a Brand-New Day

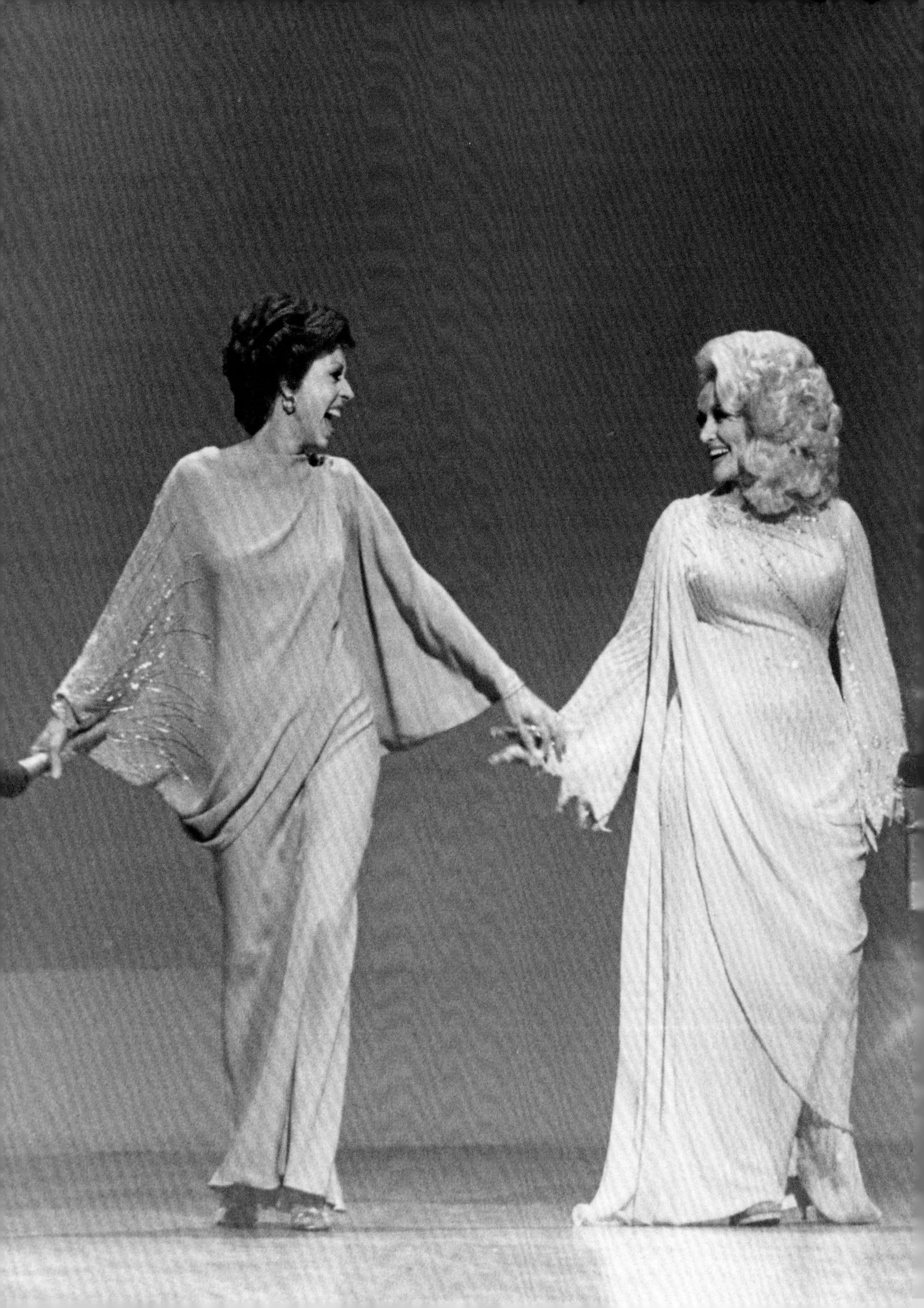

Like the previous year, I waited until the summer to tour again, and this time, I appeared in a few countries I had not previously visited. I did a show in New Zealand, four in Australia, four more in Japan, and one in Hong Kong, China. One of the best pieces of memorabilia I ever got was simply being on the cover of a Japanese magazine with the headline written in kanji next to my gaudy red fingernails and hoop earrings. It's funny—I make my living, in part, by writing, and I give books to kids through my Imagination Library to encourage them to read, but to this day, I have no idea what that headline says!

Of course, the people of Japan didn't know what I was saying either. When we went to Japan, I discovered I was huge there. I couldn't believe it. They love country music, and I guessed maybe they also liked short women with big boobs!

We'd worked up a great show for the tour, but there was one issue in Japan: so much of my act includes talking with people. Now, the Japanese audiences knew every word of my songs because they'd memorized them. But 95 percent of the audience appeared to have no idea what I was saying between the songs, let alone with my southern accent on top of that. We would do our songs, and they'd stomp, stomp, stomp. Then I'd talk, and there'd be silence. All the jokes I'd planned—silence.

I realized these people didn't understand what I was saying, but I figured if other people laughed, they'd laugh. So I started telling stories about the band—stuff that the band members didn't know about one another. My brother Randy was laughing the hardest about my jokes not landing, and I wanted to kick his butt right off that stage. So I started telling stories about Randy when he was little—things about him eating tobacco worms, or how he'd eat dirt. The band laughed, so the fans started laughing, and I laughed with them. It worked!

When I got back to the States, I added "Great Balls of Fire" and "Baby, I'm Burnin'" to my concerts. They gave the shows a little more tempo and gave people who liked pop music something more to enjoy. I would have loved to reach a larger audience by singing strictly country, but I realized that wasn't really possible at that time. The fact that I could go to Europe and Australia and Japan was confirmation that performing my music that fit many tastes was working.

American audiences validated that for me too. I remember one appearance at the Ohio State Fair in August 1979—a TV crew spent time with us at that concert for a documentary, and the fan footage featured all kinds of people: little kids, grandparents, bikers, gay people, and hippies, as well as my longstanding country audience. I liked knowing that I could connect with so many kinds of people and that they all felt comfortable attending a show with folks who might be very different from themselves. To this day, I hope that's what happens at my shows.

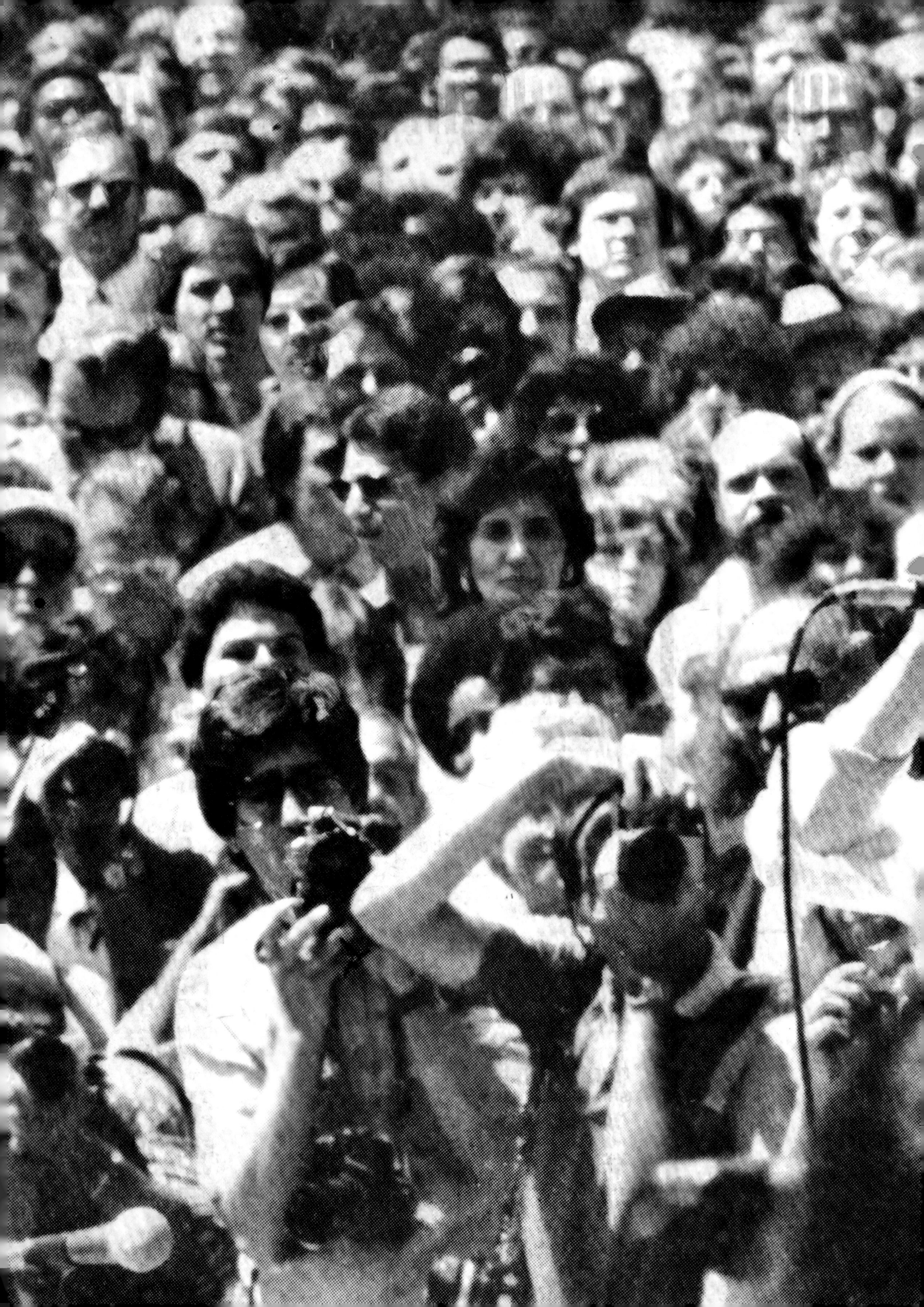

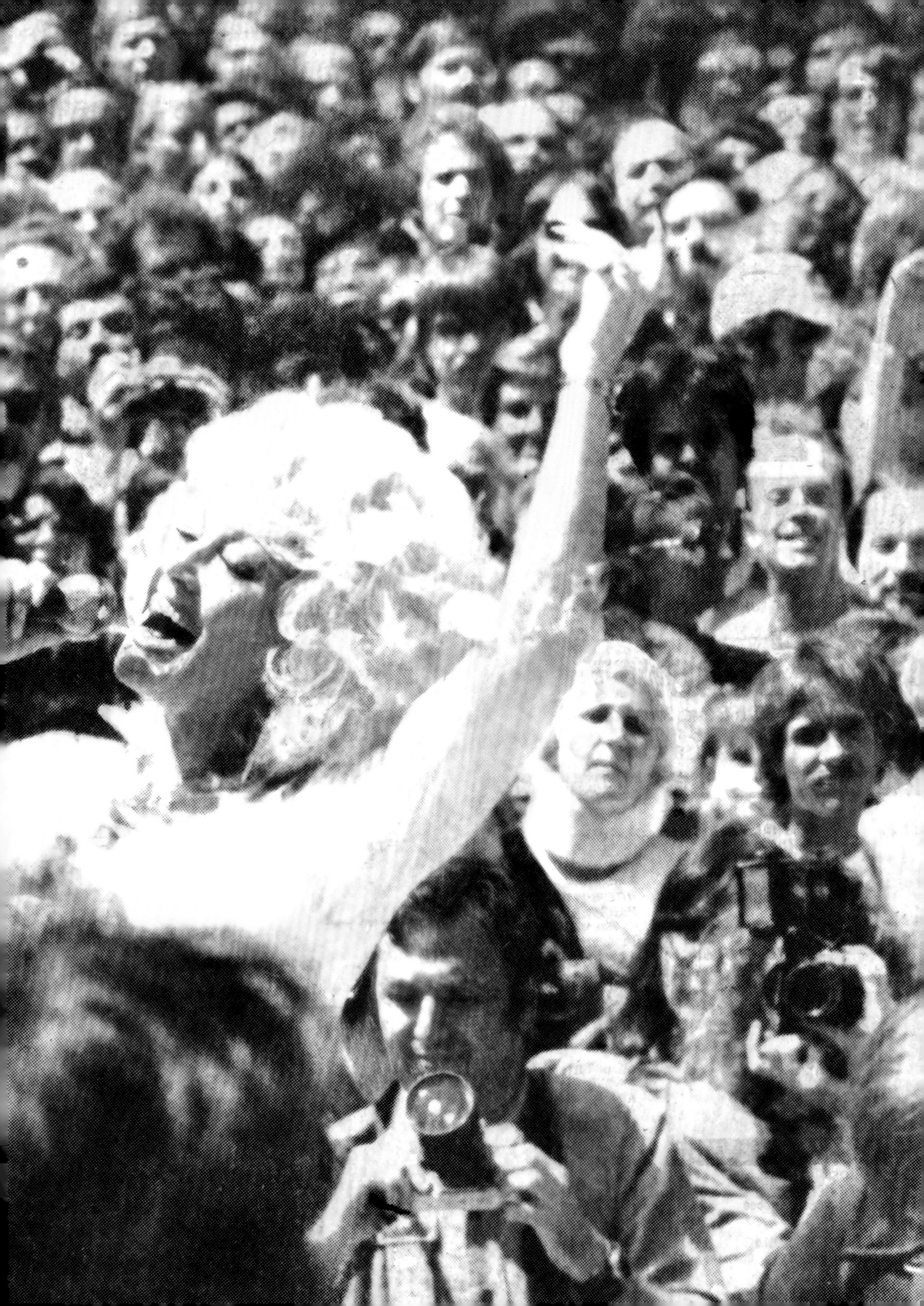

THE BIG APPLE TAKES THE CAKE

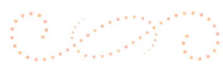

Given that I grew up in the Smoky Mountains and always talk about how proud I am of where I come from, you might be surprised to hear that I absolutely love New York City.

The roads may be uneven, the cab drivers don't always stay in their lanes, and Lord knows the smells from the subway can make their way up to the sidewalk at the worst time, just as you're walking past, but I really do love the Big Apple.

There's just an electricity there! You can do just about anything you want at any hour of the day or night, and with real estate that grew *up* instead of *out,* you can do a lot in just a few blocks. And I've found the people who live there let you be yourself, which I *really* appreciate!

I first visited New York during my senior year at Sevier County High School, when we took a chaperoned trip. There were billboards everywhere for a new musical called *Hello, Dolly!* Naturally, I told everyone the billboards must be a greeting to me!

The next time I went to New York, my friend Judy Ogle and I checked into a hotel, and I guess because of the way we looked, the staff thought we were "working girls." I was told that apparently New Yorkers felt that hookers always ran in pairs, so they presumed that's what the two of us were! We went out for a while, and by the time we got back, the staff had moved our luggage out into the hallway and proceeded to kick us out.

When I played Madison Square Garden on tour in the 1970s, we did a train-whistle concert series where I'd set up and do a half-hour performance ahead of time at a Long Island Rail Road stop to promote the show. The first two stops went off without a hitch, but when we reached the Mineola station, an employee got on the PA system and announced that we needed to cut the noise and move on. I still sang "Love Is Like a Butterfly" before they ran us off completely.

I've since played in venues all over the city: Carnegie Hall, Lincoln Plaza, the Bottom Line, the Palladium, and even the steps of City Hall, where, as I've mentioned, Mayor Ed Koch gave me a key to the city—and a kiss! Ed Koch was a character, and that day I swear he was feeling like a little kid or something! I tend to bring that out in people, I think, because I'm still a kid at heart myself.

For a time, I owned an apartment on Fifth Avenue with beautiful views of Central Park. I rode on a float twice in the Macy's Thanksgiving Day Parade, in 1975 and in 2007—and participated a third time virtually during COVID in 2020—and, of course, I spent time in the city any time I made the rounds on TV talk shows there.

It probably goes without saying that visits to the Big Apple are more normal now. The folks there have figured out that I'm not a hooker!

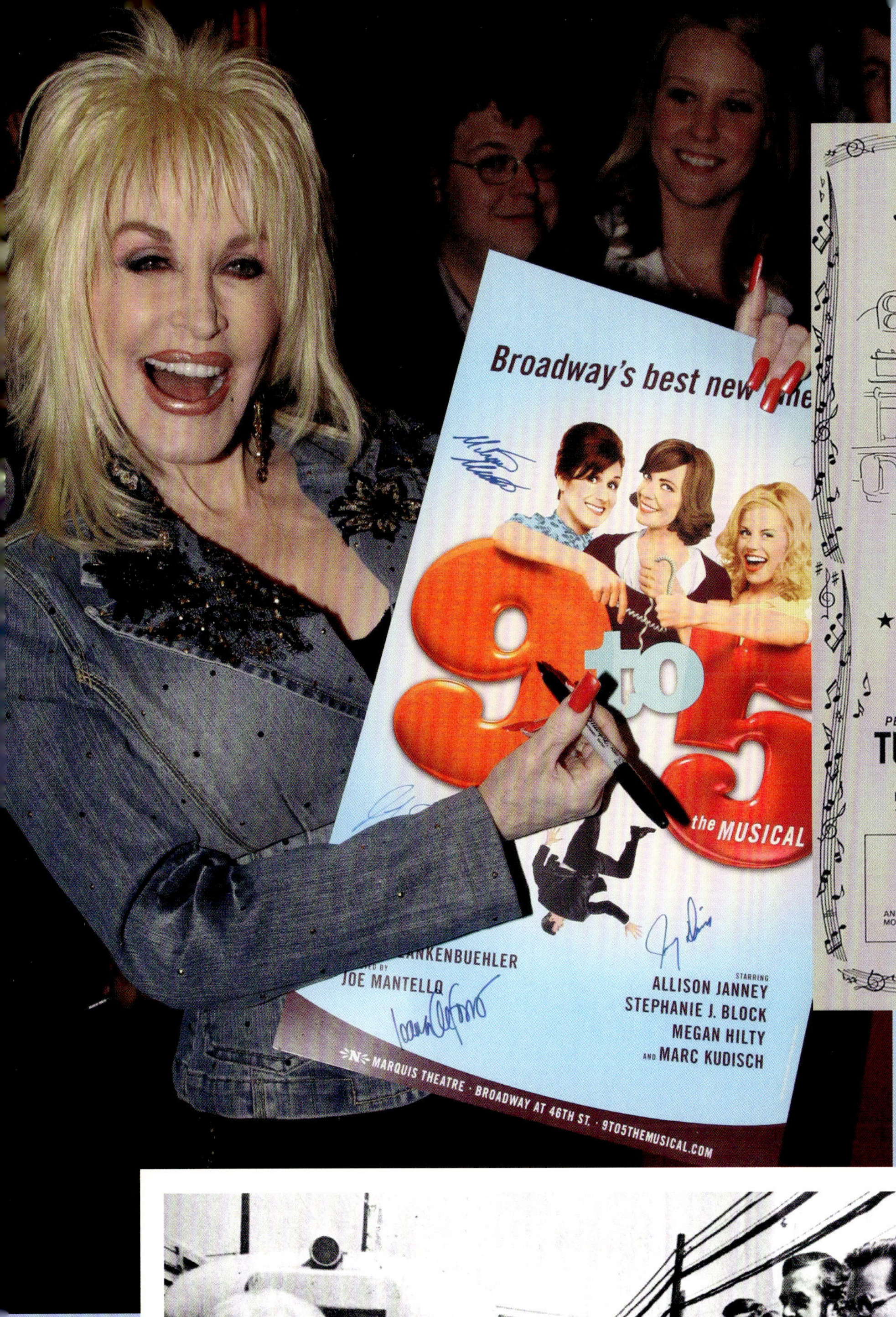

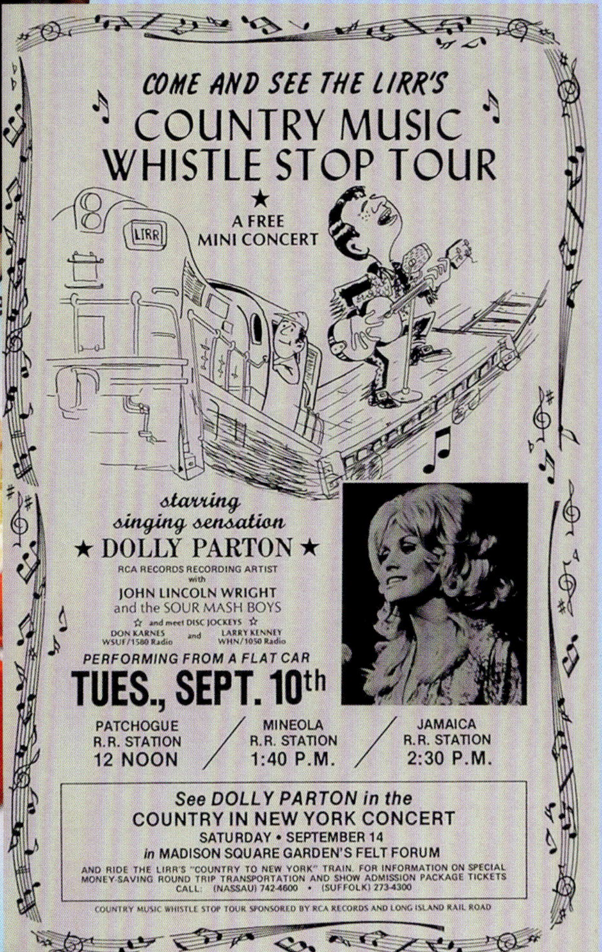

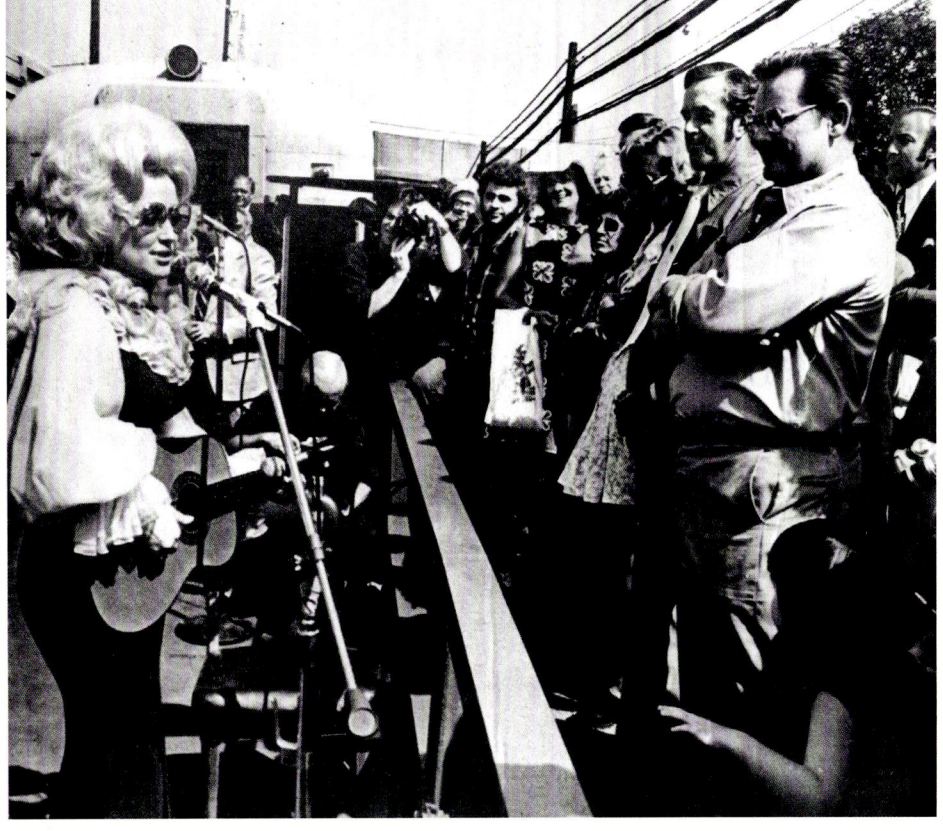

I love New York City—it's been very good to me. In the early days, I played several short concerts at the Long Island Railroad stations in a whistle-stop tour to promote an appearance at Madison Square Garden. More recently, I attended the premiere of my Tony-nominated Broadway production, *9 to 5: The Musical*. I've always loved the "city that never sleeps."

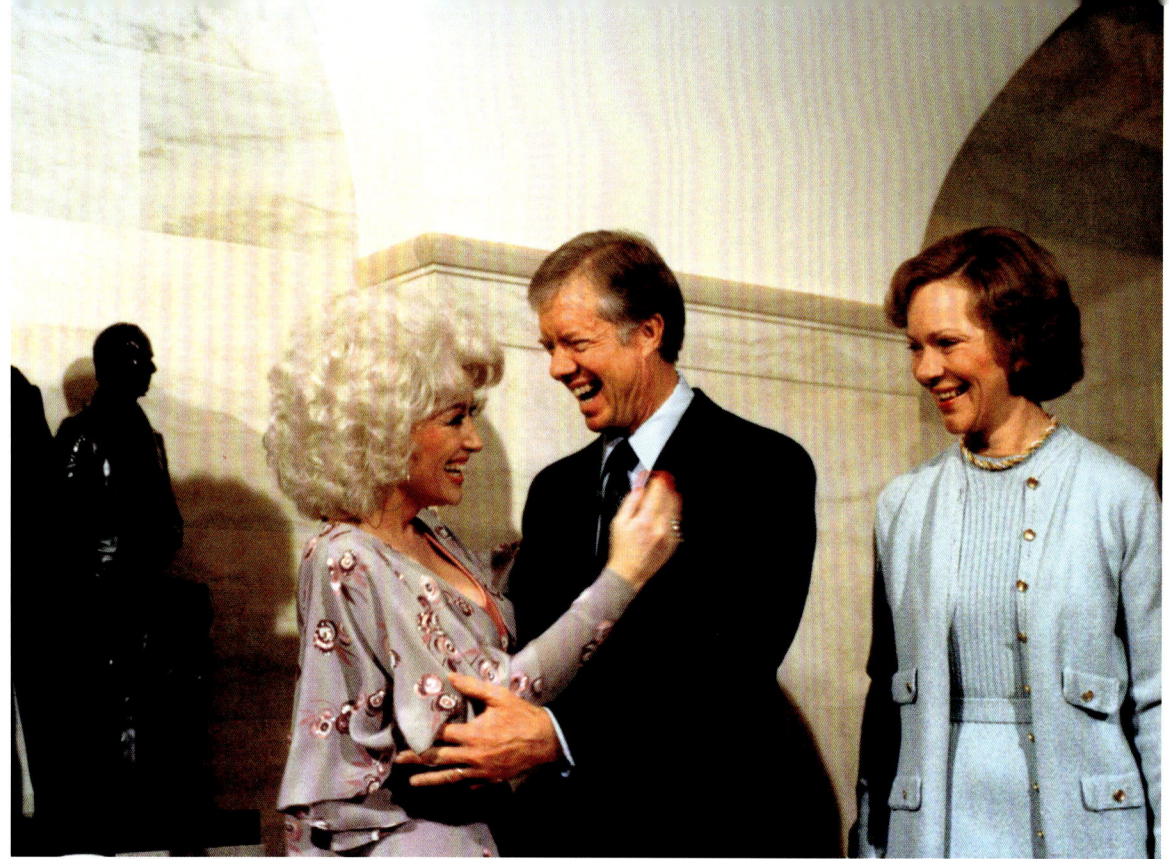

Greeting President Jimmy Carter
and First Lady Rosalynn Carter
at a luncheon at the White House.

The fall brought a few more significant concert moments. For starters, I headlined for four nights at the Universal Amphitheatre in Los Angeles. The mayor declared Dolly Parton Day in the city, Mac Davis paid me a visit, and I spent part of my days looking at scripts for the movie *9 to 5*. On the last night, Linda Ronstadt and Emmylou Harris showed up, and I surprised the crowd by bringing them out for "Even Cowgirls Get the Blues" and "The Sweetest Gift." It was one of the few times that we performed for a live audience together.

About ten days later, I cohosted *A Celebration of Country Music* with Johnny Cash, Glen Campbell, and Eddie Rabbitt at the historic Ford's Theatre in Washington, D.C. The whole cast of country performers got to have lunch at the White House before the TV taping, and during the show, I sang "I Will Always Love You" to President Jimmy Carter and his wife, Rosalynn.

I ended the decade playing a New Year's Eve show at the Resorts International in Atlantic City, New Jersey, where the high rollers paid one hundred dollars for a ticket to ring in the 1980s. Doesn't sound like much now, but one hundred dollars was a lot of money for a concert at the time—and it was certainly more than the three dollars it cost for a ticket to see Porter and Dolly in 1971!

I had seen the light of a clear blue morning when I parted ways with Porter in 1974, and five years later, I was truly living in the light of a brand-new day. That light was only growing brighter.

Star of the Show

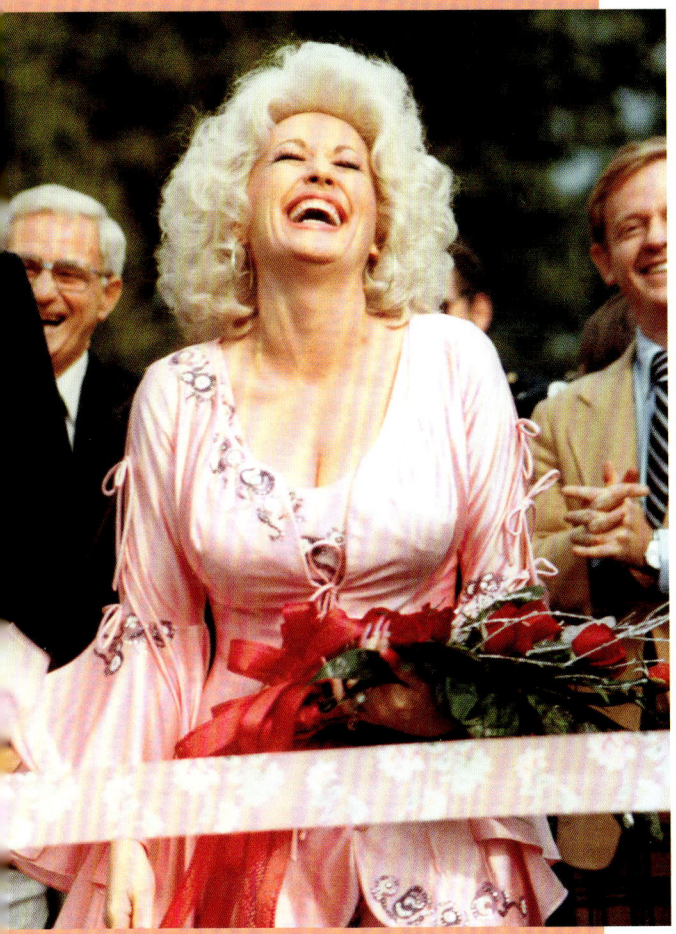

> As always its good to be back home in Sevierville Tennessee.
>
> I have been looking forward to coming back to SCHS this year to do another show. I hope the show will be enjoyable. As you know the money from the show goes into a Scholarship fund for worthy students of SCHS.
>
> I am very proud of my hometown and the people in it, and I feel very fortunate to have achieved success in the music business, which I love, and I'm very proud to contribute to my hometown of Sevierville and its people in any way I can.
>
> The Scholarship Foundation was not set up for any kind of publicity or glory for me, I look upon my help only as a part of one that I can give back to Sevier Co.
>
> There are a lot of people responsible for the Scholarship Foundation, and my help is only a small contribution.
>
> I would like to give credit and thanks to the Sevier Co. Band Boosters Club, the Sevier Co. school officials, and all the people of Sevier Co. that have taken part in this program. I personally wish to thank Louis Owens and Paul Soelberg who have worked very hard behind the scene in Nashville to make the program a better one.
>
> I also want to thank Harry Bean, the Blackwood Bros. and their band for helping with the show.
>
> I want to thank last, but not least of all, my boss and dear friend Porter Wagoner for volunteering without charge his time, talent & band (Jack Rhodes and the Wagon Masters) to help with the Scholarship Foundation fund raising show.
>
> Thanks to all of Sevier Co.
>
> As always, Dolly Parton

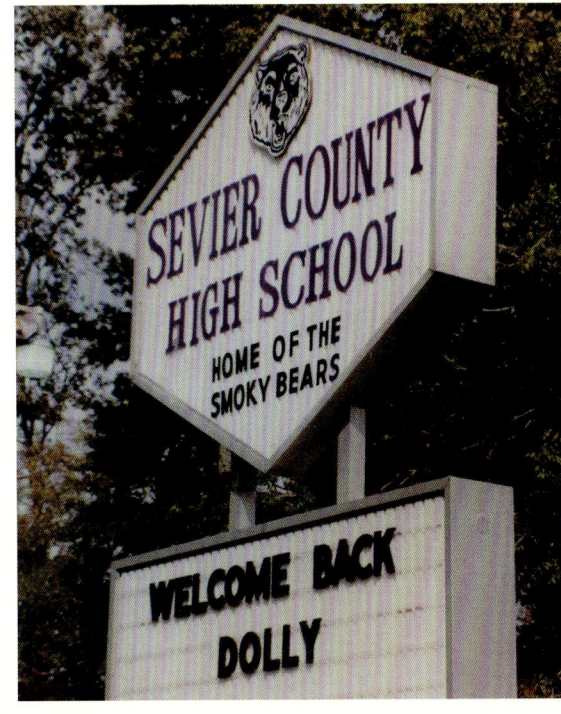

The same week that I performed for the president, I returned to Sevierville, Tennessee, for a Dolly Parton Day celebration that included the renaming of US Highway 411 as the Dolly Parton Parkway. It was a real honor—Dolly Parton Day has always meant so much to me. *Clockwise from upper left*: A scene from the ribbon-cutting ceremony, one of my handwritten speeches I've given over the years, and the sign at my alma mater, which is located on . . . Dolly Parton Parkway!

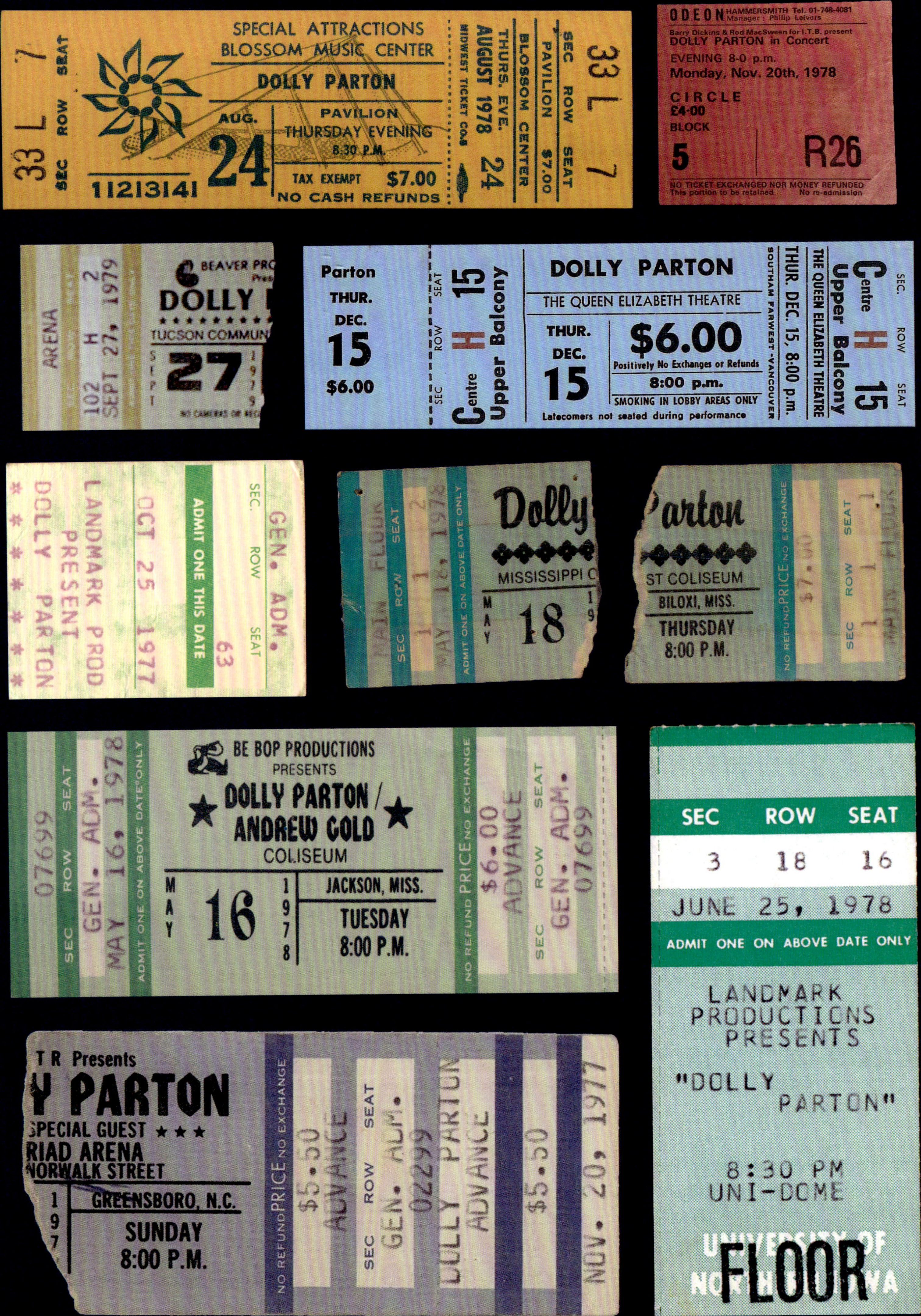

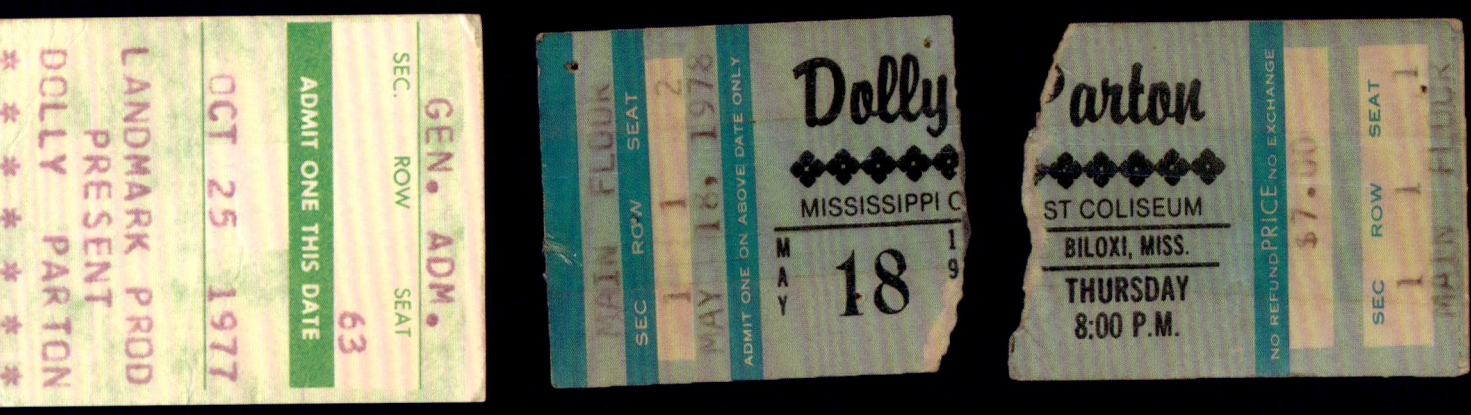
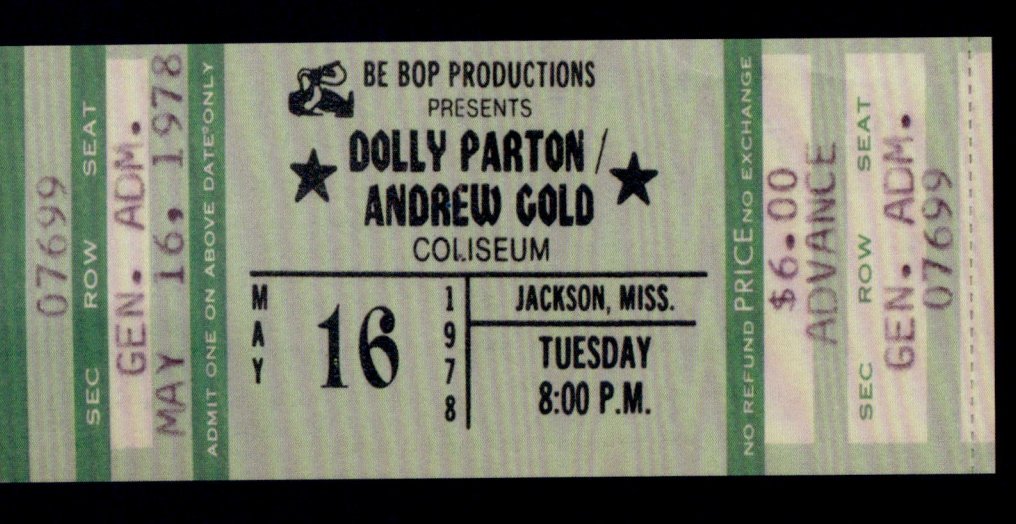

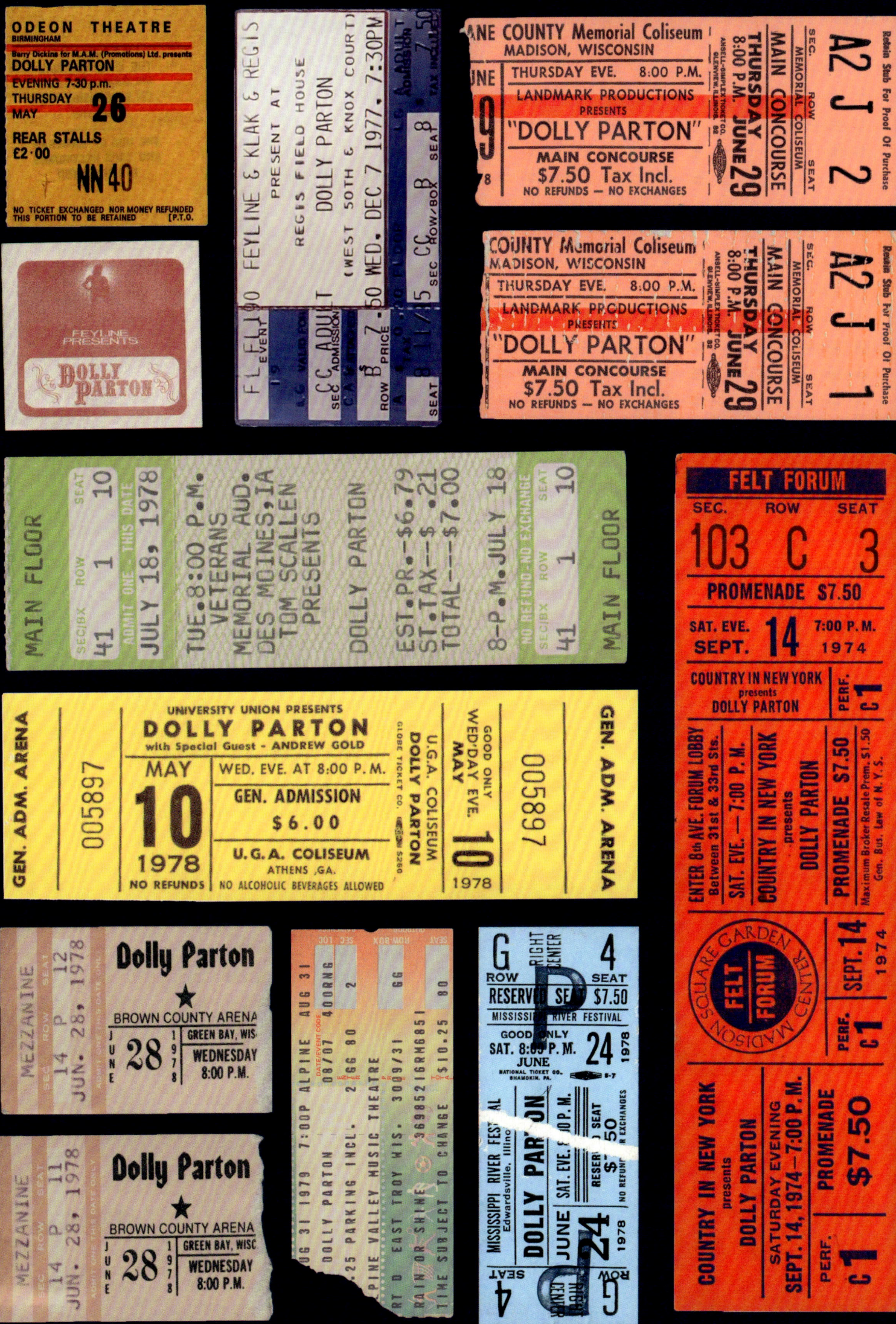

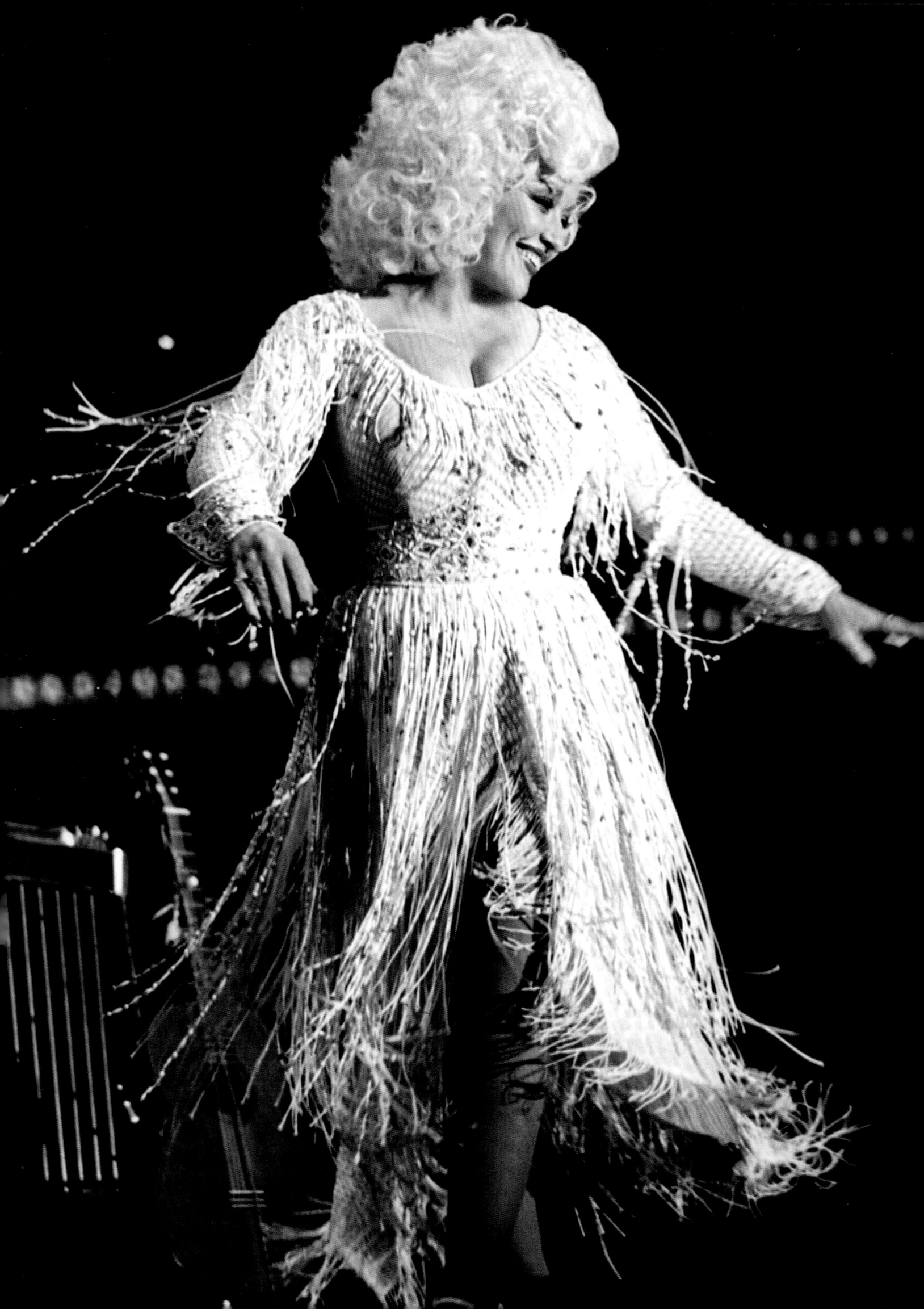

Superstar of the Show

1980-1986

1980 - 1986

Moving from country singer to pop star was one thing, appearing on the silver screen would provide Dolly with worldwide recognition on a completely different level.

Jane Fonda put her to work with a role in the 1980 movie *9 to 5*, and when that exposure was combined with the power of a no. 1 Grammy-winning, Oscar-nominated crossover single, new doors continued to open. She received more film offers, including parts in *The Best Little Whorehouse in Texas* and *Rhinestone*; became a top attraction in Las Vegas and Atlantic City; and juiced her recording career by finding a new duet partner in Kenny Rogers. Their 1983 hit "Islands in the Stream" launched a highly successful collaboration that would lead to more hits, more TV appearances, and several years of successful Kenny and Dolly concert tours.

By the mid-1980s, Dolly had gone from being the best-known woman in country music to one of the most-loved women on the planet.

—TOM ROLAND

FEBRUARY 1981
Dolly launches a Las Vegas residency at the Riviera.

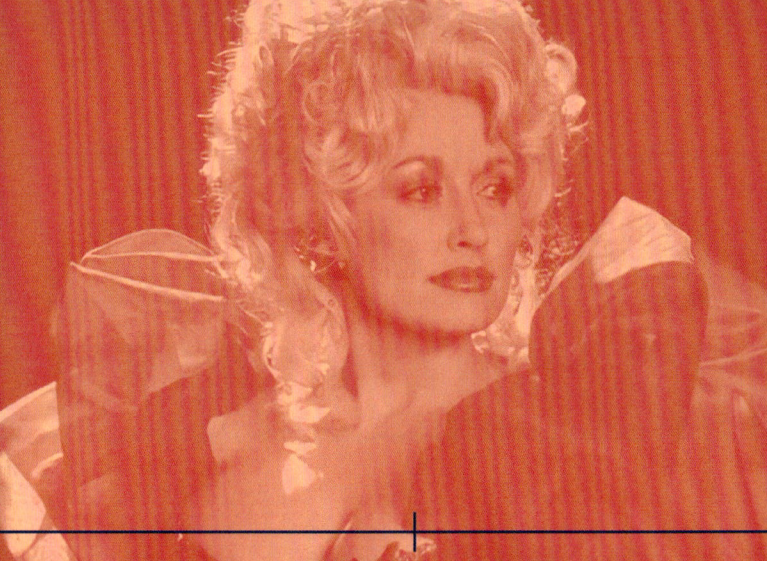

JULY 1982
Dolly stars in *The Best Little Whorehouse in Texas* with Burt Reynolds.

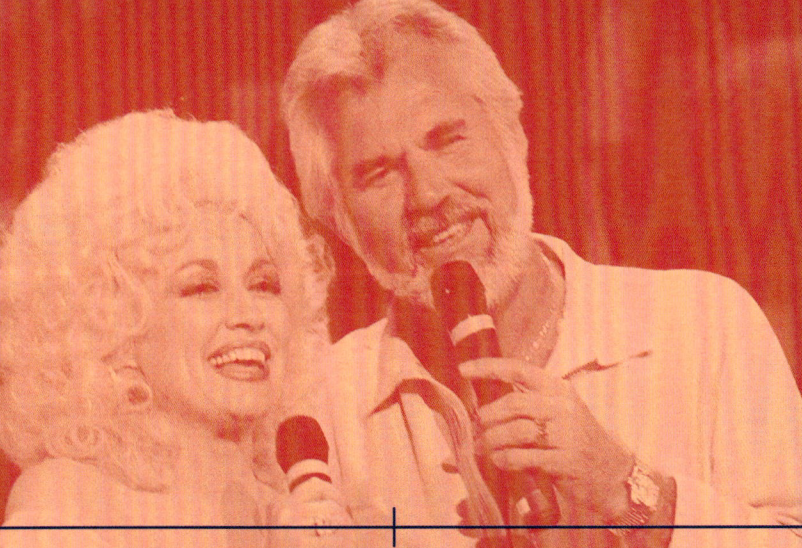

AUGUST 1983
Dolly teams with Kenny Rogers to record "Islands in the Stream." The duo rocket to no. 1 on the country, pop, and AC charts.

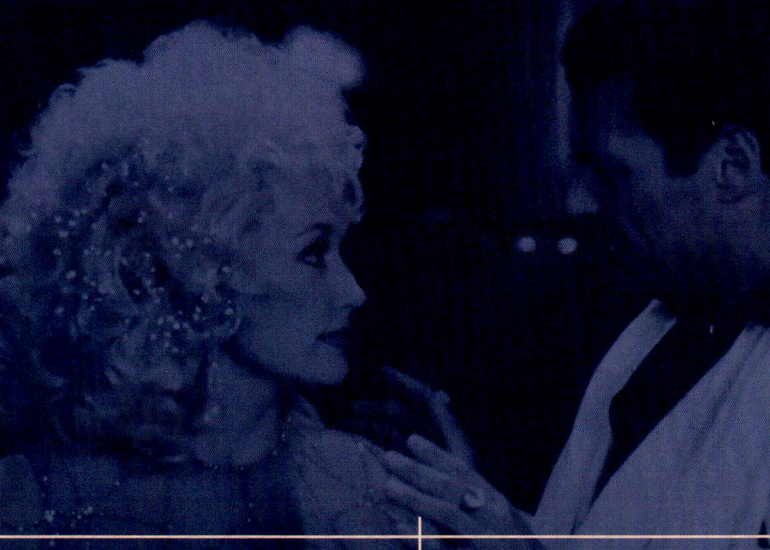

JUNE 1984
Dolly stars in *Rhinestone*. The soundtrack album produces the no. 1 hit "Tennessee Homesick Blues."

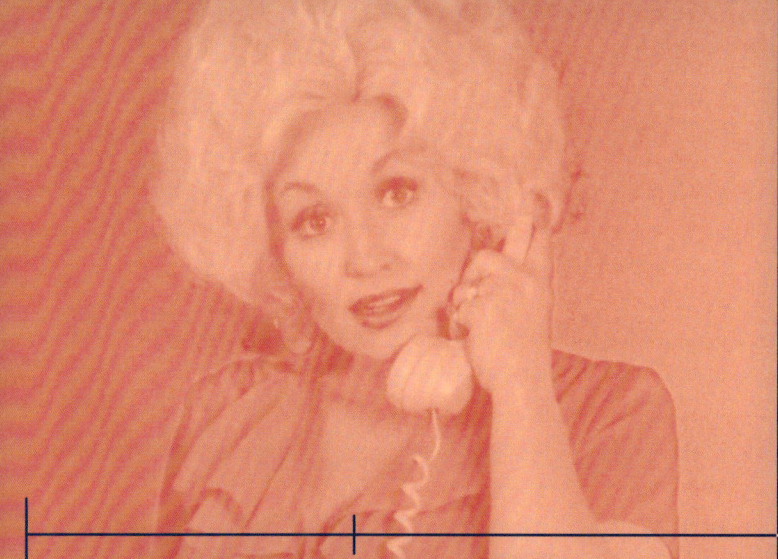

DECEMBER 1980
Dolly's first film, *9 to 5*, is released and earns her two Golden Globe nominations, as well as one Oscar nomination for the title song.

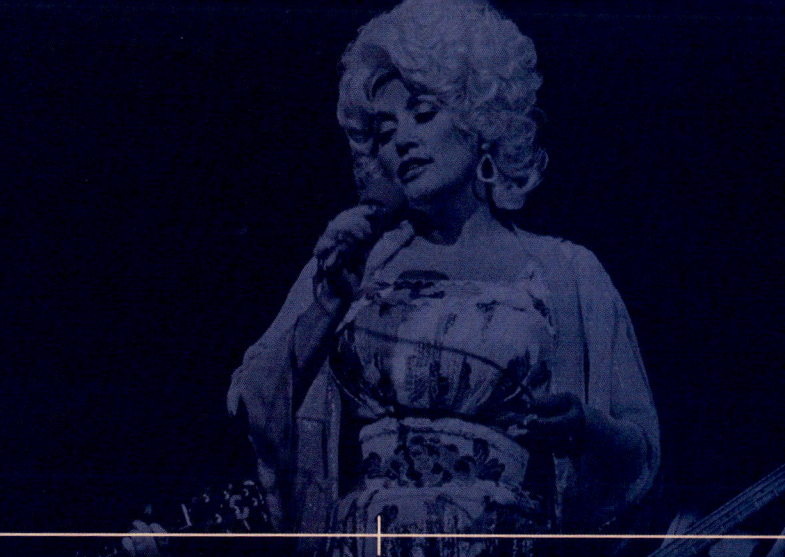

FEBRUARY 1981
The song "9 to 5" tops the country and pop charts, earning Dolly Grammys for Best Female Country Vocal Performance and Best Country Song.

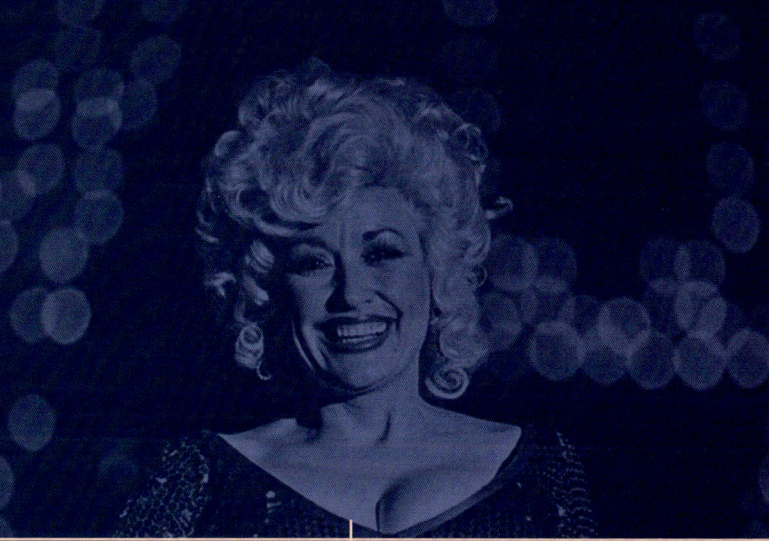

OCTOBER 1982
Dolly's remake of "I Will Always Love You" makes history by becoming the first song by the same performer to be a no. 1 hit twice.

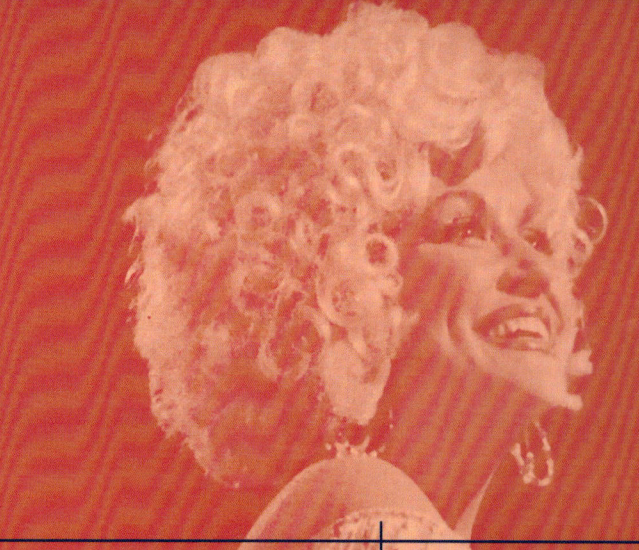

JUNE 1983
Dolly's first live concert special, *Dolly in Concert*, is filmed in London and airs on HBO.

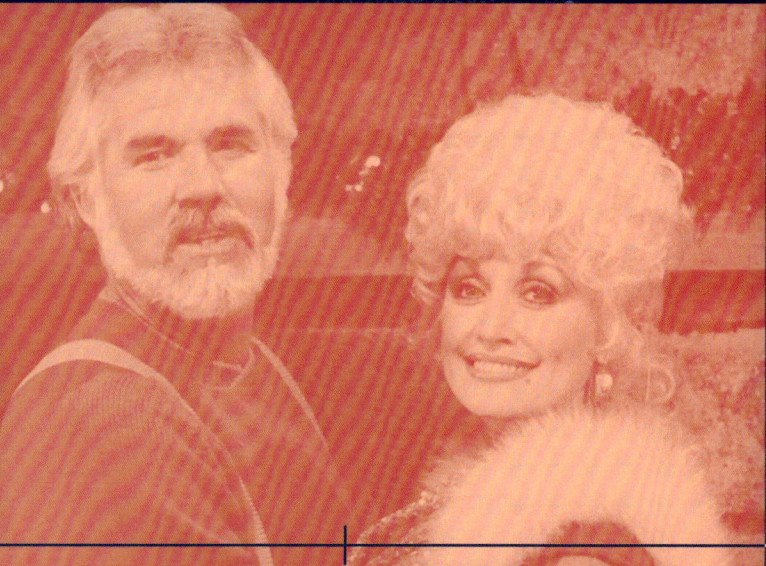

OCTOBER 1984
Dolly teams with Kenny Rogers for a multiplatinum Christmas album before launching their Real Love arena tour in 1985.

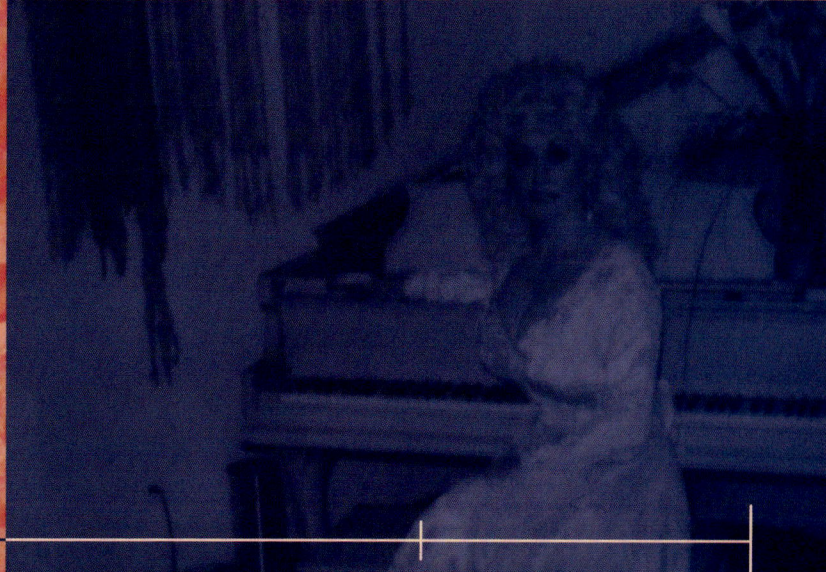

JANUARY 1985
Dolly releases *Real Love* album, which charted three top five country singles ("Real Love," no. 1; "Think About Love," no. 1; and "Don't Call It Love," no. 3).

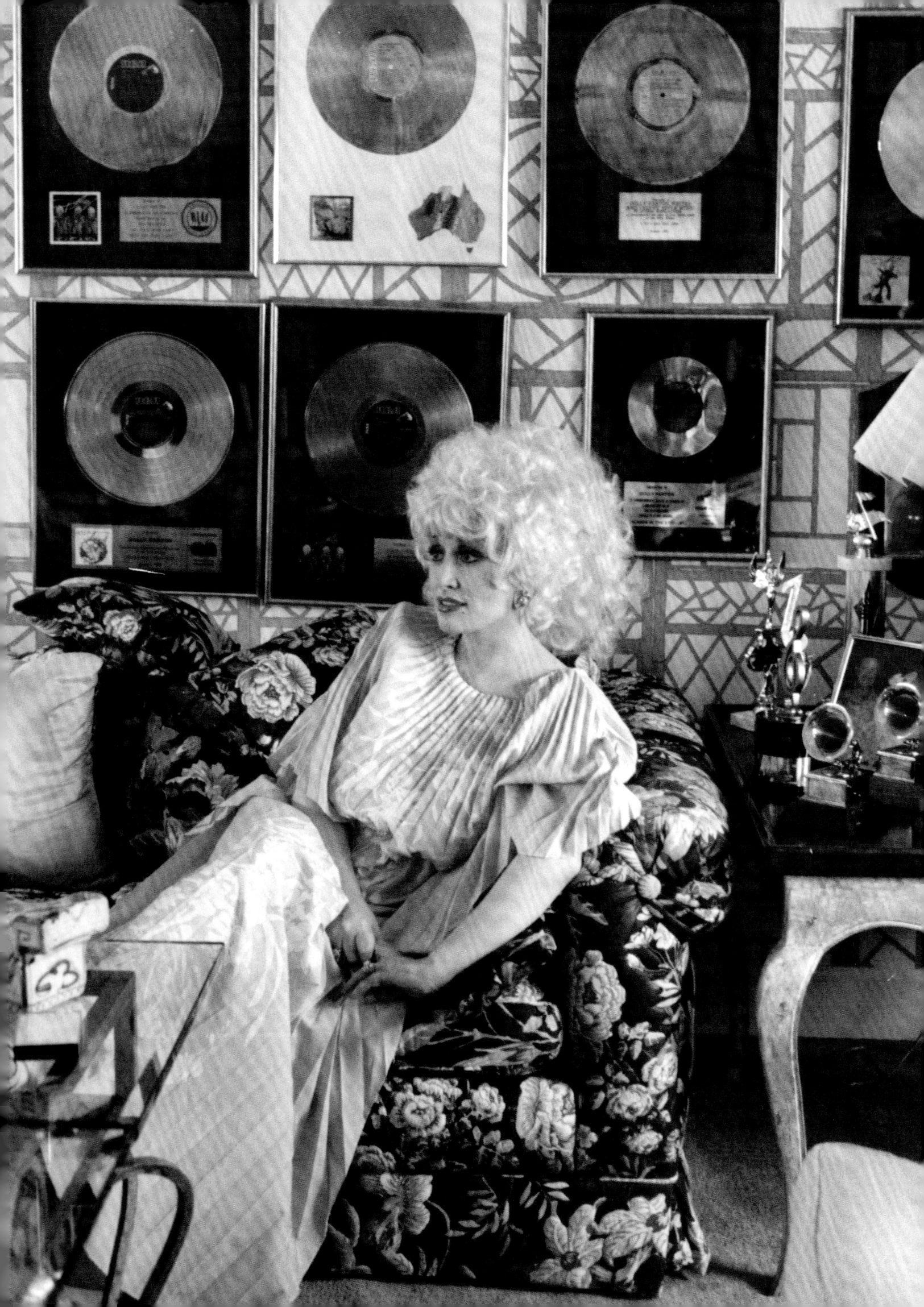

*A*s the world started a new decade on New Year's Day 1980, I launched a new stage of my career. Production began that month on *9 to 5* in Los Angeles, which kept me on a film set for about two and a half months. It gave me an opportunity to make my first appearance at the Academy Awards, where I presented the Best Original Song Score trophy with Ben Vereen. That's just one example of how working with Jane Fonda and Lily Tomlin opened me up to a world I hadn't fully explored before.

I never particularly wanted to be in the movies. I also never ruled it out. I just knew that if I was going to go down that road, it would have to come naturally, like everything else. At the time, I was fully in tune with my music and what I was doing with my touring, and although I'd been offered a few movies, I never felt inclined to do one. But Jane Fonda sent this script because she thought I'd be a fit for the role of Doralee, and given how my music career was going, she also thought I might bring in some folks who would go to see me in a movie. The script, of course, was for *9 to 5* . . . the story was great . . . and I thought, *I'll do this!*

The storyline and the opportunity got me to thinking too. I figured if I could write the theme song, it'd be even more worth doing the movie. If it was a hit, great. If it was a flop, nobody would even know. So I got with Jane and I said, "Yeah, I'd love to do it if I can write the theme song."

When it came to shooting the picture, one of the first things I said was, "I'm not an actress." And Jane said, "Well, just be yourself. Just act like you act in your songs. I believe every word you say. So just do it like you're talking to somebody." That made it easy. Because the character I played was from Texas, the accent was not much different from mine, so it was natural to become her. That's really why I took many of the film roles I took, in fact. I'm either from Texas or some Southern town in everything I've played, I think, and that allowed me to feel comfortable with the character, no matter how good an actress I am—or am not.

All the experience that I'd had on TV also helped. I made friends with the camera as a little girl working in the studio when Cas Walker started televising his shows in Knoxville. Somebody told me back then to think of the red light on the camera as eyes: "Don't ever be afraid of the camera. The camera is your friend. Just picture those eyes as someone you love, and remember that there's somebody out there watching you that you care about and that cares about you."

That stuck with me. I wasn't always comfortable on the set or in all the situations that I sang in, but when it came time to be on camera, I could focus on that.

When you make movies, though, you have to be on a spot and you're directed to move a certain way—that was different for me. You're not even supposed to look at the camera when you're in the movies. That was tough for me because I was so used to loving that camera as if it was someone I knew who cared about me.

Superstar of the Show

When filming was over, I did a little role reversal. Jane Fonda learned what it was like to be on my turf when I took her along to the Grand Ole Opry. I showed her around backstage, and then I had Jane come out to sing backup on "Applejack," a song about a small-time musician who also made apple moonshine that had been inspired by two men who taught me to play banjo when I was a girl. She had a great time, and it was a big surprise to the crowd. Although if I'm being honest, she sings about like my husband, Carl. I'm not being catty here either—she'd tell you the same thing! She said as much to a reporter that day. We took the Southern experience one step further. A day or two after her Opry debut, we headed off on my bus to the mountains, and I introduced Jane to *real* moonshine.

Filming movies takes you out of circulation from the general public, and for an entertainer like me, seeing the faces of the people you're trying to reach is energizing. So bringing Jane to the Opry was invigorating. And so was my return to Fan Fair that summer.

Fan Fair started in Nashville in 1972 as a kind of country music convention. It always includes concerts, autograph booths, and fan club parties, and sometimes it even features country music stars playing softball against one another. I was a regular during the first few Fan Fairs, but I had missed a couple at the end of the '70s, so it was fun to get back out and take pictures with the fans and get to talk to them one-on-one.

It was particularly good to see the members of my fan club, who were my most enthusiastic supporters. I was able to feel a close bond with them in part because my sister Cassie helped make it possible. She ran my fan club for years, and she used to set up the booth when I would go down and spend all day at Fan Fair. Cassie would work really hard at trying to make sure that booth was just right, and she would spend days getting it ready and setting it up. She also took a lot of pride in helping answer fan mail. It was important that the fans had a hands-on feel and sensed a close connection with me, and since they were dealing with someone from my family, when she shared news, they could say, "I know this is the truth."

In October, I performed again on the CMA Awards. I sang "Starting Over Again," which was written by Donna Summer, the disco queen, with Bruce Sudano, whom she married a couple months after it went to no. 1. They wrote it about his parents, and I suppose I liked it because it reminded me so much of my song "To Daddy." My buddy Mac Davis introduced me on the CMAs, and it might have been the first time ever that a Donna Summer song was performed live on TV with a string section *and* a steel guitar!

All that, along with a cover story in *Rolling Stone* magazine, was kind of a lead-up to the movie *9 to 5* and to the theme song that I wanted so badly for people to hear. I finally got to sing it live once the album *9 to 5 and Odd Jobs* was released. That was the working title of the album, but it really was a "working" album since all the songs were about making a living. I performed "9 to 5" three times in two days on TV—on the syndicated daytime program *The Merv Griffin Show,* on the debut episode of NBC's *Barbara Mandrell & The Mandrell Sisters,* and on the same network on *The Tonight Show* hosted by Johnny Carson. On that show, I also did a second song from the album: a cover of "House of the Rising Sun," which really is about a "working girl." That was doubly appropriate since it was already public knowledge that I'd be playing a madam in my second movie, *The Best Little Whorehouse in Texas*.

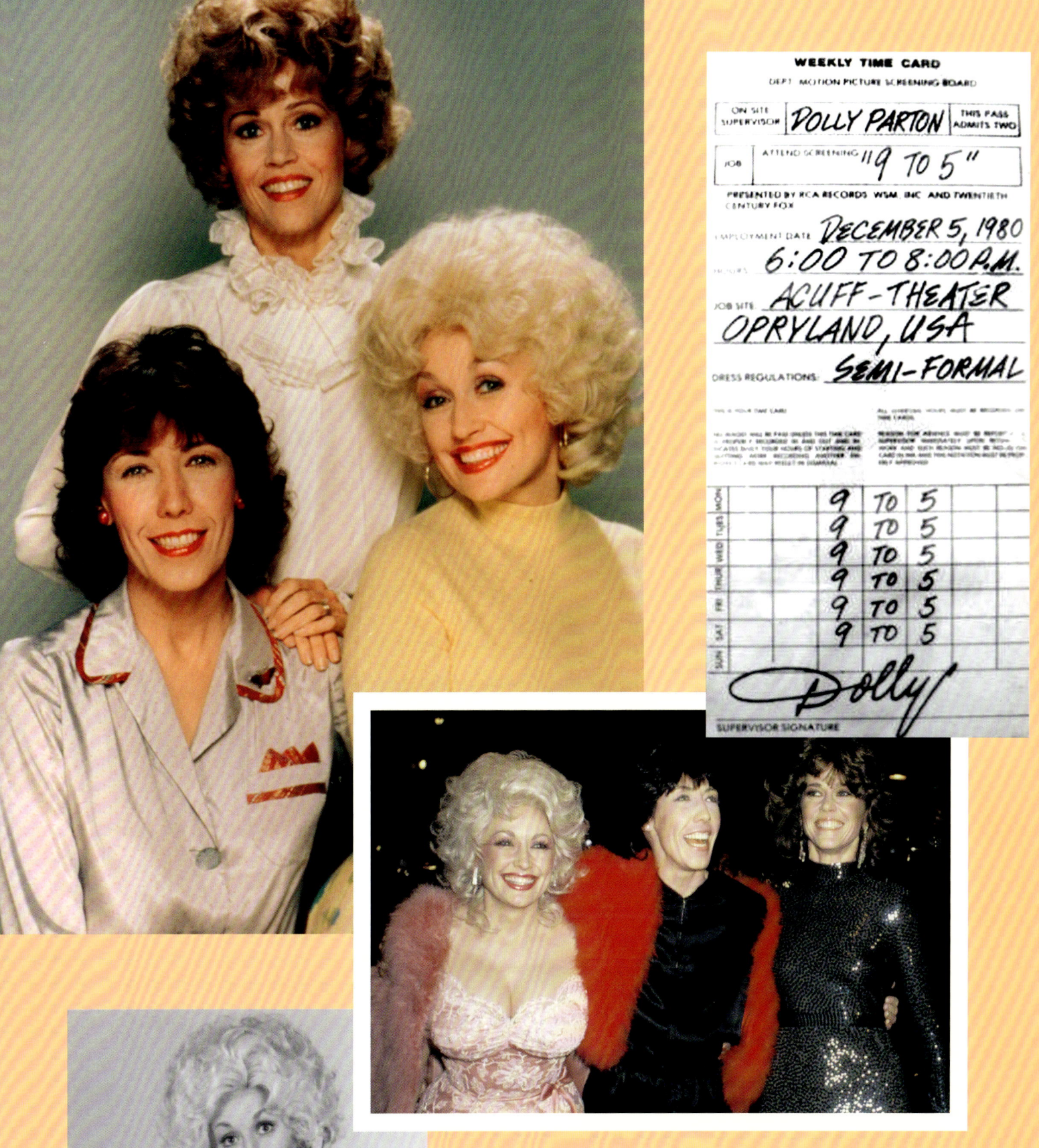

Jane Fonda saw my potential as an actress, and the opportunity to play Doralee in *9 to 5* started a new chapter in my life. *Clockwise from top left:* A formal press photo with Jane and Lily Tomlin, an invitation to the Nashville premiere of *9 to 5*, a moment from the Los Angeles premiere, and me keeping my ear to the grindstone.

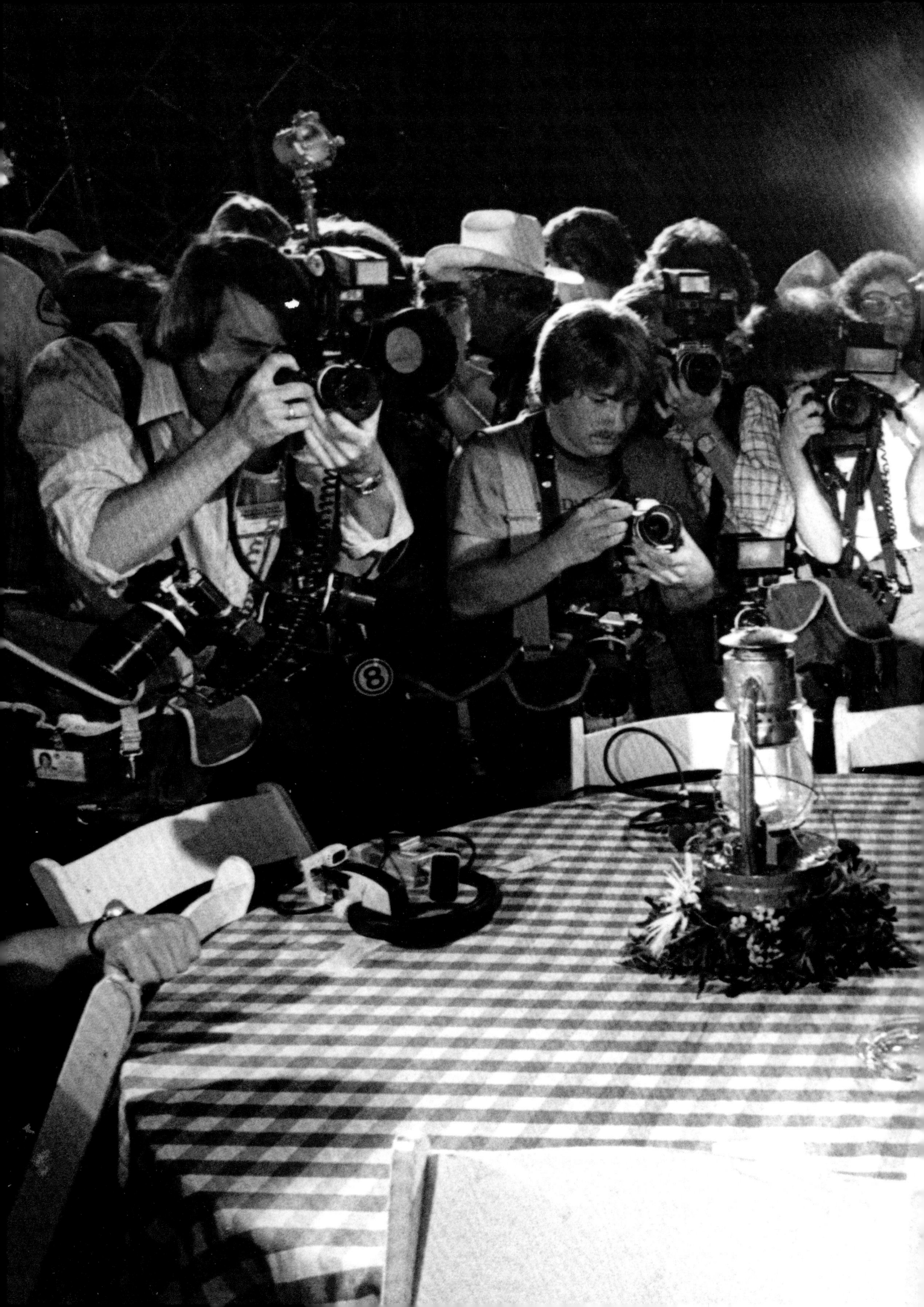

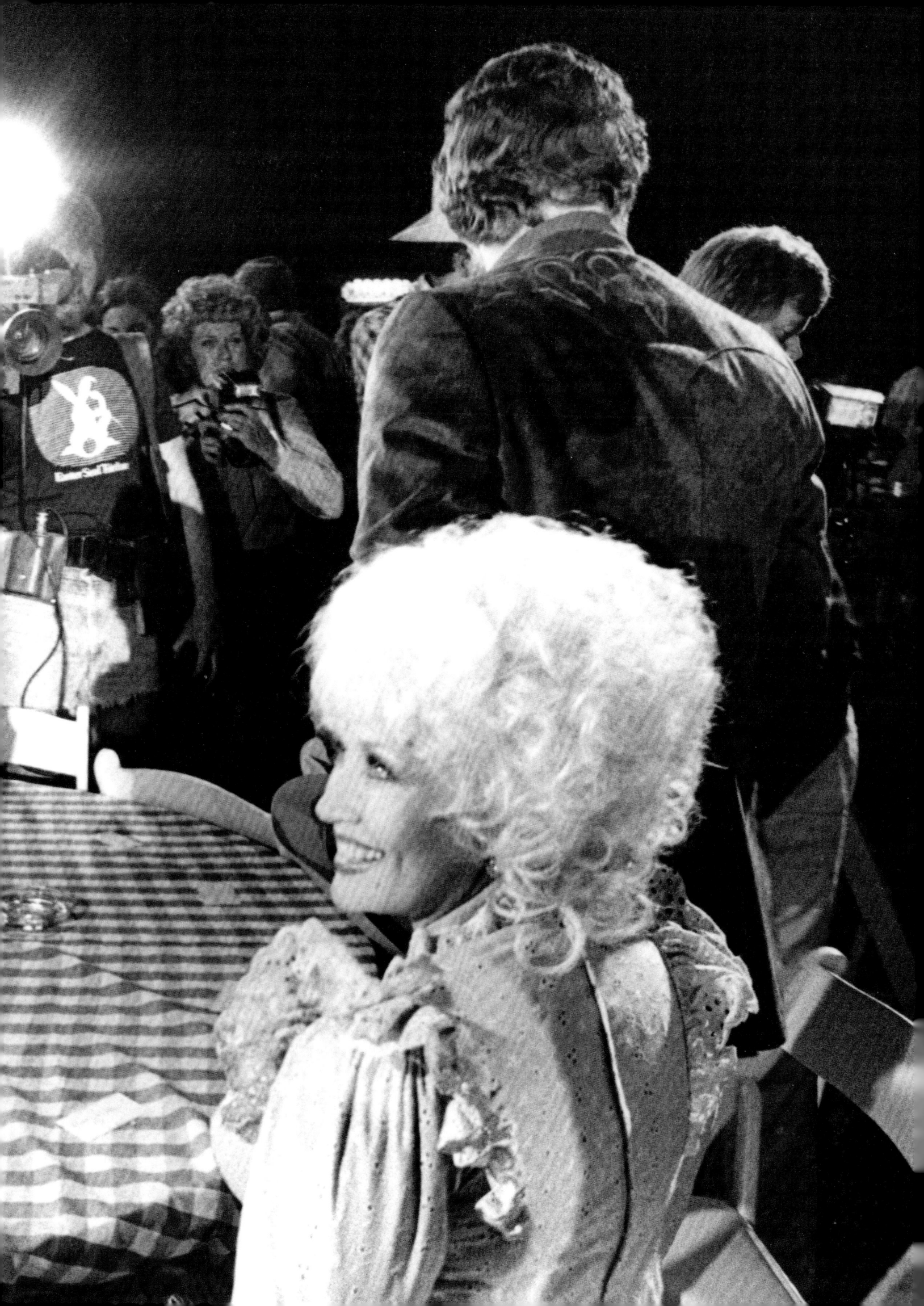

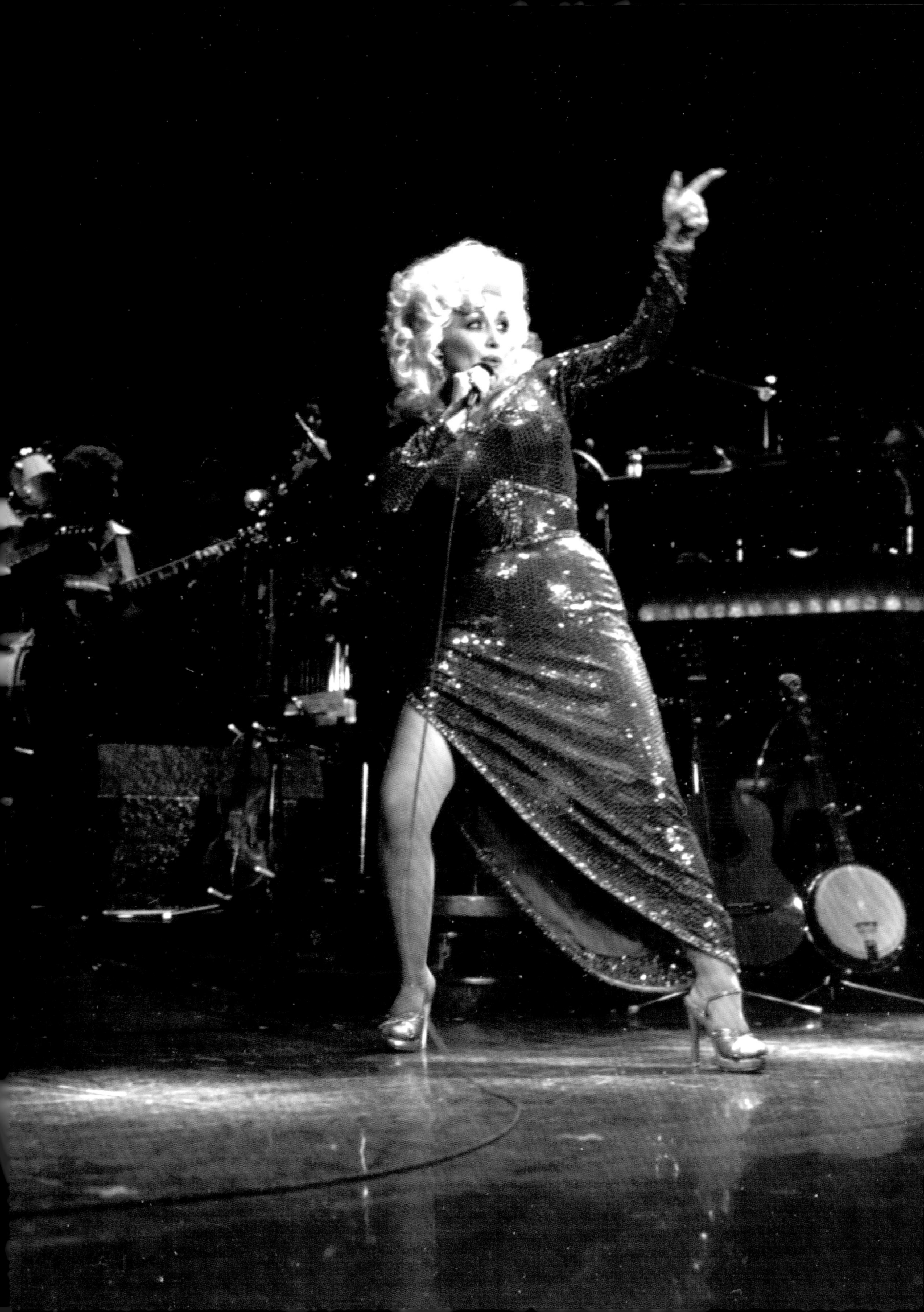

Just a few weeks later, on New Year's Eve, I performed "9 to 5" in concert for the first time at the Diplomat Hotel and Spa, a swanky thirty-six-story resort on the barrier island near Fort Lauderdale, Florida. No surprise—I held it back for the encore. That's always great when you get a chance to go out and sing a hit record for the first time and the audience really responds and starts singing the words back to you. No artist ever forgets that. It's like a confirmation: "Yeah, you know that one, don't you?" In fact, I could sort of feel people anticipating it throughout the whole show.

For most of 1981, I concentrated my concert schedule in casinos—in Atlantic City, Lake Tahoe, and Las Vegas—which allowed me to stay in one place for a bit. That set things up nicely for my work on *Whorehouse,* since the bulk of the movie's filming was supposed to take place that year. With fans coming to see me—instead of me traveling all around the country to see them—I'd be better rested and ready to memorize scripts and handle the long days. If I learned anything during *9 to 5,* it's that a movie set involves a lot of hurry up and wait. The actors are not the ones in charge. The director must coordinate the shoots, and once you're ready at six or seven in the morning, you could literally be standing around until four or five in the afternoon before the director finally says you're needed. Sometimes doing nothing will wear you out!

Playing the casinos represented a change in my thinking. Up until I accepted the Resorts booking in 1979, I had routinely declined to play them. It wasn't like anyone ever told me I shouldn't. But I had been taught when I was a kid not to gamble—and I don't, at least not with one-armed bandits! When I was growing up in the church, gambling was considered a sin, so I felt like performing at a casino must be wrong too.

But as time went on, especially after talking it over several times with Sandy Gallin, I decided it wasn't my place to judge how other people might spend their time and money. In fact, there are a lot of broken people at poker tables, and if they wanted to see Dolly Parton before or after they went and played a few hands, maybe I had something to offer them—a little bit of positivity, a little bit of gospel, and a reminder that even if blackjack treated them badly, there were people who still valued and loved them.

Once I worked all of that out in my head, I realized that I probably could have been playing casinos all along. And they would become a big part of my touring schedule in the first years of the '80s.

There are advantages to performing at casinos. For starters, they tend to book you for multiple shows—a long weekend or a whole week—and that means you get a break from all the travel for a bit. Now, there's nothing wrong with putting all those miles on the bus. Riding the road is how you get to go out and see your fans in person. But the most travel you do during a casino engagement is the trip down in the elevator to get to the stage from the hotel room. You get some rest, the pay is pretty good, and you still get to sing for people. The audience is a little different too. Instead of drawing a crowd almost entirely from a local city, casinos tend to pull in people from an entire region or even from across the country. So when those fans go home and talk about the show with their friends, it can have a wider impact than a performance at a more traditional venue.

Superstar of the Show

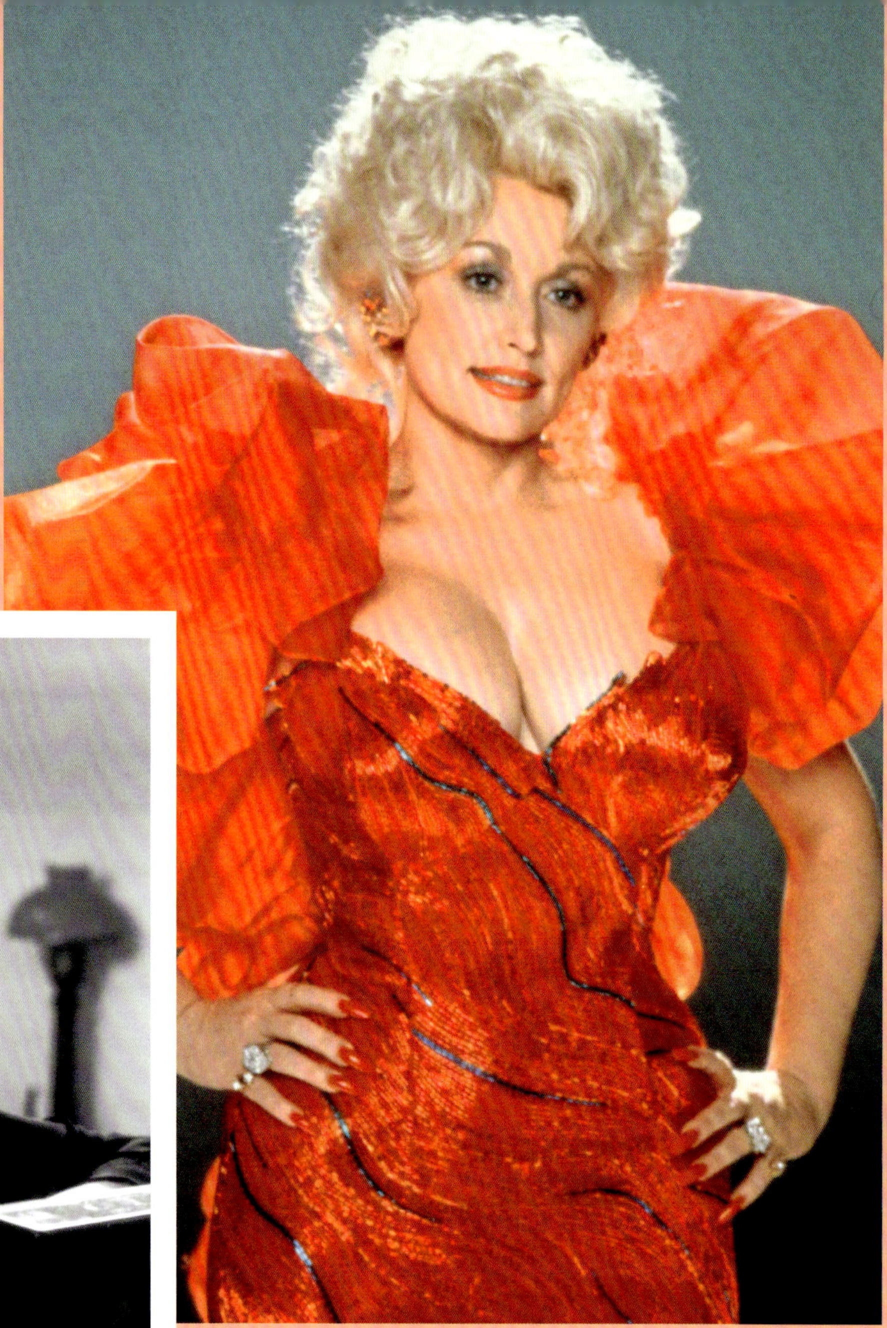

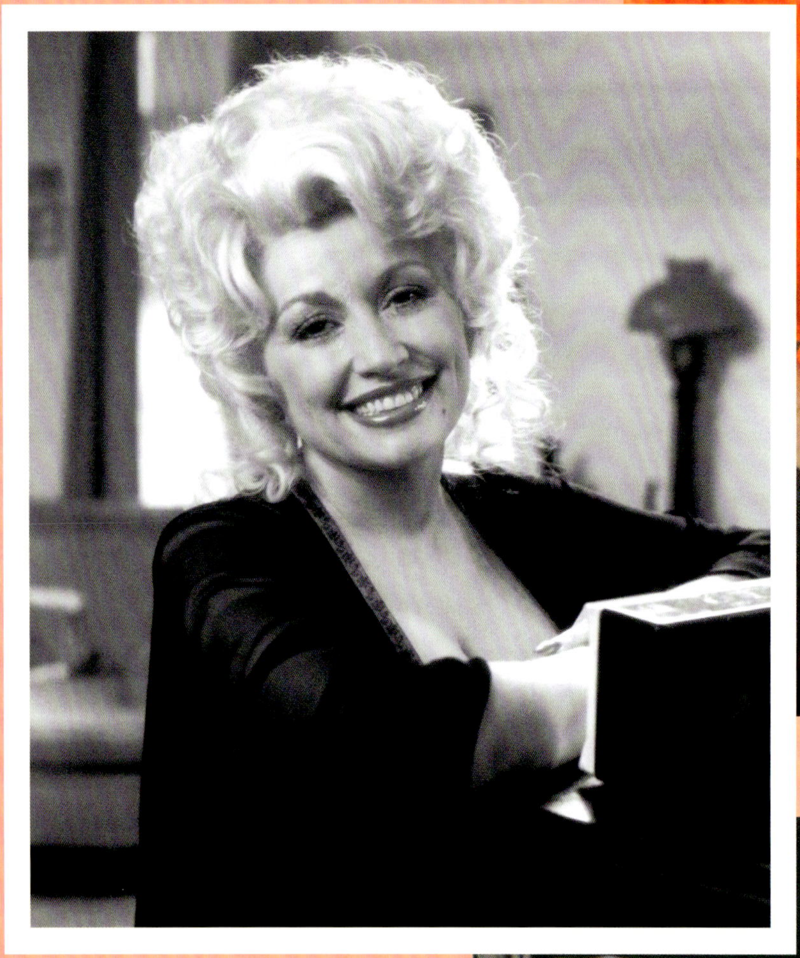

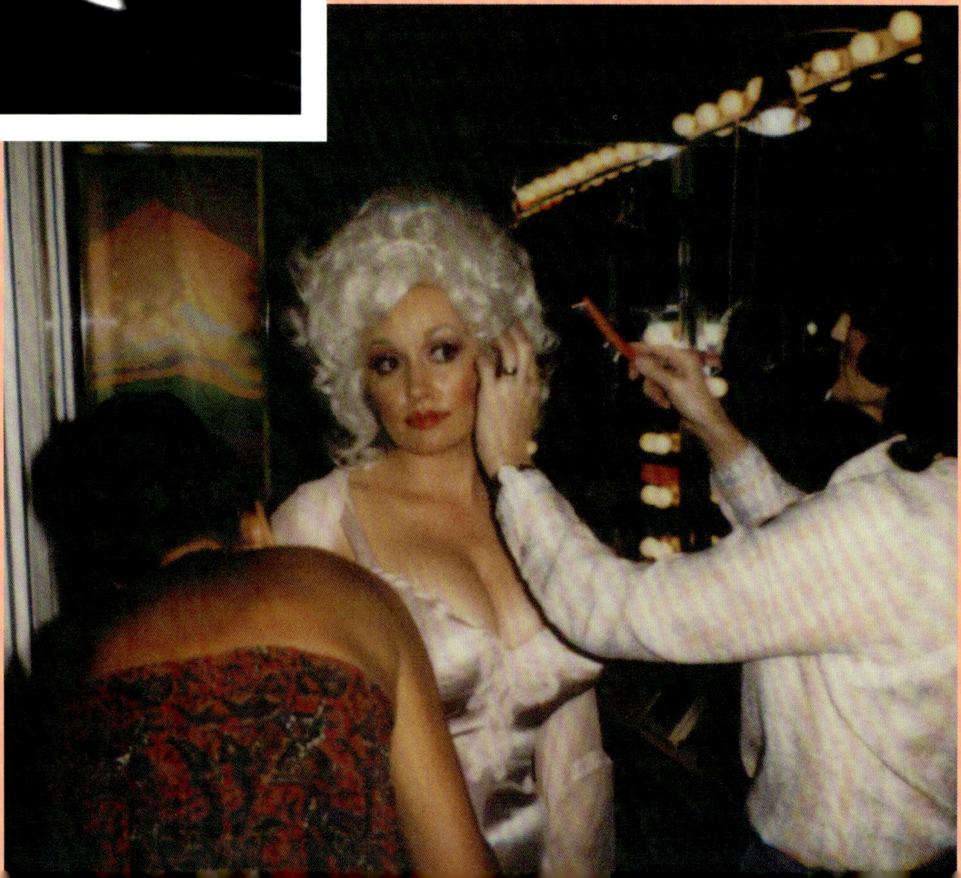

The Best Little Whorehouse in Texas was an emotional experience. Production came with a few hiccups, but in the end the movie turned out well and several friendships came out of it. Burt Reynolds and I made a good team, and Jim Nabors was a sweetheart.

Playing Las Vegas got a big buildup. The city calls itself the Entertainment Capital of the World, and I wanted to live up to that, especially after I got two Golden Globe nominations for *9 to 5*, including New Star of the Year in a Motion Picture. Since I was now one of several artists bringing country music into the bigger world of show business, I really wanted people to know that a girl from East Tennessee could hold her own on the Strip, particularly after they gave me $350,000 a week, which I was told was the best pay in the city at the time. It was a big deal that I was getting that kind of money, mostly because it meant that I was that much in demand. I took a lot of pride in that. In fact, I've been humbled by so many of the offers that we got through the years. I never totally understood it, but I always tried to make the most of it. And I know it was okay to take some pride in it—I know I worked to earn it.

Ahead of Vegas, I played a week in Tahoe, then did *The Tonight Show* again to help publicize what was supposed to be a nine-day engagement. But on opening day, my throat gave out and I had to cancel the first show.

I was devastated. It certainly wasn't the way I wanted to start. I did a couple of interviews that day in the hotel room, but when it was apparent my throat wasn't cooperating, I had to stop talking. I still did the interviews—I just answered the questions by writing on a piece of paper.

Vegas, I would discover, was always hard on my voice. I had worked so much in the '70s that it was already strained. Concert sound equipment got much better at pumping out loud volumes of sound during that period, but what the singer heard in the monitors on the floor at the front of the stage wasn't always the same mix that the audience heard. So sometimes you might sing harder than you needed to because you were trying to hear your voice above all the other instruments. Lots of singers struggled back then—I know that now. Thanks to in-ear monitors that you can tune to your own needs, that problem isn't nearly as bad now as it was in the past.

But they still haven't fixed the Vegas air. That dry climate is rough on any singer, and doing two shows a day for a week or ten days in a row is really hard.

Fortunately, we only had to delay my Vegas debut one night. I was able to sing after a day of rest and gave it everything I had. We built a castle set for the stage, and I did a costume change about two-thirds of the way through the show in the middle of the hits. I sang "But You Know I Love You," the next single scheduled for release after "9 to 5," for the first time. I did some comedy segments. I still included a gospel segment, did a couple of mountain songs, and had Gypsy Fever perform two classic country instrumentals: "Dueling Banjos" and "Orange Blossom Special." I also pulled together a medley, and even tossed in "There's No Business Like Show Business"—I gave 'em everything but the kitchen sink!

The next day, the Vegas newspaper compared me to Frank Sinatra, Paul Anka, and Wayne Newton—all the stars that had set the Vegas standard—and I felt like what I was doing was working.

Superstar of the Show

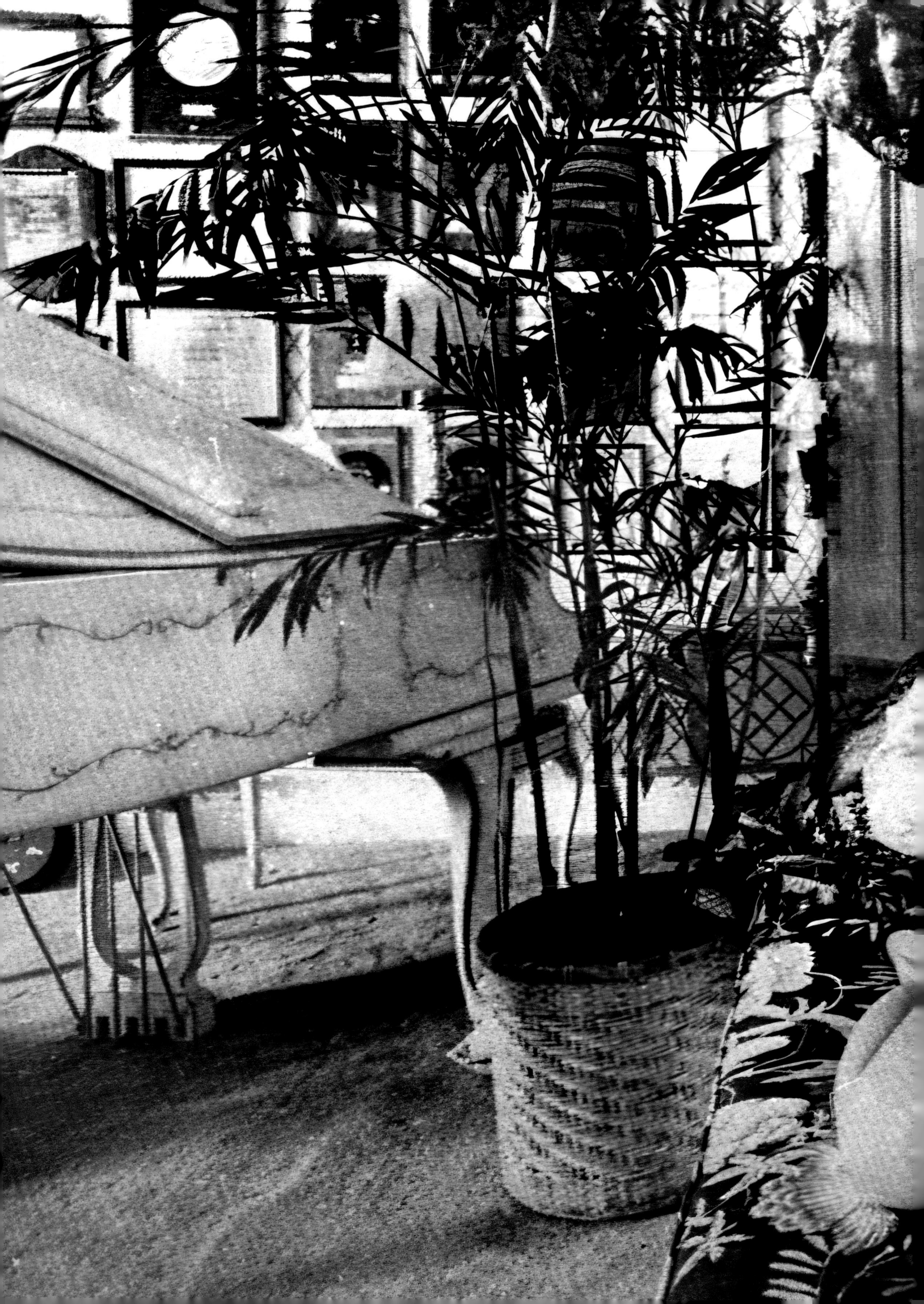

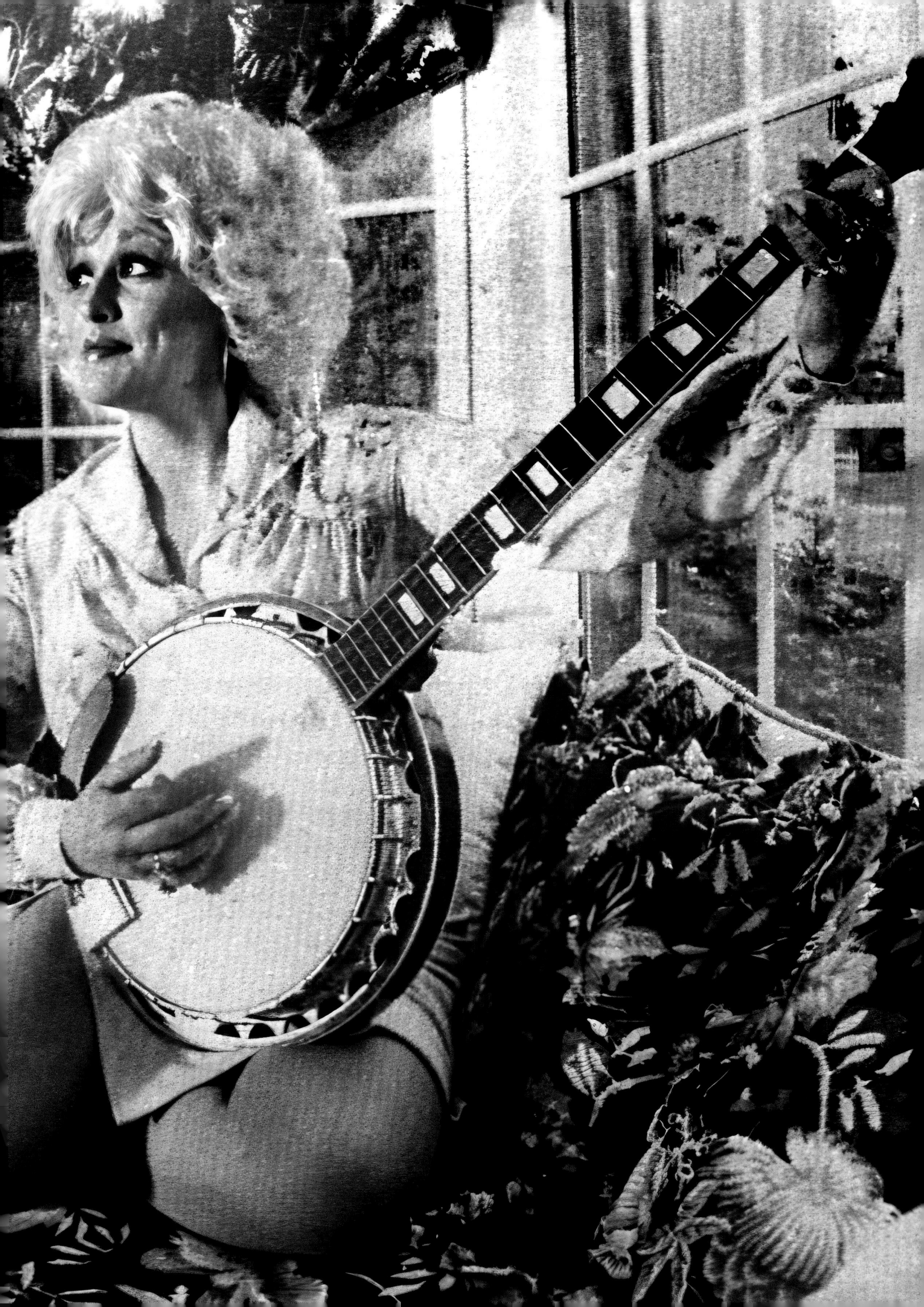

While I embraced Las Vegas, I was never totally comfortable in that setting. I don't dance, I don't like choreography, and I don't like to think about anything other than just being myself and portraying who and what I am. I've always believed in my heart—and I've proven it through the years—that being my Smoky Mountain self is what people tend to like the most. Still, there comes a time in your life when you get to be a big enough name and a drawing card, as they say, that you get all these big offers and you work to meet the moment. Of course, if you're going to go to Vegas, everybody believes that you have to have a big set. You have to have all these grandiose things going on.

The fans loved it. They seemed to understand what we were doing—that I was just trying stuff because I could. They seemed to accept that, but it was always the songs and the things that I did that were simple that got the best response, like "Coat of Many Colors."

But not every one of those simple songs worked there. Sometime in the '80s, when I was playing Vegas a lot, I sang "Me and Little Andy," this poor, pitiful song about a little girl and her little puppy dog. She dies, and the dog goes right after her. It was a beautiful song, but when I finished it, this guy hollered out from the back, "Did you have to kill the damn dog?" I decided I didn't need to be singing "Me and Little Andy" on those dates where folks may have had a little too much to drink and might be feeling tense about losing some of their money gambling, so I took it out of my Vegas show.

That wasn't the only glitzy thing on my calendar that spring. I appeared on the Academy Awards, though they were delayed by a night when President Ronald Reagan got shot. It was the right thing to do—the whole country was upset.

When the Oscars finally did take place the next night, I walked the red carpet with Mary Tyler Moore, Michael Jackson, Diana Ross, and Goldie Hawn—not that we were all hanging out together, but entertainment royalty was definitely in the house. I performed "9 to 5" with a cast of dancers—some of 'em dressed like construction workers—because my song was up for an award. I didn't win, and I wasn't too disappointed because you never know what to expect. But it was a great honor to be up there with the big boys and girls.

Not that I'm all that impressed with stars. I could see them in the audience while I was on stage that night, and though it was exciting to realize, *Oh, there, that's Jack Nicholson, oh my gosh!*, that didn't impact my performance. If the queen of England didn't scare me when we were looking at each other eye to eye, I could handle the kings and queens of Hollywood!

Willie Nelson sang "On the Road Again" that night, so it wasn't like I was the only country singer there. Country music was setting the world on fire at that point.

As it turned out, so was my acting career. Production started later that year on the film adaptation of the musical *The Best Little Whorehouse in Texas*—or, as I preferred to call it, the Chicken Ranch, since a real-life place called the Chicken Ranch inspired the story.

Of course, I loved that opportunity. I love costumes and dressing up, and I always joke that I made a better whore than a secretary. Those gaudy outfits were right up my alley—the

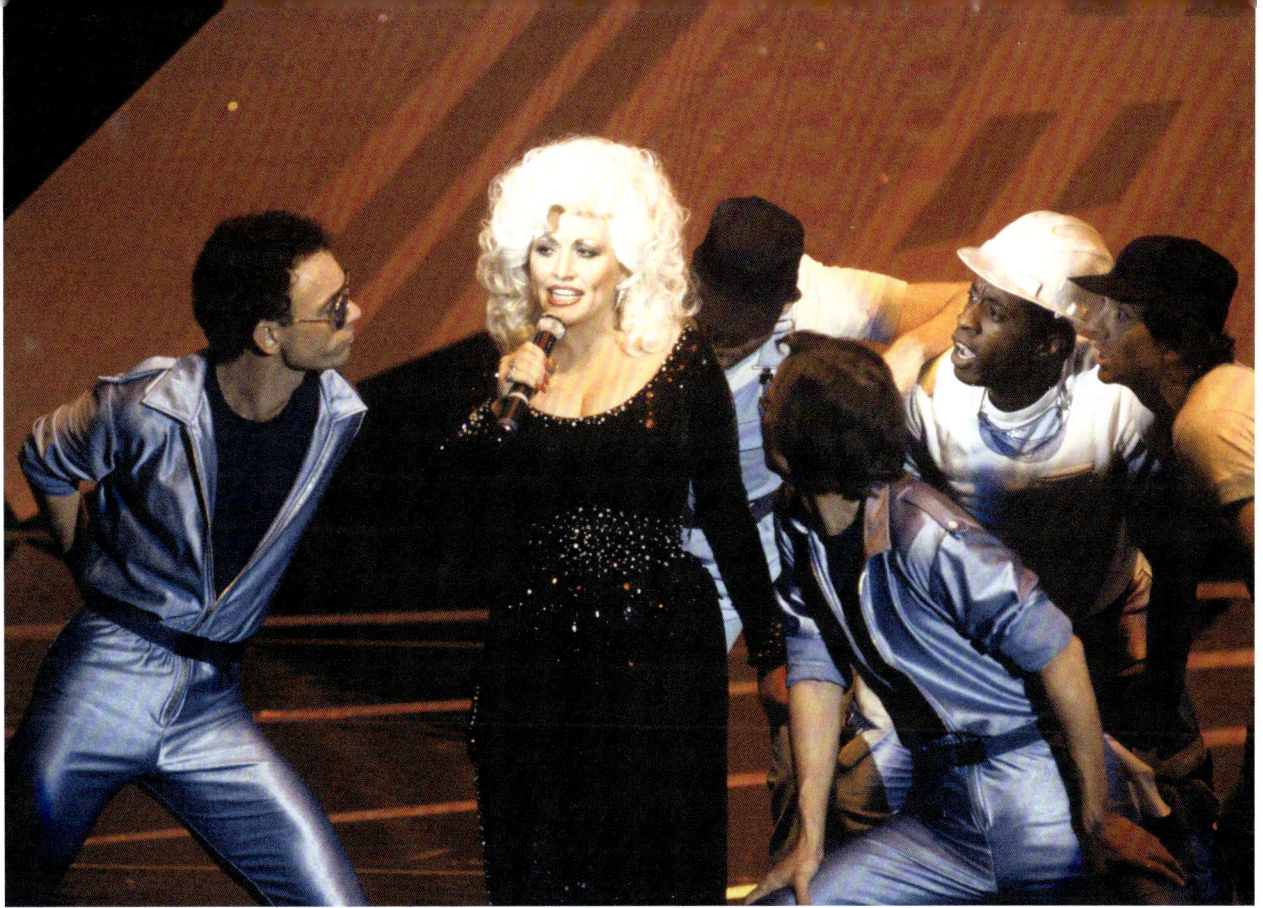

I tumbled out of bed and stumbled to the kitchen, and before the day was over, I sang "9 to 5" at the Oscars. I didn't win an award, but I'd like to think I won over the audience—not to mention the construction workers surrounding me for the production number!

big hair, the costumes, and the jewelry ... all of it! Everybody liked the idea of me and Burt Reynolds on the screen together, and I got to contribute to the soundtrack again. We did a new version of "I Will Always Love You," and as a result, some of the people who were newer Dolly fans got introduced to it for the first time.

When the Chicken Ranch production was over, I prepared to go back on the road. I loved tooling down America's highways again, seeing the faces in the crowd, and getting back on the concert stage. Through much of 1982, I didn't feel fully like myself, but I gutted it out night after night. That's what you do—the show must go on, after all.

When I got into fair season, though, things got bad. I went from feeling "not great" to feeling worse. I played a few really tough concerts—the band knew I wasn't feeling well, but I didn't let the audience know. They were coming out to escape their problems, not to get brought down by mine. But something was wrong.

My show that year at the Indiana State Fair was one of the hardest of my life. I felt horrible most of the day, and my doctor said I should not perform. But I was determined to push through it, just like I had back in Eugene all those years before. As it turned out, a storm was on its way, and a light rain fell during parts of the concert. I knew the fans were probably

Superstar of the Show

not going to get a refund for their tickets if there was an "act of God," and I wanted them to hear the songs they expected, so I declared an "act of Dolly" and rearranged my set list on the fly, putting "9 to 5" near the front of the show. The rain held off long enough that they didn't have to call off the show, and when we got to the back end of the set, I went ahead and played that song again.

No one in the audience had any idea what was happening, but shortly after the show was over, I went to the hospital and ended up being there awhile. I realized I was working myself too hard. I was not taking care of myself. I was not eating properly. I was not sleeping that well either—just go, go, go, work, work, work. God has given me the strength to really go after it, and I feel blessed to have that kind of stamina. But sometimes, you know, I kind of overdo it and go against Him, and sometimes He just has to slap me down to get me to listen: "Look now, I didn't say you had to wear yourself out. You know you need to take good care of yourself." It was clear that I had to reevaluate how I was doing everything that I was.

Carl was so supportive, and a great part of my recovery. He'd always say things like, "Hell, I've been having female problems since the day I met you—no need to make a big deal of it. You'll be fine." And I was.

I'm still a busy woman—that's never changed!—but I like to think that I've been smarter about pacing myself, eating better, and being more regimented about my sleep. And a lot of that is because that moment gave me a little "attitude adjustment." But it was needed.

Between movie work and my illness, I hadn't gotten to play for my fans nearly as much as I wanted, and as I got ready to go back on the road, I was so excited about it that I invited some of the Nashville music media to come out to rehearsals, just to have an audience and to let them see firsthand that I was really back.

The schedule would include a major performance at the Dominion Theatre in London. We filmed the concerts for an HBO special, and it seemed to go without a hitch until the final day. We were all ready to go backstage, but while the opening act—Anne Murray's brother, Bruce Murray—was still performing, Sandy Gallin came into the dressing room. He was pale and said, "We have to go right now. Just grab whatever you want to take. We have to go."

I said, "What?" I always have to know what's going on, and I kept saying, "What? What is it?" He just kept leading me out. He said, "We have to go now." He was trying not to panic me. And so then, when we got outside the building, he said, "Well, there's a bomb threat." You can bet my little high heels started spiking across the street to get back to the hotel once I heard that!

People had to be evacuated, the building had to be searched, and it was chaos all over the streets, but in the end, nothing was found. The authorities told us that it was just a prank call. Fortunately, we didn't lose a person. Everybody who had bought a ticket went right back to their seat, and we continued with the show.

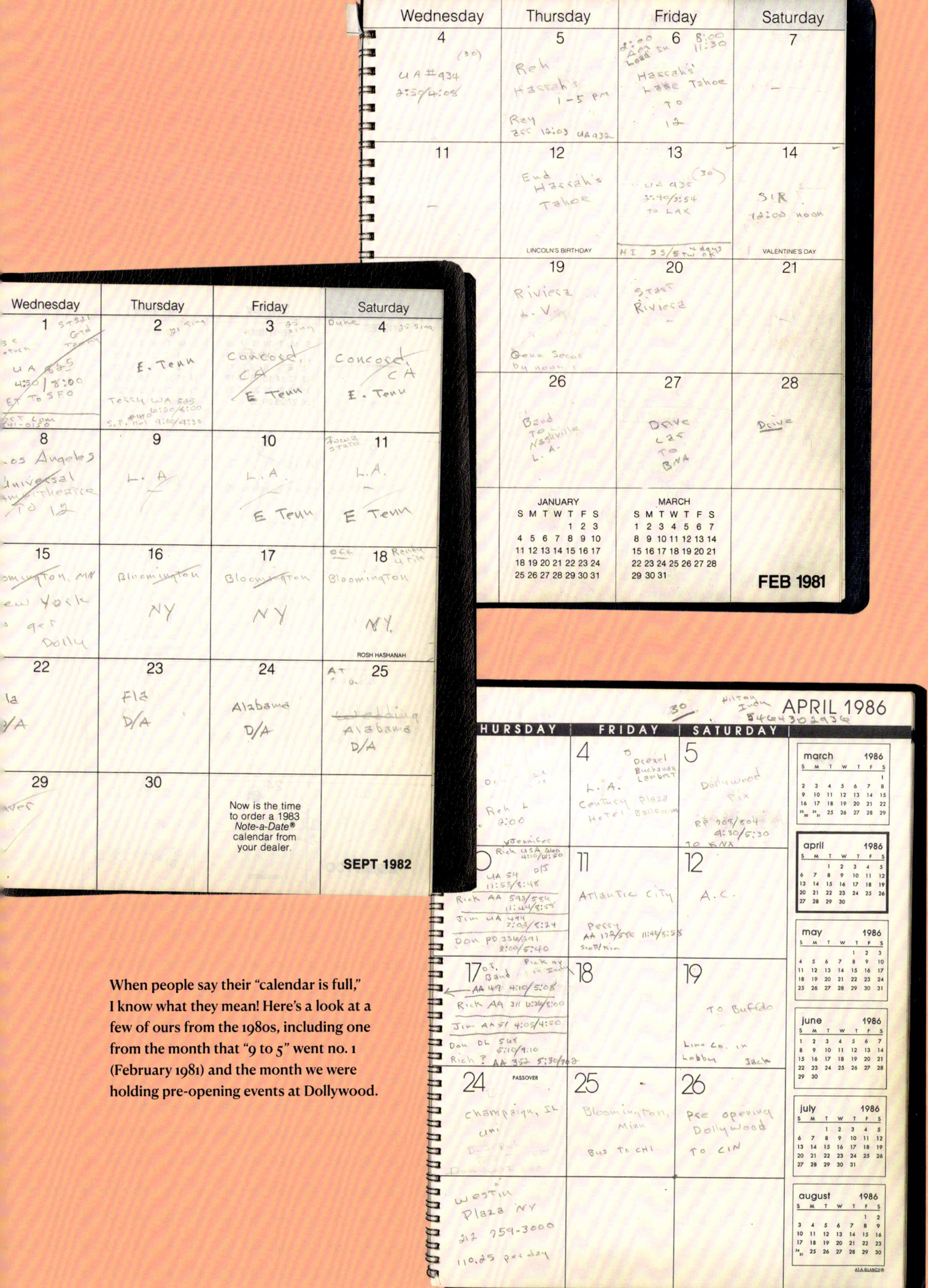

When people say their "calendar is full," I know what they mean! Here's a look at a few of ours from the 1980s, including one from the month that "9 to 5" went no. 1 (February 1981) and the month we were holding pre-opening events at Dollywood.

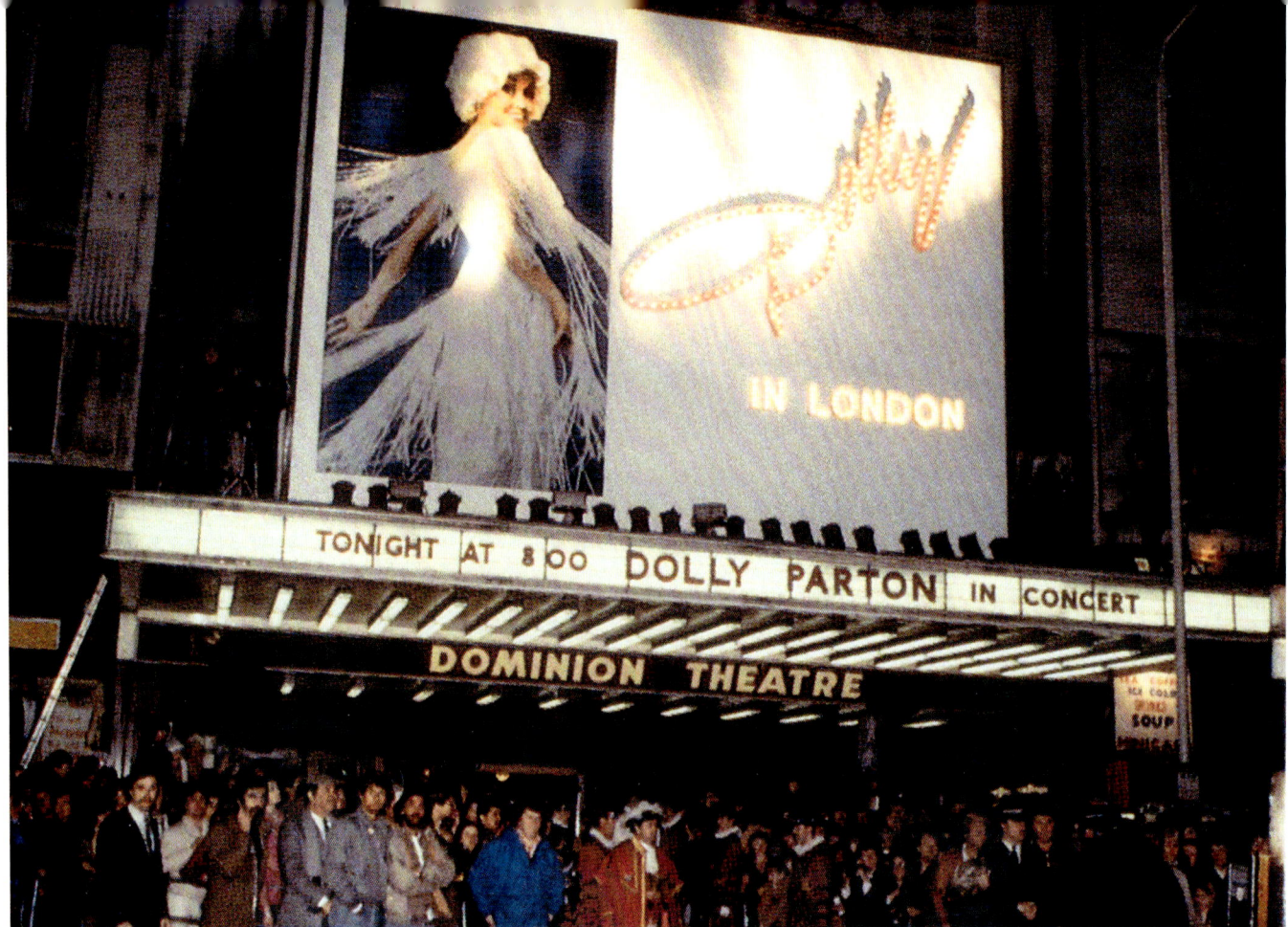

The Dominion Theatre is in the heart of London. Bringing country to a cutting-edge city was perfect for my HBO special, which drew an eclectic and enthusiastic crowd.

We might've had a few people who shouldn't have continued, though! A few of the orchestra members spent the break at a bar in the West End, and when they came back, Gregg Perry noticed that some of the notes they played were, as he put it, "interesting." Fortunately, that never came through in the TV footage.

One thing that was apparent, though, was the makeup of the audience. London's known for being very hip and in the know—a liberated city, I guess you might say—and I noticed that I had a following there that reflected that. The audience included all sorts of people! There were people with purple hair and piercings in their nose and lips right there alongside mothers and dads, kids and grandkids at that show. And there were a lot of drag Dollys in the crowd too. I remember looking out and thinking that was the craziest thing I'd ever seen—and so much fun. It was amazing to have so many different kinds of people in that audience, and I still enjoy it when I look out and see people of all kinds in the seats. It makes me smile now as much as it did then!

Beginning that summer, I filmed the movie *Rhinestone* with Sylvester Stallone. It was a great experience, even though the movie did not get great reviews. Critics were hard on Stallone because nobody wanted to see Rocky being a country star. But that movie was so great to do. That was the first time I'd really done anything since being out of commission

Star of the Show

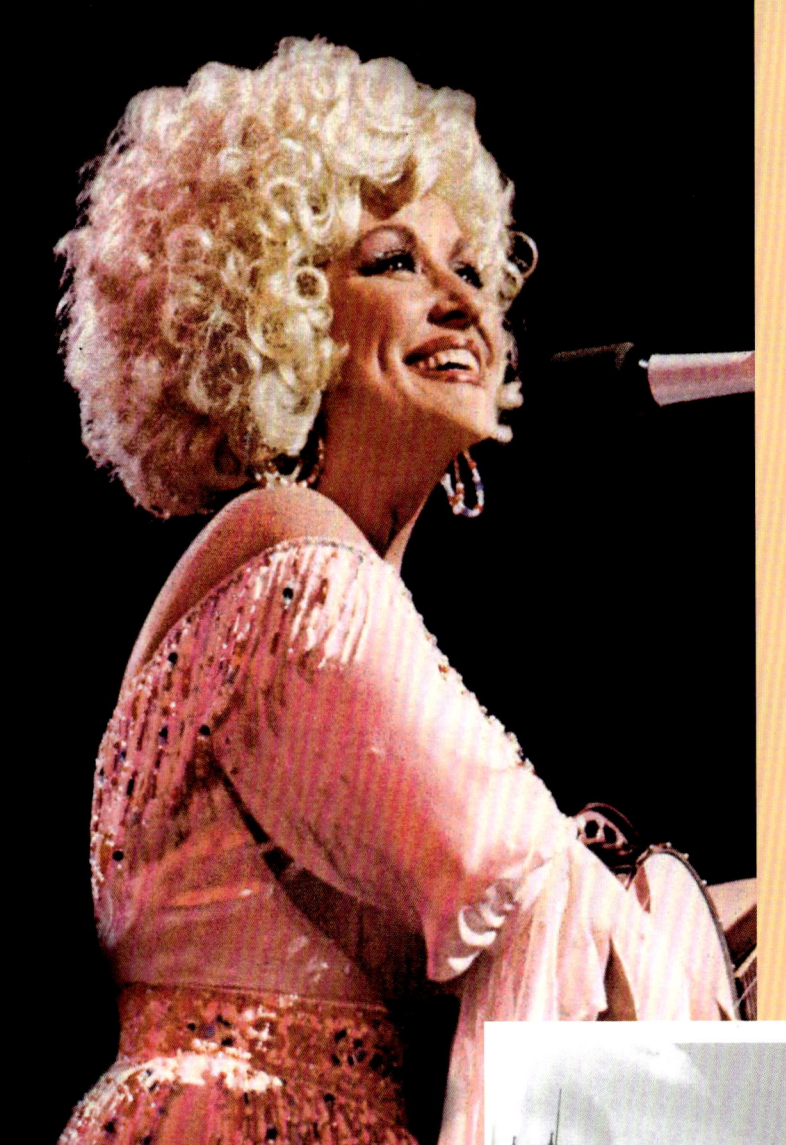

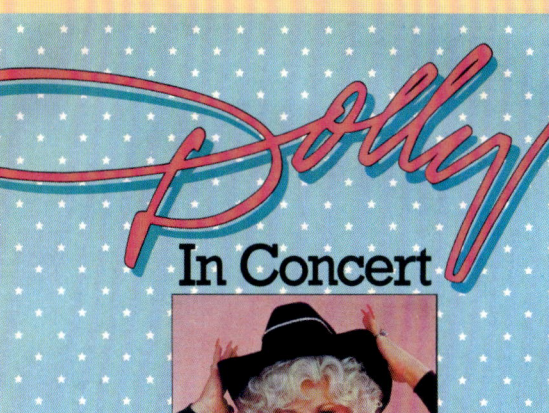

In Concert

She wrote her first song when she was four.
She made her first movie three years ago.

Now she's giving her first solo TV concert.
On HBO® and HBOnly.™

Sunday, June 19, 8PM EST

HBO

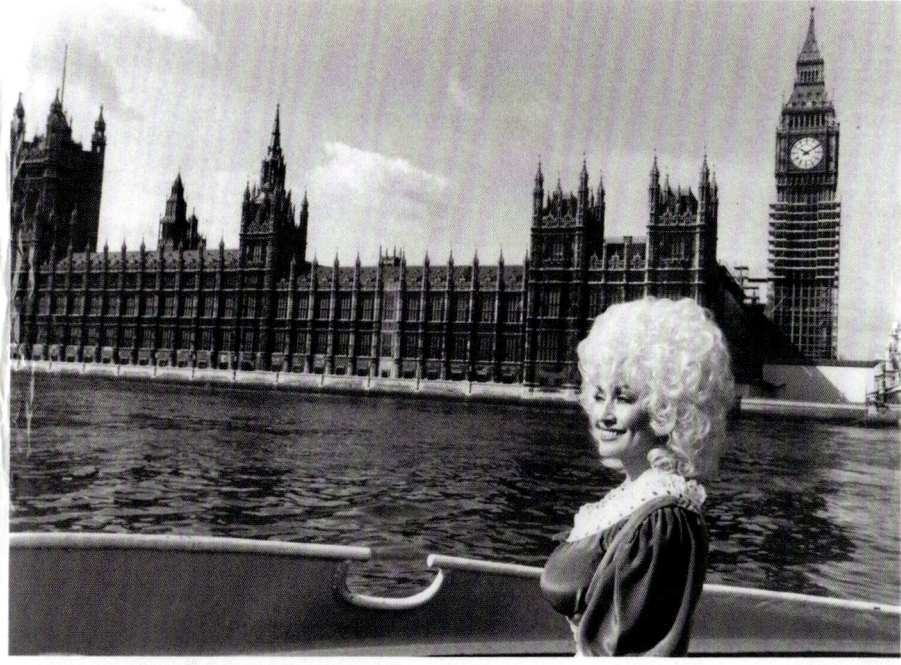

PARTON AND PARLIAMENT: Grammy Award-winning country and pop superstar Dolly Parton takes time out near the Houses of Parliament and Big Ben while in London, England, for her solo television concert debut, DOLLY IN CONCERT. The 90-minute STANDING ROOM ONLY® presentation debuts SUNDAY, JUNE 19 (8:00-9:30 p.m. ET), on Home Box Office®. HBO

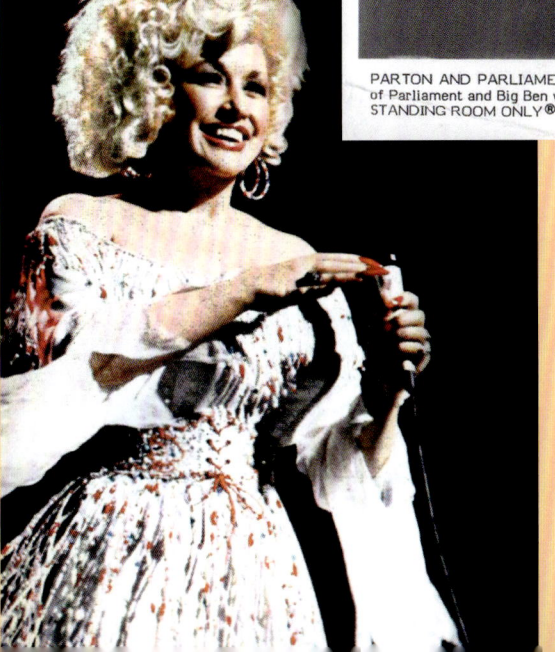

Dolly in Concert wasn't only a success—it was as fun for me as it looked!

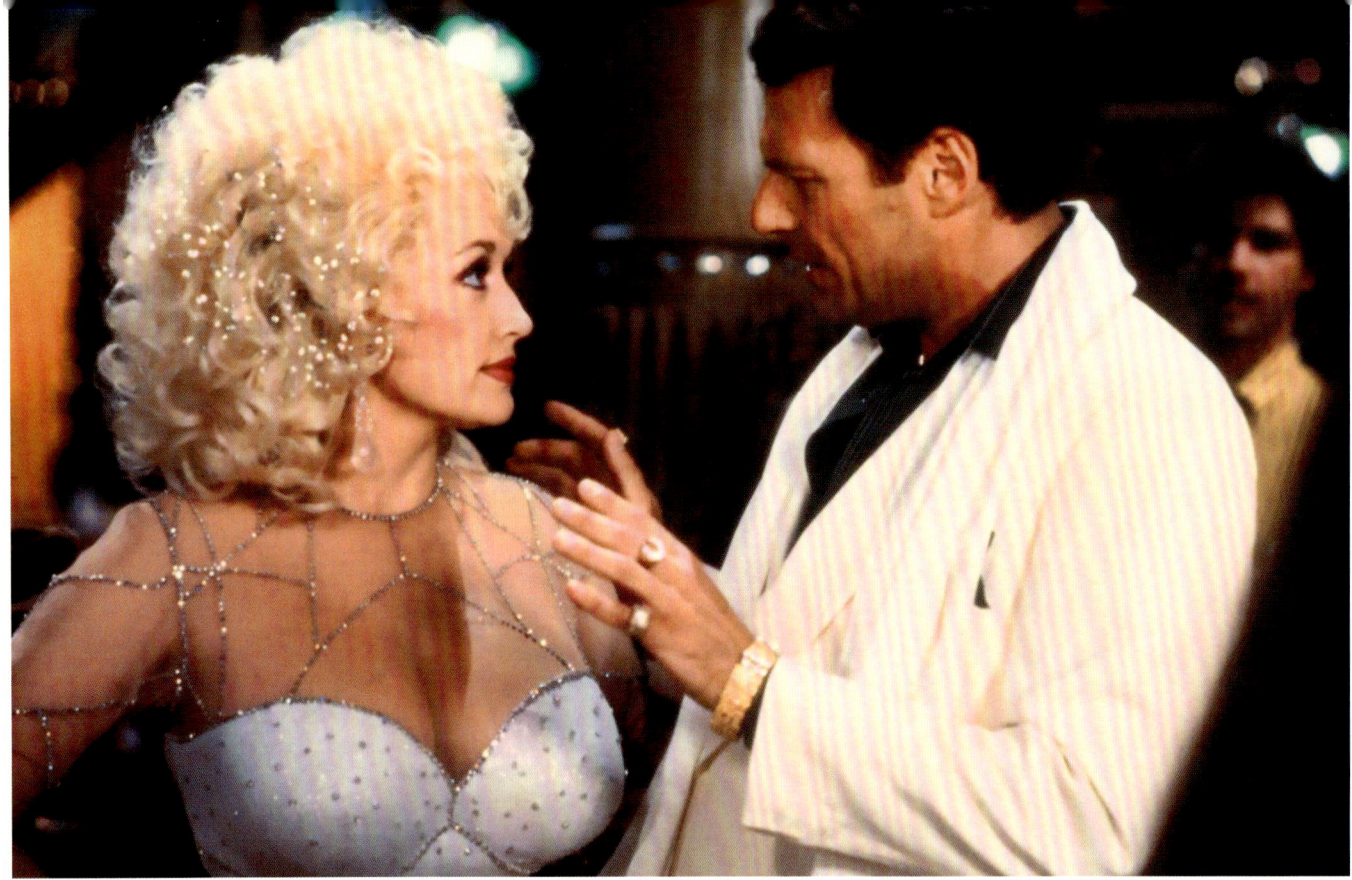

Rhinestone may not have been the biggest of my movies, but it was one of the best times I've had making one. My character, Jake, makes a bet with her club manager, Freddie (played by Ron Leibman)—and I'm grateful that everyone took a bet on *Rhinestone*.

for several months. It was really good for me, and Stallone was funny, and we just had so much fun doing it.

We shot some scenes in New York City, but I was proud to bring much of the production to Middle Tennessee. Because we did that, I was able to bring in my family. My character, Jake, was a country singer, so I used the Wild Possum Band as my band—it was made up of my uncles: Uncle Bill, Uncle Louis, Uncle Henry, and Uncle Lester. Lester was a truck driver who had also been beneficial in the early part of my career. Back then, he would send me money to buy things for the stage and stuff. We had pretty much all the Owens guys that sang, and my cousin Dwight was playing drums. I treasure that memory—and all those pictures I have of me and the family on the set of *Rhinestone*.

One of my most significant performances ever happened in the middle of shooting that movie. Kenny Rogers and I did "Islands in the Stream" on the CMA Awards that year, and it set up the next phase of my concert career, as Kenny and I went on to work on several projects together.

In November 1984, we shot the holiday TV special *Kenny & Dolly: A Christmas to Remember*, which led into a duet tour that launched just a few weeks later in Oakland, California. The format was pretty simple: I'd go out and do a fairly regular Dolly Parton solo concert. After

STAGE LOOKS
Through the Years

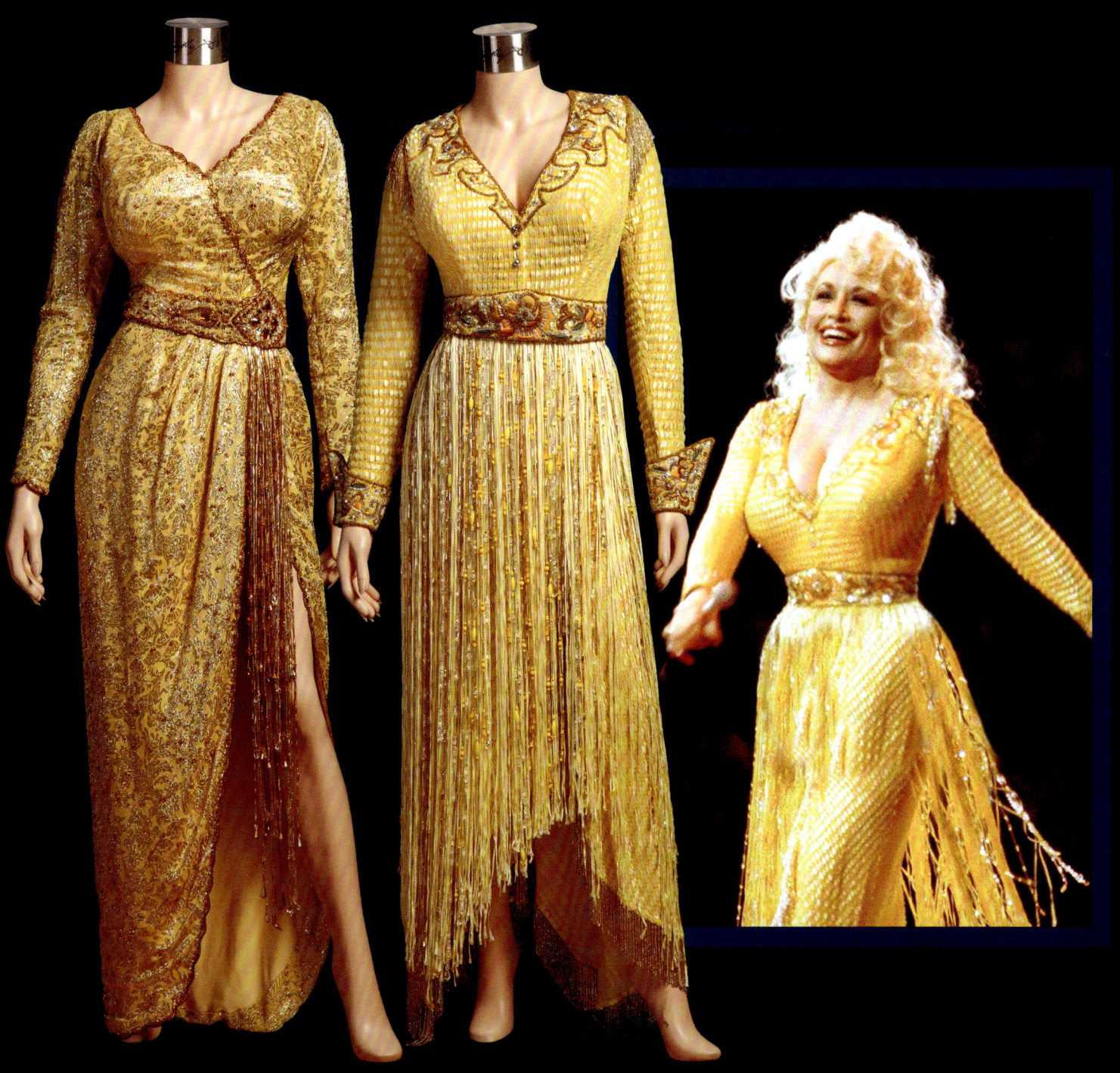

I got all "shook up" in this dress during my 1983 *Live in London* concert special!

From movie premieres to road shows, I always found a way to wear this beaded dress.

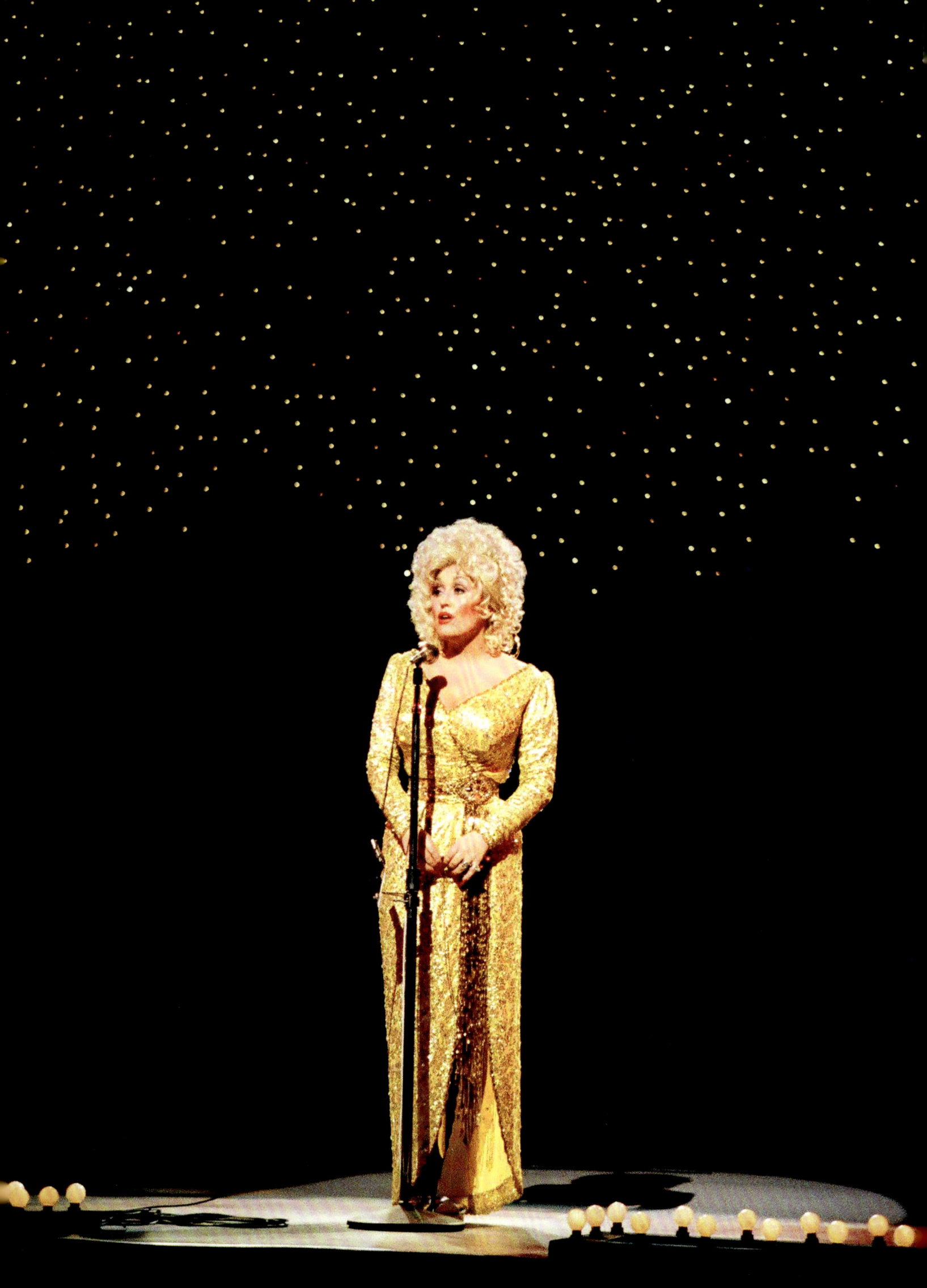

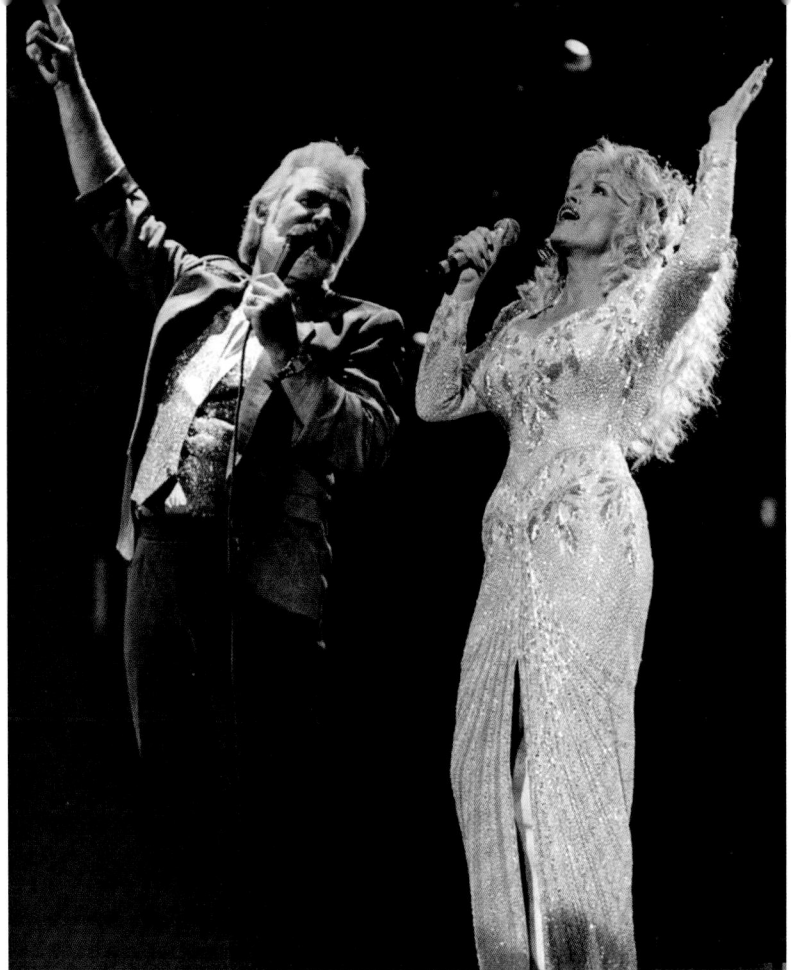

Kenny and I toured the world together from 1984 to 1990, usually performing "in the round," with the crowd on all sides of the stage. You might say that we sang "Islands in the Stream" on an island in the arena!

an intermission, he'd hit the stage and do most of a usual Kenny Rogers solo show. Then, at the finale, we took the stage together. We'd perform "We've Got Tonight," a Bob Seger song that Kenny and Sheena Easton turned into a no. 1 country hit, and I'd often change the lyrics to "We've got tonight / Who needs Sheena Easton," just to make Kenny laugh. Then we'd sing "Real Love," which Kenny recorded with me as a thank-you for taking part on "Islands in the Stream." Finally, we did "Islands" to close the show and sent everyone home happy.

We were serious about our music, and we loved how we sounded together. And I never got tired of hearing Kenny sing all the years I was with him. I would go out in the wings during his solo set and watch him perform. He was so talented, and I really loved him.

I think part of the public's attraction to us as a duo was "Islands in the Stream" itself. The song is so happy, but it's also vague. It's mostly about two people being lost in each other, although it doesn't really come out and say it directly. It kind of lets the listener arrive at that feeling, or even project something else onto the song. But the melody is so light and catchy that it's hard not to like it. And both of our voices fit it so well that I think people couldn't help but like us too. The Bee Gees really did write some great music, didn't they?!

Superstar of the Show

Spotlight

KENNY ROGERS: "OLD FRIENDS"

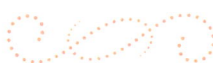

When I met up with the Gambler, we were both on a similar path.

Kenny Rogers was a guest on my syndicated TV show in 1976, and he showed up on set in a satin-like jumpsuit and large tinted sunglasses—he looked more like the man who had sung on the psychedelic pop hit "Just Dropped In (To See What Condition My Condition Was In)" than the country crooner he was becoming.

He had left his band, The First Edition, the year before and was trying to make it in country music. He sang "Love Lifted Me"—the first single he recorded after signing solo in Nashville—on *Dolly*. I knew the kind of stress he was under, since I was still in a career-building process myself—establishing a new solo identity after making a change and leaving Porter Wagoner.

We felt so comfortable together from the start. We did a gospel song, "He's Got the Whole World in His Hands," in front of the audience that day. We also had a bright idea (or maybe it was an "eye"-dea) to do a medley of songs with the word "eye" in the title. We started off with "Spanish Eyes," a pop standard that was a hit in the mid-1960s for Al Martino. I showed up in a Mexicali-flavored yellow outfit and used a lacy fan to hide my smile and play coy. And I talked to Kenny with a Spanish accent—"Sí, sí, señor"—that made him laugh and sort of stumble a little. The medley also included Chuck Berry's "Brown-Eyed Handsome Man" plus "Blue Eyes Crying in the Rain," which had been a hit for Willie Nelson the previous year.

That little comedy piece for "Spanish Eyes" set the stage for our musical relationship. I would be a little goofy, or act flirty or naive, and Kenny kind of played the straight man for my jokes. He had a great sense of humor, and we got along famously every time we were together, on stage and in the studio.

In 1983, he was working on an album that The Bee Gees' Barry Gibb was producing, and Kenny got a little bored with a song they were recording. I happened to be in the studio at the same time, and they asked if I'd put my voice on it. The song was "Islands in the Stream"—it went to no. 1 on the pop, adult contemporary, and country charts, sold several million copies, and set us on a path to do a series of duets over the years.

From 1984 to 1990, I toured more with Kenny than without him. We always had that silly Jerry Lewis/Dean Martin kind of rapport between songs, but our voices fit together seamlessly.

People speculated for years that we were a couple—or that we *should* be a couple—and to this day, I don't know if they were serious or just projecting some Hollywood-type behind-the-scenes scandal on us. There was some flirtatiousness about our relationship on stage, of course, but I always thought of him like a brother.

Kenny was one of the most important people in my entertainment life—that's undeniable—and our professional relationship lasted for several decades. When he asked me in 2013 to sing on "You Can't Make Old Friends," I was there in a heartbeat. It summarized our connection very well, and it earned us a Grammy nomination.

I always will love Kenny Rogers like the musical brother he was to me.

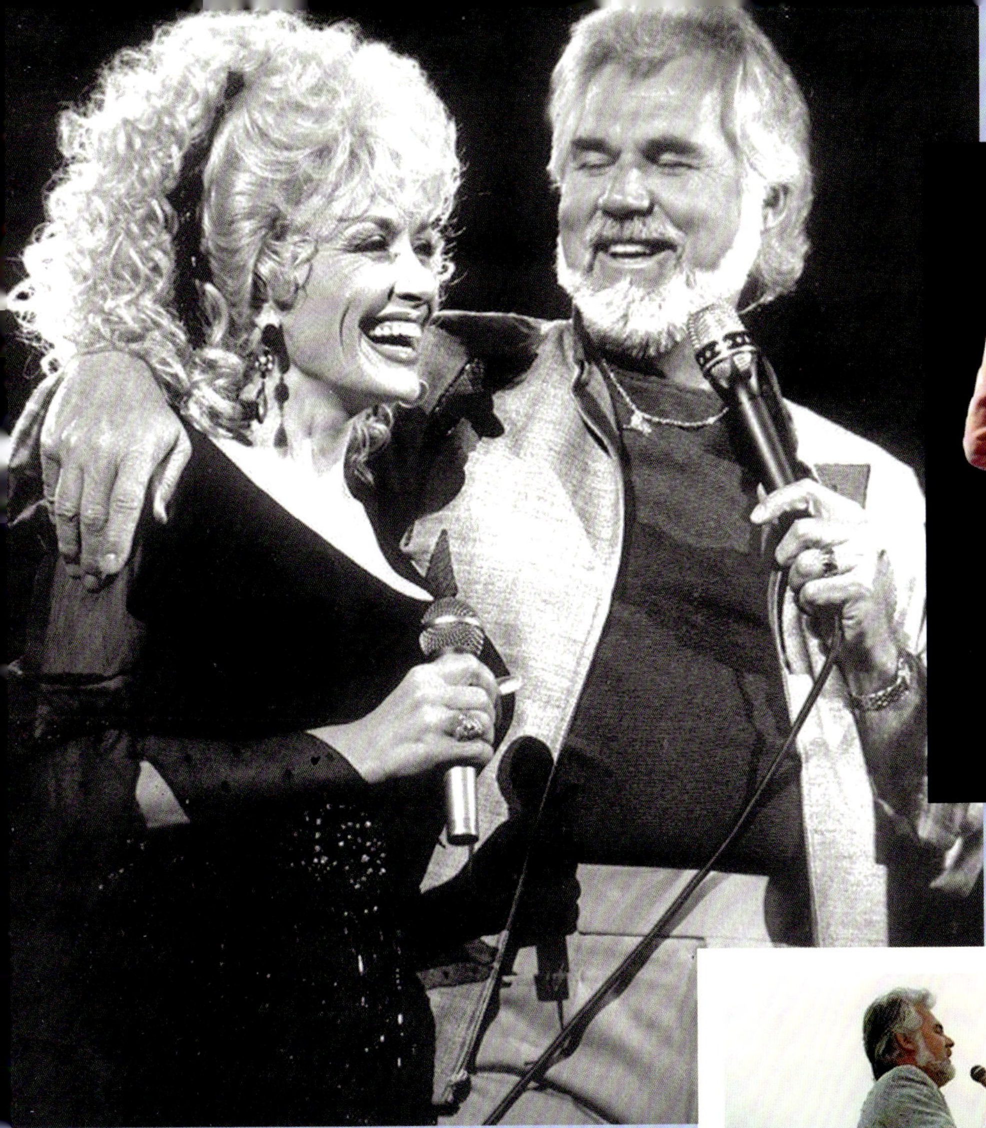

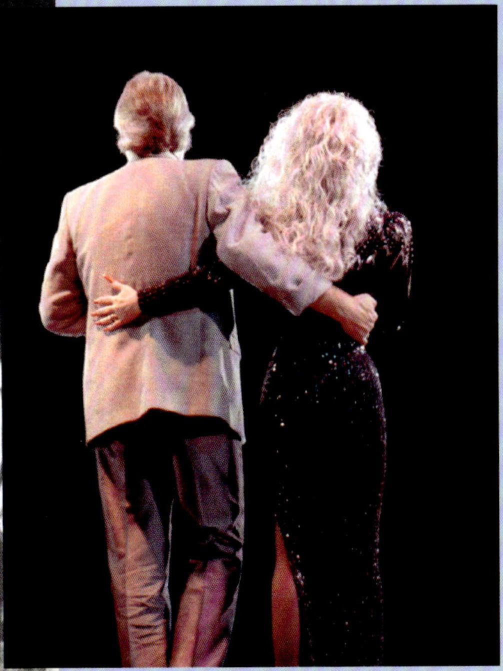

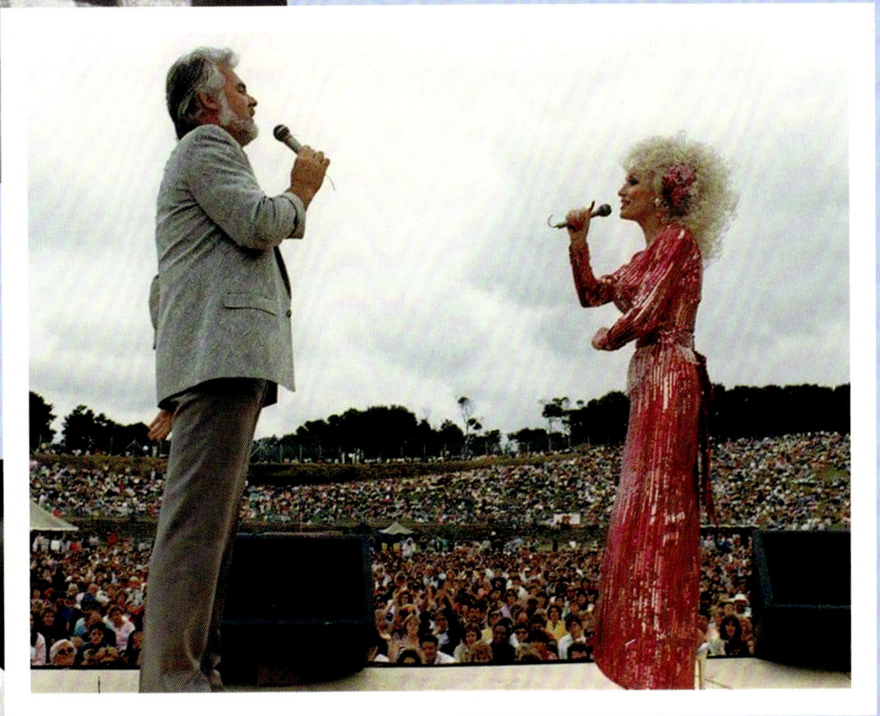

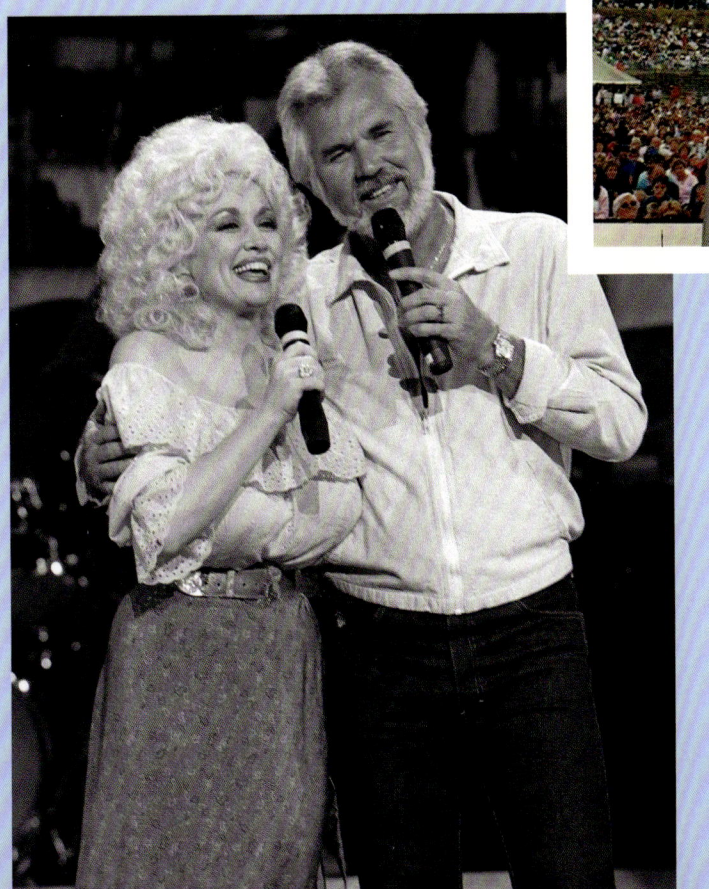

Kenny and I worked magic together—all these years later, I'm still not sure what the secret to it was. Maybe it's because we were already established as artists in our own right before we ever sang a duet together. Maybe that provided the foundation for a musical partnership that was based on mutual strength and appreciation. But I do know this: we had the best time doing all of it.

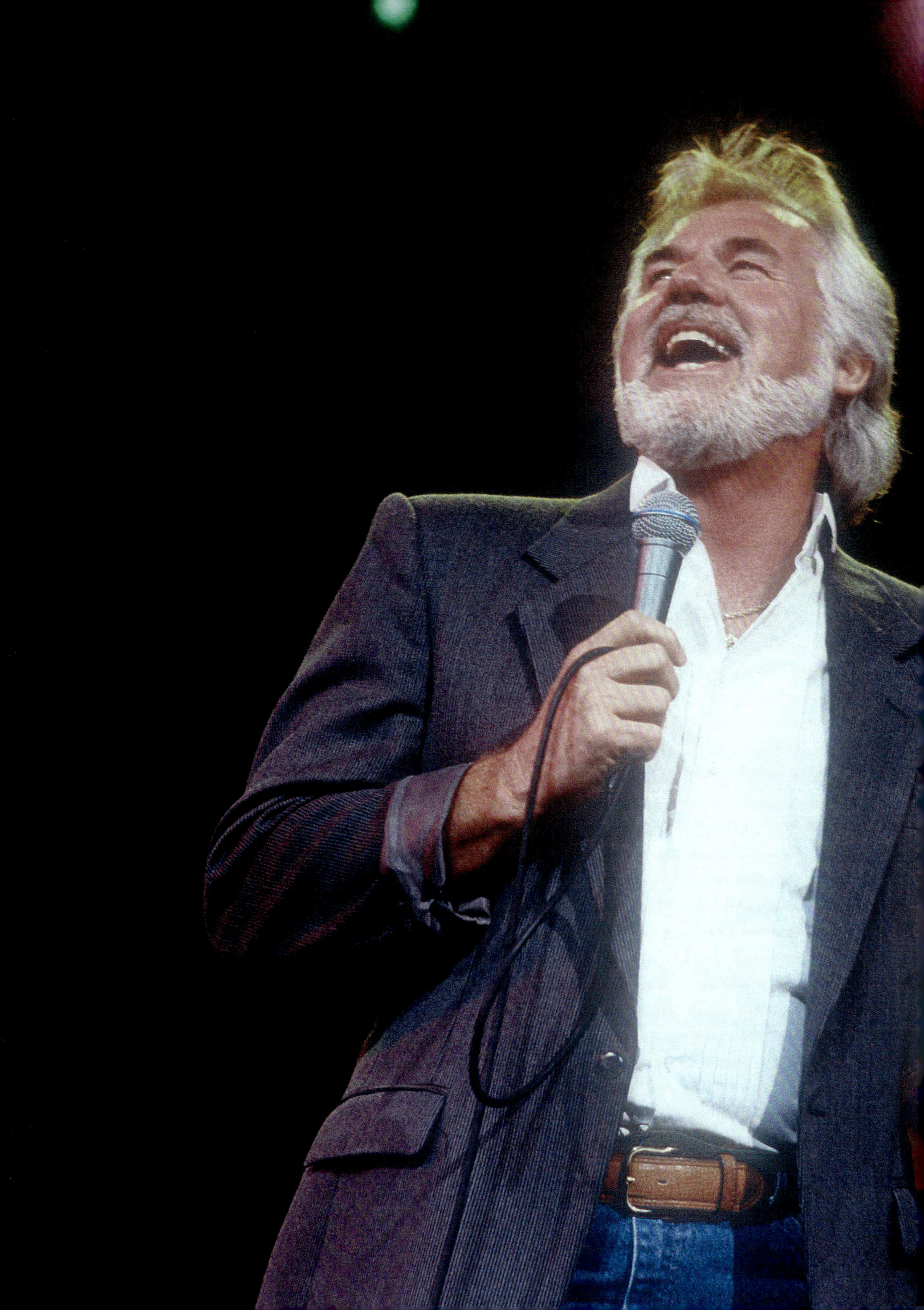

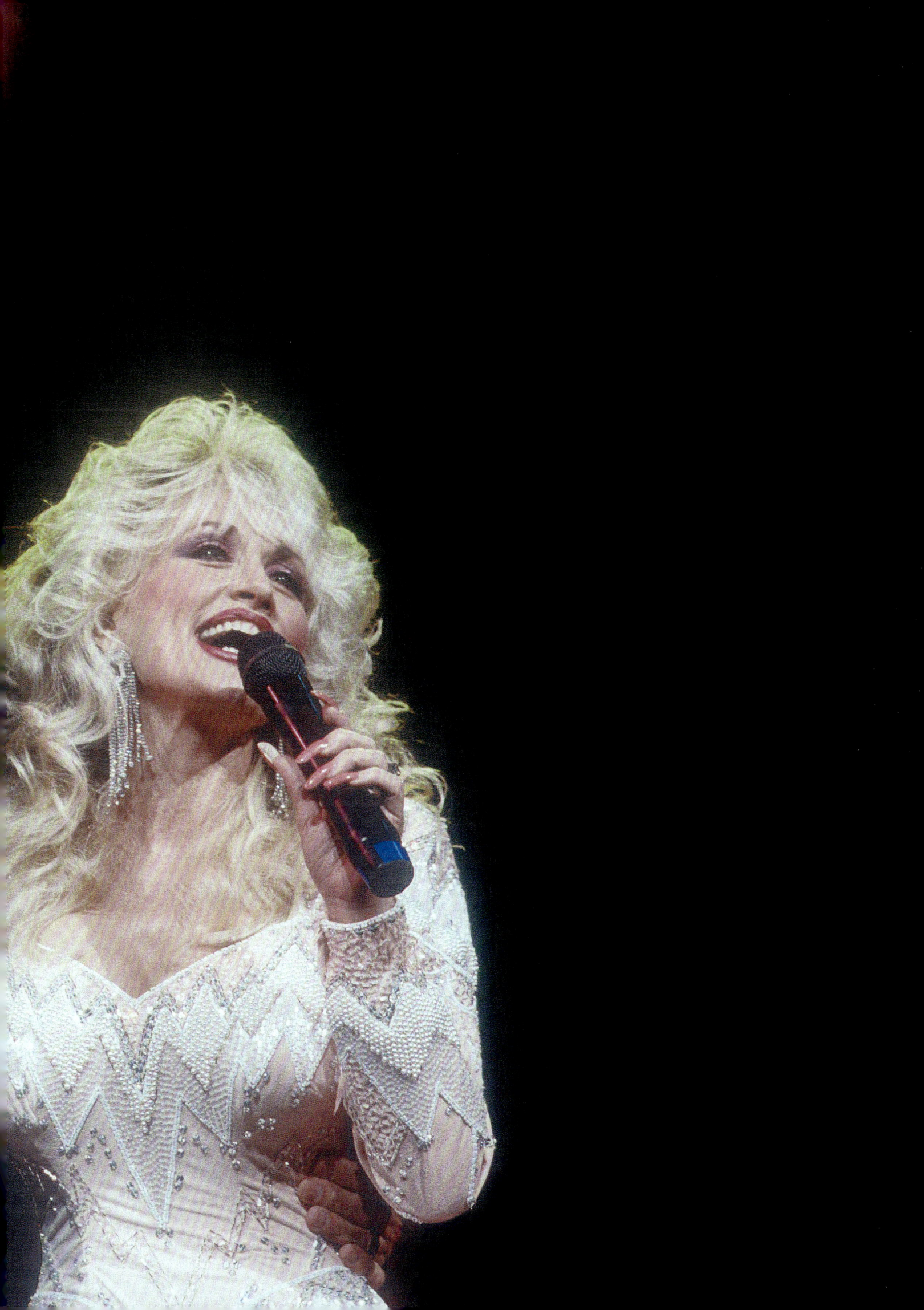

```
BURNING                4/13/86
JOLENE
TWO DOORS
COAT
APPALACHIAN
TENN HOMESICK
APPLEJACK
CROSS
THINK ABOUT LOVI
GOSPEL
ANDY
ISLANDS
HERE YOU COME
9-5
I WILL
```

Hits, gospel, mountain songs, and much more—this is a set list from a 1986 show at the Golden Nugget in Atlantic City, New Jersey.

Since I'd toured for so long with Porter Wagoner, going out on the road with Kenny was a breeze. I was prepared for a lot of it, but things were definitely different now. For one thing, we both had our own operations, and we showed up to the venue separately, rather than traveling together. So we were equals instead of him being an employer and me being his employee.

Plus, we were closer in age—both in life and in our careers. Porter had been nineteen years older than me, enough of a difference that he could've been my father. Kenny was only eight years older, so he was more like a big brother. And just like I got started as Porter's protégé, Kenny kicked off his career as part of Kenny Rogers and the First Edition. Since we were both in ensembles at the beginning of our careers, I think we were both equipped when it came to sharing the spotlight.

We were like two high-school kids when we were together. He couldn't get nothing on me, and I couldn't get nothing on him. But we would pull things on each other on stage—just crazy stuff. I'd write something on my forehead, and because I usually had bangs, I'd be right in his face and then I'd lift my bangs up. It'd be some awful something I had written just to get him tickled. They were fun little things that we'd do, little personal pranks. And I think that easygoing relationship between us showed—it sure seemed to entertain the fans.

That was particularly true in Washington State. We played the Tacoma Dome early in the tour, and it literally went so well that we were invited back to the same venue four weeks later, and that show sold out too. I started to think that it would be fun to open a venue of my own—and soon I would.

Star of the Show

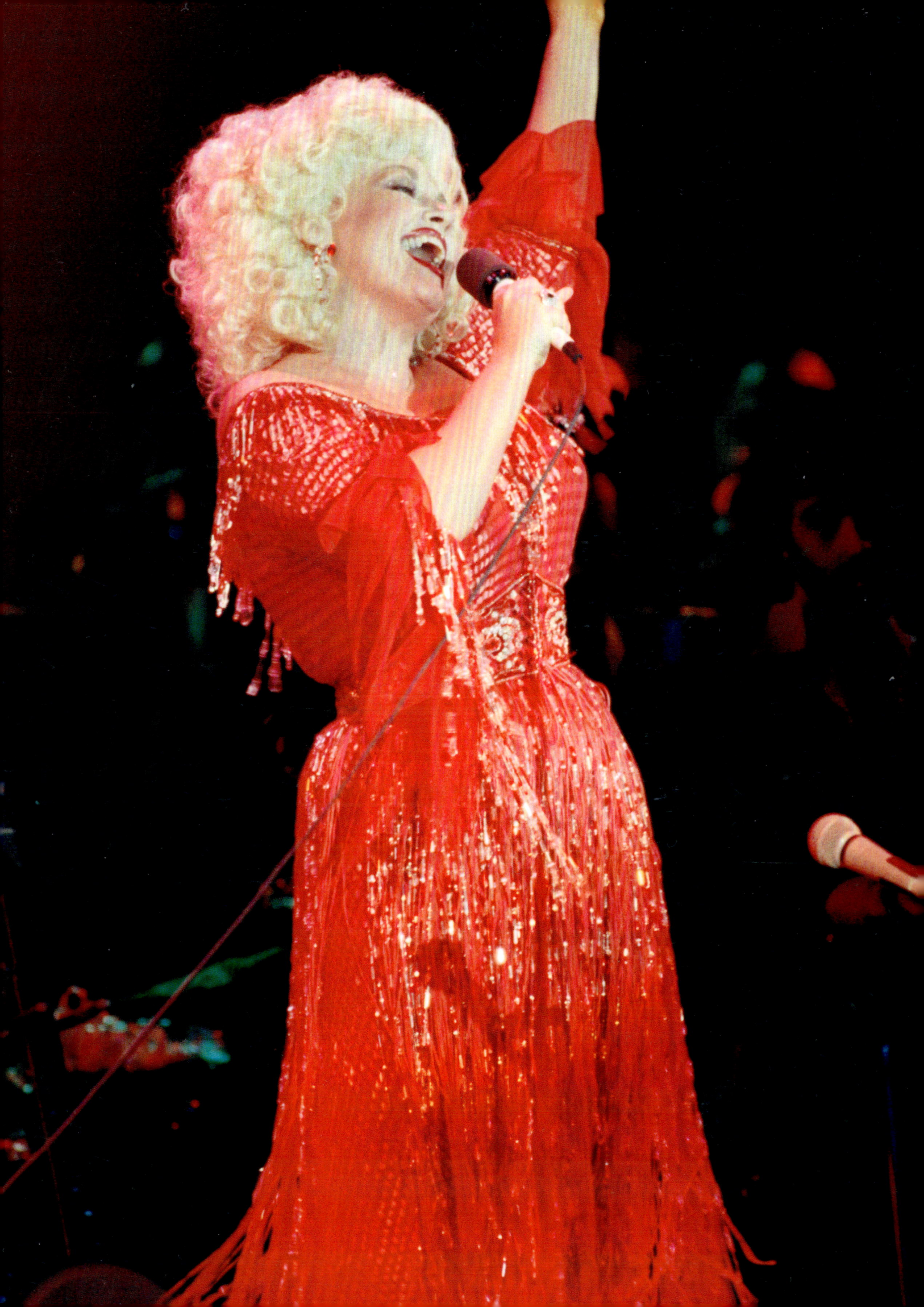

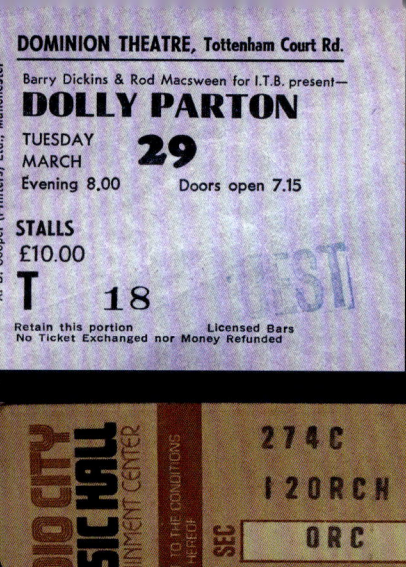
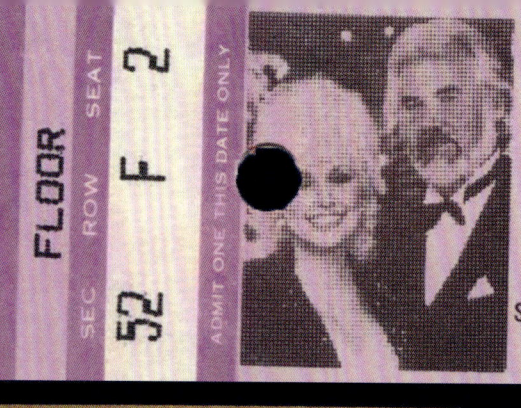
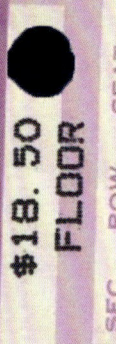
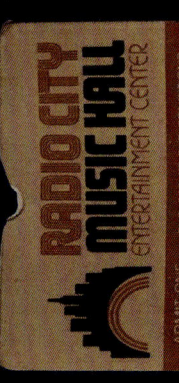
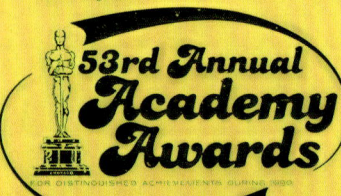
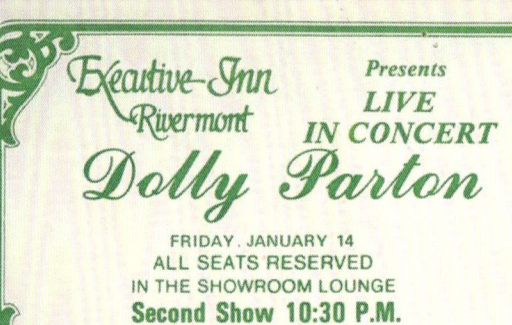
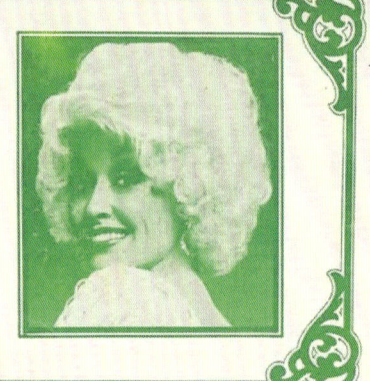
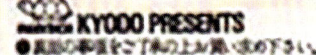

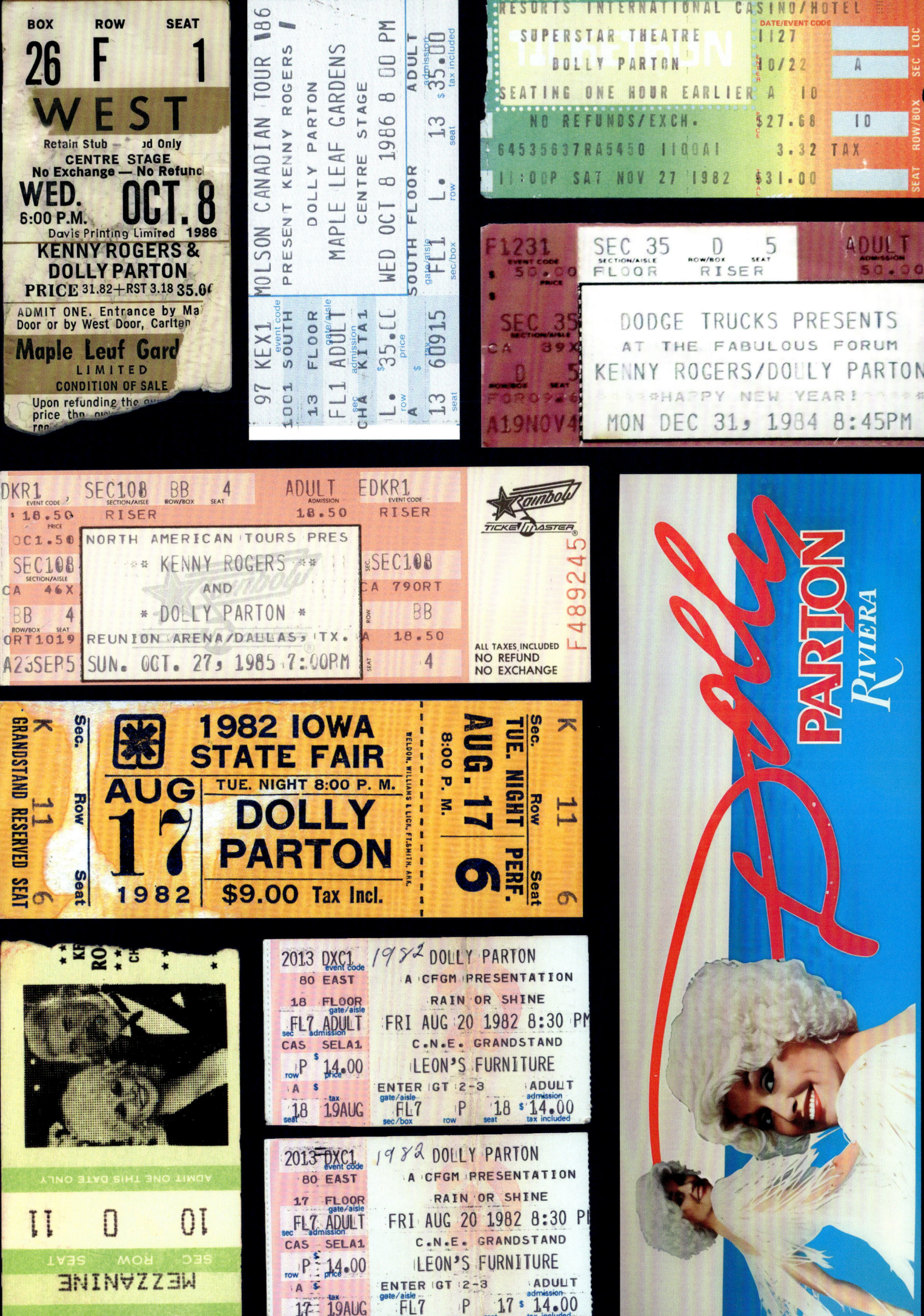

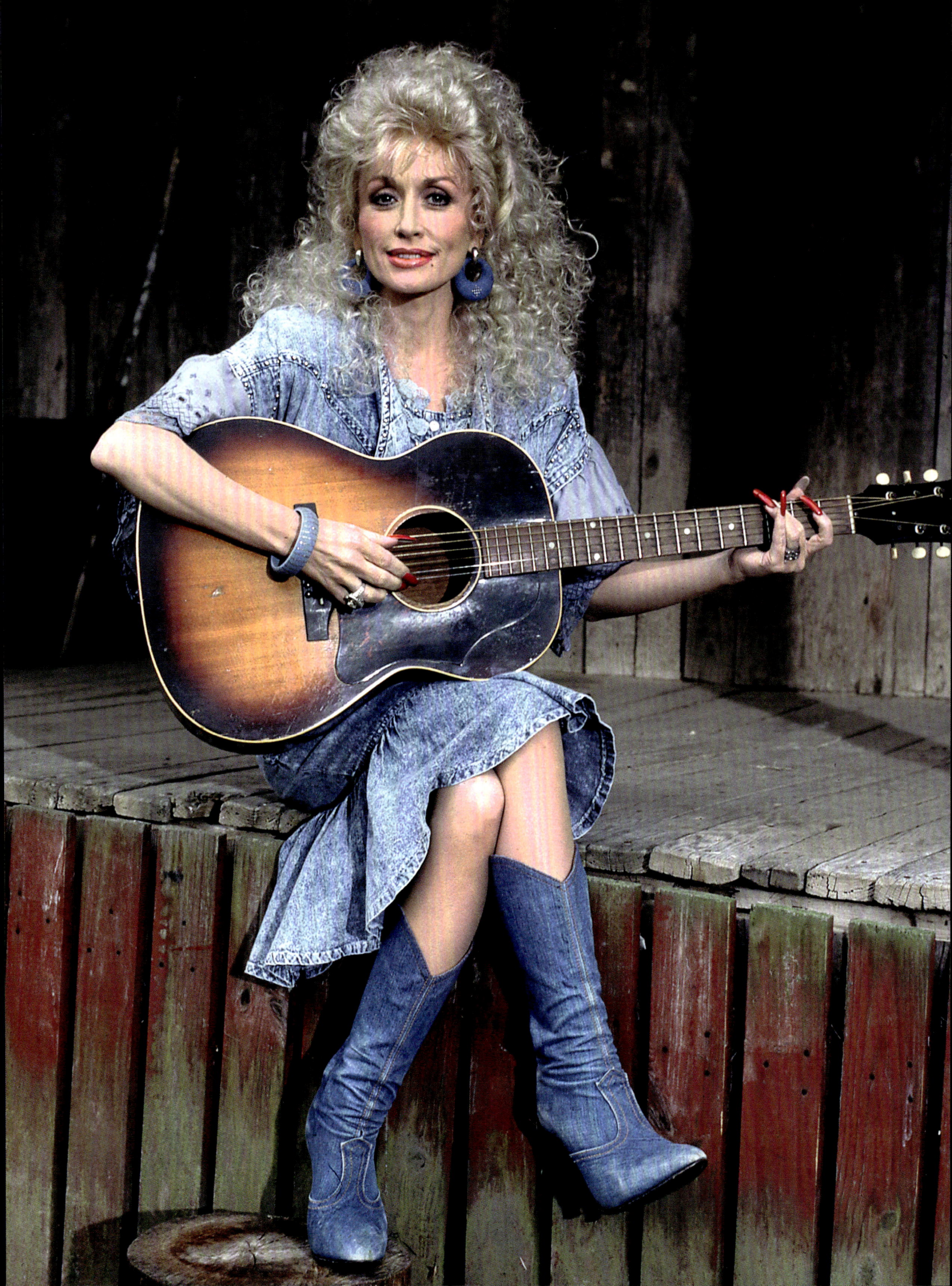

From
Hollywood
to
Dollywood

1986-1998

1986 – 1998

Life in the public eye is one big roller-coaster ride. It's difficult to get to the top, and it's even harder to stay there. But Dolly was never afraid to take a risk with her popularity, and in 1986, she rode the roller coaster down a new track, establishing a theme park, Dollywood, in the Smoky Mountains, where she grew up.

It was one of several new formats she tackled during a period that saw her testing her limits. She engaged in precision harmony with the *Trio* album, a project with Linda Ronstadt and Emmylou Harris that leaned into the mountain and bluegrass sounds of Dolly's past. In the same period, she moved into prime-time TV with the *Dolly!* variety show on ABC. She also joined an all-star cast in the 1989 movie *Steel Magnolias* and gave one of her most impactful performances ever with "He's Alive" on the CMA Awards.

The chances Dolly took during this period in her career were highly unconventional, and they helped her stand out even further from every other woman in entertainment.

—TOM ROLAND

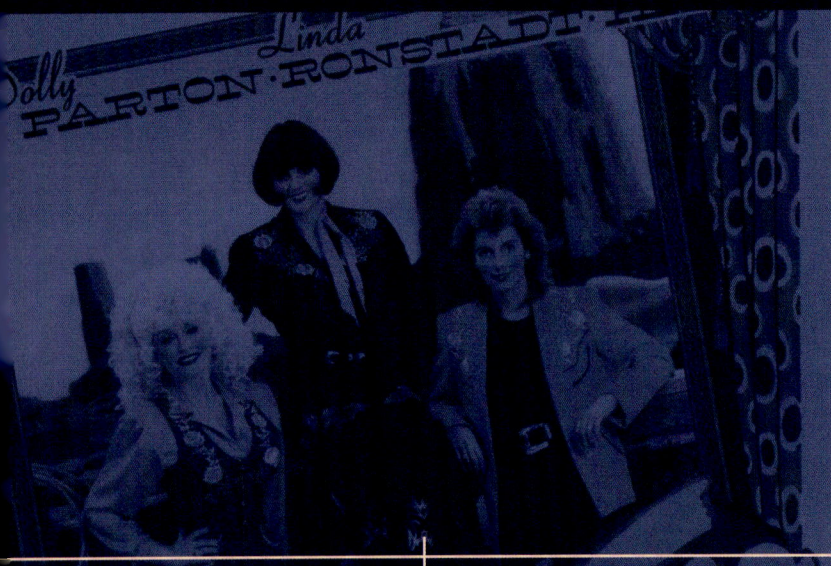

MARCH 1987
Trio, with Emmylou Harris and Linda Ronstadt, is released. It is a Top 10 pop album that wins a Grammy, the ACM Album of the Year award, and the CMA Vocal Event of the Year award.

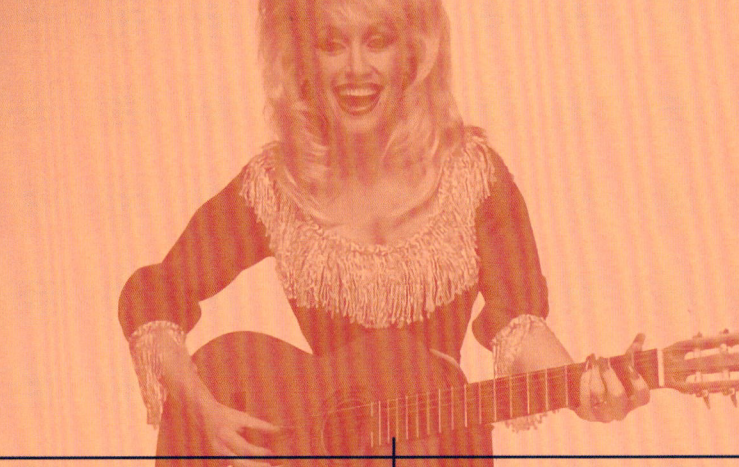

SEPTEMBER 1987
Dolly debuts on network television with the launch of *Dolly!*, an ABC prime-time variety series, setting the record for highest rated premiere of a new series.

FEBRUARY 1993
Dolly releases *Slow Dancing with the Moon*, which is quickly certified platinum. Her tour of the same name takes her across America.

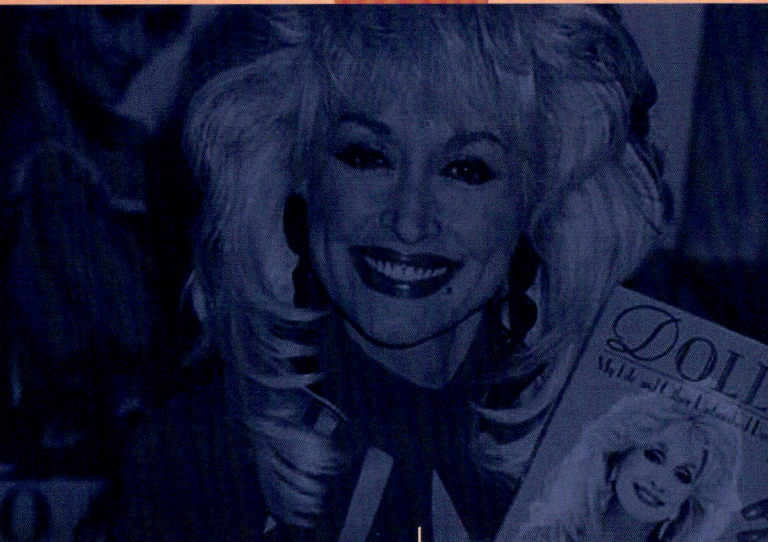

SEPTEMBER 1994
Dolly releases her autobiography, *Dolly: My Life and Other Unfinished Business*, which is a *New York Times* bestseller.

MAY 1986
Dollywood, a theme park co-owned by Dolly, opens in Pigeon Forge, Tennessee.

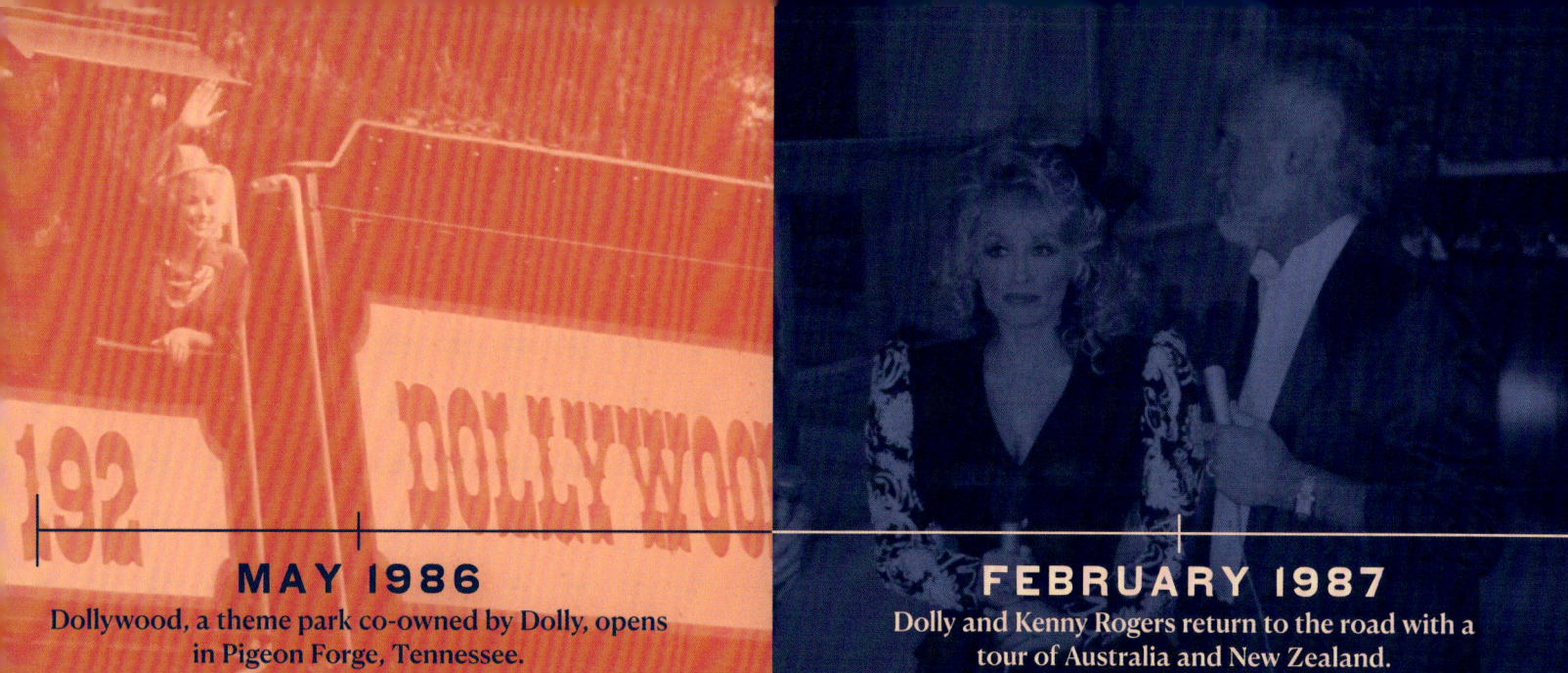

FEBRUARY 1987
Dolly and Kenny Rogers return to the road with a tour of Australia and New Zealand.

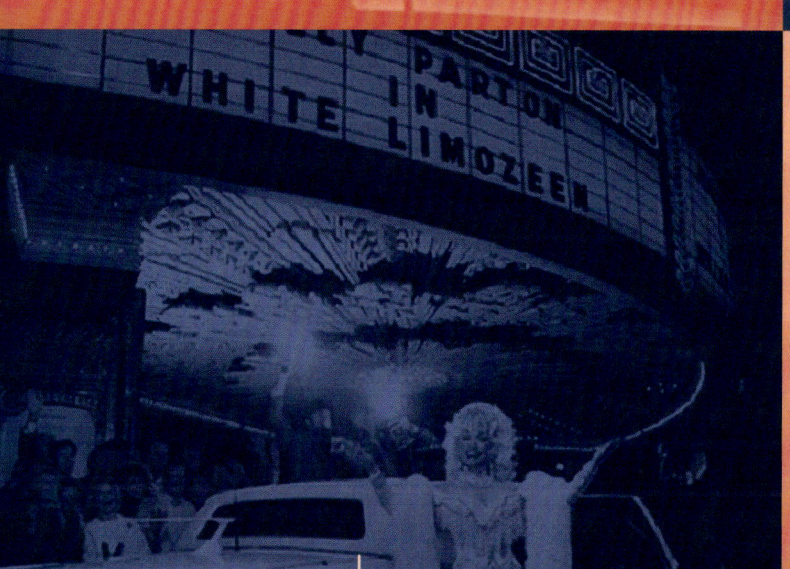

MAY 1989
Dolly releases *White Limozeen*, and the album goes gold and produces two no. 1 hit singles. She launches her biggest solo tour in a decade.

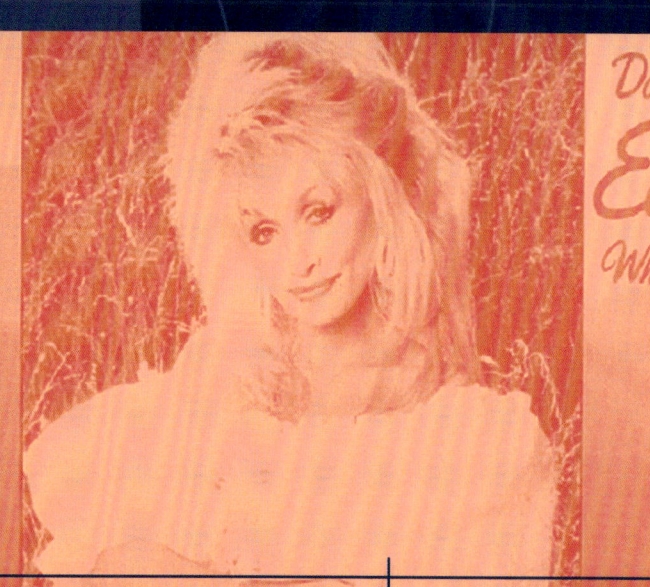

MARCH 1991
The album *Eagle When She Flies* gives Dolly another no. 1 hit: "Rockin' Years," with Ricky Van Shelton. The album also goes no. 1 and is certified platinum.

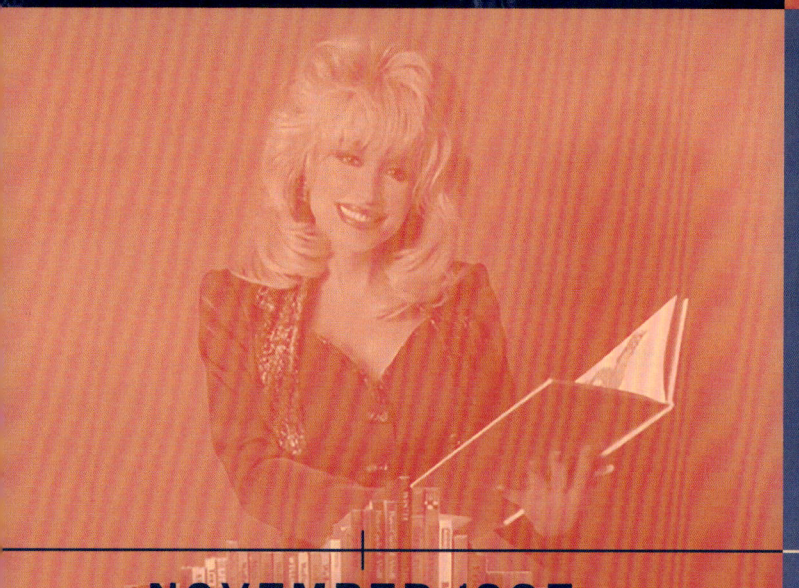

NOVEMBER 1995
Dolly launches the Imagination Library, providing books to children up to age five. By 2025, it expands to five countries, distributing over 270 million books.

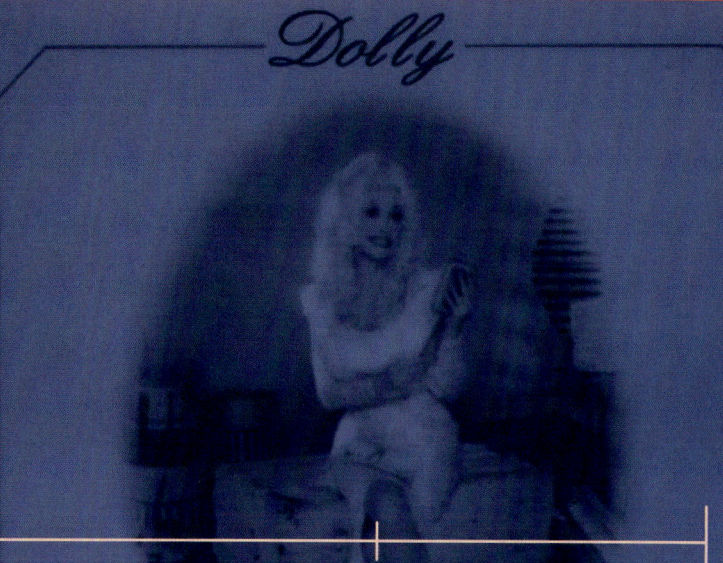

SEPTEMBER 1996
Dolly releases an album of covers, *Treasures*, and films a CBS TV concert special of the same name.

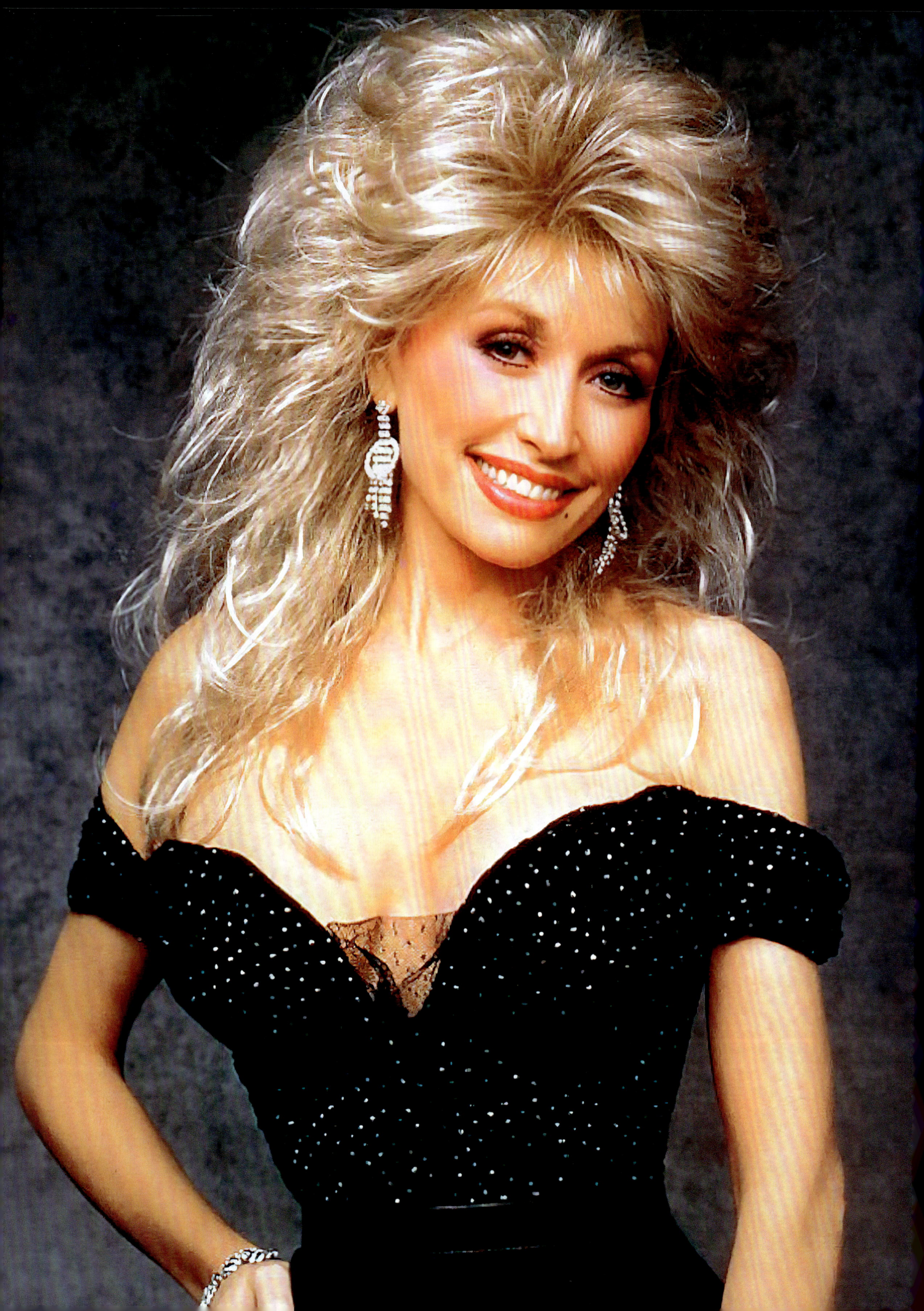

*B*y the middle of the 1980s, I'd fulfilled many of my dreams. I'd become a successful singer-songwriter, toured the world, and starred in a handful of movies. If I needed any proof that my star was shining pretty brightly, I could find it in the tabloids—they found a way to write about me just about every week! If someone started talking about "Dolly," unless they had an Aunt Dolly, by then a lot of people figured the "Dolly" they were talking about was me!

When artists reach that point, every one of them has decisions to make. There's a huge amount of work involved—and sacrifices to make—if you want to stay on top, and it takes a toll. Chances are you don't *have* to work after that point—or, at least, you don't have to work as much. That brings up a question that's familiar to everyone: Now what?

One option is to retire early and relax. That wasn't an option for me! I had bigger dreams that I wanted to see come to life. And that takes work—dreams don't necessarily come true on their own.

Slowing down wasn't—and still isn't— easy for me. I've never been interested in playing it safe. I enjoy taking risks and love learning and trying new things, and the year that I turned forty was a good time to do even more of that. Maybe I'd expand the business of Dolly a little bit! I planned to keep touring and making music, but I was ready to try some things I hadn't done before.

One of the first things I wanted to do was to finally record a full album with Linda Ronstadt and Emmylou Harris. We'd talked about it for almost ten years—ever since they'd guested on my syndicated show *Dolly*—but all three of us were busy with our own solo careers, we traveled in different circles, and life kept taking us in different directions. But we got around to recording what came to be known as the *Trio* album. It took a lot of commitment to clear our schedules and the datebooks of the people around us, but we finally did it.

Each of us brought something different to what was a really collective sound. Linda is a powerful singer, Emmylou has a voice full of shimmer and sorrow, and you can always pick me out on the high end in our harmonies.

They say there's nothing like family harmonies—that nobody can sing together quite like close relatives. And that's often true because brothers and sisters usually have some similarity in the sounds of their voices, and they typically share a lot of musical influences. It's hard to get any closer. But the Trio had that too! You'd have thought we'd been singing together our whole lives. Our voices really did combine to make some special music. It was such a beautiful sound.

There was another dream I'd been hoping for that was a long time coming: Dollywood, which opened in May 1986. We'd broken ground on the park in Pigeon Forge, Tennessee, in 1985, and I was excited to watch it all come together. I knew Dollywood had great potential, but I never could have fully envisioned then all that it has become today. I'd gotten the idea from the Hollywood sign in Los Angeles. That sign was intended to represent something magical and entertaining, and after I changed the *H* to a *D* in my mind, the result—Dollywood—called for some sort of country entertainment.

I'd first talked about the idea on *The Barbara Walters Special* a couple of years before. I'd said that I was thinking about building a theme park in my home county, and the Herschend family, who owned Silver Dollar City, came to me and said, "Well, you know, we don't need to have two parks in this area. Let's just go into business together and make it everything that we can make it." We met at my Denver, Colorado, Real Love Tour date to discuss my ideas, and we worked it out so that Dollywood expanded on the existing Silver Dollar property. The Herschends have been the best partners for forty-plus years—lovely people with good values, and we've had a wonderful, successful run together.

I grew up there in the Smoky Mountains, and that gave me a feel for the project. We lived so far back in the hills when I was young that we didn't get to go many places. We would go to the county fair, and I loved going to Gatlinburg when I first started getting to date. At that time, there was a theme park called Rebel Railroad in nearby Pigeon Forge. It was later renamed Goldrush Junction, and then it became Silver Dollar City, and a lot of my people worked there. In fact, Uncle Henry—John Henry III was his stage name—played the part of a bank robber on the train that went through there on the Goldrush Junction and Rebel Railroad. He later worked at Dollywood in the Family Kinfolk show.

When I started picturing what the park might look like, I realized I'd like to have a place everybody would enjoy, like Silver Dollar City, but on a larger scale and kind of Dollyized—something that reflected my dreams and imagination.

To transform Silver Dollar City into Dollywood, we expanded it, and I started remaking it in a way that would capture and preserve my Smoky Mountain memories. The area drew four million tourists a year, and the rides, the shops, and the theaters were all designed to give a sense of how people in the mountains really live.

I did my homework—or, as the lawyers like to say, my due diligence—and it's turned out to be one of the greatest things I've ever done. It's provided many jobs for so many people in that part of the world, including a lot of my relatives—not just as singers or musicians but also as workers in the park.

Later, we started building the resorts and the water park, Splash Country, and we became a real vacation destination, one that's catered toward family living. The resorts have bunk beds, and there are places where parents can have a little time away from the kids if they want. It's a theme park, not an amusement park, but we do have some great rides too.

My experience as an entertainer paid off when we were putting the park together. I'd gone from being a stage performer to being a stage owner, and the venues in the park were designed with both the performers and the audience in mind. I wanted everyone to feel that they're in a safe environment. I wanted the entire audience to have a good view of what's going on. And I wanted the employees to go away and say, "Oh, I loved working at

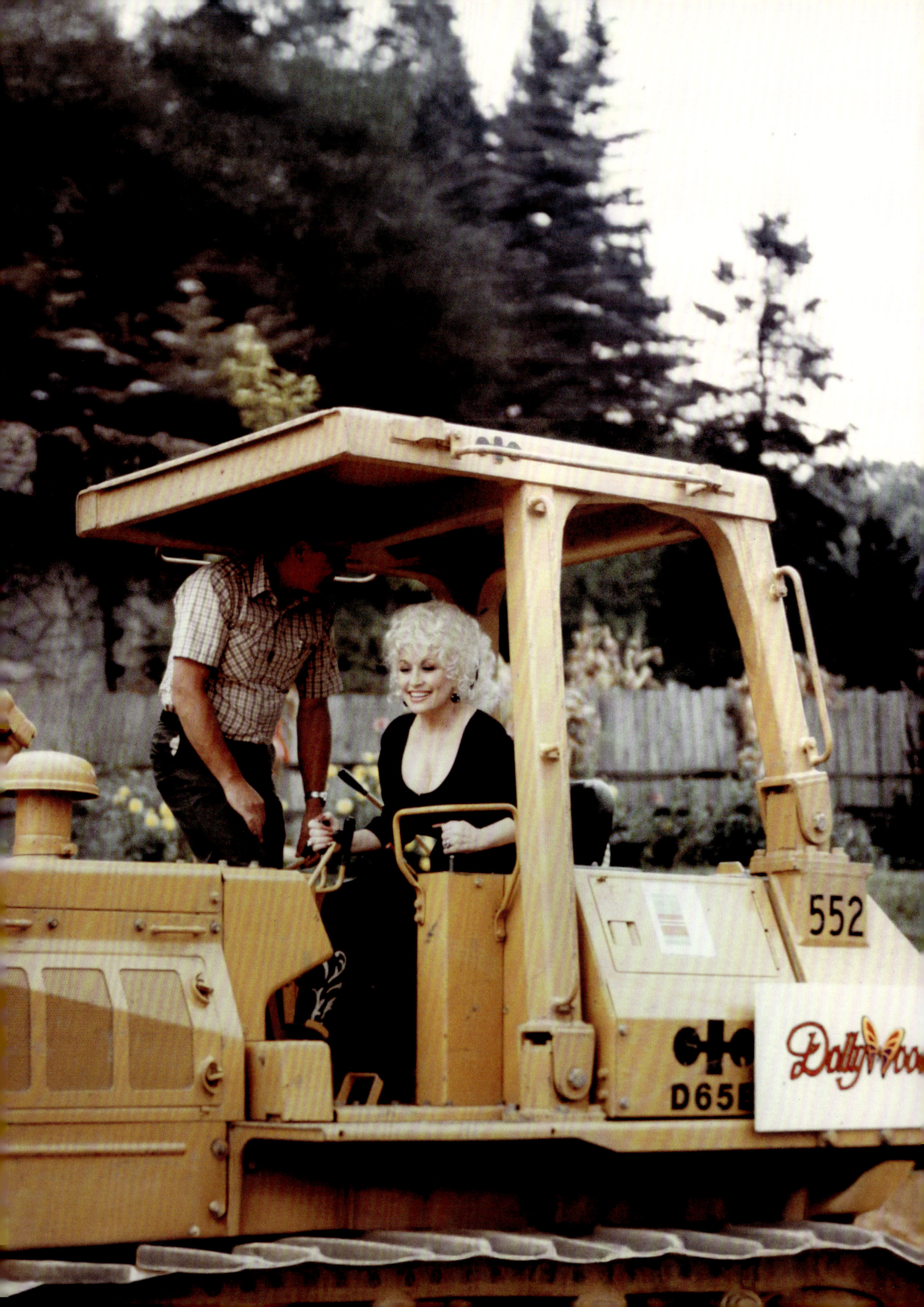

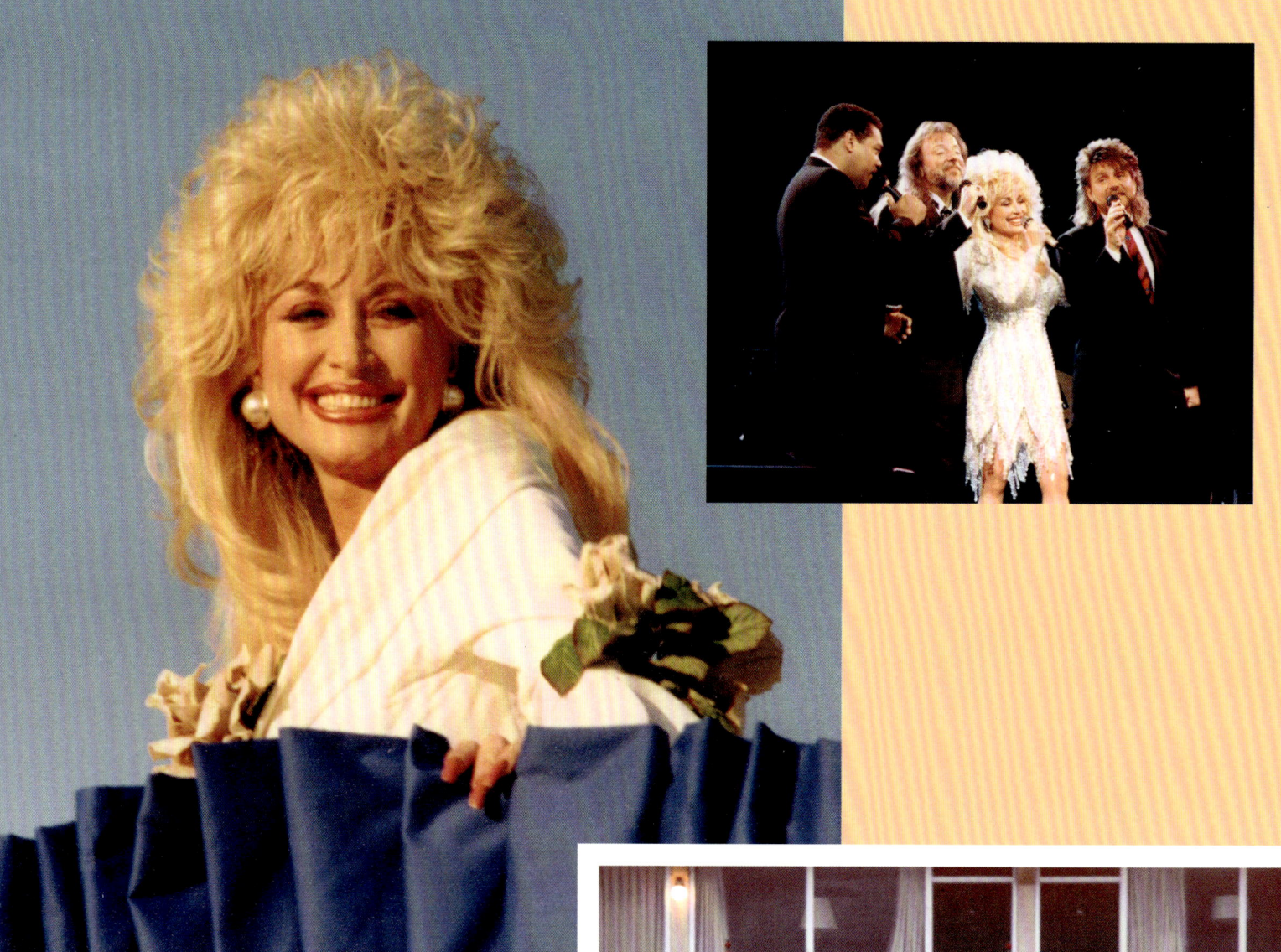

Dollywood reflects Parton's life

I was so proud when Dollywood welcomed its first guests. These moments are from over the years, including the official grand opening, where I performed a pair of concerts—one the night before the opening and one the following weekend.

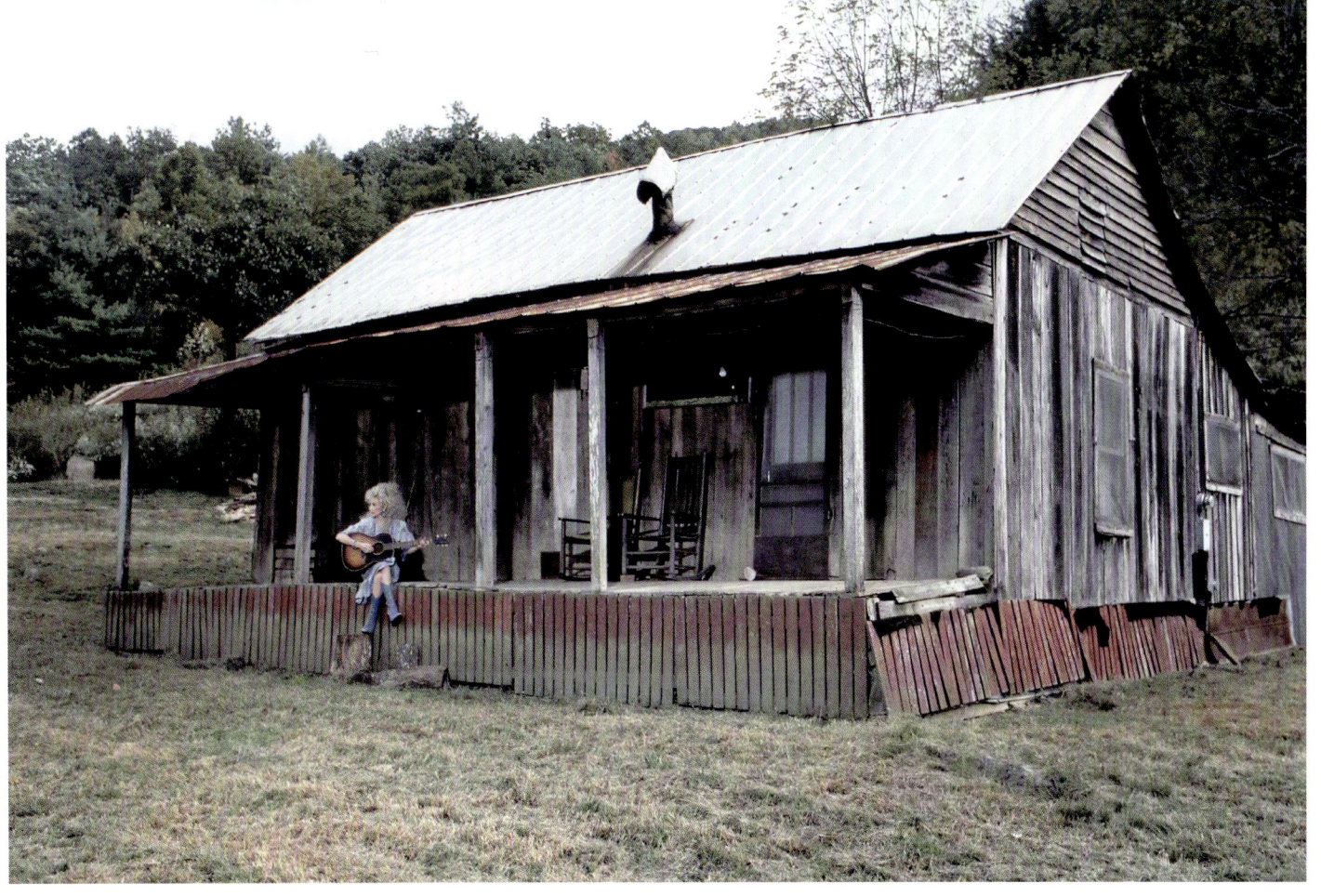

Dollywood features a replica of my real-life childhood home. But this is the original . . . and that's the front porch that I used for my first concert stage.

Dollywood. That stage is fantastic. We had the best time, and we had the best food. We had the best lighting, the best sound, the best monitor system, and the best people on stage." That's how you build a reputation.

I also used Dollywood to give visitors a sense of how Dolly would—get it? "Dolly would"?—grow into the performer she is today. The Parton Family Back Porch Theater is a replica of the house on the cover of my album *My Tennessee Mountain Home*. The porch is, of course, where I gave all those concerts for my family when I was growing up. And I planned to give a few shows there every year myself. The restaurants offered authentic food too. Aunt Granny's served dishes we would cook for guests and my siblings when we were growing up, and Apple Jack's Mill—named after my song "Applejack"—featured all kinds of menu items that were made from apples. The park also had a music hall and, naturally, a bunch of rides. Don't ask which ride is my favorite—I don't do 'em. I want people to take home a souvenir, but I don't want it to be one of my wigs!

If there were any doubts about whether it would work, they were forgotten by October of that year, when we were already announcing the first expansion of Dollywood. It had turned out to be an even bigger attraction than I'd expected, and I hired the right people—people

From Hollywood to Dollywood

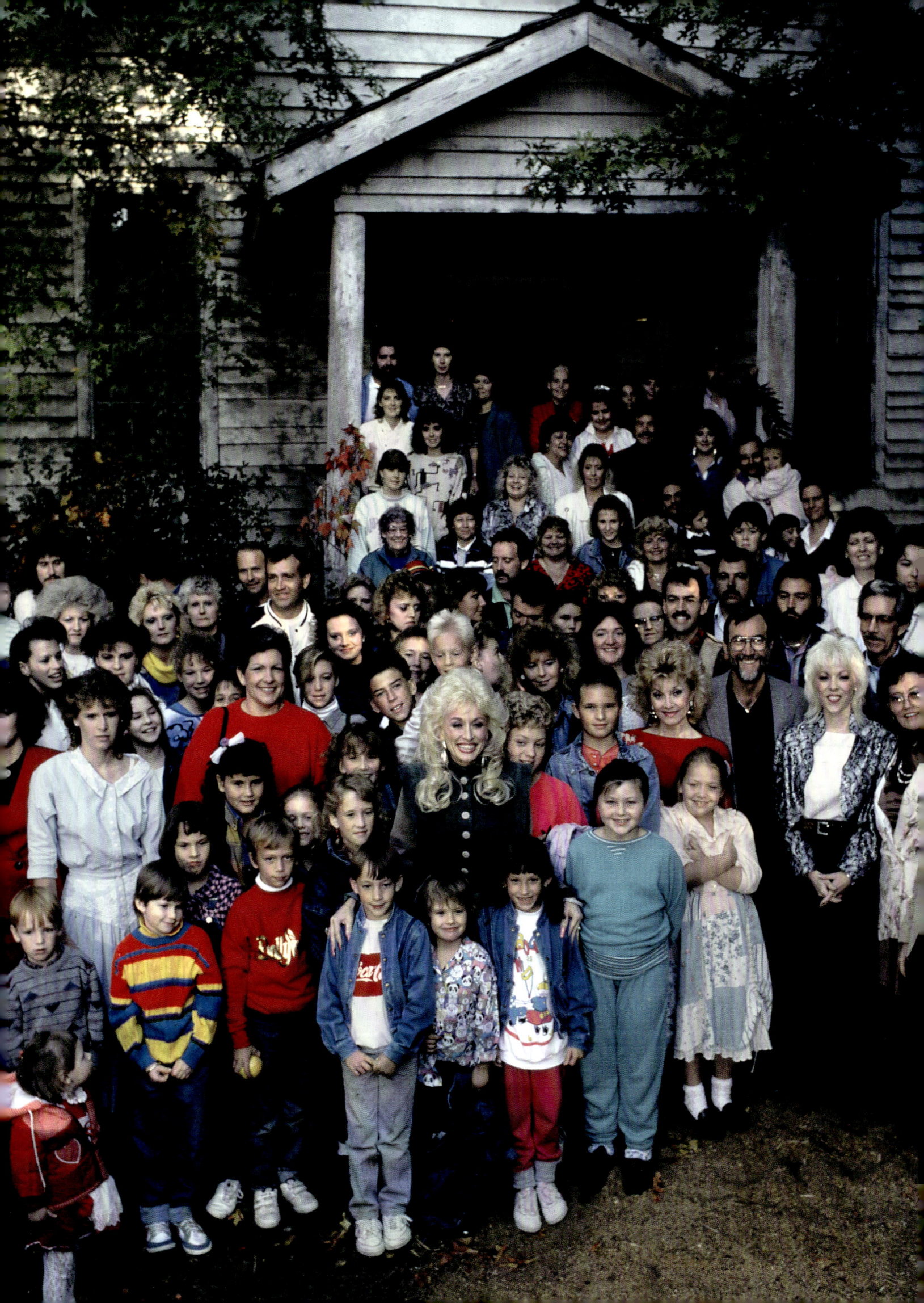

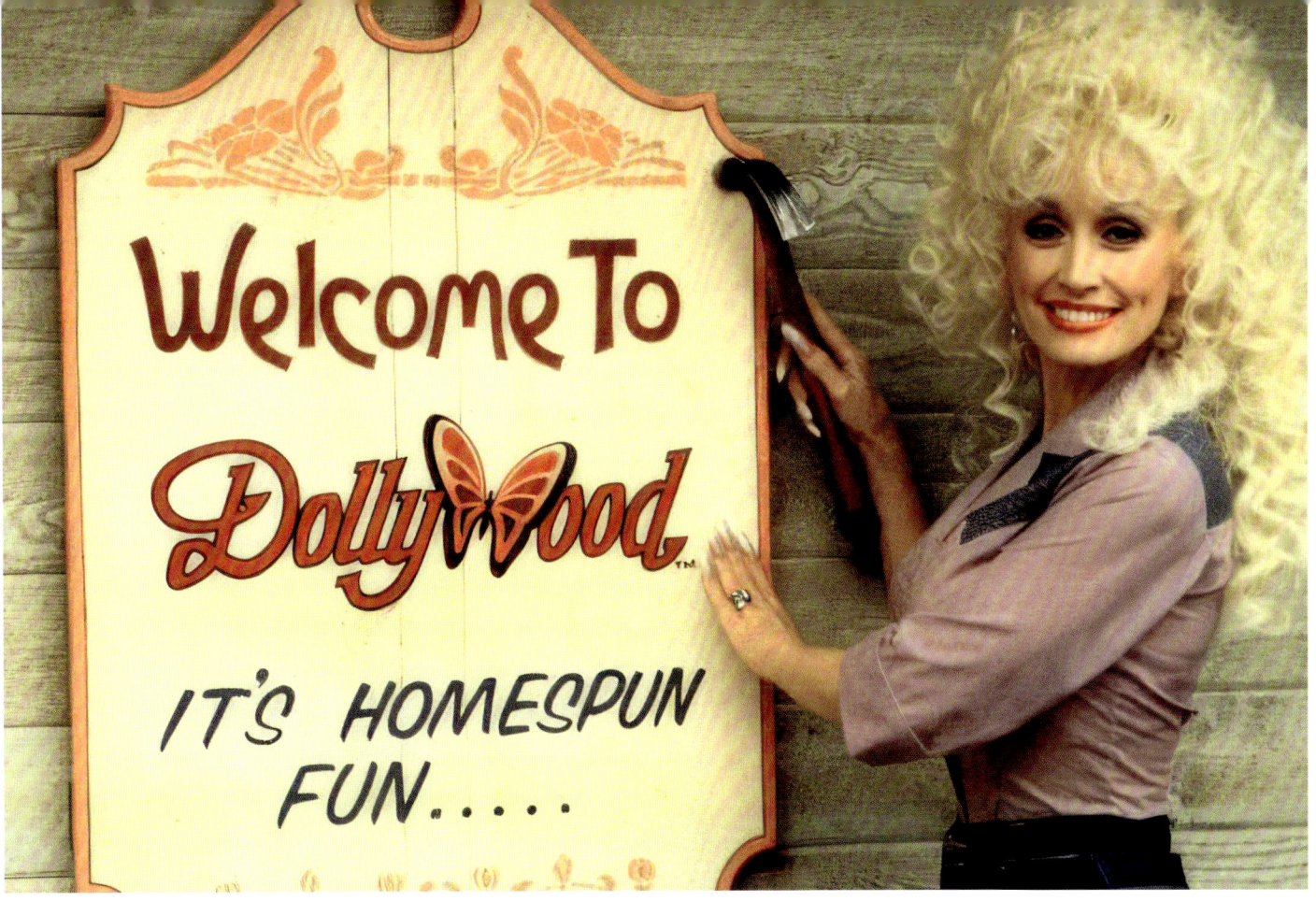

> I hammered away at guitar until I got good at it as
> a kid. I hammered away at my dreams of stardom.
> I hammered enough to be able to create Dollywood.
> And I'm still hammering.

who allowed me to take a big-picture view of the park and were able to bring my vision for a Smoky Mountain entertainment destination to life. It made me really proud and brought more money to the area where I grew up. It couldn't have been a better start.

As if recording the *Trio* album and opening the theme park weren't enough, I continued to tour and I filmed a TV movie, *A Smoky Mountain Christmas,* with Lee Majors and John Ritter.

That fall, Linda, Emmylou, and I sang one of the *Trio* songs, "My Dear Companion," publicly for the first time during the CMA Awards. Since it uses mountain-tinged harmony supported by acoustic guitar and mandolin, it fit well with the Appalachian heritage at the theme park. I can't say I planned for those two things to overlap like that—and I don't know that too many people noticed it—but I think people could still feel that I was continuing to embrace my cultural origins. I may travel around the world and do all these things, but my mountain home and the people I grew up with are never far from my thoughts—they're always in my heart.

From Hollywood to Dollywood

Spotlight

LINDA RONSTADT & EMMYLOU HARRIS:
TO KNOW THEM IS TO LOVE THEM

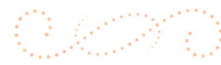

No one is more relaxed than Emmylou Harris, no one talks faster than Linda Ronstadt, and probably no one giggles more than me . . . so when you put the three of us together, we're quite the trio.

Linda and Emmylou met for the first time in 1973 when Emmy was touring with Gram Parsons and Linda was working with Neil Young. They ended up in Houston at the same time and met unexpectedly at an after-show party.

Two years later, following a session when Emmy recorded "One of These Days," the three of us were all together for the first time, and we ended up harmonizing later that day in a Beverly Hills hotel room. The sound was classic, and our ability to play off of each other came naturally. It's like we each knew which notes to take for ourselves; even our phrasing was instinctively in sync. The next year, I asked them to appear on my syndicated TV show, and we sang "The Sweetest Gift"—Linda has such power in her voice, and Emmy simply shimmers. I came in with the high harmonies, and all our tones fit together for all to hear . . . just as they had in that Beverly Hills hotel room.

Right away, we talked about making an album together—that was the era when Kenny Rogers and Dottie West were recording together, and Waylon Jennings and Willie Nelson had their duet project. We attempted to get together to record a few times but could never make our schedules work well enough to cut a whole album. Linda and I ended up singing together for more than 40,000 people at a Day on the Green concert in Oakland, California, in 1978, and all three of us harmonized in a surprise appearance during one of my Los Angeles concerts in 1979. We recorded a Christmas song, "Light of the Stable," and we all worked on Emmy's 1981 remake of "Mister Sandman." And eventually we were able to make two wonderful albums together.

The music we made remains one of the highlights of my career, and the friendships I made with Linda and Emmy are among the highlights of my life.

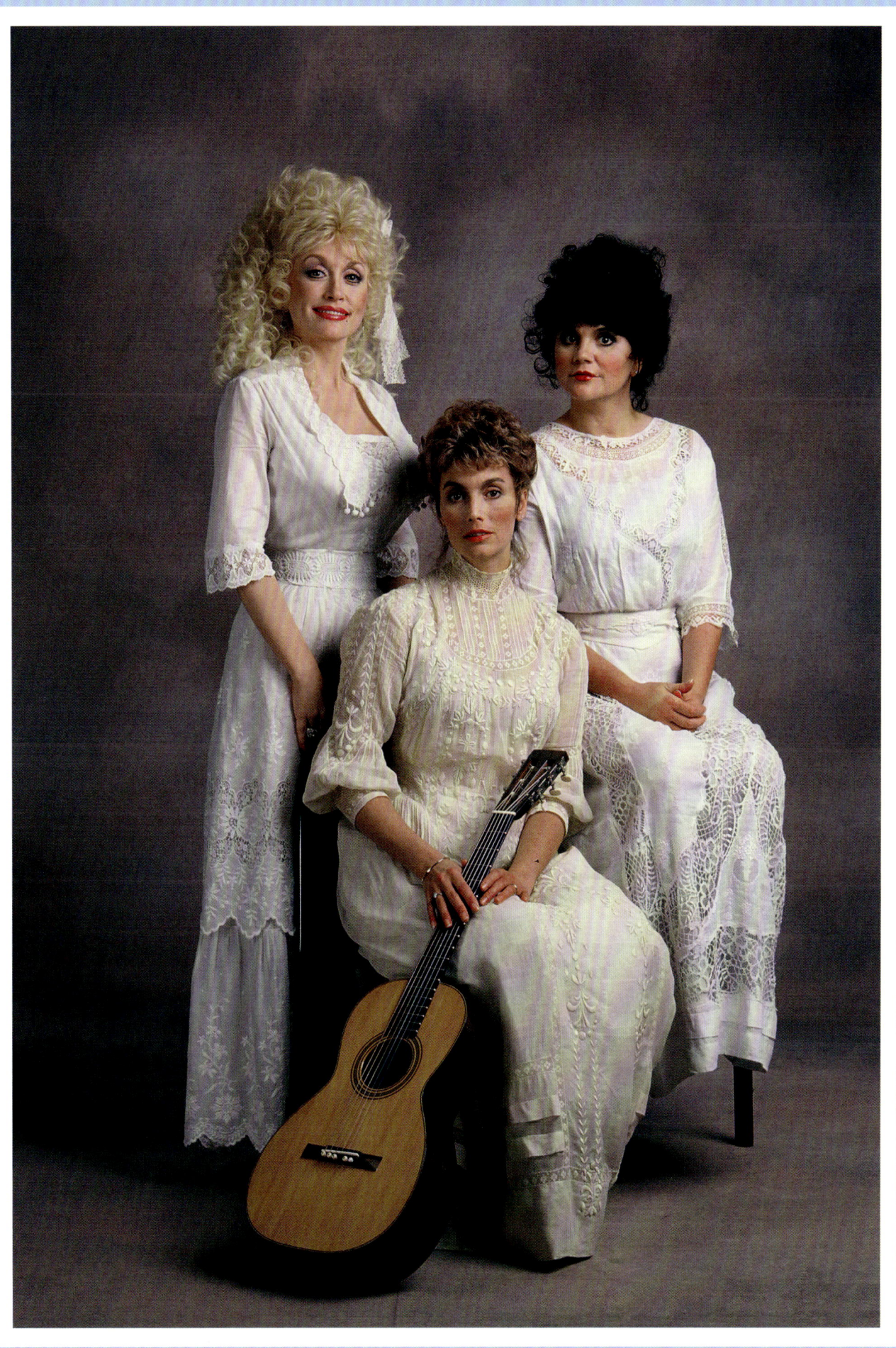

This is an alternate take (in color) of the black-and-white photo with Linda Ronstadt and Emmylou Harris that appeared in the liner notes of our *Trio* album.

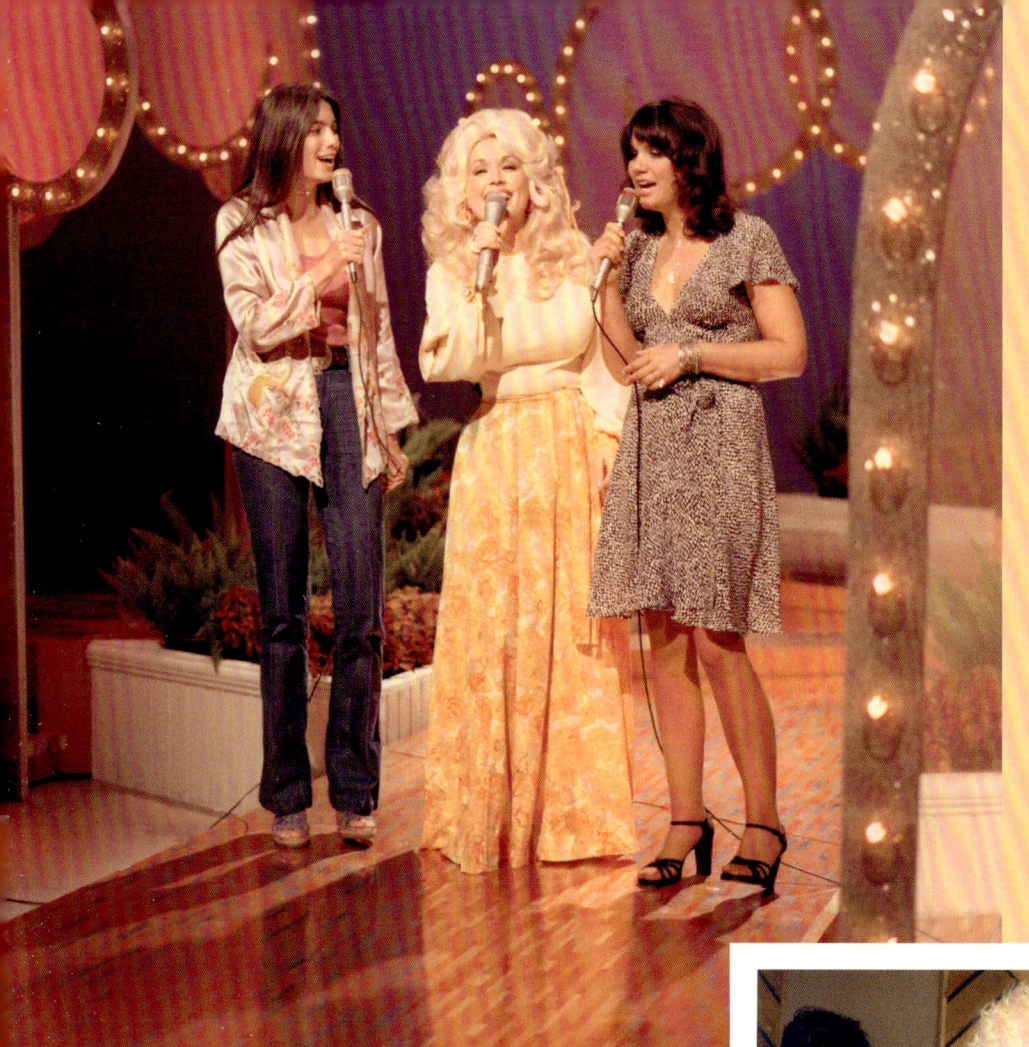

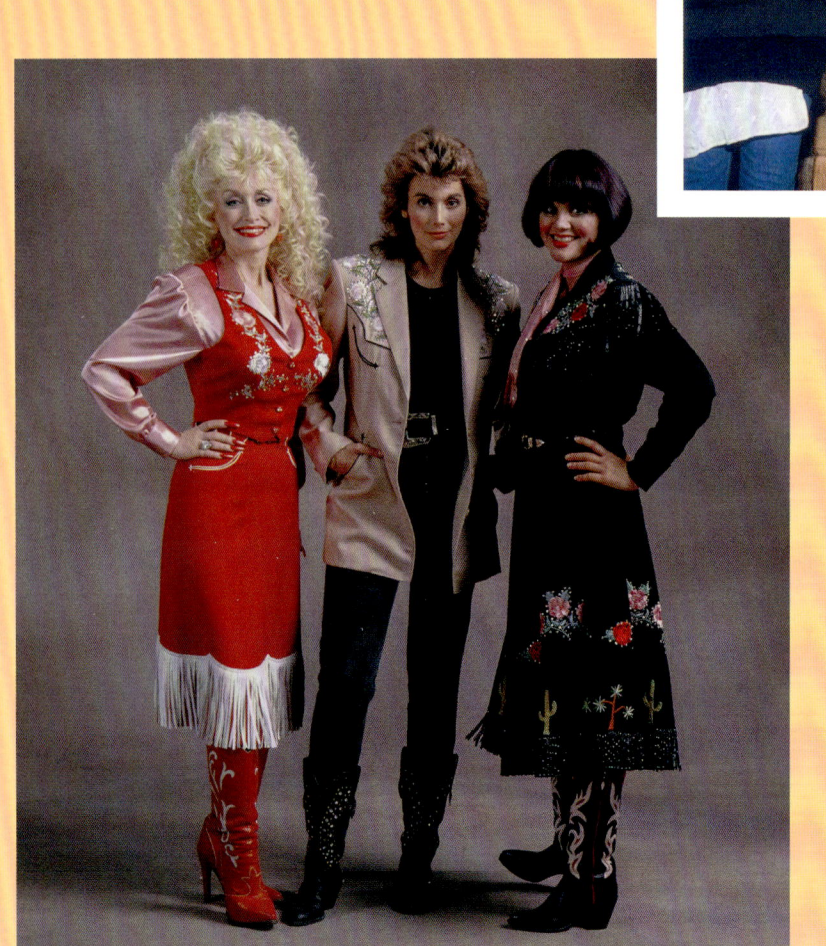

Here's a trio of looks from my time with Linda and Emmylou. *Top:* The three of us appear on the *Dolly* syndicated show in the 1970s. *Middle:* Me and some fans sporting custom-made Trio jackets. *Bottom:* Nashville designer Manuel created a Western aesthetic tailored to each of us for the *Trio* album's photo shoot.

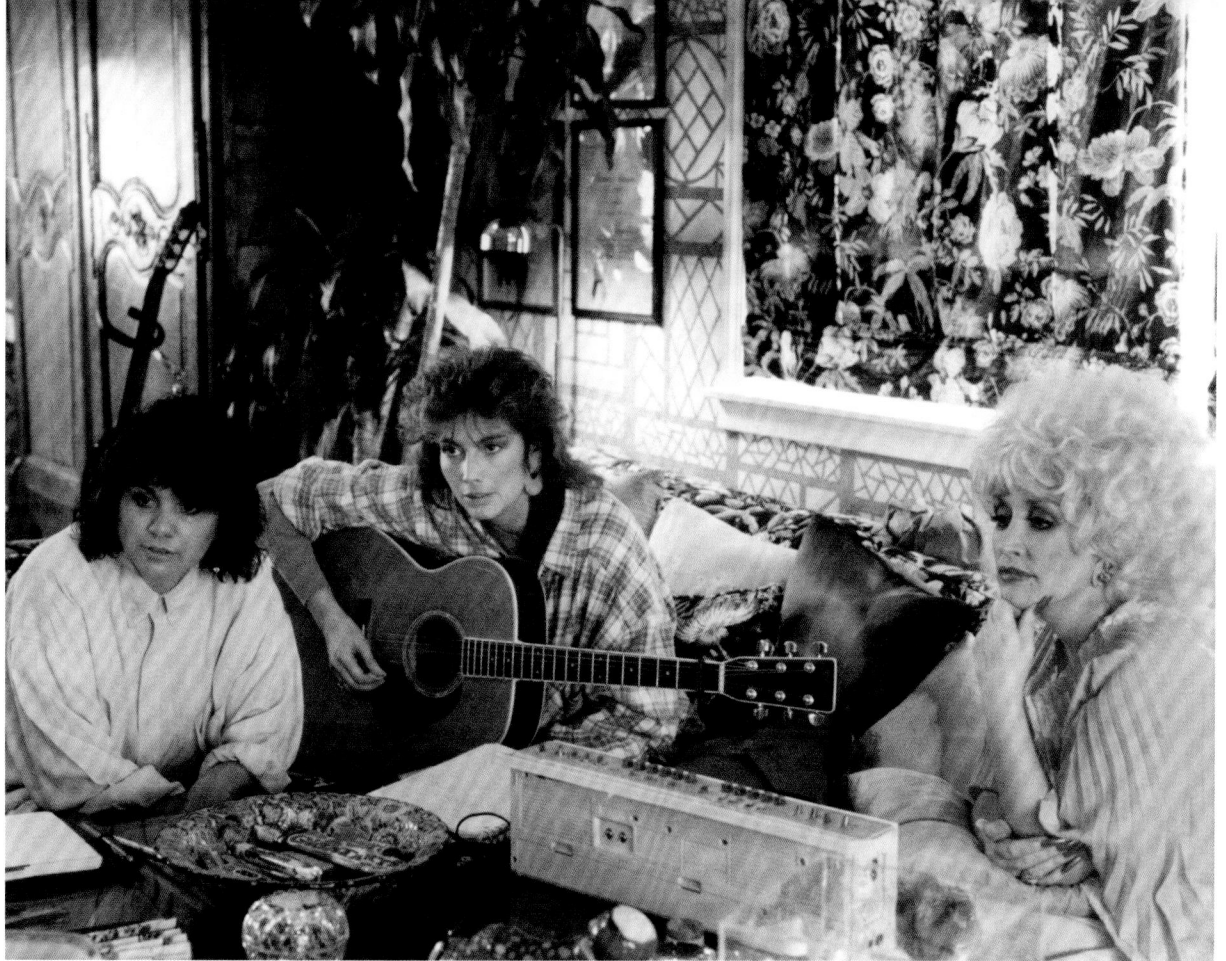

Look at that old-timey cassette player on the table in front of me! We used it on a day when Linda and Emmylou stopped by my house for a production meeting about the *Trio* album—and I still use it today!

I got to perform publicly with Linda and Emmylou a few times over the years, but it's one of my biggest career regrets that we never did a Trio tour. We certainly talked about it, but once again, our individual schedules might as well have been three different massive jigsaw puzzles, and the pieces never quite fell into place at the same time.

I did, however, have another tour with Kenny Rogers on the books in 1987. We played Australia and New Zealand eight years after my first visit there. Most country artists at the time were focused on performing in the United States. If they played internationally, they went to Canada and maybe the United Kingdom, but that was it. There were exceptions—Johnny Cash, Glen Campbell, and Charley Pride, to name a few—but most just stayed stateside at that point.

There were good reasons for that. It's expensive to tour overseas, especially if you have staging and sound equipment in addition to instruments that need to be shipped. Laws and languages and time zones are all different. It can be a real headache to put a tour together. This was particularly true in the '80s, when people didn't yet communicate via email and social media. You had to make long-distance phone calls, and they had to happen at odd times to accommodate the difference in time zones.

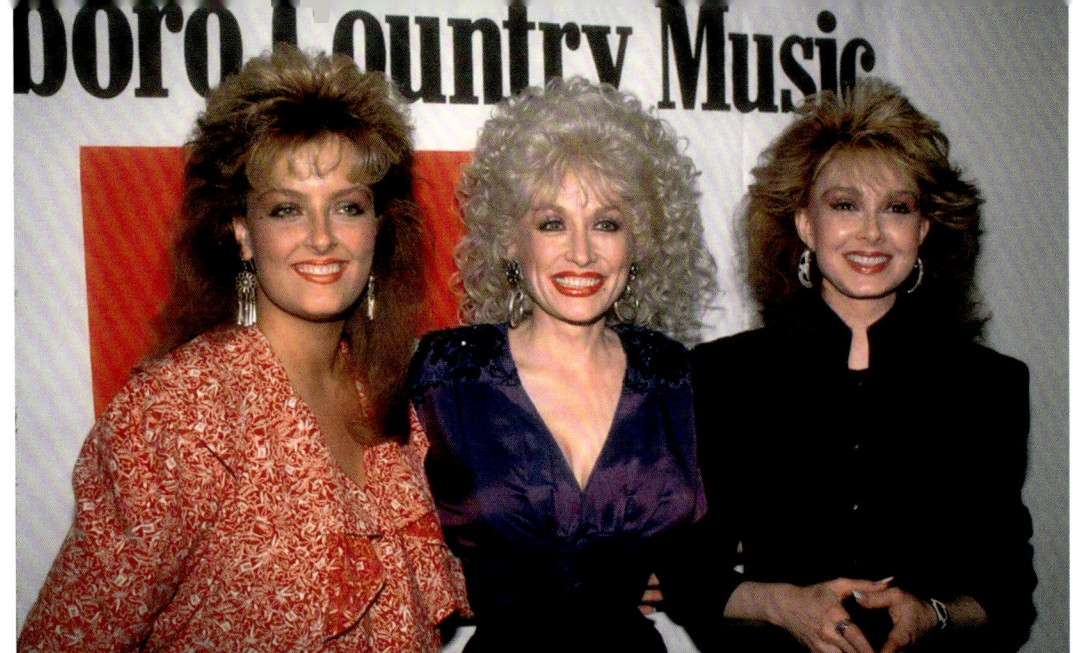

Would you look at all that hair?! That's Wynonna Judd on the left and Naomi on the right at the press conference for the Marlboro Country Music Tour in 1987, which raised money for Second Harvest Food Banks—and none of us smoked cigarettes.

It was worth all the effort though. When we got to Melbourne, the city invited residents out to the town square, and eight thousand people showed up to greet us. I yelled "Howdeee!" in my best Minnie Pearl imitation, and the mayor proceeded to present Kenny and me with keys to the city. They told us that at the time, it was the biggest turnout they'd had for any singers since The Beatles played there in 1964.

When I came back to the States, there were more collaborations on the books—just not with Kenny. Warner Bros. released the *Trio* album, and the same month, I joined Alabama and The Judds at Lincoln Center in Manhattan on the Marlboro Country Music Tour concert series.

Naomi Judd was hilarious at the press conference when she proclaimed herself to be my "biggest fan in the whole universe," and then added, "She just scatters my acorns!"

I was one of The Judds' biggest fans too. They were fresh and new when that tour came up. They played mostly acoustic music, rich in harmony, and it kind of paralleled what Emmylou and Linda and I were doing with the *Trio* album.

The Trio appropriately played a trio of songs on *The Tonight Show* around then. You could tell how serious we were from our demeanor. We set up three mic stands—no running around on the stage. We just stood there and performed our songs, soaking up the harmony as it poured out of us and enjoying the sound of the first-rate band we'd assembled. I swayed back and forth the whole time, the fringe at the hem of my red dress sashaying around my boots. Linda moved her head with each phrase in the music, and Emmylou gently tapped her left foot—though she did get kind of animated over the musicians' solo parts. We each sang lead on one song—me on "Those Memories of You," Emmylou on "To Know Him Is to Love Him," and Linda on "Hobo's Meditation."

Star of the Show

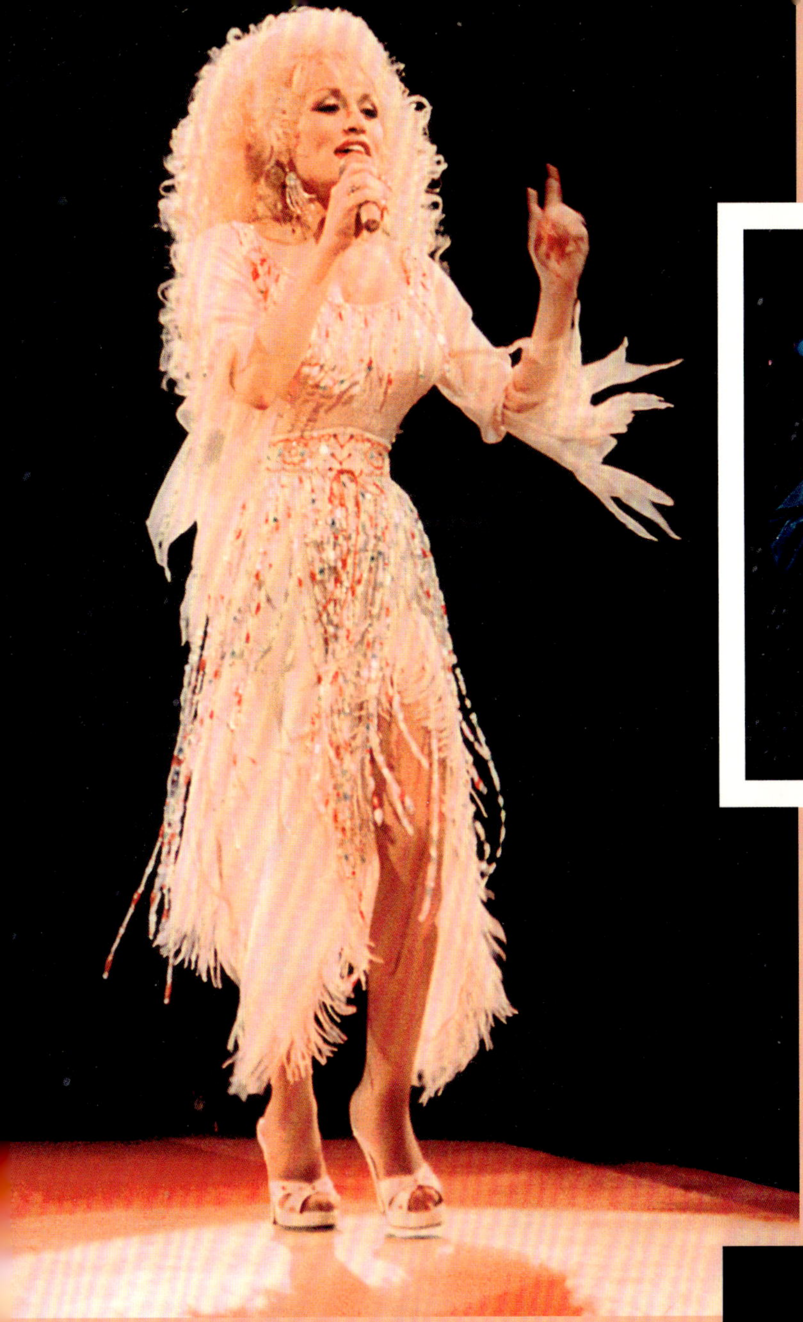

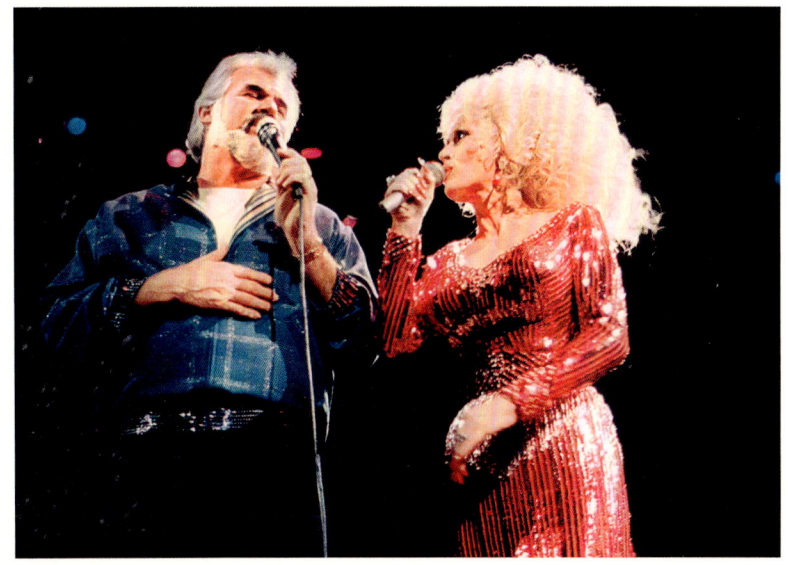

Kenny and I didn't really record that many songs together—in fact, the only full album of duets that we did was *Once Upon a Christmas*. Still, we had a real love for touring together—for a spell in the 1980s, I did almost as many shows with Kenny as I did on my own!

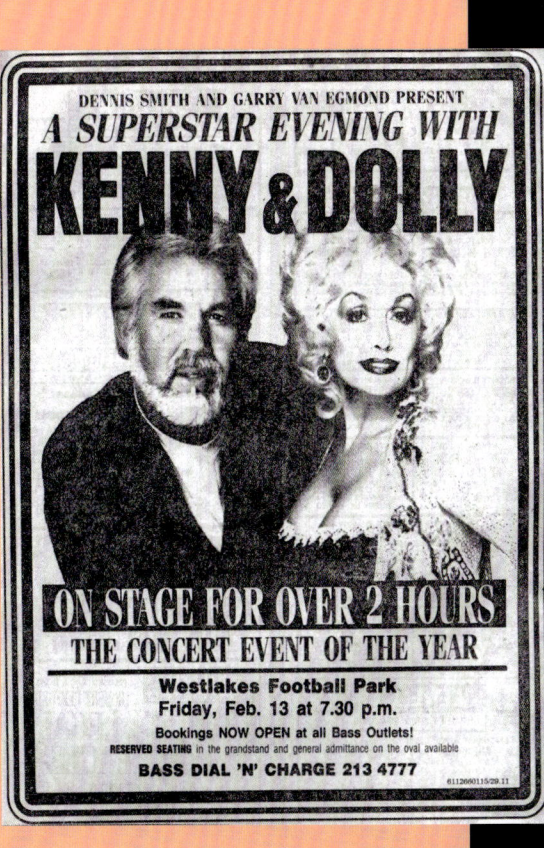

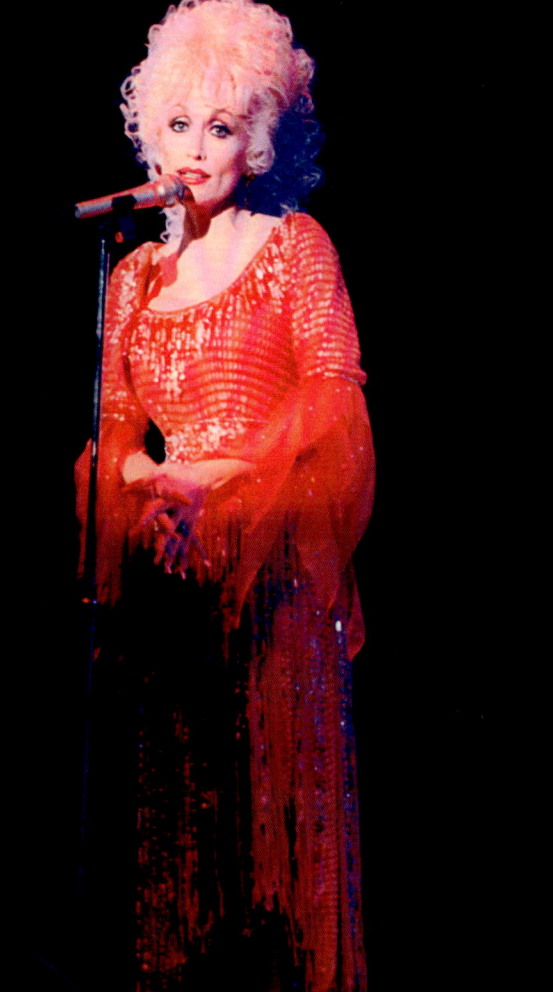

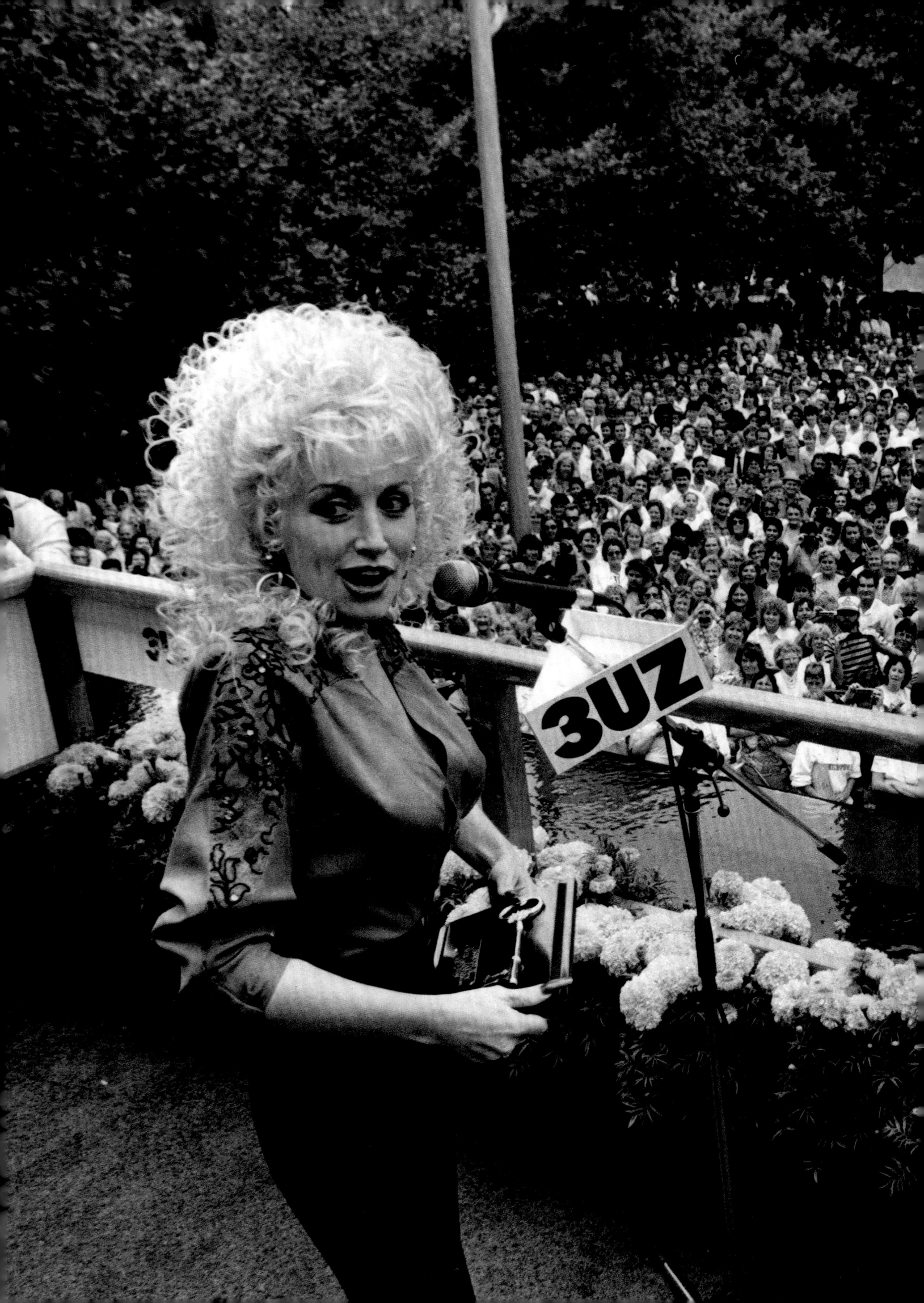

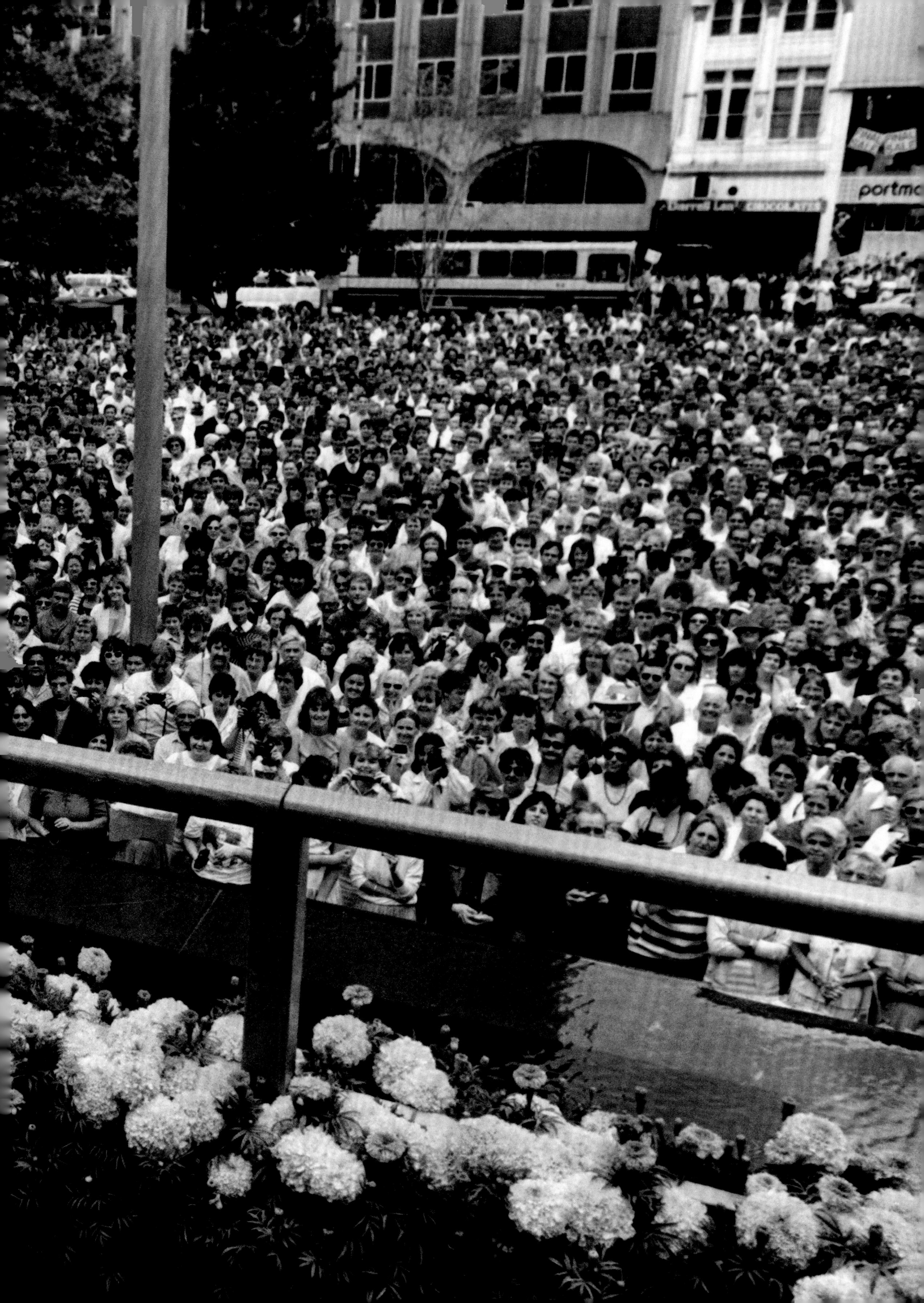

STAGE LOOKS
Through the Years

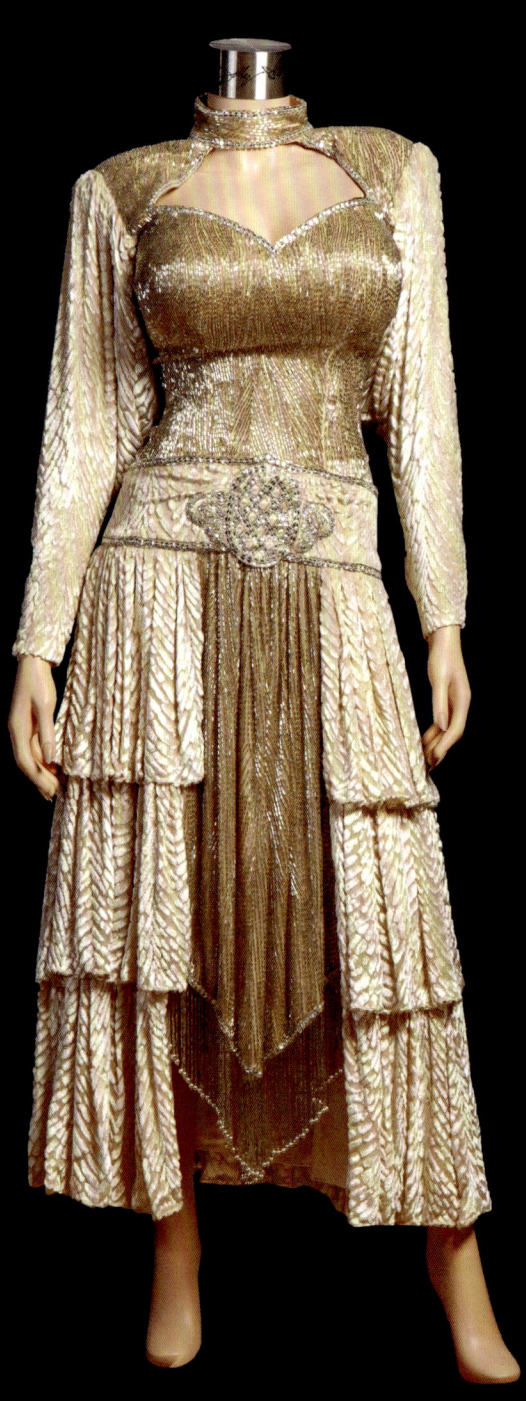

I wore this velvet Tony Chase gown on stage at the Ryman on my ABC show in 1988.

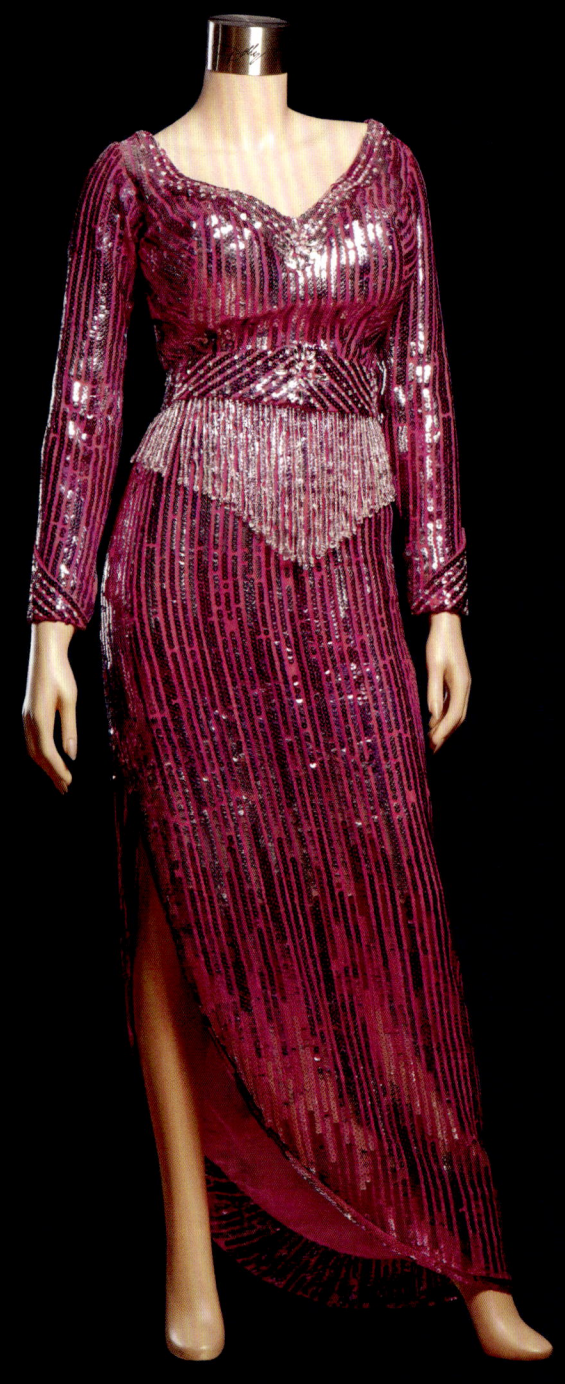

I love the '80s, I love pink, and I love this dress . . . so much so that I wore it until the sequins fell off! (If you saw me on tour with Kenny Rogers, you probably saw me in this!)

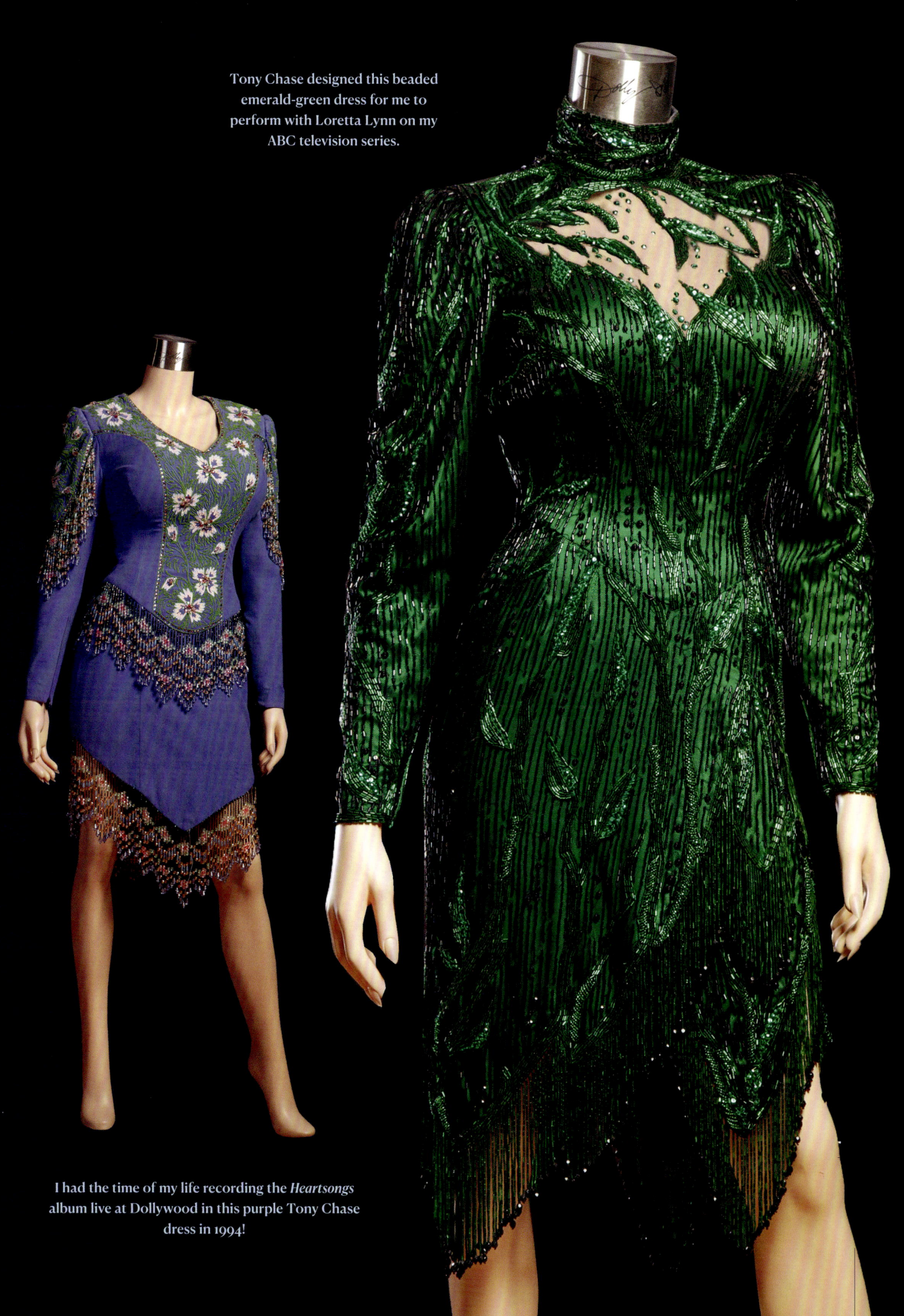

Tony Chase designed this beaded emerald-green dress for me to perform with Loretta Lynn on my ABC television series.

I had the time of my life recording the *Heartsongs* album live at Dollywood in this purple Tony Chase dress in 1994!

Dollywood opened for its second season that May, and I took part in the dedication of a Dolly statue two days later. That statue was paid for by the mighty fine people of Sevierville, and to this day it sits in the courthouse square. My daddy was prouder of that statue dedication than just about anything I'd ever done. And I was too. When your own people lift you up, well, there's no greater compliment than that. But Daddy also kept me humble. When he thought I was being too boastful about it, he told me that it was great and I might be an idol to my fans, but to the pigeons I was just another outhouse. Only later did I find out that he would clean the statue himself late at night.

The next week, I played my second show with Alabama and The Judds on that Marlboro tour, and it was particularly fun. Before the show, I got to meet the cast of *Pump Boys and Dinettes,* an off-Broadway production that was running in Chicago at the time. The show had a fantasy number called "The Night Dolly Parton Was Almost Mine," and man, talk about a fantasy! To have someone write a song about you and make it one of the highlights of a musical is a form of appreciation you don't expect.

One dream I held for years finally came true in 1987. For a long time, I'd wanted my own network variety TV show, kind of like the ones Ed Sullivan or Carol Burnett or Sonny and Cher used to host. I was excited about the possibility of getting to do something on a larger scale than the occasional TV appearances I'd made. I pictured myself doing a show that used that basic format but was true to me and true to my roots. Everybody in Hollywood seemed to be missing those variety shows that once were so huge—the time felt right to bring one back. I wasn't the only one who felt that way—some network executives thought I was hot enough at the time that we could pull it off.

I kept saying that I needed not to be doing things where I'm like a fish out of water. I am not a pop singer. I don't think comedy sketches work if the part I'm playing doesn't feel like me. But there were so many people on staff who were so excited about the show that they kept trying to make it too big. I didn't want to let them down, so we did some stuff that may not have worked for the folks watching at home. Ultimately, it was my fault, my responsibility that I let it happen.

The things we *did* get right were the guests and the music: I think they were the best part of the show.

I got Linda and Emmylou to stop by on one episode so we could do a trio of songs again—"Dear Companion," "Hobo's Meditation," and "Those Memories of You"—staged on a living room set with a cozy fireplace.

Kenny Rogers visited, and we did something I called the "Other Woman Medley," where we sang a series of songs he had recorded with other female singers: "We've Got Tonight" (Sheena Easton), "Anyone Who Isn't Me Tonight" (Dottie West), and "Don't Fall in Love with a Dreamer" (Kim Carnes). Then we capped it with one of the no. 1 songs Kenny had recorded with me, "Real Love."

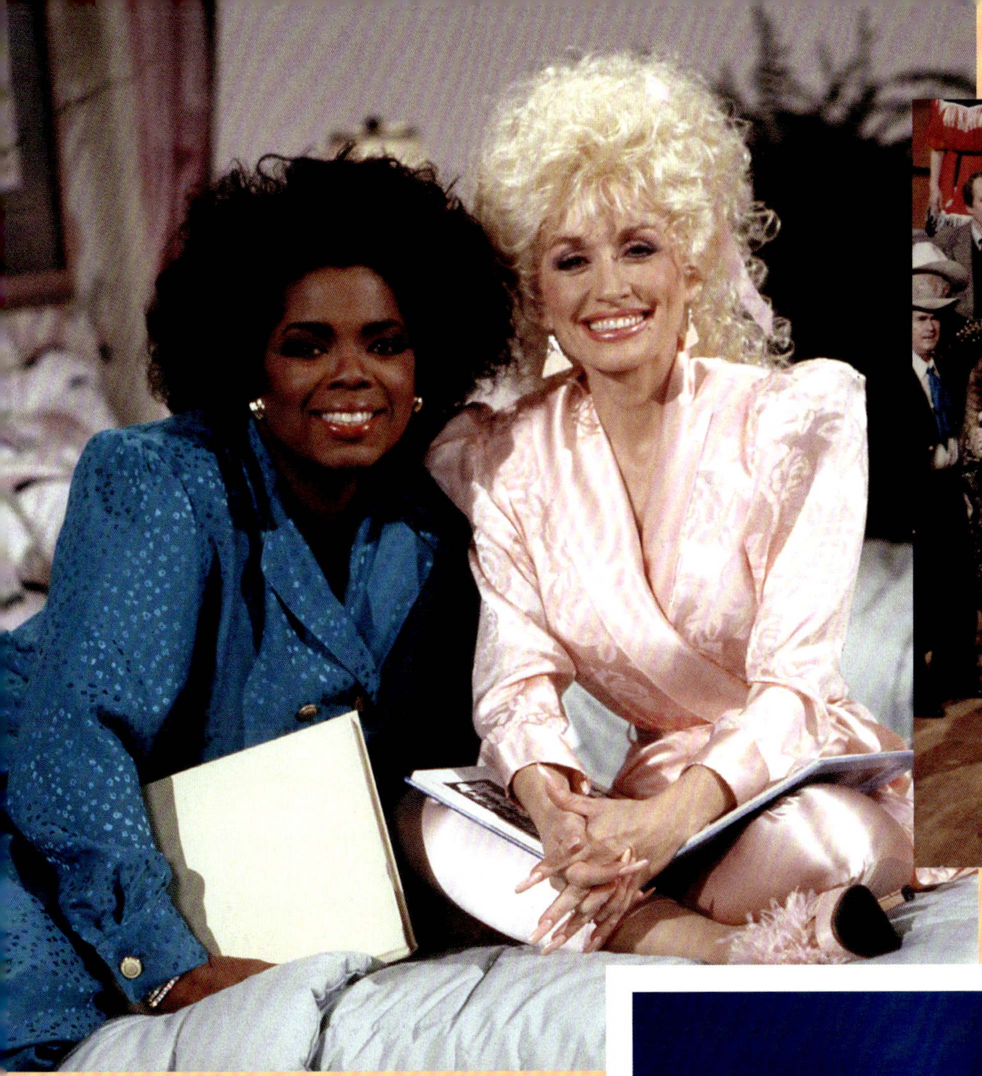

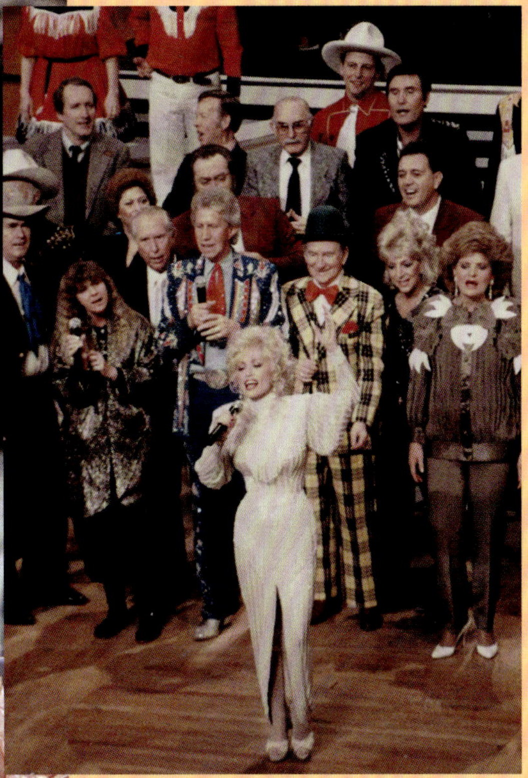

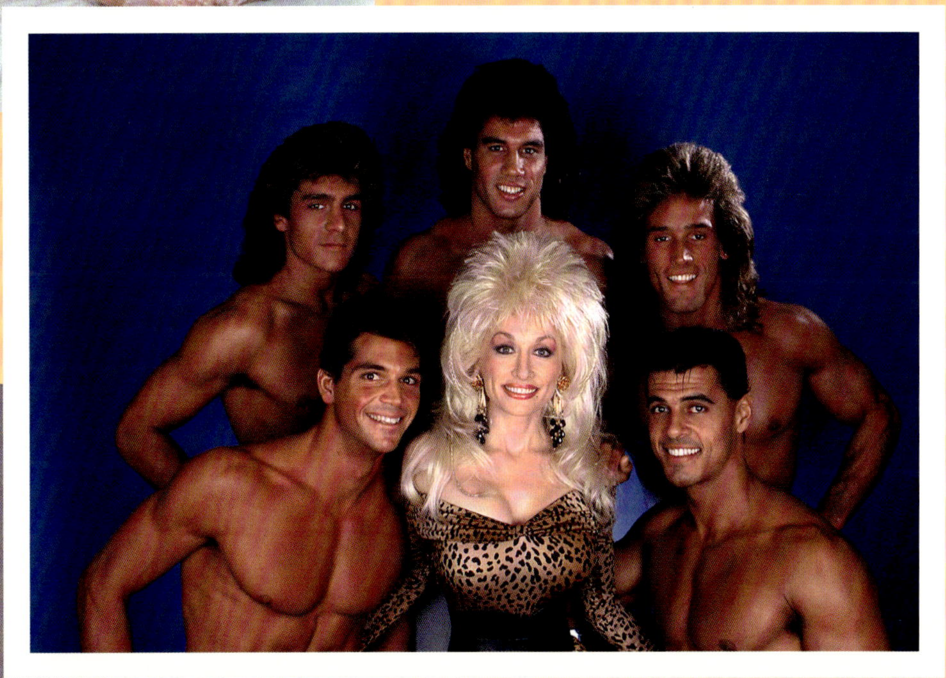

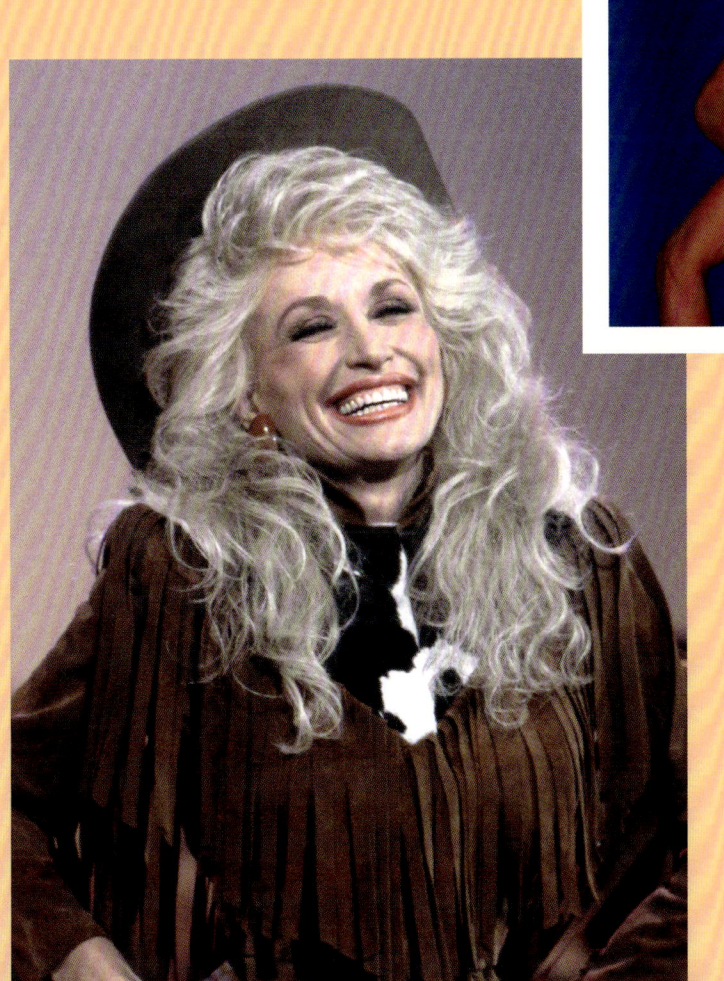

The Dolly! show on ABC went beyond music. Oprah Winfrey was a guest on one episode, my country music friends appeared, I did some acting, and I sometimes found myself surrounded by other, shall we say, "attractions" too! It was hard work, but somebody had to do it!

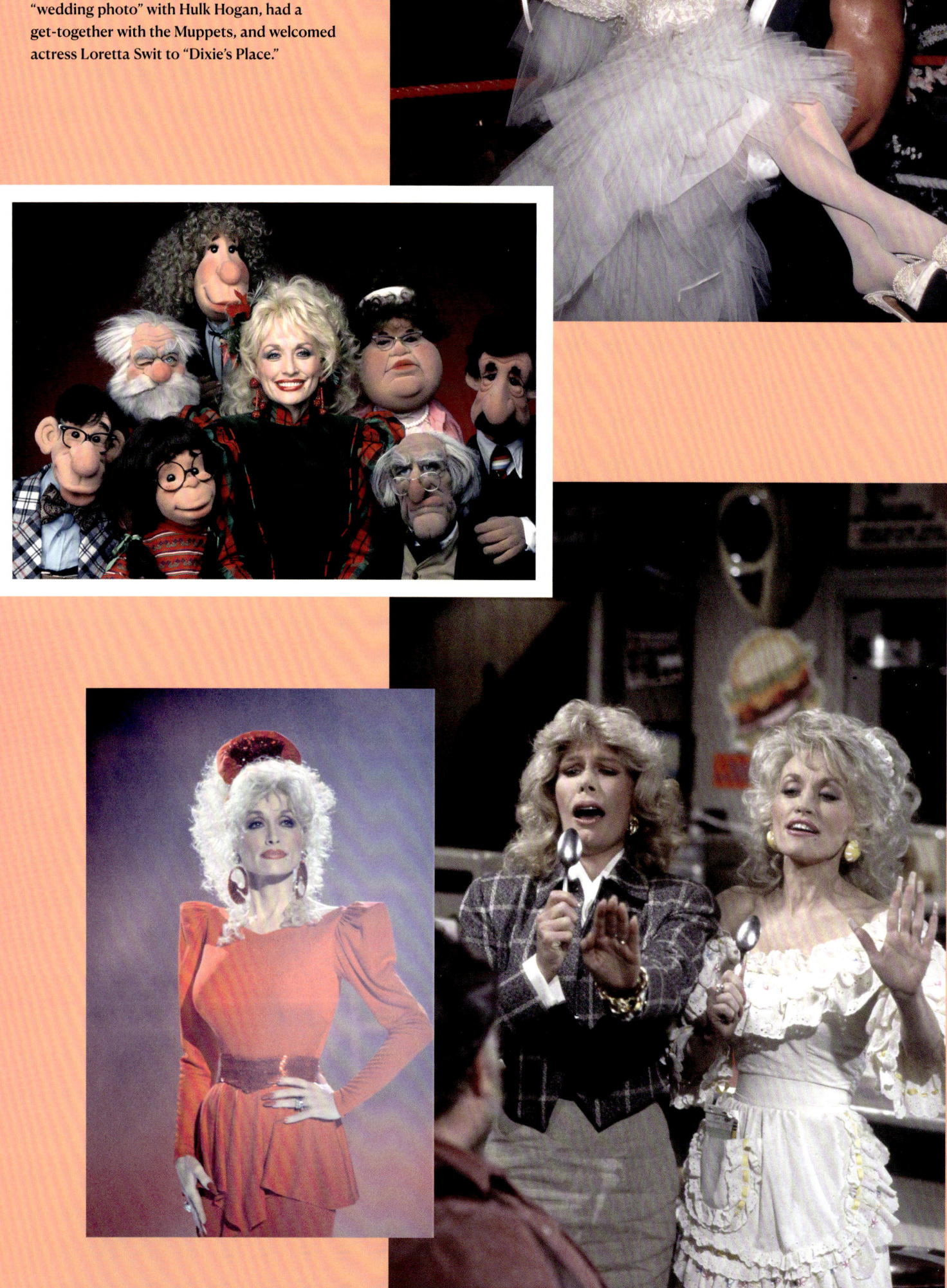

More memories of *Dolly!* I wrestled this "wedding photo" with Hulk Hogan, had a get-together with the Muppets, and welcomed actress Loretta Swit to "Dixie's Place."

Alabama visited in another episode, and Jeff Cook played banjo while we ran through Hank Williams's "I Saw the Light" in front of the fireplace. And I found a nice little harmony spot on "Mountain Music" that sounded like it was made just for me.

The most historic musical piece, of course, came when we took *Dolly!* to Nashville, and Porter Wagoner and I reunited on the stage of the Grand Ole Opry House. Porter wore a lavender rhinestone suit with a pink shirt, and we laughed our way through "The Last Thing on My Mind," "Holding On to Nothin,'" and "Daddy Was an Old-Time Preacher Man." We had our arms around each other's backs. And when we forgot the words to "Holding On to Nothin,'" we knew just how to get through it. We'd recovered from messed-up lyrics on plenty of occasions over the years—it was just like old times.

There were other musical surprises on *Dolly!* that I don't think anyone expected. Patti LaBelle visited for one show, and we sang a gospel song with a big choir behind us. The song was "Up Above My Head"—very appropriate since Patti and I both had some big, big hair above our heads. It was the '80s, after all!

One of my favorite performances came in the form of a Motown medley. The Temptations wore gold suits, Smokey Robinson showed up in a rhinestone tuxedo, and Barbara Mandrell got tuxed up too. There I was on "My Guy" with The Temptations as my backing vocal group, singing harmony with Smokey on "Ooo Baby Baby," and trading lead vocals with Barbara, Smokey, and The Temptations' Dennis Edwards on "I'm Gonna Make You Love Me."

In one of the last episodes, I made sure to do a version of "Star of the Show." It'd been released as a single in a few other countries but not in the States. It was an up-tempo song with a disco bass and a fun chorus on my 1979 album *Great Balls of Fire,* and I sang it at concerts the year that album came out. It was a perfect song to use on *Dolly!* to introduce the show's Rainbow Band: fiddler Tom Rutledge, guitarist Steve Watson, steel guitarist Al Perkins, bass player Dennis Belfield, piano player Gary Smith, keyboard player Steve Goldstein, drummer Paul Leim, and Richard Dennison on background vocals. It seemed appropriate to spotlight it on prime time.

But midway through the season, I could tell the tug of war with producers and executives about what type of show I should be doing just wasn't going to reach a mutual resolution. I was uneasy singing songs like "Someone to Watch Over Me" with a fog machine, or lounging in a bubble bath looking like I was naked. It never quite aligned with what I knew in my heart audiences wanted to see. The show wasn't renewed for a second season, but I learned a lot about the control I'd need to have in the future if I wanted to ensure my creative vision would be a success on the TV screen.

I also learned how important it was to have the right managers and lawyers negotiating on my behalf. Even though ABC didn't give us a second season, they had to pay me the full deal we'd negotiated!

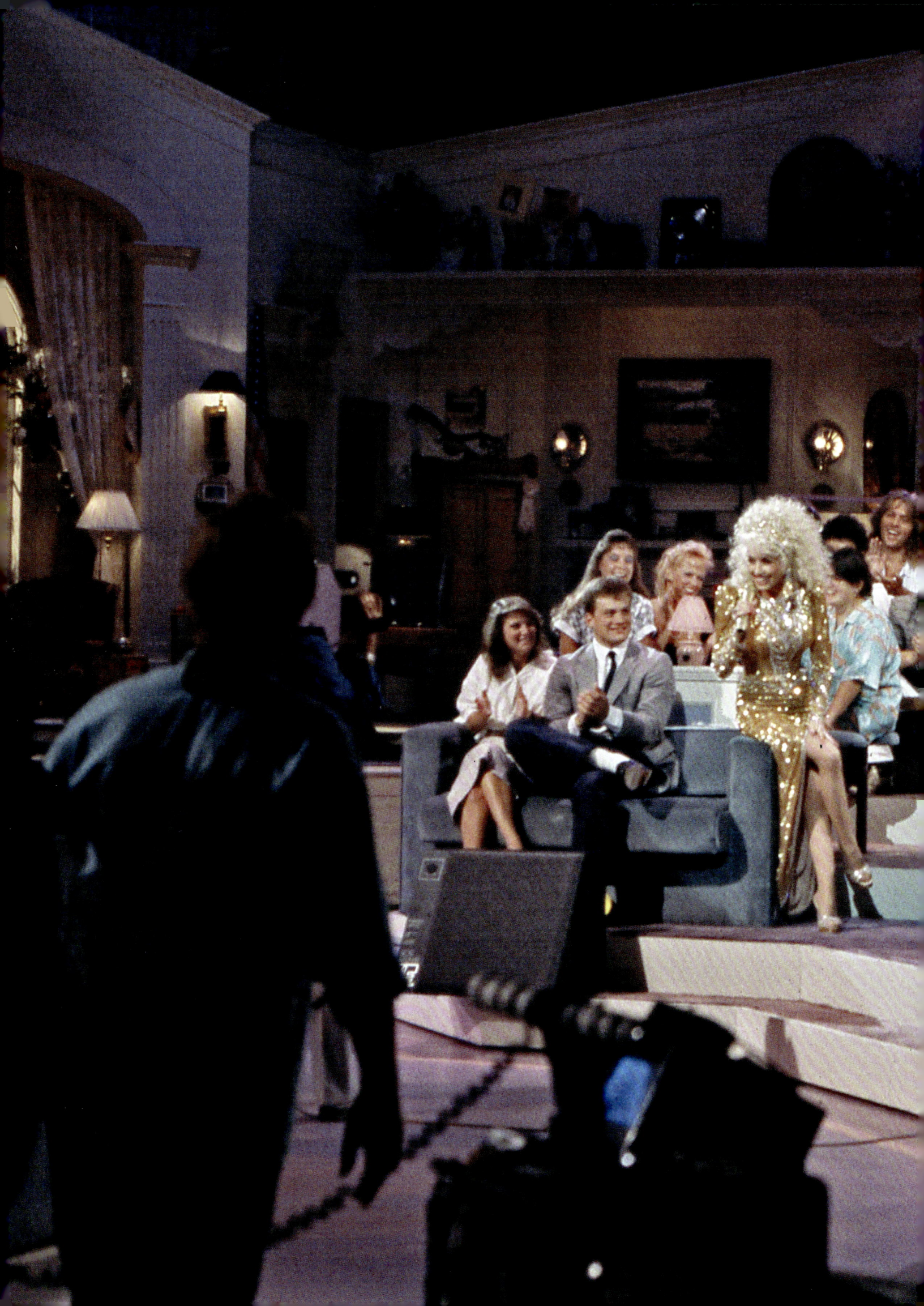

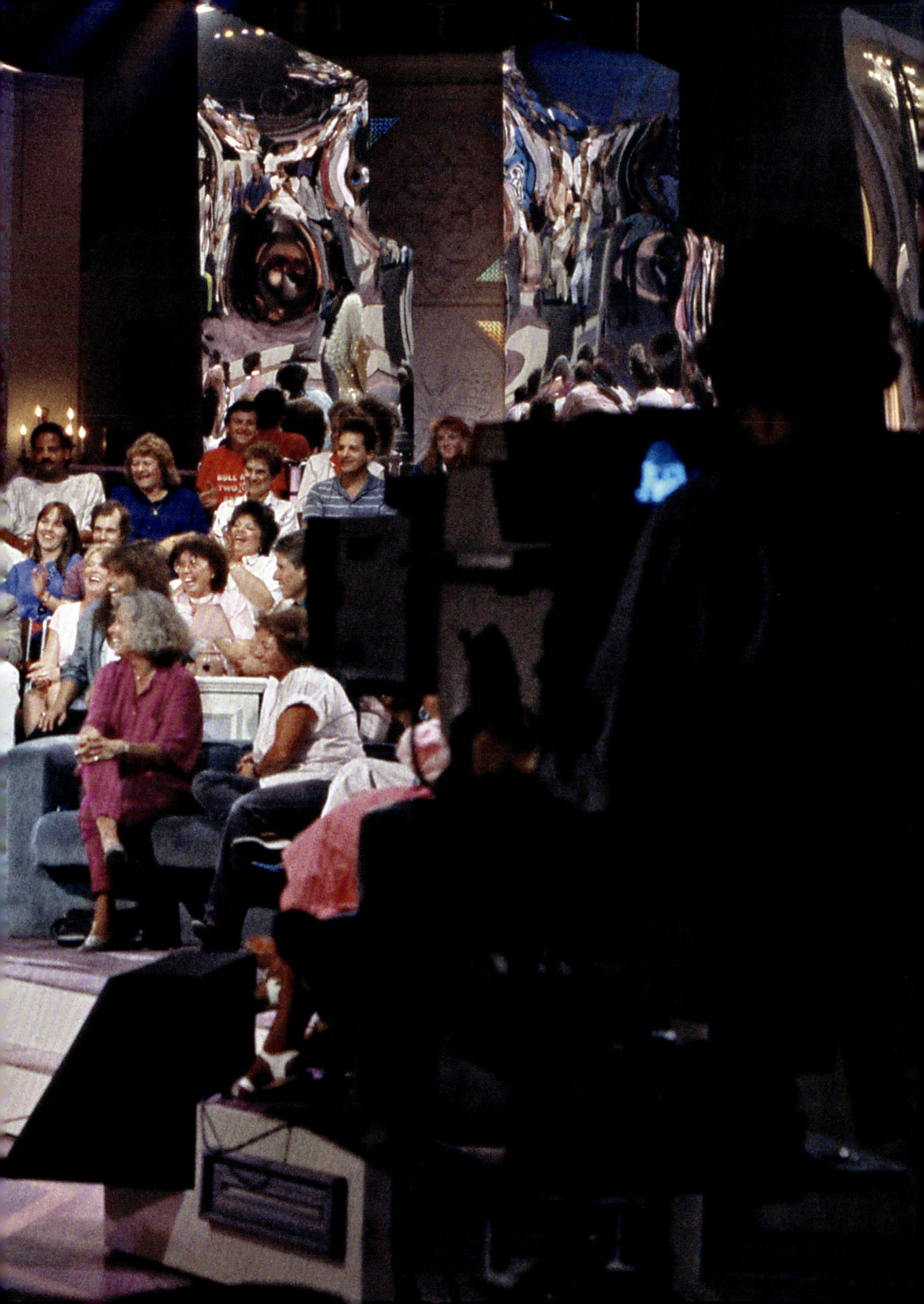

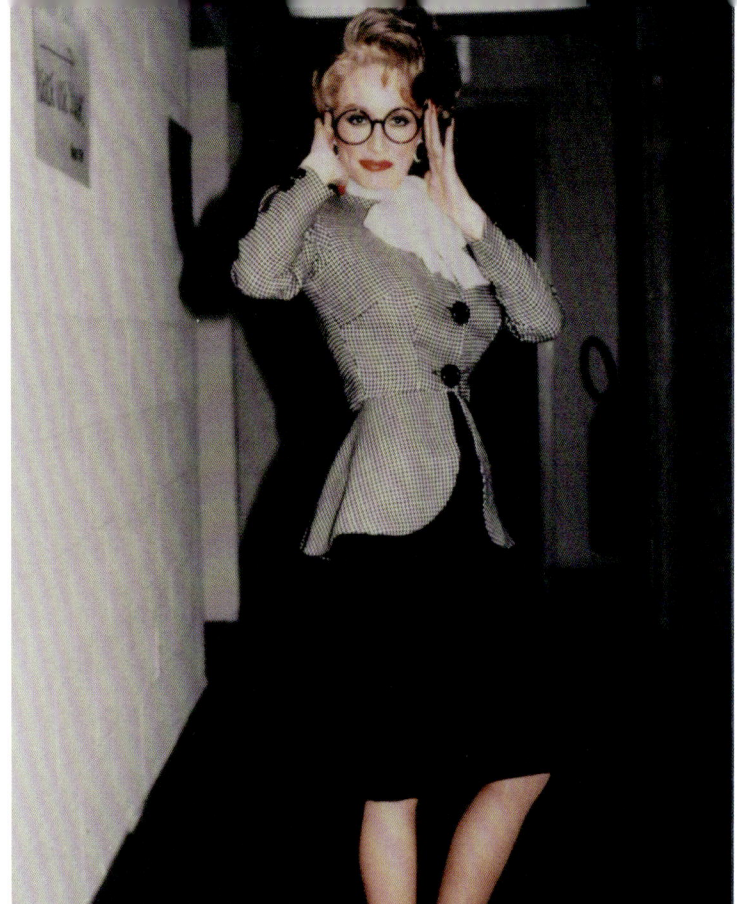

I had a lot of fun playing a teacher who taught foreign exchange students Southern-style English on my ABC series *Dolly!*

Now, understand, what I do is not about the money. It's about quality—the quality of the music; the quality of the work; the quality of the experience for the people who listen, watch, or buy a ticket and come to a show. I've always tried to say that to everybody I work with: Money's good. I want it. I need it. We all need it. But there are times when I'm not willing to sacrifice integrity and all the other things that I'd like to believe I'm about just for a dollar. I was even more adamant about that after my variety show ended.

After the whole *Dolly!* experience, it was nice to return to Dollywood. In spring 1988, when Dollywood opened for the season, we also christened a new Celebrity Theater in the park. Mickey Gilley opened for me at the first concert, and the next night, Ronnie Milsap joined me.

Filming for *Steel Magnolias* started that summer in Natchitoches, Louisiana, and I spent about three months with Julia Roberts, Shirley MacLaine, Olympia Dukakis, Daryl Hannah, and Sally Field. I had great fun with all those women. I kept saying, "The only thing I hope is we're not all PMSin' at the same time because we could kill each other!" But we got along great because we were professional women, we were grown women, and we knew what it was like to make it on our own. They had worked as hard as I had trying to get to where they were, and we all shared a mutual respect for one another.

Star of the Show

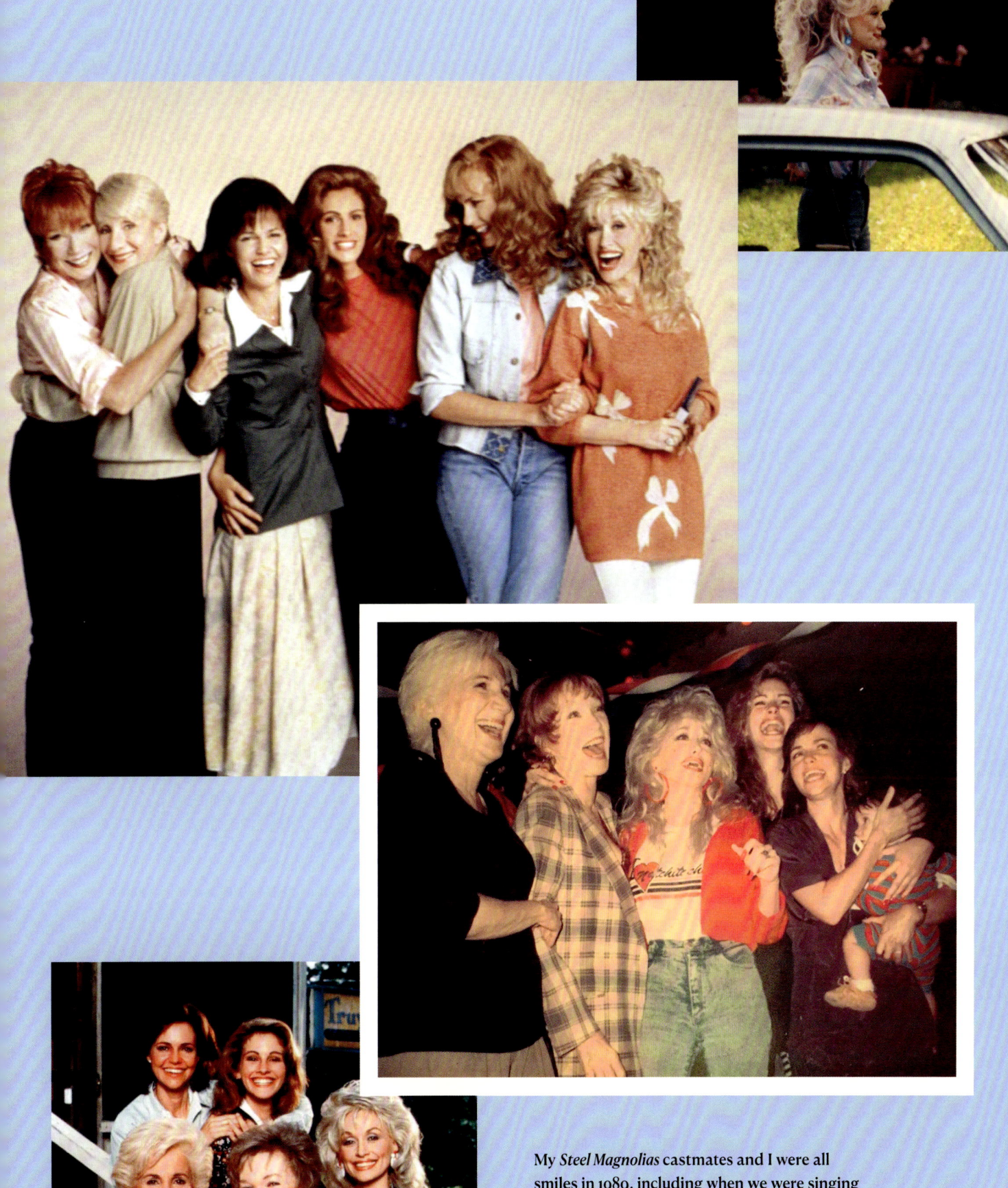

My *Steel Magnolias* castmates and I were all smiles in 1989, including when we were singing at the Northwestern Louisiana State football game in Natchitoches (middle), when I was between takes (top right), and when we were in character for studio publicity photos (top left and bottom left).

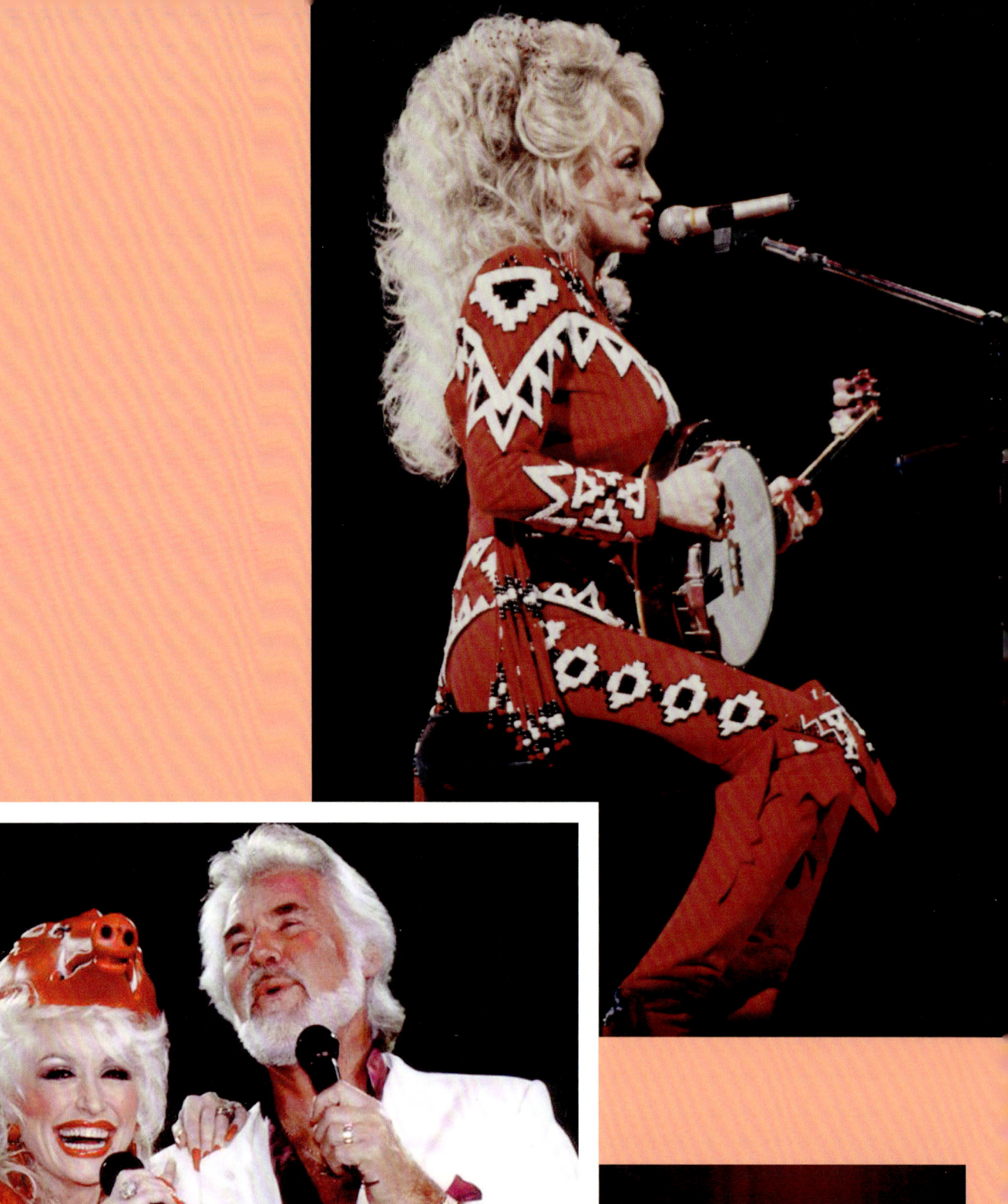

More good times on stage. *Top:* A scene from the White Limozeen Tour in 1989. *Middle:* I'm sporting an Arkansas Razorbacks mask that I surprised Kenny with at a 1990 show in Little Rock. *Bottom:* A mid-song shot from the 1993 Slow Dancing with the Moon Tour.

We also appreciated the fact that, as was the case in *9 to 5*, women were getting to do some things like this together as a community. Not to be anti-men or anything. It's just that it was a story about a mother and her daughter—M'Lynn, played by Sally Field, and Shelby, played by Julia Roberts—and it was a real-life story. It was about Robert Harling's mother and his sister, who died, just like in the movie, from complications of diabetes. So much of what happened in the film was true, and so real. And we got to bring it to life through the eyes of these wonderful women we all got to play.

The town made us all feel welcome, though it took a few weeks for them to get used to us. After all, it was Small Town, Louisiana, and here we were—a bunch of Hollywood stars and a country singer from Nashville—descending on their community and playing to the cameras on their streets and lawns and parks. The first day that I moved into a house on Parkway Drive, near the Cane River, traffic picked up on the street and a boater on the river puttered up near the house to wave. I don't think the boater meant anything bad by it, but I do need my privacy for security reasons, so I found a more secluded place to stay while we were filming. In short order, the townspeople got used to us, I think.

A local football team, the Northwestern State Demons, had their season-opening football game on Labor Day weekend, and the marching band planned to do a Dolly song for its halftime show. Ever since playing drums at football games when I was in high school, I've had a soft spot for a marching band, and when rain shut down filming for a few days, it gave us a chance to pull away from the long hours on the set. So I agreed to perform "9 to 5" with the marching band, and the whole cast made a night of it. The crowd chanted "Doll-y, Doll-y"—you'd think I'd scored a touchdown or something! The *Steel Magnolias* girls might have actually been good luck. Northwestern State won, as I recall.

That was a welcome break from the routine. We would work all day on the movie, but when we'd leave the set, there were just a couple of restaurants in town. The people were wonderful, and the food was good. It's just that it's not like Hollywood or New York, where you have a lot of options for bars or fine restaurants. We were there for three months, so anytime we got to do anything that was fun or out of the ordinary, like go to that football game, it was a nice change of pace. The people there loved us, and we loved them. And I think all of us have great memories of doing that movie—I know I sure do.

When production on the movie ended, I finished the year with more Kenny Rogers tour dates while also recording an album with Ricky Skaggs as producer. The project was *White Limozeen*. I cowrote the title track with my buddy Mac Davis, and it became the name of my next tour. To bring attention to it, I was the host and musical guest on *Saturday Night Live*—one of the earliest artists to get to pull that double duty on the show. I was happy to poke fun at myself in the monologue—heck, that's what I do—but I did tell Lorne Michaels that there were two things I wouldn't do: I wouldn't cuss, and I wouldn't make fun of Jesus.

Even though I understood the day-to-day stuff of TV by now—the cameras, the scripts, hitting your mark—*SNL* was not easy for me. I was going to host the show and be the

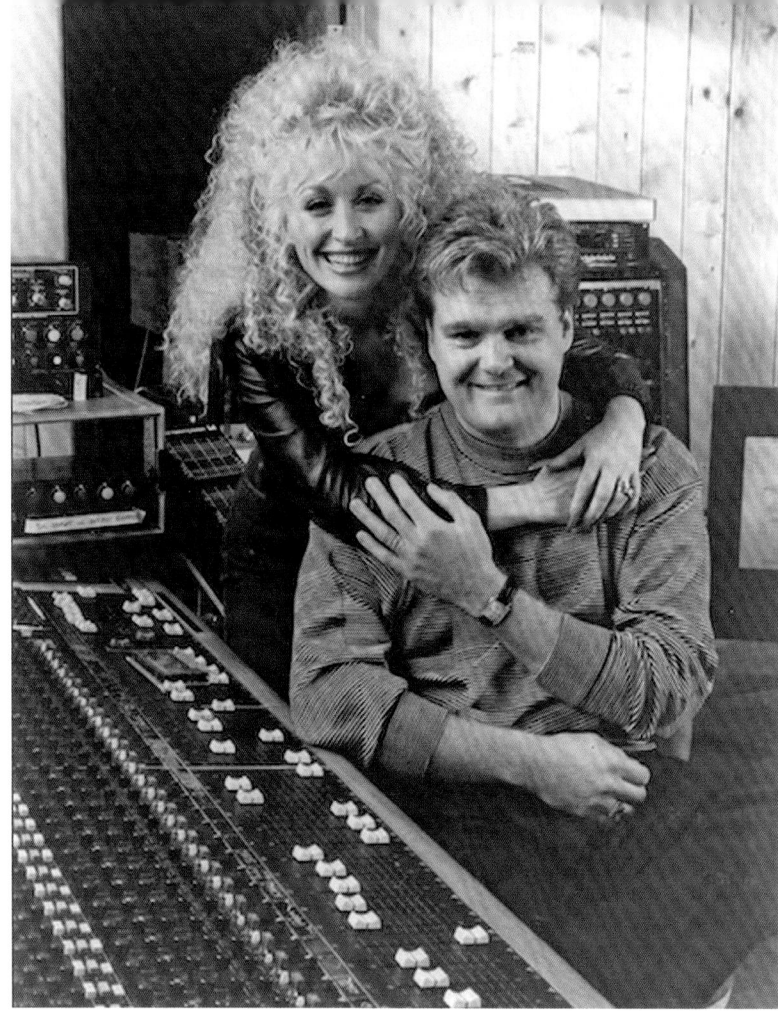

Ricky Skaggs produced my 1989 album, *White Limozeen*, and we had a lot of fun making it.

musical guest, and Tony Chase, who was my designer at the time, insisted that I have a different outfit for every song, and then I also had to change into outfits for the skits that we were doing.

The band was uncomfortable too. I had assembled a whole new group of musicians, the Mighty Fine Band, for the White Limozeen Tour, and this would be their first time playing together publicly. On national TV. In front of millions of people. Several of the musicians had never been to New York before, and after we rehearsed our musical numbers, they had three days to explore the city. They went to the Empire State Building and Central Park and a famous music store—and I went to work!

Appearing on *SNL* was the hardest job I have ever had in my life, and I've always said I'll never do that again. I will host, or I will go on as a musical guest, and then I might do a skit or something. But that week of preparing for both just about killed me—we'd rehearse everything, then they'd change the script or swap out an entire skit, and we'd rehearse all over again. I was exhausted by the end of that week when it was finally time for the show!

Adding a little extra stress, the band got new clothes for that show, but their outfits barely arrived in time. Most of the clothes didn't fit, but nobody watching knew the difference

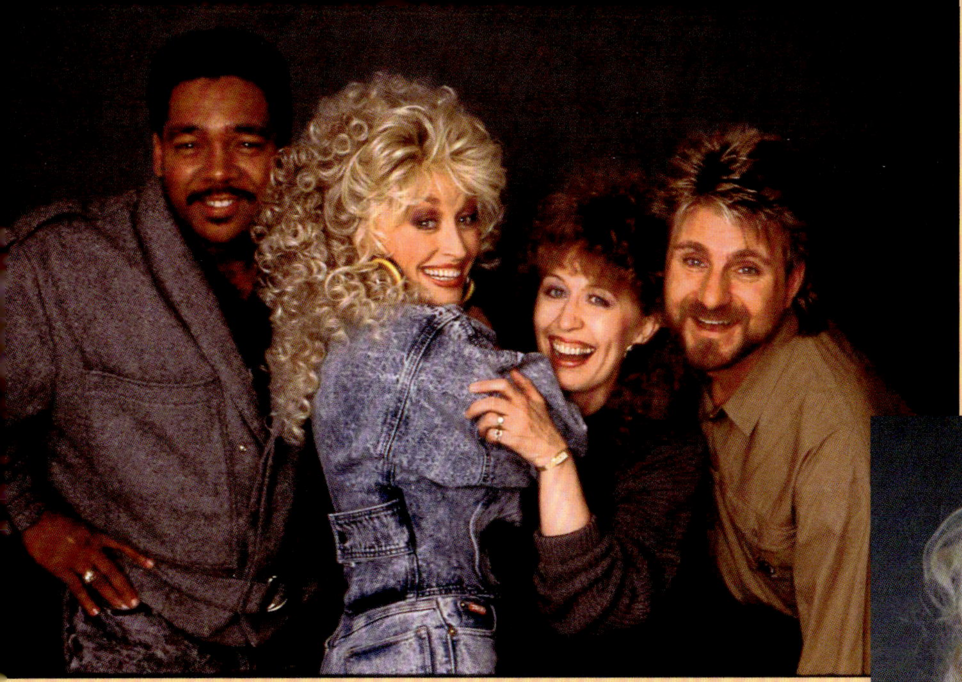

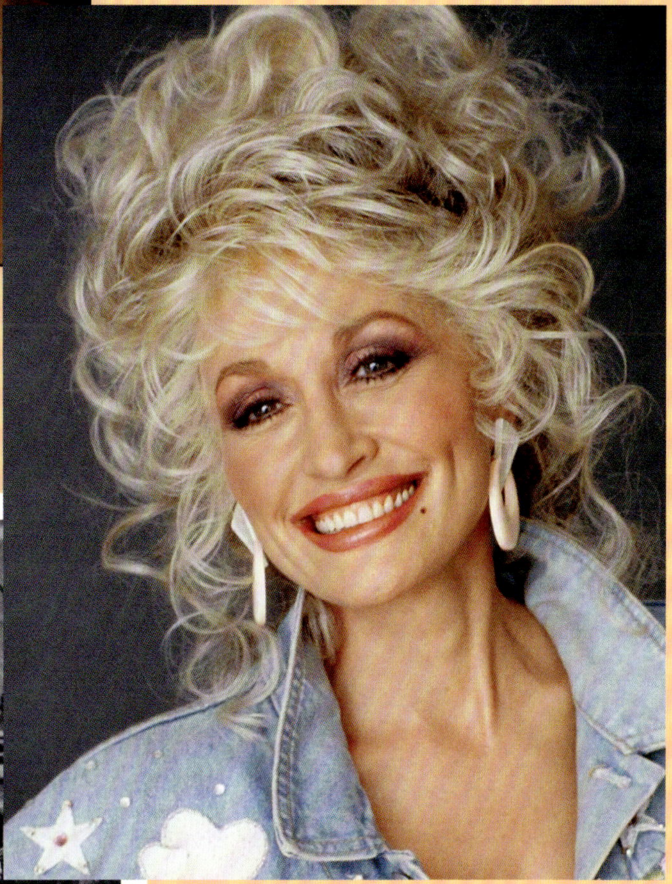

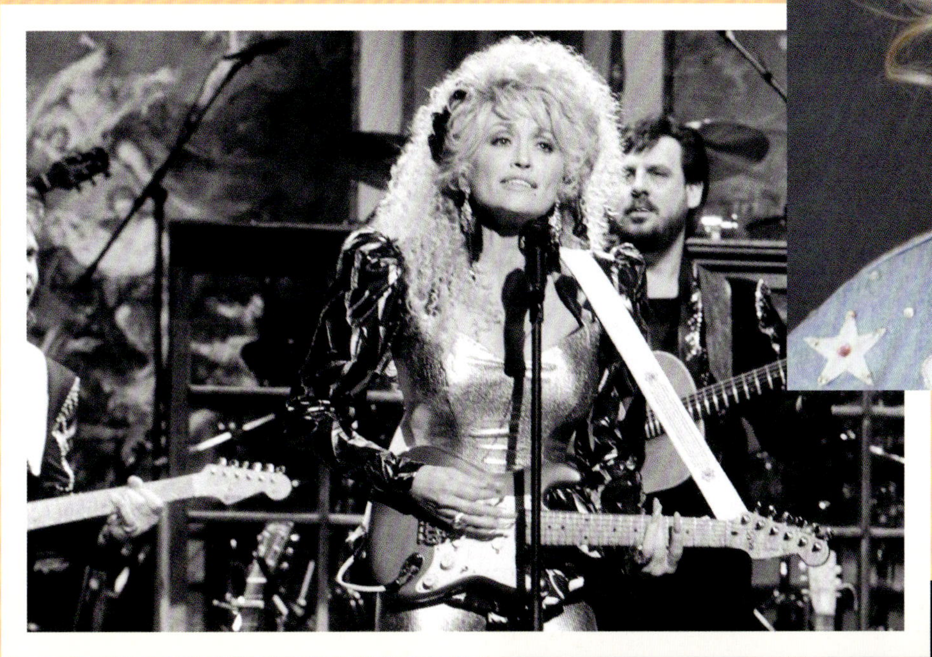

I sang "Why'd You Come in Here Lookin' Like That" and "White Limozeen" as host and musical guest on NBC's *Saturday Night Live*. *At the top:* With my backing vocal group, including Howard Smith, Jennifer O'Brien, and Richard Dennison. *Bottom:* Telling tongue-in-cheek tales about growing up in a skit called "Mountain Stories," with (from left) Dennis Miller, Nora Dunn, Phil Hartman, Dana Carvey, me, and Kevin Nealon.

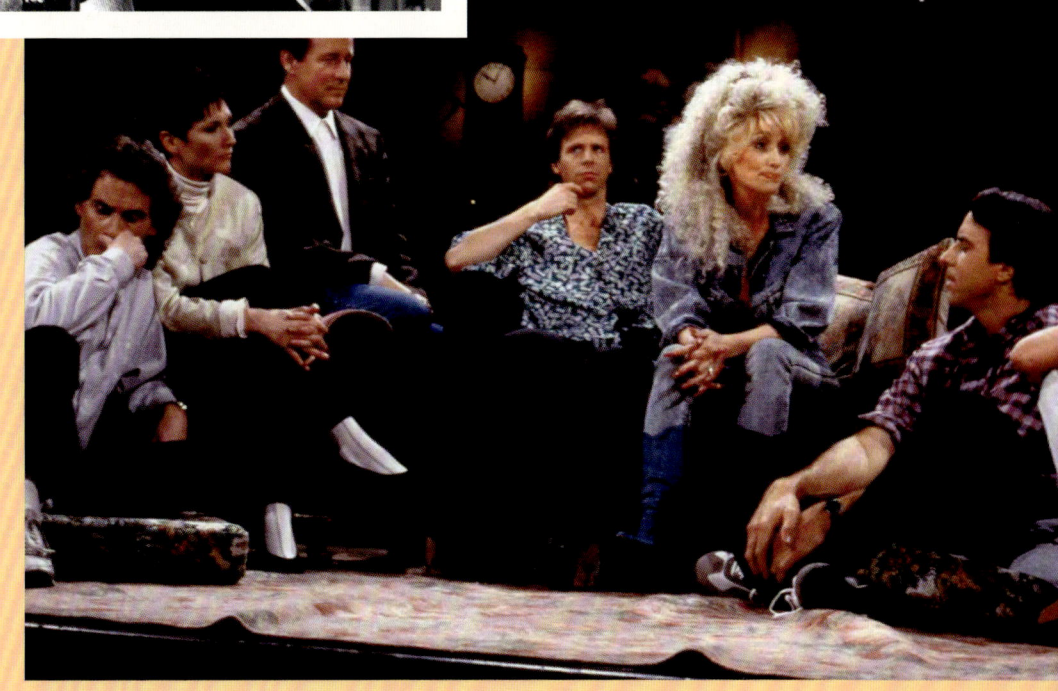

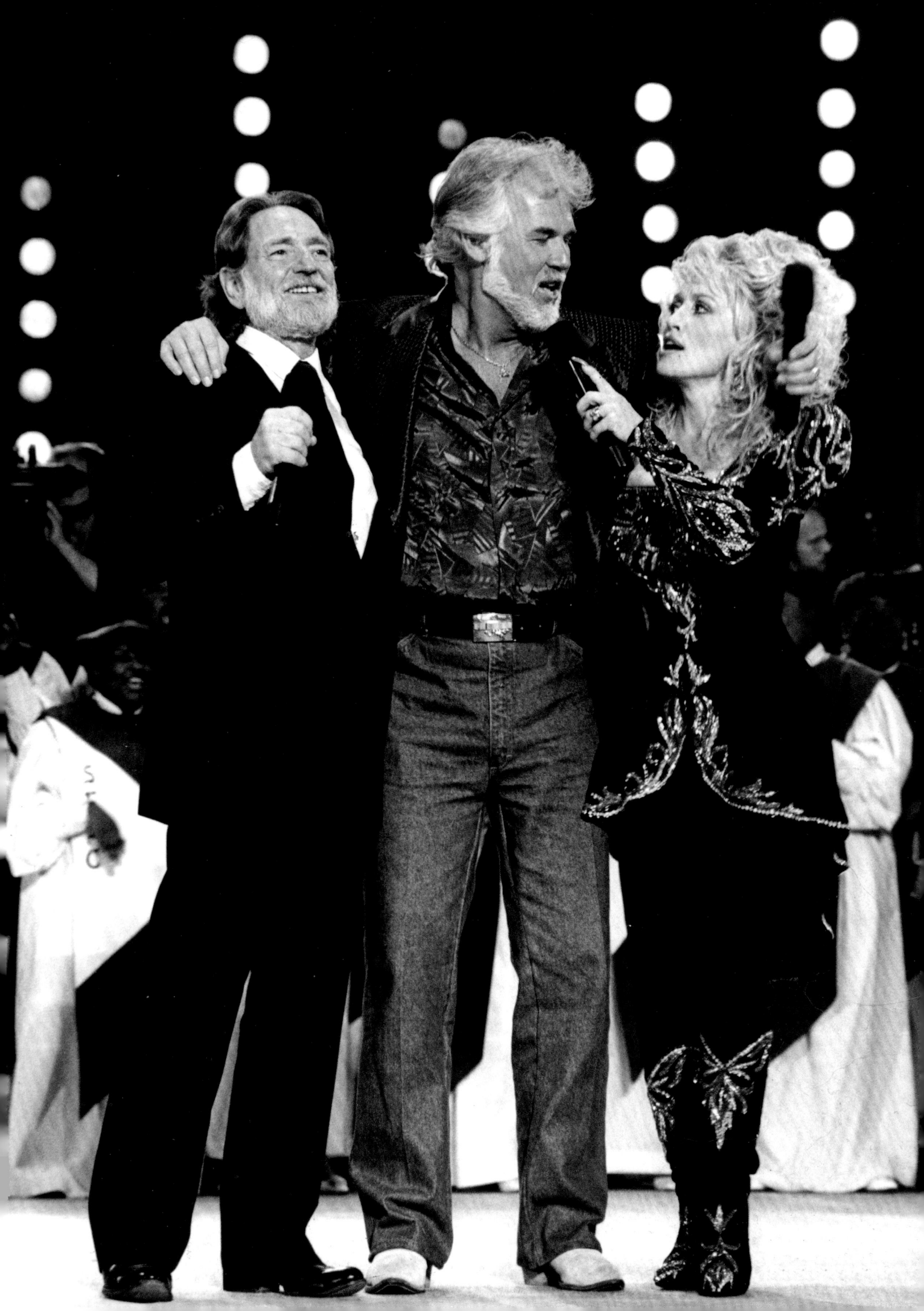

because it wasn't about the band's look. It was more important that the sound be good, and they pulled it off in fine fashion—or, to be specific, Mighty Fine fashion. I sang "Why'd You Come in Here Lookin' Like That" and "White Limozeen," and the fact that we did it well in a high-pressure situation brought our little entourage together. Most of those musicians still work with me today.

I did more television to promote *White Limozeen*, which critics billed as my return to country music more than just about any other project. I didn't feel like I'd ever stopped making country music, but . . . the bottom line is, it worked! Two of the singles went to no. 1, and the album was certified gold.

Two weeks later, Porter Wagoner joined me for a pair of concerts at the start of the new season at Dollywood. And then I teamed up with Kenny and Willie Nelson for a concert at the Johnson Space Center in Houston that was shot for a TV special, *Kenny, Dolly, and Willie: Something Inside So Strong*. It was such a big deal that Willie even wore a tie! We started off with a group version of "Lean on Me," and Willie and I sang "Coat of Many Colors" as a duet. All three of us pulled up stools to the edge of the stage and did parts of several of our songs: "Mammas Don't Let Your Babies Grow Up to Be Cowboys," "Sweet Music Man," "On the Road Again," "Two Doors Down," and "Real Love." One of the best parts about that segment was hearing very distinct artists singing other people's songs. Even though we only did maybe a verse and a chorus, each of us sang our friends' songs a little differently than they'd been sung before. It's kind of how you know somebody's a unique artist: they can take someone else's familiar song and put their own stamp on it.

That summer's White Limozeen Tour was one of my favorites. I spent a lot of time on the bus seeing the country, I was proud of the album I was promoting, and after all the time on movie sets and TV stages, it was great to be out there, just me, one-on-one with the fans. We did sort of a '50s rock 'n' roll segment in the concerts: "To Know Him Is to Love Him," "Don't Be Cruel," and "Great Balls of Fire." Kenny made a surprise appearance for "Islands in the Stream" when I played the Universal Ampitheatre in Los Angeles, and I played the Indiana State Fair with Dwight Yoakam and Clint Black. Clint actually opened a number of the shows that year, and it was exciting to see his star rise.

One of my favorite performances from my career took place on the heels of that White Limozeen Tour, and it paralleled the personal resurrection and renewed sense of purpose that I was experiencing. Carl and I had heard a song called "He's Alive" on a small radio station while we were driving from California to Nashville. The singer was a Christian artist named Don Francisco. I heard that he wrote it when he was going through a crisis and was just about to give it all up. He had gone to a hotel room and a Gideon Bible was on the table. The wind blew the Bible open, and there was a scripture that saved his life. It seems he had a spiritual experience where he realized that Jesus is a God of love, not hate. And because of that, Don was freed from a lot of his pain. And he wrote that song.

Don channeled his own sense of joy and renewal into the story of the Crucifixion and the empty tomb, and after I heard "He's Alive," I looked for an opportunity to record it.

I included it on *White Limozeen,* and though it wasn't even a single, I wanted to do it on the Country Music Association Awards show. But the producers didn't want me to sing it that night. I guess they thought it was too religious or too serious or too whatever—I don't know, but it was sort of like "The Bridge" on *The Porter Wagoner Show.* I thought, *If I'm going to sing on the show, I'm going to sing this song.* Ultimately, they did allow me to perform it on the awards show. I got to do the full five-minute version, and I completely felt the passion in the song's story while I sang it alone on the big stage at the Grand Ole Opry House.

I had a spiritual encounter that night. When I was singing "He's Alive," I was thinking about Jesus and the Crucifixion and just living that story in my mind. And that, in itself, was powerful.

But then there was an even bigger moment waiting. Jennifer O'Brien, who was one of my new singers in the Mighty Fine Band, was a member of the Christ Church Choir in Nashville, and she helped me enlist the choir for the performance. When we hit the big chorus, a proscenium lifted up and more than fifty singers were revealed in forest-green robes with yellow trim. Even though we'd rehearsed it, and I knew what was coming, I still felt chills as their voices filled the space behind me and they slowly walked forward, echoing the power and the majesty—and, most of all, the grace—in that beautiful song.

I honestly felt my spirit lifted. I felt like I was not even standing on the floor. I will always treasure that I experienced so much spiritual power in that moment—more than in anything I'd ever done before. It's really hard to describe, even to this day.

The audience, of course, didn't know the choir was coming, and I think they were all stunned for a few seconds as they sat there in their fancy clothes, but about halfway into the next chorus, the applause started right there in the middle of the song. It ended with me in my snow-white evening gown, hands held toward the sky, and all those famous cowboys stood up in appreciation. I remember one man—I think it was Little Jimmy Dickens—wiping away his tears right there on national television. To this day, the video of that performance gets reposted by people around Easter every year.

I started doing "He's Alive" in the encore every night for a period right after that.

During 1990, Kenny and I launched a North American tour, An Evening with Kenny & Dolly, that saw us hit arenas, state fairs, and casinos. I booked some solo dates, too, amid working on a Christmas album, filming the holiday TV special *Christmas at Home,* and doing preproduction for my follow-up country album to *White Limozeen.*

One of my favorite live appearances that year never appeared on an itinerary. I had a chance to go to Ireland, to a little place called Dingle on the Dingle Peninsula. I took a guy named Walter Hagan, who had been the vice president of special services at American Airlines. For years, he'd be the one to meet people like me before a flight, to take them into the special guest room away from the public to wait for the plane; he'd get us our tickets and everything. And I just fell in love with him. He took such good care of us. Walter reminded me so much of my daddy. He was an older man, and he had spent time in Ireland. He said, "I just wish so much that I could go back to Ireland and see where my mother was buried." I thought I would do something nice for him because he was so good to everybody. I said, "Well, let's go to Ireland." And we did—just a few of us went over there to support him.

There was truly a pub on every corner. You could go get drunk on a Saturday night and go pray on Sunday, and I used to kid Walter about that. There'd even be a shoe store where you could go in and get a drink. It was the craziest thing!

We went to Páidí Ó Sé's, a Kerry County pub about six miles outside of Dingle. The pub was named after its owner, who was famous in his country as a Gaelic football player and media personality, and when I walked in, it turned out that Páidí was a Dolly Parton fan. He gave me a green-and-yellow jersey that he had worn when Kerry won the 1985 championship game over Dublin—he said it still held the sweat from that title game!—and he asked me to sing for his customers.

Everyone was so friendly, and it turned out that they had two musicians, Steve and Seamus, who knew "Coat of Many Colors," so right there in front of one of the speakers, I sang an off-the-cuff version with them and had the audience join me for one last chorus. And even though it wasn't really my theme park, I welcomed everyone to "Dinglewood."

When I got back to the States, I had that green-and-yellow jersey framed. I don't know anything about Gaelic football, but I was touched that Páidí had gifted me that memorabilia from his own life, and I've had it in my house all these years. That's how special that moment was.

While I performed a few shows on the road in 1991, much of that year found me in front of the cameras. I was all over television promoting my *Eagle When She Flies* album and filming the TV movie *Wild Texas Wind*. I also filmed another movie, *Straight Talk*, where I played an unconventional Chicago talk radio host, Dr. Shirlee. I made another CMA Awards appearance, performing "Eagle When She Flies," a song I had originally written for *Steel Magnolias*, though the director had decided against using it. That year, President George H. W. Bush became the first—and, so far, the only—commander in chief to attend the CMAs, and he sat right there in the front row. No pressure, right? It was an honor to sing for a president, but I dedicated the song that night to First Lady Barbara Bush: "And she's a sparrow when she's broken / But she's an eagle when she flies."

To promote the 1992 release of *Straight Talk,* I launched a tour of the same name and gave it to the audience straight—and pointed! Madonna had incorporated a cone bra into her wardrobe on the Blonde Ambition Tour in 1990, and this blonde had her own ambition to have fun with that! As I've always said, I don't believe that less is more—*more* is more! And my brassiere was bigger and pointier than Madonna's. And just to make sure everyone was in on the joke, I sang a little of "Like a Virgin" in that bit too. It was actually part of a long segment—like twenty minutes—where we explored the history of music. I had Jimmy Mattingly, our fiddler, do a send-up of Billy Ray Cyrus's "Achy Breaky Heart." To this day, Jimmy remembers being extremely embarrassed when he went to the front of the stage and shook his pelvis and realized that Elizabeth Taylor and Liza Minnelli were right in front of him!

From Hollywood to Dollywood

TOUR MERCH
Through the Years

When you experience a special moment in life, you want to find a way to remember it forever—I know I do! And that's the case when you attend a concert. If you want to hang on to a souvenir of some sort, it used to be that you at least had your ticket stub. But somewhere along the way, someone came up with the idea of offering something more—and I'm glad they did. Tour merchandise gave me and my team another way to be creative, to have fun, and to come up with ways—beyond the great show we knew we were going to give—to provide people another means of remembering the experience and the event. And boy did we come up with some good ones! Between all our shows and all our tours, there must be enough of these items to fill a museum all their own!

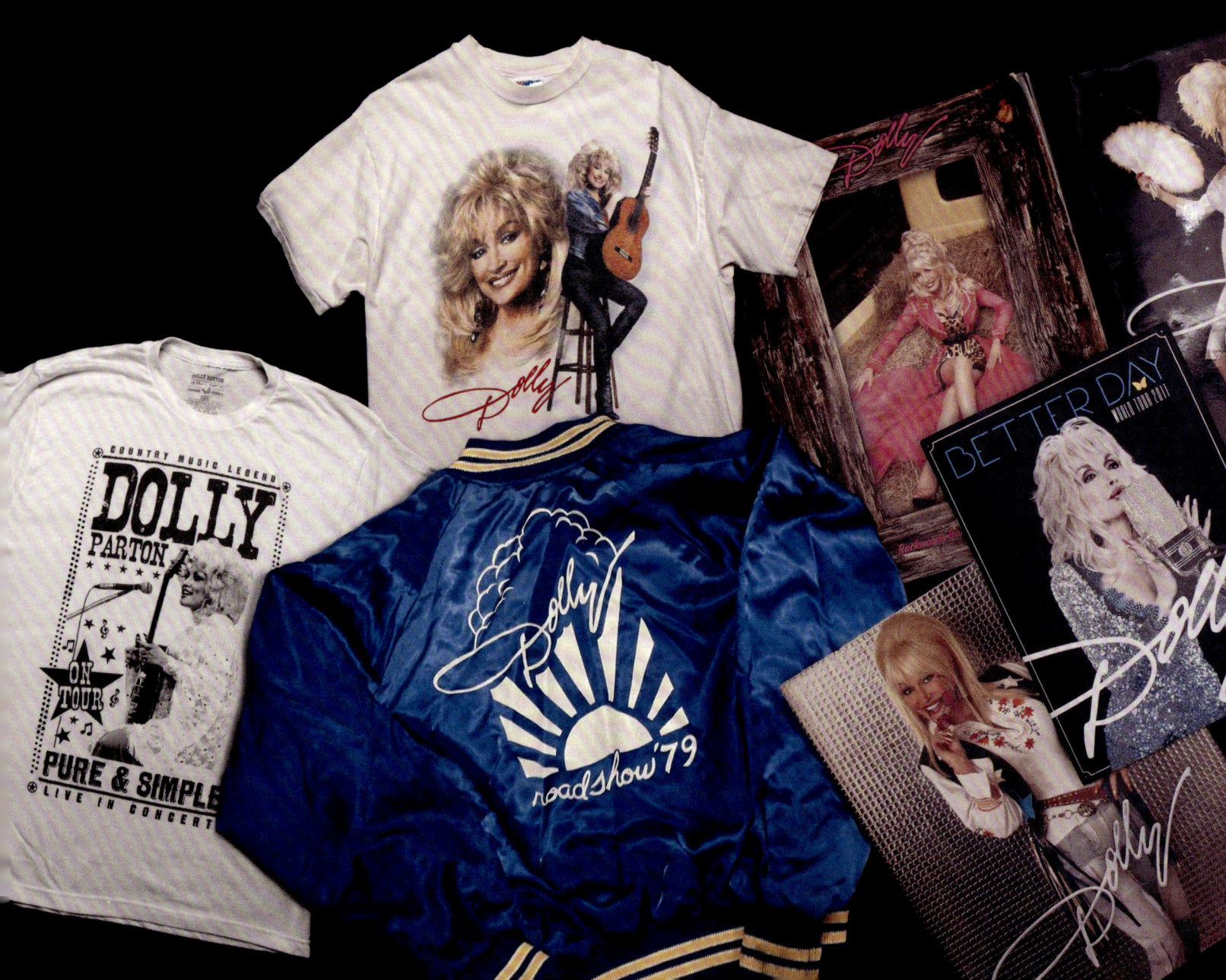

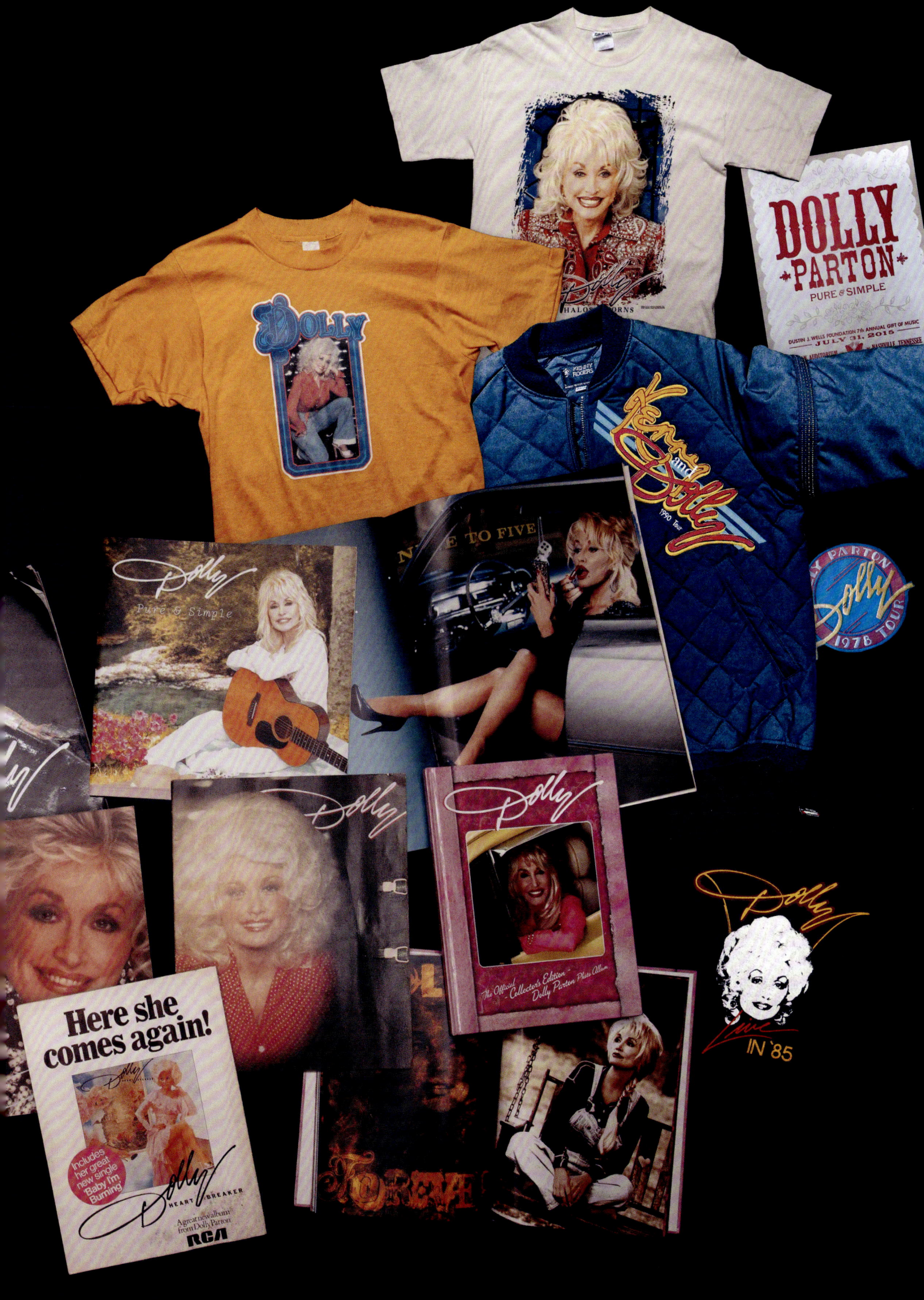

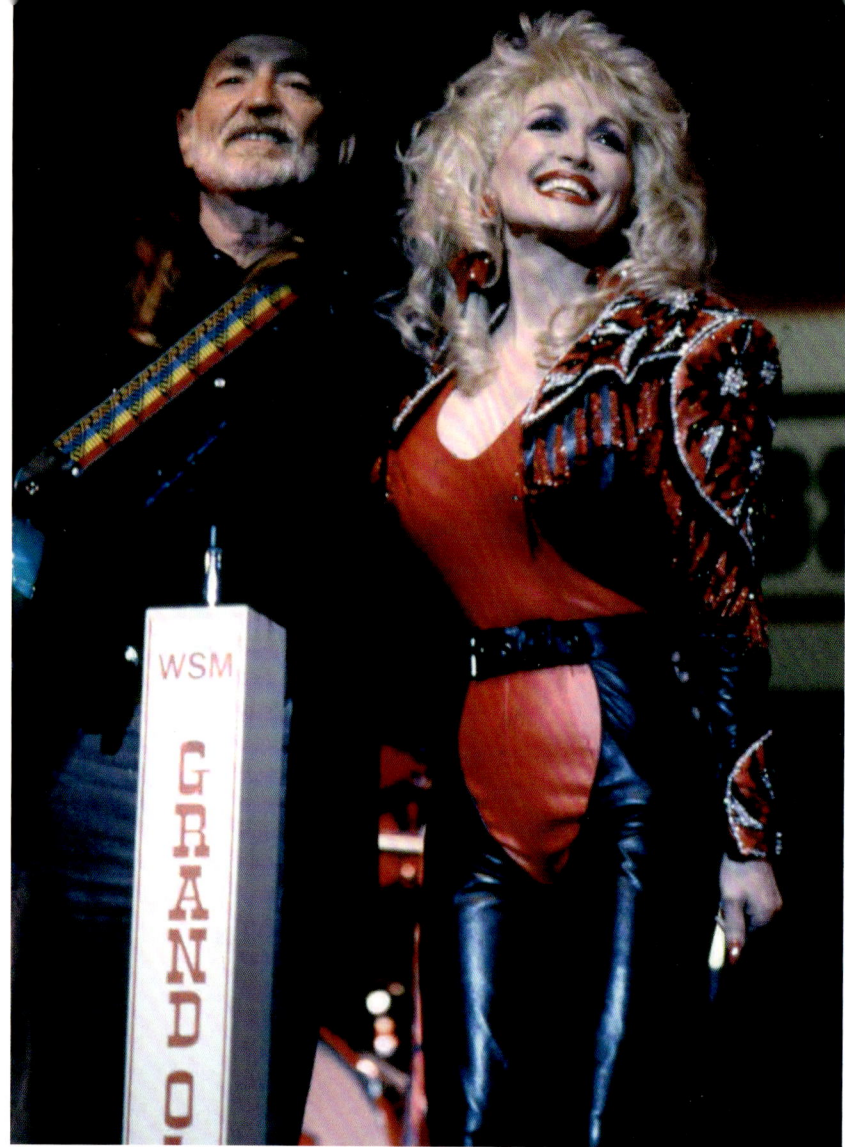

Who doesn't love and appreciate Willie Nelson?!
He's one of a kind!

We had one of my background singers, Howard Smith, dangle some beads on a pair of sunglasses to approximate Stevie Wonder. And I had my two female singers, Jennifer O'Brien and Vicki Hampton, join me near the end to do "He's a Rebel," a 1960s hit by the girl group The Crystals.

Little did I know that another pop star was going to change my life by the end of that year. Whitney Houston did a dramatic version of "I Will Always Love You" for the film *The Bodyguard*. I didn't even recognize it at first when I heard it on the radio! But since I had written it by myself and owned all the publishing rights, the sales and the radio airplay of Whitney's version created a huge windfall. I was also proud to present Whitney with a Grammy for her rendition in 1994. I've said it many times—I will always love Whitney and what she did with my little song.

Star of the Show

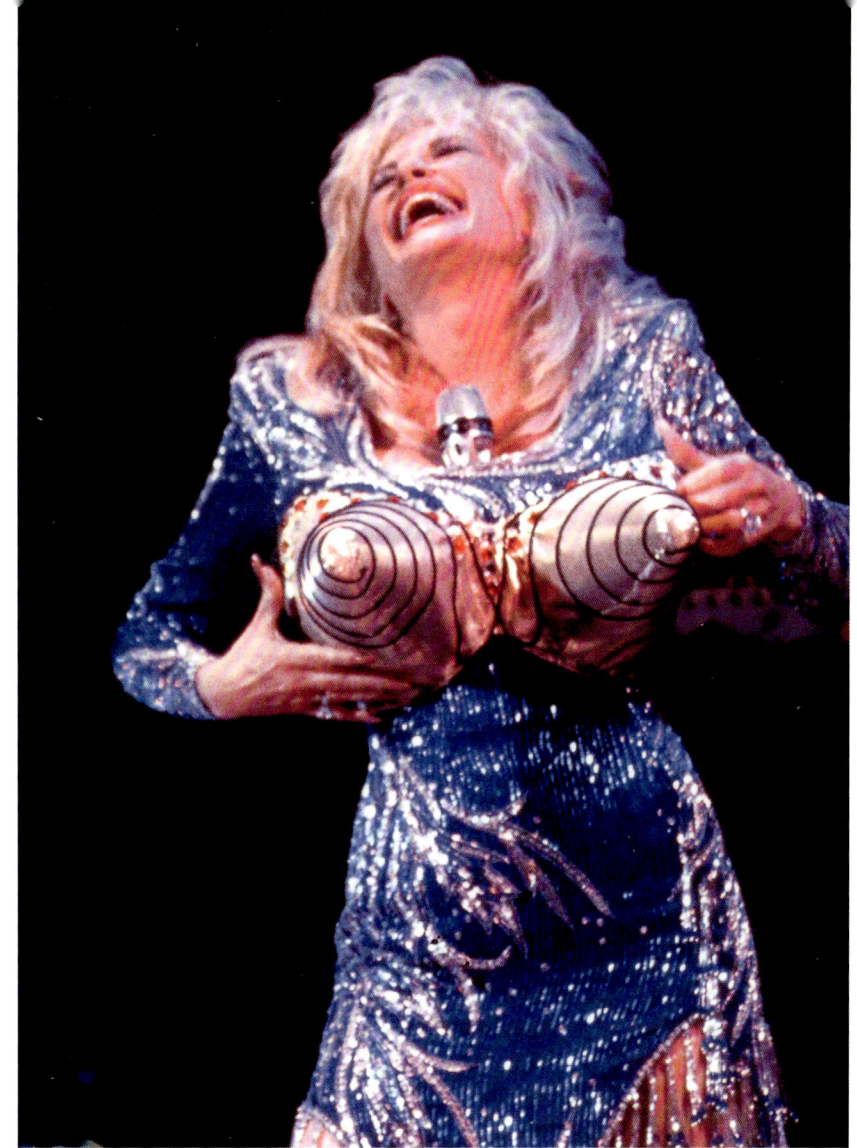

During the Straight Talk Tour we did a fun segment spotlighting music through the decades. When we got to one of Madonna's songs, I had some fun sporting my "Ma-Dolly' bra," which played up attire she was wearing onstage at that time.

In May 1993, Sony Music held a benefit for Lincoln Center—the same venue where I'd performed with Alabama and The Judds—and I joined Barbra Streisand, Neil Diamond, and Billy Joel for a special benefit concert. A couple nights later, I played Carnegie Hall as part of a multi-concert marketing effort called Country Takes Manhattan, which led to Fiftieth Street, alongside Radio City Music Hall, being renamed in my honor. Clint Black, Waylon Jennings, Willie Nelson, Trisha Yearwood, and Billy Ray Cyrus all played at different venues in New York that same week. We definitely brought country to the Big Apple: I piped in the sound of crickets to get people in the right mood, and a couple of members of my band started the show by playing a backwoods version of "Hello, Dolly!"

But the *real* country stuff happened away from New York City. In July, I played for more than forty thousand people at the Big Valley Jamboree in Saskatchewan. And in September, when I performed at the Tulare County Fair in California, you could see people bungee jumping in

From Hollywood to Dollywood

the distance. No way I was trying that! There's an old saying, "Screw your wig on tight," and I didn't plan on testing my screws! I loved playing all those fairs and festivals, and my Slow Dancing with the Moon Tour in 1993 took me all over North America, like always. Looking back on all the years of touring now makes me realize how fortunate I've been to perform for so many generations. In all honesty, it is probably why I have such a diverse fan base today.

During the 1993 CMA Awards, I teamed with Tammy Wynette and Loretta Lynn on "Silver Threads and Golden Needles"—it was kind of my second version of the Trio. I am so happy we did the *Honky Tonk Angels* album that same year. Tammy and Loretta were my girlfriends, and we kinda came up in the business together. Now that they are both gone, being able to listen to that record brings back so many great memories.

As 1994 dawned, I decided to take a break from touring and focus on television projects and business ventures, and I finished writing my autobiography, *Dolly: My Life and Other Unfinished Business,* which was released in January of that year. I also recorded a live album, *Heartsongs,* from Dollywood in 1994. It features Alison Krauss, Rhonda Vincent, Irish group Altan, Suzanne Cox of the Cox Family, Carl Jackson, and many more. I also performed with James Ingram at the 1994 Oscars.

When Dollywood had its season opener in 1995, we kicked it off with a benefit concert, and I got to share the stage with two of the artists I'd listened to when I was a teenager: Jerry Lee Lewis and Carl Perkins.

But the most important stage I worked on that year didn't involve lights or musicians or instruments. I launched a book program. The Imagination Library was inspired by my family dynamics. My daddy never did learn to read, and while he did all right in his life, he could have had a richer life and protected himself better if he had gained that skill. I know in my life, I could not have become the star of the show without learning how to write—which, of course, goes hand in hand with knowing how to read. And I guarantee you that knowing how to read has helped me steer clear of some really bad contracts over the years!

I also got to take full advantage of one of my favorite times of the year, Christmas, with a pair of prime-time TV specials in 1996. The first, *Dolly Parton: Treasures,* was an insider look at my album *Treasures,* which featured covers of songs from the 1960s, '70s, and '80s.

A few weeks later, I had the leading role in the TV movie *Unlikely Angel,* though the earthly part of my character wasn't really unlikely at all. I played Ruby Diamond, who was a country star—not much of a stretch, right? What made it different was that Ruby died and went to Heaven, but Saint Peter—who was played by Roddy McDowall—told Ruby she needed to bring a family together before Christmas if she was to be allowed past the pearly gates. It was an appropriate message for the holidays and a good reminder of what's really important in life.

That message resonated with me, because I was starting a new era in my career—one focused on going inward, reexamining my heart, and returning to my roots.

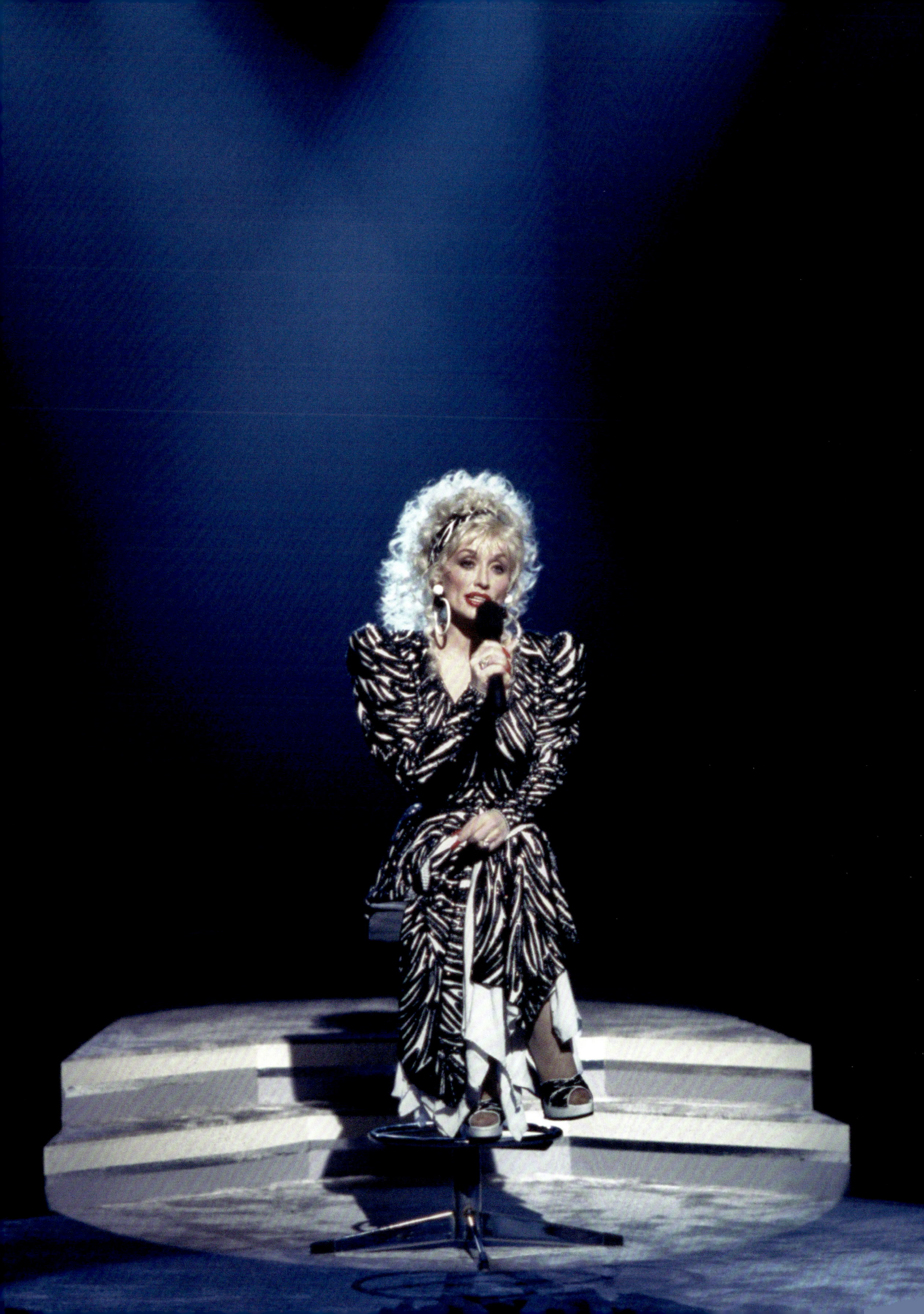

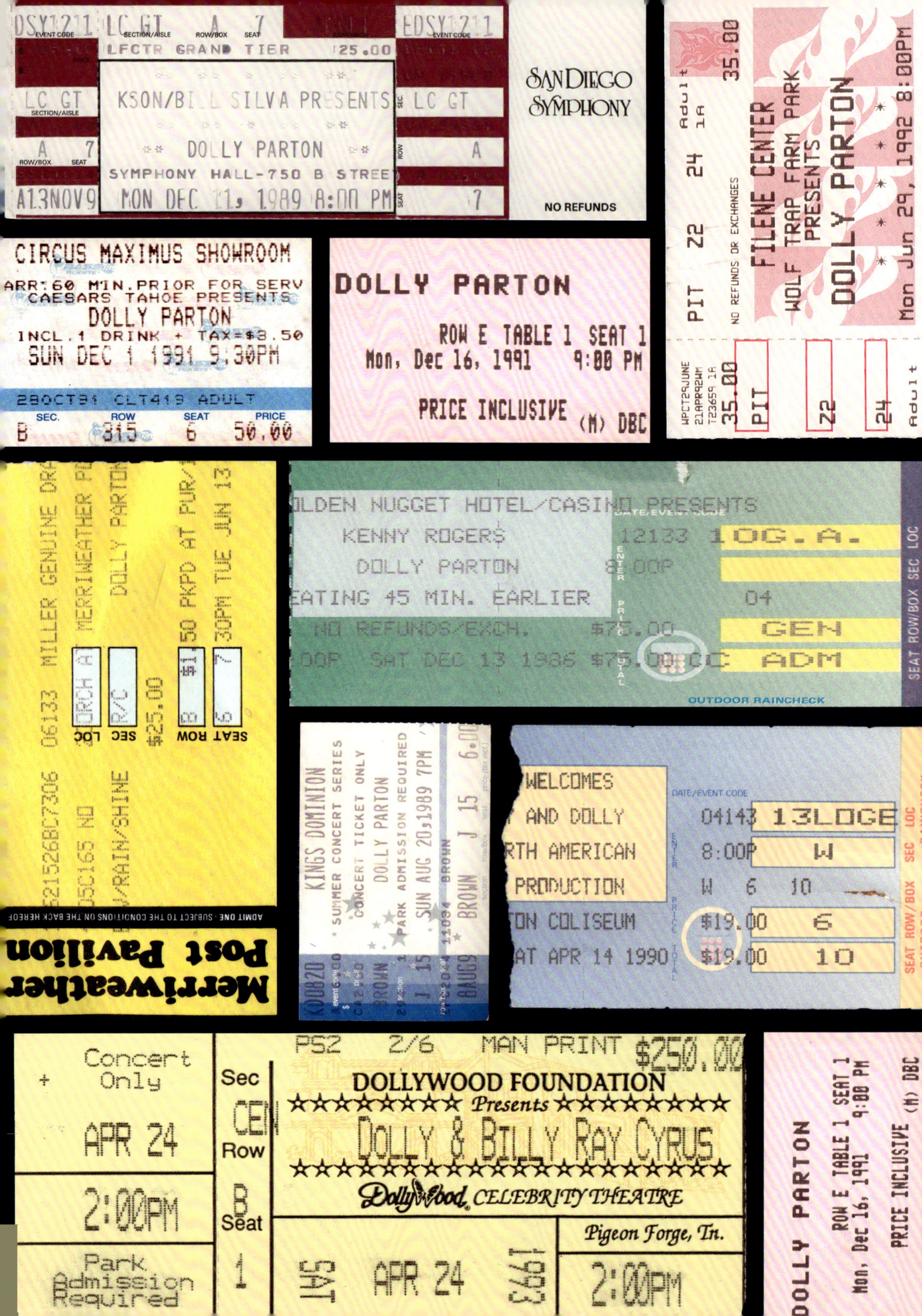

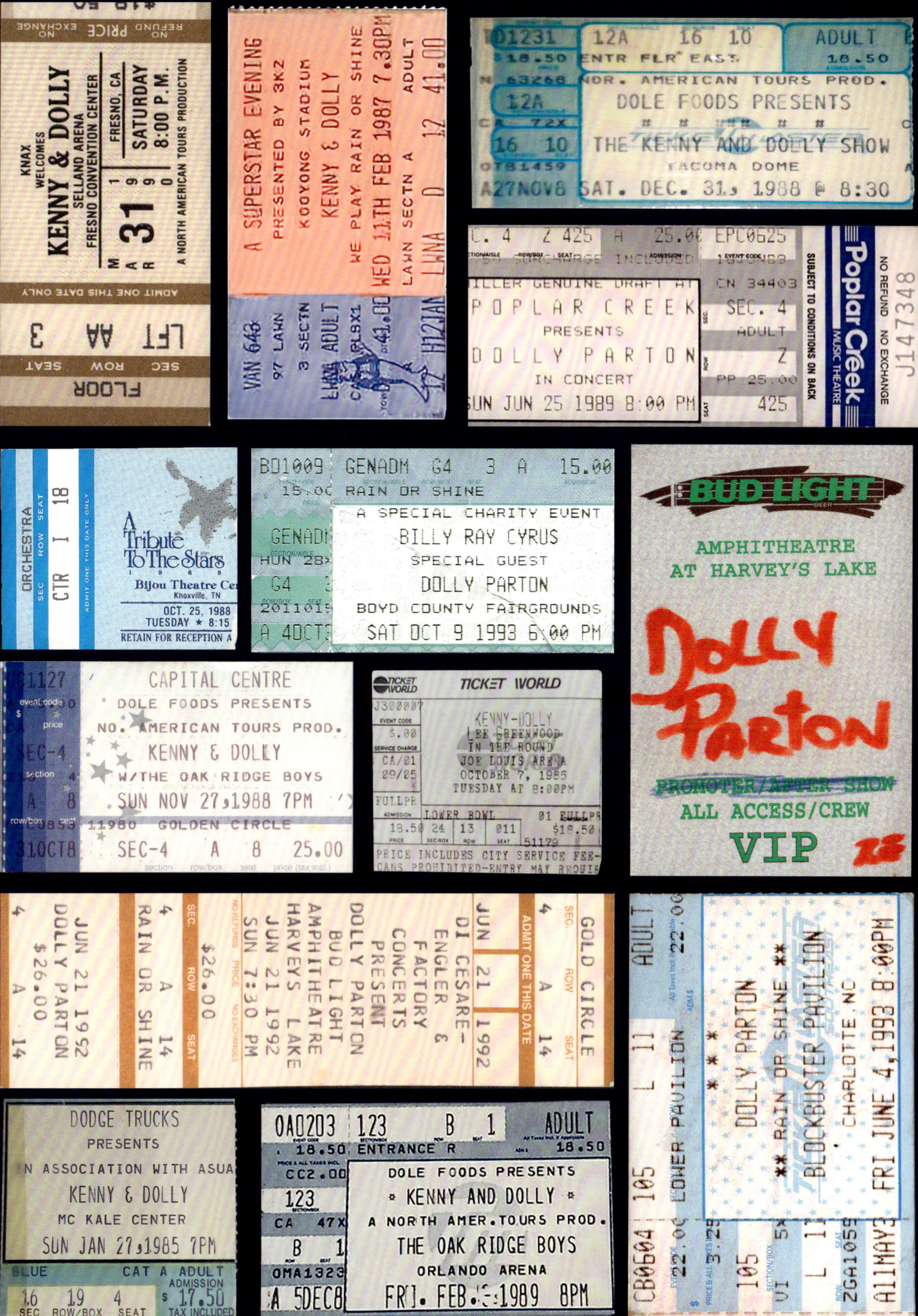

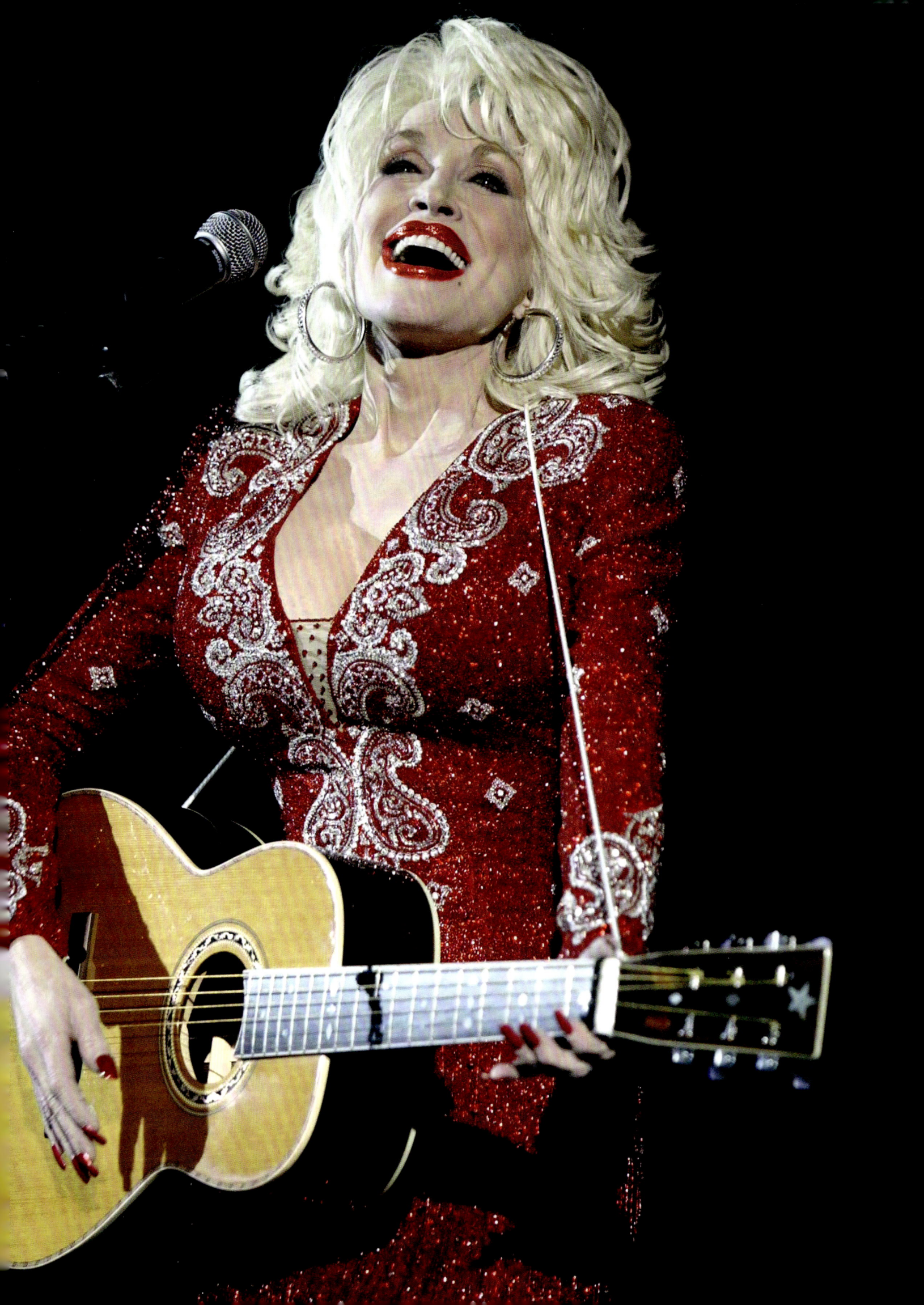

Returning to My Roots

1998-2005

1998 – 2005

From the outset of her career, Dolly always said that she would never leave her Tennessee roots behind—she was simply taking them with her on her journey. If there was any doubt about how successfully she had navigated her way, her 1999 induction into the Country Music Hall of Fame proved how deeply the rest of the industry valued her contributions.

That honor arrived at a moment when she was reaffirming her core values as a country musician and as a caring citizen. She recorded albums that revisited the bluegrass music and traditional country that had launched her stardom, and she headlined Nashville for the first time as a solo performer. And in the wake of 9/11, she reflected on her patriotism with a star-spangled appearance in front of the US Capitol during the 2003 installment of the annual PBS special *A Capitol Fourth* and doubled down on that sentiment with the album *For God and Country*.

Despite the nostalgic nature of this stage in her journey, the title of her 2005 no. 1 country single with Brad Paisley, "When I Get Where I'm Going," would be prophetic: Dolly had more stages ahead.

—TOM ROLAND

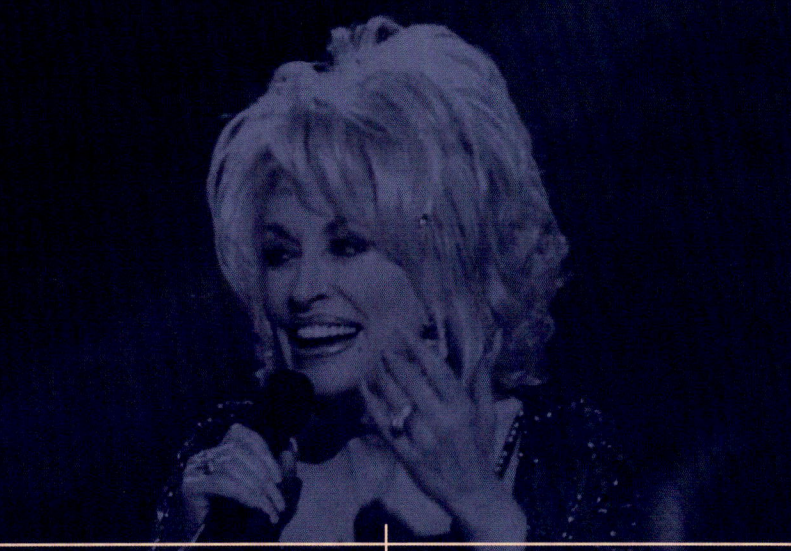

SEPTEMBER 1999
Dolly is inducted into the Country Music Hall of Fame.

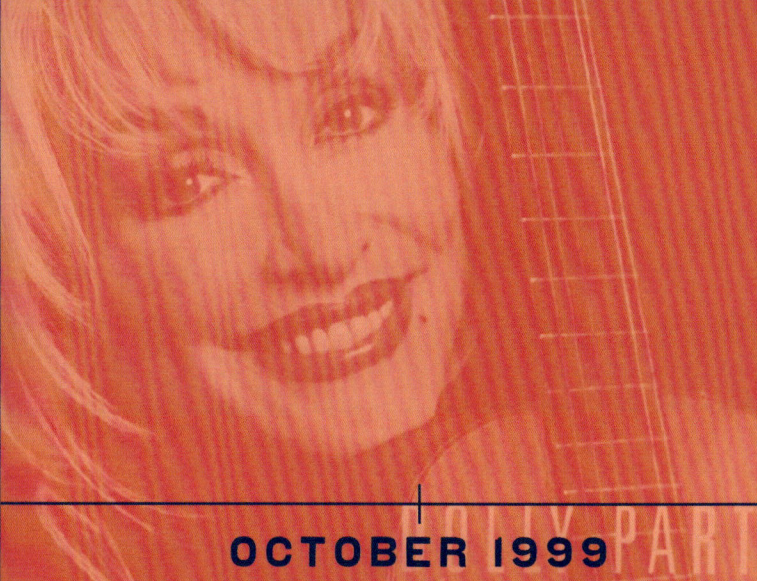

OCTOBER 1999
Dolly's first bluegrass album, *The Grass Is Blue*, is released to great critical acclaim and wins the Grammy for Best Bluegrass Album.

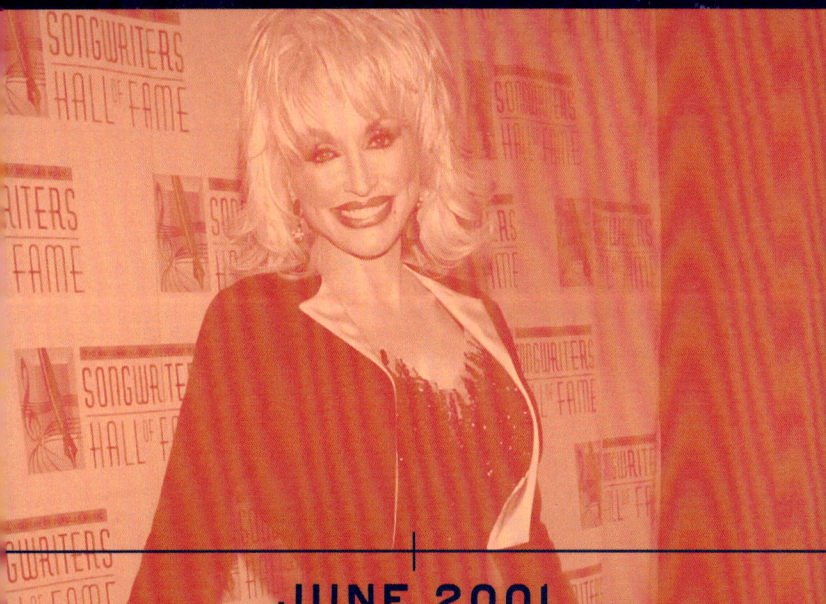

JUNE 2001
Dolly is inducted into the Songwriters Hall of Fame.

JULY 2002
Dolly releases a third bluegrass-influenced album, *Halos & Horns*, and goes on tour for the first time in a decade.

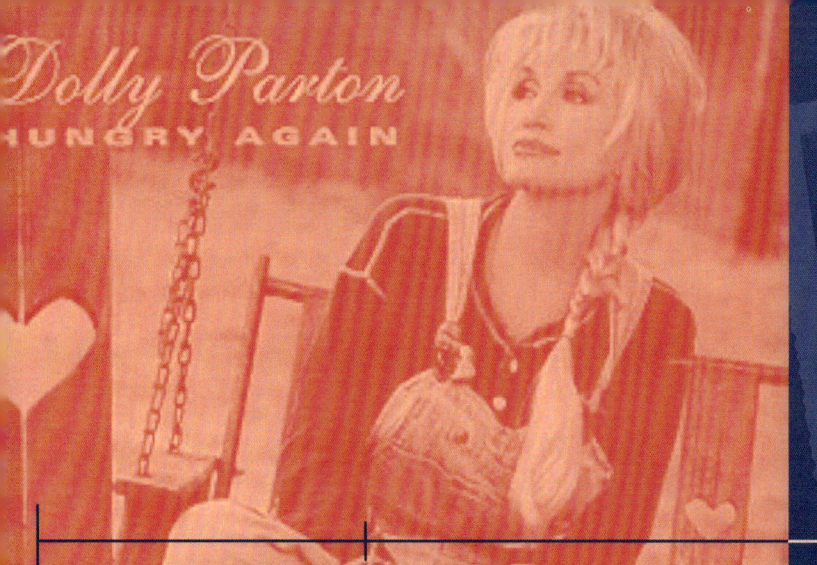

AUGUST 1998
Dolly releases *Hungry Again* and launches an aggressive promotional campaign, appearing in European media for the first time in a decade.

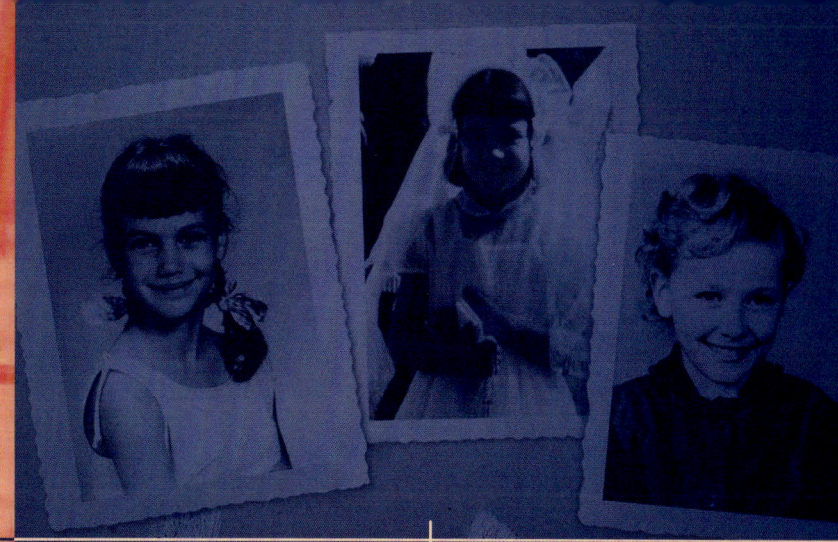

FEBRUARY 1999
Dolly collaborates with Linda Ronstadt and Emmylou Harris on *Trio II*, which is certified gold.

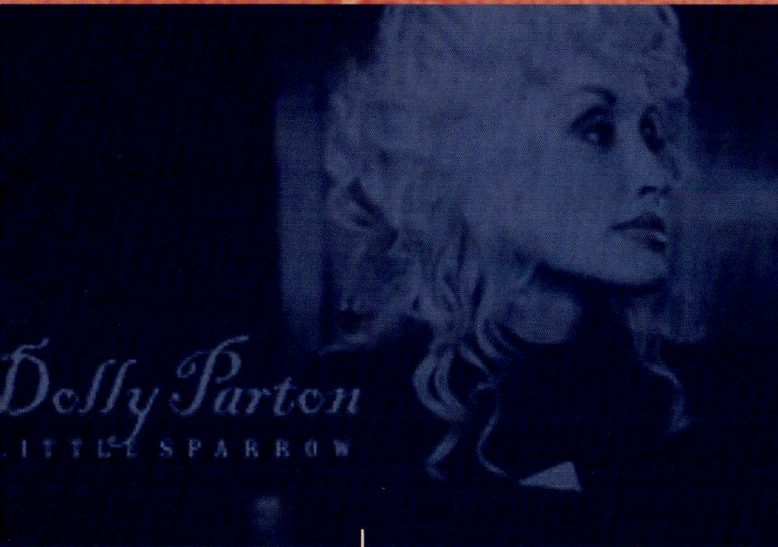

JANUARY 2001
Dolly releases *Little Sparrow*, a bluegrass and folk album. It wins a Grammy for Best Country Female Vocal Performance for "Shine."

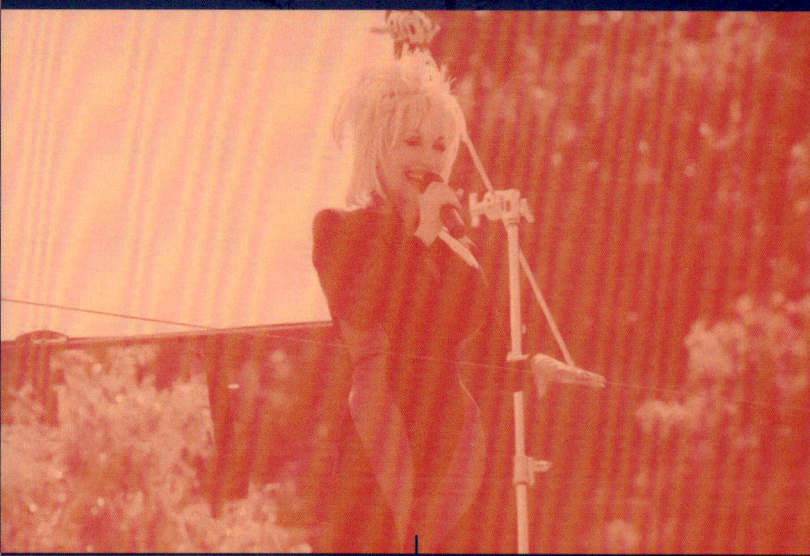

MAY 2001
Splash Country opens as part of her Dollywood theme park.

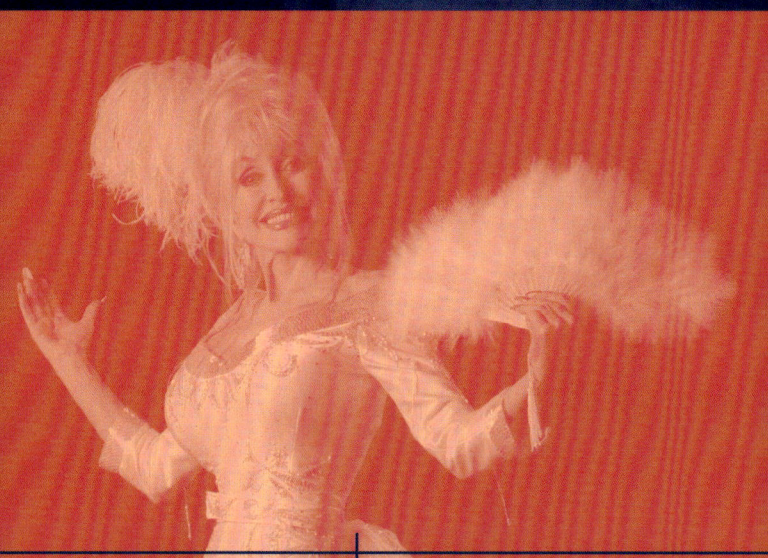

OCTOBER 2004
Dolly launches her Hello, I'm Dolly arena tour.

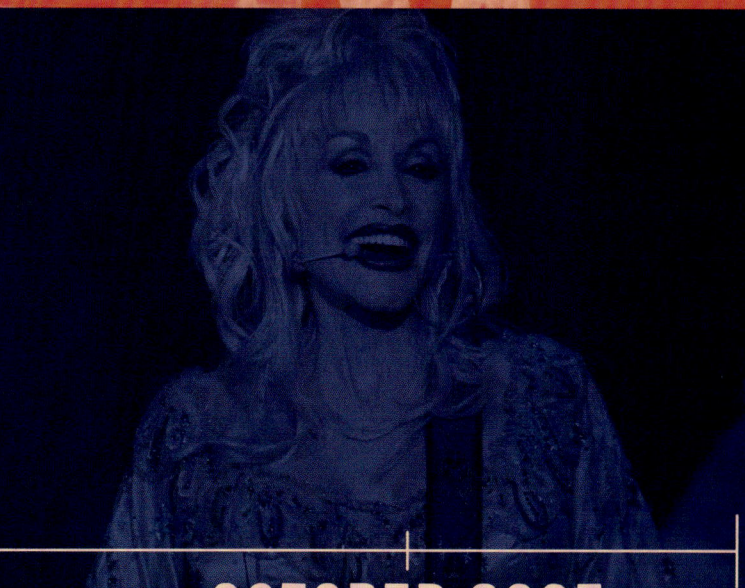

OCTOBER 2005
Dolly releases an album of covers, *Those Were The Days*, and launches the Vintage Tour.

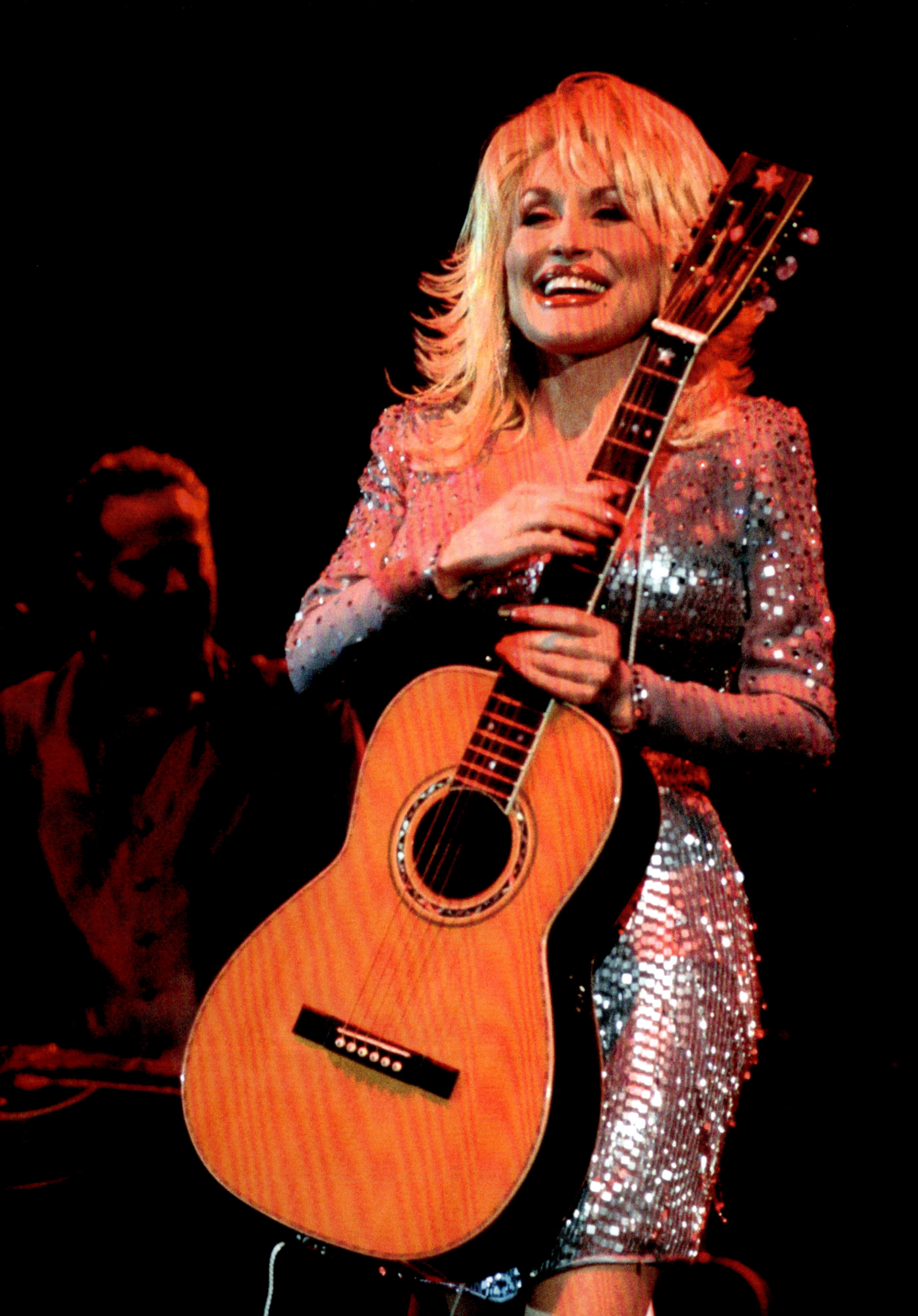

In 1998, I launched what turned out to be a new era of my career with the album *Hungry Again*. I'd spent so many years expanding the sound of my music and chasing opportunities beyond the concert stage that this more stripped-down album probably surprised a lot of people. But after decades of experimenting with other genres, I wanted to touch base with the country, bluegrass, and mountain music that had formed my roots. I went up to my mountain home for weeks, cut my nails short, fasted, and wrote all the songs for the album. As I commented at the time, it was like I had to get rich so I could afford to sing like I was poor again!

Hungry Again starts off with the title track, an acoustic ballad about a couple trying to return to the emotional excitement they felt in the beginning of their relationship: "Bring back the passion we had back then" is one of the key desires expressed in the chorus. My cousin Richie Owens co-produced the album, and we had bluegrass singer Rhonda Vincent and her brother Darrin Vincent, of the duo Dailey & Vincent, supply background vocals on that first song. The sound was like going home, which made sense because I actually did go home to record it. "Shine On" was recorded with several of my family members at the House of Prayer in East Tennessee, where my grandfather was a pastor.

At that time, I was looking for something I could do musically that would come naturally to me—something that felt easy, good, and pure. And, of course, I know I'm at my best when I do mountain songs, country songs, and bluegrass songs. That's what really fits my voice better than anything else I do, and it represents my natural self, so I started writing some of those things and made a point to do stuff I wanted to do.

That's what I did in my albums for the next several years. I was able to sing a lot of songs, like "Little Sparrow," that I wrote based on songs from the old days—songs like Mama used to sing. I write a lot in that vein, and I enjoy that, but I also pulled a lot of old country songs in, and I did some covers from other fields of music. But I countrified them and made them fit my voice and my style. I'm real proud of those records.

You don't make much money doing bluegrass music unless you have a following, so when somebody makes a bluegrass album, you know they love the music. You're never going to get rich from that high lonesome sound—not even the biggest names like Bill Monroe and the great people who invented it did. They got by, barely, by the skin of their banjos, but I loved it, because that music really has always been in my heart.

In 1999, I teamed with Linda Ronstadt and Emmylou Harris again on *Trio II,* starred in the Lifetime TV movie *Blue Valley Songbird,* and tapped my family's musical history in the TNN special *Dolly Parton's Precious Memories*.

Appropriately, as I went back to my country core, the industry gave me what may be its biggest stamp of approval at the end of 1999. I was inducted into the Country Music Hall of Fame during the CMA Awards, which meant that I'd have a bronze plaque at the Hall of Fame and Museum, right alongside all the people who had influenced me or become my friends—people like the Carter Family, Willie Nelson, Loretta Lynn, Johnny Cash, and Patsy Cline.

Words can't express how it feels to be in the same hall with Hank Williams and all those people. You feel a part of something great. You feel a part of something big. You feel a part of something necessary and real. And they were the same kind of people that I am. They grew up the same way. They were from the same dirt and the same cornfields.

In the early years, they used to surprise new Hall of Fame members with the news in the middle of the awards, but sometime in the early '90s, they started announcing the inductees in advance. So I knew going into the show that it would be one of the most important nights of my life. It was like I "went to hillbilly heaven"—that's what I told the crowd that night. But I worked that night too. I premiered "Train, Train," a song from my new bluegrass album, *The Grass Is Blue,* which was released a month after the awards. I also filled in on the CMAs for my friend Patty Loveless, who was out of the country, and sang "My Kind of Woman/My Kind of Man" with Vince Gill.

The Hall of Fame induction was a nice way to end the millennium. I started the next century with a concert that was also a return to my roots. Believe it or not, I had never headlined a solo show in Nashville, and it seemed appropriate to demonstrate my appreciation for the city that had helped launch me into the big time by starting off the new century in that same town.

New Year's Eve is a major night for entertainers. People are in a party mood, and there are lots of opportunities to take the stage and lead the celebration no matter where you are. Prior to that, I'd worked New Year's Eve at least fourteen different times.

But that year was a little different. The year 2000 was called Y2K, and it had the world in a state of concern. Computer programs had been designed in a way that made it unclear how they would behave when the first two numbers of the year turned from nineteen to twenty. There were some concerns that there would be power outages in spots all over the country, and I decided I didn't want to risk having the lights go out while I was on stage! So instead of playing New Year's Eve, I did a New Year's *Day* concert at the Opryland Gaylord Hotel.

It was a fun way to welcome a new century, and extra special since it was the place I called home. Also, I wasn't actually touring at the time. Instead, I was focusing on getting new business things started, running production companies, and putting TV specials into motion. Alison Krauss came out and sang a few songs with me, Steve Wariner opened the show, and the band included mandolin player Chris Thile, who would soon start making waves with Nickel Creek, his bluegrass band. I got to sleep at home with Carl on my first night of the 2000s even though I'd just put on a full show!

As it turned out, none of the technological glitches that had been predicted came true, though the turnover to 2000 did make a lot of people look inward, including me. As I moved forward, I was determined to concentrate on creative ventures and business decisions that made a difference in new ways. And so, in the first months of the new decade, I performed at a few events that were important to the music community, particularly the

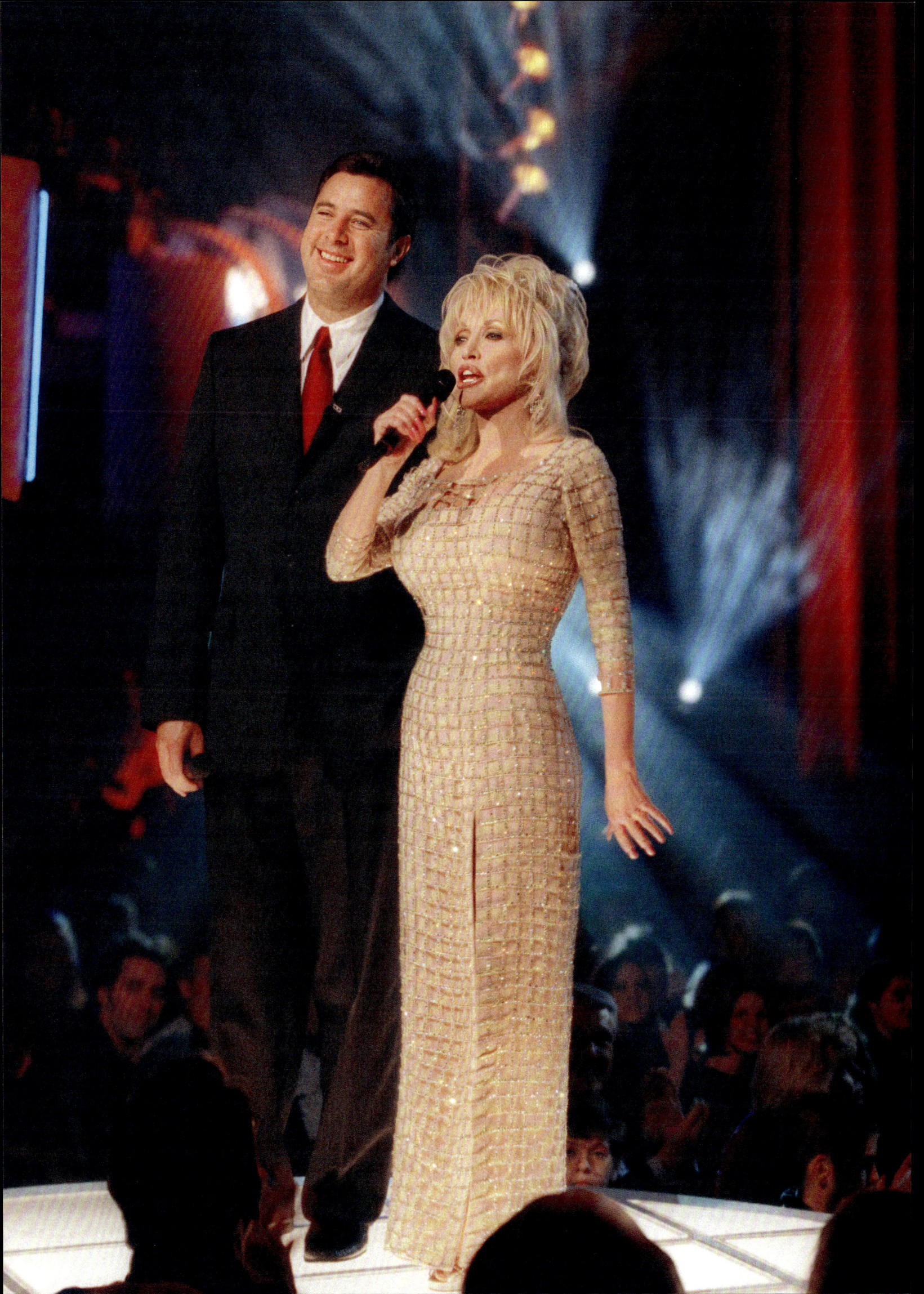

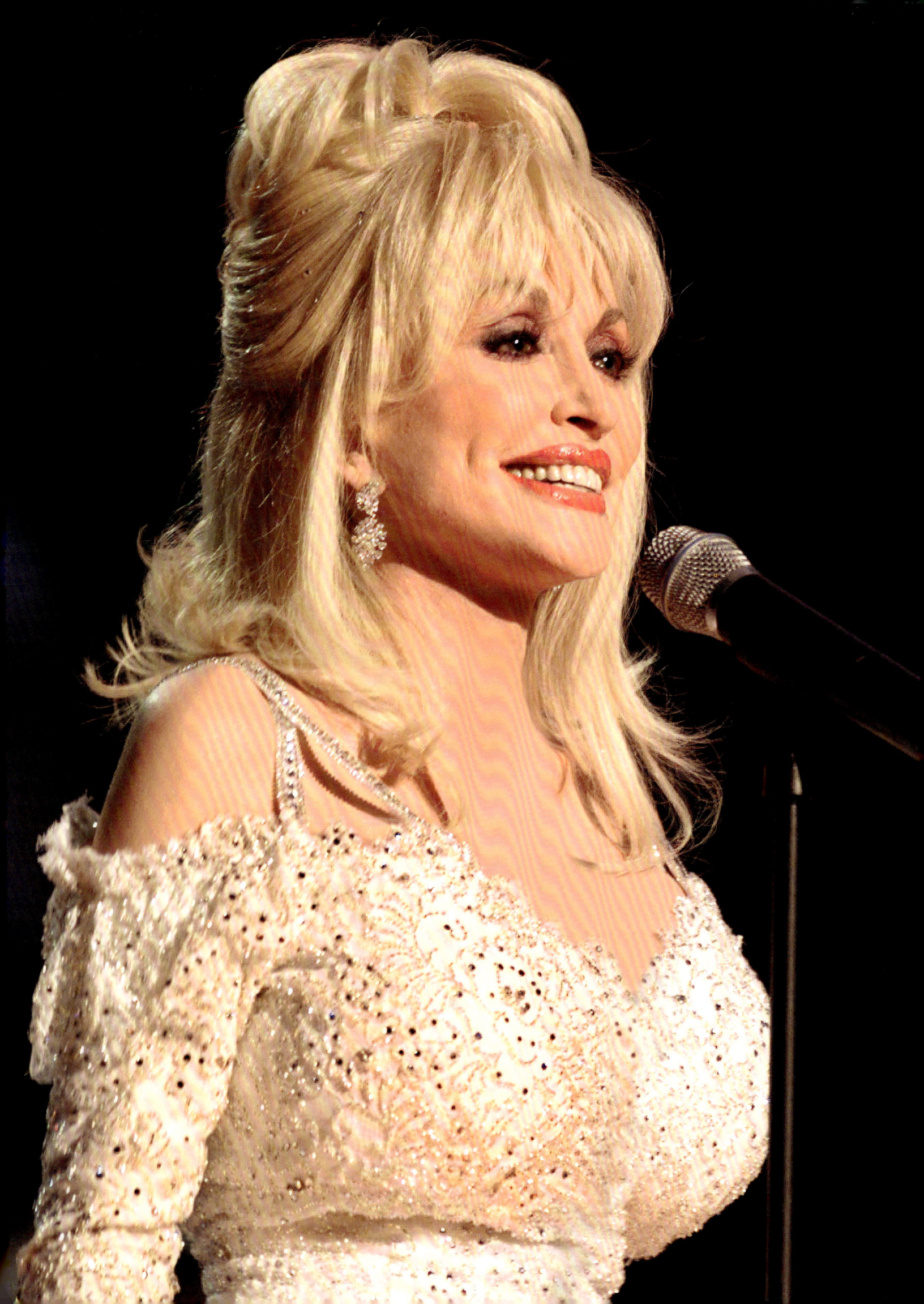

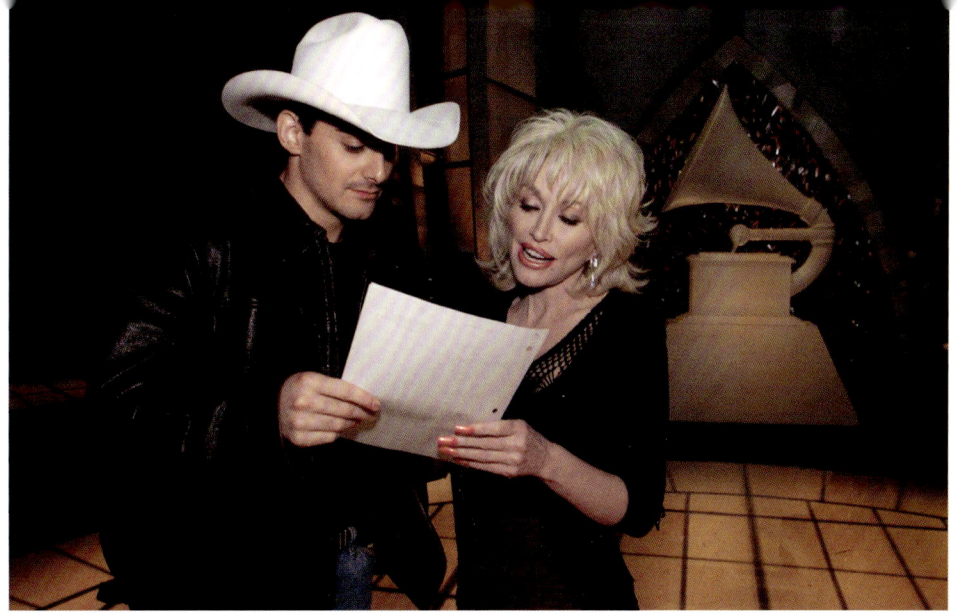

I loved performing with Brad Paisley at the Grammy Awards in 2001, where we sang Billy Joel's "Travelin' Prayer." A few years later, we teamed up again on the award-winning duet "When I Get Where I'm Going."

Nashville community. I did the Dove Awards and hosted the thirty-fifth annual Academy of Country Music Awards, where I sang a bluegrass version of Billy Joel's "Travelin' Prayer." Once again, Alison Krauss was there to play fiddle when I performed on a CBS special that I hosted with Vince Gill to celebrate the Opry's seventy-fifth anniversary.

Plus, there was a TV appearance with Bette Midler on her sitcom, *Bette,* in which she played a fictional star—who happened to be named Bette. Well, I came on to the real-life set to make an appearance on her make-believe show, and if that's confusing, just think of it all as a TV parody. Anyway, I sat with a rod and reel, fishing alongside Bette, who was dressed up as a mermaid. We sang "Islands in the Stream" together—and Bette, by the way, did great harmonies—while she flipped and flopped and flapped her fishy mermaid tail in my face. At some point, she leaned over on a palm-tree prop, and from there on out, the fictitious TV stage became a fictitious disaster.

In the months after that, I did "Travelin' Prayer" again on the Grammy Awards in 2001, but I changed up the arrangement for the performance by having Nickel Creek, Brad Paisley, and members of my own band back me up. And I made my first appearance at MerleFest, a festival celebrating roots music named after guitarist Merle Watson, the son of pioneering acoustic musician Doc Watson.

I was kind of skeptical about doing a full-blown, purebred bluegrass festival like MerleFest. Doc Watson was one of the greatest guitar players ever. I did get to know Doc, and I did get to sing a song with him. I'd done so many crossover records through the years that I thought they might boo me or walk out or something, like they'd done to Bob Dylan when he'd gone electric. I put together a band that featured some of the musicians from *The Grass Is Blue* and *Little Sparrow,* including Dobro player Jerry Douglas and mandolin player Sam Bush (the same guy who had played at the fiddling championship in 1974 where Porter Wagoner and I gave our last official concert as a duo). And the crowd was

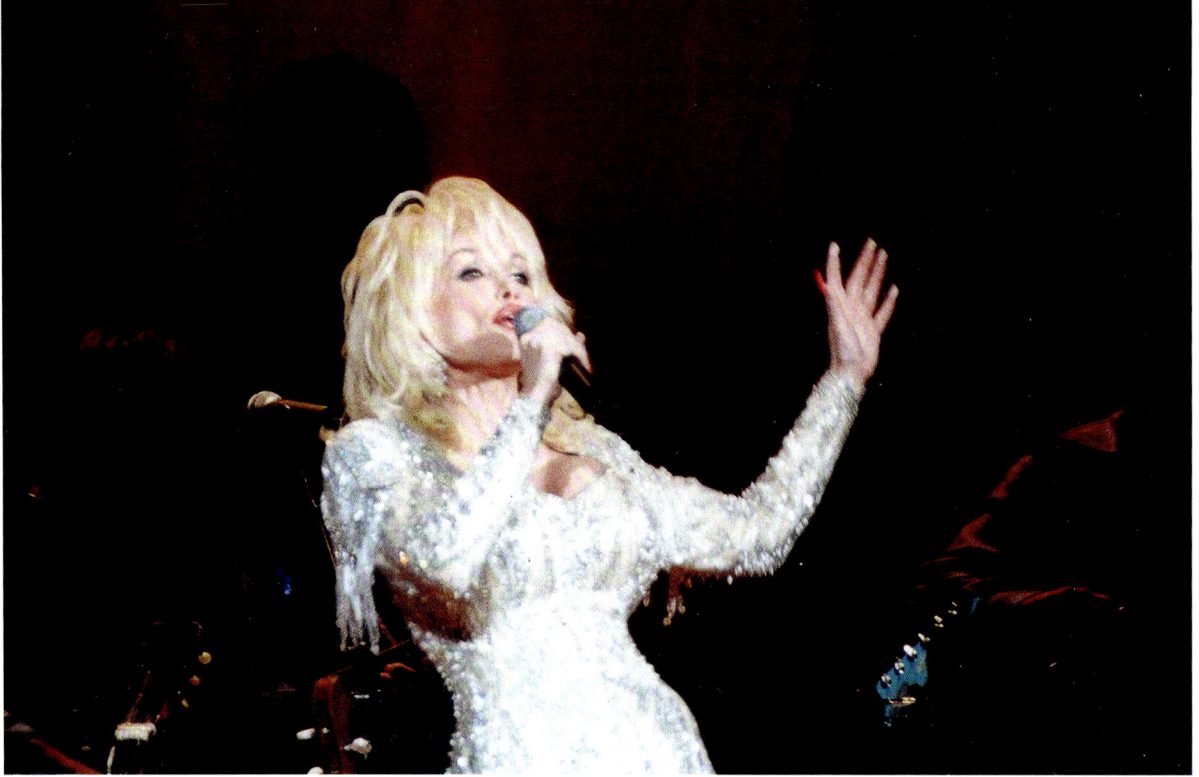

I headlined Nashville's Ryman Auditorium for the first time in my career in 2002. The balcony seats are great—and it looks like I'm making eye contact with the audience at that level!

so supportive that instead of playing forty-five minutes, I stayed on stage for more than an hour. Obviously, my fears of those bluegrass traditionalists walking out on me were unfounded; they even appreciated my version of "Shine," a song that was originated by the alternative rock band Collective Soul.

But I didn't just stick to American roots music during that time. When Dollywood opened its sixteenth season in April 2001, we hosted a Festival of Nations that ran for about a month. Groups came from all over the world, bringing their music, their culture, and their food. That first year, we had performers from Kenya, Trinidad, Ukraine, Bulgaria, Russia, Ireland, and the Czech Republic—to name just some of the countries that were represented—and I helped launch the event by singing "9 to 5" with a group from Eastern Europe known as the Stavropol Cossacks. The Festival of Nations was so well received that we made it an annual event for years, and it ended up running for about three months every summer.

One of my most satisfying Dollywood moments came during the 2018 Festival of Nations, when the African choral group Ladysmith Black Mambazo joined the celebration. They had come to fame when Paul Simon did his *Graceland* album—that's certainly when I'd become aware of them too. I decided I had to find that group, and when I did, I had them sing on a Cat Stevens song, "Peace Train," that I recorded for my album *Treasures* in the 1990s. It's one of my favorite things that I ever recorded, but it took twenty years before our schedules finally lined up and we could do that song together live. Cat Stevens's original version is from the 1970s, but what "Peace Train" says fits every era. To be able to share it with the vocalists from Ladysmith Black Mambazo at Dollywood was a special moment.

STAGE LOOKS
Through the Years

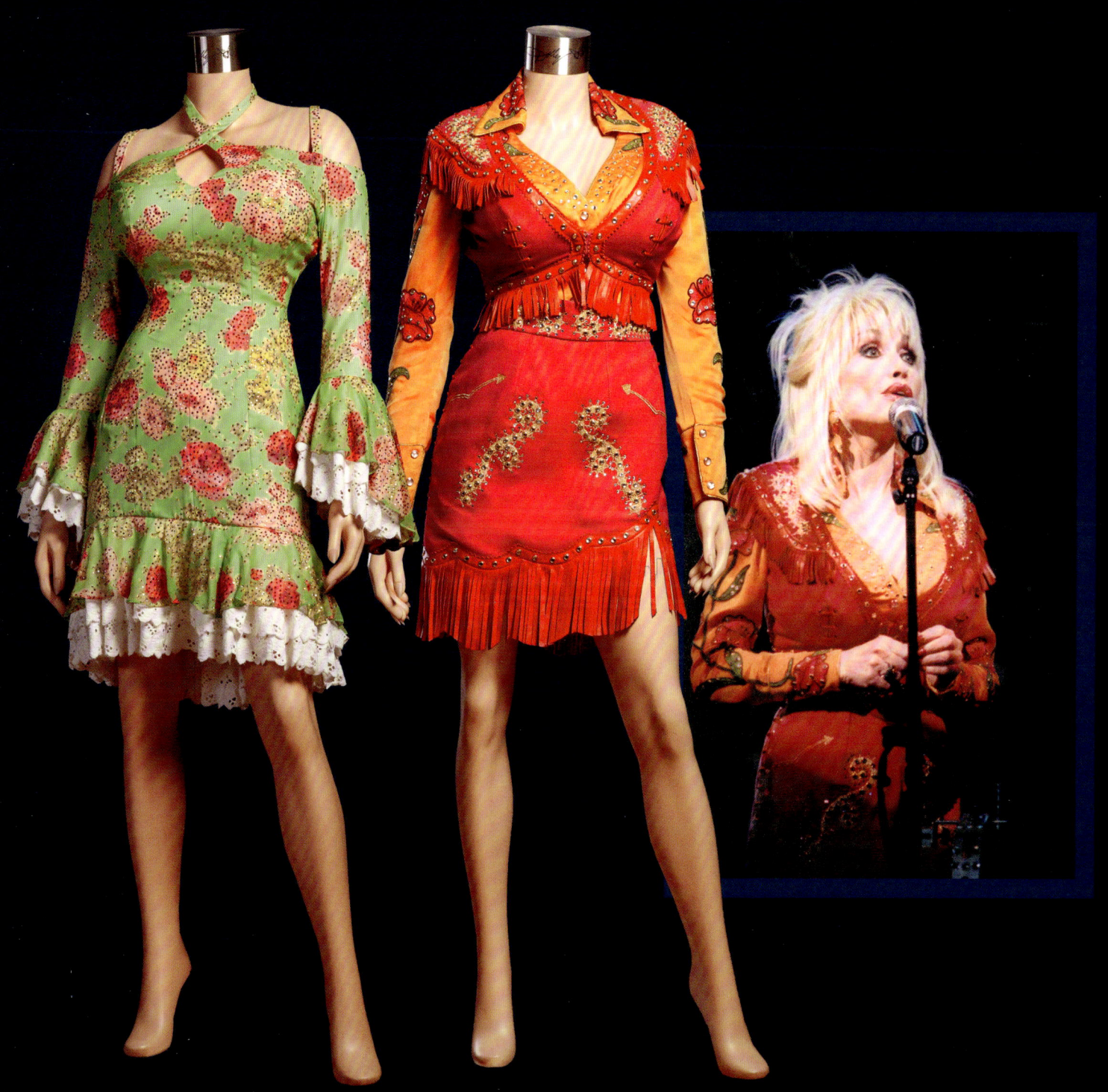

My longtime designer Robért Behar created this floral dress that became a staple in my Halos & Horns Tour wardrobe.

For a special performance in Texas, Robért also designed this Western-inspired ensemble.

One of my most difficult performances ever had international overtones that same year. When 9/11 happened, I was on a farm in East Tennessee, and a lot of people were there making a video for one of the rides at Dollywood. Many of them—the lighting and sound experts and the producers—had come down from New York to work on it. There was an old farmhouse on the property that had one television and one phone, and when we were shooting the video, somebody came out to the set and told us that the World Trade Center had been attacked and all these people were dying. Of course, we all were shocked and dismayed, but it was different for those people who'd come down from New York. Their families were there—their kids, their wives, their *everything* was there. These were the days before cell phones were widely used, and the New Yorkers were absolutely freaking out. They were running into the house, trying to see the TV, trying to get on that one phone.

The 9/11 terrorist attacks made it challenging for a lot of people to go outside. Churches, shopping malls, concert venues—every public place went into lockdown or tightened their security, afraid there might be more attacks. There's an old saying: "When you least expect it, expect it!" Well, we didn't know what to expect, and nobody wanted to get caught flat-footed.

In the middle of the fear and sadness that hit America, I kind of thought that if we all went into hiding, the other side won. As a public person, I believe that when things are at their worst, I need to be at my best. So the performers at my Stampede dinner theater still went out and did their sold-out show the evening of September 11. The cast and the audience were all in tears, but as hard as that was, I think everybody just needed a place where it was okay to put their broken hearts out on display. On September 12, I wrote a song, "Color Me America," that incorporated a little bit of "America the Beautiful." And in December 2001, I went out on stage at Dollywood singing it and hoping I could lift a few people up—or at least make them feel not so down by giving them a night out where we all got to sing and nobody had to worry about getting hurt.

A few months later, in May 2002, I did a benefit in Minneapolis for 9/11 victims that was organized by President Bill Clinton and Senator Bob Dole. America had pulled together after the attack—at least for a bit—and that point couldn't have been made much more obviously than by having two leading members of the Democratic and Republican parties working together just five years after they'd battled each other in a presidential campaign. It was my first show with a new band, The Blueniques, that included some of the Kingdom Heirs, a band that played at Dollywood, plus a few other East Tennessee musicians. Jimmy Mattingly put that band together, and they were great—great singers, great players. I still think The Blueniques is a great name for a bluegrass band!

A funny thing happened in the middle of these benefits and one-off shows. I kind of realized that after spending a long period of time doing a limited amount of travel, I needed to be out on the road with the people. When you are a true wanderer and a musician who loves touring, you're not only loving the music and loving the idea of getting out on stage and performing, you're also enjoying seeing the world. You like seeing the countryside, hearing

2002 SET LIST

(Blueniques)
Orange Blossom Special
Train, Train
Grass Is Blue
Mountain Angel
Shine
Little Sparrow
Rocky Top
TN Mtn. Home/Coat
Appalachian Memories
Applejack
Marry Me
Down From Dover
*We Irish (in Ireland)
*First Time Home (in Scotland)
Halos and Horns
I'm Gone
Dagger Through The Heart
If
9 to 5
Jolene
A Capella (Islands In The Stream/Here You Come Again/
           Why'd You Come In Here/Two Doors Down)
{Intro Band}
I Will Always Love You
{Encore} Stairway to Heaven

> This is a setlist from the European dates of my Halos & Horns Tour. We had a ball playing the hits, some of my bluegrass material, and some of my covers like "Stairway to Heaven." To make it even more special, I got to debut my ode to Ireland, "We Irish," at the shows in Belfast and Dublin!

the sound of the wheels on the road, the smell of diesel. It's like an addiction, in a way. It becomes a part of you, and it's exciting. It's a thing you can't explain unless it's in your blood, and I sometimes think diesel is in my veins. It always has been.

I hadn't done a full-blown tour for almost a decade, and now with this new rootsy music, I was itching to go out and take my Tennessee mountain home around the world. That had always been my goal, but in those early years, I'd found that if I blended crossover music into the mix at my shows, I had a chance to reach a larger audience. That's what I did, it worked, and I don't regret it a bit. But by 2002, there was no pressure on me to make hits to get on the radio. I could pretty much play concerts that featured music I wanted to make for me, and—fingers crossed—I believed the real Dolly Parton fans would be there with me. I added a few select covers alongside my new rootsy compositions and my familiar hits for these concerts and headed out on the road, hoping that audiences would respond.

Still, I wasn't entirely convinced that I would like touring again, so I made a relatively small commitment. I knew that if I was going on the road again, it would be strictly on my terms: maybe eight or ten shows a month, just enough to keep my toe in the water, the diesel in my veins, and the fans in my sights.

Returning to My Roots

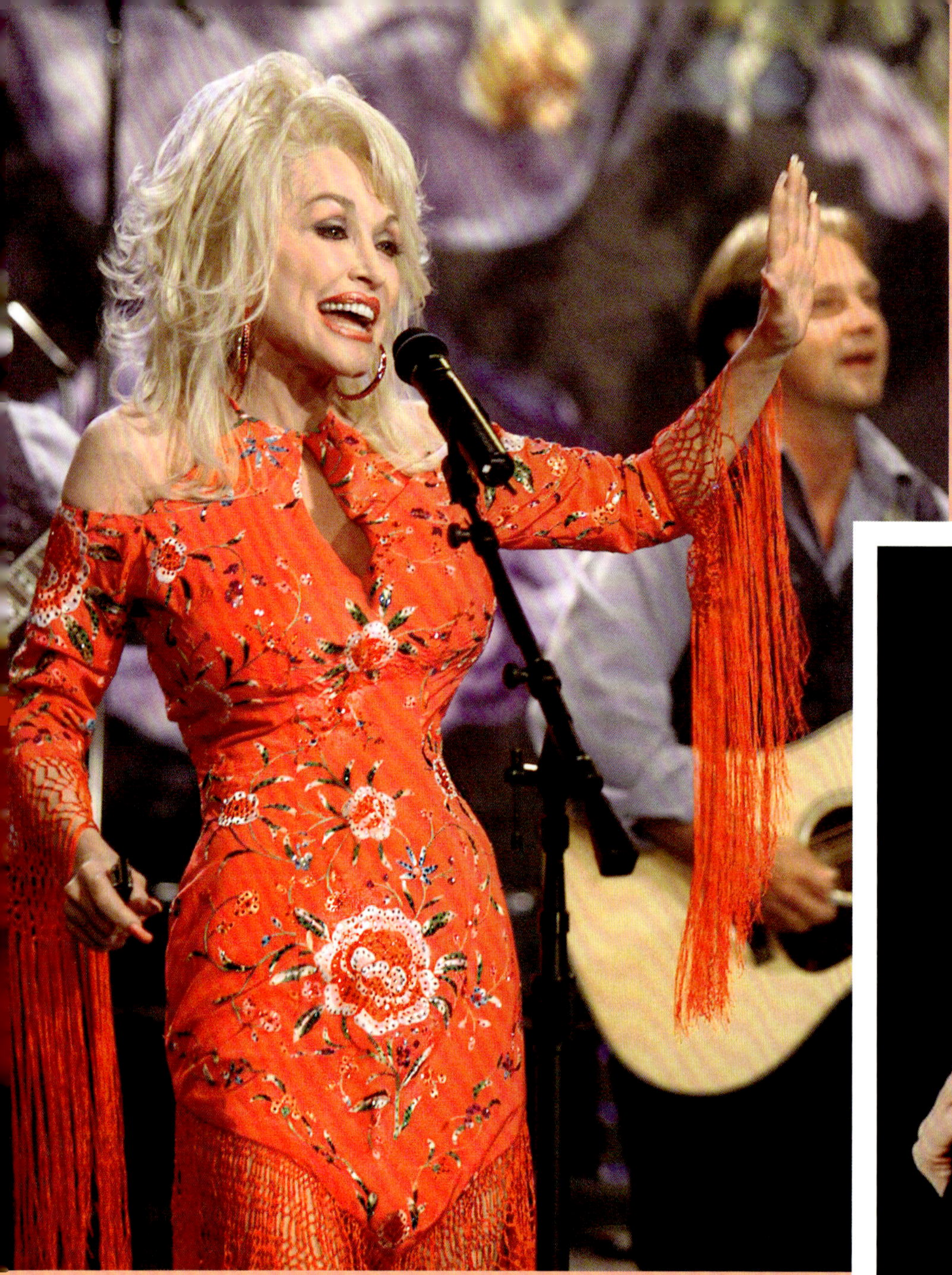

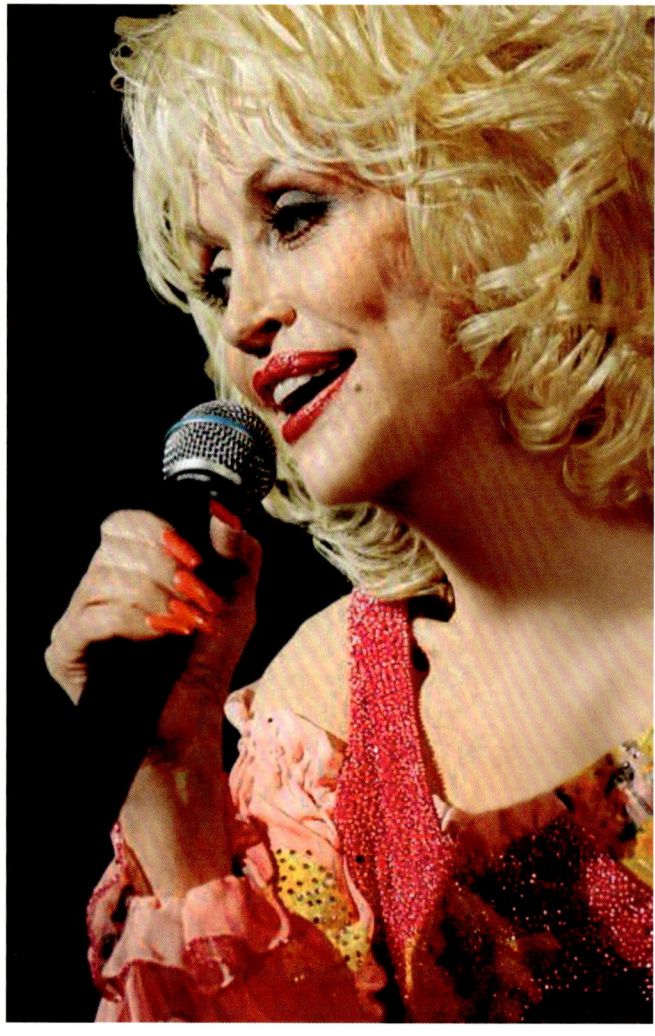

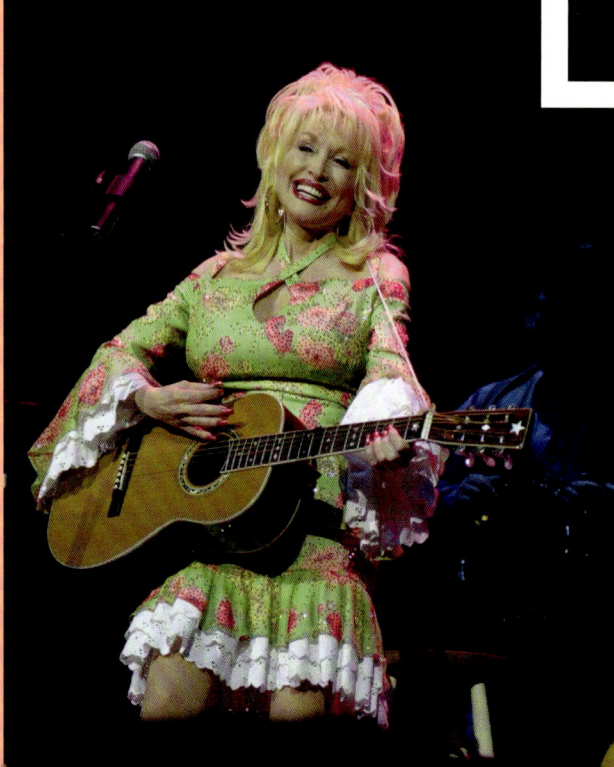

More moments from the Halos & Horns Tour, including performances on *The Tonight Show*, at the Los Angeles House of Blues, and in Scotland.

We launched the Halos & Horns Tour in a familiar venue, Irving Plaza, right there in the media capital of Manhattan. We figured that would bring some press attention and help get me back in the country headlines along with Rascal Flatts and Toby Keith and Kenny Chesney, who were dominating country radio at the time. For the first time, I headlined a concert at the Ryman Auditorium in Nashville, the place where I'd been inducted into the Grand Ole Opry. We played bluegrass versions of "Shine" and "9 to 5" and threaded in more traditional songs right along with some of my hits, and it was one of those highlight moments when you're filled with gratitude because you realize you're doing what you were called to do.

A few weeks later, I played the House of Blues on the Sunset Strip in Los Angeles. I was so excited I went outside and started greeting people in the line waiting to get into the club.

At the end of the tour's North American leg, I tacked on an extra show at the Washington Pavilion of Arts and Science in Sioux Falls, South Dakota, where we raised $118,000 for a United Way campaign that brought books to the kids in the city's school system, in conjunction with my Imagination Library. In just seven years, the library program had grown substantially from its original operation in Sevier County, Tennessee. It was now reaching fifty thousand kids in a dozen states from Maine to California, including Kansas, Georgia, South Dakota, and the Carolinas.

In November 2002, I recruited the Nashville Christ Church Choir again, just like I had in 1989, for a special awards show performance. We sang "Hello God," another song that I wrote after 9/11, on the CMA Awards stage. I believe that our relationship with God is reflected in the way we treat our brothers and sisters—not just the ones in our family but all the citizens of the world. You get it: that whole "Love thy neighbor as thyself" thing. That's what "Hello God" is, and when you hear thirty-six voices backing you up on that kind of song, it's just stirring.

It was almost as if that song set the stage for the next month, when I took the Halos & Horns Tour to the United Kingdom and Ireland. Combined with the dates we'd already done in the United States, it ended up being an important tour because it reminded me how much I'm renewed and energized anytime I can connect with people in person.

In fact, getting back on stage was such a great experience that I brought The Blueniques together on December 12 and 13 to record my *Live and Well* album. I played dulcimer on "My Tennessee Mountain Home," banjo on "Applejack," and harmonica on "I'm Gone." Now here's what really takes talent: playing the harmonica without smearing your lipstick! I also dedicated "Jolene" to some Dolly Parton drag queens I'd seen before the show, and even changed one of the lines to "I cannot compete with you, drag queens"! Every once in a while someone rags on me about my acceptance of drag, but I don't care what they're dragging as long as they're dragging it to my show! I love everybody.

I also did my version of "Stairway to Heaven," the Led Zeppelin song. It works really well with fiddle, Dobro, and mandolin—I think so, anyway—and I suspect some folks in the

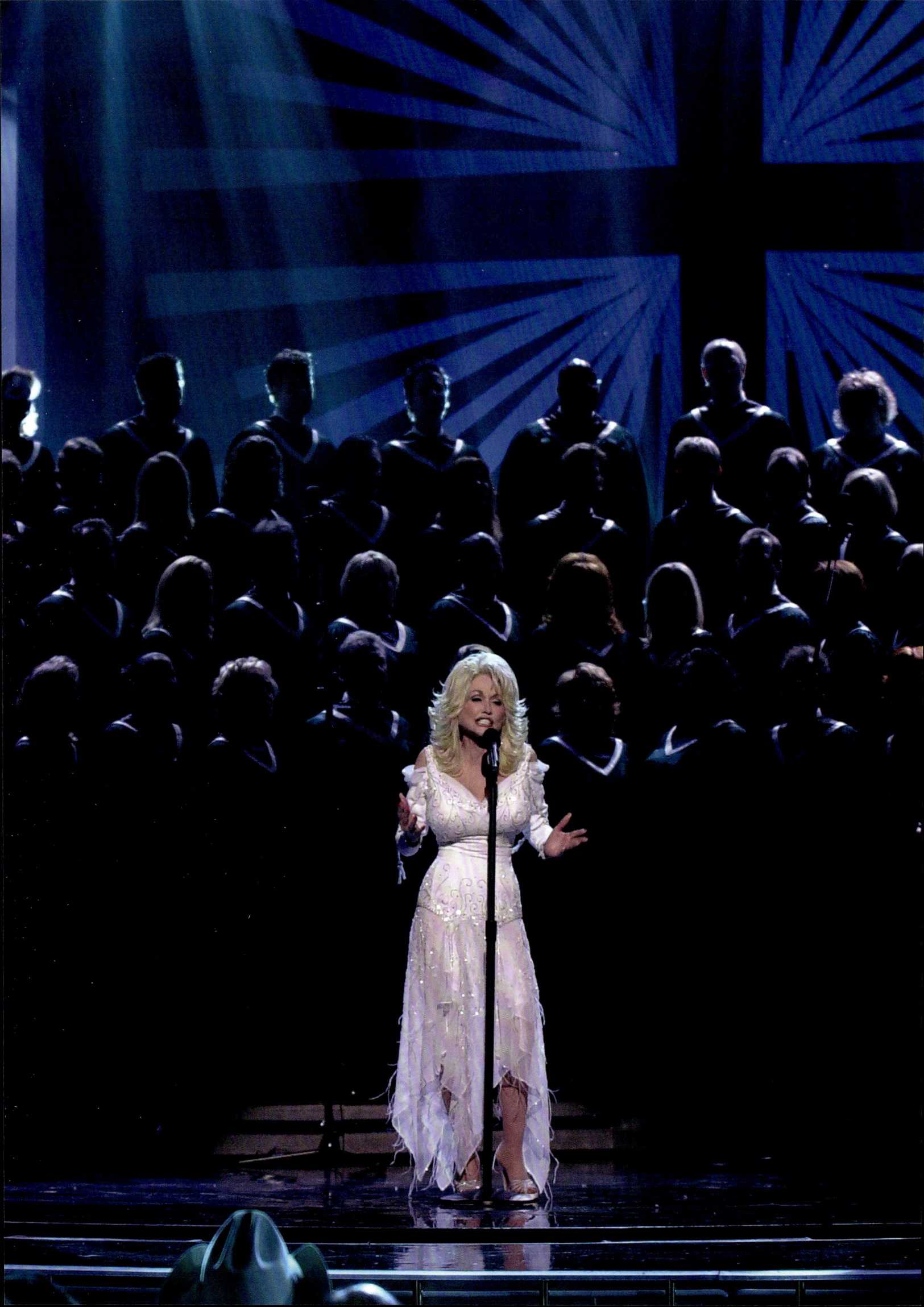

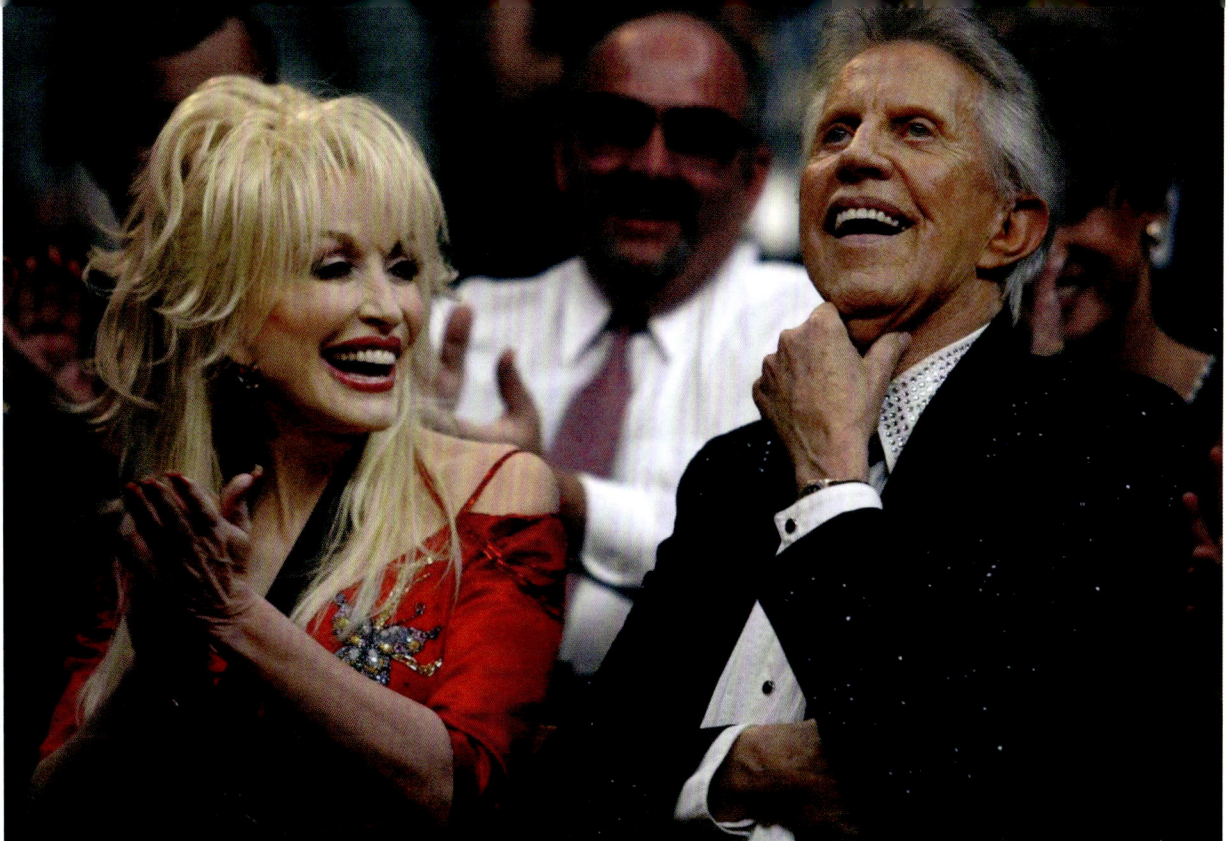

It was an honor to be part of the ceremony when Porter Wagoner was officially inducted into the Country Music Hall of Fame. He could still make everyone smile and laugh!

crowd were surprised when I pulled that song out of the hat during that tour. It has that reference about the "two paths" you can take, so I like to think it's a song about making spiritual choices, but it's extremely abstract. I suppose it can mean just about anything you want it to. Fortunately, just a few weeks before we cut the *Live and Well* album, Robert Plant attended my concert at the Point in Dublin and came backstage to tell me how much he liked my version of his song. That was especially rewarding, since I'd taken liberties with some lyrical ad-libs to fashion my interpretation of his song. As a songwriter, I really appreciated that he did that.

One real privilege that comes with becoming a veteran in your field is the opportunity to tell some of the people who were part of your story just how much they meant to you. At the CMA Awards in 2002, I was proud to announce that Porter Wagoner would be a new member of the Country Music Hall of Fame. Then, in May 2003, I attended his medallion ceremony and performed "Just Someone I Used to Know" as part of his induction.

In July 2003, I got all dressed up like a sexy version of a USO girl, or maybe a patriotic Betty Boop, in a red, white, and blue dress with matching red, white, and blue shoes, to perform on the annual PBS special *A Capitol Fourth*. The show is held on the West Lawn of the Capitol, right out on the National Mall, with the Washington Monument in the background. I sang "Light of a Clear Blue Morning," which seemed like an appropriately uplifting song as we still worked our way past the events of 9/11. And "9 to 5" was a great

Returning to My Roots

It's awe-inspiring to honor America by singing to an audience on the National Mall, near the Washington Monument. The top two photos are from rehearsals, and the bottom one shows how much I loved dressing up as a USO girl to be patriotic!

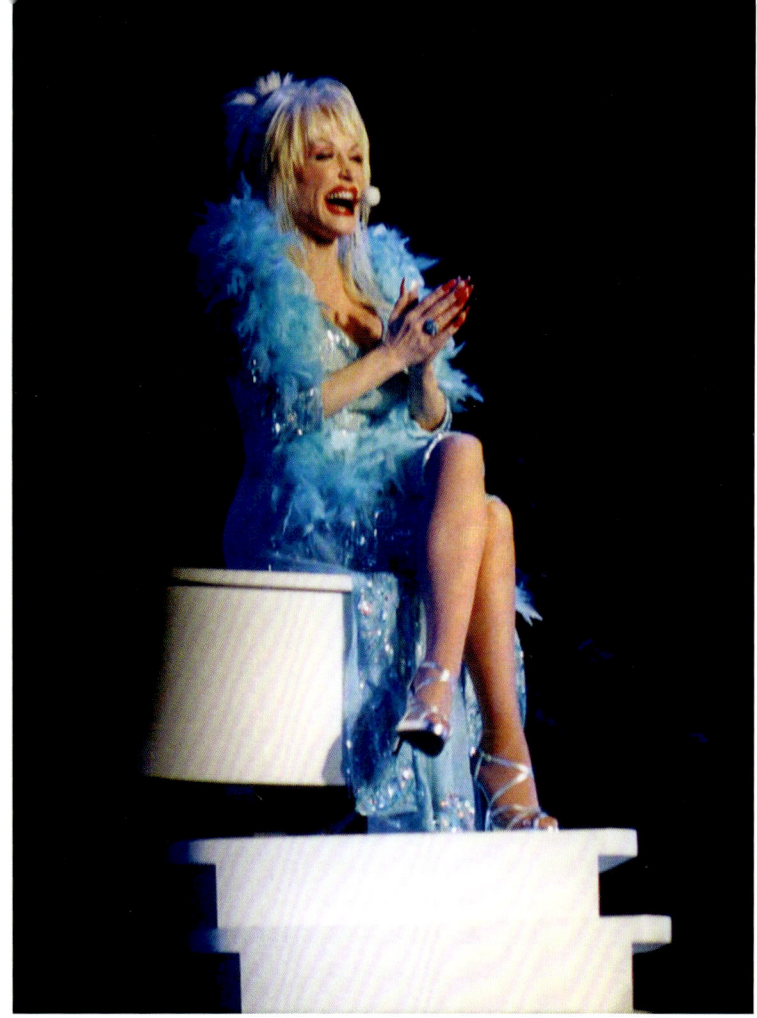

This is me—sitting on top of the world!

song to pull out for all the hardworking Americans from Boston to San Diego. It also fit with the patriotic project I'd released around that time called *For God and Country*.

It all made me proud to be an American. I always have been, of course, but that album and singing at the Capitol like that made me realize again how lucky we really are.

I was surprised a few months later when I taped a *CMT Crossroads* episode with Melissa Etheridge at the Sony Television Studios in Los Angeles. Melissa was great—that didn't surprise me. What did surprise me was how awesome the blend of our voices was. She has that very identifiable scratch, and mine is much more innocent, and kind of fluttery at times. I knew, after working up "Stairway to Heaven" and "Shine," that we could put a really great country spin on her songs "Come to My Window" and "Bring Me Some Water"—and we did. But I didn't realize just how nicely our very different voices would fit together. Melissa was so supportive on stage too. I never had a doubt that she was happy to be there. And I'm sure no one who watched the show on TV over Thanksgiving weekend doubted that either!

My first solo album back in 1967 had been titled *Hello, I'm Dolly*, playing off the Broadway musical and movie. Throughout my career, newspapers and talk show hosts had used the "Hello, Dolly" pun, and finally, in 2004, I named a series of thirty concerts the

Returning to My Roots

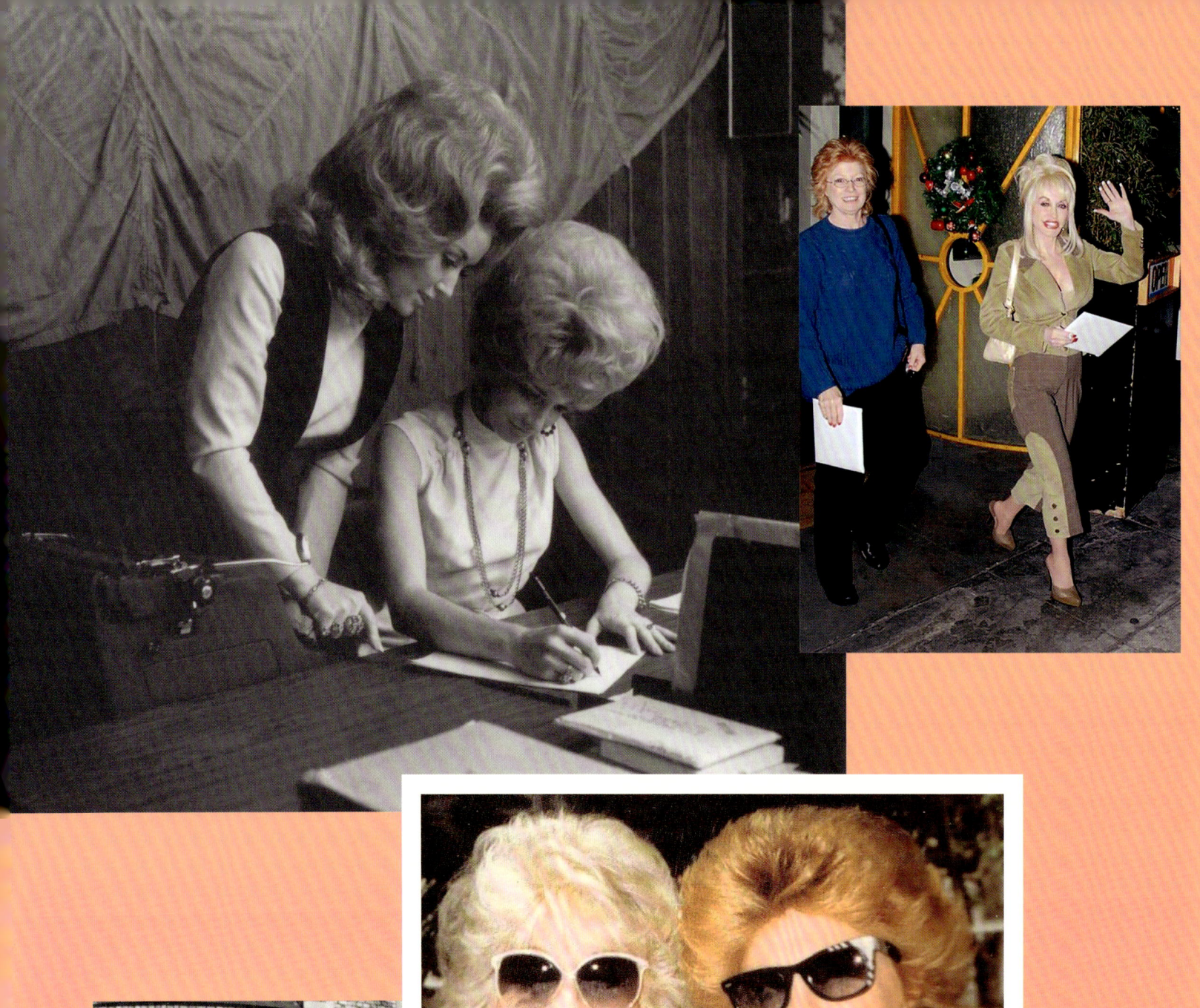

I may have been returning to my roots musically, but I've always had a little bit of Tennessee with me at every point in my career, thanks to my best friend, Judy Ogle. She traveled with me, worked as my assistant, and was there for anything I needed. We had so many adventures and so many laughs—and I can't imagine my years on the road (or my life)—without her!

Hello, I'm Dolly Tour. I wore plumage during part of the show that made some people think of one of Barbra Streisand's famous outfits in the movie, and the set included a staircase that looked just a little like the steps that Barbra walked down when she made her grand entrance in the film.

That part was unusual for me. I hate steps. I always say, "If I'm going to have steps, put a railing on it!" That's because with my boobs so big and my high heels, I'm always scared I'm going to fall right down those steps. So I don't know whose big idea that was! But we made it work. We also had a puppet of Kenny Rogers for the duet songs, and I sat on the piano during part of the show and sang with a martini in one hand—well, a martini *glass*, to be specific—and one of those long plastic cigarette holders that you picture an old-time starlet using.

Part of the reason I was able to pull off some of that staging was because it was the first concert tour where I used a headset. Think about it—we used to be tied to a mic stand, and then we were able to pull the mic off the stand and walk across the stage with it in one hand. What do you do with the other hand? A lot of times I'd just wrap the cord around my left hand and keep going. But now with a headset, I had the ability to move around even more and to make more gestures with both hands free.

I debuted the headset at the start of that tour, in Greenville, South Carolina, and for my road musicians, I used a young bluegrass band, The Grascals. It was actually an outgrowth of my previous band, The Blueniques, as it was formed by two of the guys from that lineup, Terry Eldredge and Jimmy Mattingly. On that tour I enjoyed playing "Me and Bobby McGee" as part of my set list. In fact, I called the guitar I used to perform it with "Bobby McGee," and it's one of my favorites to perform with!

In 2005, I sang classic pop and rock hits, like "Blowin' in the Wind," "Crimson and Clover," and "If I Were a Carpenter" on the Vintage Tour. In another part of my career, I might have tried to do those songs with a real pop flair, but now I Dollyized them, adapting them to the country sounds that were part of my upbringing. And they were a hit! All those great songs were featured on my album *Those Were the Days,* released that same year.

I felt nostalgic doing those old songs on the Vintage Tour. It was one of my favorites of all my shows because I love those songs. They are the kinds of songs that helped shape and mold me as a singer and as a writer and as a younger person because they came along when I was in my teens and early twenties. At that age, you're not going to just listen to older songs and artists. If you're a thriving teenager, you're going to get out and listen to whoever the hot artists of the moment are. And I was no different.

Even as a singer, you want to know what other people are doing. You want to know what they like in case you get a chance to write a song for them, or you're writing for other artists who are feeling the influence of the times.

Returning to My Roots

Through the Years

Every time I hit the road, I had a band with me. And once I went out on my own—after traveling and touring with Porter—they were *my* bands . . . musicians who could best support what I was doing at the time. As my career took different paths, so did my music . . . and so did my bands. The lineups and the faces changed, but other things did not. I always took a lot of pride in them—I still do. I expected a lot from them, but only because the fans deserved the best. And all of them delivered—for me and for the people who spent their hard-earned money on tickets to see us. I'll always be grateful for that.

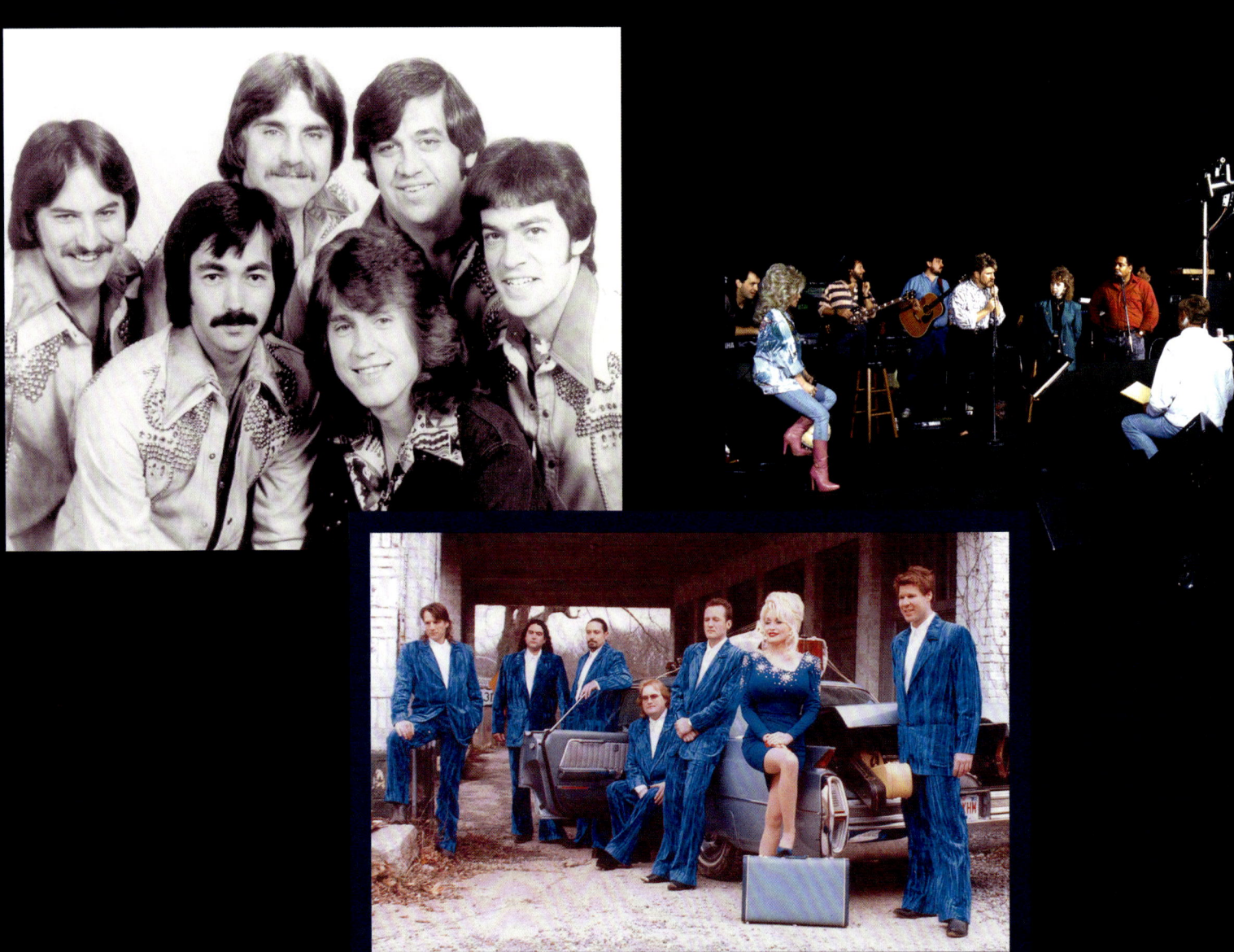

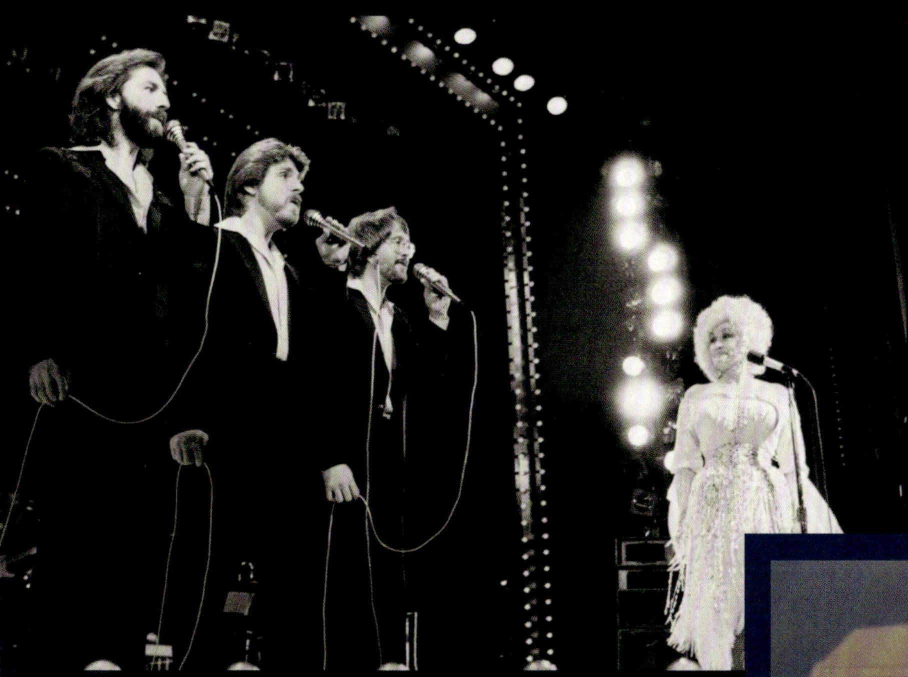

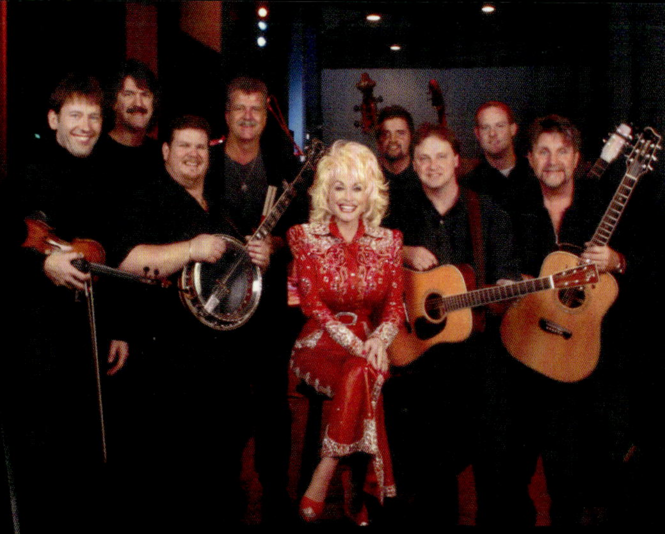

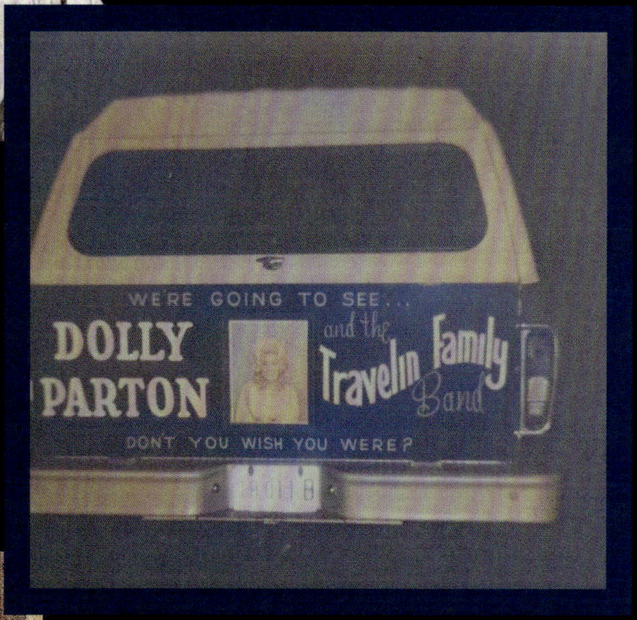

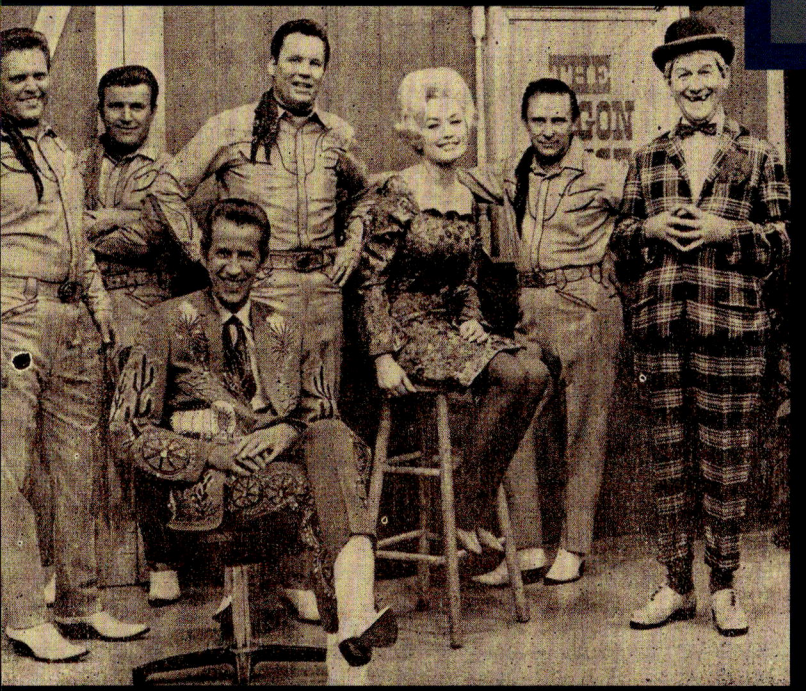
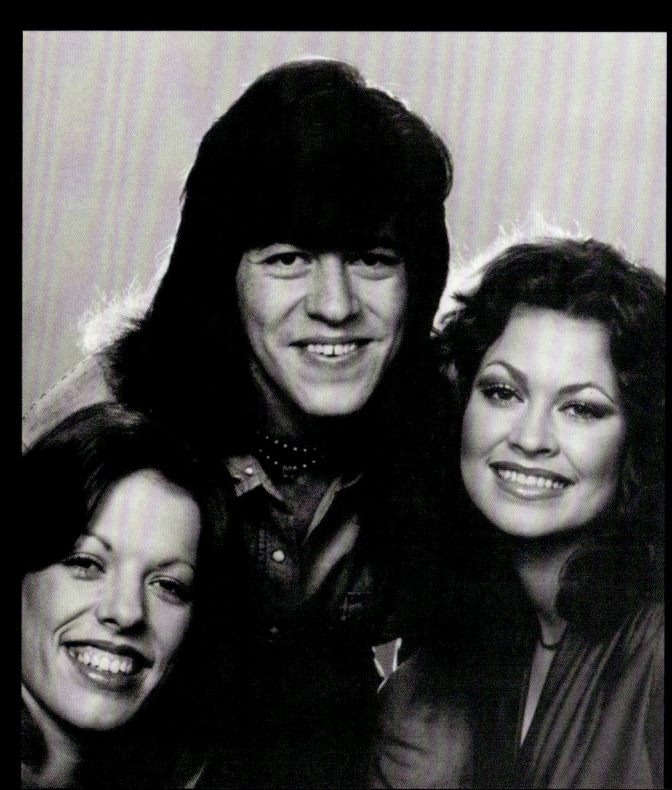

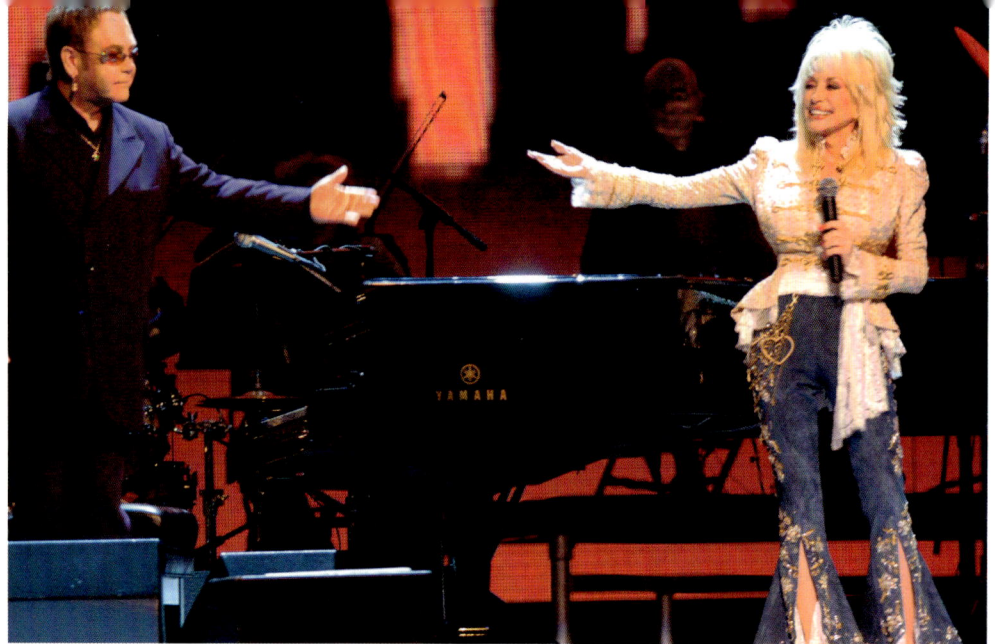

It was an honor to welcome Elton John to the
CMA Awards for our 2005 performance of
John Lennon's "Imagine."

I loved the costumes I wore on that tour too. I enjoyed getting to dress in some of those vintage clothes. And we all loved that tour because everybody in the band knew those old songs, and there wasn't a one that the audience didn't know and sing along to.

One of the highlights of that tour came when we drew about two hundred thousand people— my largest live audience ever—at the Hardly Strictly Bluegrass Festival, an annual free public event in San Francisco's Golden Gate Park. Here we were, singing "Where Have All the Flowers Gone?" and "Crimson and Clover" just walking distance from Haight-Ashbury, the neighborhood at the heart of 1967's Summer of Love.

That November, I did more than cover a pop song—I sang one right alongside a major music icon. It was the only time—so far, anyway—that the CMA Awards were held in New York City. It was at Madison Square Garden, and I stood next to Elton John, who was dressed in royal purple, at the piano for a duet of "Turn the Lights Out When You Leave" in a medley with "Imagine."

Singing "Imagine" with a British superstar like Elton turned out to be another case of foreshadowing in my career. I'd played all over the world by that point, but the next part of my live career was about to be bigger—and even *more* global—than anything I'd done to date.

Star of the Show

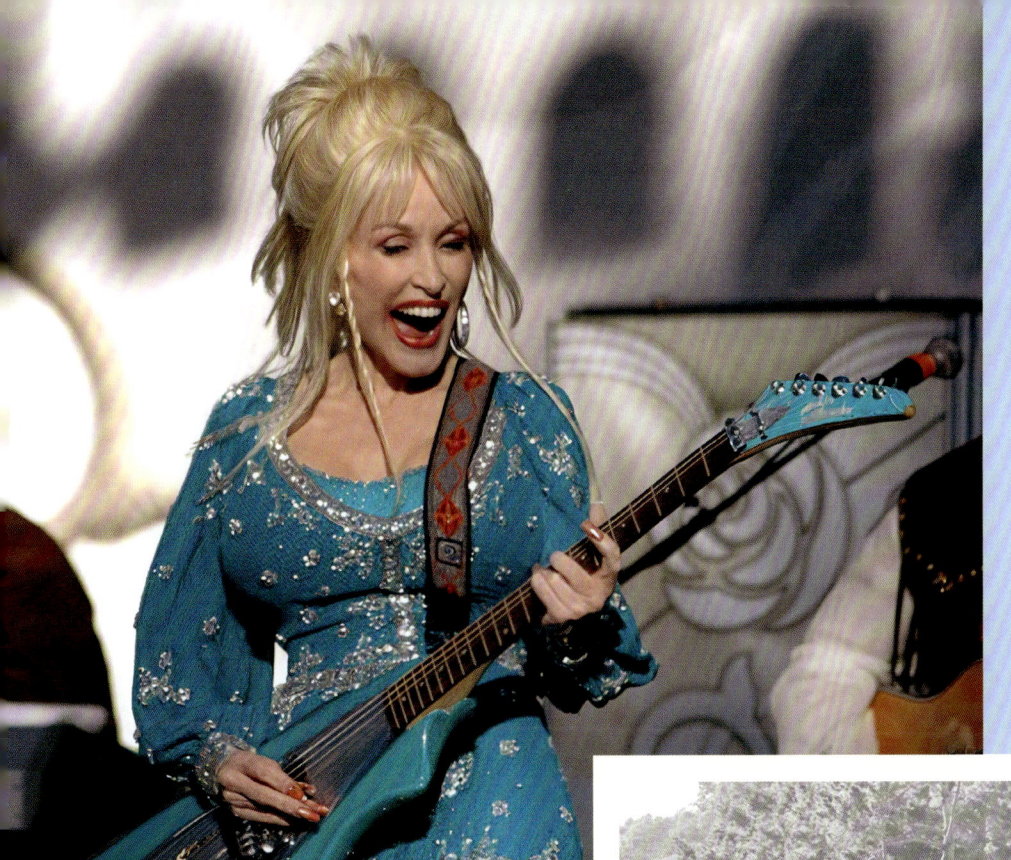

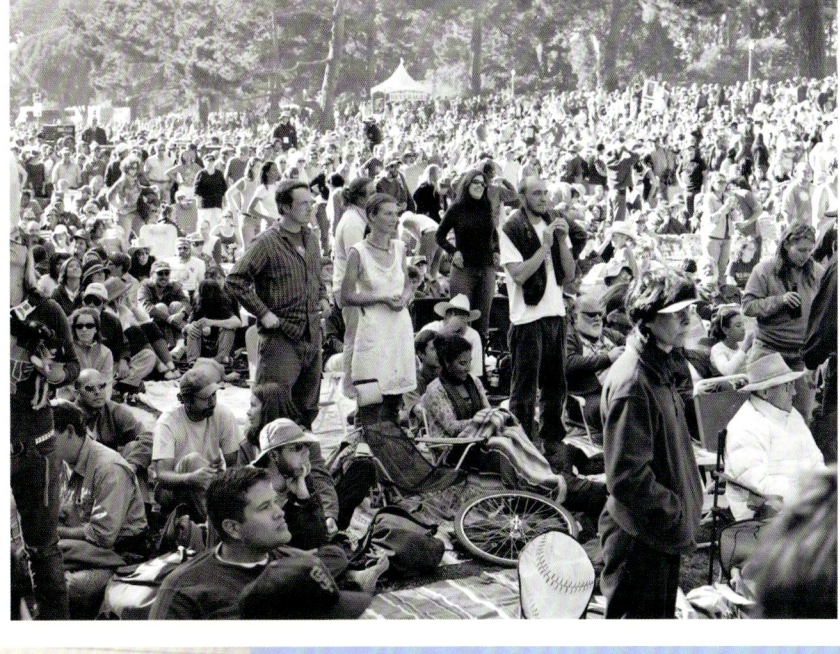

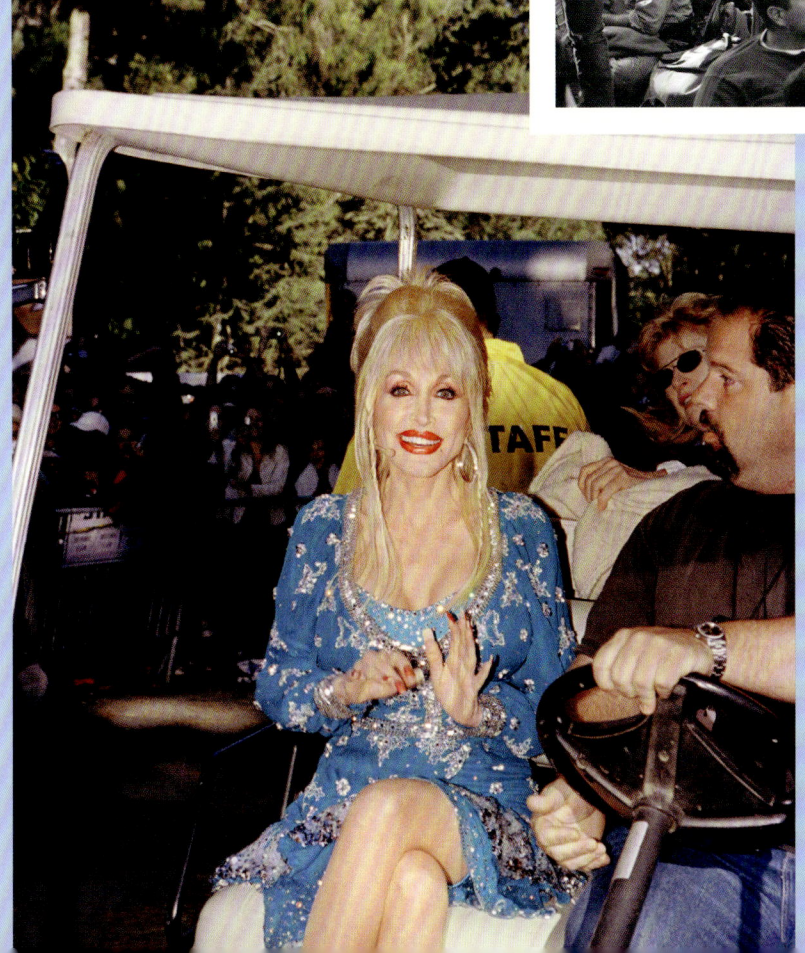

In 2005, I played to one of my biggest audiences ever at the Hardly Strictly Bluegrass Festival in San Francisco. We were on the Vintage Tour at the time, incorporating music from the 1960s and '70s, so I wanted to wear something that had just a touch of the earthy vibe from that era but still looked good with a little bit of bling!

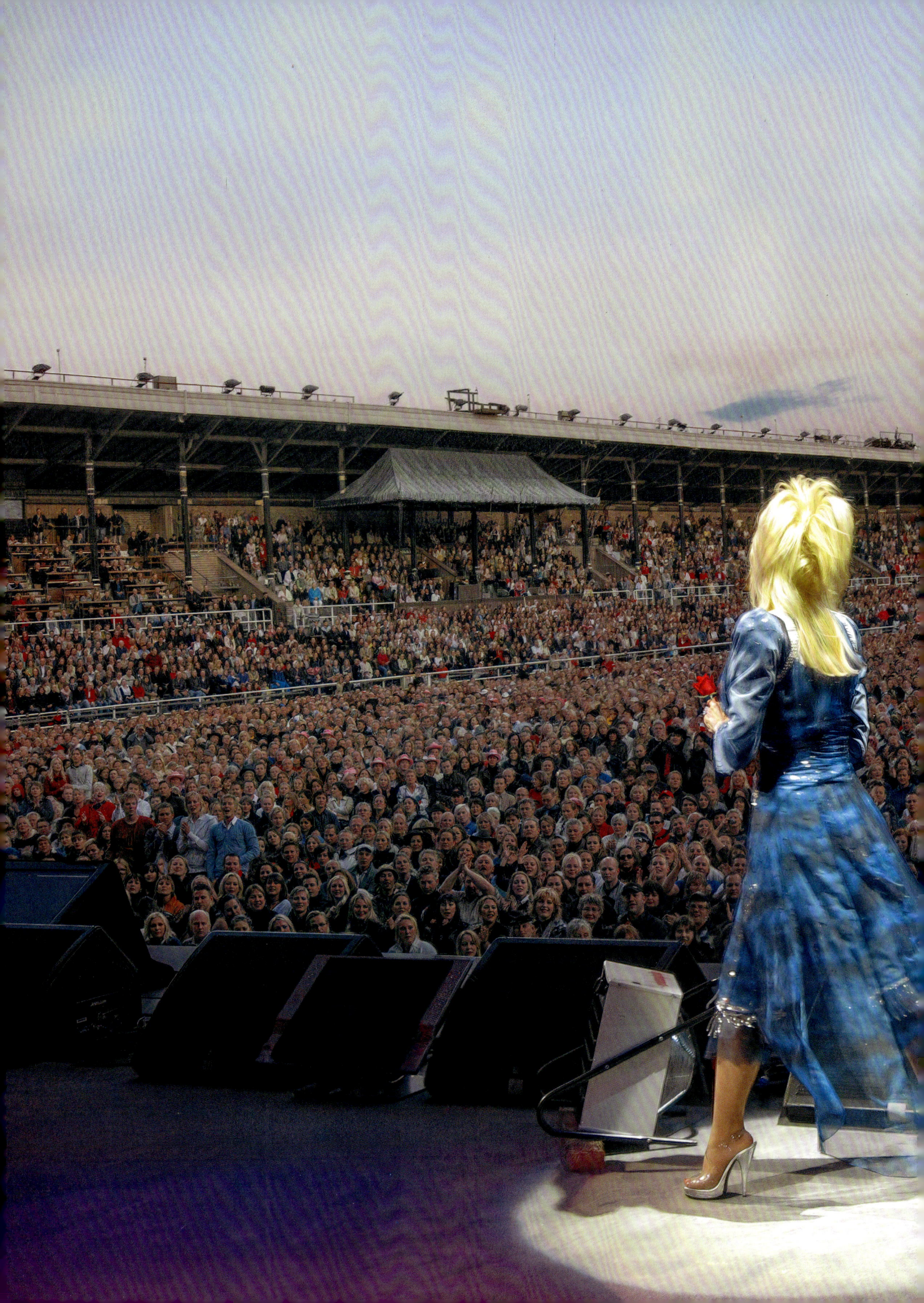

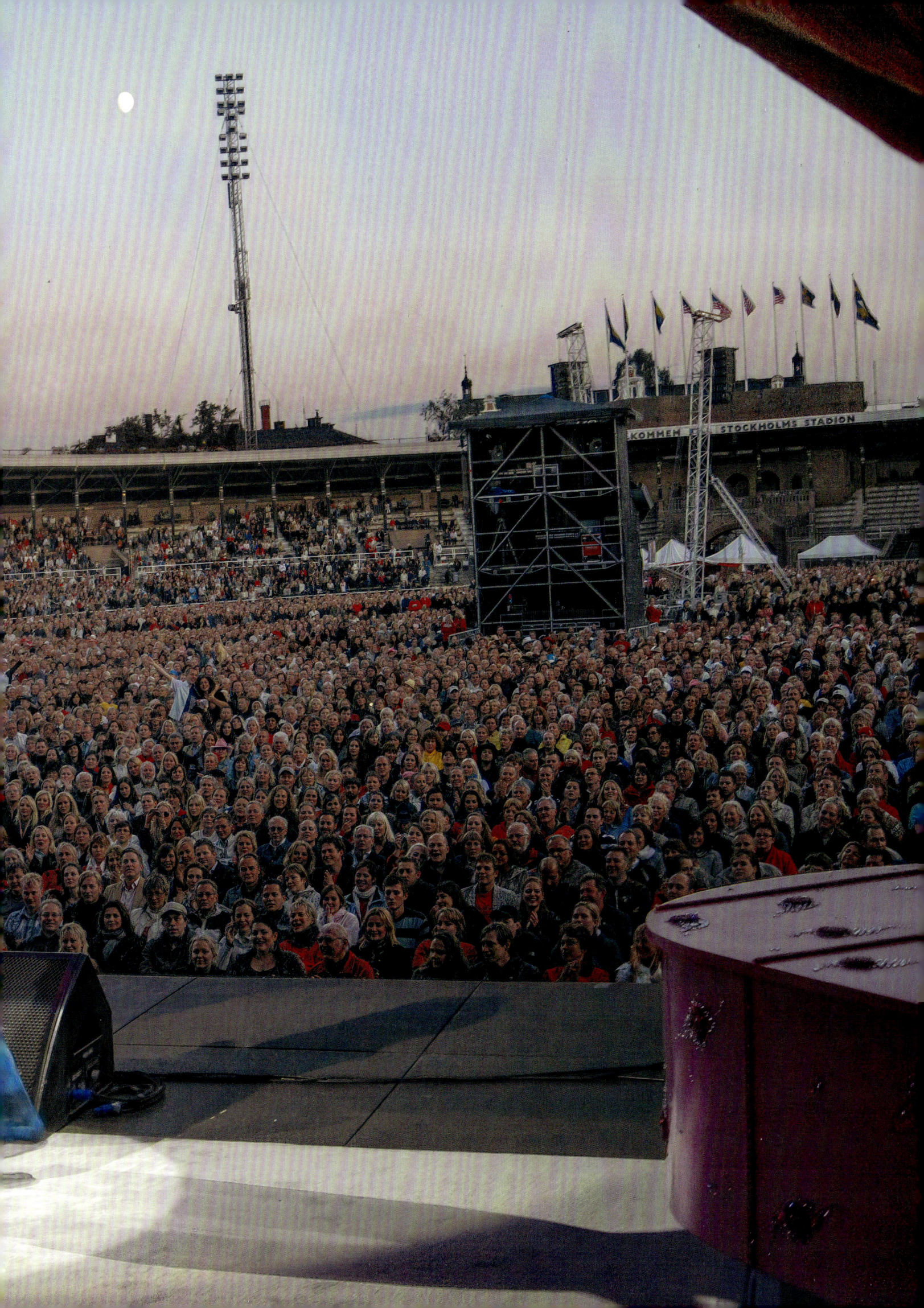

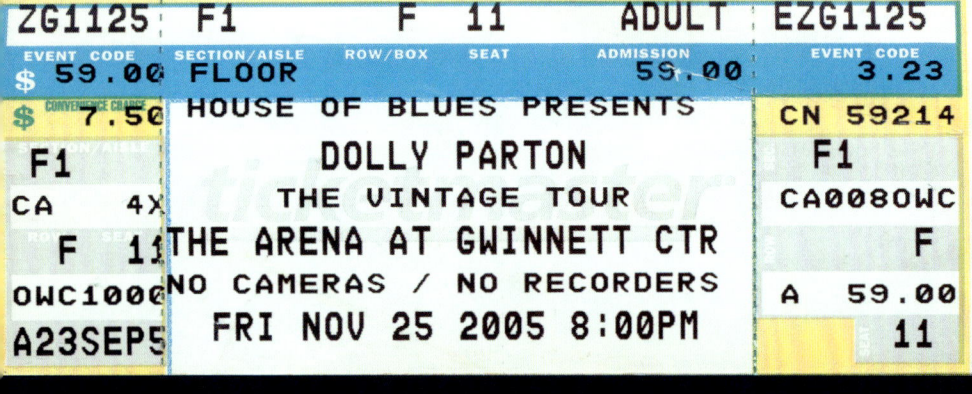
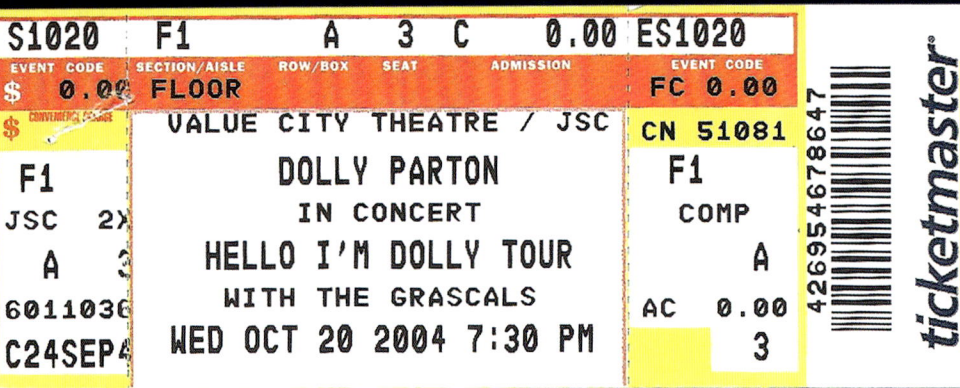
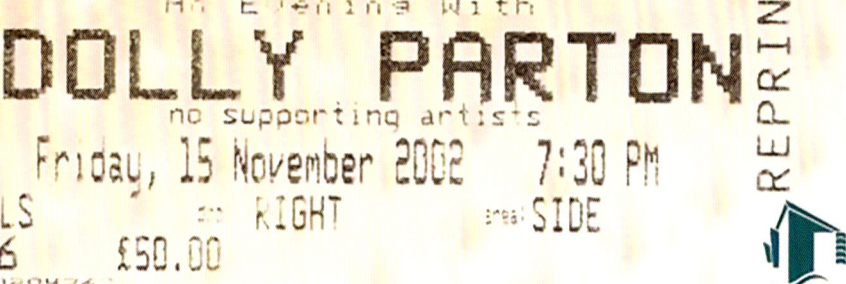

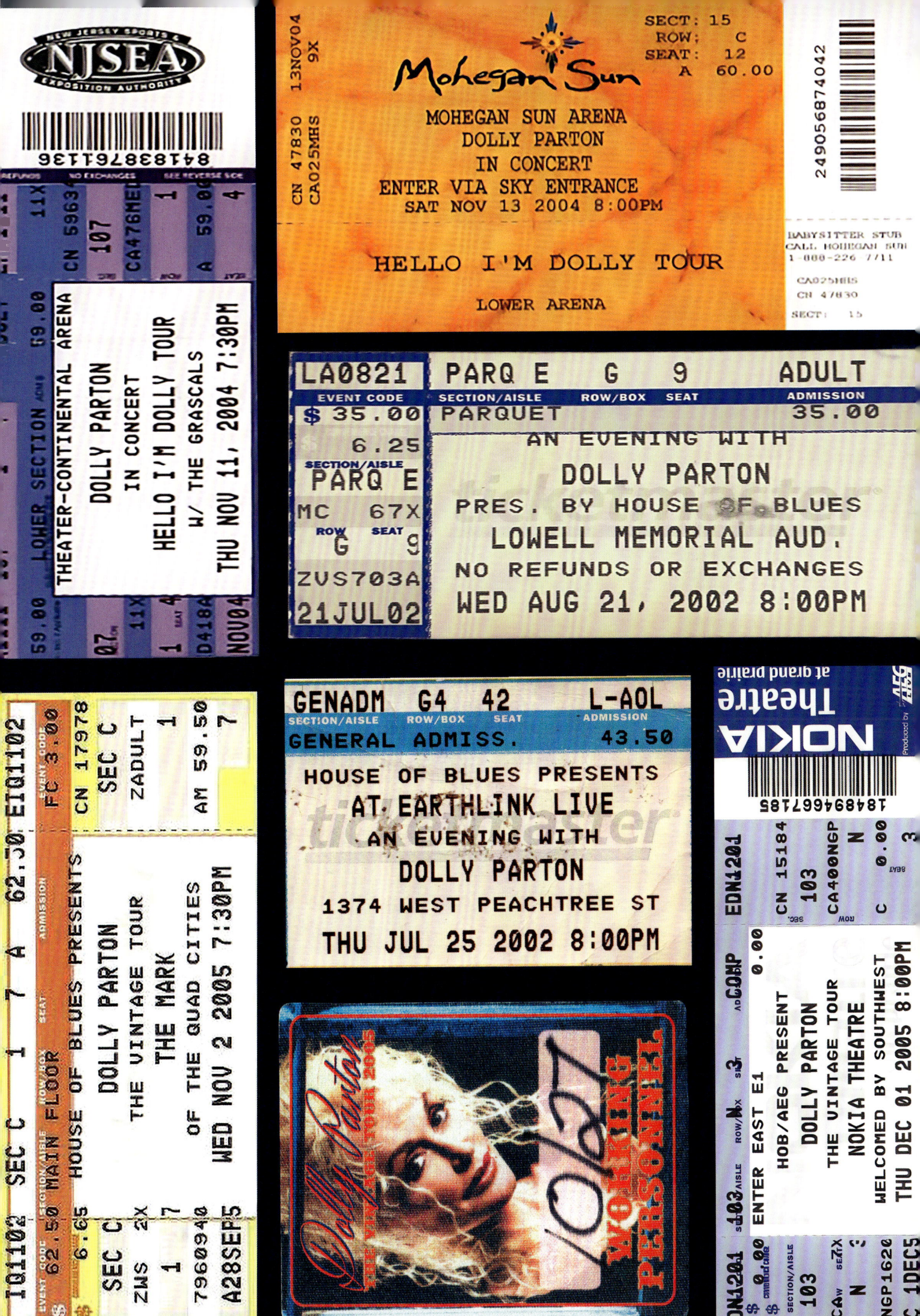

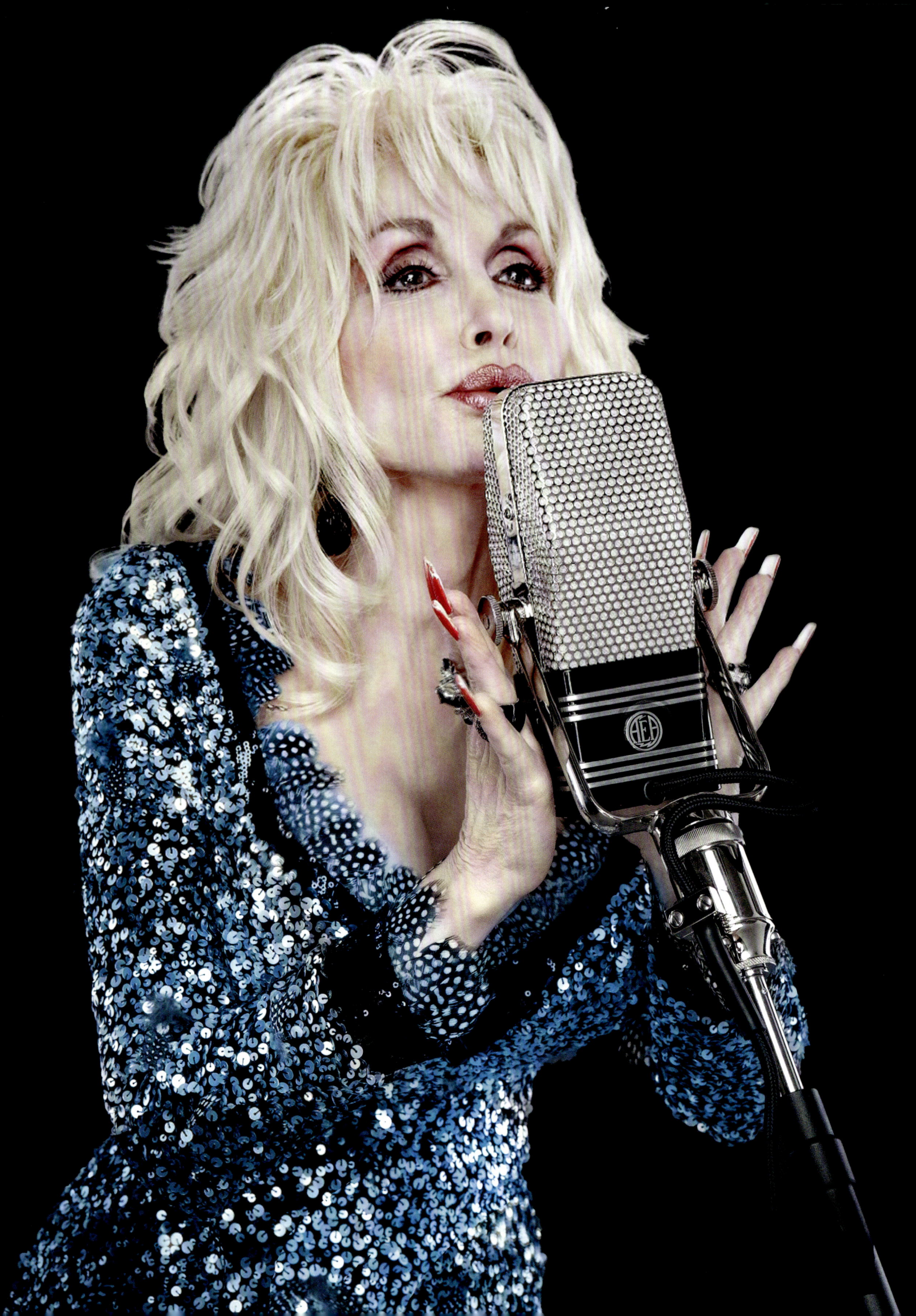

Better Days, Pure & Simple

2005-2016

2005–2016

It's a sign of Dolly's timelessness that she's had multiple songs become standards, including "Jolene," "Coat of Many Colors," "Here You Come Again," "9 to 5," "Islands in the Stream," and "I Will Always Love You." They're enduring works, and combined with her endearing presence as well as her endless optimism, they've made her a symbol of strength, resilience, and creativity that's transcended the muck and mire of everyday life.

Combining this legacy with her new works, Dolly defied the odds by launching the most successful period of her concert career in her fifties. On successive tours beginning in the 2000s, she consistently sold out arenas and stadiums as a solo artist, solidified her status as a global superstar, and played for the biggest international audience of her career, drawing more than 180,000 fans to her performance at the Glastonbury Music Festival in 2014.

Between becoming a regular at some of the world's most iconic venues and taking Broadway by storm with *9 to 5: The Musical,* Dolly made it clear that no stage was off limits.

—TOM ROLAND

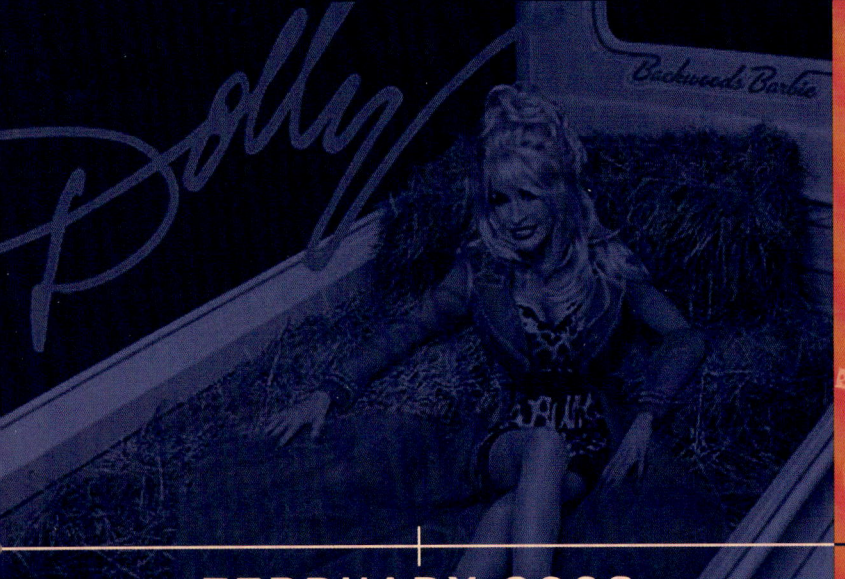

FEBRUARY 2008
Dolly releases *Backwoods Barbie* and embarks on a world tour of the same name across North America and Europe.

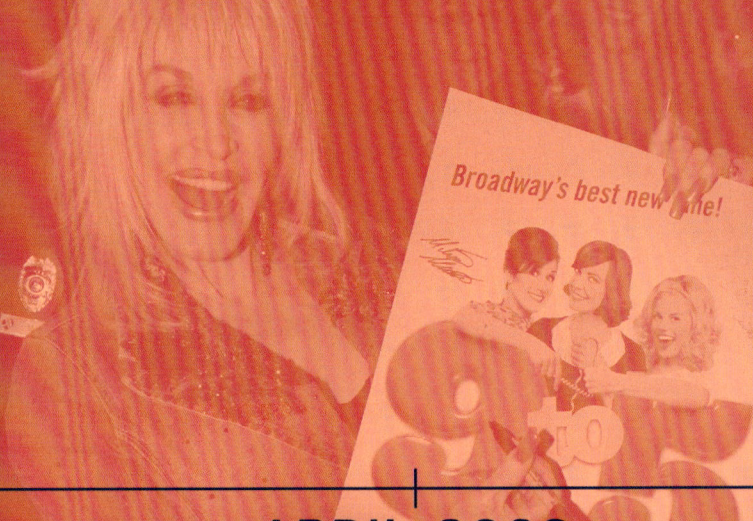

APRIL 2009
9 to 5: The Musical, for which Parton wrote the music and which she co-produced, premieres on Broadway. It continues to tour the world.

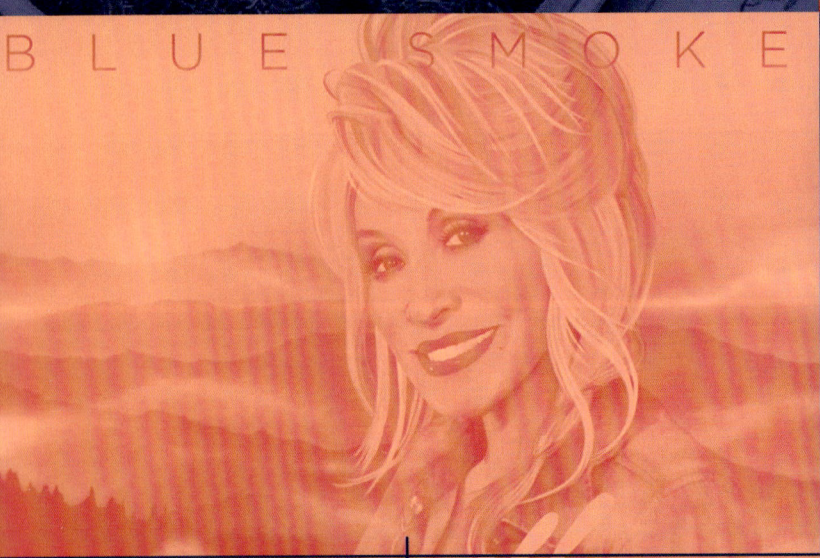

JANUARY 2014
Dolly releases *Blue Smoke* and launches a world tour of the same name, traveling across North America, Europe, Australia, and New Zealand.

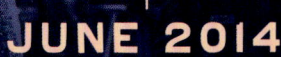

JUNE 2014
Dolly performs for the biggest international crowd of her career—more than 180,000 people at the UK's Glastonbury Festival.

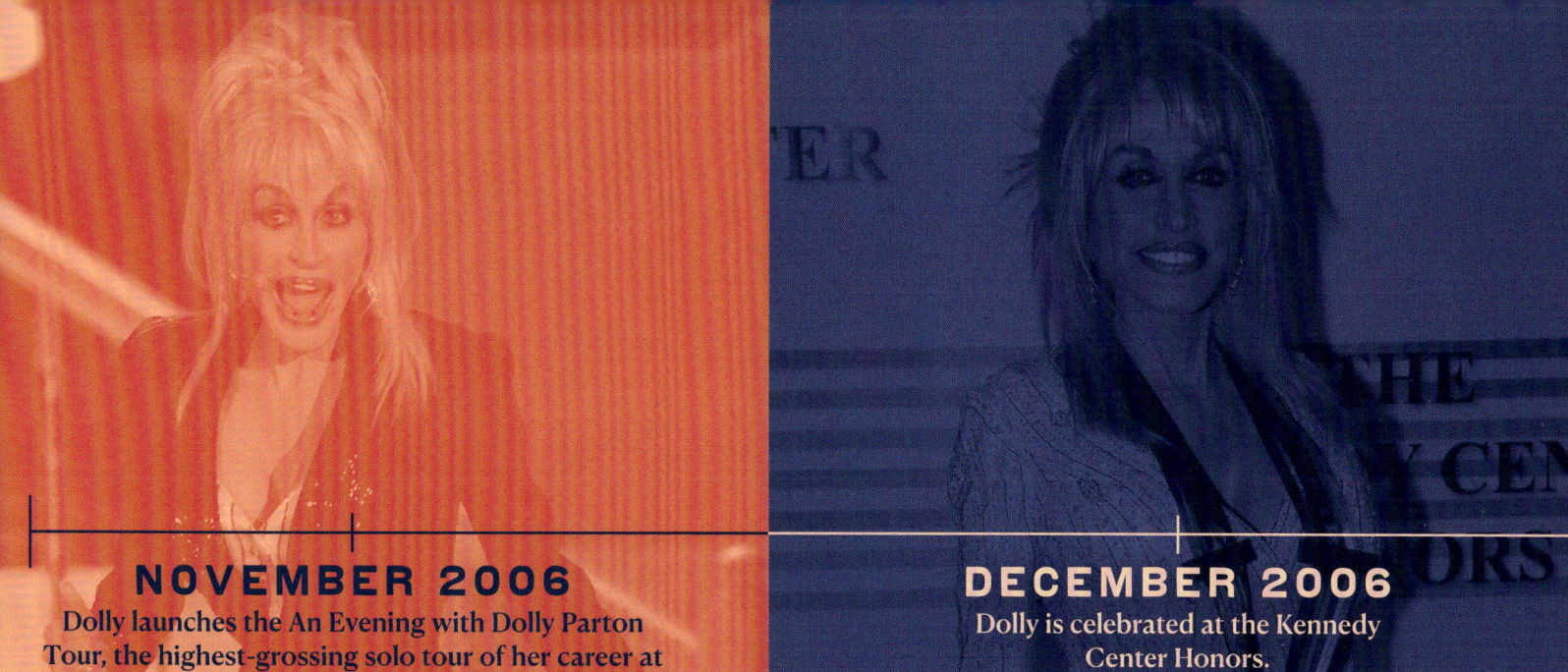

NOVEMBER 2006
Dolly launches the An Evening with Dolly Parton Tour, the highest-grossing solo tour of her career at that time.

DECEMBER 2006
Dolly is celebrated at the Kennedy Center Honors.

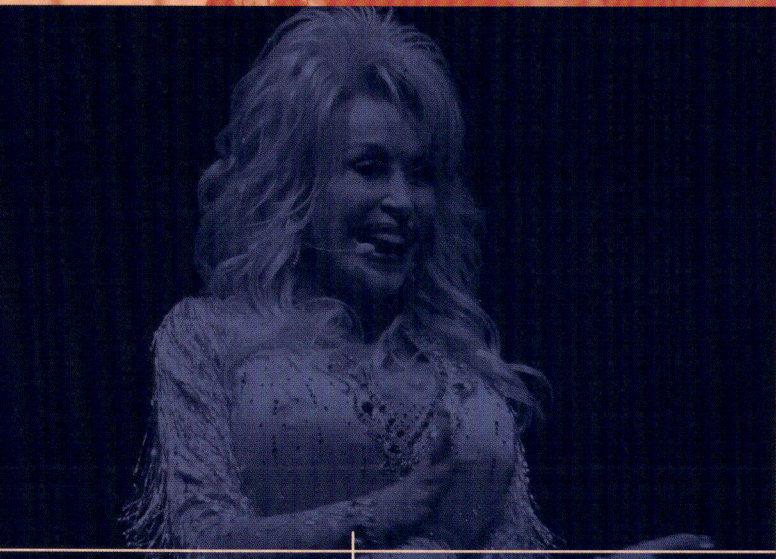

JULY 2011
Dolly launches the Better Day World Tour to support her album of the same name. The tour travels across North America, and to Europe and Australia.

JANUARY 2012
Dolly returns to the big screen, costarring with Queen Latifah in *Joyful Noise*.

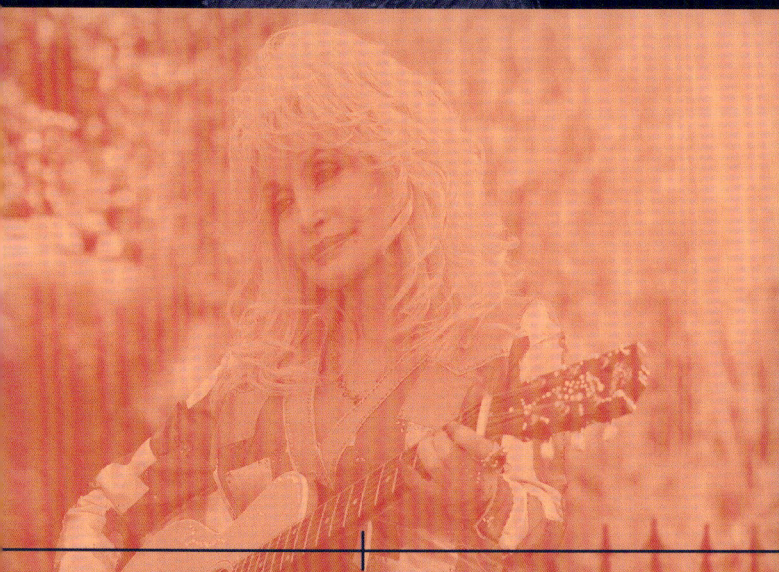

DECEMBER 2015
Dolly produces *Coat of Many Colors*, a top-rated TV film for NBC.

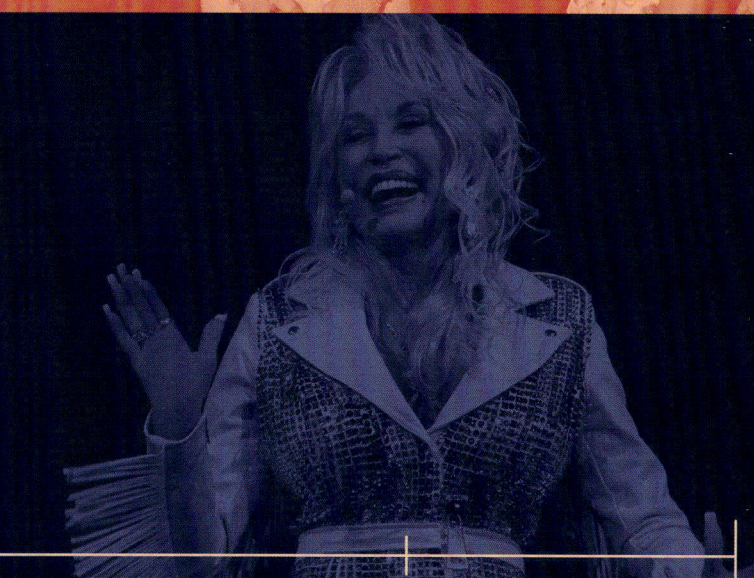

AUGUST 2016
Dolly releases *Pure & Simple*, an album that debuts at no. 1, two months after launching a tour of the same name, which becomes her highest-grossing North American arena tour.

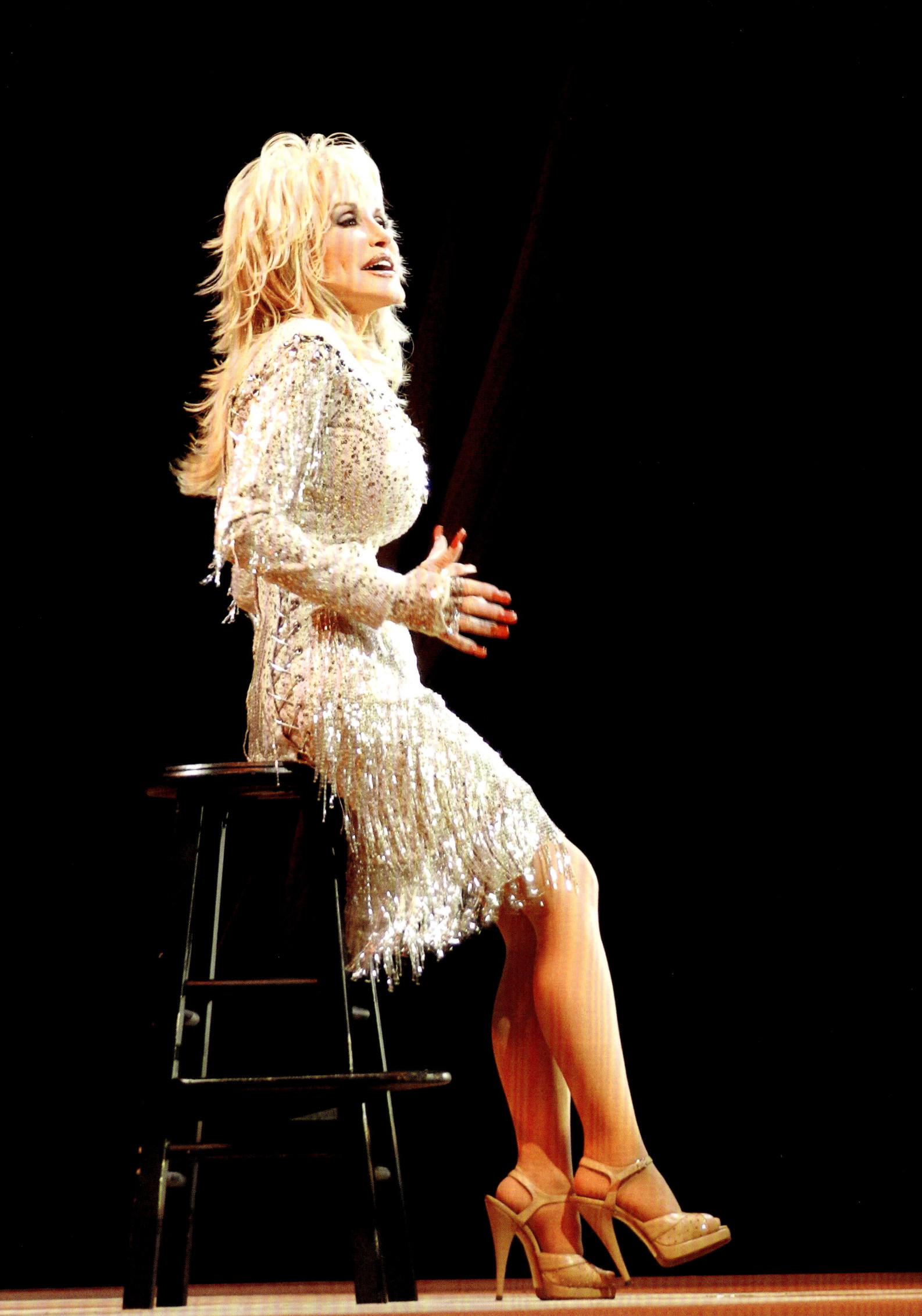

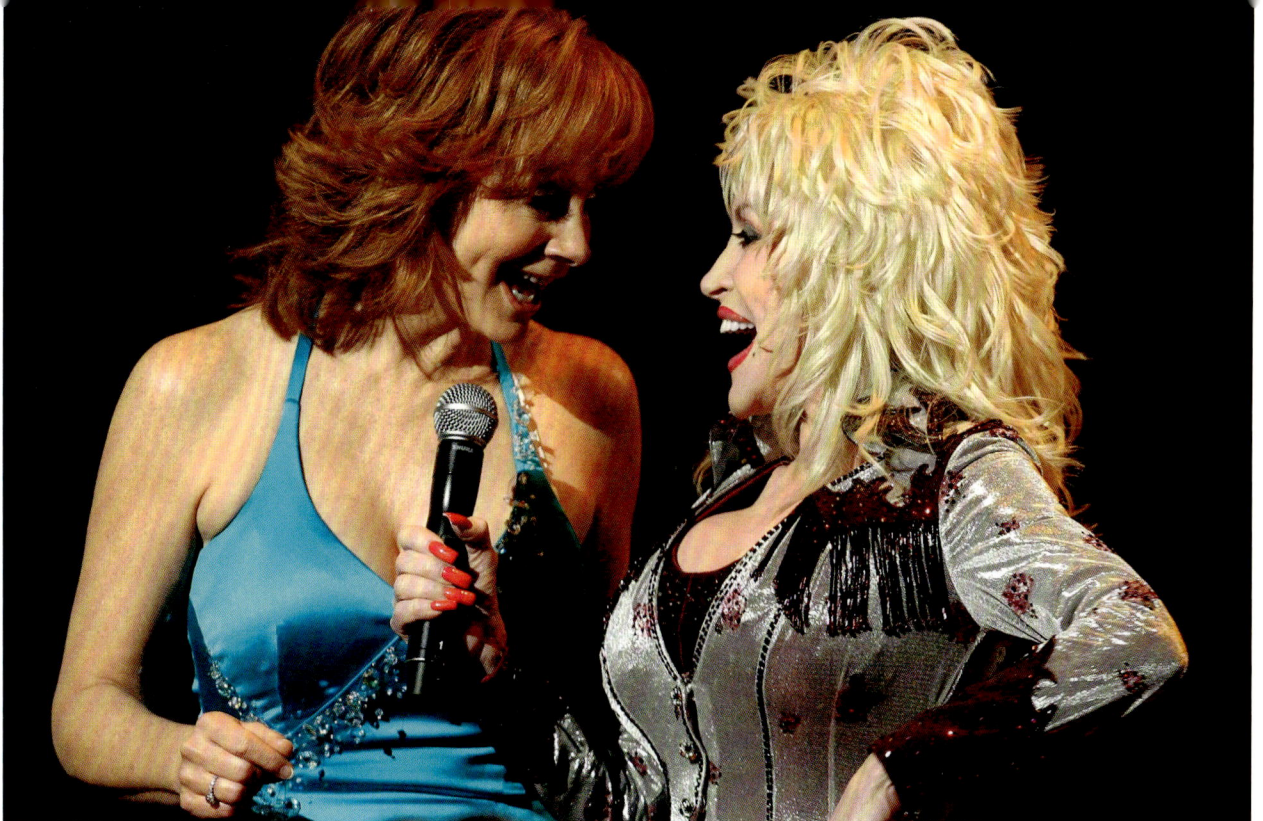

Reba McEntire is one of my closest friends in the music business. We've recorded together and acted together, and if there's anyone in country music who knows what it takes to be the "Star of the Show," it's Reba.

𝓜ost music careers have a shelf life. The business managers who work with recording artists plan their investments around the idea that an artist's financial peak will last only three to five years. After that, their fan base is established, and they tend to work a specific set of venues for a modest income.

I'd been aware of this since the time I started, and during the early 2000s, it seemed like most of the music business had decided that's what was going to happen to me.

Instead, I hit the best period of my touring life nearly forty years into my career on the national stage. I ended up selling out strings of arenas and even stadiums on three different continents at an age when many of my peers start thinking about winding things down. Best of all, I could dictate my own calendar. I'd tour when I wanted to and carve out time to pursue my interests on other stages too.

A lot of the setup for that was happening behind the scenes during 2006. Meanwhile, I was already picking and choosing the meaningful moments when I'd take part in public events, sometimes with artist friends.

For starters, I joined Keith Urban at the Country Radio Seminar (CRS) in February. CRS is an industry convention where radio programmers from all over the United States visit Nashville for three intense days of educational panels and networking parties, making it one of the most important country music business gatherings on the calendar every year.

Better Days, Pure & Simple

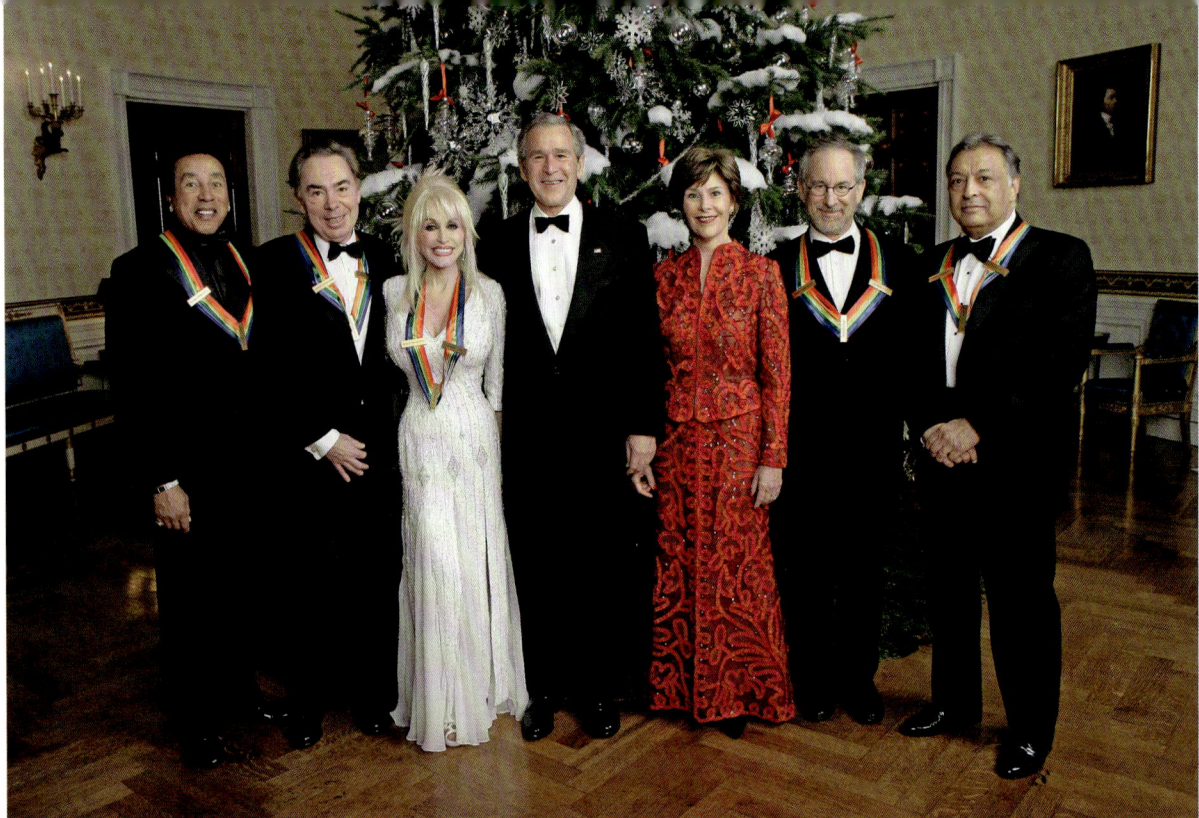

That medal is quite an honor—a Kennedy Center Honor! *From left:* Smokey Robinson, Andrew Lloyd Webber, me, President George W. Bush, First Lady Laura Bush, Steven Spielberg, and Zubin Mehta.

Keith gave a performance for the broadcasters, and he wanted to make it something special that they couldn't see every day. He asked if I would join him for a couple of songs, so we did "Jolene" and "Two Doors Down." He also brought Pat Green and Ronnie Dunn out for collaborations. Keith's talent, level of creativity, and thoughtfulness as a human being were a great reminder that the genre continues to be in good hands.

A bit later that year, I also had the honor of receiving my second Oscar nomination, for my song "Travelin' Thru," which I performed at the 2006 Academy Awards.

In September, I made my first guest appearance on Disney Channel's *Hannah Montana*. Miley Cyrus is my goddaughter, and she quickly became the hottest thing in the youth market after that TV series launched. I took part for personal reasons, but it ended up being a good career move, too, since kids who weren't even born when I was having my biggest hits suddenly became Dolly Parton fans. And it renewed some of their parents' interest in me too!

In October, I teamed up with my longtime friend Reba McEntire for "How Blue" during the *CMT Giants: Reba* TV special, and in December 2006 I attended a great concert where I didn't actually perform but my music filled the room. I was among those saluted at the Kennedy Center Honors, and I got to enjoy seeing and hearing other people sing my songs. Shania Twain did "Coat of Many Colors," Carrie Underwood teamed with Kenny Rogers on "Islands in the Stream," Alison Krauss joined Suzanne Cox and Cheryl White for "Jolene,"

Star of the Show

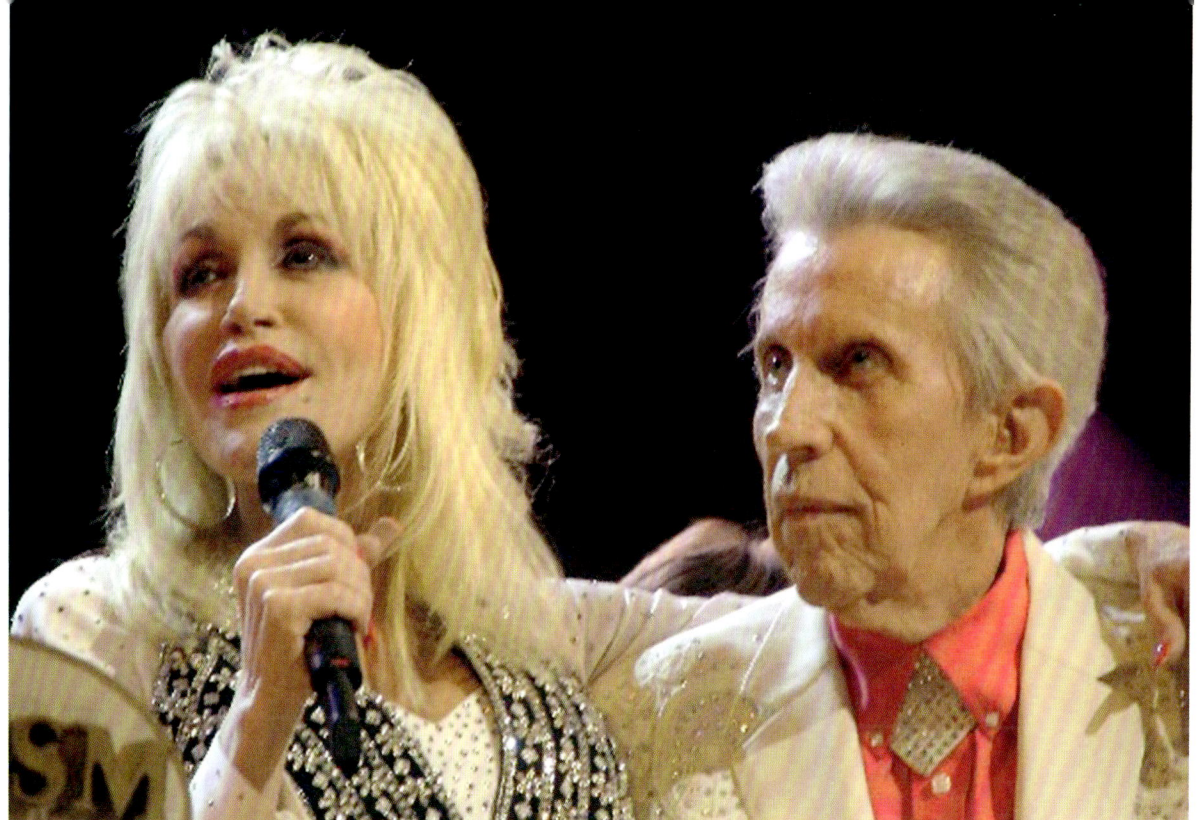

When the Grand Ole Opry celebrated Porter's fiftieth anniversary with the show, we sang together in public for the last time. It was a special night.

and Vince Gill did a sweet version of "I Will Always Love You." Reba was there to host the segment and presented me with the official honor. We have always been there for each other in key moments throughout the past several decades, and that was a special one.

While those events were happening publicly, I went through some serious retooling of my business situation behind the scenes. I had been managing myself for several years at that point, and I was happy with many of my accomplishments during that period. But let's face it: some of the details involved in business—like scheduling, keeping up with technological changes, and handling paperwork—aren't fun. I realized those functions were taking up time that I could be using for other creative ventures.

Meanwhile, Live Nation—the company that organized and produced my tours at that time—asked an executive named Danny Nozell to go through the books and see if there were ways to cut costs and increase revenues. Danny had been the manager for a heavy metal band called Slipknot and some other crazy-ass rock bands that, to be honest, might've scared me to death. I'm sure they were great artists and had their own following, but some of that stuff was so dark that it was worlds away from me.

On the surface, Danny and I might seem like an odd match. But he's good at what he does, and he not only found ways to make my shows more profitable but also took a hard look at some of the marketing around my previous tours. He was convinced that there were Dolly Parton fans who weren't being reached, who would come out to the shows if they

Better Days, Pure & Simple

knew about them further in advance. Kent Wells, my guitarist and the producer of some of my best albums, thought Danny would be a good addition to the team, and I agreed.

But Danny also presented a challenge. He wanted to do a tour without any opening acts, and he wanted to book my current show—An Evening with Dolly Parton—in big venues. Great big venues. It put a lot of pressure on me, and I'll admit I was nervous. Danny assured me it would be a positive experience and that I could do it. That was easy for him to say—he was playing with *my* money! If it didn't go as he promised, I could lose millions of dollars. I told him we could go forward, but if it didn't work, he'd be fired. And I told Kent I'd fire him too. Kent had always had my back, and I thought that would encourage him to keep an eye on whatever Danny was doing. I might've fired Danny, but not Kent!

As it turned out, none of that was necessary. Danny's a big believer in underpromising and overdelivering, and that's exactly what he did. He promised we'd make money, basing his figures on the most conservative estimate, and we made more than he'd projected. The entire tour sold out. We were getting revitalized—brushing the dust off the star, so to speak . . . polishing, it maybe. Or just adding some "shine" back to it!

Danny also talked me into going back to Europe. I had done a small number of shows in the United Kingdom and Ireland in 2002 and others years before, but I wasn't in a mood to do it again. The fans were great—I loved the people who came to the shows there—but the experience had been frustrating in some ways. I wasn't happy with the transportation on that 2002 trip, and at every stop, I'd have to oversee dozens of pieces of luggage being moved into a hotel room late at night, only to get up early and have all that luggage taken right back out and loaded back up around 5:00 a.m. In the United States, I had much more control, could use a tour bus, and didn't have to spend much time in hotel rooms. Further complicating that overseas trip, I'd had some paperwork problems that created delays when I tried to come back to the States. So I wasn't excited about going back, but Danny asked me to trust him on that too.

I gave him some time to put together a European package, and he completely surprised me. For starters, it was a bigger tour than the previous trip: eleven dates in the United Kingdom and Ireland, plus ten more shows in parts of Europe where I hadn't performed in decades. I hadn't played a concert in Denmark, Sweden, or the Netherlands since 1978 or in Norway since 1979, and I'd *never* played in Finland.

One of the key pieces was travel. We'd be crossing international borders repeatedly, and the idea of being stuck on a bus while we dealt with potential passport dramas didn't appeal to me at all.

Danny found a way to sidestep all of that. He knew the owner of a private coach company, and he hired them to build two custom buses to use in Europe. His idea was that we'd use them in conjunction with a private plane.

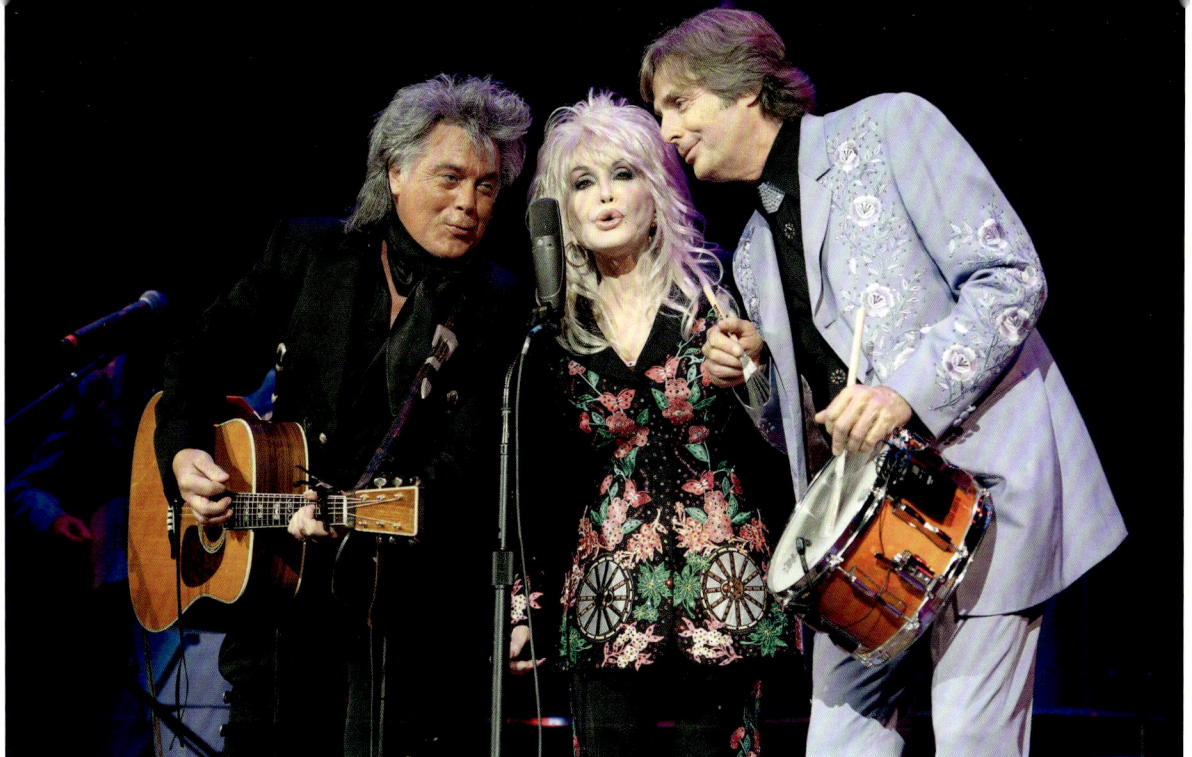

Marty Stuart, me, and "Handsome Harry" Stinson—of Marty's Fabulous Superlatives—singing "Jolene" on Marty's Late Night Jam at the Ryman Auditorium in Nashville.

As far as I was concerned, the plane was out of the question. My daddy would never have spent that kind of money, so why would I? But Danny insisted that my daddy was never in my position to worry about such things—and besides, he was going to get the promoters to pay for the plane. I'll be darned if he didn't!

Once I consented, it was the best experience I'd ever had in tour accommodations. The buses were the first two entertainer buses built in Europe with a shower and tub—that's what Danny told me, anyway! And he had them both stocked with items from my home—everything from cosmetics and food to blankets—so I felt completely at ease in my surroundings.

The plane and the buses worked in tandem to get me around. When the tour started in Horsens, Denmark, I got off the plane and headed straight for the first bus, which transported me from the airport to Forum Horsens, the site of the concert. There was no hotel. I slept on the bus, and I didn't even use the venue's dressing room. I changed clothing and did my makeup on the bus, like I'd done for years in the past, so there was no need to haul all the luggage in and out.

After the second show at Forum Horsens, the bus took me back to the airport, where I got on the private plane and flew to Bergen, Norway. There, the identical bus was waiting to take me to that city's concert stadium. That was the setup for the entire tour.

An Evening with Dolly Parton became one of the Top 10 country tours of the year, according to *Billboard*'s Boxscore.

Better Days, Pure & Simple

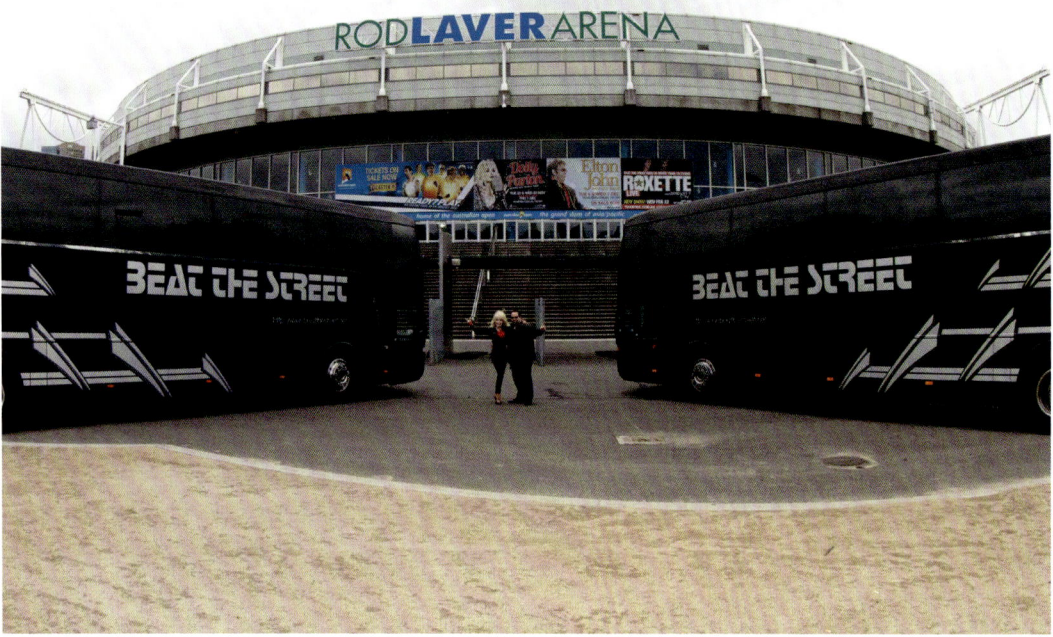

My manager, Danny Nozell, had two buses customized for our European and Australian tours in 2011 and 2014, allowing me to feel at home on the other side of the world. Here we are in front of the arena in Melbourne, Australia, where we played both of those years.

Danny's plan took advantage of the best parts of road life. I actually sleep better on the bus than in any house I've ever lived in or any other bed I've ever slept in. I've heard other artists say that too. I guess you get used to it, and for me, I know that when I'm on the bus, I'm doing what I love. The modern buses have come a long way too. They're built so that when they're parked, the side of the main cabin can pull out farther, creating a whole living room. I can live on the bus, and I can drive right up to the venue where we're playing. I go in and do a rehearsal, I get back on the bus in the parking lot at the venue, I take a nap, I get ready, and I eat supper, or I'll go in and eat with the band because they always have catering in the auditorium. As soon as that show's over, I get right back on that bus, start slinging clothes and hair everywhere, jump in that bed, and I'm ready to go again.

One unexpected development from that visit to Europe came during the first two dates. The promoters in Denmark told Danny that he needed to sell pink cowboy hats with the Dolly logo on them. He fought them on the idea. Danny said, "Why? That's tacky. Looks cheap." They said, "Trust us, we want the pink cowboy hats."

And I'm telling you, everybody bought those hats—the women *and* the men. They just loved those pink cowboy hats. And me being a girl and all, I love pink too. We sold between five and ten thousand hats during those two days at the Forum!

I have no idea why people were associating me with pink or with the hats. I'd worn a few outfits in that color, but it wasn't a dominant shade in my clothing palette. And since I'm not really a western girl, and hats would hide the wigs that are so much a part of my fashion, the cowboy hats were a surprise too. But they helped make the concerts a celebration, and I'll support a celebration any day of the week!

Star of the Show

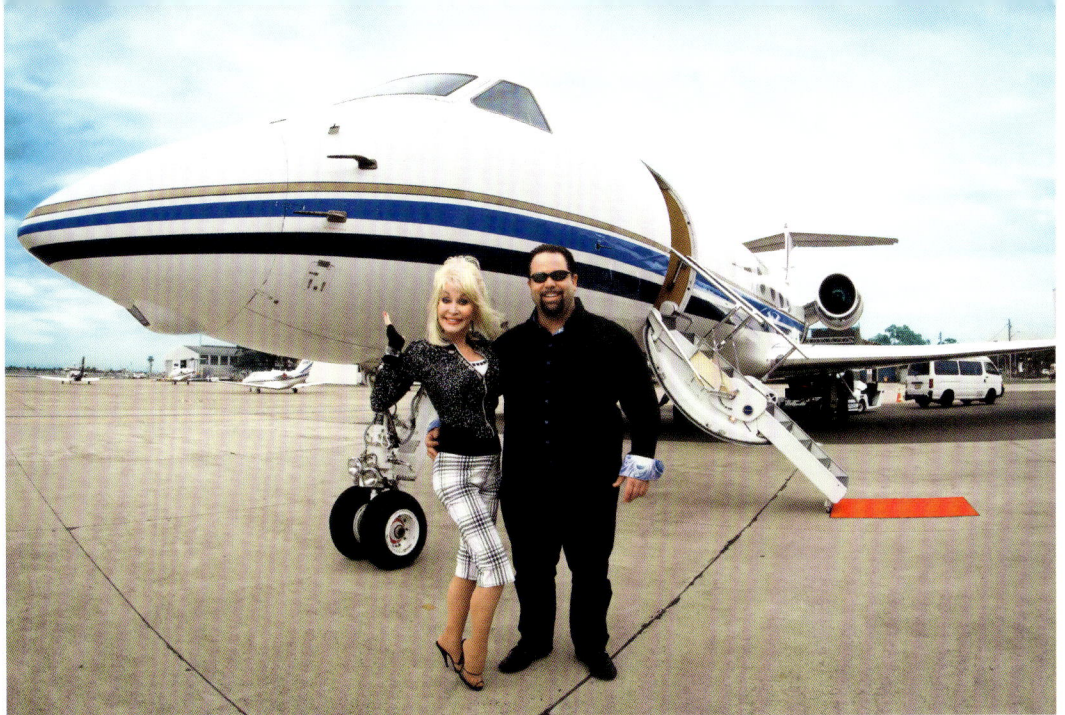

Danny and I prepare to take flight on a private plane between concerts overseas. Notice the red carpet at the foot of the staircase—I didn't ask for that, but it's a nice touch!

I got back to the States in time for the season's grand opening at Dollywood and to help celebrate Porter's fiftieth anniversary on the Grand Ole Opry. Porter and I sang "Just Someone I Used to Know" with Patty Loveless providing harmonies, and I just had to do "I Will Always Love You" in honor of Porter, who had inspired it. I was really happy that we got to celebrate Porter that way. He was diagnosed with lung cancer soon after, and in October, I was with Porter's family when he passed away.

Porter's funeral was held at the Grand Ole Opry House, and I led the room in a round of "I Saw the Light." It's always sad to lose a friend, but it was comforting to know that we'd healed all of our differences, and I was very thankful for the years I'd spent on the road with him, and I still am.

One by-product of Porter's funeral was another major change in my team. I had private security for years, beginning with Larry Seaver—a distant cousin of Baseball Hall of Famer Tom Seaver—in the late 1970s. Larry ended up marrying my sister Cassie, and their son, Bryan Seaver, followed his daddy into security after he served with the military in Iraq. He'd worked as a bodyguard for prime ministers and other heads of state in Rwanda, Haiti, Poland, and Tanzania, and he oversaw security when the Christian rock band Stryper was on tour in Brazil. I knew Bryan could handle any issues that came up at a funeral, and I really wanted a family member nearby at an event where I knew I would be emotional.

Bryan and Danny hit it off that day, and as a result, Bryan became the head of my security team. The company that was handling that role at the time was primarily focused on the concert site, but Bryan looked after me in other situations, too, and he paid greater attention to the safety of the band and crew. There's a saying, "If you take care of the crew, they'll take care of you," and the people who work for me on the road get good accommodations and daily meals from five-star chefs. We definitely take care of 'em!

Here's how much Bryan takes care of me. In the first few years he worked with me, he accompanied me to a conference at the Loews Vanderbilt Plaza. We were walking down a hallway when the door to one of the rooms opened. A guy with scruffy facial hair and blue jeans walked out, took one look at me, and *rushed my way*!

Bryan jumped in his path, pushed him up against the wall, and held him there by his chest and his throat.

I started laughing. "Bryan, let him go! *That's Kevin Costner!*"

Bryan relaxed, but he didn't let Kevin off the hook. "You should know better," Bryan told him. "You're the bodyguard!"

He was right, of course. Kevin had played a security guard for Whitney Houston's character in the movie that featured her singing "I Will Always Love You," and here was *my* security guard pinning him against a wall, thinking he was a threat. You can't make up that kind of thing!

When Bryan joined the team, I was already preparing for the release of my *Backwoods Barbie* album the next year, and as it turned out, I used a lot of pink on the cover. I don't know that those pink hats back in Denmark had much to do with that, but they might have been in my subconscious. Mostly, though, the pink was just representing more of a girlie thing. But when the *Barbie* movie came out a few years later, "Barbie Pink" was everywhere—maybe it started with me!

When I rolled out the Backwoods Barbie Tour that year, I took a seat at the piano and sang a version of "The Grass Is Blue" that was inspired by Norah Jones's version of the song. I'd originally recorded it with guitar and Dobro among the key instruments, but this live version took on a little more of a gospel feel with my three background singers—Richard Dennison, Vicki Hampton, and Jennifer O'Brien—there at my side. I also made my first appearance at the Greek Theatre in the hills of Los Angeles. It's an outdoor venue that—because it's in Southern California—almost always has great weather. And I'll tell you, the smells are great, too—the scent of garlic fries wafts up from the concession stand right next to the stage!

During the European part of the schedule, we bumped up the venue size once more. The shows were all in arenas and soccer stadiums, and we sold out everywhere we went. Here we were, forty years into my career and still climbing higher mountains. I couldn't have been more grateful—and more inspired to keep finding new avenues for my creative spirit.

The ticket sales were good, and the concerts themselves were rewarding too. The ballads might have surprised a lot of people, because it's hard to make slow songs feel intimate in a big room like that. But when they do connect, being in the bigger space makes it even more powerful. To hear ten or fifteen thousand people sing "I Will Always Love You" will give you chills. When they all light up their phones or flick their BICs—whatever they're doing—and they're swaying back and forth, it's a very solemn, sacred kind of moment to see.

I'll never forget one concert at the Marquee in Cork, Ireland, which had been postponed at the last minute the previous year because of some problems with the lighting system. When we returned, there were eighty thousand people on hand for an outdoor show, and they got pummeled with rain. It was like Dollywoodstock in Ireland—lots of mud but also lots of music and a crowd that sang every note through the bad weather.

I swapped in some different cover songs during that Backwoods Barbie Tour, kicking it off at the Roxy, a historic club on the Sunset Strip in Los Angeles that has hosted shows by Bruce Springsteen, Prince, David Bowie, and Lenny Kravitz. I did "She Drives Me Crazy" by the Fine Young Cannibals, and I sang the John Denver crossover hit "Thank God I'm a Country Boy," although I switched it to "Thank God I'm a Country Girl" while a "Backwoods Ken"—my creative director, Steve Summers—danced behind me in overalls.

While that tour was in progress, I was preparing to launch my music onto another stage: Broadway. I wrote some new songs for *9 to 5: The Musical*. That's a whole different world than the one I'm used to in the music business.

To have those characters come to life, I had to be all of them while I was writing. I even had to be Mr. Hart, the male chauvinist pig, but I got such a kick out of doing it. When I was writing the Mr. Hart part, I wrote a lot of it out at my lake house, where I had a little stairway with a banister running alongside it. I remember when I was writing, I'd come down the stairs and try to pretend I was Mr. Hart singing. I'd get such a kick out of myself that I would laugh out loud. And I thought, *God, if somebody was to see me doing this, they'd think I'd lost my mind.*

The first performance of the musical took place in Los Angeles during September 2008. When technical problems delayed the start, I stood up in the audience and kept some energy going in the room with a few jokes and stories and off-the-cuff performances of "9 to 5" and "I Will Always Love You."

From there, the production went to Broadway, where it picked up four Tony nominations, including one for me for Best Original Score. I sang "9 to 5" with the cast at the opening of the Tonys—another of those things most folks might never expect a girl from the Smoky Mountains to ever get to do. Heck, I would've never imagined getting to perform at the Tonys either—let alone being nominated for one! A year after its run in New York, the musical went on a North American tour of about thirty cities during 2010 and 2011 and has since been staged in the United Kingdom, Australia, and New Zealand.

Around this same time, the University of Tennessee in Knoxville called, saying they wanted to give me an honorary doctorate during the school's graduation exercises in

MY COACH OF MANY COLORS

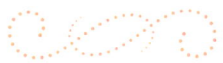

Over the years, I've had to learn to travel well.

When I was a little girl, I would get motion sick just riding on the school bus, so being a musician who plays lots of one-nighters miles apart has been challenging, to say the least!

We didn't have a car when I was growing up—we were too poor for that. I had to get used to riding a bus—there really wasn't much of a choice; it was too far to walk! I used what public transportation existed there in East Tennessee, and at age ten, I rode all the way to Lake Charles, Louisiana, with my grandma Rena to meet up with my Uncle Bill and record my first single, "Puppy Love."

I got my own bus in 1974 after I went out on my own. I will never forget the feeling. It was as if you've been waiting for a baby your whole life and never thought you were going to have one, and then all of a sudden you wound up pregnant. "Oh, you got the baby that you always wanted!" And I did!

We put the words "Traveling Family Band" in the slot above the front windshield that indicated the destination of the bus, and we all did our share of cutting up on that vehicle. We played a lot of Password and other games, and Don Warden and I would do a lot of the band's paperwork while the bus rolled down the highways.

I would write songs on the bus sometimes, too, particularly after a show when the adrenaline was still going and it was quiet and I couldn't sleep. The thing about that setup, though, is that when the wheels of the bus go round and round, they make a certain sound, and it forces you to write in the same key all the time so the guitar and the melody don't clash with the tone of those tires.

At the start of 1977, I got a new bus, and we changed the destination sign from "Traveling Family Band" to "The Wild Bunch." I called it my Coach of Many Colors, though it wasn't nearly as colorful as that coat Mama made me. The inside was kind of burgundy with a butterfly motif, and it had a reel-to-reel tape deck on the wall above one of the windows so I could listen to song demos. There was a butterfly on the tail end of the exterior, but you had to be a real insider to know that that butterfly meant it was my bus—with me on board.

Over time, I became very comfortable on the bus—the motion sickness from my youth eventually went away, and I got a better setup. By the time I hit the road for the White Limozeen Tour in 1989, I had two buses: one for me and one for the Mighty Fine Band. Mine had a private bath and a queen-size bed, and the rest of the accommodations were a step up too! It had a CD player, a VCR, and a TV. And with two buses instead of one, there was room for more stage outfits and more wigs—I practically had a rolling walk-in closet!

I still wrote songs at night after shows, and during that tour, if I didn't have time to do an interview during the day, I'd have a journalist send me questions, and I'd record the answers from my bed while we traveled down the road.

Buses have gotten even more luxurious in the last couple of decades. They're built with a pull-out option that allows you to make the bus a little wider when you arrive at your destination. It feels so much less cramped and more like a living room up front.

It all sounds extravagant, but even with the advances that have been made over the years, many aspects of touring today are still the same as they were when I started. You spend a lot of time away from home on those metal contraptions. Anything that can make it feel more like home naturally makes me feel more comfortable, and that makes it easier to be in the right mindset to put on a great performance.

Traveling well is key to being the star of *any* show. Trust me—I've learned.

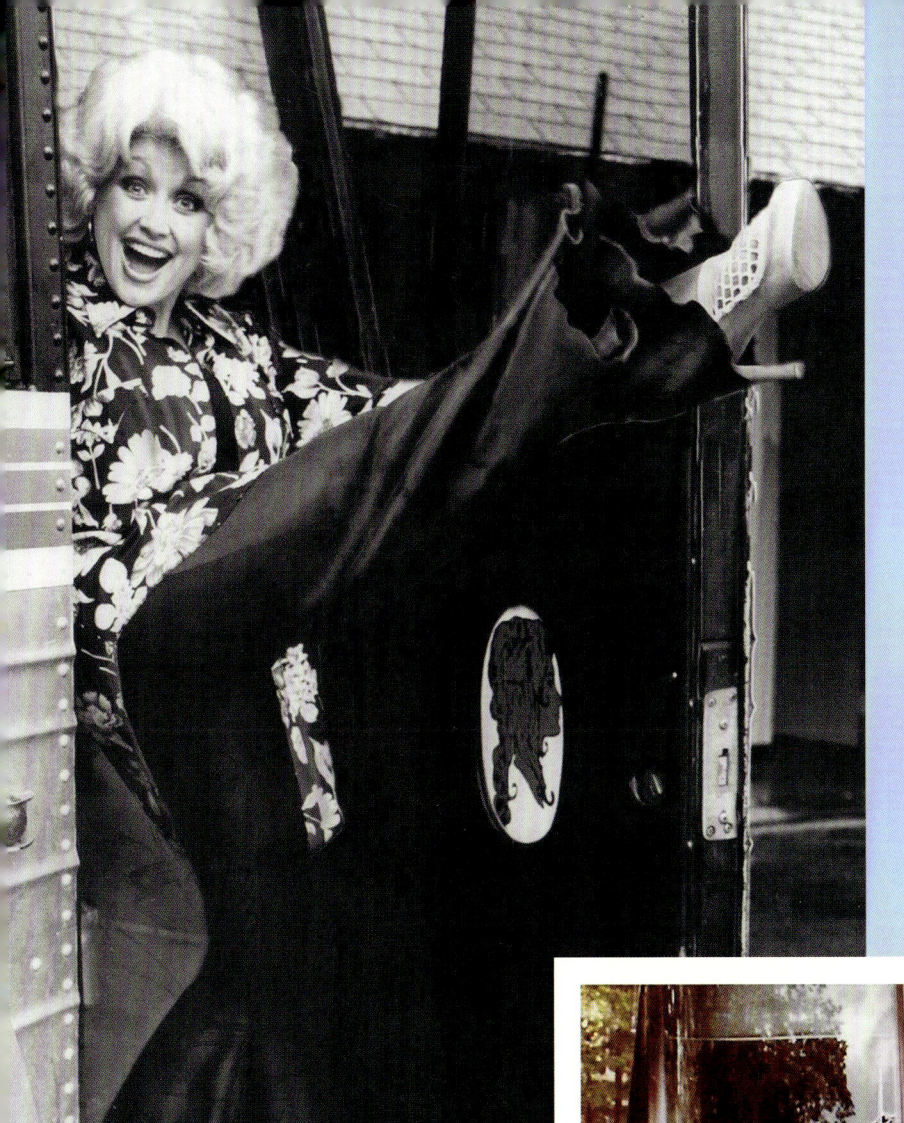
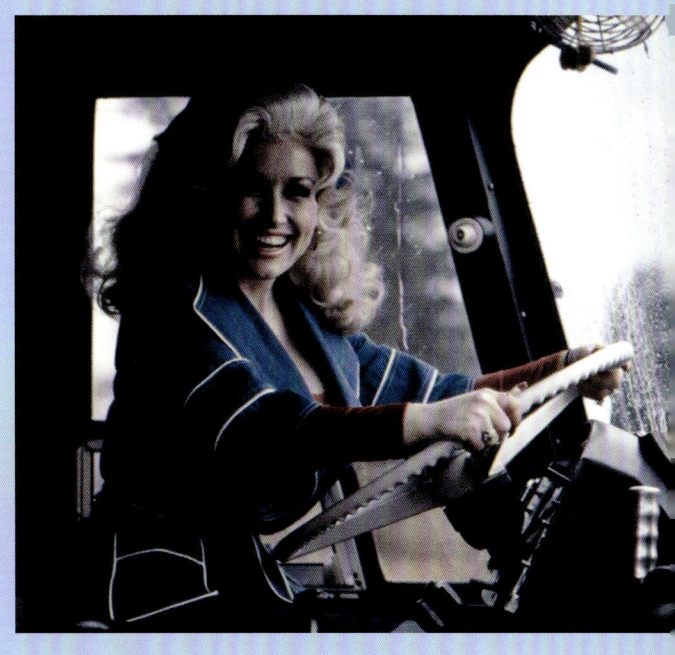
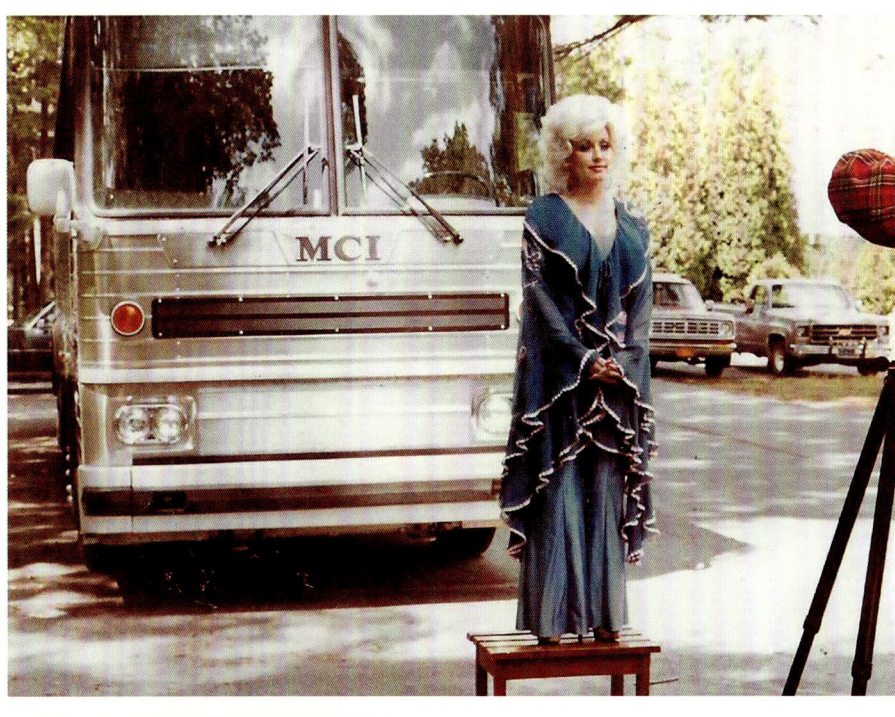
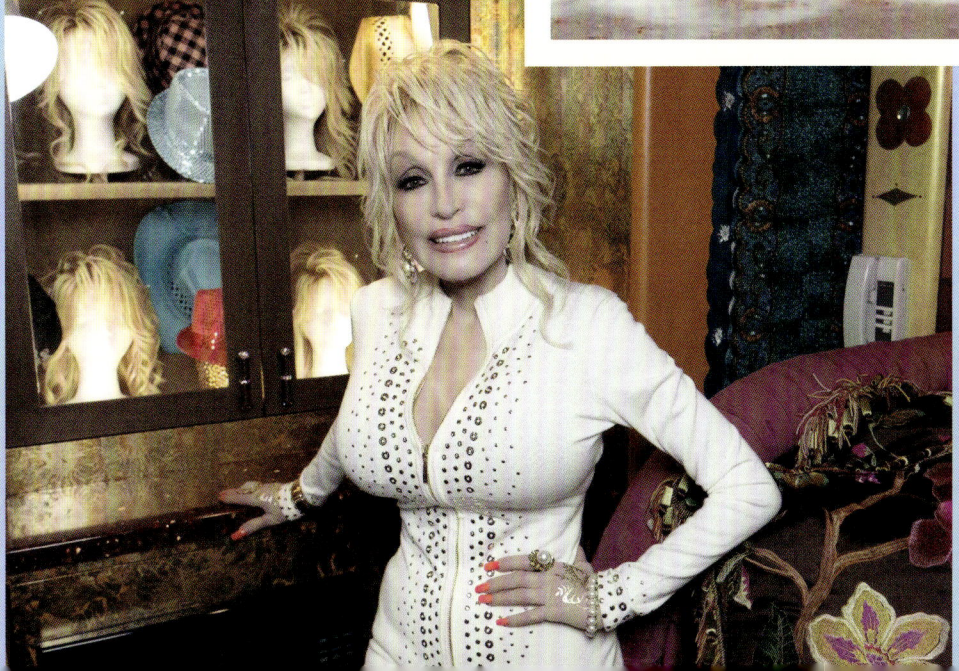

I grew to love riding the bus! The top three photos all feature my first home on wheels, which I dubbed my "Coach of Many Colors." Here's me kicking up my heels, taking the wheel, and standing on the smallest stage since childhood. And, yes, I really did drive the bus (once or twice), but I didn't ever try to back it up! *Left:* As the buses changed and became more luxurious for artists, I had an entire wig cabinet built for convenience.

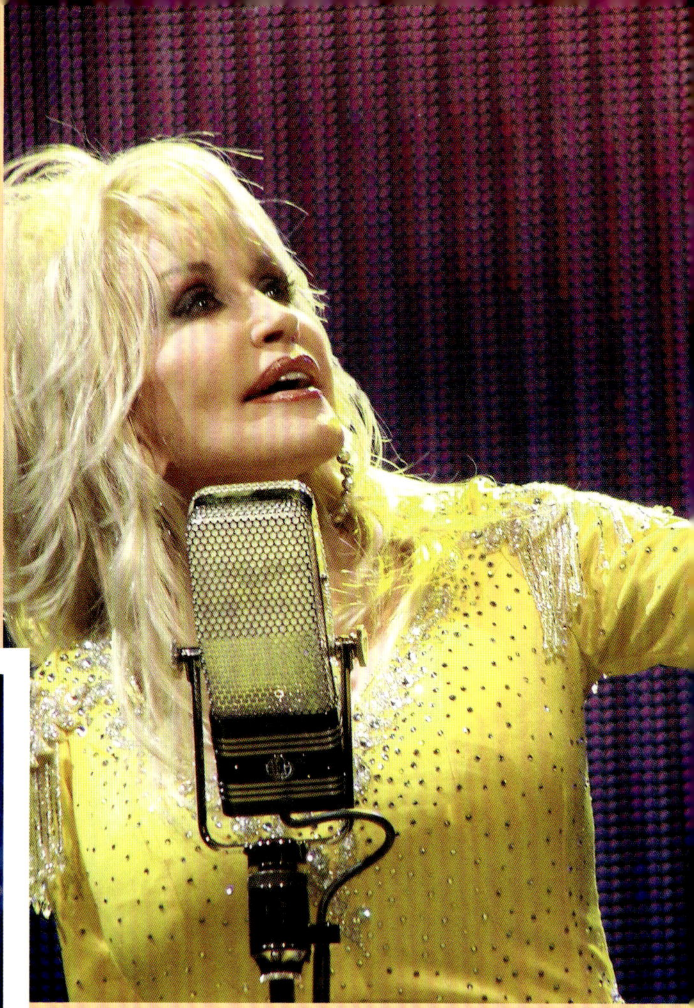

The Better Day World Tour was one of my most ambitious—in addition to playing across the United States, I spent a month in Europe and more than three weeks in Australia.

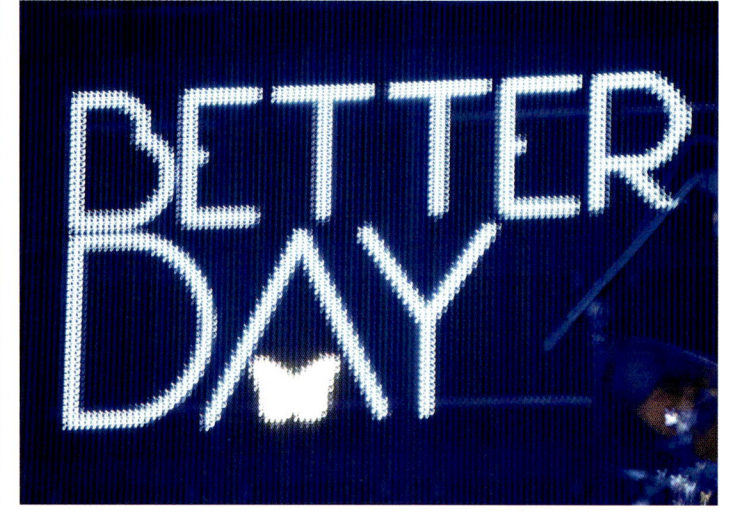

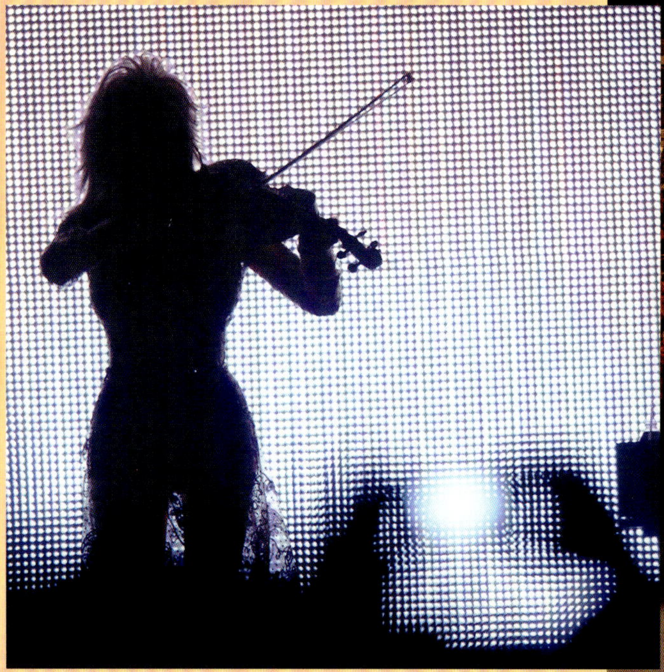

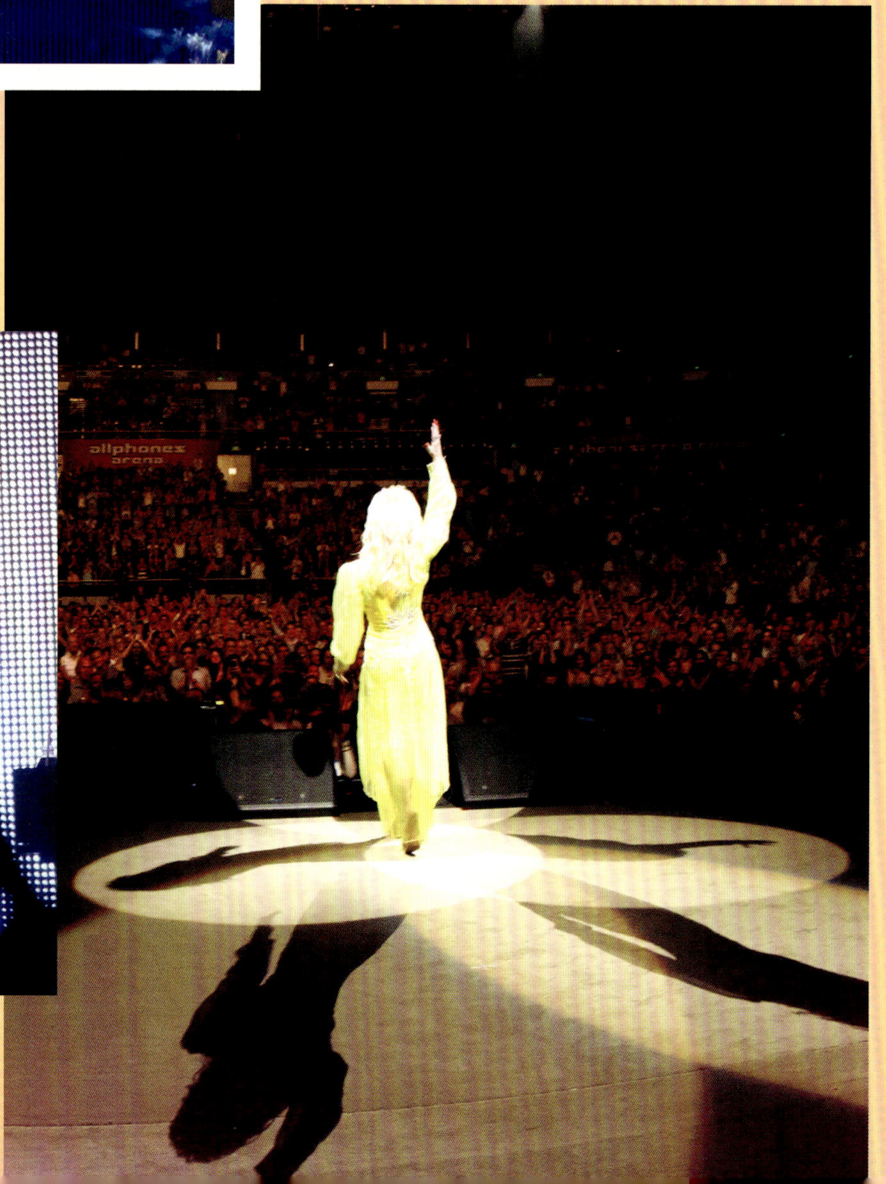

2009. Being called Dr. Dolly—Double D—was a big deal! I didn't go far enough in school to get a college degree—I barely made it through high school—so I knew that was as close as I was ever going to get to that. It was really something to think, *Here I am, you know, just a country girl, receiving a doctorate degree in music at the University of Tennessee.* What an honor.

I put music to work in the ceremony too. When I gave the commencement speech, I incorporated a few quotes from "I Will Always Love You," and before the day was through, I led everyone in the school's theme song, "Rocky Top," and publicly performed "Try," the theme song for Imagination Library, for the first time.

A month later at Dollywood, when four hundred Girl Scouts received a new Coat of Many Colors patch that supported helping other people, I surprised them by singing the song that gave the patch its name. It's so rewarding to have a song that meant so much to me play a positive role in the lives of a new generation. Equally rewarding was the thought that Dollywood has become a venue where these kinds of events could happen. A year later, I rounded up Kenny Rogers, Billy Ray Cyrus, and Miley Cyrus to shoot a Hallmark Channel special, *Dolly Celebrates 25 Years of Dollywood*.

I was happy to work with yet another fellow artist when I performed at Marty Stuart's Late Night Jam at the Ryman Auditorium in 2011. Marty held that concert with a rotating guest list every year on the eve of the CMA Music Festival in Nashville, and there are so many events going on during that four-day festival that he decided the best way to find a hole in people's schedules was to hold it at 10:30 p.m.—thus the Late Night name. I typically get out of bed around three in the morning, so it's fair to say I was pushing it to make that fit into my routine. But it was definitely worth the effort. I got to hang out with Marty's wife, my friend Connie Smith, at the same venue where we used to cut up when it hosted the Opry in the 1960s. I wore an outfit with lots of rhinestones and sang "Coat of Many Colors" and "I Will Always Love You," with Marty and Harry Stinson, the drummer in Marty's band The Fabulous Superlatives, providing harmony.

A few weeks later, I launched the Better Day World Tour in Knoxville at Thompson-Boling Arena on the campus of the University of Tennessee, the same place where I received the honorary doctorate. I wrote all twelve of the songs on the album that the tour was named for—in fact, I had only one co-writer on the whole project: Mac Davis and I worked together on "Country Is as Country Does." The album was intended to provide a bit of uplift at a time when a lot of people were suffering from the economy, so during that tour, I did some cheery-sounding covers: Katrina and the Waves' "Walking on Sunshine," Tina Turner's "River Deep—Mountain High," and The Beatles' "Help!"—to hopefully get people feeling good on their night out.

A couple of events from that tour stood out because they were happening for the first time. When you're new, all kinds of "firsts" keep happening, and it's quite a rush. But as you put a few miles on the bus, it's harder to find something you haven't done before. So doing something for the first time after a while is particularly rewarding.

STAGE LOOKS
Through the Years

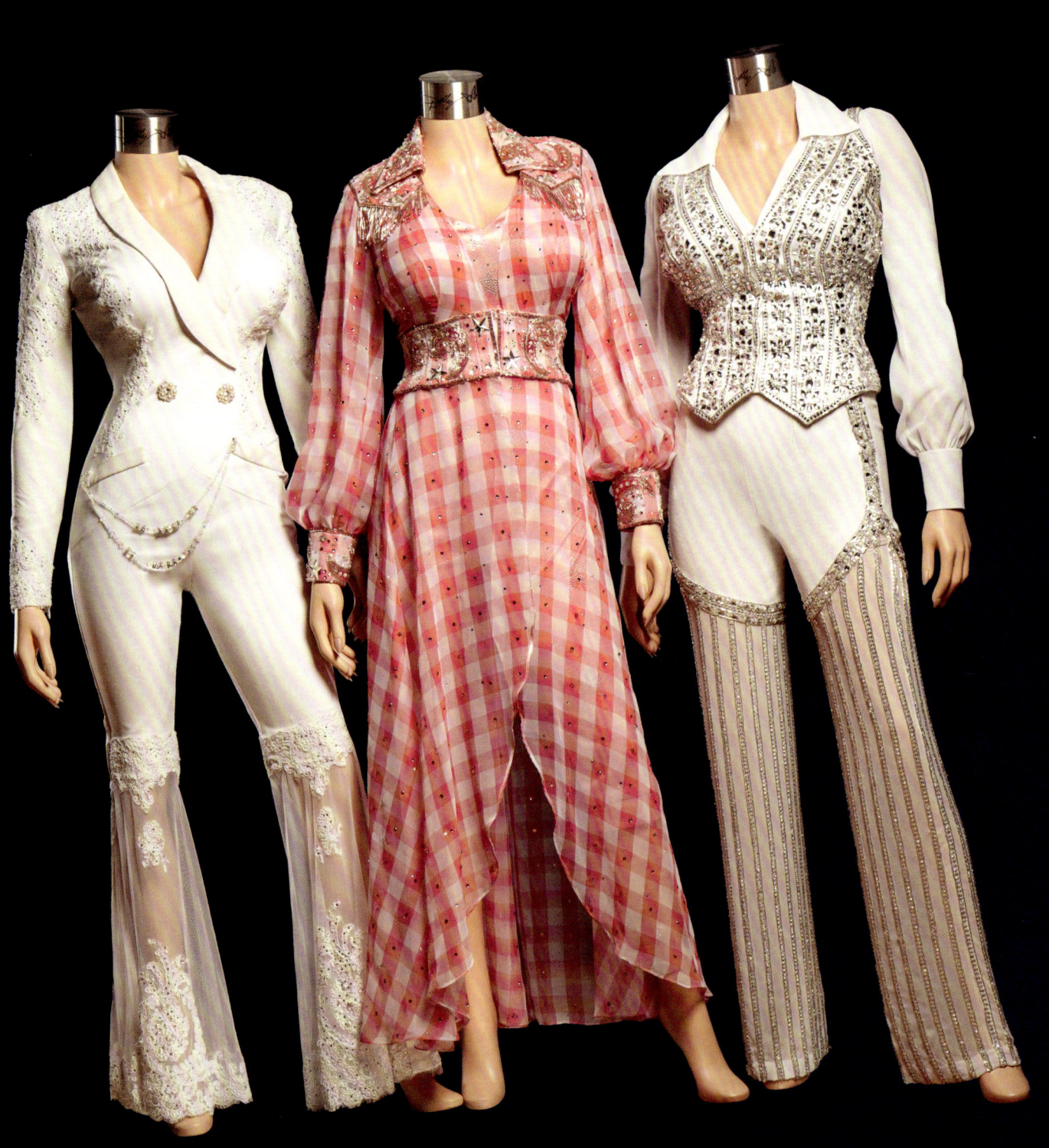

I wanted to wear white for my performance at the Mother Church (the Ryman), and this white Robért

I felt like a Backwoods Barbie in this pink gingham look Robért designed for me.

I had 180,000 rhinestones—well, almost!—for a crowd of 180,000 at Glastonbury.

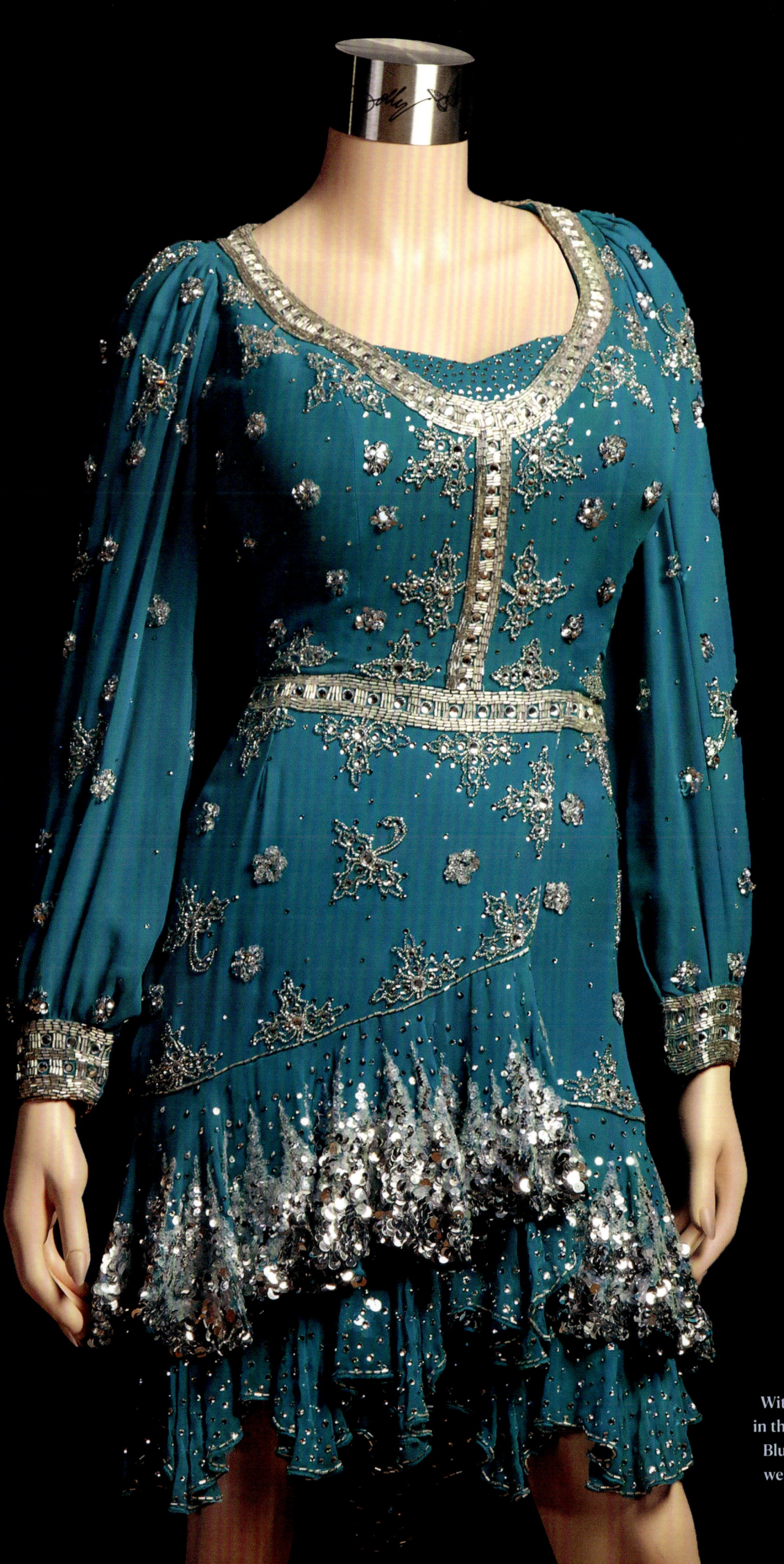

With more than 200,000 people in the crowd at the Hardly Strictly Bluegrass Festival, I thought I'd wear teal to this really big deal!

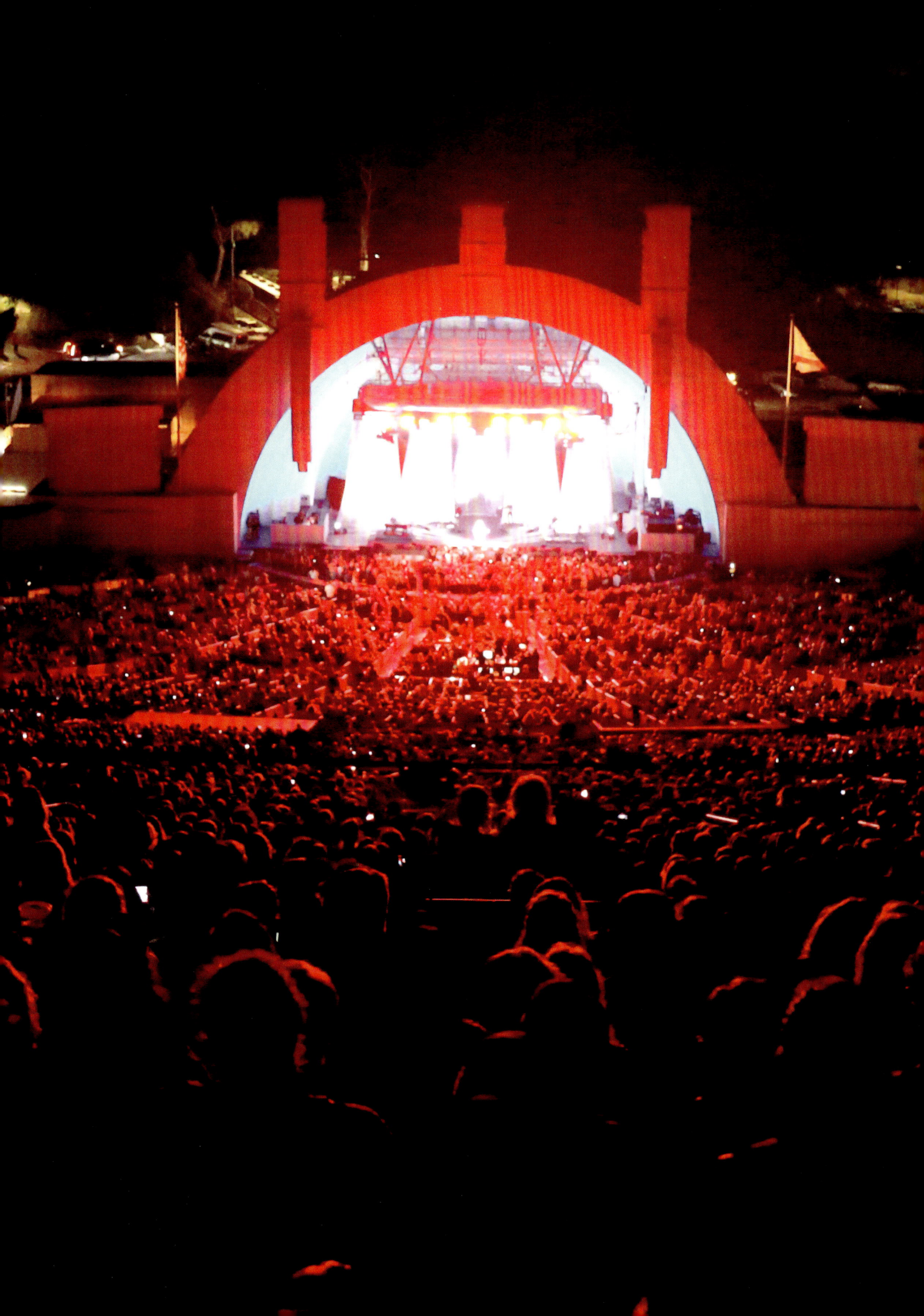

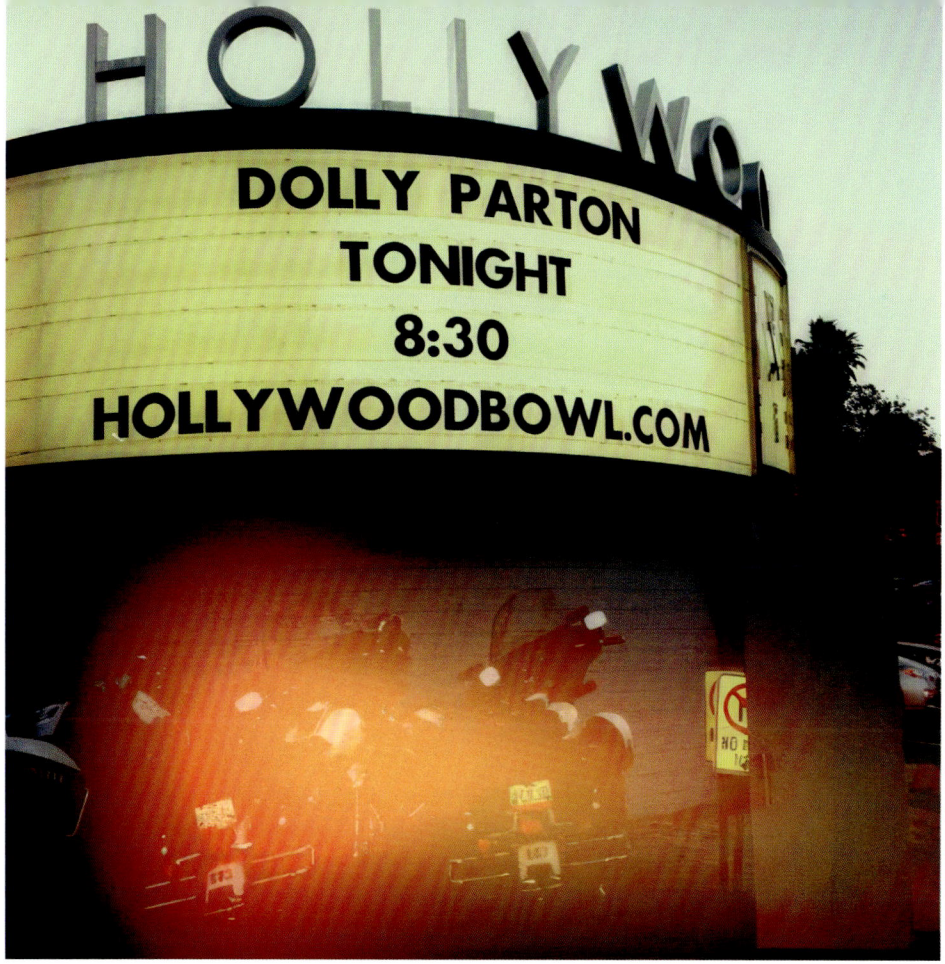

Left: The audience stretches up the hill at the iconic Hollywood Bowl. *Above:* Even the marquee looks classic!

For starters, I got to see my name on the marquee at the Hollywood Bowl for the first time when I did a two-night, sold-out stand there. It's a massive outdoor venue right off the Hollywood Freeway that seats eighteen thousand people and has an extraordinary live-music history. All the biggies have played there: The Beatles, Garth Brooks, Johnny Cash, Ella Fitzgerald, Tony Bennett, James Brown, and Willie Nelson, just for starters. It was impressive to sit on that stage and look up at the audience in the seats dotting a natural hillside. There were more people in that venue than lived in my hometown, but somehow, playing music on a little make-believe porch in the cool night air felt a lot like when I sang with the tobacco-stick mic stand on the porch in Locust Ridge. I'd come a long way by doing what I'd always done. I was just doing it on a bigger stage.

When I returned to Australia on that tour, another first was using the same travel setup Danny had rigged up for me in Europe, with a private plane and two buses. In fact—and Danny had to pull a few strings to do it—they were transported by ship around the Cape of Good Hope in South Africa to get to Australia.

Better Days, Pure & Simple

I didn't want to go if I couldn't bring my own bus, which is like my little home on wheels. There was a big tiff with the Australian government until the federal transport minister, Anthony Albanese, figured out how to make it happen. Danny had literally written it into the contract that I had to travel on my own buses, and the promoter came back at some point and told Danny that he just couldn't make it happen. But Danny is so good at sticking up for me—he was prepared to call off the tour, even though it was sold out, and ended up on the phone with the prime minister before it was all over. I knew it was a problem—the bus is oversized in both length and width for a lot of the roads in Australia, and it's heavy, to boot. Danny had a few alterations made on the buses to meet some of those standards, and he let the Australian government plot out the routes for the buses to minimize any damage to the roads.

When it came time for the Blue Smoke Tour in 2014, I talked to more than one hundred media outlets in four hours—*The Tennessean* documented it—and set up a good run, starting with some West Coast dates, then flying Down Under before another one-month run in the United Kingdom and Europe. (The buses came with me again!)

The best coverage of that year surrounded a couple of concerts that featured surprise appearances by Bon Jovi guitarist Richie Sambora. He joined me on stage on June 27 at the O2 Arena in London to play on "Lay Your Hands on Me." And two days later, he returned for another unannounced walk-on at the Glastonbury Festival.

The Glastonbury show turned out to be one of the biggest days of my professional life, and it was totally unexpected. There were 180,000 people in the audience at that concert, almost four times the crowd size from the Day on the Green festival I'd played in Oakland back in the 1970s.

The response I received from the crowd meant even more to me because it was the one concert on that tour that made me apprehensive. Promoters had been asking me to play Glastonbury for years, and I kept turning them down because I didn't think the crowd would appreciate me based on some of the other artists they tended to book. I mean, Metallica headlined the day before I performed! I wasn't sure the fans would want to listen to a quiet song of mine like "Coat of Many Colors."

As it turned out, the response was over the top. It was still daylight when I went on stage and through most of my set, and seeing that many people standing out there that close together was impressive—even a little overwhelming. First of all, I'm claustrophobic, and I would have died if I'd been surrounded by that many people so close around me without knowing I had an easy way out of there! You can bet I was glad I was on stage, not down in that crowd (even though they looked like they were having lots of fun). But that packed crowd was incredible.

I'd also always heard that Glastonbury was a big pile of mud because it rains a lot. I decided I'd write something for the occasion, "The Mud Song," to surprise the audience. It was a sing-along, and they got into it quickly. I told them, "Look, you can't fool me. The rain did

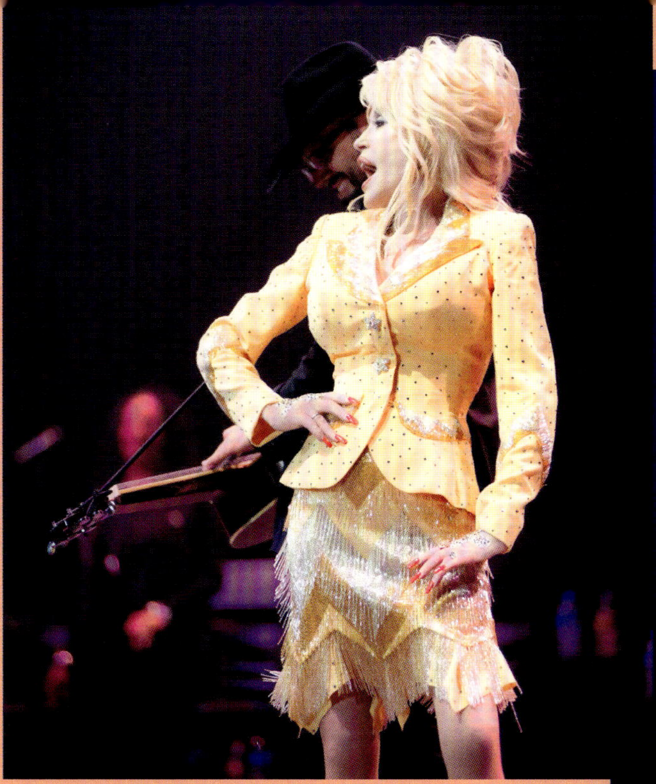

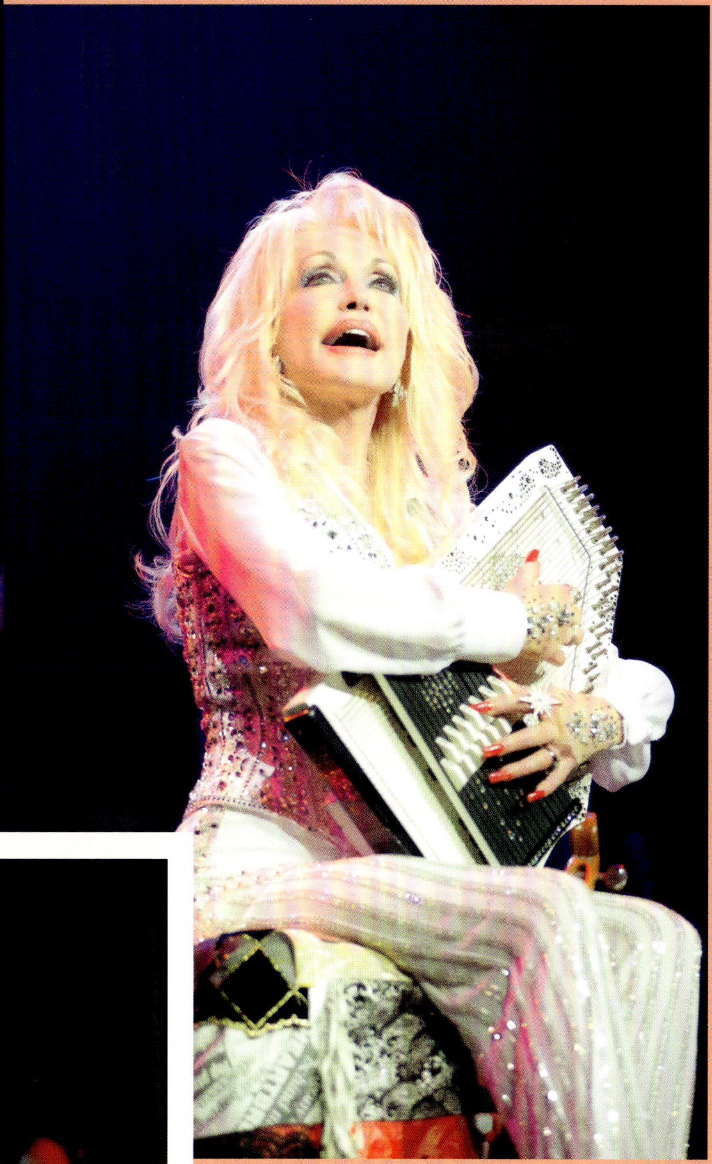

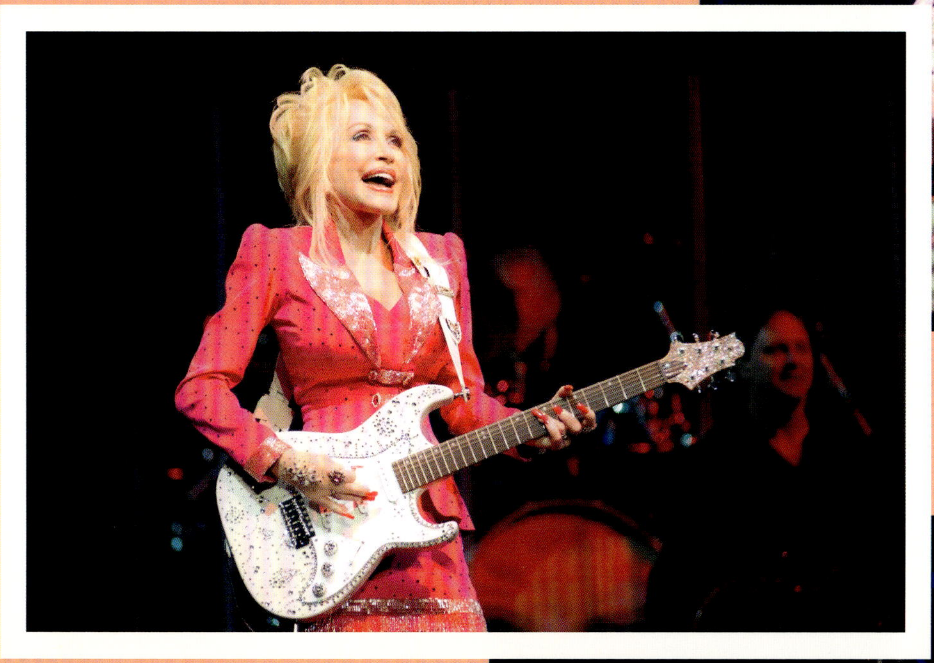

I pack a ton of instruments when I tour—including autoharp and electric guitar—but I'm quite comfortable working hands-free too! *Right:* The view of the stage from the soundboard, where the crew oversees what the audience hears, as well as the sound that's fed into the in-ear plugs of everyone on stage.

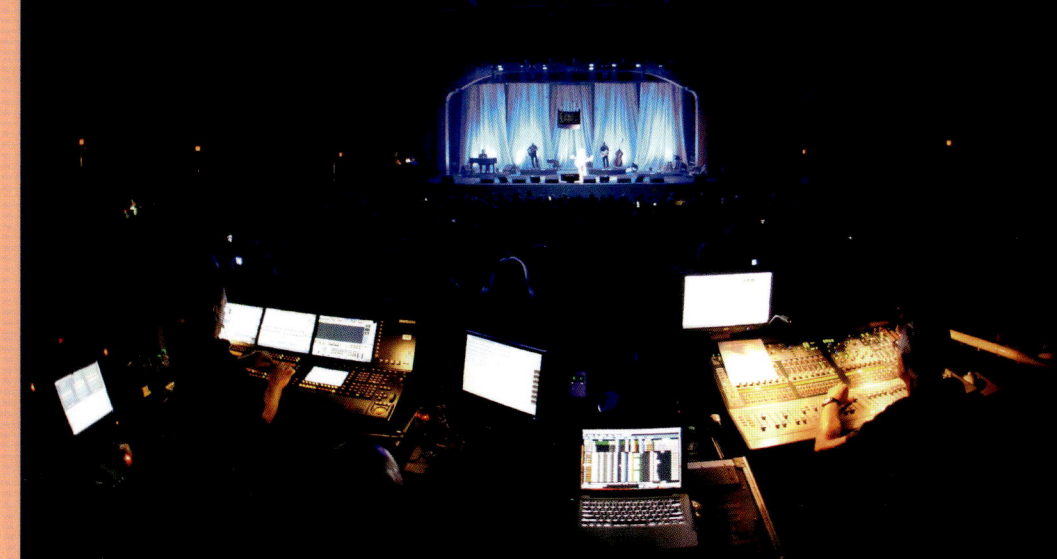

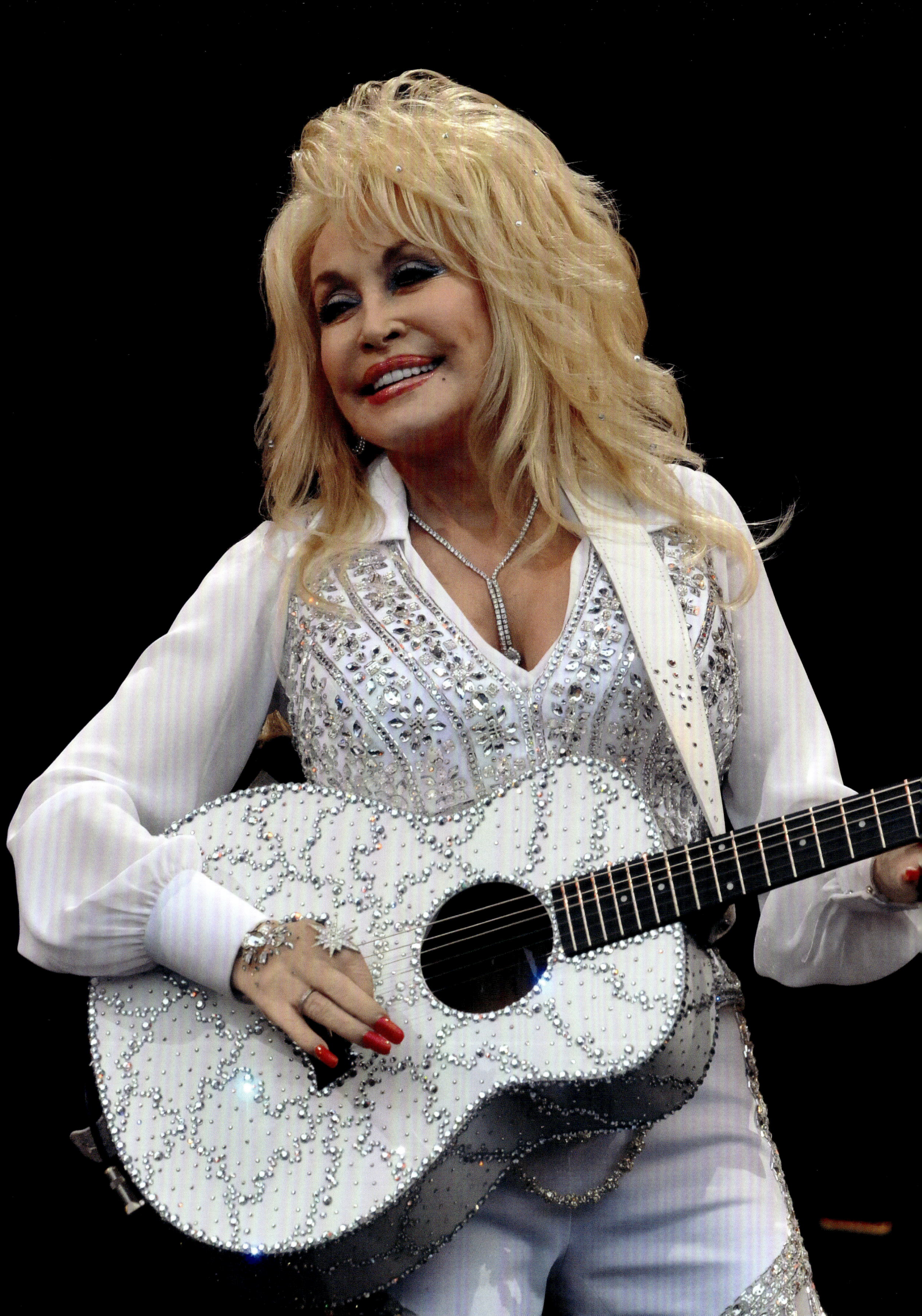

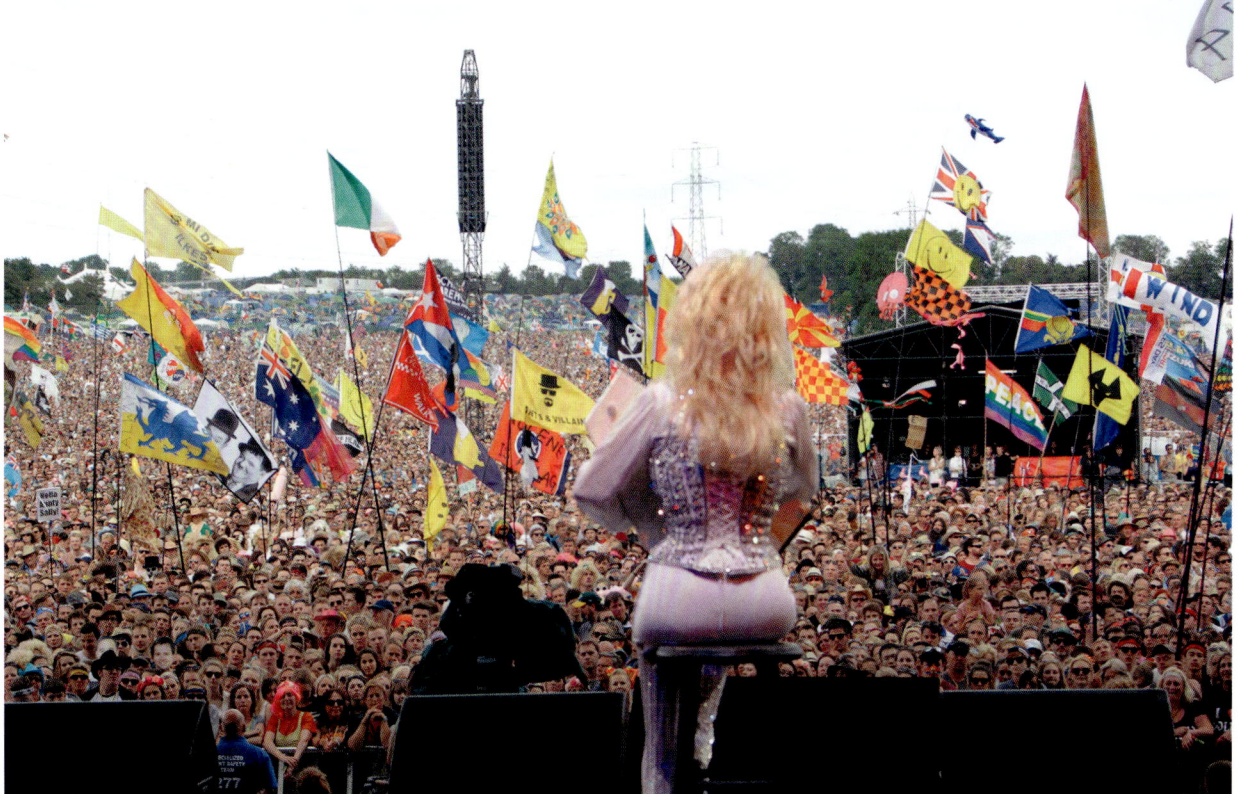

The Glastonbury Music Festival was the biggest international concert I ever gave, and many of the fans brought flags to celebrate their hometowns and favorite causes—or to help mark their location if anyone in their group got lost in the crowd.

not cause that mud. With you people standing that close together, I know you can't get to a bathroom, so I know that's pee!" Boy, did they holler at that one. It might have been true! Either way, I had a lot of fun with that audience.

Now, I didn't get in that mud, mind you. I love to wear white, and that's what I wore that day. It was a challenge for my crew. When I visited the media tent prior to the show, they had to lay out wooden planks ahead of me to keep my heels from sinking into the muck.

I wore different shoes while I was walking on the plank up to the stage, and I pulled my pants legs up to keep them out of the mud. But there was no mud on stage, so when we got up there, I slid the pants legs down, put a different pair of shoes on, and went for it. They're all pros, so if you watch video of that show today, I can promise you won't see a speck of mud on my outfit!

I knew it would be a different show right from the start. Not only did people show up in big numbers and sing along to all the hits, but a media outlet had organized a dance prior to my appearance, and when I launched into "Jolene," people were doing these synchronized steps—right there in the mud!—and having a big ol' time of it. Sometimes people say a concert was "triumphant." In a lot of cases, that ends up seeming like a lot of hype. But 180,000 people traipsing through the mud in Glastonbury to see a girl from the Smoky Mountains—that *really* felt triumphant.

Better Days, Pure & Simple

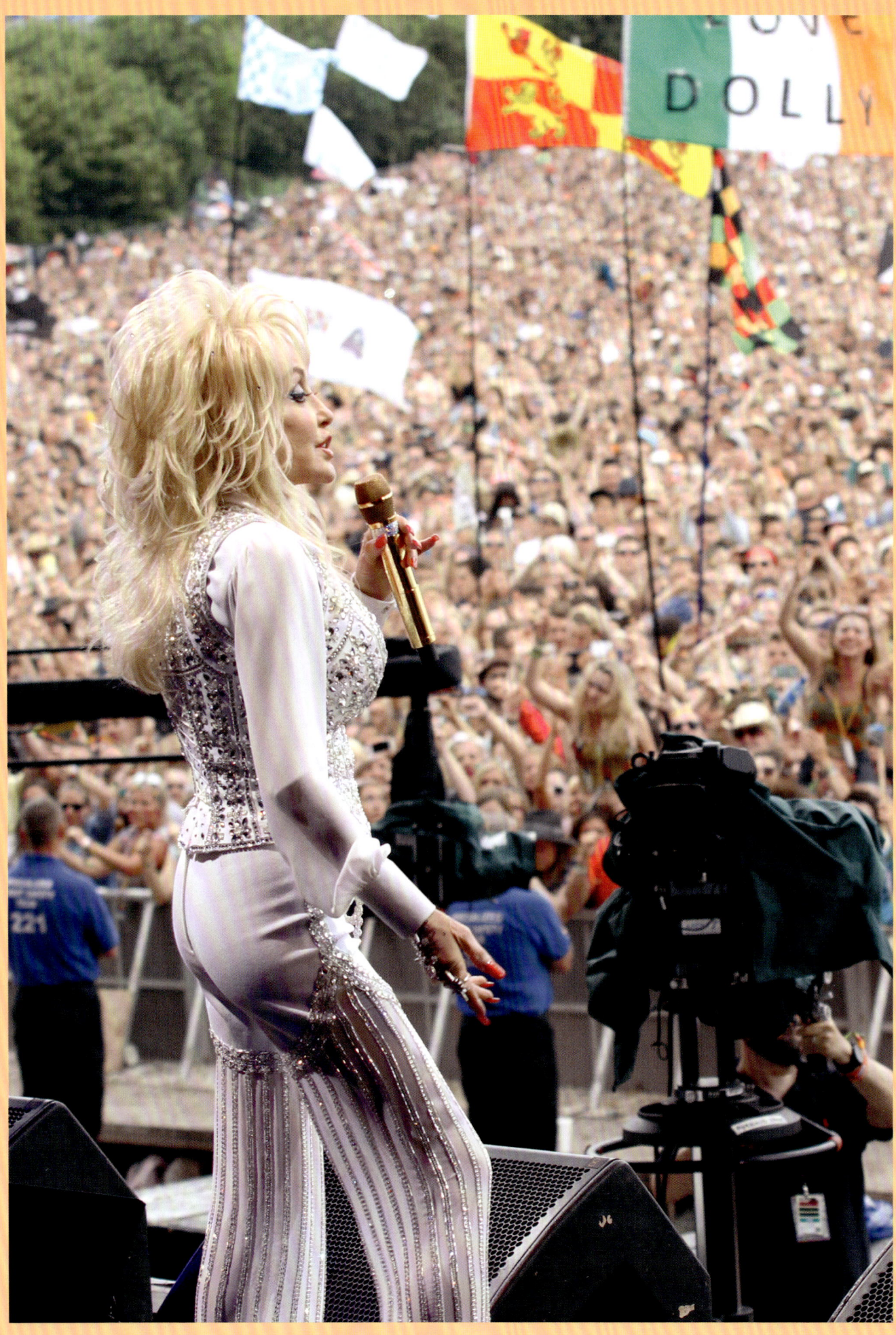

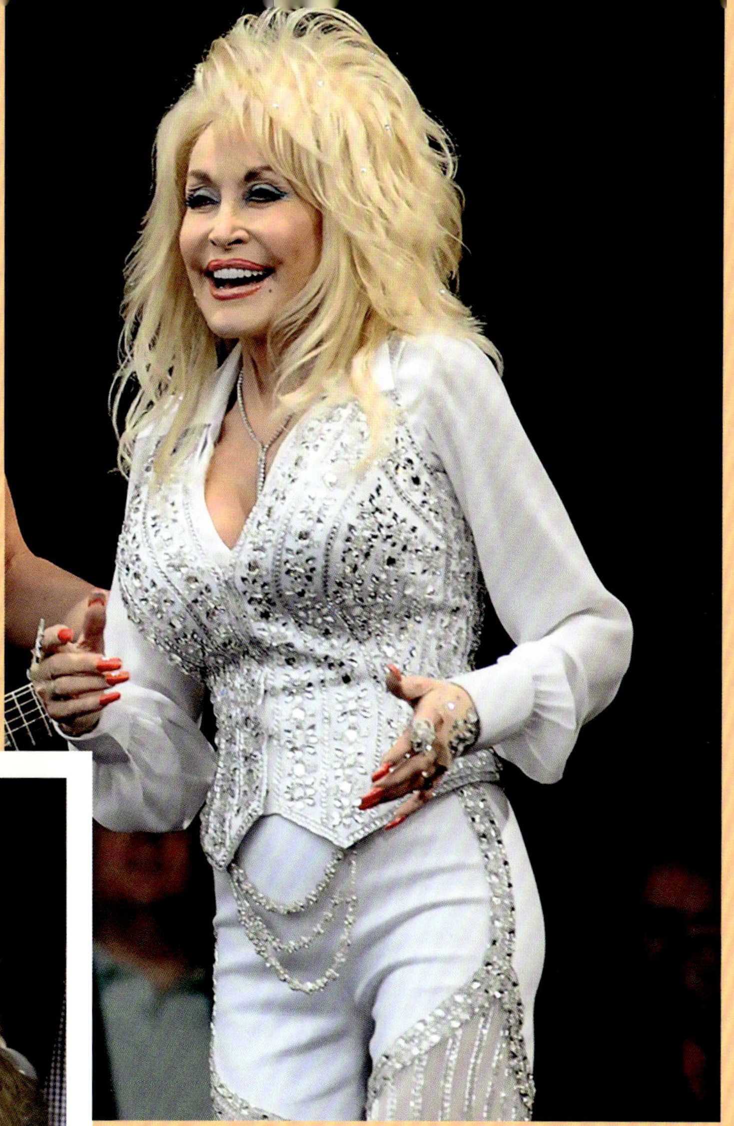

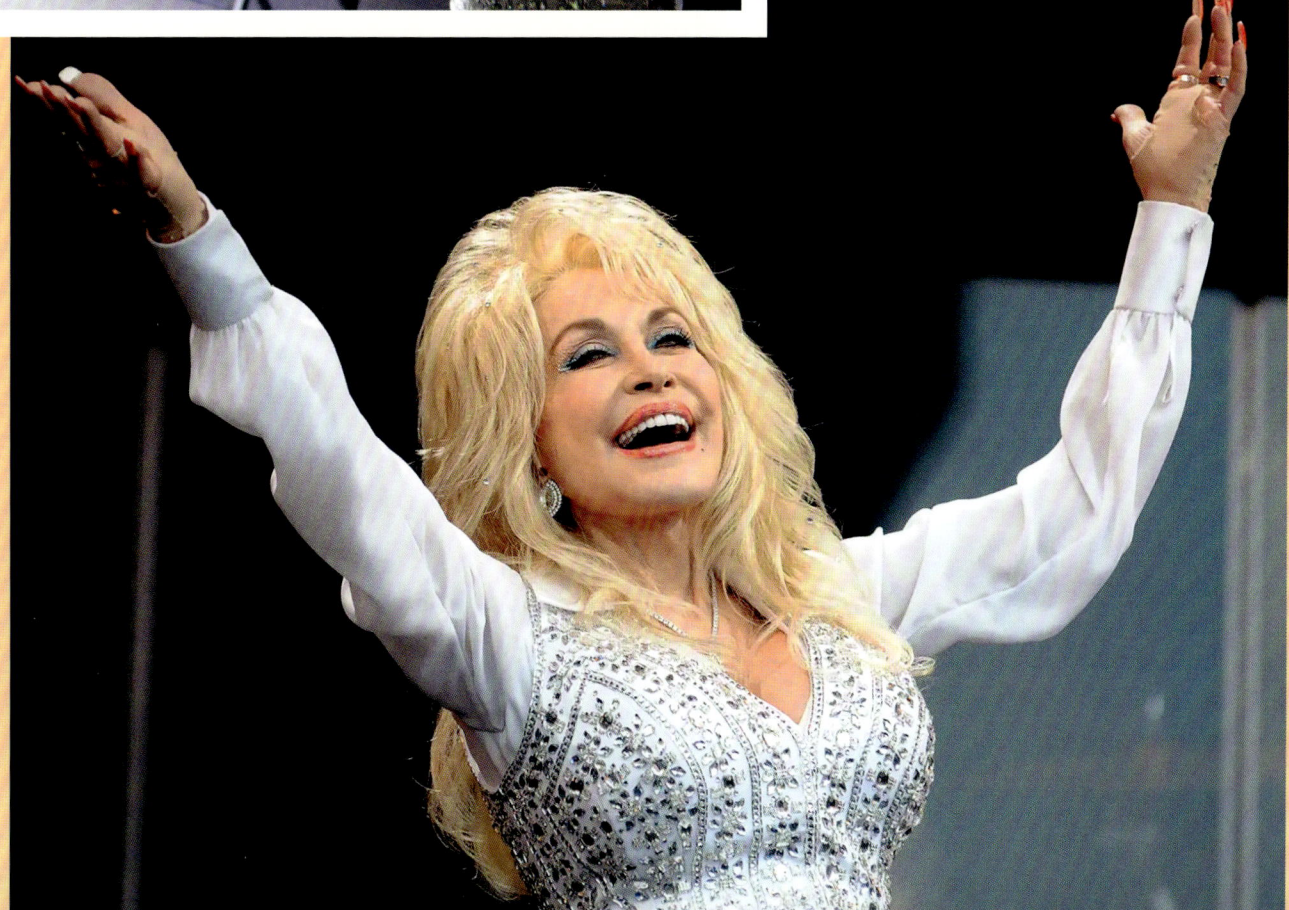

Left: How's that for a crowd? The view from the stage at the Glastonbury Music Festival.
Right and below: I had to get a sneak peek at the audience. The whole thing became one big celebration.

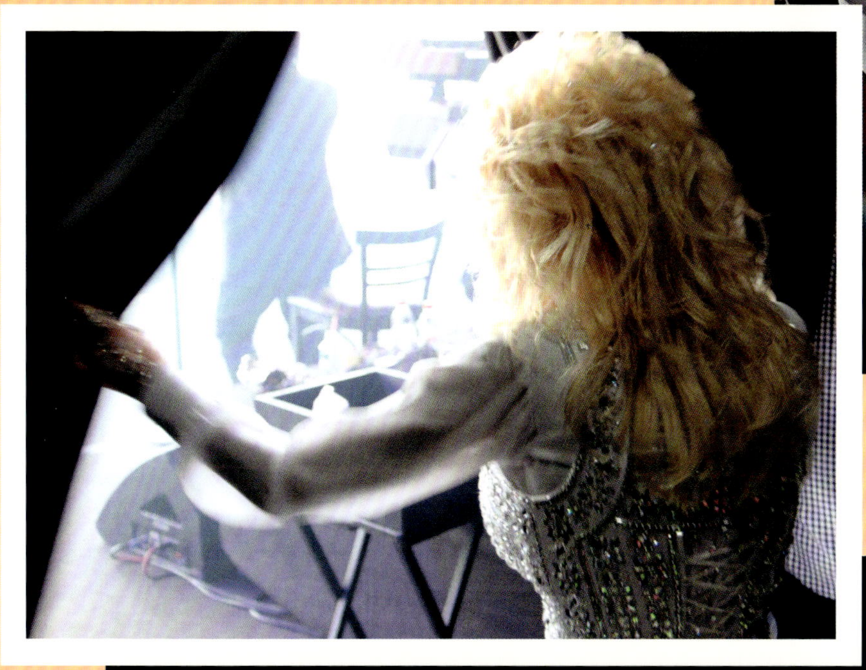

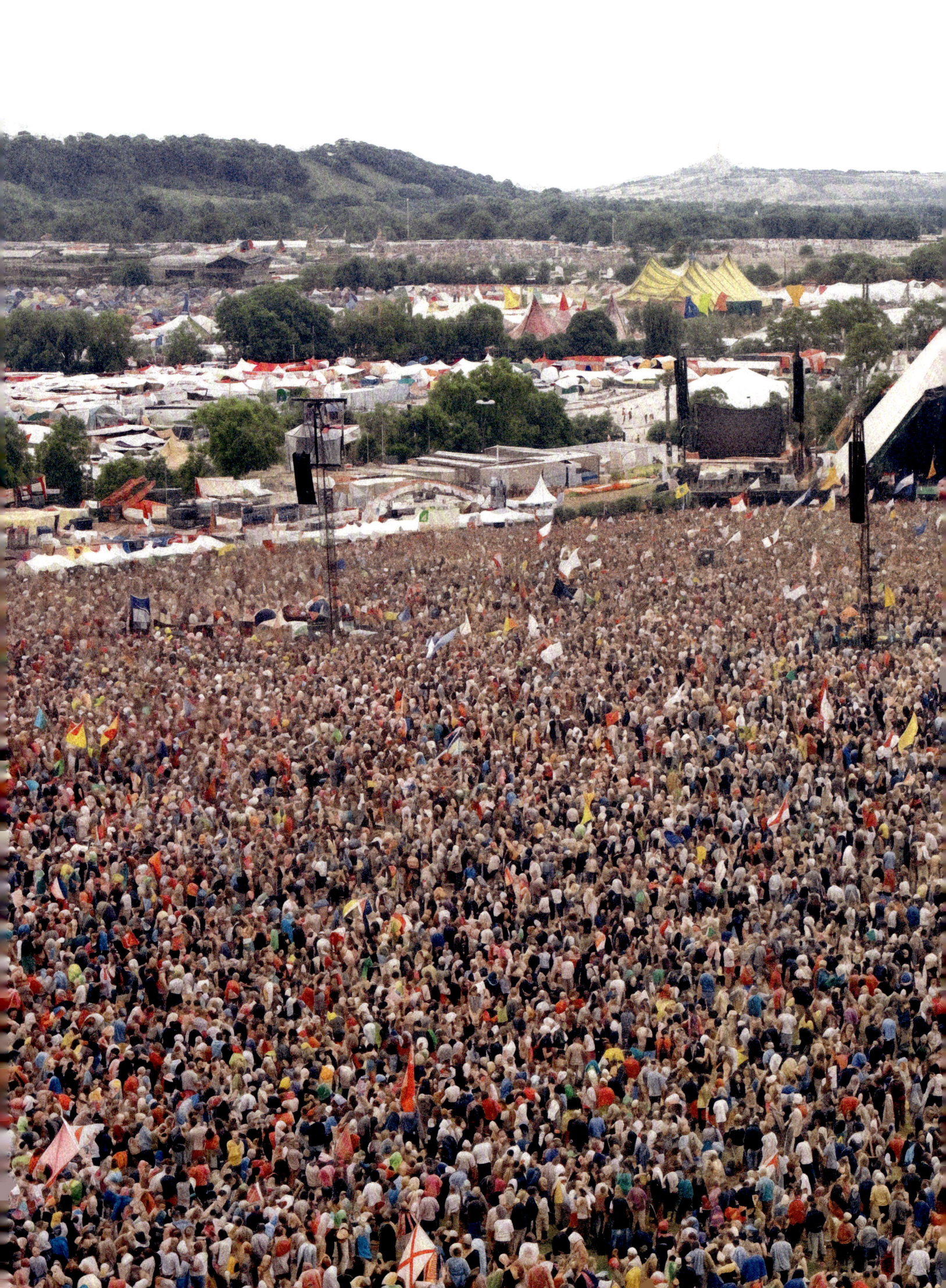

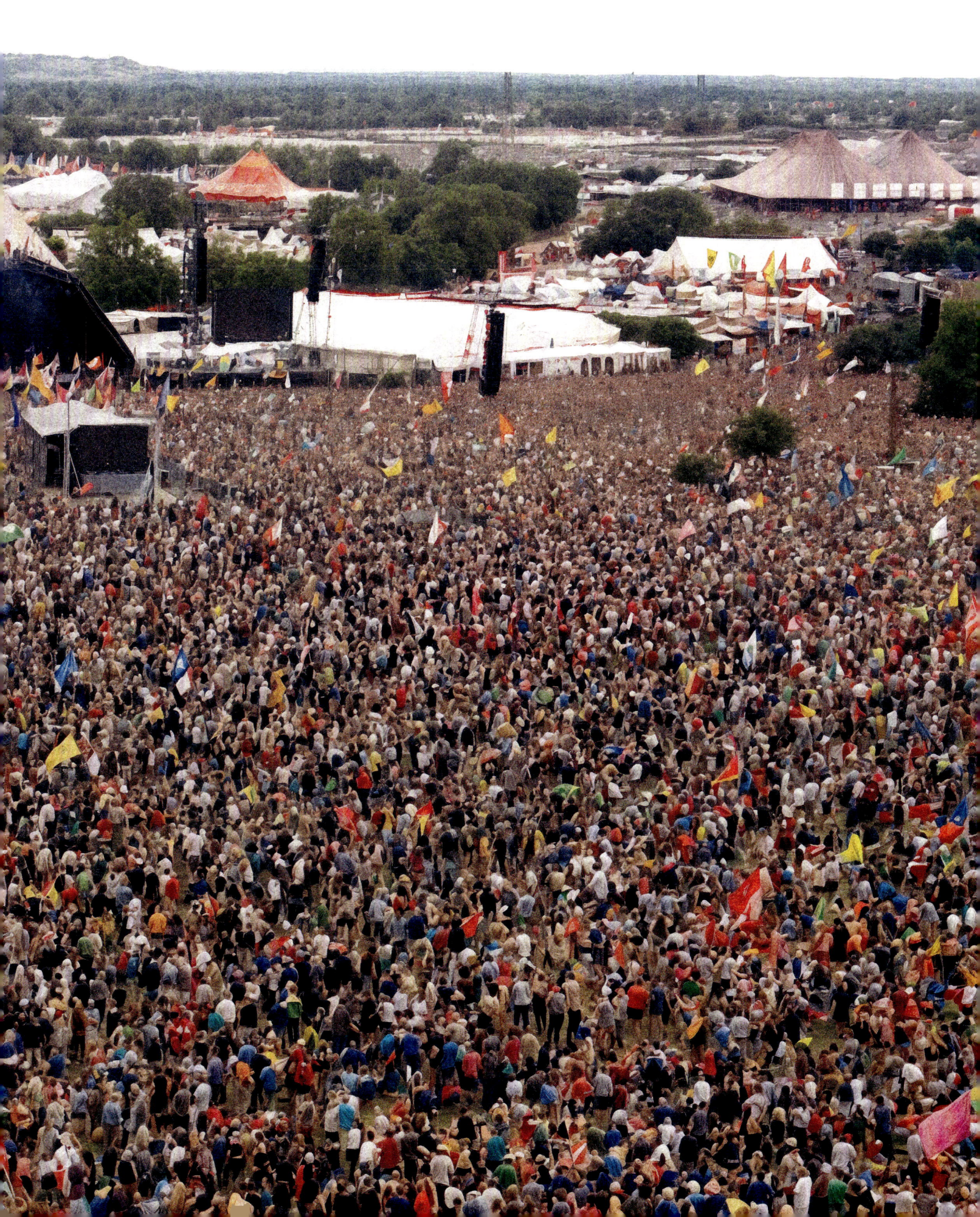

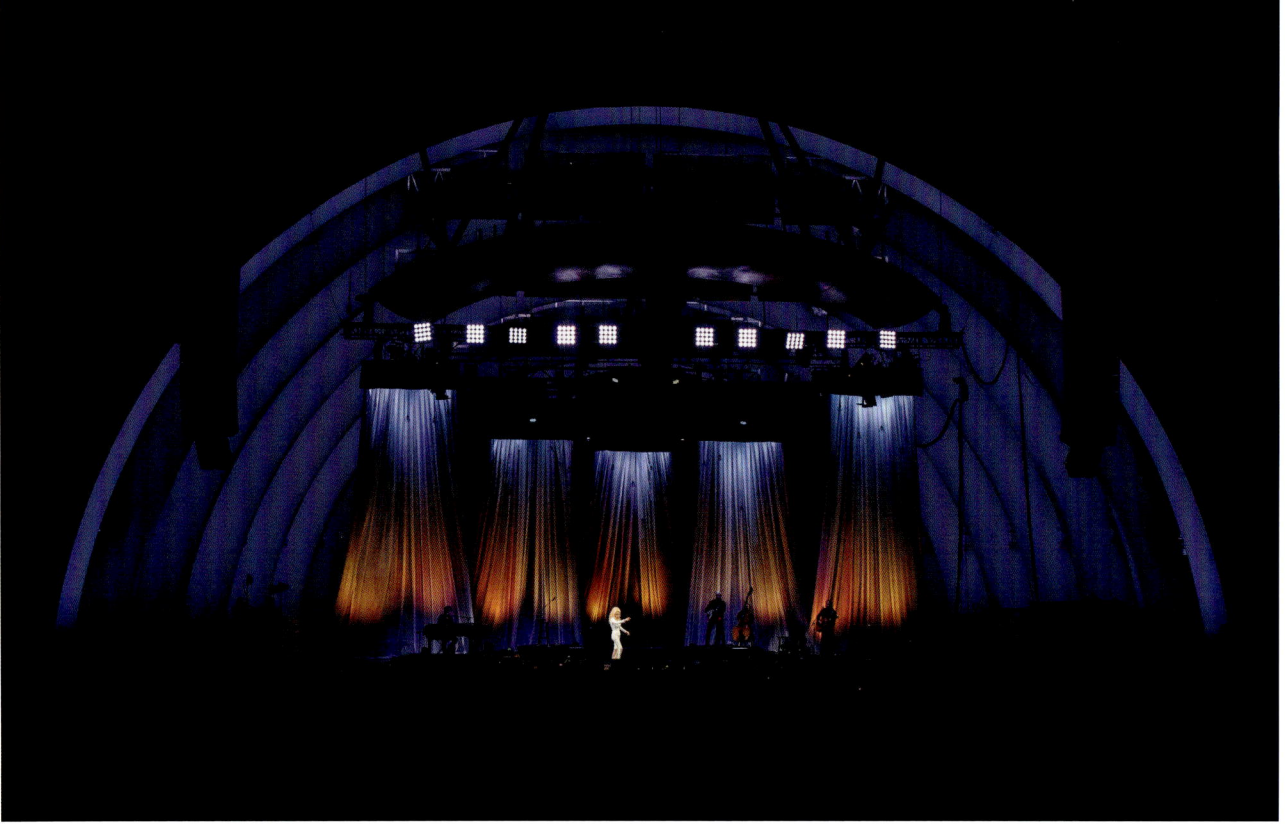

As much as I like to dress up, I usually prefer a modest production. *Above:* The stage at the Hollywood Bowl shows how a little lighting can accomplish a lot.

As big as Glastonbury was, there was no sense in ever trying to top it. When I went back on the road two years later, I set up the Pure & Simple Tour to go along with my *Pure & Simple* album, which was inspired by my Ryman shows and my fiftieth anniversary with my husband, Carl. That release was a basic back-to-my-roots kind of sound applied specifically to love songs, and I even remade a couple of the duets I wrote when I was with Porter Wagoner: "Say Forever You'll Be Mine" and "Tomorrow Is Forever."

After spending most of the previous tour out of the country, this one stayed entirely in North America. It covered sixty cities, making it the biggest concert tour I'd conducted in more than twenty-five years. Before it launched in June, I went to Las Vegas in April for the Academy of Country Music (ACM) Awards. The ACM gave me the Tex Ritter Award, which honors performers for sharing country music in the movies and on TV. Katy Perry presented me with the award for my NBC movie *Coat of Many Colors,* and she joined me to perform some of my hits for the national TV audience. The backdrop was one of the nicest I ever worked with. It featured patchwork patterns to keep the visuals interesting while we sang "Coat of Many Colors," it spelled out our first names in Vegas neon as Katy and I performed "Jolene," and it backed us with a wall of clocks when we did "9 to 5."

I liked to joke about the Pure & Simple Tour that I wasn't really all that pure, but I could be pretty simple.

Star of the Show

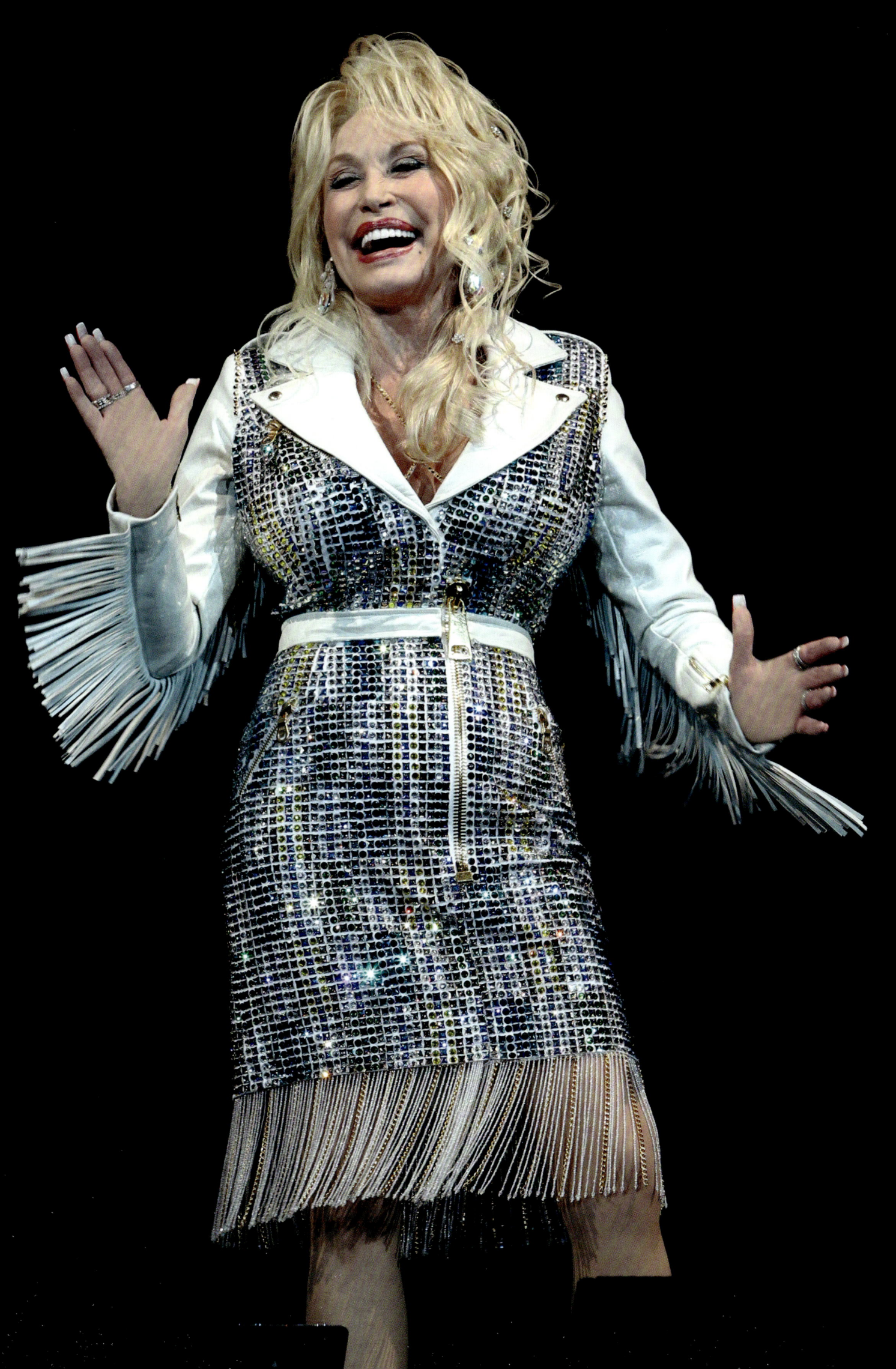

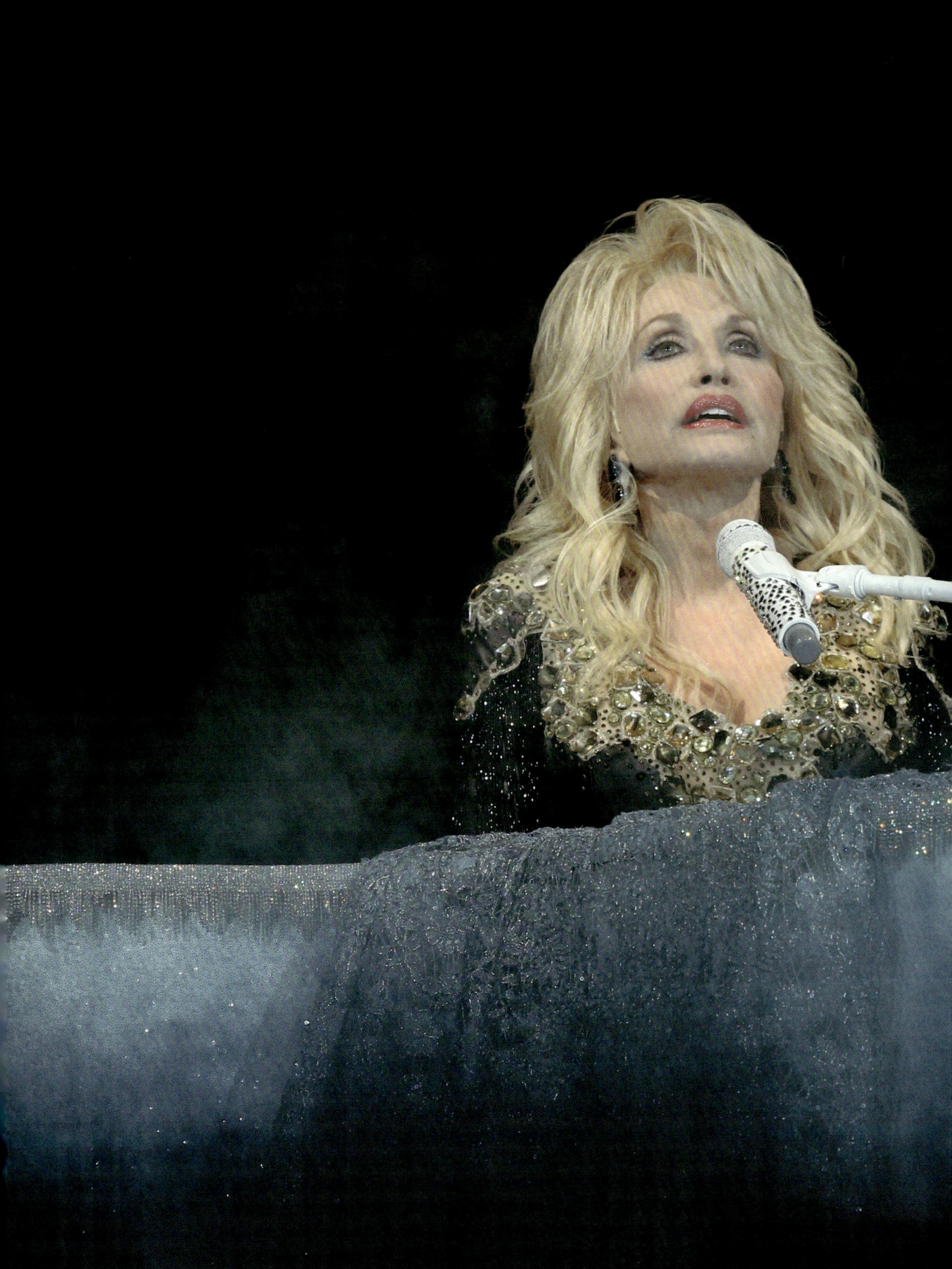

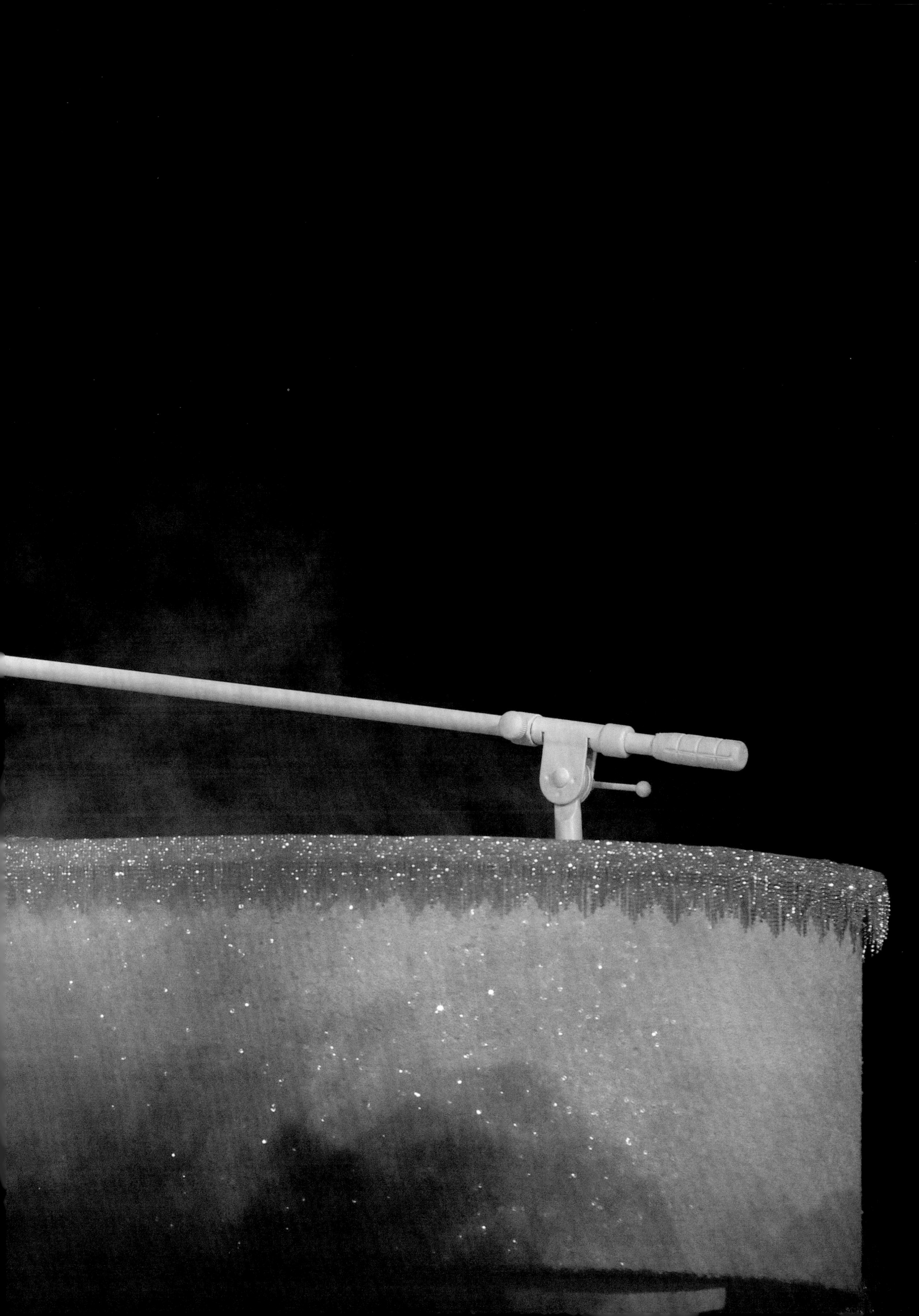

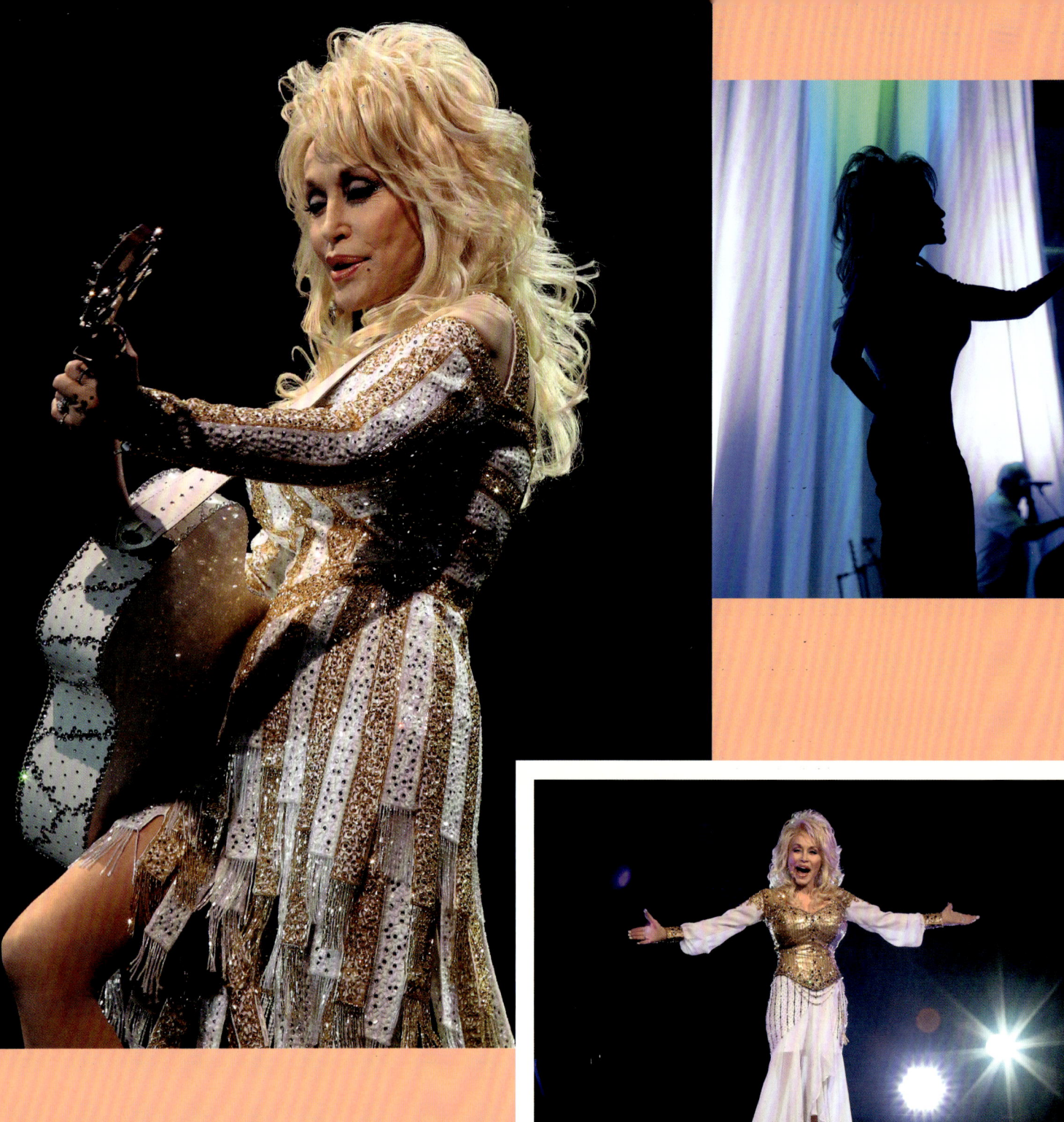

The Pure & Simple Tour featured a smaller band but still showcased my dreams and big ambitions. It's rewarding to think back on those simple days on the front porch in the Smoky Mountains and then see the pure joy in these photos of me at home in my role as the star of the show.

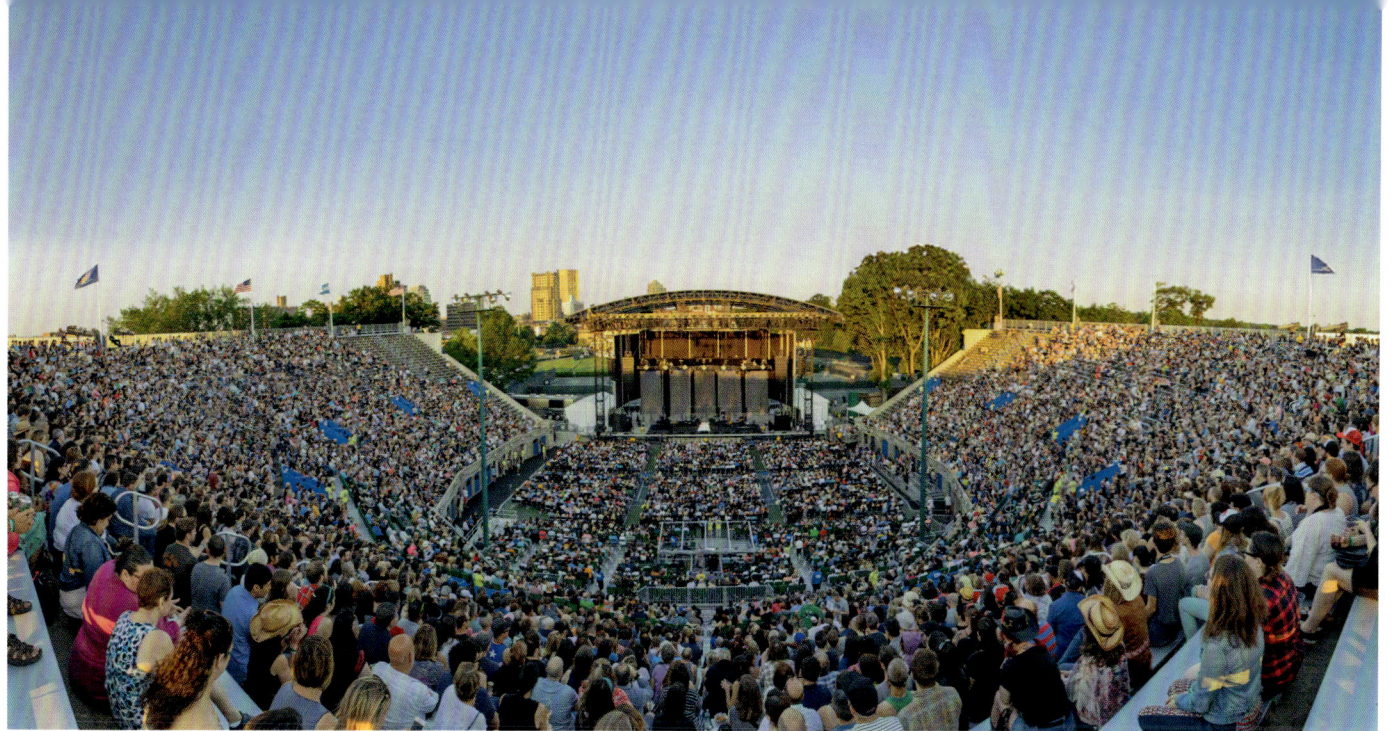

I've always had a special place in my heart for the Big Apple, and I was so excited to play Forest Hills in 2016. It was a beautiful night in a beautiful venue!

That said, the way the tour developed was purely on a "wink" and a prayer. We didn't have anything planned, but Danny thought we should announce we'd be heading out for a string of concerts in North America. We had more than fifty reporters on hand for a press conference in Nashville, and we unveiled the tour. Actually, we kind of made things up. When they asked where we were playing, I looked at Danny, and he just started naming places: New York, California, Texas, Minnesota, North Carolina, and Canada. We announced it would run from May through December and extend to more than sixty shows.

My booking agents were in shock. They had no idea we were planning a new round of shows. Funny thing is, that press conference was how we got the tour booked. Promoters started calling, asking if they could get in on it. And all the places we named? We did at least one concert in every one of the states Danny had named, as well as Canada.

True to the tour name, those live shows were exactly as advertised: simple. The set was built around a front porch, and the shows started with the sound of crickets. There were just four people on the stage: me, keyboard player Richard Dennison, guitarist Kent Wells, and bass player Tom Rutledge. We didn't have all the big group sounds, and we didn't have the big drum sounds, although I love all that stuff. We had a little drum machine, and if we needed drums on anything, we could play a bit of that. It kind of took me back to the early days. It reminded me of the Traveling Family Band and my early shows after I left Porter.

On one of our tour dates, Garth Brooks had the whole crew out for a party. He and Trisha Yearwood have a great house and barns and arcades and game rooms. I think we had a day off, and I remember all of us spending hours and hours there. We had the best time.

Better Days, Pure & Simple

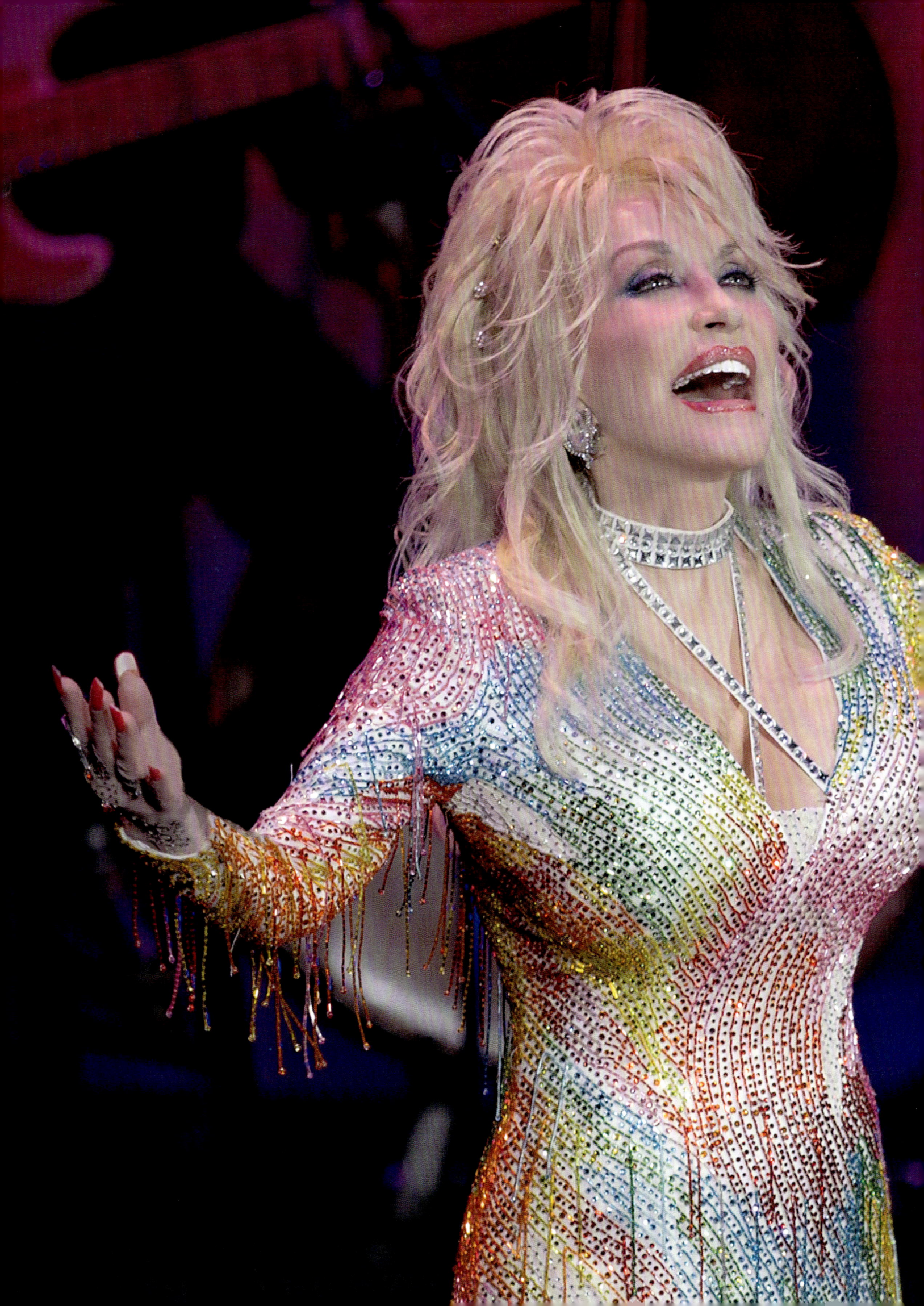

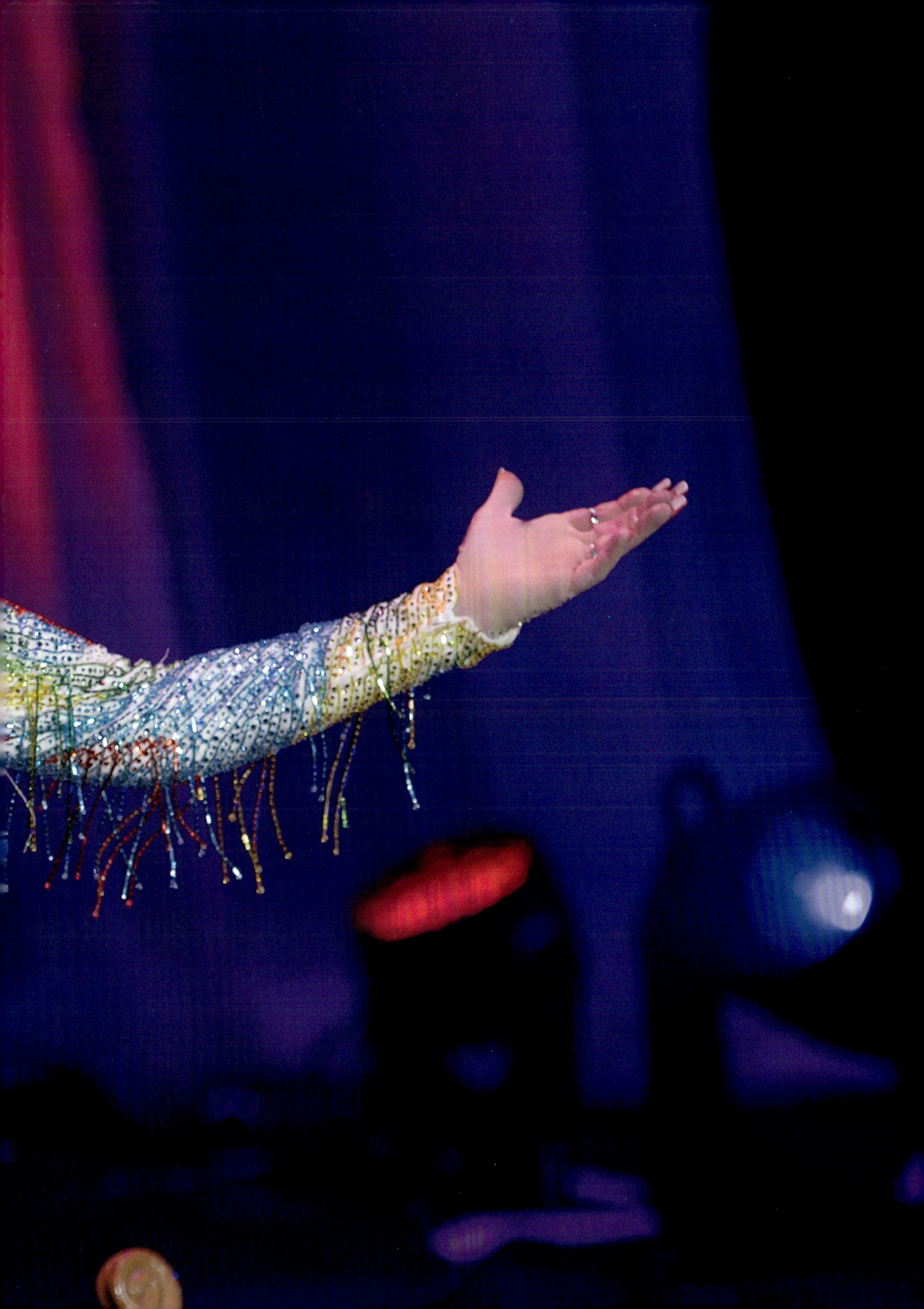

My sister Rachel loves Trisha Yearwood. Rachel is who I wrote the *Good Lookin' Cookin'* cookbook with, and she said, "If you're going up there, I want to know what Trisha's kitchen is like." I think Trisha was out of town, but Garth took me in his golf cart up to the house, and it was impressive. She's got a great kitchen.

The tour also included two nights at the prestigious Hollywood Bowl in a return engagement, five years after I'd played there the first time. It's always fun playing those outdoor theaters at night. You can feel the cool evening air, you can see the people, and there's a feeling of freedom. You can also see beyond the crowd, out into the sky. You feel such an openness.

The Pure & Simple Tour closed on a high note. Randy Travis came out and met up with the whole crew backstage on the last night. Anytime you see one of your fellow musicians—particularly someone as great as Randy Travis, who has gone through what he has gone through as an artist—show up like that, it's very special. To think that he wanted to come backstage and watch the show is more memorable than the fact that it was the final night of the tour.

I was doing so much at the time that wrapping a tour didn't feel like a big deal at all, in fact. My NBC holiday movie *Dolly Parton's Christmas of Many Colors* aired, and that same night, I sang on the TV special *Christmas in Rockefeller Center*.

But what was really weighing on my heart in that moment—more than Christmas and more than my concert tour or anything else—was a major wildfire. It broke out in the Smoky Mountains and quickly grew, expanding to burn a lot of land in the Smokies and damaging parts of Gatlinburg. It threatened Dollywood, and people I knew lost their homes or their valuable memories. The whole area was devastated.

It made me so sad. But it also made me want to help. These were my people who were suffering; that was the place I called home. I pulled together a telethon, *Smoky Mountains Rise: A Benefit for the My People Fund,* with Chris Stapleton, Big & Rich, Reba McEntire, Jamey Johnson, and Chris Young, among others. Kenny Rogers dropped by to sing "Islands in the Stream" with me, and the whole thing raised $13 million for people whose worlds were torn apart.

That was one of those events where I was able to use the stage to make a difference. That's always been important to me, but it would become an even bigger motivator in the years that followed, as I found still more new stages to conquer.

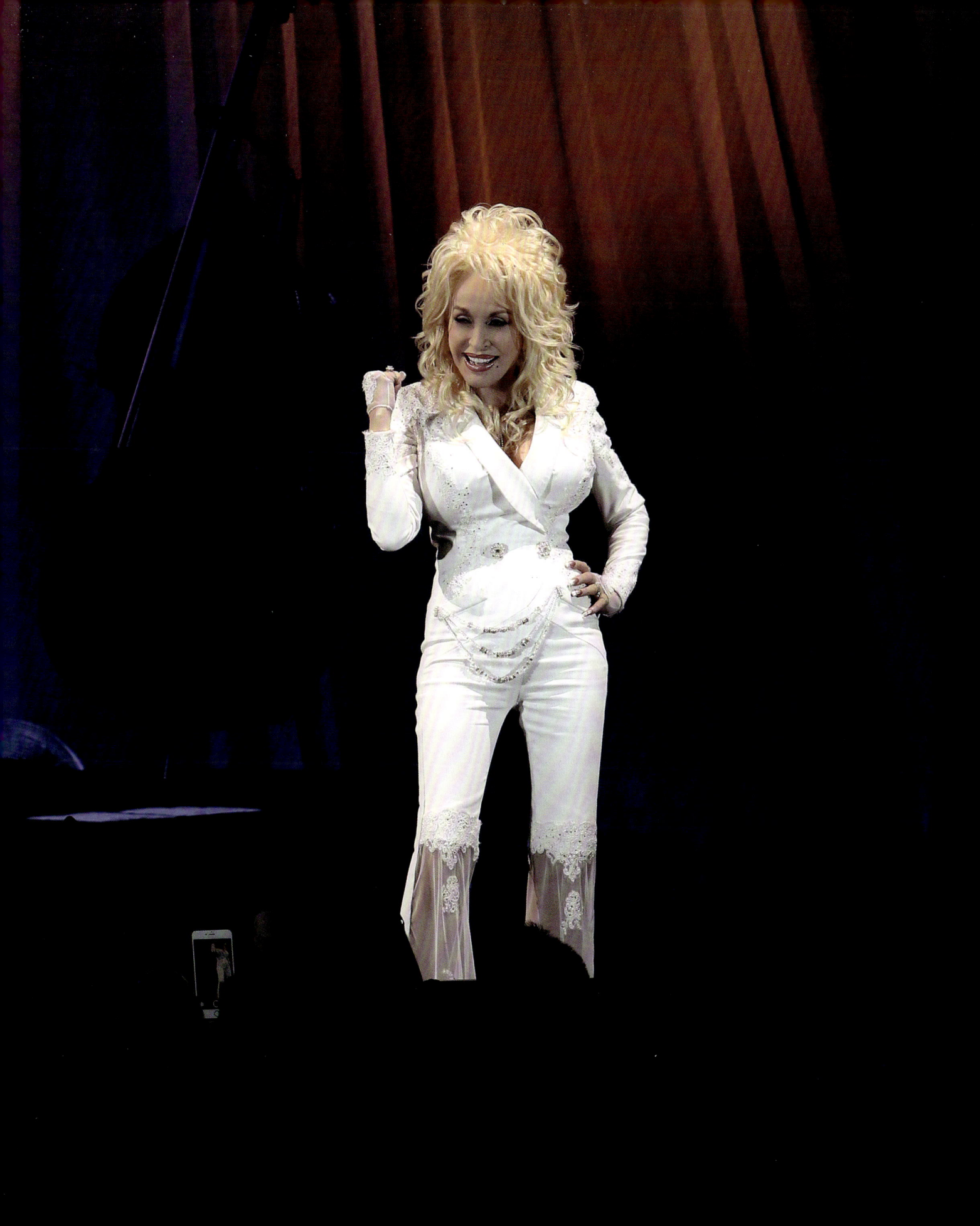

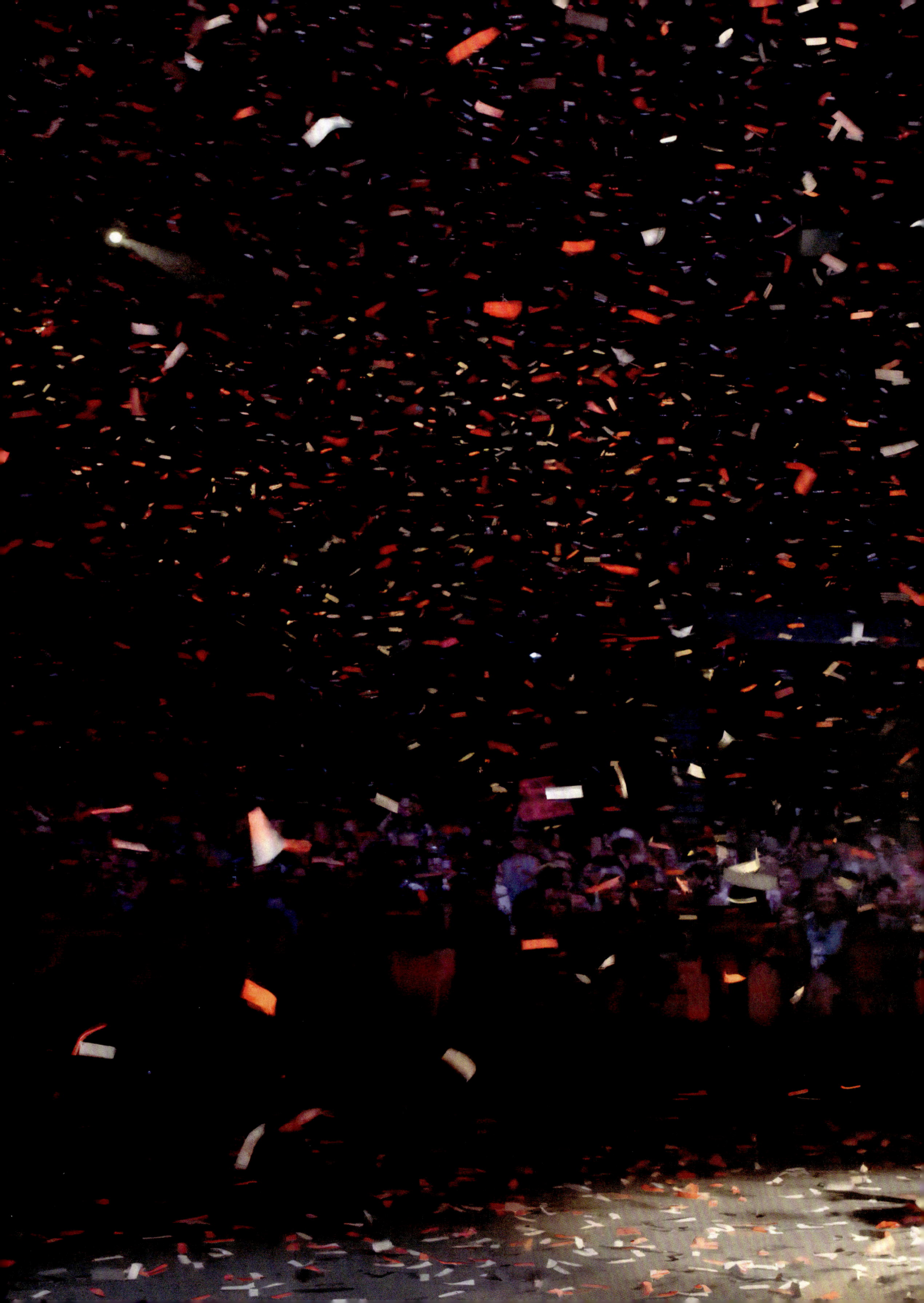

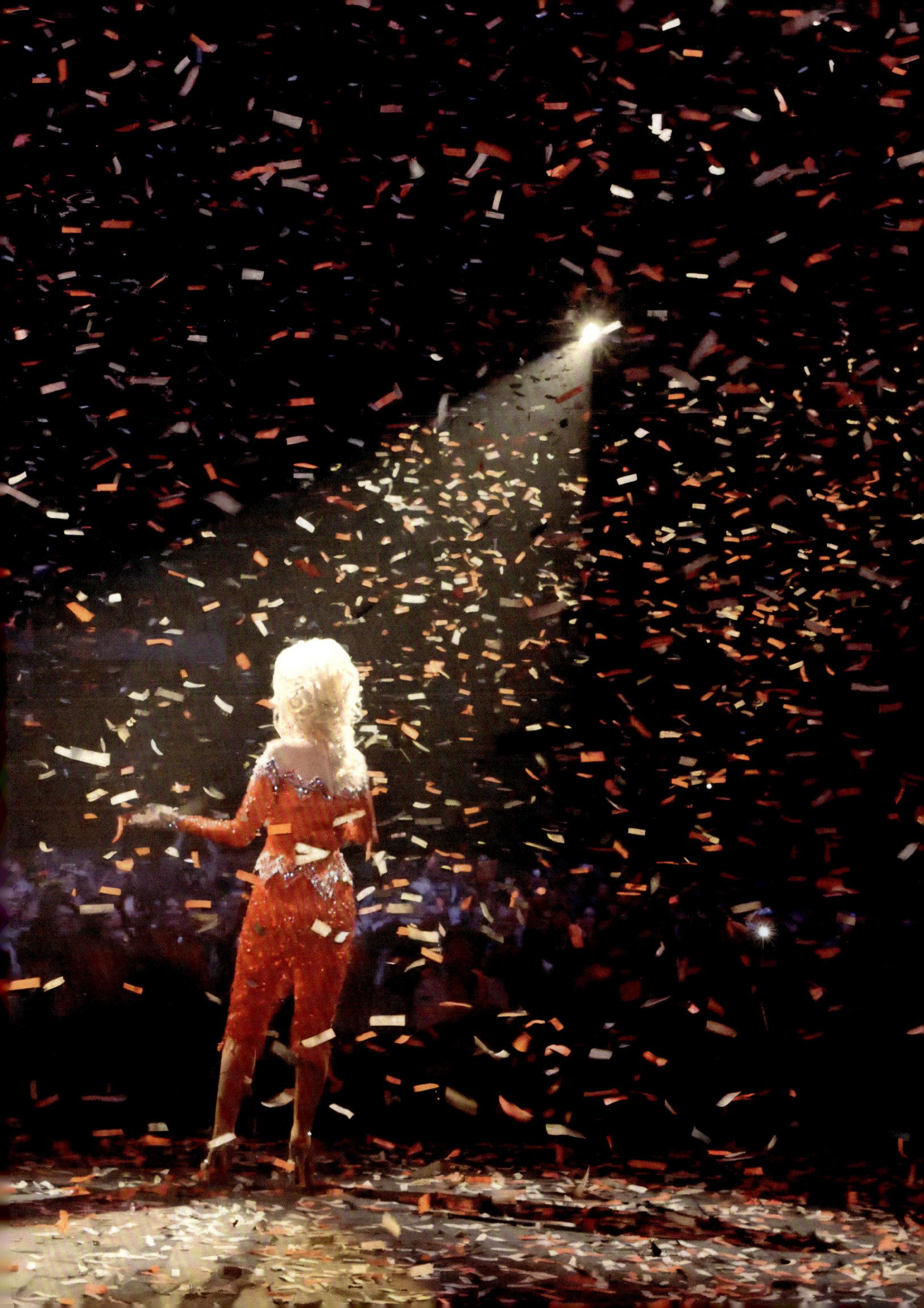

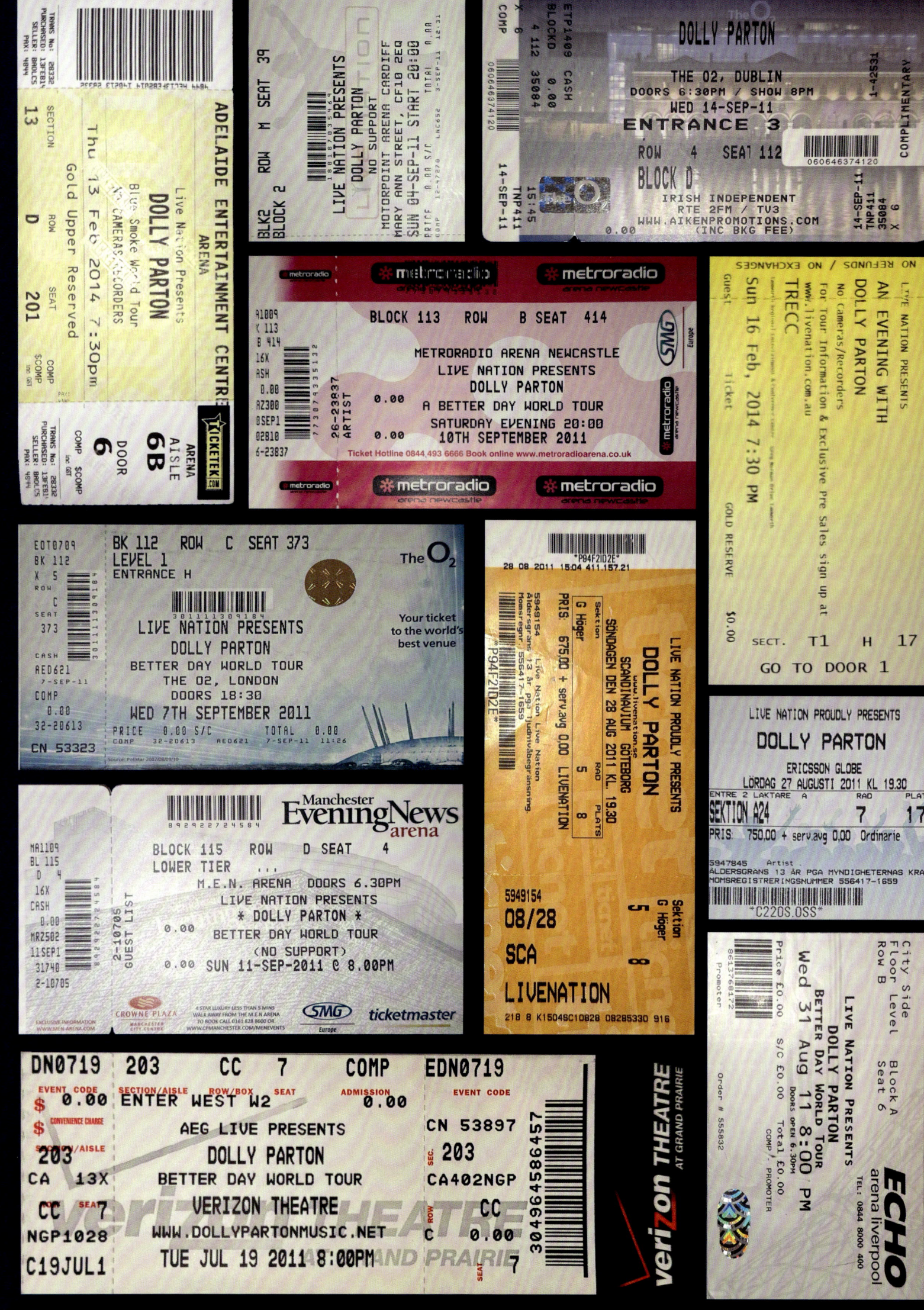

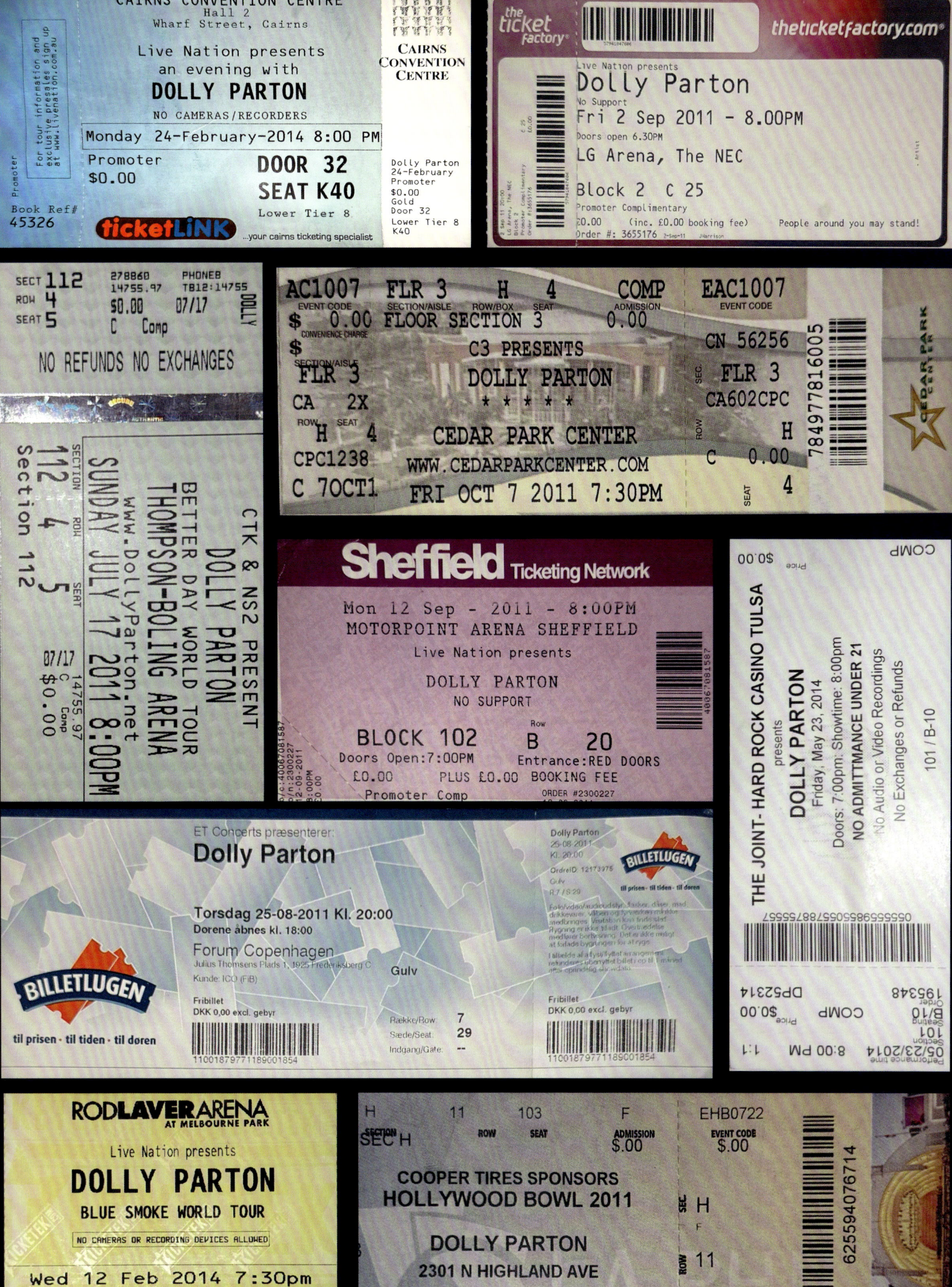

Starring Dolly Parton

CONCERTS, APPEARANCES,
AND PERFORMANCES
FROM 1957-2025

3/19 to 3/20/71 Sam Houston Coliseum, Houston, TX
3/26/71 Griswold Center, Decatur, IL
3/27/71 Grand Ole Opry, Nashville, TN
3/28/71 Davenport Masonic Temple, Davenport, IA
4/10/71 Civic Center, Philadelphia, PA
4/17/71 Roanoke Civic Center, Roanoke, VA
4/24/71 Grand Ole Opry, Nashville, TN
4/30/71 Vets Memorial Coliseum, Dayton, OH
5/8/71 War Memorial Auditorium, Syracuse, NY
5/15/71 Grand Ole Opry, Nashville, TN
5/21/71 Memorial Auditorium, Greenville, SC
5/22/71 Greensboro Coliseum, Greensboro, NC
5/23/71 Asheville City Auditorium, Asheville, NC
5/28/71 Dorton Arena, Raleigh, NC
5/29/71 Cripple Creek, Lancaster, PA
5/30/71 Ontelaunee Park, Hazelton, PA
6/4/71 Madison Square Garden, New York, NY
6/6/71 Dolly Parton Day, Sevierville, TN
6/11/71 Fairgrounds Coliseum, Jackson, MS
6/12/71 Mid-South Coliseum, Memphis, TN
7/8/71 *The David Frost Show*, New York, NY
7/17/71 Rockdale Jamboree, Ashland, KY
7/22/71 Thomas Johnson High School, Frederick, MD
7/23/71 Delmarva Hall, Salisbury, MD
7/25/71 Mocking Bird Hill Park, Anderson, IN
7/29/71 Jackson Coliseum, Jackson, TN
7/30/71 BlueGrass Fair, Lexington, KY
8/7/71 Grand Ole Opry, Nashville, TN
8/8/71 Lucas County Fair, Maumee, OH
8/11/71 Gouveneur and St. Lawrence County Fair, Syracuse, NY
8/14/71 Chemung County Fair, Elmira, NY
8/15/71 Ponderosa Park, Salem, OH
8/18/71 Ozark Fair, Springfield, MO
8/19/71 Illinois State Fair, Springfield, IL
8/20/71 Tri-County Speedway, Cincinnati, OH
8/22/71 Missouri State Fair, Moberly, MO
8/26/71 Fairbury Park, Fairbury, IL
8/27/71 Columbiana County Fair, Salem, OH
8/29/71 Buck Lake Ranch, Angola, IN
8/30/71 Garfield Park, Indianapolis, IN
9/2/71 Stark County Fair, Canton, OH
9/3/71 Charleston Municipal Auditorium, Charleston, WV
9/4/71 Christiana High School, Wilmington, DE
9/5/71 Montgomery County Fair, Dayton, OH
9/6/71 Juniata Fair, Everett, PA
9/10/71 Crossroads Music Park, Kings Mountain, NC
9/11/71 Grand Ole Opry, Nashville, TN
9/15/71 Western Fair, London, ON
9/16/71 St. Mary's County Fairgrounds, Leonardtown, MD
9/17/71 York Fair, York, PA
9/18/71 Wheeling Jamboree, Wheeling, WV
9/19/71 Eastern States Exposition-The Coliseum, Springfield, MA
9/22/71 Adair County Fair, Columbia, KY
9/23/71 Ashland County Fair, Ashland, OH
9/25/71 Porter Wagoner Boulevard Dedication Event, West Plains, MO
10/2/71 Ottumwa Coliseum, Ottumwa, IA
10/3/71 KRNT Theater, Des Moines, IA
10/9/71 Grand Ole Opry, Nashville, TN
10/10/71 CMA Awards, Nashville, TN
10/16/71 Grand Ole Opry, Nashville, TN
10/20/71 Boliver County Exposition Hall, Cleveland, MS
10/29/71 Salem Civic Center, Salem, VA
11/6/71 Grand Ole Opry, Nashville, TN
11/9/71 Overton High School Gym, Nashville, TN
11/14/71 New Prairie Junior High School, South Bend, IN
11/19/71 Jaffa Mosque, Tyrone, PA
11/20/71 Consistory Auditorium, Freeport, IL
11/21/71 Casey High School, Terre Haute, IN
11/27/71 Municipal Auditorium, Atlanta, GA
12/10/71 Washington High School Gym, Washington, NC
12/11/71 Kenan Memorial Auditorium, Kenansville, NC
12/18/71 Grand Ole Opry, Nashville, TN
12/28/71 Cumberland County Memorial Arena, Fayetteville, NC
12/30/71 Municipal Auditorium, Birmingham, AL
12/31/71 Macon Coliseum, Macon, GA

1972

1/7/72 Carolina Coliseum, Columbia, SC
1/8/72 Greenville Memorial Auditorium, Greenville, SC
1/9/72 Greensboro Coliseum, Greensboro, NC
1/15/72 Municipal Auditorium, Columbus, GA
1/22/72 Grand Ole Opry, Nashville, TN
1/29/72 Grand Ole Opry, Nashville, TN
1/30/72 Stevensen High School, Detroit, MI
2/4/72 Old South Jamboree, Covington, LA
2/5/72 Pascagoula–Jackson County Fair, Pascagoula, MS
2/6/72 Rapides Parish Coliseum, Alexandria, LA
2/7/72 Mayfair Center, Tyler, TX
2/11/72 Civic Auditorium, Portland, OR
2/14/72 Lane County Fairgrounds, Eugene, OR
2/16/72 Kennewick Gym, Richland, WA
2/17/72 Spokane Coliseum, Spokane, WA
2/18/72 Falls Civic Center, Great Falls, MT
2/19/72 Jubilee Auditorium, Calgary, AB
2/20/72 Queen Elizabeth Theater, Vancouver, BC
2/26/72 Grand Ole Opry, Nashville, TN
3/4/72 Grand Ole Opry, Nashville, TN
3/11/72 William Woods Campus Auditorium, Fulton, MO
3/15/72 Municipal Auditorium, Manhattan, KS
3/17/72 Springfield Shrine House, Springfield, MO
3/18/72 Municipal Auditorium, Sioux City, IA
3/19/72 Corrigan Hall, Emmitsburg, IA
3/22/72 Sioux Falls Coliseum, Sioux Falls, SD
3/23/72 City Music Hall, Omaha, NE
3/24/72 Salina Memorial Hall, Salina, KS
3/25/72 Convention Hall, Wichita, KS
3/26/72 Memorial Building, Kansas City, MO
4/5/72 Walkway of Stars, Nashville, TN
4/7/72 Eau Claire Auditorium, Eau Claire, WI
4/8/72 University of Wisconsin, Platteville, WI
4/12 to 4/15/72 Fan Fair, Nashville, TN
4/15/72 Grand Ole Opry, Nashville, TN
4/22/72 Natchez Trace Inn, Tupelo, MS
4/28/72 Peterstown High School, Beckley, WV
4/29/72 Grand Ole Opry, Nashville, TN
5/5/72 Memorial Auditorium, Wichita Falls, TX
5/7/72 Amusement Park, Mountain Home, AR
5/10 to 5/11/72 Country Radio Seminar, Nashville, TN
5/12/72 West Edgecome Auditorium, Rocky Mount, NC
5/12/72 *Hee Haw* (TV appearance; airs)
5/13/72 Raleigh County Armory, Beckley, WV
5/20/72 Grand Ole Opry, Nashville, TN
5/27/72 Cripple Creek, Lancaster, PA
6/1/72 Holston High School, Damascus, TN
6/2/72 E. C. Glass High School, Lynchburg, VA
6/3/72 Bluegrass Park, Camp Springs, NC
6/4/72 Watermelon Park, Berryville, VA
6/8/72 Richmond Civic Hall, Richmond, IN
6/17/72 Grand Ole Opry, Nashville, TN
6/18/72 Country Shindig, Tuscumbia, MO
6/27/72 Bramwell Street Fair, Bramwell, WV
7/22/72 Grand Ole Opry, Nashville, TN
7/26/72 Harrison County Fair, Dover, OH
7/27/72 Bramwell Street Fair, Bramwell, WV
7/28/72 Midway Amusement Park, Jamestown, NY
7/30/72 Sunset Park, Lancaster, PA
8/3/72 Northern Wisconsin State Fair, Chippewa Falls, WI
8/4/72 Marion County Fair, Salem, IL
8/6/72 Auglaize County Fair, Lima, OH
8/9/72 Gouveneur High School, Gouveneur, NY
8/10/72 Thomas Johnson High School, Frederick, MD
8/11/72 Wood County Fair, Bowling Green, OH
8/12/72 Washington Junior High School, Pittsburgh, PA
8/13/72 Ponderosa Park, Salem, OH
8/14/72 Holiday Hall, Decatur, IL
8/15/72 Frontier Jamboree, Marceline, MO
8/16/72 Interstate Fair, Coffeyville, KS
8/19/72 Grand Ole Opry, Nashville, TN
8/24/72 Appalachian District Fair, Johnson City, TN
8/26/72 Malden High School, Molden, MO
9/2/72 Grand Ole Opry, Nashville, TN
9/10/72 Old Plantation Park, Lakeland, FL
9/15/72 Memorial Hall, Dayton, OH
9/16/72 The Taft, Cincinnati, OH
9/21/72 St. Joseph Fair, Centerville, MI
9/22/72 Municipal Auditorium, Charleston, WV
9/30/72 Auditorium Theater, Rochester, NY
10/1/72 Masonic Auditorium, Scranton, PA
10/6/72 War Memorial Auditorium, Syracuse, NY
10/7/72 Kleinhans Music Hall, Buffalo, NY
10/14/72 Grand Ole Opry, Nashville, TN
10/16/72 CMA Awards, Nashville, TN
10/20/72 RCA Luncheon, Nashville, TN
10/21/72 Grand Ole Opry, Nashville, TN
10/29/72 Symphony Hall, Boston, MA
11/1/72 Southeast Louisiana University, Hammond, LA
11/3/72 Wego Country Opry, Westwego, LA
11/4/72 Grand Ole Opry, Nashville, TN
11/11/72 Dolly Parton Day, Sevierville, TN
11/16/72 Cherokee High School Auditorium, Canton, GA
11/17/72 Reidland High School, Paducah, KY
11/18/72 Jackson Coliseum, Jackson, TN
11/19/72 Jefferson City Senior High School, Jefferson City, MO
12/3/72 Sports & Convention Center, Frankfort, KY
12/8/72 Municipal Auditorium, San Antonio, TX
12/9/72 Fair Park Coliseum, Lubbock, TX
12/10/72 Civic Center Coliseum, Amarillo, TX
12/16/72 Grand Ole Opry, Nashville, TN
12/29/72 The Arena, Duluth, MN
12/30/72 Dane County Coliseum, Madison, WI
12/31/72 Veterans Memorial Auditorium, Des Moines, IA

1973

1/6/73 Grand Ole Opry, Nashville, TN
1/20/73 Grand Ole Opry, Nashville, TN
1/26/73 Louisville Convention Center, Louisville, KY
1/27/73 Grand Ole Opry, Nashville, TN
2/3/73 Grand Ole Opry, Nashville, TN
2/8/73 Pensacola Municipal Auditorium, Pensacola, FL
2/9/73 Three Arts Center, Columbus, GA
2/10/73 Dothan Civic Center, Dothan, AL
2/16/73 Kennewick High School, Richland, WA
2/18/73 Goodman Gymnasium (Catawba College), Salisbury, NC
2/27/73 Civic Center, El Paso, TX
3/1/73 Golden Hall, San Diego, CA
3/2/73 Long Beach Auditorium, Long Beach, CA
3/3/73 Bakersfield Civic Center, Bakersfield, CA
3/4/73 Selland Arena, Fresno, CA
3/7/73 Redding Civic Auditorium, Redding, CA
3/8/73 Stockton Civic Auditorium, Stockton, CA
3/9/73 Berkeley Community Theater, Oakland, CA
3/10/73 San Jose Civic Auditorium, San Jose, CA
3/24/73 Grand Ole Opry, Nashville, TN
3/29/73 Keith Albee Theater, Huntington, WV
3/30/73 Granite Falls High School Gym, Granite Falls, NC
3/31/73 TC Robertson High School, Asheville, NC
4/1/73 Charlotte Park Center, Charlotte, NC
4/12/73 Shrine Mosque, Springfield, IL
4/13/73 Joplin Memorial Hall, Joplin, MO
4/14/73 Topeka Municipal Auditorium, Topeka, KS
4/15/73 St. Joseph Auditorium, St. Joseph, MO
4/20/73 Austin Peay Municipal Stadium, Clarksville, TN
4/23/73 Tarkio College, Tarkio, MO
4/25/73 Sioux Falls Coliseum, Sioux Falls, SD
4/26/73 Municipal Auditorium, Sioux City, IA
4/27/73 Memorial Hall, Salina, KS
4/28/73 Century II Concert Hall, Wichita, KS
4/29/73 Civic Center, Little Rock, AR
5/4/73 Lakeland Community College, Willoughby, OH
5/5/73 Packard Music Hall, Warren, OH
5/6/73 Honeywell Center, Wabash, IN
5/19/73 Grand Ole Opry, Nashville, TN
5/25/73 Raleigh County Armory, Beckley, WV
5/26/73 Shindig at Cripple Creek, Lancaster, PA
5/30/73 Lonesome Pine Raceway, Coburn, VA
6/6/73 Fan Fair, Nashville, TN
6/9/73 Grand Ole Opry, Nashville, TN
6/10/73 Fiddler's Championship-Concert, Nashville, TN
7/21/73 Grand Ole Opry, Nashville, TN
7/28/73 Municipal Auditorium, Atlanta, GA
7/31/73 Western Kentucky State Fair, Hopkinsville, KY
8/2/73 Bramwell Street Fair, Bramwell, WV
8/4/73 Harrison County Fair, Cordin, IN
8/8/73 *That Good Ole Nashville Music* (films), Nashville, TN
8/9/73 North Central Missouri Fair, Trenton, MO
8/11/73 Grand Ole Opry, Nashville, TN
8/12/73 Ponderosa Park, Salem, OH
8/21/73 Appalachian Fair, Kingsport, TN
8/23/73 Steuben County Fair, Elmira, NY
8/31/73 Six Flags Over Mid-America, St. Louis, MO
9/1/73 Grand Ole Opry, Nashville, TN
9/8/73 Grand Ole Opry, Nashville, TN
9/11/73 Wayne County Fair, Wooster, OH
9/13/73 *Rowan & Martin* TV special (airs)
9/14/73 Raleigh Memorial Auditorium, Raleigh, NC
9/15/73 Macon Coliseum, Macon, GA
9/21/73 Cumberland County Memorial Arena, Fayetteville, NC
9/22/73 Memorial Auditorium, Greenville, SC
9/28/73 Jackson Coliseum, Jackson, MS
9/29/73 Rapides Parish Coliseum, Alexandria, LA
9/30/73 Civic Center, Lake Charles, LA
10/6/73 Grand Ole Opry, Nashville, TN
10/13/73 Cordell Hull Dam Dedication Ceremony, Carthage, TN
10/13/73 Grand Ole Opry, Nashville, TN
10/14/73 Porter Wagoner Golf Championship, Nashville, TN
10/15/73 CMA Awards, Nashville, TN
10/20/73 RCA Breakfast, Nashville, TN
10/27/73 Grand Ole Opry, Nashville, TN
11/24/73 Grand Ole Opry, Nashville, TN
12/1/73 Grand Ole Opry, Nashville, TN
12/7/73 Timberlake Concert Hall, Lynchburg, VA
12/14/73 Murfreesboro Middle School, Murfreesboro, TN
12/15/73 Green Central High School, Snow Hill, NC

1974

1/5/74 Grand Ole Opry, Nashville, TN
1/12/74 Dobyns-Bennett High School, Johnson City, TN
1/13/74 Bluefield Auditorium, Bluefield, WV
1/18/74 Texarkana College Auditorium, Texarkana, TX
1/19/74 Monroe Civic Center, Monroe, LA
1/20/74 Municipal Auditorium, El Dorado, AR
1/24 to 1/25/74 Albert Thomas Convention Center, Houston, TX
1/26/74 San Angelo Municipal Auditorium, San Angelo, TX
2/6/74 Toledo Masonic Auditorium, Toledo, OH
2/7/74 Dayton Memorial Hall, Dayton, OH
2/8/74 Veterans Memorial Hall, Columbus, OH
2/9/74 Taft Theater, Cincinnati, OH
2/10/74 Stanbaugh Auditorium, Youngstown, OH
2/14/74 McMahon Auditorium, Lawton, OK
2/15/74 Civic Center, Oklahoma City, OK
2/16/74 Tulsa Assembly Center, Tulsa, OK
2/17/74 Music Hall, Hot Springs, AR
2/19/74 Porter Wagoner and Dolly Parton press conference, Nashville, TN
2/21/74 Knoxville Civic Auditorium, Knoxville, TN
2/22/74 North Hall Auditorium, Memphis, TN
3/1/74 Country Radio Seminar, Nashville, TN
3/2/74 Grand Ole Opry, Nashville, TN
3/6/74 Symphony Hall, Phoenix, AZ
3/7/74 Oxnard Auditorium, Oxnard, CA
3/8/74 Sacramento Memorial Auditorium, Sacramento, CA
3/9/74 *The Burt Reynolds Late Show* (airs)
3/9/74 Redding Civic Auditorium, Redding, CA
3/10/74 Bakersfield Civic Center, Bakersfield, CA
3/14/74 San Jose Civic Auditorium, San Jose, CA
3/15/74 Selland Arena, Fresno, CA
3/16/74 Grand Ole Opry, Nashville, TN
3/17/74 Community Center, Tucson, AZ
3/28/74 Civic Auditorium, Grand Rapids, MI
3/29/74 IMA Auditorium, Flint, MI
3/30/74 Masonic Auditorium, Detroit, MI
3/31/74 Old Central Auditorium, Battle Creek, MI
4/2/74 Vanderbilt University-UTK Game special ceremony, Nashville, TN
4/5/74 Joplin Memorial Hall, Joplin, MO
4/6/74 Kansas Memorial Hall, Kansas City, MO
4/15 to 4/17/74 Opryland USA, Nashville, TN
4/18/74 Mitchell Corn Palace, Mitchell, SD
4/19/74 Salina Memorial Hall, Salina, KS
4/20/74 Kemper Military Field House, Booneville, MO
4/24/74 *Country Comes Home* (TV special; NBC)
4/27/74 Cobb County Fairgrounds (Wendy Bagwell benefit concert), Atlanta, GA
5/1/74 Amarillo Civic Center, Amarillo, TX
5/3/74 Ector Coliseum, Odessa, TX
5/4/74 Abilene Civic Center, Abilene, TX
5/10/74 Pershing Auditorium, Lincoln, NE
5/11/74 Sioux City Municipal Auditorium, Sioux City, IA
5/12/74 Hammond Civic Center, Hammond, IN
5/16/74 Northside Junior High Gym (benefit show), Nashville, TN
5/18/74 Grand Ole Opry, Nashville, TN
6/7/74 Veterans Memorial Auditorium, Des Moines, IA
6/8/74 Belle Claire Fairgrounds, Belleville, IL
6/9/74 Davenport Masonic Temple, Davenport, IA
6/12 to 6/14/74 Fan Fair, Nashville, TN
6/15/74 Grand Ole Opry, Nashville, TN
6/15 to 6/16/74 Fan Fair, Nashville, TN
6/16/74 Grand Masters Fiddling Contest, Opryland, Nashville, TN
7/5 to 7/6/74 Grand Ole Opry, Nashville, TN
7/12 to 7/13/74 Grand Ole Opry, Nashville, TN
8/1/74 McLean County Fair, Bloomington, IL
8/10/74 Ozark Empire Fair, Springfield, MO
8/16 to 8/17/74 Grand Ole Opry, Nashville, TN
8/18/74 Allen County Fair, Salem, OH
8/20/74 West Virginia State Fair, Lewisburg, WV
8/21/74 WBAP Country Gold 4th Anniversary Party, Arlington Stadium, Ft. Worth, TX
8/23/74 Sweeney Gymnasium, Santa Fe, NM
8/25/74 Anaheim Convention Center, Anaheim, CA
8/26/74 Country Gold Anniversary, Ft. Worth, TX
8/28/74 Washington Fairgrounds, Walla Walla, WA
8/30/74 Redding Civic Auditorium, Redding, CA
8/31/74 Oregon State Fair, Albany, OR
9/1/74 *Muscular Dystrophy Telethon*, Labor Day (airs)
9/6/74 Asheville Civic Center, Asheville, NC
9/10/74 Whistle Stop, New York, NY
9/14/74 Felt Forum at Madison Square Garden, New York, NY
9/20/74 Akron Civic Center, Akron, OH
9/22/74 Lansing Civic Center, Lansing, MI
9/28/74 Virginia State Fair, Danville, VA
9/29/74 Opera House, Spokane, WA
10/7/74 *Nashville North with Ian Tyson* (Canada TV appearance; airs), Calgary, AB
10/8/74 Dade County Shrine Fair, Ft. Walton Beach, FL
10/10/74 Chilhowee High School, Chilhowee, VA
10/11/74 Municipal Auditorium, Lafayette, LA
10/14/74 CMA Awards, Nashville, TN
10/20/74 Mid-South Coliseum, Memphis, TN
10/24/74 Bell Auditorium, Aiken, SC
10/25/74 Knoxville Civic Coliseum, Knoxville, TN
10/26/74 Municipal Auditorium, Charleston, WV
10/27/74 Hayfield Secondary School, Woodbridge, VA
11/2/74 Holiday Lake Park, Spartansburg, SC
11/8/74 *The Wilburn Brothers Show* (airs)
11/8 to 11/9/74 Stardust, Waldorf, MD
11/17/74 Buddie Boswell's Union Mill, St. Joseph, MO
11/18/74 *Nashville North with Ian Tyson* (Canada, 2nd appearance; airs)
11/23/74 The Arena, Saskatoon, SK
11/24/74 Center for the Arts, Regina, SK
11/25/74 Jubilee Auditorium, Edmonton, AB
11/26/74 Southern Alberta Jubilee, Calgary, AB
11/27/74 Opera House, Spokane, WA
11/29/74 Queen Elizabeth Ballroom, Vancouver, BC
12/1/74 Portland Civic Auditorium, Portland, OR
12/21/74 WESC Radio Salute to Dolly Parton, Greenville, SC

1975

1/3/75 Grand Ole Opry, Nashville, TN
1/4/75 Grand Ole Opry, Nashville, TN
1/5/75 Market Square Arena, Indianapolis, IN
1/10/75 Mid-South Coliseum, Memphis, TN
1/11/75 Monroe Civic Center, Monroe, LA
1/15/75 *In Concert* TV special (films), Nashville, TN
1/17/75 Roberts Stadium, Evansville, IN
1/18/75 Louisville Convention Center, Louisville, KY
1/24/75 Salem Roanoke Civic Center, Salem, VA
1/25/75 Cumberland County Memorial Arena, Lumberton, SC
1/26/75 Market Square Arena, Indianapolis, IN
1/31/75 Dothan Civic Center, Dothan, AL
2/1/75 Municipal Auditorium, Atlanta, GA
2/2/75 Birmingham Municipal Auditorium, Birmingham, AL
2/8/75 Rapides Parish Coliseum, Alexandria, LA
2/12/75 *Dinah!* TV appearance (airs)
2/14/75 LSU Assembly Hall, Lafayette, LA
2/15/75 *Hee Haw* (airs)
2/20/75 Sevier County High School, Sevierville, TN
2/22/75 Greensboro Coliseum, Burlington, NC
2/23/75 The Mosque, Richmond, VA
2/24/75 Salem Civic Center, Salem, VA
2/28/75 Curtis Hixon Hall, Tampa, FL
3/1/75 Dorton Arena, Raleigh, NC
3/2/75 West Palm Beach Auditorium, Palm Beach, FL
3/3/75 *Nashville North with Ian Tyson* (Canada, 3rd appearance; airs)
3/7/75 Civic Center, Lake Charles, LA
3/8/75 Mobile Municipal Auditorium, Mobile, AL
3/14/75 Dobyns-Bennett Dome, Kingsport, TN
3/15/75 Dorton Arena, Raleigh, NC
3/22/75 Columbia Coliseum, Columbia, SC
3/29/75 Wembley Arena, London, England
3/30/75 Scandinavium, Gøteborg, Sweden
4/11/75 Henderson County Junior College, Athens, TX
4/12/75 Dekalb Rodeo, Dekalb, TX
4/19/75 Tarrant County Convention Center, Worth, TX

fold out

5/3/75 Disney World, Orlando, FL
5/5/75 Dade County Youth Fair, Miami, FL
5/18/75 Woody's, Nova, OH
5/23/75 West Florence High School Gym, Florence, SC
6/28 to 6/29/75 Franklin County Fairgrounds, Richmond, IN
7/3/75 Kentucky Lake Music Barn, Clarksville, TN
7/4/75 Assumption High School, Assumption, IL
7/5/75 Six Flags, St. Louis, MO
7/6/75 Ponderosa Park, Salem, OH
7/11/75 Myrtle Beach Convention Center, Myrtle Beach, SC
7/25 to 7/26/75 Grand Ole Opry, Nashville, TN
7/27/75 Tombstone Junction, Middlesboro, KY
7/29/75 Lucas County Fair, Port Clinton, OH
7/31/75 Elkhart County 4 to H Fair, South Bend, IN
8/2/75 Summer Music Festival, Manasquan, NJ
8/5/75 Chemung County Fair, Elmira, NY
8/8/75 Sullivan County College, Loch Sheldrake, NY
8/9/75 Canaan Fair, West Lebanon, NH
8/16/75 Muskingum County Fair, Zanesville, OH
8/17/75 Sunset Park, State College, PA
8/20/75 *The Porter Wagoner Show* (TV appearance; airs)
8/23/75 DuQuoin State Fair, DuQuoin, IL
8/24/75 Buck Lake Ranch, South Bend, IN
8/26/75 Minnesota State Fair, Minneapolis, MN
8/27/75 Busch Stadium, Indianapolis, IN
8/28/75 *Candid Camera* (airs)
8/29/75 Old Settlers Festival, Chillicothe, MO
9/1/75 *Muscular Dystrophy Telethon*, Labor Day (airs)
9/12/75 Jenkins High School Gym, Jenkins, KY
9/15/75 *Grand Ole Country* TV appearance (airs)
9/18/75 Ashland County Fair, Ashland, OH
9/19 to 9/20/75 Mid-South Fair, Memphis, TN
9/22/75 Hillsdale Fair, Hillsdale, MI
9/26/75 Studio Theater, Hamilton, OH
9/27/75 Bloomsburg Fair, Bloomsburg, PA
9/28/75 Mt. Vernon High School, Mt. Vernon, VA
10/1/75 Ambassador Theater, St. Louis, MO
10/2/75 Memorial Centre, Kingston, ON
10/4/75 Brantford Civic Center, Brantford, ON
10/10/75 Ambassador Theater, St. Louis, MO
10/11/75 Hazard Kentucky, Hazard, KY
10/12/75 BMI Awards, Nashville, TN
10/13/75 CMA Awards, Nashville, TN
10/18/75 Grand Ole Opry, Nashville, TN
10/24/75 Von Braun Center, Huntsville, AL
10/25/75 Grand Ole Opry, Nashville, TN
10/26/75 Texas Prison Rodeo, Huntsville, TX
10/31/75 Grand Ole Opry, Nashville, TN
11/1/75 Jaycees County Fair, Hattiesburg, MS
11/7/75 Memorial Hall, Dayton, OH
11/8/75 Veterans Memorial Hall, Columbus, OH
11/9/75 Masonic Auditorium, Toledo, OH
11/11/75 *Grand Ole Opry at 50!* (TV special)
11/14/75 Auditorium Theater, Rochester, NY
11/16/75 Masonic Temple, Scranton, PA
11/21/75 War Memorial Syracuse, Syracuse, NY
11/22/75 Taft Theater, Fairfield, OH
11/23/75 Whiting Auditorium, Flint, MI
11/27/75 Macy's Thanksgiving Day Parade
11/28/75 *Country Music Hit Parade* (airs)
11/28 to 11/29/75 Grand Ole Opry, Nashville, TN
12/1/75 Drendel Auditorium, Hickory, NC
12/5/75 Morris Auditorium, South Bend, IN
12/13/75 Little Nashville Opry, Nashville, IN
12/14/75 Hickory High School, Hickory, NC

1976

1/5 to 1/8/76 Harrah's, Lake Tahoe, NV
1/10/76 North Lenoir High School Gym, Kinston, NC
1/11/76 Raleigh Memorial Auditorium, Raleigh, NC
1/13/76 *That Good Ole Nashville Music* (airs)
1/20/76 *Dinah!*, TV show (airs)
1/24/76 Cumberland Memorial Arena, Fayetteville, NC
1/31/76 Exposition Center, Waukesha, WI
2/1/76 Arie Crown Theater, Chicago, IL
2/2/76 *Hill Country Sounds*, TV show (airs)
2/7/76 Florida State Fair, Tampa, FL
2/13/76 Winston Salem Memorial Coliseum, Winston to Salem, NC
2/14/76 Salem-Roanoke Civic Center, Salem, VA
2/23 to 2/24/76 Two Rivers Plaza, Grand Junction, CO
2/26/76 Spokane Opera House, Spokane, WA
2/27/76 Portland Civic Auditorium, Portland, OR
2/28/76 Seattle Opera House, Seattle, WA
2/29/76 The Ranier Theater, Tonasket, WA
3/2/76 Jubilee Auditorium, Edmonton, AB
3/4/76 Centennial Concert Hall, Winnipeg, MB
3/5/76 Centennial Auditorium, Saskatoon, SK
3/6/76 Center for the Arts, Regina, SK
3/7/76 Jubilee Auditorium, Calgary, AB
3/12/76 East Burke High School, Hickory, NC
3/13/76 Municipal Auditorium, Charleston, WV
3/24/76 *Captain Kangaroo* TV appearance (airs)
3/26/76 Erwin Junior High School, Salisbury, NC
3/27/76 Wheeling Jamboree, Wheeling, WV
3/28/76 Freedom Hall, Louisville, KY
4/4/76 Memorial Gym, Kokomo, IN
4/9/76 Waco Convention Center, Waco, TX
4/10/76 Tarrant County Convention Center, Ft. Worth, TX
4/18/76 Wembley Music Fest, London, England
4/19/76 Scandinavium, Göteborg, Sweden
4/24/76 West Florence High School Gym, Florence, SC
4/25/76 Ketron High School, Kingsport, TN
4/30/76 Webster Auditorium, Webster, IA
5/1/76 Illinois Country Opry, Decatur, IL
5/4/76 Centennial Hall, Juneau, AK
5/5/76 Hering Auditorium, Fairbanks, AK
5/8/76 Conroy Bowl, Honolulu, HI
5/22/76 Grand Ole Opry, Nashville, TN
5/28 to 5/29/76 Grand Ole Opry, Nashville, TN
6/3/76 Chambersburg High School, Chambersburg, PA
6/4/76 Roman Forum, West Patterson, NJ
6/5/76 Concerts at the Dam, Bruceton Mills, WV
6/6/76 Sunset Park, West Grove, PA
6/10/76 *The Mac Davis Show* (airs)
6/10/76 Fan Fair, Nashville, TN
6/12/76 Grand Ole Opry, Nashville, TN
7/11/76 Buck Lake Ranch, Angola, IN
7/16 to 7/17/76 Hotel El Rancho, Sacramento, CA
Fall 1976 *Dolly* TV variety series (syndicated; films)
10/1/76 Donk's Theater, Newport News, VA
10/2/76 Bloomsburg Fair, Bloomsburg, PA
10/8/76 Ark-La-Miss Industrial Fair, Monroe, LA
10/9/76 LanierLand Music Park, Cummings, GA
10/11/76 CMA Awards, Nashville, TN
10/19/76 High Point Theater, High Point, NC
10/23/76 Grand Ole Opry, Nashville, TN
11/1/76 Myrtle Beach Convention Center, Myrtle Beach, SC
11/5/76 Auditorium Theater, Rochester, NY
11/6/76 Kleinhaus Music Hall, Buffalo, NY
11/7/76 Masonic Temple, Scranton, PA
11/20/76 Massey Hall, Toronto, ON
11/21/76 Front Row, Cleveland, OH
12/26/76 *Midnight Special* (airs)
12/28/76 *New Harvest . . . First Gathering* album release party at the Bistro, Los Angeles, CA

1977

Spring 1977 *Dolly* TV variety series (syndicated; films)
1/15/77 Oxnard Civic Auditorium, Oxnard, CA
1/16/77 DeAnza College, Cupertino, CA
1/19/77 *The Tonight Show with Johnny Carson*, Los Angeles, CA
1/21/77 Waco Convention Center, Waco, TX
1/22/77 Municipal Auditorium, San Antonio TX
1/23/77 Paramount Theater, Austin, TX
1/25/77 Brownwood Coliseum, Brownwood, TX
1/26/77 San Angelo Coliseum, San Angelo, TX
1/28/77 Lubbock Municipal Auditorium, Lubbock, TX
1/29/77 Civic Center, Albuquerque, NM
1/31/77 American Music Awards, Los Angeles, CA
2/17/77 *The Tonight Show with Johnny Carson*, Los Angeles, CA
2/19/77 Grammy Awards, Los Angeles, CA
2/20/77 Taylor County Coliseum, Abeline, TX
2/21/77 Lloyd Noble Center, Norman, OK
2/22/77 Hearnes Multi-Purpose Building, Columbia, MO
2/24/77 Hammons Student Center, Springfield, MO
2/27/77 Anaheim Convention Center, Anaheim, CA
3/1/77 Paramount theater, Oakland, CA
3/2/77 Golden Hall, San Diego, CA
3/3 to 3/5/77 Celebrity Theater, Phoenix, AZ
3/6/77 Cerebral Palsy Telethon, Corpus Christi, TX
3/8/77 RKO Theater, Davenport, IA
3/9/77 Veterans Memorial Auditorium, Green Bay, WI
3/10/77 Performing Arts Center, Milwaukee, WI
3/11/77 Dane County Coliseum, Madison, WI
3/12/77 Bradley University, Peoria, IL
3/13/77 W. K. Kellogg Auditorium, Battle Creek, MI
3/16/77 Greensboro Coliseum, Greensboro, NC
3/17/77 Roanoke Auditorium, Roanoke, VA
3/19/77 Freedom Hall Civic Center, Johnson City, TN
3/20/77 Municipal Auditorium, Charleston, WV
4/15 to 4/16/77 The Roxy, Los Angeles, CA
4/20/77 Stockton Memorial Auditorium, Stockton, CA
4/21 to 4/23/77 The Boarding House, San Francisco, CA
4/25 to 4/26/77 Ebbets Field, Denver, CO
4/27/77 *Mac Davis: Sounds Like Home*, TV special (airs)
4/28 to 4/29/77 Ivanhoe Theater, Chicago, IL
4/30/77 Donahue, Chicago IL
4/30 to 5/1/77 Carowinds, Charlotte, NC
5/2 to 5/3/77 Great Southeast Music Hall, Atlanta, GA
5/3/77 Peaches Record Store in-store signing, Atlanta, GA
5/5/77 Freedom Hall, Louisville, KY
5/6/77 Civic Auditorium, Knoxville, TN
5/7/77 Birmingham Civic Center, Birmingham, AL
5/9 to 11/77 *The Mike Douglas Show* (4-day cohost takeover; films), Philadelphia, PA
5/12 to 5/14/77 Bottom Line, New York, NY
5/17/77 King's Theatre, Glasgow, Scotland
5/18/77 *Musikladen* TV show (films) and other media interviews, Hamburg, Germany
5/19 to 5/25/77 media interviews, London, England
5/26/77 The Odeon, Birmingham, England
5/27/77 *The Mike Douglas Show* (airs)
5/27/77 The Empire, Liverpool, England
5/28/77 Rainbow Theater, London, England
5/28/77 *The Russell Harty Show* (films and airs)
6/20 to 6/25/77 Oakdale Music Theater, Oakdale, CT
6/27 to 7/2/77 O'Keefe Center, Toronto, ON
7/4 to 7/9/77 South Shore Music Circus, Cohasset, MA
7/11 to 7/17/77 Valley Forge Music Fair, Devon, PA
7/18 to 7/23/77 Colonie Coliseum, Latham, NY
7/25 to 7/31/77 Painters Mill, Owings Mills, MD
8/7/77 Holland International Speedway, Holland, NY
8/8/77 Allentown Fair, Allentown, PA
8/9/77 The Mosque Theater, Richmond, VA
8/10/77 Chrysler Hall, Newport News, VA
8/13/77 Auditorium Theater, Rochester NY
8/15/77 O'Shaunessy Auditorium, St. Paul, MN
8/16/77 Wisconsin State Fair, Milwaukee, WI
8/17/77 Duluth Auditorium, Duluth, MN
8/18/77 Iowa State Fair, Des Moines, IA
8/19/77 Morris Civic Auditorium, South Bend, IL
8/20/77 Ohio State Fair, Columbus, OH
8/23 to 8/26/77 Indiana State Fair, Indianapolis, IN
8/28/77 Rialto Theater, Joliet, IL
8/29 to 8/30/77 Mill Run Theater, Niles, IL
8/31/77 Valparaiso University Theater, Valparaiso, IN
9/2/77 Michigan State Fair, Detroit, MI
9/5/77 Colorado State Fair, Colorado Springs, CO
9/15/77 The Rock Music Awards, Los Angeles, CA
9/17/77 Grand Ole Opry, Nashville, TN
10/1/77 Grand Ole Opry, Nashville, TN
10/5/77 *Pop! Goes the Country* (airs)
10/10/77 CMA Awards, Nashville, TN
10/12/77 Dixon Myers Hall, Memphis, TN
10/13/77 Sevier County High School, Sevierville, TN
10/14/77 Dothan Civic Center, Dothan, AL
10/16/77 Georgia Tech Coliseum, Atlanta, GA
10/18/77 Houston Music Hall, Houston, TX
10/20 to 10/21/77 St. Bernard Civic Auditorium, New Orleans, LA
10/23/77 Pabst Theater, Milwaukee, WI
10/25/77 Paramount Theater, Cedar Rapids, ID
10/27/77 Mayo Civic Auditorium, Rochester, NY
10/28/77 Mary E. Sawyer Auditorium, La Crosse, WI
10/29/77 Wausau West Fieldhouse, Wausau, WI
11/1/77 Glacier Arena, Traverse City, MI
11/2/77 Auditorium Theater, Chicago, IL
11/4/77 Kiel Opera House, St. Louis, MO
11/5/77 Memorial Hall, Salina, KS
11/6/77 Civic Center, Sioux Falls, SD
11/8 to 11/10/77 American Royal Rodeo, Kansas City, KS
11/11/77 Western Hall, Western Illinois University, Macomb, IL
11/13/77 Southern Illinois University, Carbondale, IL
11/15/77 Northern Kentucky University, Cincinnati, OH
11/16/77 University of Northern Alabama, Florence, AL
11/17/77 Tully Gym, Tallahassee, FL
11/19/77 Jacksonville State University, Jacksonville, FL
11/20/77 Greensboro Coliseum, Greensboro, NC
11/22/77 Tower Theater, Philadelphia, PA
12/1/77 Abilene Civic Center, Abilene, TX
12/2/77 Panther Hall, Ft. Worth, TX
12/3/77 Oklahoma Music Hall, Oklahoma City, OK
12/4/77 Wichita Falls Auditorium, Wichita Falls, TX
12/6/77 Two Rivers Plaza, Grand Junction, CO
12/6/77 *Barbara Walters Special* (airs)
12/7/77 Regis College, Boulder, CO
12/8/77 Terrace Ballroom, Salt Lake City, UT
12/10/77 Arlington Theater, Santa Barbara, CA
12/11/77 Marin Veterans Auditorium, San Rafael, CA
12/12/77 Memorial Auditorium, Sacramento, CA
12/13/77 Civic Center, Redding, CA
12/14/77 *The Tonight Show with Johnny Carson*, Los Angeles, CA
12/15/77 Vancouver Exhibition Hall, Vancouver, BC
12/16/77 Paramount Northwest Auditorium, Seattle, WA
12/17/77 Opera House, Spokane, WA
12/18/77 Paramount Theater, Portland, OR

1978

1/16/78 American Music Awards, Los Angeles, CA
1/22/78 *50 Years of Country Music*, TV special (airs)
3/4/78 Radio & Records Convention, Dallas, TX
3/5/78 Houston Livestock Rodeo, Houston, TX
3/18 to 3/20/78 NARM Convention, New Orleans, LA
4/2 to 4/5/78 *The Cher Special*, TV special (films), Los Angeles, CA
5/5/78 Charleston Civic Center, Charleston, WV
5/6/78 Apple Blossom Festival, Winchester, VA
5/8/78 Hampton Coliseum, Hampton, VA
5/9/78 Track Coliseum, Wilmington, NC
5/10/78 Stegman Coliseum—University of Georgia, Athens, GA
5/11/78 Frances Marion Gym, Florence, SC
5/12/78 Asheville Civic Center, Asheville, NC
5/13/78 Charlotte Coliseum, Charlotte, NC
5/15/78 Troy Stadium, Troy, AL
5/16/78 Jackson Coliseum, Jackson, MS
5/17/78 Boutwell Auditorium, Birmingham, AL
5/18/78 Mississippi Coliseum, Biloxi, MS
5/19/78 Florida Junior College, Jacksonville, FL
5/20/78 Sunrise Music Theater, Sunrise, FL
5/21/78 Lakeland Civic Center, Lakeland, FL
5/23/78 Montgomery Civic Center, Montgomery, AL
5/24/78 Bell Auditorium, Augusta, GA
5/25/78 Atlanta Civic Center, Atlanta, GA
5/26/78 Von Braun Civic Center, Huntsville, AL
5/28/78 Oakland Coliseum (A Day on the Green), Oakland, CA
6/10/78 Dallas Memorial Auditorium, Dallas, TX
6/11/78 LaCentre Civique (Lake Charles Civic Center), Lake Charles, LA
6/15/78 Municipal Auditorium, San Antonio, TX
6/23/78 Hammons Student Center, Springfield, MO
6/24/78 Mississippi River Fest, Edwardsville, IL
6/25/78 Uni-Dome, Cedar Falls, IA
6/27/78 The Arena, Duluth, MN
6/28/78 Brown County Arena, Green Bay, WI
6/29/78 Dane County Coliseum, Madison, WI
6/30/78 Summerfest, Milwaukee, WI
7/1/78 Trumbull County Fair, Cortland, OH
7/15/78 Hara Arena, Dayton, OH
7/16/78 Auditorium Theater, Chicago, IL
7/17/78 Palmer Auditorium, Davenport, IA
7/18/78 Veterans Memorial Auditorium, Des Moines, IA
7/19/78 Civic Auditorium, Fargo, ND
7/22/78 Edmonton Coliseum, Edmonton, AB
7/24/78 Klondike Days, Ottawa, ON
7/26 to 7/27/78 Cheyenne Frontier Days, Cheyenne, WY
7/28/78 Rushmore Plaza Civic Center, Rapid City, SD
7/29/78 Montana State Fair, Great Falls, MT
7/30/78 Municipal Auditorium, Minot, ND
7/31/78 Buffalo Days, Regina, SK
8/11/78 Hershey Park, Hershey, PA
8/12/78 Garden State Arts Center, Holmdel, NJ
8/13/78 Merriweather Post Pavilion, Columbia, MD
8/16/78 Civic Auditorium, Pine Bluff, AR
8/18 to 8/20/78 Kentucky State Fair, Louisville, KY
8/21/78 City Hall Free Concert, New York, NY
8/22/78 The Palladium, New York, NY
8/22/78 Studio 54 Honors Dolly, New York, NY
8/24/78 Blossom Music Center, Cleveland, OH
8/25/78 Canadian Expo Show, Toronto, ON
8/26/78 Stanley Theater, Pittsburgh, PA
8/27/78 Ohio State Fair, Columbus, OH
8/28/78 Pine Knob Music Theatre, Birmingham, MI
8/30/78 Minnesota State Fair, St. Paul, MN
8/31/78 Municipal Auditorium, Sioux City, IA
9/1/78 Nebraska State Fair, Lincoln, NE
9/2/78 Gross Memorial Coliseum, Hays, KS
9/3/78 Colorado State Fair, Pueblo, CO
9/13/78 *The Tonight Show with Johnny Carson*, Los Angeles, CA
9/29/78 *Midnight Special* (host; airs)
9/30/78 Mid-South Fair, Memphis, TN
10/6 to 10/7/78 Central Washington State Fair, Yakima, WA
10/9/78 CMA Awards, Nashville, TN
10/13/78 WKBK Radio Station, in-studio visit and signing, Buffalo, NY
10/26/78 Sevier County High School, Sevierville, TN
10/30/78 Royal Dublin Society Theater, Dublin, Ireland
11/1/78 London press conference, London, England
11/2/78 Chateau Neuf, Oslo, Norway
11/3/78 Scandinavium, Gothenburg, Sweden
11/4/78 Concert House, Stockholm, Sweden
11/5/78 European Interviews, Copenhagen, Denmark
11/6/78 Tivoli Theater, Copenhagen, Denmark
11/7/78 European Interviews, Lund, Sweden
11/7/78 Olympian Scandanavian, Lund, Sweden
11/8/78 Sportshaus, Vejli, Denmark
11/9/78 Offenbach Sladhalle, Frankfurt, Germany
11/10/78 Concert Hall, Amsterdam, Netherlands
11/11/78 *Parkinson* (TV show; airs), London, England
11/12/78 DenHaag, Congresgebouw
11/13 to 11/14/78 media interviews, Paris, France
11/15/78 Conference Center, Brighton, England
11/16/78 Gaumont Theater, Ipswich, England
11/17/78 Coventry Theater, Coventry, England
11/18/78 Oxford Theater, Oxford, England
11/19/78 Empire Theater, Liverpool, England
11/20/78 Odeon Hammersmith, London, England
12/12/78 International Radio and TV Christmas Benefit, Hilton Hotel, New York, NY
12/28/78 *Dolly and Carol* press conference, Nashville, TN

1979

1/5 to 10/79 *Dolly and Carol in Nashville* (films), Nashville, TN
5/1/79 Dollar General Press Event, Scottsville, KY
7/7/79 Neal S. Bloisdell Arena, Honolulu, HI
7/11/79 Auckland Hall, Auckland, New Zealand
7/13/79 Australian press conference, Sydney, Australia
7/15/79 *Countdown with Ian Molly Meldrum* (Australia, TV show)
7/16/79 Festival Hall, Melbourne, Australia
7/17/79 Australian Media Interviews, Sydney, Australia
7/18/79 Hordern Pavilion, Sydney, Australia
7/21/79 AC Hall, Hong Kong, China
7/23 to 7/25/79 Japan press conference and media interviews, Tokyo, Japan
7/26/79 Mainichi Hall, Osaka, Japan
7/27/79 Skimin Kaikan Hall, Nagoya, Japan
7/30/79 Nakano Sun Plaza Hall, Tokyo, Japan
7/31/79 Shinjuku Kosei to Nenkin Hall, Tokyo, Japan
8/13/79 Garden State Arts Center, Holmdel, NJ
8/14/79 New York State Arts Festival, Saratoga Springs, NY
8/15/79 Hopkins Center, Dartmouth College, Hanover, NH
8/16/79 Wolf Trap, Vienna, VA
8/18 to 8/19/79 Carowinds, Charlotte, NC
8/21/79 Roanoke Civic Center, Roanoke, VA
8/23/79 Stanley Theater, Pittsburgh, PA
8/25/79 Indiana State Fair, Indianapolis, IN
8/26/79 Ohio State Fair, Columbus, OH
8/27/79 DuQuoin State Fair, DuQuoin, IL
8/29/79 Centennial Hall, Toledo, OH
8/30/79 Blossom Music Center, Akron, OH
8/31/79 Alpine Valley Music Theater, Milwaukee, WI
9/2/79 Red Rocks Amphitheater, Denver, CO
9/4/79 *Music Fair Japanese*, TV show (airs)
9/10/79 Metronome Award Event, Nashville, TN
9/15/79 Selland Arena, Fresno, CA
9/19/79 *The Tonight Show with Johnny Carson*, Los Angeles, CA
9/21 to 9/24/79 Universal Amphitheater, Los Angeles, CA
9/26/79 Symphony Hall, Phoenix, AZ
9/27/79 Tucson Community Center, Tucson, AZ
9/28/79 PanAm Center, Las Cruces, NM
9/29/79 Greyhound Arena, Roswell, NM
10/2/79 White House Luncheon with President Jimmy Carter, Washington, DC
10/2/79 *A Country Music Celebration at Ford Theater* (films), Washington, DC
10/4/79 Dolly Parton Parkway Dedication, Sevierville, TN
10/4/79 Sevier County High School, Sevierville, TN
10/9/79 CMA Awards, Nashville, TN
Fall/Winter 1979 *9 to 5*, movie (films)

12/22/79 Grand Ole Opry, Nashville, TN
12/24/79 *Mac Davis: A Christmas Special with Love*, TV special (airs)
12/27 to 12/31/79 Resorts International, Atlantic City, NJ

1980

4/14/80 Academy Awards, Los Angeles, CA
Spring/Summer 1980 *9 to 5*, movie (filming continues)
5/10/80 Grand Ole Opry, Nashville, TN
6/11/80 Fan Fair, Nashville, TN
10/13/80 CMA Awards, Nashville, TN
11/11/80 *The Mike Douglas Show* (films), Los Angeles, CA
11/17/80 *The Merv Griffin Show* (airs), Los Angeles, CA
11/18/80 *The Tonight Show with Johnny Carson*, Los Angeles, CA
11/18/80 *Barbara Mandrell and the Mandrell Sisters* (airs), Los Angeles, CA
11/23/80 The *Today* show (from Dallas, TX), Dallas, TX
11/24/80 *The Phil Donahue Show* (from Dallas, TX), Dallas, TX
12/5/80 *9 to 5* Nashville premiere, Opryland Hotel, Nashville, TN
12/10/80 *9 to 5* Hollywood premiere, Los Angeles, CA
12/12/80 *9 to 5* New York City premiere, Sutton Theater, New York, NY
12/15/80 *9 to 5* Dallas premiere, Loews Anatole Hotel, Dallas, TX
12/31/80 The Diplomat, Hollywood, FL

1981

1/22/81 *The Mike Douglas Show* (airs)
1/31/81 Golden Globe Awards, Los Angeles, CA
2/2/81 *Lily Sold Out*, TV special (airs)
2/6 to 2/12/81 Harrah's, Lake Tahoe, NV
2/17/81 *The Tonight Show with Johnny Carson*, Los Angeles, CA
2/22 to 2/26/81 Riviera Hotel, Las Vegas, NV
3/12/81 Country Radio Seminar, Nashville, TN
3/27/81 Dade County Youth Fair, Miami, FL
3/30/81 Academy Awards, Los Angeles, CA
4/2 to 4/4/81 Riviera Hotel, Las Vegas, NV
4/15 to 4/17/81 Riviera Hotel, Las Vegas, NV
4/30 to 5/6/81 Riviera Hotel, Las Vegas, NV
5/29 to 5/31/81 Resorts International, Atlantic City, NJ
6/5 to 6/7/81 Resorts International, Atlantic City, NJ
6/11 to 6/17/81 Riviera Hotel, Las Vegas, NV
6/25 to 7/1/81 Riviera Hotel, Las Vegas, NV
7/19/81 Vegas Entertainer of the Year Awards (airs)
7/26/81 Fred Foster Roast, Opryland Hotel, Nashville, TN
8/17 to 8/23/81 Resorts International, Atlantic City, NJ
Summer/Fall 1981 *The Best Little Whorehouse in Texas*, movie (films)
10/12/81 CMA Awards (via satellite), Austin, TX
11/1/81 BMI Awards, Los Angeles, CA
12/20/81 *All-Star Garden Party for Burt Reynolds* (airs), 1982

1982

6/14 to 6/18/82 *Good Morning America* (on location; special segments), New York, NY
6/20/82 Tree International (Sony Publishing) press conference, Nashville, TN
6/24/82 *The Tonight Show with Johnny Carson*, Los Angeles, CA
7/10/82 *The Best Little Special in Texas* (films), Pflugerville, TX
7/11/82 *The Best Little Whorehouse in Texas* Austin premiere, Austin, TX
7/12/82 *The Best Little Whorehouse in Texas* press event, Atlanta, GA
7/15/82 *The Best Little Whorehouse in Texas* Miami premiere, Miami, FL
7/22/82 *The Best Little Whorehouse in Texas* Nashville premiere, Nashville, TN
8/1/82 *The Late Late Breakfast Show* (UK; via satellite with performance)
8/6 to 8/8/82 Front Row Theater, Cleveland, OH
8/13 to 8/15/82 Front Row Theater, Cleveland, OH
8/16/82 *The Best Little Special in Texas* (airs)
8/17/82 Iowa State Fair, Des Moines, IA
8/20/82 Canadian Exhibition Hall, Toronto, ON
8/21/82 Ohio State Fair, Columbus, OH
8/22/82 Indiana State Fair, Indianapolis, IN
11/10/82 Nashville press conference, Nashville, TN
11/14/82 *PM Magazine* (airs)
11/19 to 11/21/82 Resorts International, Atlantic City, NJ
11/26 to 11/28/82 Resorts International, Atlantic City, NJ
12/1 to 12/2/82 South Africa Press, Pretoria, South Africa
12/8 to 12/12/82 Sun City Resort, Pretoria, South Africa
12/14/82 *Barbara Walters Special* (airs)

1983

1/5 to 1/8/83 Carlton Theater, Bloomington, MN
1/13 to 1/14/83 Executive Inn, Owensboro, KY
2/12/83 Mayfair Music Hall (Mike Post Special Event), Santa Monica, CA
3/25/83 *Wogan* (UK; airs), London, England
3/27 to 3/29/83 *Dolly in London*, Dominion Theater (films), London, England
4/10/83 *Dolly Meets the Kids* (films; airs 9/17; HBO)
6/4/83 *Solid Gold* (airs)
6/11/83 *Solid Gold* (airs)
6/18/83 *Solid Gold* (airs)
6/19/83 *Dolly in London* premiere (HBO)
Summer/Fall 1983 *Rhinestone*, movie (films)
9/24/83 Dr. Robert F. Thomas Foundation Charity Event, Gatlinburg, TN
9/27/83 *Live . . . And in Person*, TV special (airs)
10/8/83 Carousel Ball Benefit, Denver, CO
10/10/83 CMA Awards, Nashville, TN
12/5/83 *Alvin and the Chipmunks* (airs)

1984

2/9/84 *Rhinestone* press party, Los Angeles, CA
3/3/84 Country Radio Seminar, Nashville, TN
3/4 to 3/8/84 *The Great Pretender* promotional press tour (six cities)
4/9/84 Academy Awards, Los Angeles, CA
6/10/84 *Rhinestone* Hollywood premiere, Los Angeles, CA
6/14/84 Hollywood Walk of Fame Ceremony, Los Angeles, CA
6/15/84 *The Tonight Show with Johnny Carson*, Los Angeles, CA
6/17/84 *Rhinestone* Nashville premiere, Roy Acuff Theater, Nashville, TN
6/20/84 *Rhinestone* New York City premiere, Coronet Theater, New York, NY
6/27/84 *Good Morning America*, New York, NY
9/8/84 Dr. Robert F. Thomas Foundation Charity Event, Sevierville, TN
10/8/84 CMA Awards, Nashville, TN
10/10/84 BMI Awards, Nashville, TN
11/14/84 A Night at the Races benefit concert, Los Angeles, CA
11/15 to 11/17/84 *Kenny & Dolly: A Christmas to Remember* (films), Los Angeles, CA
12/2/84 *Kenny & Dolly: A Christmas to Remember* (airs)
12/7 to 12/10/84 *The Winning Hand*, TV special (films), Nashville, TN
12/28/84 Oakland Coliseum, Oakland, CA
12/29/84 Cow Palace, San Francisco, CA
12/31/84 LA Forum, Los Angeles, CA

1985

1/4/85 Sports Arena, San Diego, CA
1/11 to 1/12/85 Pacific Coliseum, Vancouver, BC
1/13/85 Tacoma Dome, Tacoma, WA
1/18/85 Thomas & Mack Center, Las Vegas, NV
1/20 to 1/21/85 Selland Arena, Fresno, CA
1/23 to 1/24/85 ASU Activity Center, Tempe, AZ
1/26/85 University Of New Mexico Arena, Albuquerque, MN
1/27/85 McHale Center, Tucson, AZ
2/3/85 McNichols Arena, Denver, Colorado
2/5/85 Salt Palace, Salt Lake City, UT
2/22 to 2/23/85 Littlejohn Coliseum, Clemson, SC
2/24/85 Reynolds Coliseum, Raleigh, NC
3/1/85 Freedom Hall, Louisville, KY
3/2/85 Charlotte Coliseum, Charlotte, NC
3/3/85 Charleston Civic Center, Charleston, WV
3/5/85 Juvenile Diabetes Research Benefit Concert at Waldorf Astoria, New York, NY
4/13/85 Portland Coliseum, Portland, OR
4/13/85 *Kenny & Dolly: Real Love*, HBO special (films), Portland, OR
4/14/85 Tacoma Dome, Tacoma, WA
7/14/85 *Kenny & Dolly: Real Love* premiere (HBO)
8/18/85 Pontiac Silverdome, Detroit, MI
8/28/85 Spectrum, Philadelphia, PA
8/29/85 Nassau Coliseum, Union Dale, NJ
8/30/85 Meadowlands, East Rutherford, NJ
10/18/85 Dollywood Groundbreaking Event, Pigeon Forge, TN
10/24/85 The Arena, St. Louis, MO
10/26/85 The Summit Arena, Houston, TX
10/27/85 Reunion Arena, Dallas, TX
11/2/85 Superdome, New Orleans, LA
11/3/85 Frank Erwin Center, Austin, TX
11/7/85 Rupp Arena, Lexington, KY
11/21/85 *Grand Ole Opry 60th Anniversary*, TV special (films), Nashville, TN
11/24/85 The Omni, Atlanta, GA
11/27/85 Dollywood press conference, Pigeon Forge, TN
11/30 to 12/1/85 The Centrum Arena, Worcester, MA
12/2/85 Broome County Arena, Binghampton, NY
12/6/85 Kemper Arena, Kansas City, MO
12/7/85 Market Square Arena, Indianapolis, IN

1986

1/14/86 *Grand Ole Opry 60th Anniversary*, TV special (airs)
2/14 to 2/16/86 Golden Nugget, Las Vegas, NV
2/28/86 Universal Amphitheater, Los Angeles, CA
3/14/86 *A Musical Homecoming*, TV special (airs)
4/8/86 *Good Morning America*, New York, NY
4/9/86 *Larry King Live*, New York, NY
4/11 to 4/13/86 Golden Nugget, Atlantic City, NJ
4/15 to 4/16/86 National Association of Broadcasters Convention, Dallas, TX
4/20/86 Memorial Auditorium, Buffalo, NY
4/21/86 Rosemont Horizon, Chicago, IL
4/24/86 Assembly Hall, Champagne, IL
4/25/86 Met Center, Bloomington, MN
4/27/86 Riverfront Coliseum, Cincinnati, OH
5/2/86 Dollywood Grand Opening, Pigeon Forge, TN
5/2/86 McCarter Hollow Amphitheater, Pigeon Forge, TN
5/3 to 5/5/86 Dollywood Grand Opening, Pigeon Forge, TN
5/9/86 McCarter Hollow Amphitheater, Pigeon Forge, TN
5/15 to 5/17/86 Golden Nugget, Las Vegas, NV
5/18/86 *60 Minutes* (Australia; airs)
5/30/86 *The Tonight Show with Johnny Carson*, Los Angeles, CA
Summer 1986 *A Smoky Mountain Christmas*, TV movie (films)
6/7/86 *PM Magazine* (airs)
6/9/86 Music City News Country Awards, Nashville, TN
6/11/86 Dollywood Special Appearance, Pigeon Forge, TN
6/28/86 Dollywood Special Appearance, Pigeon Forge, TN
7/5/86 VP Fair, St. Louis, MO
7/15 to 7/16/86 Coliseum, Vancouver, BC
7/21 to 7/22/86 Northlands Coliseum, Edmonton, AB
7/23/86 Olympic Saddledome, Calgary, AB
8/4/86 Royal Ottawa Country Fest, Ottawa, ON
8/7 to 8/9/86 Golden Nugget, Las Vegas, NV
8/10/86 Mid-State Fair, Paso Robles, CA
8/17/86 University Of New Brunswick Arena, Moncton, NB
8/18 to 8/19/86 Halifax Metro Centre, Halifax, NS
9/18 to 9/20/86 Golden Nugget, Las Vegas, NV
9/27/86 State Farm Private Performance, Las Vegas, NV
10/7/86 Joe Louis Arena, Detroit, MI
10/8/86 Maple Leaf Arena, Toronto, ON
10/9/86 Montreal Forum, Montreal, QB
10/13/86 CMA Awards, Nashville, TN
10/17 to 10/19/86 Golden Nugget, Atlantic City, NJ
10/30/86 Mid-South Coliseum, Memphis, TN
10/31/86 Jefferson Civic Center, Birmingham, AL
11/1/86 MTSU Arena, Murfreesboro, TN
11/9/86 *Disney World 15th Anniversary Special* (airs)
12/4 to 12/7/86 Golden Nugget, Atlantic City, NJ
12/10/86 *The Tonight Show with Johnny Carson*
12/12 to 12/14/86 Golden Nugget, Atlantic City, NJ
12/14/86 *A Smoky Mountain Christmas* premiere (ABC)
12/31/86 Harrah's, Lake Tahoe, NV

1987

1/7/87 The *Today* show, New York, NY
1/13/87 *Late Night with David Letterman*, New York, NY
1/29 to 1/30/87 Perth Entertainment Centre, Perth, WA
1/30/87 The *Today* show, Perth, WA
2/2/87 *The Oprah Winfrey Show* (airs)
2/3 to 2/4/87 Myer Music Bowl, Melbourne, VT
2/8/87 Hobart Arena, Hobart, TS
2/11/87 Yooyong Center, Melbourne, VT
2/13/87 Westlake Park, Adelaide, SA
2/15/87 King George V Park, Canberra, ACT
2/16 to 2/18/87 Sydney Entertainment Centre, Sydney, NSW
2/20 to 2/21/87 Sydney Entertainment Centre, Sydney, NSW
2/22 to 2/24/87 Brisbane Entertainment Centre, Brisbane, QL
2/27/87 Brisbane Entertainment Centre, Brisbane, QL
3/1/87 Auckland City Arena, Auckland, NZ
3/8/87 Marlboro Country, Lincoln Center, New York, NY
3/13/87 *The Tonight Show with Johnny Carson*, Los Angeles, CA
4/1/87 *Late Night with David Letterman*, New York, NY
4/23 to 4/25/87 Golden Nugget, Las Vegas, NV
5/1/87 *Good Morning America*, Pigeon Forge, TN
5/1/87 *PM Magazine/Hour Magazine/Evening Magazine*, Pigeon Forge, TN
5/2/87 Dollywood Grand Opening, Pigeon Forge, TN
5/3/87 Dollywood Grand Opening/Sevierville Statue Dedication, Pigeon Forge, TN
5/10/87 Marlboro Country, Rosemont Horizon, Chicago, IL
5/10/87 *Cover Story*, TV appearance (airs)
5/22 to 5/23/87 Golden Nugget, Atlantic City, NJ
6/8/87 *Nighlife with David Brenner*, New York, NY
6/9/87 The *Today* show, New York, NY
6/28/87 Marcus Amphitheater, Milwaukee, WI
7/2 to 7/4/87 Golden Nugget, Vegas, NV
Fall 1987 *Dolly!*, ABC variety series (films)
9/1/87 *Good Morning America*
9/26 to 9/27/87 Dollywood Harvest Festival, Pigeon Forge, TN
10/1/87 *Good Morning America*, New York, NY

1988

Spring 1988 *Dolly!*, ABC variety series (films)
2/20/88 Grand Ole Opry, Nashville, TN
3/13/88 People's Choice Awards
3/29/88 *Rainbow* London press conference, London, England
3/30/88 *Aspel & Co.* (UK TV appearance), London, England
4/18/88 Retinitis Pigmentosa Foundation Benefit Concert, New York, NY
4/29 to 5/1/88 Dollywood Grand Opening, Pigeon Forge, TN
Summer 1988 *Steel Magnolias*, movie (films)
7/16/88 Northwestern State University, Natchitoches, LA
9/3/88 Turpin Stadium, Natchitoches, LA
10/10/88 CMA Awards, Nashville, TN
10/20/88 The Meadowlands, East Rutherford, NJ
10/25/88 East Tennessee Hall of Fame, Bijou Theater, Knoxville, TN
10/25/88 Dollywood Fall Festival, Pigeon Forge, TN
10/26/88 East Tennessee Teachers Association (guest speaker), Pigeon Forge, TN
11/4/88 Kemper Arena, Kansas City, KS
11/5/88 Civic Center, Peoria, IL
11/6/88 The Met Center, Bloomington, MN
11/26/88 Carrier Dome, Syracuse, NY
11/27/88 Capital Center, Landover, MD
12/19/88 *Bob Hope Christmas Special* (airs)
12/31/88 Tacoma Dome, Tacoma, WA

1989

2/3/89 Orlando Arena, Orlando, FL
3/24/89 *Crook & Chase*, Nashville, TN
3/27/89 *Nashville Now*, Nashville, TN
4/7/89 *Live! With Regis & Kathie Lee*, New York, NY
4/7/89 The *Today* show, New York, NY
4/11/89 *Live at Five*, New York, NY
4/11/89 *Late Night with David Letterman*, New York, NY
4/12/89 *The Pat Sajak Show*, New York, NY
4/15/89 *Saturday Night Live*, New York, NY
4/17/89 *Larry King Live*, New York, NY
4/28 to 4/30/89 Dollywood Grand Opening, Pigeon Forge, TN
5/2/89 *Something Inside So Strong*, TV show (films), Houston, TX
5/12 to 5/15/89 IBM Convention, Royal Playhouse, West Palm Beach, FL
5/19/89 Bayfront Arena, St. Petersburg, FL
5/20/89 *Something Inside So Strong*, TV show (airs; NBC)
5/23 to 5/24/89 Sunrise Music Theater, Sunrise, FL
5/26/89 Leon Civic Center, Tallahassee, FL
5/27/89 Civic Center, Pensacola, FL
5/30/89 Chastain Park, Atlanta, GA
6/2/89 Von Braun Civic Center, Huntsville, AL
6/3/89 Convention Center, Arkansas State University, Jonesboro, AR
6/13/89 Merriweather Post Pavilion, Columbia, MD
6/15/89 Riverside Theater, Milwaukee, WI
6/17/89 Swiss Villa Amphitheater, Springfield, MO
6/20/89 Fox Theater, St. Louis, MO
6/22/89 Sandstone Amphitheater, Bonner Springs, KS
6/24/89 Jackson Civic Center, *Miss Tennessee Pageant* (airs), Jackson, TN
6/25/89 Poplar Creek, Chicago, IL
6/30/89 Palace Theater, Cleveland, OH
7/2/89 Pine Knob Music Theater, Detroit, MI
7/12 to 7/13/89 Universal Amphitheater, Los Angeles, CA
7/15/89 Irvine Meadows Amphitheater, Laguna Hills, CA
7/18/89 Concord Pavilion, Concord, CA
7/20/89 Park West, Salt Lake City, UT
7/22/89 Fiddler's Green Amphitheater, Denver, CO
7/25/89 Six Flags Over Texas, Arlington, TX
7/28 to 8/5/89 Golden Nugget, Las Vegas, NV
8/9/89 Lake Compounce, Bristol, CT
8/11/89 Kingswood Music Theater, Toronto, ON
8/13/89 Cumberland Civic Center, Old Orchard Beach, ME
8/16/89 Great Woods Amphitheatre, Mansfield, MA
8/18/89 Indiana State Fair, Indianapolis, IN
8/20/89 Kings Dominion, Richmond, VA
8/23/89 Six Flags Over Texas, Dallas, TX
9/3/89 Pacific National Exhibition Fair, Vancouver, BC
9/7/89 Jubilee Auditorium, Calgary, AB
9/15/89 RIAA Awards, Washington Hilton, Washington, DC
9/22 to 9/24/89 Caesars, Stateline, NV
9/29 to 10/1/89 Trump Castle, Atlantic City, NJ
10/9/89 CMA Awards, Nashville, TN
11/1/89 The *Today* show, New York, NY
11/5/89 *Steel Magnolias* New York premiere, New York, NY
11/8/89 *Steel Magnolias* Hollywood premiere, Los Angeles, CA
11/10/89 *Steel Magnolias* Natchitoches premiere, Natchitoches, LA
11/13/89 *The Oprah Winfrey Show*, Chicago, IL
11/22/89 *The Tonight Show with Johnny Carson*, Los Angeles, CA
11/27/89 *CBS This Morning*, New York, NY
11/30/89 *The Phil Donahue Show*, Chicago, IL
12/3/89 Portland Civic Center, Portland, OR
12/4/89 Paramount Theater, Seattle, WA
12/6/89 BSU Pavilion, Boise, ID
12/9/89 L.I.F.E. Christmas Show, Universal Amphitheater, Los Angeles, CA
12/11 to 12/12/89 Symphony Hall, San Diego, CA
12/13/89 Centennial Hall, Tucson, AZ
12/26 to 12/27/89 Golden Nugget, Las Vegas, NV
12/31/89 Caesars, Lake Tahoe, NV

1990

1/1/90 Caesars, Lake Tahoe, NV
1/1/90 *Designing Women* (airs; cameo)
1/21/90 Arco Arena, Sacramento, CA
2/8/90 Olympic Saddledome, Calgary, AB
2/9/90 Northlands Coliseum, Edmonton, AB
2/10/90 Saskplace, Saskatoon, SK
2/13/90 McNichols Arena, Denver, CO
2/21/90 *Kenny & Dolly: Love Is Strange* tour press conference, Las Vegas, NV
2/22 to 2/27/90 The Mirage, Las Vegas, NV
3/23 to 3/25/90 Trump Castle, Atlantic City, NJ
3/27/90 National Dropout Convention, Nashville, TN
3/31/90 Selland Arena, Fresno, CA
4/1/90 Sports Arena, San Diego, CA
4/5/90 The Dove Awards, Nashville, TN
4/8/90 Greensboro Coliseum, Greensboro, NC
4/12/90 Charleston Civic Center, Charleston, WV
4/13/90 Reynolds Coliseum, Raleigh, NC
4/14/90 Hampton Coliseum, Hampton, VA
4/15/90 Roanoke Civic Center, Roanoke, VA
4/19/90 Carolina Coliseum, Columbia, SC
4/20/90 Memorial Coliseum, Jacksonville, FL
4/21/90 Miami Arena, Miami, FL
4/22/90 Orlando Arena, Orlando, FL
4/27/90 *Good Morning America* (via satellite)
4/28 to 4/29/90 Dollywood Grand Opening, Pigeon Forge, TN
5/3/90 Memorial Coliseum, Fort Wayne, IN
5/4/90 Riverfront Coliseum, Cincinnati, OH
5/5/90 Charlotte Coliseum, Charlotte, NC
5/6/90 Capital Center, Landover, MD
5/9/90 The Arena, St. Louis, MO
5/10/90 T. H. Barton Coliseum, Little Rock, AR
5/11/90 Mid-South Coliseum, Memphis, TN
5/19/90 Civic Center, Philadelphia, PA
5/21/90 *The Arsenio Hall Show* (airs), Los Angeles, CA
6/2/90 Sea World, Orlando, FL
6/9/90 Alabama's June Jam, Ft. Payne, AL
7/19 to 7/22/90 Trump Castle, Atlantic City, NJ
8/5/90 WE Fest, Detroit, MI
8/9 to 8/12/90 Caesars, Lake Tahoe, NV
8/16 to 8/17/90 Mid-State Fair, Paso Robles, CA
8/21/90 Pacific National Exhibition Centre, Vancouver, BC
8/23/90 Oregon State Fair, Salem, OR
8/28/90 Casper Events Center, Casper, WY
8/29/90 Salt Palace, Salt Lake City, UT
9/1/90 *Jerry Lewis MDA Labor Day Telethon* (airs)

1957

/4/57 Fifth Anniversary Hillbilly Homecoming, Knoxville, TN

1958

/25/59 Grand Ole Opry, Nashville, TN

1959

pring 1959 Fountain City Parking Lot Concert, Knoxville, TN

1965

0/4/65 Music Operators of America Convention, Chicago, IL
0/15/65 Jerry G & Company performance, Lawton, OK
2/12/65 Toys for Tots Concert, Knoxville Coliseum, Knoxville, TN

1966

/15/66 *UpBeat Show,* Cincinnati, OH
/19/66 Country DJ Convention, Nashville, TN
/30/66 Oak Grove Night Club, Knoxville, TN
0/1/66 WIVK Show, Knoxville, TN
0/20/66 BMI Awards, Nashville, TN

1967

/3/67 *The Bobby Lord Show* (syndicated), Boqualusta, LA
/7/67 National Guard Armory (WPLO radio show), Jackson, GA
/8/67 *The American Swingaround* (TV appearance), Chicago, IL
/4/67 Skymart Opening, Morristown, TN
/16/67 *The Wilburn Brothers Show* (syndicated), Nashville, TN
/1/67 Summer County Lake, Richmond, VA
/20/67 C. M. Taylor Motors, WKPT autograph session, Kingsport, TN
/20/67 Civic Auditorium, Kingsport, TN
/5/67 Hornersville Gym Watermelon Festival, Hornersville, AR
/11 to 8/13/67 Imperial Ballroom, Tampa, FL
/18/67 Disneyland, Anaheim, CA
/26/67 Lakeview Club, College Station, TX
all 1967 to Spring 1974 *The Porter Wagoner Show* (syndicated; TV series regular)
/15/67 Starland Arena, Roanoke, VA
/20/67 San Angelo City Auditorium, San Angelo, TX
/21/67 Brownwood Coliseum, Brownwood, TX
/26/67 Civic Auditorium, Kingsport, TN
/27/67 Battle High School, Bristol, TN
/30/67 Louisiana Hayride, Ponchatoula, LA
0/1/67 *The Cas Walker Show,* Knoxville, TN
0/7/67 Inaugural Dolly Parton Day, Sevierville, TN
0/7/67 Grand Ole Opry, Nashville, TN
0/14/67 Grand Ole Opry, Nashville, TN
0/19 to 10/20/67 Country Radio Seminar, Nashville, TN
0/21/67 RCA Breakfast, Municipal Auditorium, Nashville, TN
0/24/67 Vance Junior High School, Bristol, TN
0/25/67 Shelby City Park, Shelby, NC
1/1/67 Monroe Junior High Auditorium, Monroe, WI
1/3/67 Stanley Theater, Jersey City, NJ
1/10/67 Hershey Sports Arena, Hersey, PA
1/11/67 Bushnell Auditorium, Hartford, CT
1/17/67 Capitol Theater, Ottawa, ON
1/25/67 Grand Ole Opry, Nashville, TN
2/1/67 Civic Auditorium, Kingsport, TN
2/16/67 TN Metro Fire Dept. Benefit Concert, Nashville, TN
2/23/67 Grand Ole Opry, Nashville, TN
2/29/67 KOKE Holiday Spectacular, Municipal Auditorium, Austin, TX
2/30/67 KBER Grand Ole Opry, San Antonio, TX
2/31/67 Hirsch Youth Center, Shreveport, LA

1968

/4/68 Ponchatoula Hayride, Ponchatoula, LA
/6/68 Grand Ole Opry, Nashville, TN
/12/68 Jaycee Civic Center, Paducah, KY
/13/68 Grand Ole Opry, Nashville, TN
/18/68 Topeka Municipal Auditorium, Topeka, KS
/19/68 Joplin Memorial Hall, Joplin, MO
/20/68 Pershing Auditorium, Lincoln, NE
/21/68 Memorial Building, Kansas City, KS
/22/68 Harris Community Club, Lake Park, IA
/23/68 Sioux Falls Coliseum, Sioux Falls, SD
/24/68 Sioux City Municipal Auditorium, Sioux City, IA
/25/68 Salina Memorial Hall, Salina, KS
/26 to 1/27/68 Cotillion Ballroom, Wichita, KS
2/2/68 Memorial Auditorium, Greenville, SC
2/3/68 Civic Coliseum, Knoxville, TN
2/4/68 City Auditorium, Asheville, NC
2/11/68 Indianapolis Coliseum, Indianapolis, IN
2/17/68 Columbia Township Auditorium, Columbia, SC
2/24/68 WPLO Shower of Stars, Atlanta, GA
2/25/68 Lake Norman Music Hall, Terrell, NC
3/1/68 Morristown Plaza, Morristown, TN
3/2/68 Municipal Auditorium, Birmingham, AL
3/3/68 Monroe Civic Center, Monroe, LA
3/9/68 Grand Ole Opry, Nashville, TN
3/14/68 Rocky Mount Senior High School, Rocky Mount, NC
3/16/68 T-Bird Country, Danville, VA
3/22/68 Sports Center, Owensboro, KY
3/24/68 Cincinnati Music Hall, Cincinnati, OH
3/31/68 Mosque Theater, Richmond, VA
4/1/68 Memorial Auditorium, Raleigh, NC
4/12/68 Civic Auditorium, Albuquerque, NM
4/13/68 Liberty Hall, El Paso, TX
4/15/68 Lincoln Junior High School, Abilene, TX
4/16/68 BHS Auditorium, Freeport, TX
4/17/68 Memorial Auditorium, Wichita Falls, TX
4/18/68 San Angelo Coliseum, San Angelo, TX
4/19/68 Tri-State Fair Coliseum, Amarillo, TX
4/20/68 City Auditorium, Colorado Springs, CO
4/23/68 Municipal Auditorium, Lubbock, TX
4/24/68 Clifford Hope Auditorium, Garden City, KS
4/26/68 Phoenix Giants Baseball Park, Phoenix, AZ
4/28/68 Swing Auditorium, San Bernardino, CA
4/29/68 Convention Center Theater (KEAP Radio Show), Fresno, CA
5/1/68 *The Tonight Show with Johnny Carson*
5/3/68 The Strand (KLOC Radio Show), Modesto, CA
5/4/68 Shrine Auditorium, Los Angeles, CA
5/5/68 National Guard Armory (KRAS Radio Show), Salinas, CA
5/6/68 Circle Star Theater, Oakland, CA
5/8/68 Valley Music Hall (KSOP Radio Show), Salt Lake City, UT
5/10/68 McMahon Auditorium, Lawton, OK
5/12 to 5/13/68 Municipal Auditorium, San Antonio, TX
5/18/68 Grand Ole Opry, Nashville, TN
5/25/68 Grand Ole Opry, Nashville, TN
6/1/68 Grand Ole Opry, Nashville, TN
6/2/68 Music Park, Anderson, IN
6/14/68 Fairgrounds Coliseum, Jackson, MS
6/15/68 Mid-South Coliseum, Memphis, TN
6/16/68 Roberts Stadium, Evansville, IN
7/4/68 Camden Park, Huntington, WV
7/6/68 Grand Ole Opry, Nashville, TN
7/11/68 Bryan Civic Auditorium, Bryan, TX
7/12/68 Harleton Football Field, Longview, TX
7/13/68 Panther Hill Ballroom, Ft. Worth, TX
7/14/68 Municipal Auditorium "Louisiana Hayride," Shreveport, LA
7/18/68 Murray Fair, Murray, KY
7/21/68 Buck Lake Ranch, Angola, IN
7/28/68 Macon County Fair, Macon, GA
7/29/68 Delaware County Fair, Muncie, IN
7/30/68 *The Ralph Emery Show,* Nashville, TN
8/1/68 Lincoln County Fair, Wausau, WI
8/3/68 Fon du Lac County Fair, Fon du Lac, WI
8/7/68 Fayette County Fair, Connersville, IN
8/9/68 Ozark Empire Fair, Springfield, MO
8/10/68 Carson Hall, Paducah, KY
8/11/68 Frontier Ranch, Columbus, OH
8/17/68 Greensboro Coliseum, Greensboro, NC
8/18/68 The Mosque, Richmond, VA
8/23/68 Garfield Park, Indianapolis, IN
8/24/68 Grand Ole Opry, Nashville, TN
8/25/68 Chautauqua Park, Franklin, OH
8/26/68 Green County Fair, Johnson City, TN
8/30/68 Memorial Auditorium, Greenville, SC
8/31/68 Civic Coliseum, Knoxville, TN
9/1/68 Berryville Bluegrass Festival, Berryville, VA
9/2/68 New York State Fair, Syracuse, NY
9/7/68 Grand Ole Opry, Nashville, TN
9/12/68 Eastside Speedway, Waynesboro, VA
9/13/68 American Theater, Roanoke, VA
9/14/68 Convention Hall, Philadelphia, PA
9/15/68 Eastern States Exposition, The Coliseum, Springfield, MA
9/20/68 Myrtle Beach Convention Center, Myrtle Beach, SC
9/21/68 Charlotte Coliseum, Charlotte, NC
9/26/68 Rapides Parish Coliseum, Alexandria, LA
9/27 to 9/28/68 Texas Western Fair, Ft. Worth, TX
10/4 to 10/5/68 Municipal Auditorium, Orlando, FL
10/6/68 War Memorial Auditorium, Ft. Lauderdale, FL
10/8/68 Green Acres Pony Track, Jay, FL
10/12/68 Grand Ole Opry, Nashville, TN
10/18/68 CMA Awards, Nashville, TN
10/19/68 Grand Ole Opry, Nashville, TN
10/26/68 Grand Ole Opry, Nashville, TN
10/27/68 Foremost Dairy Division, Springfield, MO
10/30/68 Civic Center Music Hall, Oklahoma City, OK
11/8/68 Columbia Township Auditorium, Columbia, SC
11/16/68 Consistory Auditorium, Freeport, IL
11/22/68 Mayo Civic Auditorium, Rochester, MN
11/23/68 Veterans Memorial Coliseum, Cedar Rapids, IA
11/24/68 Memorial Auditorium, Burlington, IA
11/29/68 McElroy Auditorium, Waterloo, IA
11/30/68 Minneapolis Auditorium, Minneapolis, MN
12/1/68 KRNT Theater, Des Moines, IA
12/8/68 Tipton Building, Tipton, IN
12/18/68 Henry Clay Auditorium, Lexington, KY
12/27/68 Austin Municipal Auditorium, Austin, TX
12/28/68 Municipal Auditorium, Shreveport, LA
12/29/68 KBER Grand Ole Opry Show, San Antonio, TX
12/31/68 North Side Coliseum, Ft. Worth, TX

1969

1/3/69 Old South Jamboree, Walker, LA
1/4/69 Ponchatoula Hayride, Ponchatoula, LA
1/11/69 Grand Ole Opry, Nashville, TN
1/16/69 Arlington Firehouse, Grand Prairie, TX
1/18/69 Lufkin High School, Lufkin, TX
1/24/69 Memorial Auditorium, Greenville, SC
1/25/69 Civic Auditorium, Knoxville, TN
1/26/69 Mosque Auditorium, Richmond, VA
1/31/69 Albemarle High School Auditorium, Charlottesville, VA
2/2/69 Fairmont Theater, Fairmont, WV
2/8/69 Grand Ole Opry, Nashville, TN
2/15/69 Grand Ole Opry, Nashville, TN
2/16 to 2/18/69 San Antonio Stock Show & Rodeo, San Antonio, TX
2/19/69 Alabama Cattlemen's Association Luncheon, Montgomery, AL
2/21/69 E. C. Glass High School, Lynchburg, VA
2/22/69 Greensboro Coliseum, Greensboro, NC
3/1/69 Bangor Auditorium, Bangor, ME
3/1/69 *The Jim Clayton Show* (syndicated)
3/2/69 Braintree Arena, Boston, MA
3/8/69 Grand Ole Opry, Nashville, TN
3/9/69 Masonic Temple, Davenport, IA
3/12/69 Grammy Awards at National Guard Armory, Nashville, TN
3/15/69 Louisville Convention Center, Louisville, KY
3/16/69 Music Hall, Cincinnati, OH
3/20/69 DeGraffenreid Auditorium, Russellville, KY
3/22/69 Grand Ole Opry, Nashville, TN
3/23/69 Kiel Auditorium, St. Louis, MO
3/27/69 DeGraffenreid Auditorium, Russellville, KY
3/29/69 Memorial Coliseum, Winston Salem, NC
3/30/69 City Auditorium, Asheville, NC
4/11/69 Charleston Civic Center, Charleston, WV
4/13/69 Indianapolis Coliseum, Indianapolis, IN
4/18/69 Civic Auditorium, Kingsport, TN
4/20/69 Gowdy Baseball Field, Fort Benning, GA
4/24/69 Dade County Auditorium, Miami, FL
4/26/69 Orlando Sports Stadium, Orlando, FL
4/27/69 Curtis Hixon Auditorium, Tampa, FL
5/2/69 Sportatorium, Dallas, TX
5/5/69 Municipal Auditorium, Austin, TX
5/7/69 Albuquerque Civic Auditorium, Albuquerque, NM
5/8/69 Lubbock Municipal Auditorium, Lubbock, TX
5/9/69 Convention Center, Ft. Worth, TX
5/10/69 Municipal Auditorium, Shreveport, LA
5/11/69 Civic Center Auditorium, Oklahoma City, OK
5/16/69 Viroqua Senior High Gym, Eau Claire, WI
5/18/69 Convention Center, Ft. Worth, TX
5/22/69 Moody Civic Center, Galveston, TX
5/24/69 Grand Ole Opry, Nashville, TN
5/31/69 Grand Ole Opry, Nashville, TN
6/1/69 Music Park, Anderson, IN
6/8/69 Chautauqua Park, Dayton, OH
6/11/69 Omaha Civic Auditorium, Omaha, NE
6/12/69 Pershing Auditorium, Lincoln, NE
6/13/69 Joplin Memorial Hall, Joplin, MO
6/15/69 Kansas Memorial Building, Kansas City, KS
7/4/69 Camden Park, Huntington, WV
7/5/69 Grand Ole Opry, Nashville, TN
7/18/69 Civic Center, Salisbury, MD
7/19/69 Cumberland Raceway, Cumberland, MD
7/22/69 Reading Fair, Reading, PA
7/23/69 Milwaukee Arena, Milwaukee, WI
7/27/69 Mockingbird Hill Park, Anderson, IN
7/30/69 Delaware State Fair, Wilmington, DE
8/2/69 Ottawa County Fair, Holland, MI
8/8/69 Fairgrounds, Tulsa, OK
8/9/69 Ozark Empire Fair, Springfield, MO
8/15/69 Delaware County Fair, Walton, NY
8/17/69 Ponderosa Park, Salem, OH
8/22/69 Lake County Fair, Crown Point, IN
8/23/69 DuQuoin State Fair, Carbondale, IL
8/24/69 Missouri State Fair, Moberly, MO
8/26/69 North Dakota State Fair, Minot, ND
8/27/69 Minnesota State Fair, Minneapolis, MN
8/31/69 Sunset Park, West Grove, PA
9/1/69 Juniata County Fair, Chambersburg, PA
9/6 to 9/7/69 Saginaw Fair, Saginaw, MI
9/12/69 American Theater, Roanoke, VA
9/13/69 Dorton Arena, Raleigh, NC
9/14/69 Blue Grass Park, Riedsville, NC
9/15/69 Montgomery County Fair, Gaithersburg, MD
9/20/69 WBAY Auditorium, Green Bay, WI
9/21/69 Buckeye Lake Park, Buckeye Lake, OH
9/24 to 9/25/69 McElroy Green Park, Waterloo, IA
9/28/69 Rolling Green Park, Selinsgrove, PA
10/4/69 Grand Ole Opry, Nashville, TN
10/7/69 Sauk Rapids Auditorium, St. Cloud, MN
10/9/69 Dane County Coliseum, Madison, WI
10/11/69 Grand Ole Opry, Nashville, TN
10/18/69 Grand Ole Opry, Nashville, TN
10/25/69 Greensboro Coliseum, Greensboro, NC
10/26/69 Mosque Auditorium, Richmond, VA
11/1/69 Tulsa Assembly Center, Tulsa, OK
11/2/69 Civic Center Music Hall, Oklahoma City, OK
11/13/69 Fitchburg Theater, Fitchburg, MA
11/14/69 City Hall Auditorium, Portland, ME
11/16/69 Mt. Vernon High School, Alexandria, VA
11/22/69 Mid-South Coliseum, Memphis, TN
11/23/69 Louisiana Hayride, Ponchatoula, LA
11/29/69 Silver Spurs, Warren, OH
12/6/69 Grand Ole Opry, Nashville, TN
12/13/69 Grand Ole Opry, Nashville, TN
12/15/69 *The Mike Douglas Show* (films), Philadelphia, PA
12/20/69 Grand Ole Opry, Nashville, TN
12/25/69 *An Old Time Country Christmas* (special airs)
12/27/69 Century II Convention Hall, Wichita, KS
12/28/69 Municipal Auditorium, Topeka, KS
12/31/69 Omaha Music Hall, Omaha, NE

1970

1/1/70 KC Kansas Memorial Building, Kansas City, KS
1/2/70 Memorial Building, Joplin, MO
1/4/70 KRNT Theater, Des Moines, IA
1/10/70 Veterans Memorial Coliseum, Cedar Rapids, IA
1/11/70 Medina Temple, Chicago, IL
1/18/70 Indianapolis Coliseum, Indianapolis, IN
1/24/70 Civic Coliseum, Knoxville, TN
1/30/70 Civic Arena, Pittsburgh, PA
1/31/70 Louisville Convention Center, Louisville, KY
2/1/70 Cincinnati Music Hall, Cincinnati, OH
2/14/70 Grand Ole Opry, Nashville, TN
2/16 to 2/19/70 San Antonio Stock Show & Rodeo, San Antonio, TX
2/21/70 Grand Ole Opry, Nashville, TN
2/28/70 Olde South Jamboree, Walker, LA
3/7/70 Kleinhans Music Hall, Buffalo, NY
3/13/70 Memorial Hall, Lima, OH
3/18/70 *Hee Haw,* Nashville, TN
3/18/70 Bangor Auditorium, Bangor, ME
3/22/70 Bushnell Memorial Hall, Hartford, CT
3/28/70 Grand Ole Opry, Nashville, TN
4/2/70 Kitchner Memorial Auditorium, Kitchner, ON
4/3/70 Nazareth College, Rochester, NY
4/4/70 Memorial Hall, Dayton, OH
4/5/70 Dallastown High School Auditorium, York, PA
4/9/70 Memorial Auditorium, Burlington, VT
4/11/70 War Memorial, Syracuse, NY
4/16/70 WBAY Auditorium, Green Bay, WI
4/19/70 Fairmont Theater, Fairmont, WV
4/25/70 Sevier County High School—*A Real Live Dolly* album recording, Sevierville, TN
5/1/70 Charleston Civic Center, Charleston, WV
5/7/70 West Palm Beach Auditorium, West Palm Beach, FL
5/8/70 Curtis Hixon Hall, Tampa, FL
5/9/70 Macon Coliseum, Macon, GA
5/15/70 Cumberland County Memorial Coliseum, Fayetteville, NC
5/16/70 Winston Salem Coliseum, Winston Salem, NC
5/22/70 Memorial Auditorium, Greenville, SC
5/23/70 Dorton Arena, Raleigh, NC
5/24/70 City Auditorium, Asheville, NC
5/29/70 Greenville Memorial Auditorium, Greenville, SC
5/30/70 Grand Ole Opry, Nashville, TN
6/5/70 Albemarle High School Auditorium, Charlottesville, VA
6/6/70 Salisbury Civic Center, Salisbury, MD
6/7/70 Sunset Park, West Grove, PA
6/10/70 Newberry's Valley Plaza (autograph session), Poplar Bluff, MO
6/10/70 Poplar Bluff High School Stadium, Poplar Bluff, MO
6/11/70 Scottsboro Junior High School, Scottsboro, AL
7/11/70 Grand Ole Opry, Nashville, TN
7/12/70 Mockingbird Hill Park, Anderson, IN
7/15/70 Howard County Fair, Cresco, IA
7/18/70 Wheeling Jamboree, Wheeling, WV
7/25/70 Bluegrass Park, Reidsville, VA
7/29/70 Marion County Fair, Salem, IL
8/1/70 Veterans Memorial Coliseum, Saginaw, MI
8/9/70 Buck Lake Ranch, Angola, IN
8/11/70 Great Bedford Fair, Bedford, PA
8/14/70 Fairgrounds Coliseum, Jackson, MS
8/15/70 Mid-South Coliseum, Memphis, TN
8/22/70 Grand Ole Opry, Nashville, TN
8/24/70 West Virginia State Fair, Lewisburg, WV
8/27/70 Iowa State Fair, Des Moines, IA
9/5/70 Grand Ole Opry, Nashville, TN
9/7/70 Ontelaunee Lake, Allentown, PA
9/8/70 *The Mike Douglas Show* (films), Philadelphia, PA
9/11/70 E.C. Glass High School, Lynchburg, VA
9/12/70 Hampton Roads Coliseum, Hampton Roads, VA
9/19/70 Grand Ole Opry, Nashville, TN
9/20/70 Civic Center, Geneva, IL
9/21/70 McAlister Auditorium, Lexington, KY
9/26/70 Dade County Auditorium, Miami, FL
10/1/70 Wards Drug Store Grand Opening, Ft. Worth, TX
10/2 to 10/3/70 Panhandle South Plains Fair, Lubbock, TX
10/5/70 Municipal Auditorium, Austin, TX
10/10/70 Grand Ole Opry, Nashville, TN
10/13/70 BMI Country Awards
10/14/70 CMA Awards, Nashville, TN
10/15/70 WSM Luncheon & Spectacular, Nashville, TN
10/16/70 CMA Banquet, Nashville, TN
10/17/70 Grand Ole Opry, Nashville, TN
10/19/70 The *Today* show (from Nashville; airs)
10/19/70 Interstate Fair, Pensacola, FL
10/25/70 Roberts Stadium, Evansville, IN
10/29/70 Middlesboro High School, Middlesboro, KY
10/30 to 10/31/70 Municipal Auditorium, Birmingham, AL
11/6/70 Morris Civic Auditorium, South Bend, IN
11/11/70 Kings College Gym, Wilkes Barre, PA
11/13/70 Salem-Roanoke Civic Center, Salem, VA
11/28/70 Municipal Auditorium, Atlanta, GA
12/5/70 The Coliseum, Columbia, SC
12/12/70 Dobyns-Bennett Gym, Kingsport, TN
12/?/70 Grand Ole Opry, Nashville, TN
12/26/70 Grand Ole Opry, Nashville, TN
12/30/70 Sioux Falls Coliseum, Sioux Falls, SD
12/31/70 Century II Convention Hall, Wichita, KS

1971

1/1/71 Century II Convention Hall, Wichita, KS
1/2/71 Springfield Mosque, Springfield, MO
1/3/71 Memorial Building, Kansas City, MO
1/9/71 Grand Ole Opry, Nashville, TN
1/16/71 Grand Ole Opry, Nashville, TN
1/22/71 Low Country, Orangeburg, SC
1/23/71 WIVK Shindig, Civic Center, Knoxville, TN
1/29/71 Baker Civic Center, Baker, LA
2/6/71 Grand Ole Opry, Nashville, TN
2/13/71 Florida State Fair, Tampa, FL
2/20/71 Charlotte Coliseum, Charlotte, NC
2/25/71 Gregg County Fairgrounds, Longview, TX
2/26/71 Panther Hall, Ft. Worth, TX
2/27/71 Assembly Center, Tulsa, OK
2/28/71 Civic Center Music Hall, Oklahoma City, OK
3/7/71 Mosque Auditorium, Richmond, VA
3/13/71 Grand Ole Opry, Nashville, TN
3/16/71 Grammy Awards, Nashville NARAS Banquet, Nashville, TN

continued

7/28/17 My People special appearance, Pigeon Forge, TN
8/15/17 I Believe in You press conference, Nashville, TN
8/18 to 8/19/17 Dollywood Summer Fest, Pigeon Forge, TN
8/23/17 ACM Honors, Nashville, TN
9/15/17 Variety Women in Film & TV Event, Los Angeles, CA
9/16/17 NBC Pre-Emmy Party
9/17/17 Emmy Awards, Los Angeles, CA
9/18/17 *Pickler & Ben* (TV show), Nashville, TN
9/22/17 Grand Ole Opry, Nashville, TN
9/30/17 Ashdown, AR Benefit Concert
Fall 2017 *Dolly Parton's America* podcast taping, Nashville, TN
10/8/17 SiriusXM, Music City Theater, Nashville, TN
10/9/17 Radio interviews (SiriusXM; *The Bobby Bones Show*, etc.)
10/13/17 Vanderbilt Children's Hospital press event, Nashville, TN
10/16/17 *The View*, New York, NY
10/16/17 *The Dr. Oz Show*, New York, NY
10/16/17 *The Today* show, New York, NY
10/16/17 *Fox & Friends*, New York, NY
10/17/17 *The Chew*, New York, NY
10/17/17 *Sprout House: A Day with Dolly*, TV special (films), New York, NY
10/25/17 *All In for the Gambler*, Bridgestone Arena (films), Nashville, TN
10/30/17 The *Today* show (airs), Nashville, TN
10/31/17 *The Harry Connick Jr. Show* (airs)
10/31/17 The *Today* show (Halloween episode; pretaped)
11/3 to 11/5/17 Dollywood Smoky Mountain Christmas, Pigeon Forge, TN

2018

2/27/18 Library of Congress Imagination Library 100 Million Book Event, Washington, DC
2/28/18 *Nightline* (films), New York, NY
2/28/18 *Good Morning America*, New York, NY
3/1/18 *Nightline* (airs)
3/16 to 3/18/18 Dollywood Grand Opening, Pigeon Forge, TN
5/5 to 5/6/18 Dollywood's Flower & Food Festival, Pigeon Forge, TN
5/7/18 Dolly Parton Sevier County Senior Center dedication, Pigeon Forge, TN
5/15/18 Music Biz Conference, Nashville, TN
5/17/18 Vanderbilt Children's Hospital Butterfly Garden dedication, Nashville, TN
5/24/18 LA Press Club Awards, Los Angeles, CA
Summer/Fall 2018 *Heartstrings* TV movies filmed (Netflix 8-part series)
6/9/18 Dolly Parton's Pirate's Voyage Grand Opening, Pigeon Forge, TN
8/3/18 Dollywood appearance, Pigeon Forge, TN
8/4/18 Dollywood Wildwood Grove Press Conference, Pigeon Forge, TN
8/11/18 Dolly Parton Excellence in Leadership Award Ceremony at Country Music Hall of Fame, Nashville, TN
8/17/18 *9 to 5: The Musical* UK Promotional Content Capture, Nashville, TN
9/18/18 *9 to 5: The Musical* UK Press Day (various outlets), Nashville, TN
10/8/18 Radio Interviews (SiriusXM; *The Bobby Bones Show; American Country Countdown*)
10/22/18 HFPA Press Event and Performance—*Dumplin'*, Los Angeles, CA
11/9 to 11/11/18 Dollywood Smoky Mountain Christmas, Pigeon Forge, TN
11/18/18 Dolly Parton's Smoky Mountain Christmas Carol at Ordway, St. Paul, MN
11/20/18 *Trio: Complete Collection* Satellite Media Tour
11/27/18 Imagination Library 1st Statewide Program Recognition with Gov. Haslam & Gov. Lee at Governor's Mansion, Nashville, TN
11/29/18 *Dolly Parton: The Making of a Soundtrack*, TV special premiere
11/29/18 *The Tonight Show with Jimmy Fallon*, New York, NY
11/30/18 The *Today* show, New York, NY
12/4/18 *Dumplin'* press junket (with Jennifer Aniston), Los Angeles, CA
12/5/18 *Good Morning America* (airs)
12/5/18 *The Late Late Show with James Corden*, Los Angeles, CA
12/5/18 *The Ellen DeGeneres Show*, Los Angeles, CA
12/6/18 *The Talk*, Los Angeles, CA
12/6/18 *Dumplin'* Los Angeles Premiere, Los Angeles, CA

2019

1/28/19 Media Day (Spotify; Apple Music; BBC), Nashville, TN
2/4/19 Grammy Museum Exhibit Grand Opening, Los Angeles, CA
2/8/19 Grammy MusiCares Person of the Year (event), Los Angeles, CA
2/10/19 *CBS Sunday Morning* (airs)
2/10/19 Grammy Awards, Los Angeles, CA
2/16 to 2/19/19 *9 to 5: The Musical* London media junket (various outlets), London, England
2/18/19 *Lorraine* (airs)
2/19/19 *The One Show* (airs), London, England
2/19/19 *9 to 5: The Musical* London premiere, London, England
3/2/19 North Carolina Imagination Library statewide celebration at Marbles Kids Museum, Raleigh, NC
3/15 to 3/17/19 Dollywood Grand Opening, Pigeon Forge, TN
3/29/19 The *Today* show, New York, NY
4/4/19 *We Are HEAR* filming with Linda Perry, Sheryl Crow, and Grimes, Nashville, TN
4/14/19 THEA Awards (virtual)
5/10/19 Dollywood Wildwood Grove Launch Event, Pigeon Forge, TN
5/11 to 5/12/19 Dollywood Summer Festival, Pigeon Forge, TN
6/6/19 Frizzel Chicken Farmhouse and Comedy Barn, Pigeon Forge, TN
6/7/19 Dolly Parton's Pirates Voyage Grand Opening, Pigeon Forge, TN
6/8 to 6/9/19 Dollywood Summer Fest, Pigeon Forge, TN
Summer 2019 *Christmas on the Square* TV movie films (Netflix)
Summer 2019 *Dolly Parton's America* podcast launch
7/27/19 Newport Folk Festival, Newport, RI
8/5/19 National Conference of State Legislature at Music City Center, Nashville, TN
9/4/19 Dollywood appearance, Pigeon Forge, TN
9/21/19 Smoky Mountain Burlesque at Bijou Theatre, Knoxville, TN
Fall 2019 *Christmas at Dollywood* TV movie films
10/12/19 Grand Ole Opry, Nashville, TN
10/28/19 *Heartstrings* media day (various outlets), Pigeon Forge, TN
10/29/19 *Heartstrings* Dollywood premiere, Pigeon Forge, TN
10/30/19 Dollywood appearance, Pigeon Forge, TN
11/5/19 We Are Family Foundation event, New York, NY
11/8/19 *Christmas at Dollywood* (films)
11/10/19 *A Life on the Road with Brian Johnson* (airs)
11/12/19 *Dolly Parton: Here She Comes Again!* (TV special airs)
11/12/19 *Good Morning America* (via satellite), Nashville, TN
11/13/19 CMA Awards, Nashville, TN
11/20/19 *The Tonight Show with Jimmy Fallon*, New York, NY
11/20/19 The *Today* show, New York, NY
11/21/19 *Late Night with Seth Meyers*, New York, NY
11/22/19 *The View*, New York, NY
11/22/19 *Heartstrings* (Netflix 8-part series premiere)
11/28/19 *Dolly: 50 Years at the Opry* (TV special; airs)
12/5/19 *A Smoky Mountain Christmas Carol* Musical (premiere), Boston, MA
12/8/19 *Christmas at Dollywood* (TV movie premiere)
12/23/19 The *Today* show (airs)

2020

1/30/20 The Gift of Music Benefit Concert, Ryman Auditorium, Nashville, TN
3/2/20 American Greetings Content Capture, Nashville, TN
4/2/20 *The Library That Dolly Built* (documentary premiere)
5/2/20 *RuPaul's Drag Race* (airs)
5/18/20 A Night of Covenant House Stars (virtual)
7/7/20 PaleyFest *Heartstrings* panel (virtual)
8/6 to 8/7/20 *There Was Jesus* media days (with Zach Williams; various outlets), Nashville, TN
8/10/20 Williams Sonoma Collection content shoot and media day, Nashville, TN
8/11 to 8/14/20 *A Holly Dolly Christmas* media days (various outlets), Nashville, TN
8/17/20 *A Holly Dolly Christmas* media day (various outlets), Nashville, TN
Fall 2020 *A Holly Dolly Christmas* TV special (films), Nashville, TN
10/5/20 Toronto Santa Claus Parade performance (virtual)
10/6 to 10/8/20 *Songteller* Media Days (various outlets), Nashville, TN
10/9/20 *The Graham Norton Show* (airs; virtual)
10/21/20 *The Late Show with Stephen Colbert* (airs; virtual)
11/16 to 11/20/20 *A Holly Dolly Christmas* media days (various outlets), Nashville, TN
11/13/20 *The Oprah Conversation* (airs)
11/22/20 *Christmas on the Square* (Netflix premiere)
11/26/20 Macy's Thanksgiving Day Parade (virtual), New York, NY
12/2/20 Rockefeller Tree Lighting Special (virtual), New York, NY
12/5/20 *A Holly Dolly Christmas* (TV special; airs), New York, NY

2021

2/9/21 *The Tonight Show with Jimmy Fallon* (virtual), Nashville, TN
4/7/21 *Dolly Parton: A MusiCares Tribute* (Netflix special premiere)
4/18/21 ACM Awards (virtual)
5/9/21 Latin Grammy Awards (virtual)
5/12/21 *Good Morning America* (special broadcast), Pigeon Forge, TN
7/12/21 Dolly Beauty Media Day (various outlets), Nashville, TN
7/17/21 Media Day (various outlets), Nashville, TN
7/20/21 *Run, Rose, Run* Album Listening Party, Nashville, TN
7/27/21 *Good Morning America* (via satellite)
7/27/21 HSN (via satellite), Nashville, TN
7/28/21 *Watch What Happens LIVE!* (via satellite)
8/12/21 *9 to 5: The Musical* Australian media day, Nashville, TN
8/15/21 *Scent From Above* Commercial Shoot, Nashville, TN
9/9/21 Media Day (various outlets), Nashville, TN
9/19/21 Emmy Awards (virtual)
9/25/21 *Kenny Rogers: All In for the Gambler* (TV special premiere)
10/24/21 Komen Foundation Kiss Cancer Goodbye Benefit (CMA Theater), Nashville, TN
10/28/21 *Baking with Dolly* (ConAgra) content capture, Nashville, TN
10/29/21 Media Day (various outlets), Nashville, TN
11/7/21 HSN (via satellite), Nashville, TN
12/8 to 12/10/21 *Run, Rose, Run* media day (various outlets), Nashville, TN

2022

2/10/22 T-Mobile Superbowl Ad (airs)
3/6/22 *CBS Sunday Morning* (airs)
3/6/22 *Run, Rose, Run* media day (various outlets), Las Vegas, NV
3/7/22 *Good Morning America*, Las Vegas, NV
3/7/22 ACM Awards, Las Vegas, NV
3/10 to 3/12/22 Dollywood Grand Opening, Pigeon Forge, TN
3/18/22 SXSW Live from Austin, special performance, Austin, TX
3/25/22 *Run, Rose, Run* media day (various outlets), Nashville, TN
4/9/22 University of Mississippi Donor Dinner (Imagination Library), Oxford, MS
4/10/22 University of Mississippi Foundation Award event, Oxford, MS
5/2/22 *Grace & Frankie* (TV series cameo; premieres)
5/3/22 Dolly Parton Excellence in Leadership Award presentation to Gov. and First Lady Haslam at Tennessee State Museum, Nashville, TN
5/5/22 Imagination Library Statewide Celebration (Arkansas), Little Rock, AR
5/5/22 Imagination Library Statewide Celebration (Delaware), Wilmington, DE
5/9/22 Walmart Meeting, Bentonville, AR
5/20/22 Media Day (various outlets), Nashville, TN
6/26/22 HeartSong Lodge Groundbreaking, Pigeon Forge, TN
7/15/22 Media Day (various outlets), Nashville, TN
7/21/22 *The Orville* (cameo appearance; airs)
8/5/22 Big Bear Mountain groundbreaking and press conference, Pigeon Forge, TN
8/9/22 Imagination Library Statewide Celebration (Ohio), Columbus, OH
8/9/22 Imagination Library Statewide Celebration (West Virginia), Charleston, WV
Summer 2022 *Dolly Parton's Mountain Magic Christmas* (TV movie films)
10/17/22 Carnegie Medal of Philanthropy, New York, NY
11/5/22 Rock & Roll Hall of Fame Induction Ceremony, Los Angeles, CA
11/7/22 LA Media (*The Kelly Clarkson Show; NYE Special* promos; *Rockstar* preview), Los Angeles, CA
11/12/22 The Jeff Bezos Courage & Civility Award Ceremony, New York, NY
11/30/22 *The Tonight Show with Jimmy Fallon*, New York, NY
12/1/22 *The Kelly Clarkson Show* (airs)
12/1/22 The *Today* show (airs)
12/1/22 *Dolly Parton's Mountain Magic Christmas* (TV movie premiere)
12/2/22 Media Day (various outlets), Nashville, TN
12/3 to 12/4/22 HSN (via satellite), Nashville, TN
12/31/22 *Miley & Dolly's New Year's Eve Party* (TV special; airs live), Miami, FL

2023

3/12 to 3/14/23 Dollywood Grand Opening, Pigeon Forge, TN
4/23/23 ACM Awards Promotional content day, Nashville, TN
4/28/23 ACM Awards media day, Nashville, TN
5/10/23 *Rockstar* press conference, Dallas, TX
5/11/23 ACM Awards, Dallas, TX
5/12/23 Dollywood Big Bear Mountain Grand Opening, Pigeon Forge, TN
5/20/23 NBC Olympics commercial shoot ("We Are the Champions"), Nashville, TN
6/29/23 *Rockstar* European press conference, London, England
6/29 to 6/30/23 *Rockstar* Global media day (various outlets), London, England
6/30/23 *The One Show* (in-studio), London, England
7/19/23 *Amazon Music: The Walk in With Mo Heart* (film), Nashville, TN
7/20/23 *Apple Music: What Would Dolly Do?* (4 episodes), Nashville, TN
7/31/23 Dollar General Convention, Nashville, TN
8/3 to 8/4/23 *Rockstar* media day (various outlets), Nashville, TN
8/7/23 *Behind the Seams* media day (various outlets), Nashville, TN
8/8/23 *Rockstar* Media Day (various outlets), Nashville, TN
8/10 to 12/23 *Good Lookin' Cookin'* content and photo shoot day, Nashville, TN
8/14/23 Imagination Library Statewide Celebration (Kansas), Topeka, KS
8/15/23 Imagination Library Statewide Celebration (Washington), Tacoma, WA
8/17/23 *Rockstar* media day (various outlets), Nashville, TN
8/21 to 8/22/23 *Baking with Dolly* (ConAgra) content day, Nashville, TN
8/28/23 Marty Stuart's Congress of Country Music Concerts, Philadelphia, MS
8/30/23 *Rockstar* media day (various outlets), Nashville, TN
8/31/23 *Rockstar* Cracker Barrel Commercial Shoot, Nashville, TN
9/1/23 *Behind the Seams* media day (various outlets), Nashville, TN
9/9/23 Golden Ticket Awards, Pigeon Forge, TN
9/21/23 ConAgra Corporate Headquarters Town Hall, Chicago, IL
9/25/23 Dallas Cowboys & Salvation Army Commercial Content Capture, Nashville, TN
9/26 to 9/29/23 *Rockstar* media day (various outlets), Nashville, TN
10/3 to 10/4/23 *Rockstar* media day (various outlets), Nashville, TN
10/10/23 *Rockstar* media day (various outlets), Nashville, TN
10/11/23 Nashville Songwriters Hall of Fame International Event, Nashville, TN
10/13/23 HSN (via satellite), Nashville, TN
10/16/23 *Rockstar* media day (various outlets), Nashville, TN
10/17/23 *Behind the Seams* media day (various outlets), Nashville, TN
10/17/23 *The View* (virtual) airs
10/19/23 *Person to Person with Norah O'Donnell* Special (airs)
10/25 to 10/26/23 *Rockstar* media day (various outlets), Nashville, TN
10/27/23 *Behind the Seams* Lipscomb University Exhibit Grand Opening, Nashville, TN
11/3 to 11/4/23 HeartSong Lodge press conference and dedication, Pigeon Forge, TN
11/7/23 *Rockstar* media day (various outlets), Nashville, TN
11/7/23 *Dolly Parton: From Rhinestones to Rock & Roll* (special airs)
11/15/23 *The Howard Stern Show* (via satellite), Nashville, TN
11/15/23 *Dolly: Rockstar—A Global Theatrical Event* (premiere)
11/15/23 *Rockstar* media day (various outlets), Nashville, TN
11/16/23 *Rockstar* press conference live stream event, Nashville, TN
11/17/23 *Rockstar* media day (various outlets), Nashville, TN
11/18/23 UT Vols vs. Georgia College game-day special appearance, Knoxville, TN
11/23/23 Dallas Cowboys Thanksgiving Day Halftime Show Performance, Dallas, TX
11/27/23 *The Drew Barrymore Show* (airs)

2024

Winter 2024 *Dolly Parton Presents Doggy Parton's Pet Gala* (films), Nashville, TN
1/23 to 1/24/24 *Baking with Dolly* (ConAgra) Media Day, Nashville, TN
2/22/24 *Dolly Parton Presents Doggy Parton's Pet Gala* (TV special; airs)
3/8 to 3/11/24 Dollywood Grand Opening, Pigeon Forge, TN
4/5/24 Dolly Wines content day, Nashville, TN
4/30/24 *God, Family and Show Business* (online special taping), Nashville, TN
5/24/24 Dollywood Dolly Parton Experience Grand Opening, Pigeon Forge, TN
5/28 to 30/24 Smoky Mountain DNA Performance Filming, Bijou Theater, Knoxville, TN
6/10/24 CMA Music Fest press conference, Nashville, TN
6/17 to 6/18/24 *Good Lookin' Cookin'* media day (various outlets), Nashville, TN
7/2/24 *Good Lookin' Cookin'* media day (various outlets), Nashville, TN
7/15/24 Dolly Beauty content capture, Nashville, TN
7/30/24 Home Chef and *Good Lookin' Cookin'* content capture, Nashville, TN
8/9/24 HSN (via satellite) and TalkShopLive
8/13 to 8/14/24 *Baking with Dolly* (ConAgra) content capture, Nashville, TN
8/21/24 ACM Honors (virtual)
8/27/24 Imagination Library Statewide Celebration (Kentucky), Lexington, KY
8/27/24 Imagination Library Statewide Celebration (Missouri), Kansas City, MO
9/9/24 *Good Lookin' Cookin'* Media Day (various outlets), Nashville, TN
9/11/24 Home Chef and *Good Lookin' Cookin'* Media Day (various outlets), Nashville, TN
9/11/24 *Dolly Parton—Threads: My Songs in Symphony* content day, Nashville, TN
9/16/24 Kendra Scott content capture, Nashville, TN
9/17/24 *Good Lookin' Cookin'* media day (various outlets), Nashville, TN
9/20/24 Tennessee Tourism and Dollywood content day, Nashville, TN
10/4/24 Walmart Meeting, Bentonville, AR
10/4/24 Hurricane Helene Donation press conference (with Walmart), Newport, TN
10/16/24 Dolly Wines media day (various outlets), Nashville, TN
10/16/24 Country Music Hall of Fame & Museum Exhibit content day, Nashville, TN
10/17/24 Dolly Wines media day (various outlets), Nashville, TN
10/17/24 Dolly Beauty media day (various outlets), Nashville, TN
10/18/24 *Still Working 9 to 5* documentary release
10/21/24 Kendra Scott Media Day (various outlets), Nashville, TN
11/6/24 Smoky Mountain DNA, etc., media day (various outlets), Nashville, TN
11/25/24 Celebrate with Dolly media day (various outlets), Nashville, TN
12/4/24 *Billy the Kid Comes Home for Christmas* media day (various outlets), Nashville, TN

2025*

1/28/25 Musical Fisher Center Press Conference and ticket on-sale, Nashville, TN
2/6/25 *Good American* production day, Nashville, TN
3/13 to 3/14/25 Dollywood Grand Opening Weekend, Pigeon Forge, TN
3/19/25 *Good American* media day, Nashville, TN
3/20/25 *Threads: My Songs in Symphony* Nashville premiere, Nashville, TN
4/3/25 Kendra Scott production day, Nashville, TN
5/2 to 5/3/25 Dollywood 40th Anniversary events, Pigeon Forge, TN
5/8/25 E. W. "BUD" Wendell Award Luncheon, Music City Center, Nashville, TN
5/19/25 Country Music Hall of Fame & Museum Exhibit Opening, Nashville, TN
5/21/25 ConAgra Media Day and Guinness World Record Presentation, Nashville, TN

**Performances updated through May 2025*

9/5/90 Market Square Arena, Indianapolis, IN
9/6/90 MSU Breslin Center, Lansing, MI
9/13 to 9/18/90 The Mirage, Las Vegas, NV
10/10 10/16/90 *Christmas at Home*, TV special (films), Pigeon Forge, TN
10/21/90 Carson Newman College to Honorary Doctorate Degree, Jefferson City, TN
10/23/90 Sun Dome, Tampa, FL
10/24/90 Omni, Atlanta, GA
10/25/90 The Superdome, New Orleans, LA
10/27/90 Kemper Arena, Kansas City, KS
10/28/90 Bob Devany Sports Center, Lincoln, NE
10/29/90 The Target Center, Minneapolis, MN
10/31/90 War Memorial Auditorium, Rochester, NY
11/1/90 Buffalo Memorial Auditorium, Buffalo, NY
11/18/90 The Knickerbocker, Albany, NY
12/6 to 12/11/90 The Mirage, Las Vegas, NV
12/14/90 *The Tonight Show with Johnny Carson*
12/20/90 *Late Night with David Letterman*
12/21/90 *CBS This Morning*
12/21/90 *Christmas at Home* (airs; ABC)
12/28/90 The Kirby Center, Wilkes Barre, PA
12/29/90 Etess Arena, Trump Taj Mahal, Atlantic City, NJ
12/31/90 Riverside Theater, Milwaukee, WI

1991

Winter 1991 *Wild Texas Wind*, TV movie (films)
1/14 to 1/15/91 Governor Ann Richards Inauguration, Austin, TX
2/7/91 *Babes*, TV series (airs; cameo)
4/26 to 4/28/91 Dollywood Grand Opening, Pigeon Forge, TN
5/8/91 *The Tonight Show with Johnny Carson*, Los Angeles, CA
5/30/91 *The Oprah Winfrey Show* (airs live), Chicago, IL
Summer 1991 *Straight Talk*, movie (films), Chicago, IL
9/21/91 *Into the Night with Rick Dees*, Los Angeles, CA
9/23/91 *Wild Texas Wind*, TV movie premiere (ABC)
9/26 to 9/28/91 Dollywood Fall Festival, Pigeon Forge, TN
10/1/91 CMA Awards, Nashville, TN
10/25/91 *Disney World's 20th Anniversary Celebration* (airs)
11/15/91 Dollywood Smoky Mountain Christmas, Pigeon Forge, TN
11/22/91 Portland Civic Auditorium, Portland, OR
11/23/91 Paramount Theater, Seattle, WA
11/24/91 Hult Center, Eugene, OR
12/1/91 Caesars, Lake Tahoe, NV
12/12 to 12/17/91 The Mirage, Las Vegas, NV
12/29 to 12/31/91 Caesars Atlantic City Hotel & Casino, Atlantic City, NJ

1992

2/14/92 Gavin Convention Center, San Francisco, CA
2/26/92 Dolly Trolley Dedication, Nashville, TN
2/28/92 Sunrise Musical Theater, Sunrise, FL
2/29/92 Ruth Eckerd Hall, Clearwater, FL
3/6/92 King Center, Melbourne, FL
3/9/92 *Straight Talk* press conference, Atlanta, GA
3/12/92 *Straight Talk* press conference, San Francisco, CA
3/13/92 Marin Vets Memorial Auditorium, San Rafael, CA
3/15/92 Sacramento Community Center Theater, Sacramento, CA
3/19/92 *The Arsenio Hall Show* (airs), Los Angeles, CA
3/24/92 *Straight Talk* press conference, Kansas City, MO
3/25/92 *Conversations with Burt Reynolds* (films), Nashville, TN
3/27/92 *Straight Talk* press conference, Nashville, TN
3/30 to 3/31/92 *Straight Talk* press conference, Chicago, IL
4/1/92 *Straight Talk* press event, Chicago, IL
4/1/92 *Larry King Live*, New York, NY
4/2/92 *Late Night with David Letterman*, New York, NY
4/3/92 *Good Morning America*, New York, NY
4/3/92 *The Oprah Winfrey Show* (airs)
4/3/92 *Straight Talk* press conference, New York, NY
4/8/92 *The Tonight Show with Johnny Carson*, Los Angeles, CA
4/23/92 *Conversations with Burt Reynolds* (airs)
4/24 to 4/26/92 Dollywood Grand Opening, Pigeon Forge, TN
5/3/92 *Bob Hope's America: Red, White & Blue Celebration* (films)
5/16/92 *Bob Hope's America: Red, White & Blue Celebration* (airs)
6/1/92 *Crook & Chase* (airs)
6/3/92 *The Wogan Show* (UK; airs)
6/5/92 Brady Theater, Tulsa, OK
6/6/92 Country Days, Farmington, MO
6/12/92 Fox Theater, St. Louis, MO
6/14/92 Poplar Creek, Chicago, IL
6/19/92 Meadow Brook Music Festival, Oakland, CA
6/20/92 Landmark Theater, Syracuse, NY
6/21/92 Harvey's Lake Amphitheater, Wilkes Barre, PA
6/22/92 Dolly Parton's Stampede Grand Opening, Myrtle Beach, SC
6/25 to 6/27/92 The Mirage, Las Vegas, NV
6/29/92 Wolf Trap, Vienna, VA
7/1/92 Ferrel Center, Baylor University, Waco, TX
7/3/92 The Cynthia Woods Mitchell Pavilion, The Woodlands, TX
7/4/92 Sea World of Texas, San Antonio, TX
7/10/92 Ocean City Convention Center, Ocean City, MD
7/11/92 Carowinds, Charlotte, NC
7/12/92 Ponderosa Park, Salem, OH
7/16/92 Chastain Park, Atlanta, GA
7/17/92 Classic Amphitheater, Virginia Beach, VA
7/24/92 Broome County Veterans Memorial Arena, Binghampton, NY
7/25/92 Mann Music Center, Philadelphia, PA
7/26/92 Great Woods Amphitheater, Boston, MA
7/31/92 Orange County Speedway, Middletown, NY
8/1/92 I. C. Light Amphitheatre, Pittsburgh, PA
8/2/92 Garden State Arts Center, Holmdel, NJ
8/6/92 Aquafest, Austin, TX
8/7/92 Municipal Auditorium, Shreveport, LA
8/8/92 Mudd Island Amphitheater, Jackson, MS
8/9/92 Chastain Park, Atlanta, GA
8/20 to 8/25/92 The Mirage, Las Vegas, NV
9/3 to 9/6/92 Caesars Tahoe, Stateline, NV
9/18/92 Riverbend Music Theater, Cincinnati, OH
9/20/92 Braden Auditorium, Bloomington, IL
9/30/92 CMA Awards, Nashville, TN
10/19/92 *Celebrities Offstage* (special; airs; TNN)
11/13/92 Dollywood Smoky Mountain Christmas, Pigeon Forge, TN
11/14/92 An Evening of Elegance, Dr. Robert F. Thomas Benefit, Gatlinburg, TN
11/18/92 Life Gala, Universal Amphitheater, Los Angeles, CA

1993

1/13/93 *CMA Honors*, TV special (films), Nashville, TN
1/29 to 1/30/93 Caesars, Lake Tahoe, NV
2/6/93 *CMA Honors*,TV special (airs)
2/25 to 2/28/93 Palace Theater, Cleveland, OH
3/1/93 *The Joan Rivers Show* (airs), New York, NY
3/2/93 *Live! With Regis & Kathie Lee*, New York, NY
3/4/93 Country Radio Seminar, Nashville, TN
3/5/93 *The Tonight Show with Jay Leno*, Los Angeles, CA
3/10/93 *The Phil Donahue Show* (films), Chicago, IL
3/11/93 Veterans Memorial Coliseum, Columbus, OH
3/13/93 Stanley Performing Arts Center, Utica, NY
3/14/93 Eastman Theater, Rochester, NY
3/15/93 *Larry King Live*, New York, NY
3/16/93 *The Today* show, New York, NY
3/16/93 *Late Night with David Letterman*, New York, NY
3/18/93 Chef Atkins Party at BMI, Nashville, TN
3/24/93 Anderson Civic Center, Anderson, SC
3/25/93 University of Florida Theater, Gainesville, FL
3/26/93 Tampa Bay Performing Arts Center, Tampa, FL
3/27/93 Sunrise Music Theater, Fort Lauderdale, FL
3/29/93 Mariott Marco Island Theater, Marco Island, FL
4/1 to 4/8/93 The Mirage, Las Vegas, NV
4/16 to 4/17/93 Holiday Star Theater, Merrillville, IN
4/18/93 University of Illinois Amphitheater, Champaign, IL
4/20/93 *The Beverly Hillbillies*, movie (films; cameo)
4/23 to 4/25/93 Dollywood Grand Opening, Pigeon Forge, TN
4/28/93 Civic Center, Orlando, FL
4/30/93 Louisville Gardens, Louisville, KY
5/3/93 *The Arsenio Hall Show* (airs), Los Angeles, CA
5/7/93 *The Phil Donahue Show* (airs)
5/10/93 Sony Music Anniversary, New York, NY
5/11/93 Planet Hollywood Handprint Ceremony, New York, NY
5/14/93 Country Takes Manhattan, Carnegie Hall, New York, NY
5/16/93 Cambria County War Memorial, Johnstown, PA
5/17/93 Eastman Theater, Rochester, NY
5/26 to 5/30/93 The Fox Theater, Detroit, MI
6/4/93 Verizon Wireless Center, Charlotte, NC
6/5/93 Martin Luther King Jr. Arena, Savannah, GA
6/7/93 TNN/Music City News Country Awards, Nashville, TN
6/10 to 6/15/93 The Mirage, Las Vegas, NV
6/18/93 Country Jam USA, Grand Junction, CO
6/19 to 6/20/93 Kersge Auditorium, Interlochen, MI
6/25/93 Country Jam USA, Grand Junction, CO
6/27/93 Cal Farley Coliseum, Amarillo, TX
7/1/93 Century II Civic Center, Wichita, KS
7/2/93 Civic Center Music Hall, Oklahoma City, OK
7/3/93 Smirnoff Music Center, Dallas, TX
7/5/93 VP Fair, St Louis, MO
7/10/93 Music Mansion Theater Groundbreaking, Pigeon Forge, TN
7/10/93 Sunset Music Festival, Pigeon Forge, TN
7/15/93 Olympic Saddledome, Calgary, AB
7/16/93 Country Jamboree, Edmonton, AB
7/17/93 Big Valley Jamboree, Craven, SK
7/21/93 Midland Theater, Kansas City, MO
7/23/93 Rodeo Arena, Dodge City, KS
7/24/93 Municipal Auditorium, Sioux City, IA
7/25/93 Country Jam, Eau Claire, WI
7/28/93 Wendler Arena, Saginaw, MI
7/30/93 Deer Creek Amphitheater, Indianapolis, IN
8/1/93 Fraze Pavilion, Dayton, OH
8/2/93 Ravinia Festival, Indianapolis, IN
8/6/93 Michigan Festival, East Lansing, MI
8/7/93 Civic Center, Erie, PA
8/8/93 Rocky Gap Festival, Cumberland, MD
8/9/93 Shea's Performing Arts Center, Buffalo, NY
8/14/93 ASU Sun Devil Stadium, Phoenix, AZ
8/29/93 Grace Pavilion, Concord, CA
9/3/93 Minnesota State Fair, Minneapolis, MN
9/4/93 Sheboygan County Fair, Sheboygan, WI
9/5/93 Canfield Fair, Canfield, OH
9/10 to 9/11/93 Caesars, Lake Tahoe, NV
9/14/93 Tulare County Fair, Tulare, CA
9/26/93 *Honky Tonk Angels* press conference, Nashville, TN
9/29/93 CMA Awards, Nashville, TN
10/9/93 Boyd County Fairgrounds, Ashland, KY
11/12/93 Dollywood Smoky Mountain Christmas, Pigeon Forge, TN
11/13 11/14/93 Beauty Confidence Collection press conference, Pigeon Forge, TN

1994

1/18/94 *The Tonight Show with Jay Leno*, Los Angeles, CA
Spring 1994 *Heaven's to Betsy*, TV series (films; never aired), Los Angeles, CA
3/1/94 Grammy Awards, New York, NY
3/21/94 Academy Awards, Los Angeles, CA
4/22 to 4/24/94 Dollywood Grand Opening, Pigeon Forge, TN
5/26/94 BMI Awards, New York, NY
6/6/94 TNN/Music City News Country Awards (via satellite), Nashville, TN
9/21/94 *Dateline* (airs)
9/24/94 *Dolly: My Life . . .* book signing, Super Crown, New York, NY
9/26/94 *The Late Night with David Letterman*, New York, NY
9/27/94 *Good Morning America*, New York, NY
9/27/94 *Live! With Regis & Kathie Lee*, New York, NY
9/27/94 *Dolly: My Life . . .* book signing, Barnes & Noble, New York, NY
9/28/94 *Dolly: My Life . . .* book signing, Super Crown, McLean, VA
9/28/94 *Larry King Live*, New York, NY
9/29/94 *Dolly: My Life . . .* book signing, Davis Kidd, Memphis, TN
10/5/94 CMA Awards, Nashville, TN
10/19/94 *On the Record with Ralph Emery* (airs)
10/31/94 *The Phil Donahue Show* (airs), Chicago, IL
11/20/94 *Dolly: My Life . . .* book signing, Books-a-Million, Birmingham, AL
11/28/94 *Dolly: My Life . . .* book signing, Hollywood, Los Angeles, CA
11/28/94 *The Tonight Show with Jay Leno*, Los Angeles, CA
11/29/94 *Dolly: My Life . . .* book signing, Brentano's, Los Angeles, CA

1995

1/22/95 *Big Dreams & Broken Hearts to Dottie West*, TV movie (cameo)
4/1/95 *Live! With Regis & Kathie Lee*, New York, NY
4/20/95 Porter Wagoner Charity Roast, Nashville, TN
4/21/95 *CBS This Morning* (via satellite), Pigeon Forge, TN
4/21/95 *The Late Show with David Letterman* (via satellite), Pigeon Forge, TN
4/21 to 4/23/95 Dollywood Grand Opening, Pigeon Forge, TN
5/14/95 *Naomi & Wynonna: Love Can Build a Bridge*, TV movie (cameo)
7/8/95 Sevier County Time Capsule Dedication, Pigeon Forge, TN
7/17/95 Dolly Parton's Stampede Grand Opening, Branson, MO
8/26/95 Grand Ole Opry, Nashville, TN
8/26/95 *Something Special* album release party, Inca Hoots, Nashville, TN
8/28/95 *CBS This Morning*, New York, NY
8/31/95 *The Tonight Show with Jay Leno*, Los Angeles, CA
9/8/95 *Music City Tonight* (TNN), Nashville, TN
10/4/95 CMA Awards, Nashville, TN
11/27 to 30/95 *Grand Ole Opry 70th Birthday Special* (films), Nashville, TN
11/9/95 Dollywood Smoky Mountain Christmas, Pigeon Forge, TN

1996

1/4/96 *Grand Ole Opry 70th Birthday Special* (host; airs)
4/3/96 *The Tonight Show with Jay Leno*, Los Angeles, CA
4/10 to 4/12/96 *Live! With Regis & Kathie Lee* (guest cohost), New York, NY
4/15/96 *Prime Time Country* (TNN), Nashville, TN
4/19 to 4/21/96 Dollywood Grand Opening, Pigeon Forge, TN
Summer 1996 *Unlikely Angel*, TV movie, (films)
Fall 1996 *Treasures*, TV special (films)
10/2/96 CMA Awards, Nashville, TN
10/11/96 National Association of Broadcasters Convention, Los Angeles, CA
11/26/96 *CBS This Morning*, New York, NY
11/26/96 *The Late Show with David Letterman*, New York, NY
11/26/96 *The Late Late Show with Tom Snyder*, New York, NY
11/26/96 *The Rosie O'Donnell Show*, New York, NY
11/28/96 *Treasures*, TV special (airs, CBS)
12/14/96 Harmony Award Presentation, Nashville Symphony, Nashville, TN
12/17/96 *Unlikely Angel*, TV film (airs, CBS)

1997

4/11/97 *Live! With Regis & Kathie Lee*, New York, NY
4/18 to 4/20/97 Dollywood Grand Opening, Pigeon Forge, TN
6/12 to 6/13/97 Dollywood Summer Fest, Pigeon Forge, TN
6/14/97 Dolly Parton's Stampede Grand Opening, Pigeon Forge, TN
8/5/97 *Porter Wagoner's 50th Anniversary Special* (airs; TNN)
9/28/97 *Get to the Heart—the Barbara Mandrell Story*, TV movie (cameo)
12/9/97 American Bus Marketplace Convention, Opryland Hotel, Nashville,TN

1998

3/26/98 *Good Morning America*, New York, NY
3/26/98 *The Late Show with David Letterman*, New York, NY
3/27/98 *The View*, New York, NY
4/2/98 *The Rosie O'Donnell Show*, New York, NY
4/9/98 Tammy Wynette Memorial Service, Nashville, TN
4/16/98 *Good Morning America* (via satellite), Pigeon Forge, TN
4/17/98 *CBS This Morning* (via satellite), Pigeon Forge, TN
4/17 to 4/19/98 Dollywood Grand Opening, Pigeon Forge, TN
6/16/98 Fan Fair, Nashville,TN
8/13/98 *Hungry Again* album release party, BMI, Nashville, TN
8/24/98 *The Tonight Show with Jay Leno*, Los Angeles, CA
8/24/98 *The Howie Mandel Show*, Los Angeles, CA
8/28/98 *The Today* show, New York, NY
8/31/98 *Live! With Regis & Kathie Lee*, New York, NY
9/2/98 *Larry King Live*, New York, NY
9/5 to 9/6/98 Dollywood Harvest Festival, Pigeon Forge, TN
9/17/98 *Hungry Again* album release party, Hard Rock Café, London, England
9/19/98 *The National Lottery* (UK TV appearance), London, England
9/19/98 *TFI Friday* (UK TV appearance), London, England
9/24/98 *Midday* (UK TV appearance), London, England
9/24/98 *Des O'Connor Tonight* (UK TV appearance), London, England
9/30/98 *Prime Time Country* (TNN), Nashville, TN
10/2/98 *Canada AM* (via satellite)
11/6 to 27/98 *CMT Showcase* (4-part series airs)
11/13/98 Dollywood Smoky Mountain Christmas, Pigeon Forge, TN
11/24/98 *Live! With Regis & Kathie Lee*, Los Angeles, CA

1999

Winter 1999 *Precious Memories* TV special (films), Nashville, TN
2/9/99 *The Tonight Show with Jay Leno*, Los Angeles, CA
2/11/99 *Trio II* press conference, New York, NY
2/11/99 *The Today* show, New York, NY
2/11/99 *Crook & Chase* (via satellite)
2/12/99 *The Rosie O'Donnell Show*, New York, NY
2/26/99 *CBS This Morning*, New York, NY
3/2/99 *Donny & Marie* (TV show), Los Angeles, CA
3/3/99 *The Howie Mandel Show*, Los Angeles, CA
3/24/99 *Live! With Regis & Kathie Lee* (guest cohost), New York, NY
3/24/99 AMVETS Awards, Vienna, VA
3/24/99 *The Late Show with David Letterman*, New York, NY
3/25/99 *Live! With Regis & Kathie Lee* (guest cohost), New York, NY
3/25/99 *Prime Time Country* (TNN), Nashville, TN
3/28/99 *Precious Memories* TV special (airs; TNN)
4/1/99 Southbank Show (UK TV appearance, via satellite)
4/16 to 4/18/99 Dollywood Grand Opening, Pigeon Forge, TN
Summer 1999 *Blue Valley Songbird* TV movie (films)
6/14/99 *Jackie's Back* TV movie (cameo; airs)
7/3/99 Opryland press conference, Y2K Concert, Nashville, TN
9/22/99 *CBS This Morning* (via satellite), Nashville, TN
9/22/99 CMA Awards, Nashville, TN
9/25/99 *The National Lottery* (UK TV appearance, remote)
10/27/99 *The Martin Short Show*, Los Angeles, CA
10/28/99 *Live! With Regis & Kathie Lee*, San Francisco, CA
10/29/99 *The Today* show (via satellite), Los Angeles, CA
10/31/99 *Blue Valley Songbird* TV film (airs; Lifetime)
11/1/99 *Donny & Marie* (TV show), Los Angeles, CA
11/2/99 *The Tonight Show with Jay Leno*, Los Angeles, CA
11/4/99 *The Grass Is Blue* Walmart album signing, Franklin, TN
11/17 to 11/18/99 Dollywood Smoky Mountain Christmas, Pigeon Forge, TN

2000

1/1/00 Opryland Millennium Concert, Nashville, TN
1/6/00 Country Music Hall of Fame Medallion Ceremony, Nashville, TN
2/28/00 *The Late Show with David Letterman*, New York, NY
2/29/00 *Live! With Regis & Kathie Lee*, New York, NY
3/22/00 Association Of American Publishers, Washington, DC
3/23/00 National Press Club, Washington, DC
4/14 to 4/16/2000 Dollywood Grand Opening, Pigeon Forge, TN
4/20/00 The Dove Awards, Nashville, TN
5/3/00 ACM Awards, Los Angeles, CA
8/19/00 Sevier County Football Championship, Sevierville, TN
9/5 to 9/7/2000 *Live! With Regis & Kathie Lee* (guest cohost), New York, NY
9/14/00 *Our Country* IMAX movie (films)
10/7/00 Stars Over Mississippi benefit concert, Amory, MS
10/14/00 Grand Ole Opry, Nashville, TN
10/19/00 IBMA Bluegrass Awards, Louisville, KY
10/25/00 *Bette* TV episode airs (special guest)
11/16/00 International Association of Amusement Parks Event, Atlanta, GA
11/23/00 *Grand Ole Opry 75th Birthday Special* (airs)
12/6/00 The Spirit Of Music Awards Dinner, New York, NY
12/16 to 12/17/2000 Dollywood Smoky Mountain Christmas, Pigeon Forge, TN

2001

1/8/01 *Top of the Pops 2*, UK TV appearance (via satellite)
1/18/01 *Austin City Limits* (films; PBS), Austin, TX
1/23/01 *The Today* show, New York, NY
1/24/01 Little Sparrow Tower Records signing, New York, NY
1/30/01 *The Late Show with David Letterman*, New York, NY
1/31/01 Joe's Pub (private media performance), New York, NY
2/1/01 *Late Night with Conan O'Brien*, New York, NY
2/16/01 *Wake Up with Wogan!*, London, England
2/16/01 *Little Sparrow* HMV signing, London, England
2/17/01 *The Parkinson Show*, London, England
2/19/01 *This Morning*, London, England
2/19/01 *Open House*, London, England
2/20/01 Grammy Awards, Los Angeles, CA
2/23/01 *Little Sparrow* Tower Records signing, Los Angeles, CA

2/23/01 *So Graham Norton*, UK TV appearance (airs), London, England
2/27/01 *The Tonight Show with Jay Leno*, Los Angeles, CA
3/24/01 *Austin City Limits* (airs; PBS)
4/6/01 Dolly Parton's Stampede special appearance, Myrtle Beach, SC
4/6 to 4/8/01 Dollywood Grand Opening, Pigeon Forge, TN
4/27/01 MerleFest press conference, Charlotte, NC
4/28/01 MerleFest, Charlotte, NC
5/2/01 *Kennedy Center Honors Lily Tomlin* (films), Washington, DC
5/19/01 Dollywood's Splash Country Grand Opening, Pigeon Forge, TN
Summer 2001 *Frank McClusky C.I.* movie (films)
6/13/01 CMT MWL, Nashville, TN
6/14/01 Songwriters Hall of Fame (induction), New York, NY
7/5/01 *LK Today*, UK television appearance (airs)
7/13/01 *Late Night with Conan O'Brien*, New York, NY
9/14/01 *Graham Norton at Dollywood* (films), Pigeon Forge, TN
12/15 to 12/16/01 Dollywood Smoky Mountain Christmas, Pigeon Forge, TN

2002

2/17/02 American Association of School Administrators, San Diego, CA
4/5 to 4/7/02 Dollywood Grand Opening, Pigeon Forge, TN
4/11/02 Dolly Parton's Stampede (Imagination Library Event), Myrtle Beach, SC
4/25/02 *SPRUNG TV* (Sweden TV; remote)
5/5/02 Country Music Hall of Fame Medallion Ceremony, Nashville, TN
5/17/02 Citizen's Scholarship of America Benefit Concert, Minneapolis, MN
7/1/02 *Graham Norton at Dollywood* (UK; airs)
7/1/02 *The Bob & Tom Radio Show* (in-studio visit; syndicated), Indianapolis, IN
7/5/02 The *Today* show, New York, NY
7/7/02 *The Late Show with David Letterman*, New York, NY
7/9/02 *The View*, New York, NY
7/9/02 *Halos & Horns* signing, Virgin Megastore, New York, NY
7/10/02 Irving Plaza, New York, NY
7/15/02 9:30 Club, Washington, DC
7/20/02 Grand Ole Opry, Nashville, TN
7/21/02 Ryman Auditorium, Nashville, TN
7/25/02 Earthlink Center Stage, Atlanta, GA
7/29/02 House of Blues, New Orleans, LA
8/3/02 Grenada Theater, Dallas, TX
8/6/02 KZLA/Los Angeles (in-studio visit), Los Angeles, CA
8/7/02 House of Blues, Los Angeles, CA
8/8/02 *The Tonight Show with Jay Leno*, Los Angeles, CA
8/13/02 Paramount Theater, Denver, CO
8/17/02 House of Blues, Chicago, IL
8/21/02 Lowell Auditorium, Lowell, MA
8/28/02 The Pageant, St. Louis, MO
8/31/02 Uptown Theater, Kansas City, MO
9/4/02 Washington Pavilion for the Arts and Science, Sioux City, SD
10/4/02 *TROS* (TV show), Amsterdam, Netherlands
10/5/02 *The Jonathan Ross Show*, London, England
10/7/02 *The Tom Morton Show*, London, England
10/8/02 *The Frank Skinner Show*, London, England
10/9/02 GMTV, Dublin, Ireland
10/9/02 *Halos & Horns* signing, HMV Dublin, Dublin, Ireland
10/10/02 *The Breakfast Show*, London, England
10/10/02 Gloria Hunningford Open House, London, England
10/11/02 GMTV, London, England
10/11/02 *The TV Show*, Amsterdam, Netherlands
10/12/02 *BINGO LOTTO!*, Stockholm, Sweden
10/13/02 *Stina Dabrowski Presents*, Stockholm, Sweden
10/14/02 *The Des O'Connor Show*, London, England
10/15/02 Tennessee Film Commission Special Performance, Los Angeles, CA
10/24/02 River Bend Centre, *Stars Over Texas* (CMT Special taping), Austin, TX
11/6/02 CMA Awards, Nashville, TN
11/8/02 *Halos & Horns* signing, HMV London, London, England
11/9/02 *Breakfast Television*, London, England
11/15/02 Bridgewater Hall, Manchester, England
11/18 to 11/19/02 Hammersmith Apollo, London, England
11/22/02 *The Gerry Kelly Show*, Belfast, Northern Ireland
11/23/02 Waterfront Hall, Belfast, Northern Ireland
11/26/02 GMTV, Glasgow, Scotland
11/26 to 11/27/02 Clyde Auditorium, Glasgow, Scotland
11/29/02 The Point, Dublin, Ireland
12/1/02 *Good Morning Sunday*, London, England
12/13 to 12/14/02 Dollywood Smoky Mountain Christmas, Pigeon Forge, TN

2003

3/3/03 *Stars Over Texas* (CMT TV special airs)
3/11/03 Lifetime Achievement—Tennessee Arts Commission, Nashville, TN
3/19/03 50th Anniversary of WIVK, Knoxville Convention Center, Knoxville, TN
4/4 to 4/5/03 Dollywood Grand Opening, Pigeon Forge, TN
4/5/03 Junior Achievement Hall of Fame Honors, Pigeon Forge, TN
5/4/03 Country Music Hall of Fame Medallion Ceremony, Nashville, TN
6/3/03 *MWL Star* (CMT TV special airs)
6/9/03 *9 to 5* Reunion Special Event, Los Angeles, CA
6/18/03 *Good Morning America* (via satellite), Orlando, FL
6/18/03 Dolly Parton's Stampede Grand Opening, Orlando, FL
6/20/03 *The Early Show* (via satellite; CBS), Pigeon Forge, TN
6/20/03 Dollywood KidsFest, Pigeon Forge, TN
6/22/03 National PTA Conference, Charlotte, NC
7/2/03 White House appearance (VIP reception), Washington, DC
7/2/03 National Zoo appearance (American Bald Eagle Foundation), Washington, DC
7/3/03 *Larry King Live*, Washington, DC
7/4/03 *A Capitol Fourth* (live concert; PBS), Washington, DC
8/9/03 *The Tonight Show with Jay Leno*, Los Angeles, CA
8/23 to 8/24/03 *The John Walsh Show* (syndicated; taping at Dollywood), Pigeon Forge, TN
9/9/03 The Dove Awards, Nashville, TN
9/11/03 *The John Walsh Show* (syndicated; airs)
9/30/03 *Women Who Rock* (Lifetime; TV special films), New York, NY
10/9/03 *The Tonight Show with Jay Leno*, Los Angeles, CA
10/13/03 *The Early Show* (CBS), New York, NY
10/20/03 *The Terry & Gabby Show* (UK; via satellite)
10/22/03 *The Oprah Winfrey Show* (films), Chicago, IL
10/23/03 *Women Who Rock* (Lifetime; TV special airs)
10/26/03 *The Mark Twain Prize* (honoring Lily Tomlin; films), Washington, DC
11/1/03 *The O'Reilly Factor* (via satellite)
11/4/03 *The Oprah Winfrey Show* (airs)
11/3/03 BMI Awards, Nashville, TN
11/5/03 *The Early Show* (via satellite; CBS), Pigeon Forge, TN
11/5/03 CMA Awards, Nashville, TN
11/11/03 *CBS Sunday Morning* (airs)
11/12/03 *The Late Show with David Letterman*, New York, NY
11/14/03 *Late Night with Conan O'Brien*, New York, NY
11/28/03 *CMT Crossroads with Melissa Etheridge* (airs), Los Angeles, CA
12/12/03 Imagination Library One-Millionth Book Celebration, Pigeon Forge, TN
12/13 to 12/14/03 Dollywood Smoky Mountain Christmas, Pigeon Forge, TN

2004

3/1/04 Reading Works Awards, Vanderbilt University, Nashville, TN
4/2 to 4/4/04 Dollywood Grand Opening, Pigeon Forge, TN
4/14/04 Living Legend Presentation, Library of Congress, Washington, DC
4/21/04 CMT Music Awards, Nashville, TN
5/5/04 *MTV: The Upfront Show* (airs)
6/9/04 CMT Greatest Love Songs, Bridgestone Arena, Nashville, TN
6/18/04 Dollywood KidsFest, Pigeon Forge, TN
8/9/04 Ryman Auditorium (with Norah Jones), Nashville, TN
8/30/04 American Legion National Convention, Opryland Hotel, Nashville, TN
9/14/04 *Live & Well* CD signing (Sam's Club), Franklin, TN
9/17 to 9/18/04 *Live & Well* CD signing (Walmart), Huntsville, AL
9/24/04 Knoxville Air Base to Airplane dedication, Knoxville, TN
9/24 to 9/26/04 Dollywood Harvest Festival, Pigeon forge, TN
10/14/04 Bi-Lo Center, Greenville, SC
10/15/04 Fox Theater, Atlanta, GA
10/16/04 Grand Casino, Biloxi, MS
10/19/04 Gund Theater, Cleveland, OH
10/20/04 Schottenstein Center, Columbus, OH
10/22 to 10/24/04 Casino Rama Resort Entertainment Centre, Toronto, ON
10/26/04 Fox Theater, Detroit, MI
10/27/04 Resch Center, Green Bay, WI
10/29/04 Exel Energy Center, St. Paul, MN
10/30/04 Qwest Center, Omaha, NE
10/31/04 Savvis Center, St. Louis, MO
11/4/04 RBC Center, Raleigh, NC
11/7/04 Joel Coliseum, Winston Salem, NC
11/8/04 CMA Awards, Nashville, TN
11/9/04 Scope Arena, Norfolk, VA
11/11/04 Continental Airlines Arena, East Rutherford, NJ
11/12/04 Caesars Atlantic City Hotel & Casino, Atlantic City, NJ
11/13/04 Mohegan Sun Arena, Uncasville, CT
11/14/04 Patriot Center, Fairfax, VA
11/17/04 Pepsi Arena, Albany, NY
11/18/04 Wachovia Spectrum, Philadelphia, PA
11/19/04 Wachovia Arena, Wilkes Barre, PA
11/20/04 Sovereign Center, Reading PA
11/21/04 Bryce Jordan Center, State College, PA
12/2/04 Frank Erwin Center, Austin, TX
12/3/04 American Airlines Center, Dallas, TX
12/5/04 Toyota Center, Houston, TX
12/7/04 Caesar's Palace, Las Vegas, NV
12/8/04 Dodge Center, Phoenix, AZ
12/9/04 Arrowhead Pond, Anaheim, CA
12/10/04 HP Pavilion, San Jose, CA
12/11/04 Hilton Theater, Reno, NV
12/12/04 ARCO Arena, Sacramento, CA
12/16/04 Idaho Center, Nampa, ID
12/17/04 Rose Garden Theater of the Clouds, Portland, OR
12/18/04 Spokane Arena, Spokane, WA
12/19/04 Everett Arena, Everett, WA

2005

3/1/05 Country Radio Hall of Fame, Nashville, TN
3/15/05 Imagination Library appearance, Nashville, TN
3/19/05 *Naomi's New Morning* (TV appearance; Lifetime), Nashville, TN
3/24/05 *Miss Congeniality 2* premieres (cameo)
4/1 to 4/3/05 Dollywood Grand Opening, Pigeon Forge, TN
4/15/05 *Reba* TV show appearance airs (special guest)
4/21/05 Give Back Your Smile Gala Event to Opryland Hotel, Nashville, TN
4/23/05 Grand Ole Opry, Nashville, TN
6/8/05 CMT Greatest Duets, Bridgestone Arena, Nashville, TN
6/9/05 CMA Music Fest press conference, Nashville, TN
6/9/05 CMA Music Fest stadium appearance, Nashville, TN
6/17/05 Dollywood KidsFest, Pigeon Forge, TN
6/28/05 *The Late Late Show with Craig Ferguson*, New York, NY
7/10/05 Station Inn, Nashville, TN
8/16/05 House of Blues, Atlantic City, NJ
8/18/05 Radio City Music Hall, New York, NY
8/19/05 Mohegan Sun Arena, Uncasville, CT
8/20/05 Mann Center, Philadelphia, PA
8/23/05 DAR Constitutional Hall, Washington, DC
8/25/05 Civic Center, Portland, ME
8/27/05 Halifax Metro Centre, Halifax, NS
8/28/05 Harbour Center, St. Johns, NB
8/31/05 Corel Centre, Ottawa, ON
9/1/05 Molson Amphitheater, Toronto, ON
9/15/05 House of Blues, Myrtle Beach, SC
9/16/05 Civic Center, Tallahassee, FL
9/18/05 BJCC Arena, Birmingham, AL
9/23/05 *The Tonight Show with Jay Leno*, Los Angeles, CA
9/24 to 9/25/05 Dollywood Fall Festival, Pigeon Forge, TN
9/30/05 Gibson Amphitheater, Los Angeles, CA
9/30/05 *Larry King Live*, Los Angeles, CA
10/1/05 House of Blues, Las Vegas, NV
10/2/05 Golden Gate Park, San Francisco, CA
10/4/05 Wells Fargo Center, Santa Rosa, CA
10/6/05 The Lecture Hall, Denver, CO
10/13/05 *Good Morning America*, New York, NY
10/15/05 *Late Night with Conan O'Brien*, New York, NY
10/17/05 *The Daily Show with Jon Stewart*, New York, NY
10/19/05 *The View*, New York, NY
10/20/05 *Those Were the Days* CD signing, Best Buy, New York, NY
10/25/05 Norton Center, Danville, KY
10/27/05 GMTV (UK; via satellite)
10/27/05 Fox Theater, Detroit, MI
10/28/05 Chicago Theater, Chicago, IL
10/29/05 Veterans Memorial Coliseum, Madison, WI
10/30/05 Milwaukee Theater, Milwaukee, WI
11/1/05 Roberts Stadium, Evansville, IN
11/2/05 MARK of the Quad Cities, Moline, IL
11/4/05 Municipal Auditorium, Kansas City, MO
11/5/05 Gateway Arena, Sioux City, IA
11/6/05 Taylor Arena, Rochester, MN
11/8/05 Ford Theater, Oklahoma City, OK
11/9/05 Mabee Center, Tulsa, OK
11/11/05 Roanoke Rapids, Randy Parton Theater Opening, Roanoke, NC
11/14/05 *CBS This Morning*, New York, NY
11/15/05 CMA Awards, New York, NY
11/24/05 *The Tony Danza Show* (airs)
11/25/05 Gwinnett Center, Duluth, GA
11/26/05 House of Blues, Orlando, FL
11/27/05 Count de Hoernle Amphitheater, Boca Raton, FL
11/28/05 Ruth Eckerd Hall, Clearwater, FL
12/1/05 Nokia Live, Grand Prairie, TX
12/2/05 Frank Erwin Center, Austin, TX
12/3/05 BJCC Arena, Birmingham, AL
12/6/05 Alltel Arena, Little Rock, AR
12/8/05 Civic Center, Tallahassee, FL
12/9 to 12/10/05 Cypress Bayou Arena, Charenton, LA
12/15/05 Bobcats Arena, Charlotte, NC
12/16/05 House of Blues, Myrtle Beach, SC
12/18/05 Turning Stone Casino, Verona, NY

2006

2/15/06 Country Radio Seminar, Nashville, TN
2/21/06 *The Tonight Show with Jay Leno*, Los Angeles, CA
2/23/06 *The Ellen DeGeneres Show*, Los Angeles, CA
2/24/06 *The Late Late Show with Craig Ferguson*, Los Angeles, CA
2/27/06 Academy Awards rehearsal, Los Angeles, CA
3/4/06 Weinstein Company pre-Oscar party, Los Angeles, CA
3/5/06 Academy Awards, Los Angeles, CA
3/30/06 *9 to 5* DVD release event, Los Angeles, CA
3/31/06 The *Today* show (via satellite)
4/4/06 *The Early Show* (CBS; via satellite), Pigeon Forge, TN
4/6 to 4/8/06 Dollywood Grand Opening, Pigeon Forge, TN
5/19/06 Southern Women In Public Service Awards, Nashville, TN
6/16/06 Dollywood KidsFest, Pigeon Forge, TN
9/15/06 Dollywood Harvest Festival, Pigeon Forge, TN
9/29/06 *Hannah Montana* TV appearance (airs)
10/26/06 *Reba: CMT Giants* (TV taping), Los Angeles, CA
11/4/06 Dollywood Smoky Mountain Christmas, Pigeon Forge, TN
11/16/06 Mohegan Sun Arena, Uncasville, CT
11/18/06 Turning Stone Casino, Verona, NY
11/20/06 Casino Rama, Toronto, ON
11/21/06 Canadian Imagination Library Event, Toronto, ON
11/21 to 11/22/06 Casino Rama, Toronto, ON
12/3/06 *Kennedy Center Honors* (films), Washington, DC
12/20/06 *The Early Show* (CBS; via satellite)
12/26/06 *Kennedy Center Honors* (airs), 2007

2007

2/14/07 Grace Pavilion, Santa Rosa, CA
2/15/07 Chumash Casino Resort, Santa Ynez, CA
2/16/07 Fantasy Springs Resort Casino, Indio, CA
2/17/07 Buffalo Bill's Arena, Primm, NV
2/26/07 *The Early Show*, New York, NY
3/6 to 3/7/07 Forum Horsens, Horsens, Denmark
3/10/07 Vestlandshallen, Bergen, Norway
3/11/07 Lofbergs Lila Arena, Karlstad, Sweden
3/13/07 Hartwell Arena, Helsinki, Finland
3/15/07 ForKvall TV Show, Oslo, Norway
3/15/07 The Spectrum, Oslo, Norway
3/16/07 The Globe, Stockholm, Sweden
3/17/07 *God kveld Norge!* TV show, Amsterdam, Netherlands
3/18/07 Ijsselhalle, Zwolle, Netherlands
3/19/07 Wembley Arena, London, England
3/20/07 The Evening News Arena, Manchester, England
3/21/07 The Arena, Newcastle, England
3/23/07 Clyde Auditorium, Glasgow, Scotland
3/24/07 The Arena, Sheffield, England
3/25/07 Wembley Arena, London, England
3/27/07 The International Arena, Cardiff, Wales
3/28/07 NEC Arena, Birmingham, England
3/30/07 The Odyssey Arena, Belfast, Northern Ireland
4/2/07 The Point, Dublin, Ireland
4/3/07 The Odyssey Arena, Belfast, Northern Ireland
4/14 to 4/15/07 Dollywood Grand Opening, Pigeon Forge, TN
4/17/07 BMI Awards, Las Vegas, NV
5/10 to 5/12/07 Fallsview Casino Resort, Niagara Falls, ON
5/19/07 Grand Ole Opry, Nashville, TN
5/20/07 Smokies Stadium, Kodak, TN
5/21/07 Sevier Medical Center Groundbreaking Ceremony, Sevierville, TN
5/21/07 Dolly Parton's Stampede 20th Anniversary Event, Pigeon Forge, TN
6/15/07 Girl Scouts Dedication Patch Ceremony, Pigeon Forge, TN
6/16 to 6/17/07 Dollywood KidsFest, Pigeon Forge, TN
6/20/07 ACM Honors, Nashville, TN
8/23/07 *Backwoods Barbie* album preview party, Los Angeles, CA
9/14/07 Dollywood Harvest Festival, Pigeon Forge, TN
9/20/07 WGAR/Cleveland Radio (in-studio visit), Cleveland, OH
9/25/07 *After Midnite with Blair Garner* (radio in-studio; syndicated), Los Angeles, CA
9/25/07 *Dancing with the Stars* (airs)
9/26/07 Dollywood Harvest Festival, Pigeon Forge, TN
10/1/07 WIVK/Knoxville Radio (in-studio visit), Knoxville, TN
10/2/07 WQYK/Tampa Radio (in-studio visit), Tampa, FL
11/8/07 Woodrow Wilson Award for Public Service, Nashville, TN
11/19/07 WKSF/Asheville Radio (in-studio visit), Asheville, NC
11/21/07 WXTU/Philadelphia Radio (in-studio visit), Philadelphia, PA
11/22/07 Macy's Thanksgiving Day Parade, New York, NY
12/5/07 Imagination Library UK Launch Event, London, England
12/5/07 Magna Science & Adventure Park (Imagination Library), Rotherham, England
12/7/07 *The Shaun Keveany Show*, London, England

2008

3/28/08 The Roxy, Los Angeles, CA
3/30/08 Park West, Chicago, IL
4/1/08 *American Idol* (airs)
4/2/08 Highline Ballroom, New York, NY
4/11 to 4/13/08 Dollywood Season Opening, Pigeon Forge, TN
4/22/08 Benedum Center, Pittsburgh, PA
4/23/08 Hershey Theatre, Hershey, PA
4/25/08 Mohegan Sun Arena, Uncasville, CN
4/26/08 Broome County Veterans Memorial Arena, Binghamton, NY
4/28/08 Patriot Center, Fairfax, VA
4/29/08 Fox Theater, Atlanta, GA
5/1/08 Radio City Music Hall, New York, NY
5/3/08 Borgata Arena, Atlantic City, NJ
5/5/08 Opera House, Boston, MA
5/7/08 Northrup Auditorium, Minneapolis, MN
5/8 to 5/9/08 Chicago Theater, Chicago, IL
5/11/08 Nokia Live, Dallas, TX
6/13/08 Stockholm Olympic Stadium, Stockholm, Sweden
6/14/08 Malmo Stadium, Malmo, Sweden
6/15/08 Viborg Stadium, Viborg, Denmark
6/17/08 Sor Arena, Kristiansand, Norway
6/19/08 Rotterdam Ahoy, Rotterdam, Netherlands
6/21/08 Live at the Marquee, Cork, Ireland
6/22/08 Nowlan Park, Kilkenny, Ireland
6/24 to 6/25/08 Odyssey Arena, Belfast, Northern Ireland
6/27/08 SECC, Glasgow, Scotland
6/28/08 Manchester Evening News Arena, Manchester, England
6/29/08 SECC, Glasgow, Scotland
7/1/08 Trent FM Arena, Nottingham, England
7/2/08 National Indoor Arena, Birmingham, England
7/4/08 Cardiff International Arena, Cardiff, Wales
7/5 to 7/6/08 The O2 Arena, London, England
7/15/08 *9 to 5: The Musical* Broadway press conference, New York, NY
8/1/08 Humphrey's Concert By The Sea, San Diego, CA
8/3/08 The Greek Theatre, Los Angeles, CA
8/4/08 ARCO Arena, Sacramento, CA
8/5/08 Hearst Greek Theater, Berkeley, CA
8/7/08 Theater Of The Clouds, Portland, OR
8/8/08 WaMu Theater, Seattle, WA
8/10/08 Opera House, Denver, CO
8/11/08 Qwest Center, Omaha, NE
8/13/08 DTE Energy Music Theatre, Detroit, MI
8/14/08 Fox Theatre, St. Louis, MO
8/16 to 8/17/08 Dollywood Summer Fest, Pigeon Forge, TN
9/9/08 *9 to 5: The Musical* Los Angeles premiere, Los Angeles, CA
9/11/08 National Assembly of State Arts Agencies, keynote speaker, Chattanooga, TN
9/19/08 *The Tonight Show with Jay Leno*, Los Angeles, CA

continued

0/22/08 *The Ellen DeGeneres Show,* Los Angeles, CA
0/2/08 WSIX/Nashville In-Studio Visit, Nashville, TN
0/2 to 10/3/08 Dollywood Harvest Festival, Pigeon Forge, TN
0/17/08 Mizner Park Amphitheater, Boca Raton, FL
0/18/08 UCF Arena, Orlando, FL
0/20/08 Ruth Eckerd Hall, Clearwater, FL
0/21/08 Veterans Memorial Arena, Jacksonville, FL
0/24/08 Chastain Park, Atlanta, GA
0/25/08 Brock Auditorium, Richmond, KY
0/26/08 Louisville Palace, Louisville, KY
1/1/08 Providence Performing Arts Center, Providence, RI
1/2/08 MGM Foxwoods Casino, Mashantucket, CT
1/5/08 BRC Center, Raleigh, NC
1/6/08 Constant Convocation Center, Norfolk, VA
1/7/08 Sovereign Center, Reading, PA
1/9 to 11/10/08 Casino Rama, Toronto, ON
1/13/08 MTS Centre, Winnipeg, MB
1/14/08 Saskatoon Credit Union Centre, Saskatoon, SK
1/17/08 Riverside Theater, Milwaukee, WI
1/18/08 Resch Center, Green Bay, WI
1/19/08 The Civic Center, Des Moines, IA
1/30/08 Dollywood Smoky Mountain Christmas, Pigeon Forge, TN

2009

2/2/09 Gospel Music Hall of Fame, Nashville, TN
2/2/09 Wildhorse Saloon, Kellie Pickler Benefit, Nashville, TN
2/9/09 *The Alan Titchmarsh Show* (UK; airs)
2/10/09 National Harbor, Temple Hills, MD
2/10/09 Press Club, Washington, DC
3/6/09 Rotary Club Convention—Imagination Library Event, Atlanta, GA
3/9/09 *33 Variations* premiere at Eugene O'Neill Theatre, New York, NY
3/27 to 3/29/09 Dollywood Grand Opening, Pigeon Forge, TN
3/31/09 Dolly Parton Unplugged (330 Sessions; CMT taping), Nashville, TN
4/13/09 *9 to 5: The Musical* preview appearance, New York, NY
4/22/09 The *Today* show, New York, NY
4/29/09 *The Late Show with David Letterman,* New York, NY
4/30/09 *9 to 5: The Musical* Broadway premiere, New York, NY
5/5/09 *9 to 5: The Musical* press day, New York, NY
5/6/09 Meet the Nominees TONY Awards junket at the Millennium Broadway Hotel, New York, NY
5/8/09 University of Tennessee Commencement Address, Knoxville, TN
5/15/09 Imagination Library Appearance, United Way, Detroit, MI
6/5/09 The Palm Restaurant Mural Unveiling, New York, NY
6/7/09 *60 Minutes* (airs)
6/7/09 The TONY Awards, New York, NY
6/13 to 6/14/09 Dollywood KidsFest, Pigeon Forge, TN
6/15/09 *I Am A Rainbow* book signing at the Opry Shop, CMHOF, Nashville, TN
7/1/09 *The Joy Behar Show* (airs)
9/2/09 Great Smoky Mountain Park 75th Anniversary Event, Gatlinburg, TN
11/8/09 Music City Walk of Fame Dedication, Nashville, TN
11/9/09 Live in London DVD release press conference, Nashville, TN
11/12/09 *Good Morning America,* New York, NY
11/12/09 *The Tonight Show with Conan O'Brien,* New York, NY
11/29/09 *Fern Britton Meets . . . Dolly Parton* (UK show airs)
12/7/09 *My Gift: A Christmas Special from Carrie Underwood* (airs)

2010

1/5/10 *GAC Master Series* (airs), 2010
1/7/10 Imagination Library Nashville Public Library Book Reading, Nashville, TN
2/9/10 *The Alan Titchmarsh Show* (UK; airs)
2/12/10 The Dolly Parton Center, LaConte Medical Center Event, Sevierville, TN
3/12/10 Trinkets & Treasures Store Grand Opening, Nashville, TN
3/26/10 Dollywood Grand Opening, Pigeon Forge, TN
3/26/10 *Fox & Friends* (via satellite), Pigeon Forge, TN
3/27/10 *CMT Insider* (via satellite), Pigeon Forge, TN
3/27 to 3/28/10 Dollywood Grand Opening, Pigeon Forge, TN
4/10/10 *Kenny Rogers: The First 50 Years* (films), Foxwoods, CT
5/7 to 5/9/10 Dollywood Grand Opening and *Dolly Celebrates 25 Years of Dollywood* (films), Pigeon Forge, TN
5/14/10 University of Tennessee Commencement Address, Knoxville, TN
5/17/10 *The Wendy Williams Show* (remote from Foxwoods, CT; airs)
5/21/10 *The Oprah Winfrey Show* (airs)
5/21 to 5/23/10 Dollywood Park, Pigeon Forge, TN
5/29/10 *The Marty Stuart Show* (RFD; airs)
6/2/10 Nashville Flood Relief Press Conference, Nashville, TN
6/11/10 Dollywood's KidsFest, Pigeon Forge, TN
6/29/10 *Good Morning America,* New York, NY
6/29/10 *The Late Show with David Letterman,* New York, NY
6/30/10 *Fox & Friends,* New York, NY
6/30/10 *Live! With Regis and Kelly,* New York, NY
6/30/10 *The Late Show with David Letterman,* New York, NY
7/3/10 *Dolly Celebrates 25 Years of Dollywood,* TV special (airs)
7/14/10 The *Today* show, New York, NY
8/23/10 *NBC Nightly News,* New York, NY
8/28/10 Applause Awards—TPAC, Nashville, TN
8/29/10 Dale Franklin Leadership Awards, Renaissance Hotel, Nashville, TN
9/15/10 *The Nate Berkus Show* (airs)
9/18/10 Grand Ole Opry, Nashville, TN
9/26/10 *9 to 5: The Musical* Nashville premiere, Nashville, TN
10/2/10 *9 to 5: The Musical* Atlanta premiere, Atlanta, GA
10/4/10 IEBA Convention, Nashville, TN
10/5/10 All for the Hall, Bridgestone Arena Nashville, TN
10/8/10 *9 to 5: The Musical* Charlotte premiere, Charlotte, NC
10/9/10 Grand Ole Opry, Nashville, TN
11/16/10 IAPPA Expo 2010, Orange County Convention Center, Orlando, FL
11/18/10 *Larry King Live,* New York, NY
11/25/10 *Live! With Regis and Kelly,* New York, NY
12/19/10 *Hannah Montana* TV appearance (airs), 2011

2011

1/19/11 *9 to 5: The Musical* Chicago premiere, Chicago, IL
Winter 2011 *Joyful Noise* (films)
3/25/11 *Good Morning America* (via satellite), Pigeon Forge, TN
3/25 to 3/27/11 Dollywood Grand Opening, Pigeon Forge, TN
4/10/11 GLAAD Awards, Los Angeles, CA
4/12/11 *The One Show,* London, England
4/13/11 *Lorraine,* London, England
4/14/11 *This Morning,* London, England
4/15/11 *Loose Women,* London, England
5/6 to 5/8/11 Dollywood Summer Fest, Pigeon Forge, TN
5/22/11 Country Music Hall of Fame Medallion Ceremony, Nashville, TN
5/27/11 *The Ellen DeGeneres Show,* Los Angeles, CA
6/3/11 Pirates Voyage Grand Opening, Myrtle Beach, SC
6/8/11 Marty Stuart's 10th Annual Late Night Jam, Nashville, TN
6/11/11 CMA Music Fest, Nashville, TN
6/16/11 Dollywood KidsFest, Pigeon Forge, TN
7/17/11 Thompson Boling Arena, Knoxville, TN
7/19/11 Verizon Theatre, Grand Prairie, TX
7/20/11 Sandia Casino, Albuquerque
7/22/11 *The Better Show,* Los Angeles, CA
7/22/11 *The Tonight Show,* Los Angeles, CA
7/22 to 7/23/11 Hollywood Bowl, Los Angeles, CA
7/24/11 Sleep Train Pavilion Concord, Concord, CA
7/27/11 Mystic Lakes Casino, Prior Lake, MN
7/28/11 Rosemont Theater, Chicago, IL
7/30/11 Oakdale Theater, Wallingford, CT
7/31/11 Wolf Trap Farm Park, Vienna, VA
8/2/11 Durham Performing Arts Center, Durham, NC
8/3/11 Verizon Wireless Amphitheater, Alpharetta, GA
8/20 to 8/21/11 SECC, Glasgow, Scotland
8/22/11 Capital FM Arena, Nottingham, England
8/25/11 Forum, Copenhagen, Denmark
8/27/11 Ericsson Globe, Stockholm, Sweden
8/28/11 Scandinavium, Gothenborg, Sweden
8/31/11 Echo Arena, Liverpool, England
9/2/11 LG Arena, Birmingham, England
9/3 to 9/4/11 Motorpoint Arena, Cardiff, Wales
9/6/11 Windsor Hall, Bournemouth, England
9/7 to 9/8/11 O2 Arena, London, England
9/10/11 Metro Radio Arena, Newcastle, England
9/11/11 *Strictly Come Dancing* (UK; airs), London, England
9/11/11 Manchester Evening News Arena, Manchester, England
9/12/11 Motorpoint Arena, Sheffield, England
9/14/11 O2 Arena, Dublin, Ireland
9/15/11 Odyssey Arena, Belfast, Ireland
9/24/11 Grand Ole Opry, Nashville, TN
10/7/11 Cedar Park Center, Cedar Park, TX
10/8/11 BOK Center, Tulsa, OK
10/10/11 Mississippi Coast Coliseum, Biloxi, MS
10/11/11 Verizon Wireless Theater, Houston, TX
10/14/11 Wild Adventure Amphitheater, Valdosta, GA
10/15/11 Ruth Eckerd Hall, Clearwater, FL
10/16/11 Van Wezel Performing Arts Hall, Sarasota, FL
10/18/11 Hard Rock Live, Hollywood, FL
10/28/11 How Sweet the Sound Finale with Queen Latifah at Staples Center, Los Angeles, CA
11/8/11 Perth Bushwood Dome, Perth, AU
11/11/11 InterContinental Arena, Sydney, AU
11/12/11 Adelaide Entertainment Center, Adelaide, AU
11/15/11 Sydney Acer Arena, Sydney, AU
11/19 to 11/20/11 Hunter Valley Hope Estate, Pokoblin, AU
11/22 to 11/23/11 Rod Laver Arena, Melbourne, AU
11/25 to 11/27/11 Entertainment Center, Brisbane, AU
11/29/11 Allphones Arena, Sydney, AU
12/1/11 Rod Laver Arena, Melbourne, AU
12/16/11 *Newsies* Broadway show, New York, NY
12/19/11 VH1 Divas Celebrate Soul Concert, New York, NY

2012

1/4/12 The *Today* show, New York, NY
1/9/12 *Joyful Noise* premiere, Los Angeles, CA
1/11/12 *The Late Show with David Letterman,* New York, NY
1/12/12 *AC360 with Anderson Cooper* (CNN), New York, NY
1/13/12 *The Tonight Show,* New York, NY
1/19/12 Gaylords Hotels Press Conference, New York, NY
3/23 to 3/25/12 Dollywood Grand Opening, Pigeon Forge, TN
3/26/12 TJ Martell Honors Gala, Hutton Hotel, Nashville, TN
4/2/12 Satellite media tour for *An Evening with Dolly Parton* DVD, Nashville, TN
4/28/12 *Dr. Steve* (airs)
5/11 to 5/13/12 Dollywood Summer Fest, Pigeon Forge, TN
5/26/12 Dollywood (surprise appearance), Pigeon Forge, TN
5/28/12 *The Bachelor* (airs)
6/16/12 Dollywood's Splash Country Appearance, Pigeon Forge, TN
8/12/12 An Evening with Dolly Parton Gold Certification press conference, Nashville, TN
11/26/12 *Nightline,* New York, NY
11/27/12 *Good Morning America,* New York, NY
11/27/12 *The Colbert Report,* New York, NY
11/28/12 *Live! With Kelly & Michael,* New York, NY
12/24/12 *Strombo, Geroge Stroumboulopoulos Tonight* (Canada; airs)
12/29/12 *Graham Goes to Dollywood* (UK; airs)

2013

1/10/13 *The Magazine* (Northern Ireland; airs), 2013
3/22 to 3/24/13 Dollywood Grand Opening, Pigeon Forge, TN
4/1/13 *60 Minutes* (Australia; films), Nashville, TN
4/17/13 The *Today* show (airs), Pigeon Forge, TN
5/10/13 Dollywood's Splash Country appearance, Pigeon Forge, TN
5/30/13 *PBS News Hour* (airs)
6/12/13 Biennial Homecoming press conference, Pigeon Forge, TN
8/16/13 The *Today* show (via satellite), Pigeon Forge, TN
8/21/13 DreamMore Resort Announcement, Pigeon Forge, TN
8/23 to 8/24/13 *A Country Christmas Story* TV movie films, Pigeon Forge, TN
9/27/13 *Good Morning America,* New York, NY
9/27/13 *Nightline,* New York, NY
10/19/13 *60 Minutes* (Australia; airs)
10/21/13 *The Queen Latifah Show* (airs), Culver City, CA
12/1/13 *A Country Christmas Story* TV movie premieres (cameo)
12/9/13 *Kenny & Dolly: An Intimate Conversation* (GAC; airs), 2014

2014

1/24/14 Aqua Caliente Center, Rancho Mirage, CA
1/25/14 Star of the Desert Arena, Primm, NV
1/26/14 Reno Events Center, Reno, NV
1/28/14 Coamerica Theater, Phoenix, AZ
2/7 to 2/8/14 Vector Arena, Auckland, NZ
2/11 to 2/12/14 Rod Laver Arena, Melbourne, AU
2/12/14 *Sunrise* (Australia; airs)
2/13/14 Adelaide Entertainment Centre, Adelaide, AU
2/15/14 Hope Estate Winery Amphitheater, Hope Valley, AU
2/16/14 Tamworth Entertainment Centre, Tamworth, AU
2/18 to 2/19/14 Qantas Credit Union Arena, Sydney, AU
2/21 to 2/22/14 Brisbane Entertainment Centre, Brisbane, AU
2/24/14 Cairns Convention Centre, Cairns, AU
2/27/14 Perth Arena, Perth, AU
3/21 to 3/23/14 Dollywood Grand Opening, Pigeon Forge, TN
4/14/14 *The Big Interview with Dan Rather* (AXS; airs)
4/18/14 Red Tent Women's Conference, Nashville, TN
4/27/14 *A Night in Nashville with Dolly Parton* (QVC), Nashville, TN
5/2 to 5/4/14 Dollywood Summer Fest, Pigeon Forge, TN
5/13/14 The *Today* show, New York, NY
5/13/14 *The Tonight Show with Jimmy Fallon,* New York, NY
5/14/14 *Imus in the Morning,* New York, NY
5/14/14 *The Wendy Williams Show,* New York, NY
5/22 to 5/23/14 Hard Rock Casino, Tulsa, OK
5/25/14 Harrah's Cherokee Casino, Cherokee, NC
5/27/14 EKU Center For The Arts, Richmond, KY
5/28/14 Thompson to Boling Arena, Knoxville, TN
5/30 to 5/31/14 Winstar Casino, Thackerville, OK
6/8/14 Echo Arena, Liverpool, England
6/10/14 The Odyssey Arena, Belfast, Ireland
6/11/14 The O2 Arena, Dublin, Ireland
6/14/14 Metro Radio Arena, Newcastle, England
6/15/14 GE Oil & Gas Arena, Aberdeen, Scotland
6/17 to 6/18/14 SSE Hydro Arena, Glasgow, Scotland
6/20/14 First Direct Arena, Leeds, England
6/21/14 Phones4U Arena, Manchester, England
6/22/14 LG Arena, Birmingham, England
6/24 to 6/25/14 Motorpoint Arena, Cardiff, Wales
6/27 to 6/28/14 O2 Arena, London, England
6/29/14 Glastonbury Festival, Somerset, England
7/2/14 Capital FM Arena, Nottingham, England
7/5/14 Lanxess Arena, Cologne, Germany
7/6/14 O2 Arena Berlin, Berlin, Germany
7/8/14 Forum, Copenhagen, Denmark
7/9/14 The Spectrum, Oslo, Norway
7/11/14 Ericsson Globe, Stockholm, Sweden
7/14/14 Piazza Grande, Locarno, Switzerland
9/30/14 The TN State Capitol, Event with Governor Bill Haslam, Nashville, TN

2015

3/20/15 Dollywood Grand Opening, Pigeon Forge, TN
5/1 to 5/2/15 Dolly Parton Homecoming Parade, Pigeon Forge, TN
5/10/15 My People Grand Opening at Dollywood, Pigeon Forge, TN
5/10/15 Dolly Parton Homecoming Parade, Pigeon Forge, TN
5/11/15 Dollywood Summer Fest, Pigeon Forge, TN
5/15/15 NBC Advertisers Upfront Appearance, New York, NY
Summer 2015 *Coat of Many Colors* TV movie films
7/31 to 8/1/15 Ryman Auditorium, Nashville, TN
8/8 to 8/9/15 Pure & Simple Benefit Concert at Dollywood, Pigeon Forge, TN
8/13/15 NBCUniversal Press Tour at Beverly Hills Hilton, Los Angeles, CA
12/2/15 *Coat of Many Colors* premiere, Los Angeles, CA
12/3/15 *The Talk,* Los Angeles, CA
12/7/15 *Home & Family* (airs), Los Angeles, CA
12/8/15 *The Voice,* Los Angeles, CA
12/9/15 The *Today* show, New York, NY
12/10/15 *Coat of Many Colors* TV movie premiere, 2016

2016

2/5/16 Movie Guide Awards Gala, Los Angeles, CA
3/7/16 Pure & Simple Tour press conference, Nashville, TN
3/24 to 3/27/16 Dollywood Season Grand Opening, Pigeon Forge, TN
4/3/16 ACM Awards, Las Vegas, NV
5/3/16 *CBS This Morning* (airs)
5/6/16 Dolly Parton Homecoming Parade, Pigeon Forge, TN
5/19/16 Dolly Parton's Lumberjack Adventures Grand Opening, Pigeon Forge, TN
5/21 to 5/22/16 *Home & Family* films, Pigeon Forge, TN
Summer 2016 *Christmas of Many Colors* TV movie films
6/3/16 Greensboro Coliseum, Greensboro, NC
6/4/16 Infinite Energy Center, Duluth, GA
6/5/16 Peace Center, Greenville, SC
6/8/16 Wolf Trap, Vienna, VA
6/10/16 Hard Rock Casino, Northfield, OH
6/11/16 Horseshoe Casino, Cincinnati, OH
6/12/16 Artpark Arena, Lewiston, NY
6/13/16 Pure & Simple press conference, Toronto, ON
6/15/16 Mann Music Center, Philadelphia, PA
6/18/16 Darlings Waterfront Pavilion, Bangor, ME
6/21/16 Wang Theatre, Boston, MA
6/22/16 Mohegan Sun Arena, Wilkes-Barre, PA
6/25/16 Forest Hills Stadium, Forest Hills, NY
6/26/16 PNC Bank Arts Center, Holmdel, NJ
6/28/16 Consol Energy Center, Pittsburgh, PA
7/17/16 Tanglewood Arena, Lenox, MA
7/19/16 US Cellular Center, Cedar Rapids, IA
7/20/16 Grand Casino Hickory, Hinckley, MN
7/22/16 Denny Sanford Premier Center, Sioux Falls, SD
7/23/16 Deadwood Mountain Center, Deadwood, SD
7/29/16 Sprint Center, Kansas City, MO
7/30/16 Scottrade Center, St. Louis, MO
8/2/16 Ohio State Fair, Columbus, OH
8/3/16 Allen County War Memorial, Fort Wayne, IN
8/4/16 Caesar's Windsor, Windsor, ON
8/7/16 Ravinia Festival, Highland Park, IL
8/9/16 North Center for Arts, Danville, KY
8/10/16 Ford Center, Evansville, IN
8/12/16 BOK Center, Tulsa, OK
8/23/16 *The Tonight Show with Jimmy Fallon,* New York, NY
8/23/16 *Fox & Friends,* New York, NY
8/24/16 The *Today* show, New York, NY
8/29/16 *Larry King Now* (airs)
9/9/16 Molson Canadian Amphitheater, Toronto, ON
9/16/16 Scotiabank Saddledome, Calgary, AB
9/17/16 Rogers Place, Edmonton, AB
9/19/16 Rogers Arena, Vancouver, BC
9/21/16 ShoWare Center, Kent, WA
9/22/16 Northern Quest Casino, Airway Heights, WA
9/25/16 Santa Barbara Bowl, Santa Barbara, CA
9/28/16 Vina Robles Amphitheatre, Paso Robles, CA
10/1 to 10/2/16 Hollywood Bowl, Los Angeles, CA
10/3/16 *Jimmy Kimmel Live,* Los Angeles, CA
10/16/16 Country Music Hall of Fame Medallion Ceremony, Nashville, TN
11/1/16 *The Voice* (taped performance), Los Angeles, CA
11/2/16 CMA Awards, Nashville, TN
11/3/16 *Christmas of Many Colors* press conference, Nashville, TN
11/15/16 LeConte Center, Pigeon Forge, TN
11/16/16 Von Braun Center, Huntville, AL
11/19/16 Spectrum Center, Charlotte, NC
11/22/16 *Christmas of Many Colors* Dollywood Premiere, Pigeon Forge, TN
11/26/16 Amalie Arena, Tampa, FL
11/27/16 BB&T Center, Sunrise, FL
11/29/16 Pensacola Bay Center, Pensacola, FL
11/30/16 Smoothie King Center, New Orleans, LA
11/30/16 *Christmas of Many Colors* TV movie premieres
11/30/16 *The Real* (airs)
12/2/16 American Bank Center, Corpus Christi, TX
12/3/16 Verizon Theatre, Grand Prairie, TX
12/5/16 NRG Arena, Houston, TX
12/6/16 Frank Erwin Center, Austin, TX
12/8/16 Tobin Center, San Antonio, TX
12/9 to 12/10/16 Global Events Center, Thackerville, OK
12/13/16 *My People Telethon,* Nashville, TN

2017

1/28/17 Screen Actors Guild Awards, Los Angeles, CA
4/21/17 Dolly Parton's Smoky Mountain Adventures Grand Opening, Pigeon Forge, TN
5/4/17 Dolly Parton Homecoming Parade, Pigeon Forge, TN
5/6 to 5/7/17 Dollywood Grand Opening, Pigeon Forge, TN
5/29/17 CMHOF, RCA Studio B, *Arnold's Country Kitchen . . . Take Me Home* (films)
7/26/17 *Dollywood to My People* (premiere), Pigeon Forge, TN
7/28/17 *Smoky Mountain Adventure Dinner Show* special appearance, Pigeon Forge, TN

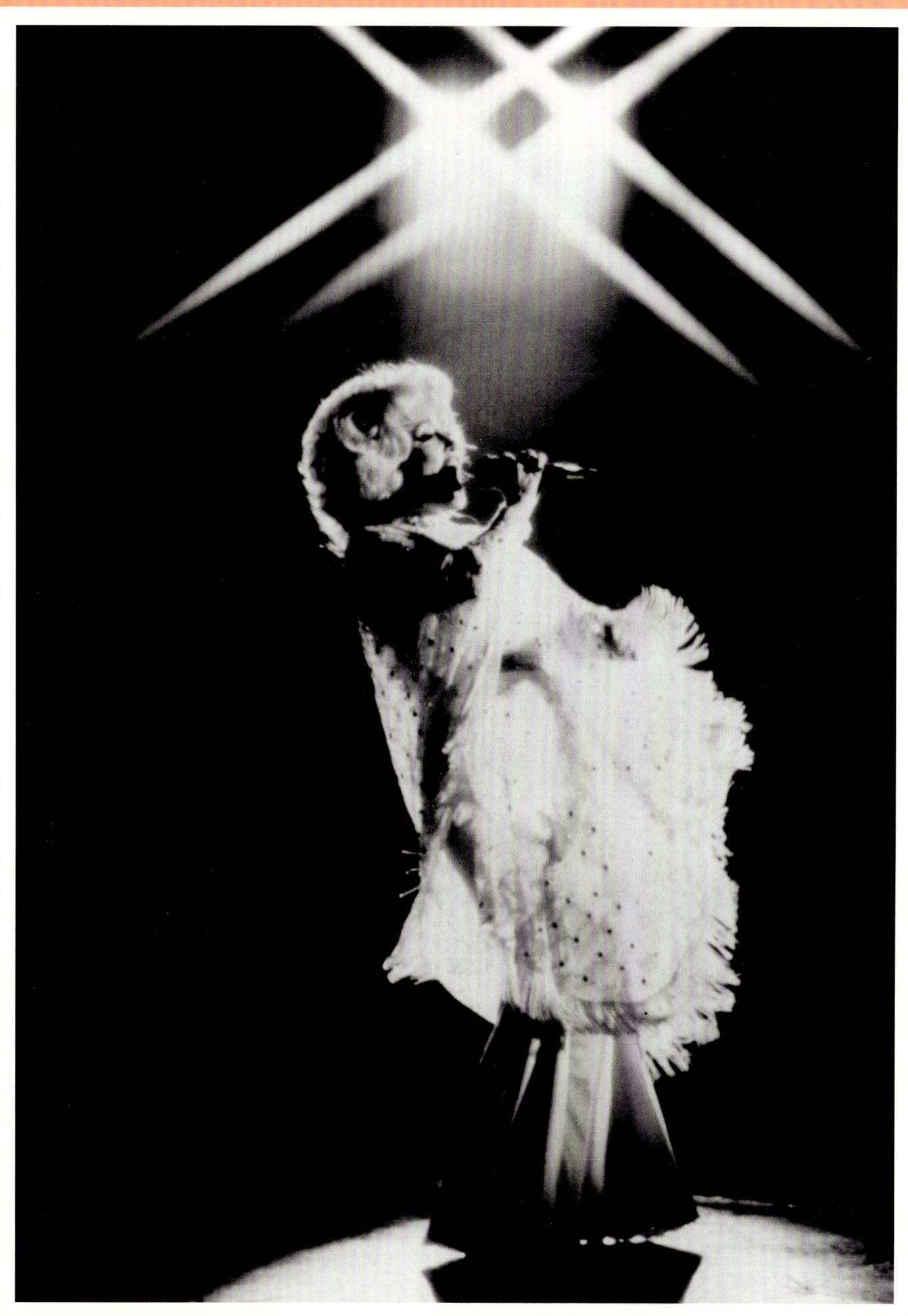

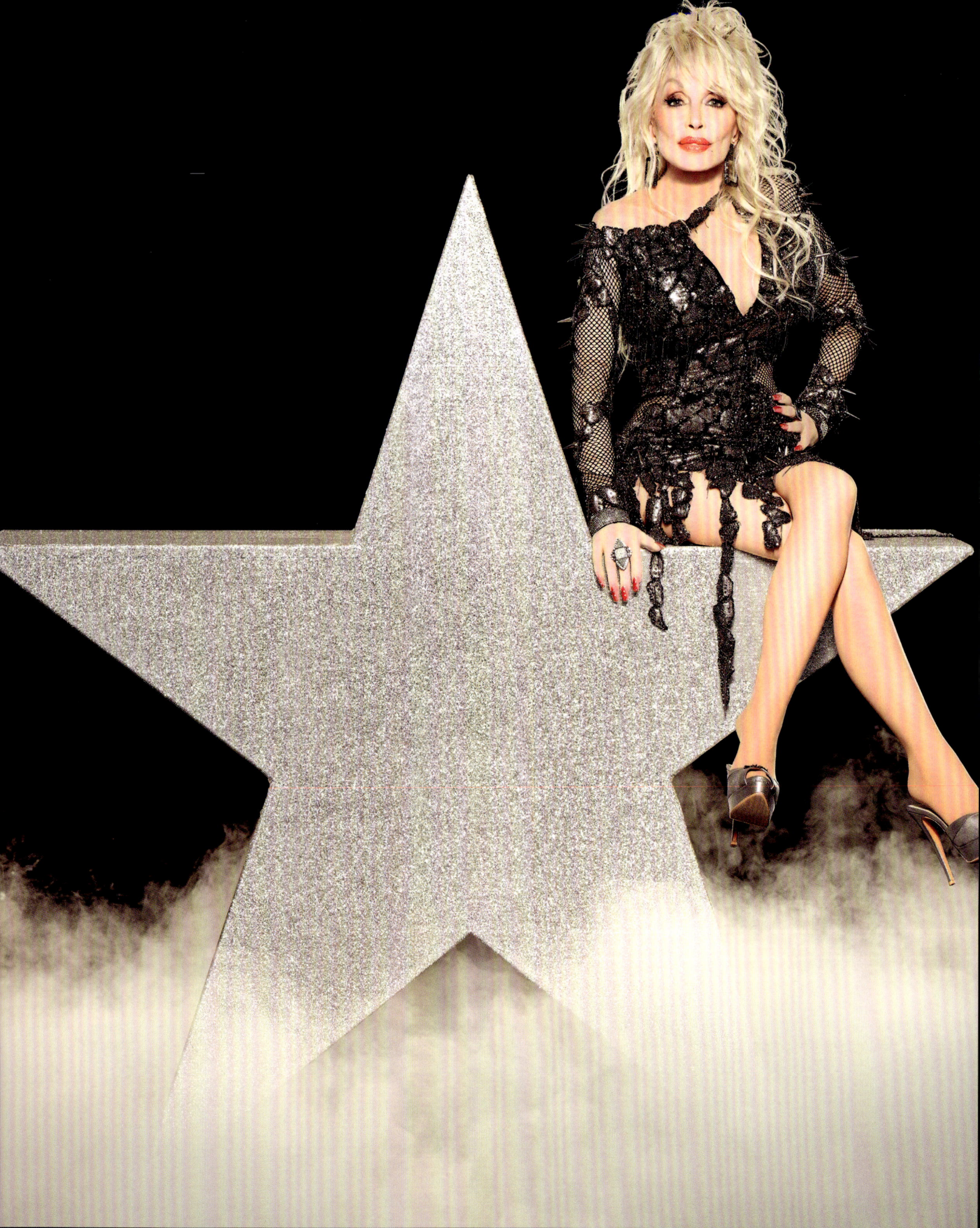

New Stages

2016 & BEYOND

2016 & BEYOND

Dolly can work any stage with two high heels and a microphone, but she's found avenues for her creativity in other venues too.

When the global pandemic hit in 2020, Dolly donated $1 million to Vanderbilt University's research efforts, contributing to the development of the Moderna vaccine.

She also built on her longtime support of reading skills through the Imagination Library and authored a series of her own bestselling books. The Rock & Roll Hall of Fame inducted her in 2022, and she responded with her gold-certified *Rockstar* album. Plus, a Thanksgiving halftime performance became one of the most-talked-about appearances of her entire career. But that wasn't everything. She also rolled out her own lines of baking goods and frozen foods, adapted her songs for orchestras, developed her life story for a Broadway musical, and more.

As long as there is a new stage to conquer, Dolly is ready for the challenge.

—TOM ROLAND

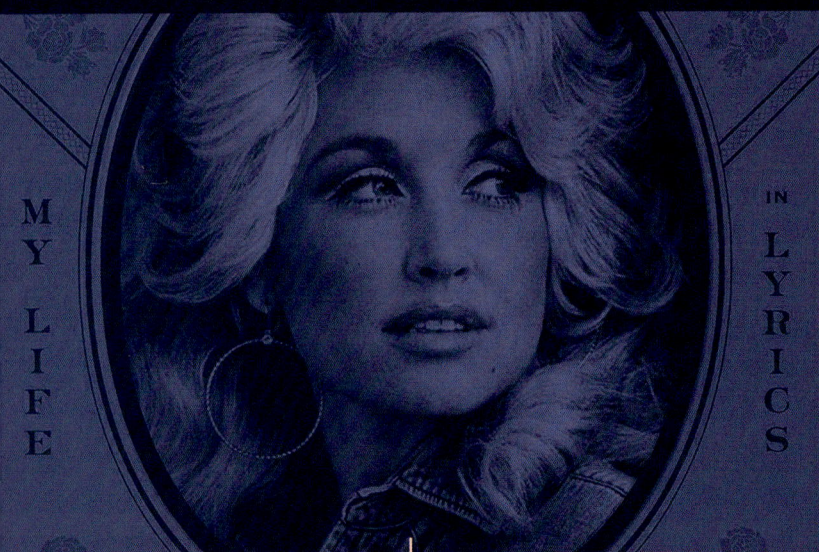

NOVEMBER 2020
Dolly releases the first book in a trilogy, chronicling her life, *Dolly Parton, Songteller: My Life in Lyrics*. It becomes a *New York Times* bestseller.

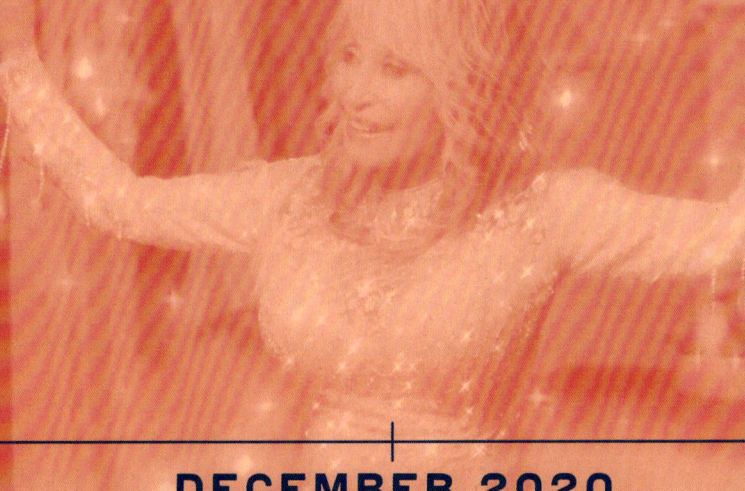

DECEMBER 2020
Dolly stars in the *Holly Dolly Christmas* TV special for CBS, based on her no. 1 holiday album, and in *Christmas on the Square* for Netflix, which wins two Emmys.

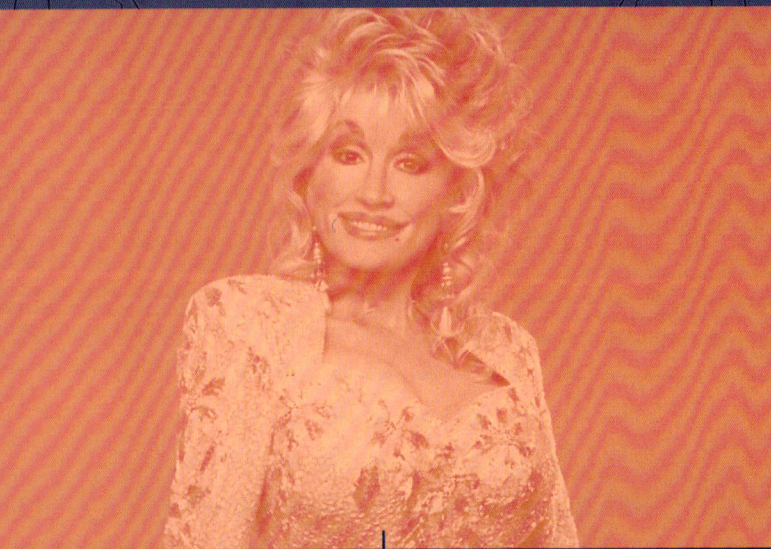

OCTOBER 2023
Dolly releases the second book in her trilogy, *Behind the Seams: My Life in Rhinestones*, which becomes a *New York Times* bestseller.

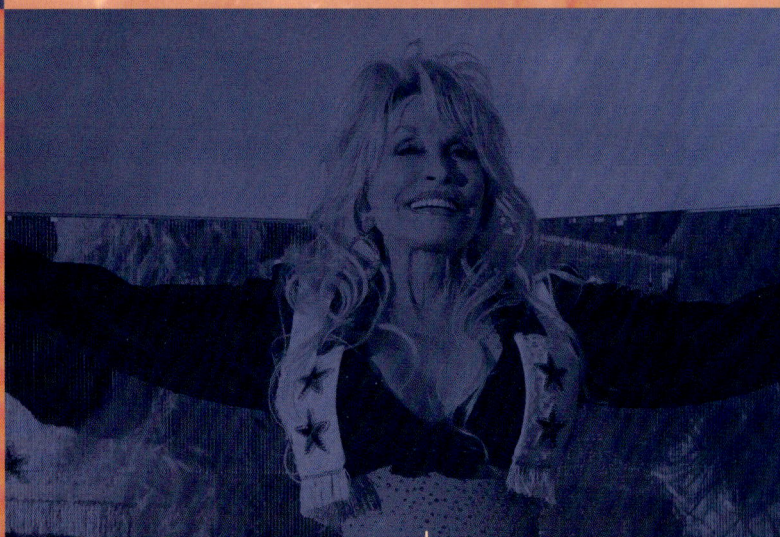

NOVEMBER 2023
Dolly performs for 42 million viewers on Thanksgiving Day during halftime of the Dallas Cowboys football game, broadcast on CBS.

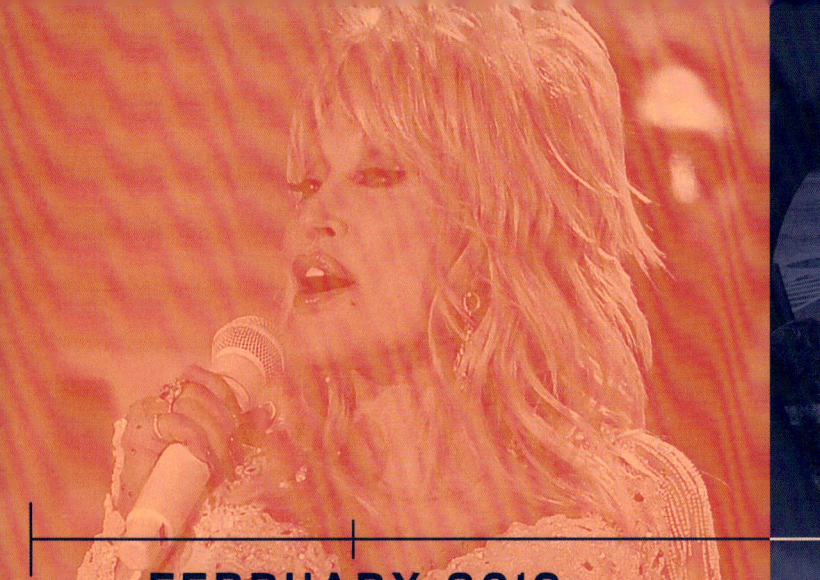

FEBRUARY 2019
Dolly is honored as the Grammy MusiCares Person of the Year. Her ten-minute performance becomes the show's highest-rated moment.

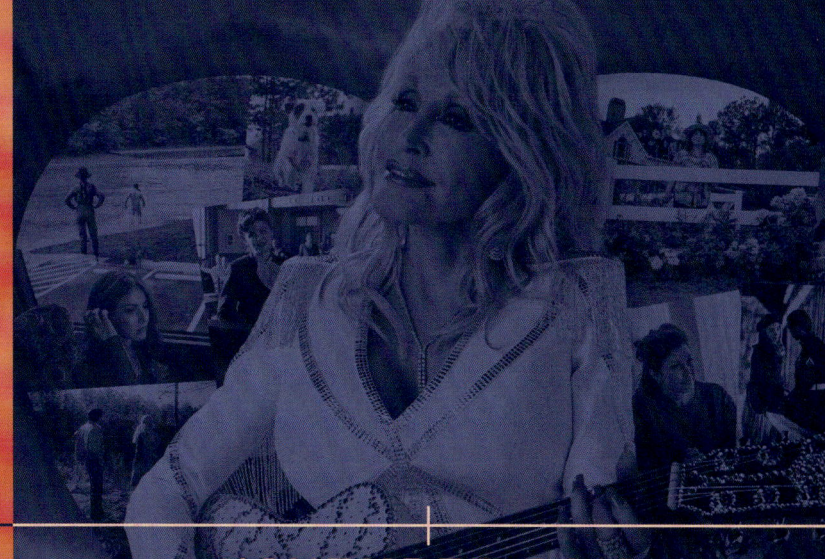

NOVEMBER 2019
Dolly produces *Heartstrings*, a miniseries of films for Netflix.

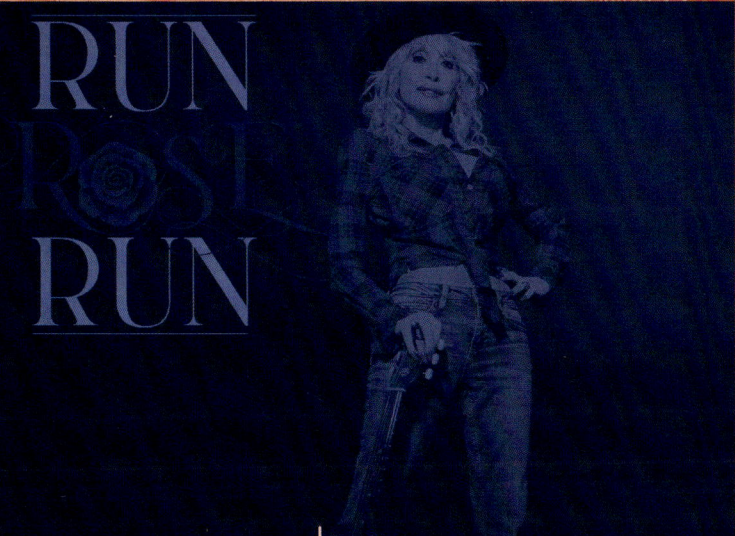

MARCH 2022
Dolly teams with James Patterson for her first novel, *Run, Rose, Run*, a no. 1 *New York Times* bestseller, and releases an accompanying album of the same name.

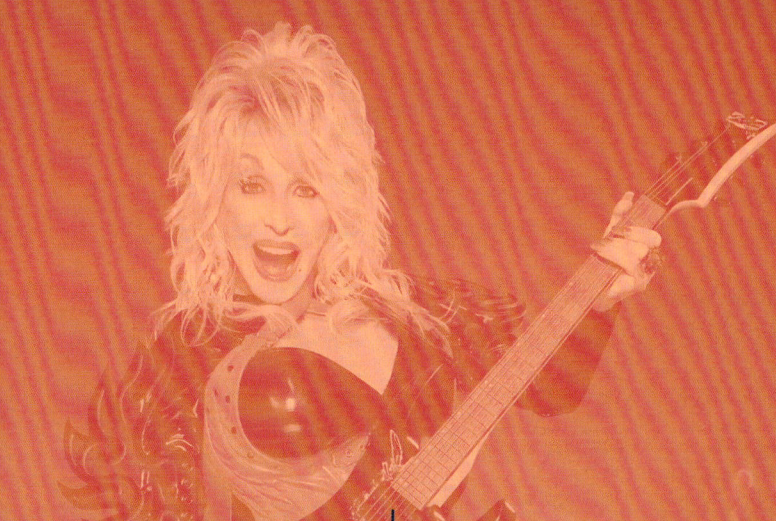

NOVEMBER 2022
Dolly is inducted into the Rock & Roll Hall of Fame, becoming the first person in the Country, Rock, Gospel, and Songwriter Halls of Fame. She releases *Rockstar* in 2023, debuting at no. 1 on six charts.

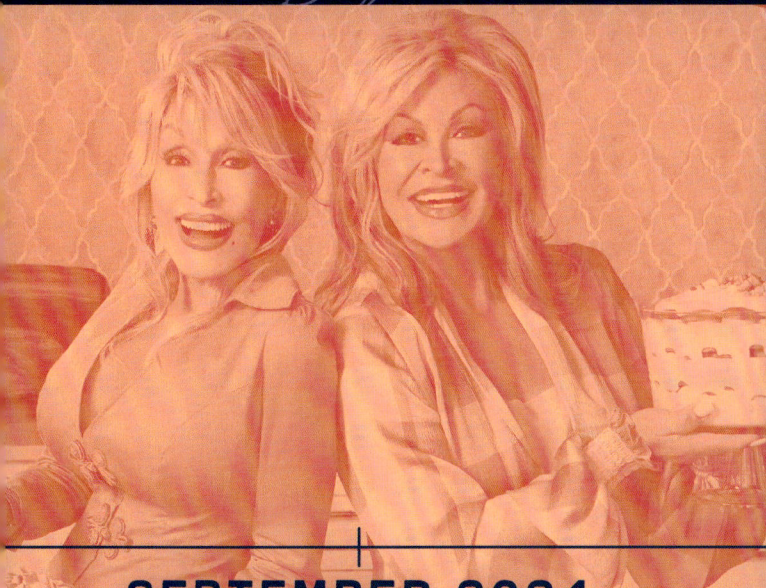

SEPTEMBER 2024
Dolly releases *Good Lookin' Cookin'* with her sister Rachel, debuting at no. 1 on the *New York Times* bestseller list.

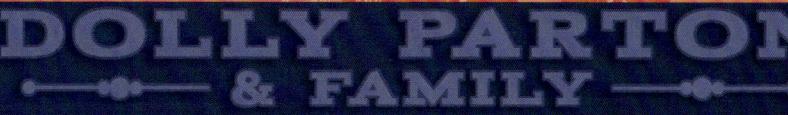
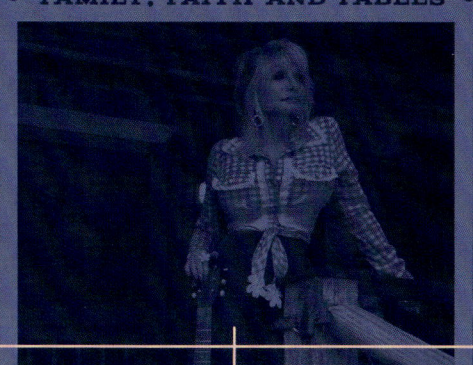
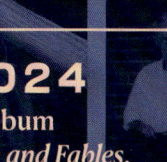

NOVEMBER 2024
Dolly releases her family album *Smoky Mountain DNA: Family, Faith and Fables*.

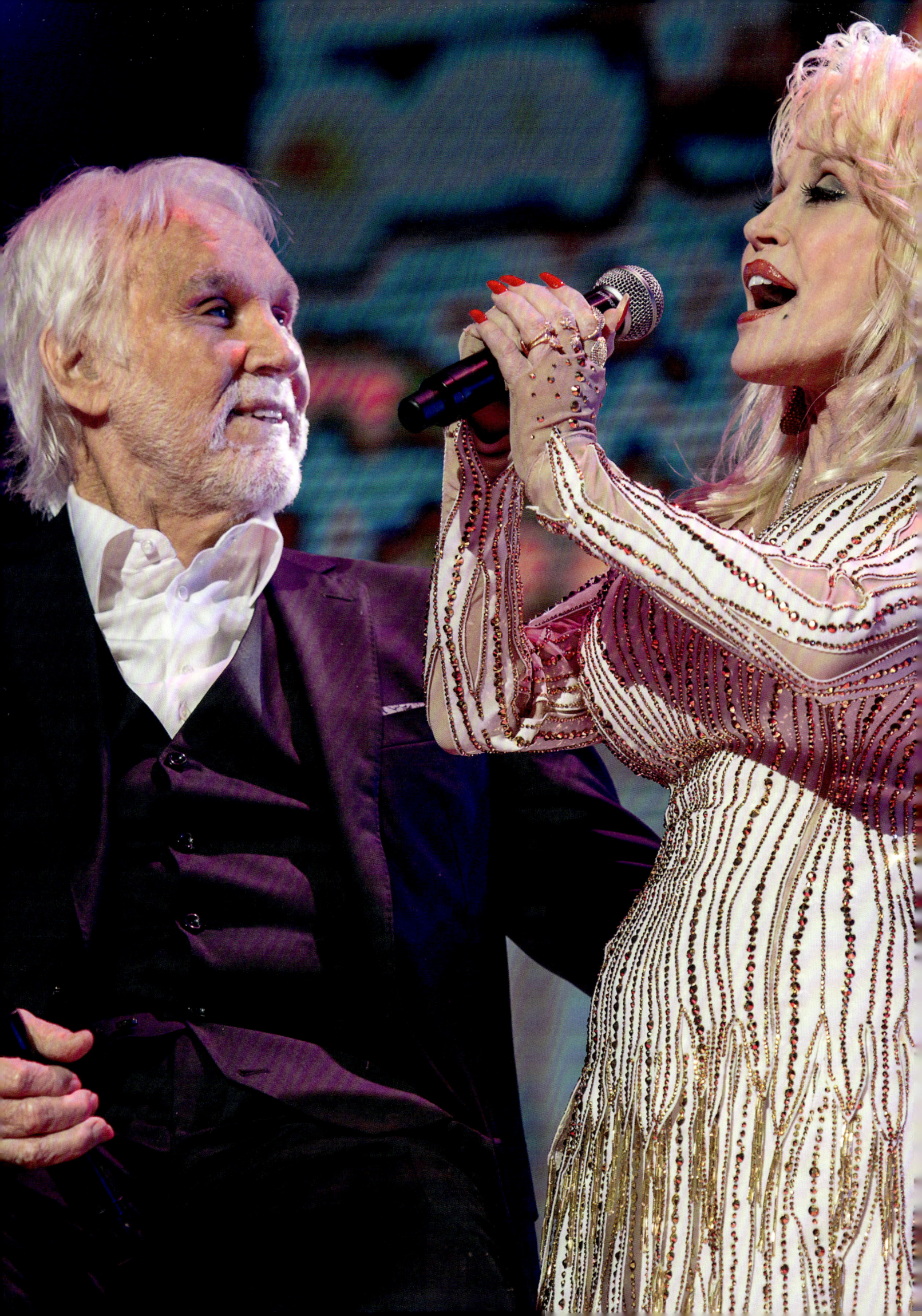

When most people think about my life on stage, they probably imagine me standing in front of a microphone singing for an audience. And they're not wrong. Those performances are at the heart of any musician's career, and they've certainly been central to mine. I treasure them all.

But something I've learned over the course of my career is that there are other "stages" available, too, if you're willing to pursue them. After the Pure & Simple Tour ended, it seemed like a good time to tackle some of those other items, so we didn't plot out another tour. We would take care of that when the sound of the bus wheels and the smell of the diesel called to me again.

Instead, I focused on other platforms and opportunities: awards-show hosting, a podcast, food lines, books, TV appearances, and concerts for special events. And at times, I invested in efforts by others to make the world a better place.

One of those first public investments after Pure & Simple came when I made a big donation to the Monroe Carell Jr. Children's Hospital at Vanderbilt in Nashville and visited with kids at the facility.

In fact, Vandy—as Vanderbilt University is often called in Music City—played a good-size role in a few of my post–Pure & Simple ventures. I'd become friends with Dr. Naji Abumrad, a surgeon and professor. Jad Abumrad, his son, had this idea to do a podcast that explored how my music connects with American culture, and it sounded so unique that I sat down with Jad beginning in November 2017 for a round of interviews. The podcast, *Dolly Parton's America,* came out in 2019, and it ended up winning a Peabody Award. Jad got the title from a University of Tennessee class in Knoxville that has taken its own scholarly approach to interpreting my place in the world. It's amusing to think that I've become an educational subject, and I so wish my parents could have witnessed that, because I think they'd be proud.

The month before I sat down with Jad, I stood on a traditional stage at Nashville's Bridgestone Arena during a concert called Kenny Rogers: All In for the Gambler. It was a tribute to Kenny as he officially retired from performing, and it boasted a huge all-star cast, including Chris Stapleton, Reba McEntire, The Judds, Lionel Richie, and Little Big Town, to name only a handful. It was one of the most emotional and meaningful things I've ever done. Many complicated feelings are involved when you know you're doing something for the last time, and sharing microphones with Kenny that night brought up a whole lot of those feelings about our musical history.

I had heard before that performance that Kenny was ill, and when we got to the song "You Can't Make Old Friends," which talks about having to leave a person behind and hoping to see them on the other side, it was all I could do to keep from getting so emotional that I couldn't finish in a professional way. In those situations, you have to find a way to put up a door or a wall to what you're feeling inside. I prefer a door because you can't get through a wall. Sometimes you need to open the door a little bit to let some of those emotions in or out. I had to close the door a few times during that show in order to not

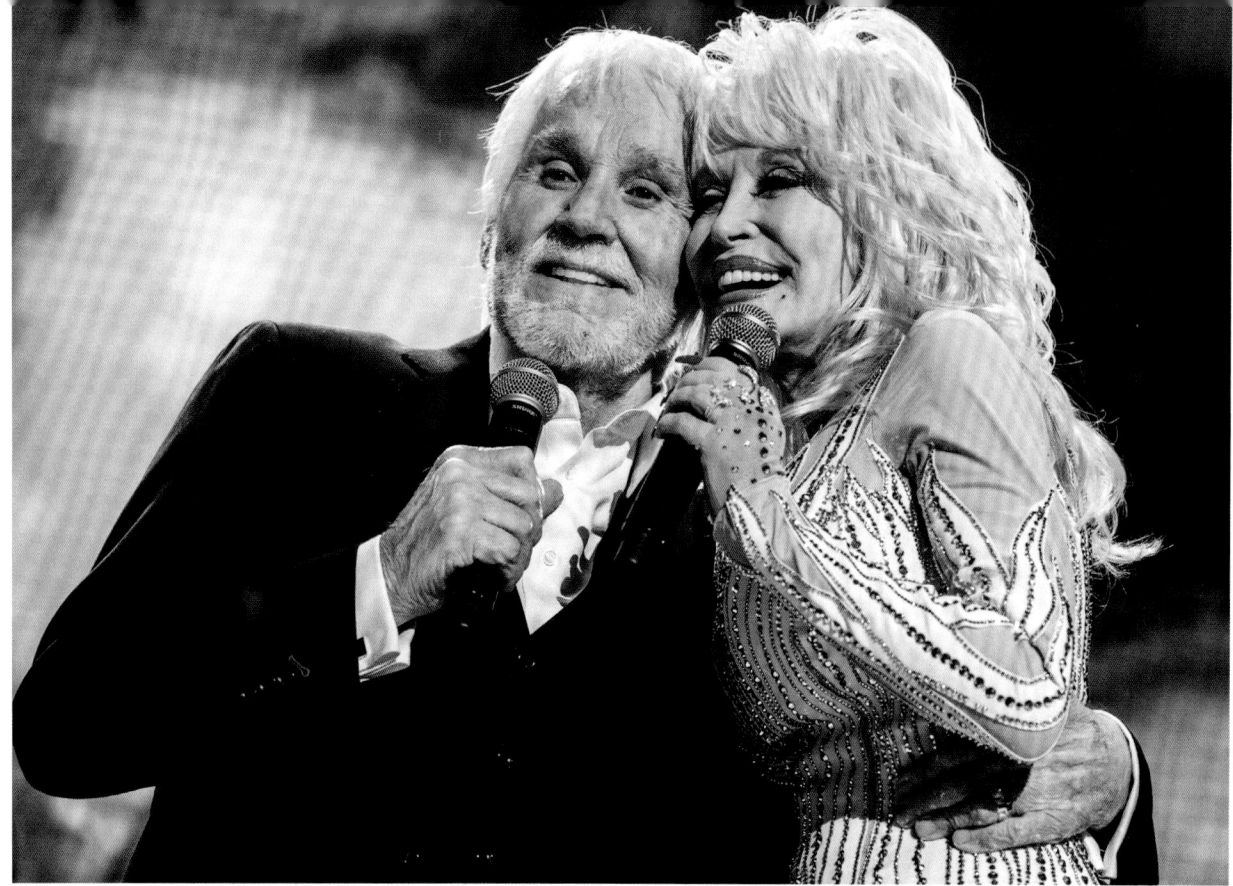

Kenny Rogers and I held it together—just barely—
during our final appearance together at the Nashville
tribute concert All In for the Gambler.

start crying. If I had, everybody would have made a big deal of it—"Dolly breaks down at Kenny's concert!"—and I don't really like that kind of stuff. Besides, it was Kenny's night. I didn't need to be taking away from any of that—I needed to be helping with that.

I serenaded Kenny with "I Will Always Love You." He and I had seen so much of the world together that the performance of that song was just as personal as the times I had sung it for Porter Wagoner. And it showed. I think you can see that door open up some, especially toward the end.

At the end, we did a mic drop and walked off stage together. That was Kenny's idea. I didn't want to do it because I know those microphones cost a fortune. Kenny said, "Who gives a rat's ass? This is the end of our show, and we're going to do it." So we did it, but I still was looking down at that mic thinking, *Oh, I hope we can still use that.*

When Kenny passed away, it was like somebody in my family had died. I grieved over him for weeks. When I think about him now, it's pleasant memories, but every once in a while, his passing will stab at me like a little knife reminding me that he's not here anymore.

The following year, my philanthropic ambitions got a fair amount of attention. The Library of Congress held an event to celebrate my Imagination Library as we reached 100 million

Star of the Show

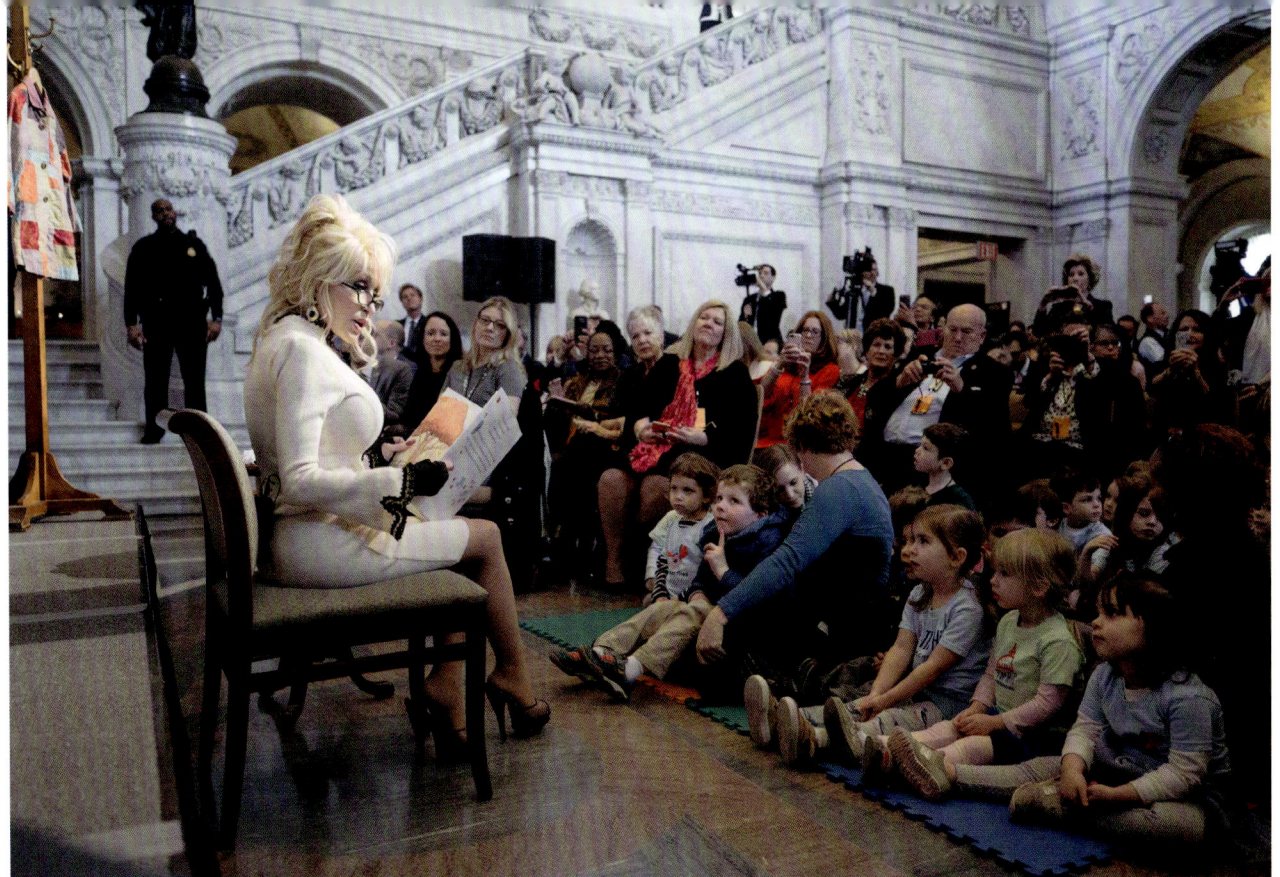

In 2018, I was honored to celebrate at the Library of Congress the 100 millionth book given away by my Imagination Library. I read to a group of kids at the event, though I bet none of them really knew they were part of a milestone moment!

books donated to children. Few things will expand a young mind more than a book. Reading gives kids the opportunity to see what the world and its people are like in places they've never been, or to visit worlds that don't even exist. Over the years, the Imagination Library grew from a statewide initiative in Tennessee to a national one, and it's been further adopted in Canada, the United Kingdom, Northern Ireland, and Australia. Jumping from 1 million to 100 million books distributed in fourteen years was incredibly rewarding. And in the next six years, the program passed 250 million books! Since the Library of Congress milestone, at least eight individual states have held their own Imagination Library events, which is a great way to make sure that parents are reminded about the program and that their children benefit from it.

Since I'm passionate about giving away books, it's not a big surprise that I'd end up writing some too. Even back in the 1970s, I was already plotting that I would become an author later on, and I've ended up writing quite a bit! There've been some children's books, including *I Am a Rainbow* and several Billy the Kid books, named after Danny Nozell's dog, my adopted goddog. I got a chance to work with James Patterson on *Run, Rose, Run,* an opportunity that came out of nowhere. It was a great experience, and when the book was released, it debuted at no. 1 on the *New York Times* bestseller list and stayed there for weeks. Then when I got a chance to write *Good Lookin' Cookin'* with my sister Rachel, it also became a

New Stages

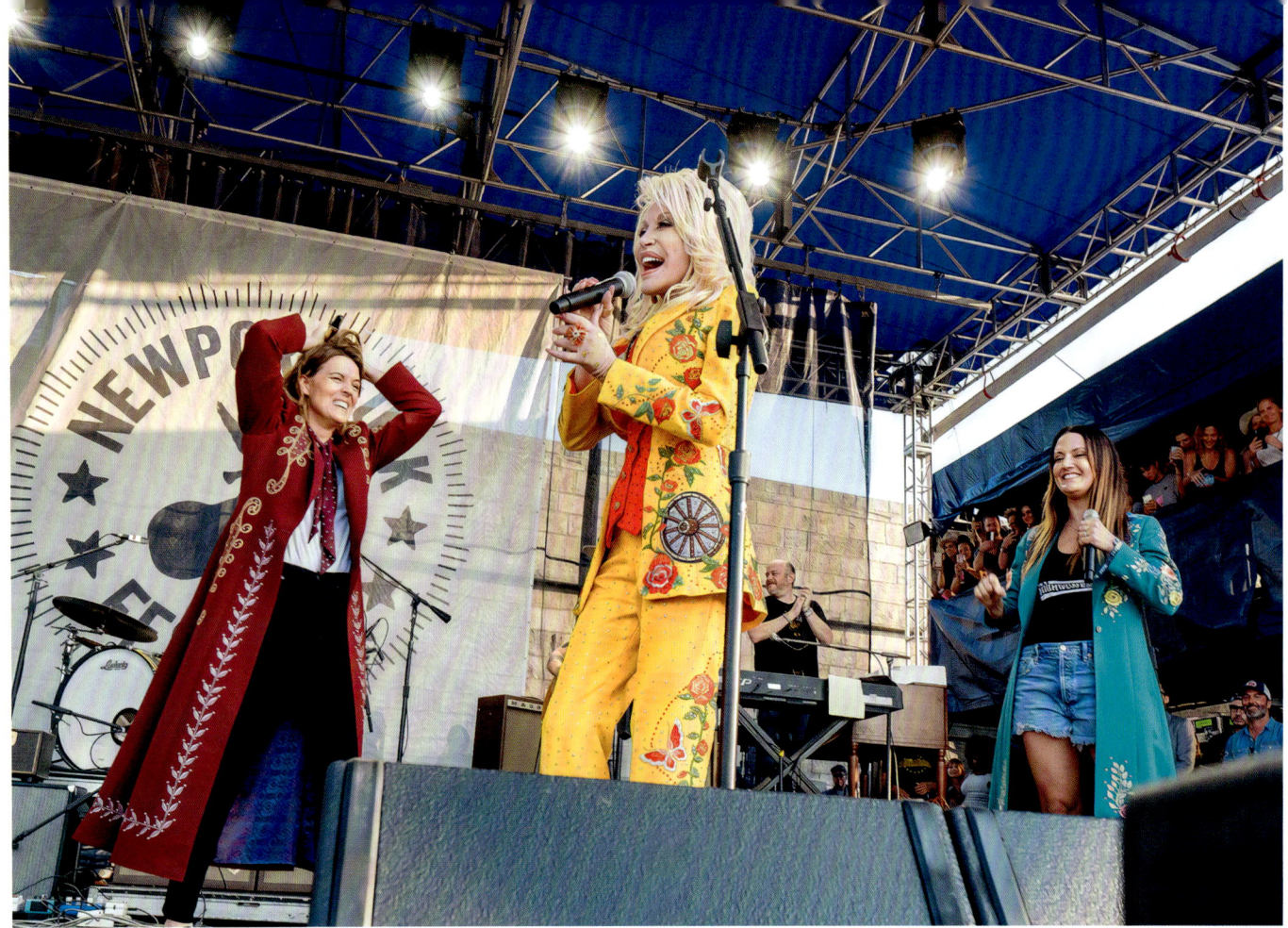

We shocked the crowd at the Newport Folk Festival when I popped out from backstage in wagon wheels and sunshine. With me are Highwomen Brandi Carlile (left) and Natalie Hemby.

New York Times bestseller. We took great pride in that cookbook, plus we had a great time writing it. It's wonderful when you get a chance to do something with someone you love.

We had *Dolly Parton, Songteller: My Life in Lyrics,* which was about my songwriting and where my songs came from, and *Behind the Seams: My Life in Rhinestones,* which looked at my fashion history. Those two, along with *Star of the Show,* have given me a chance to share a nice little trilogy of stories about my life in show business.

In May 2018, the city of Sevierville renamed a senior facility the My People Senior Activity Center and dedicated it to my parents. Around the same time, I returned to Vanderbilt to visit patients and observe the dedication of the Hannah Dennison Butterfly Garden, named after my niece, who recovered from pediatric leukemia.

Another opportunity to do something good came when I was asked to write the theme song for *Dumplin',* a movie about a girl with body-image issues. The character, Willowdean, is obsessed with Dolly Parton music, and the producers suggested I work with Linda Perry, who was producing new versions of some of my older songs for the film's soundtrack. Linda and I hit it off so well that we ended up writing five new songs for it, and one of

Star of the Show

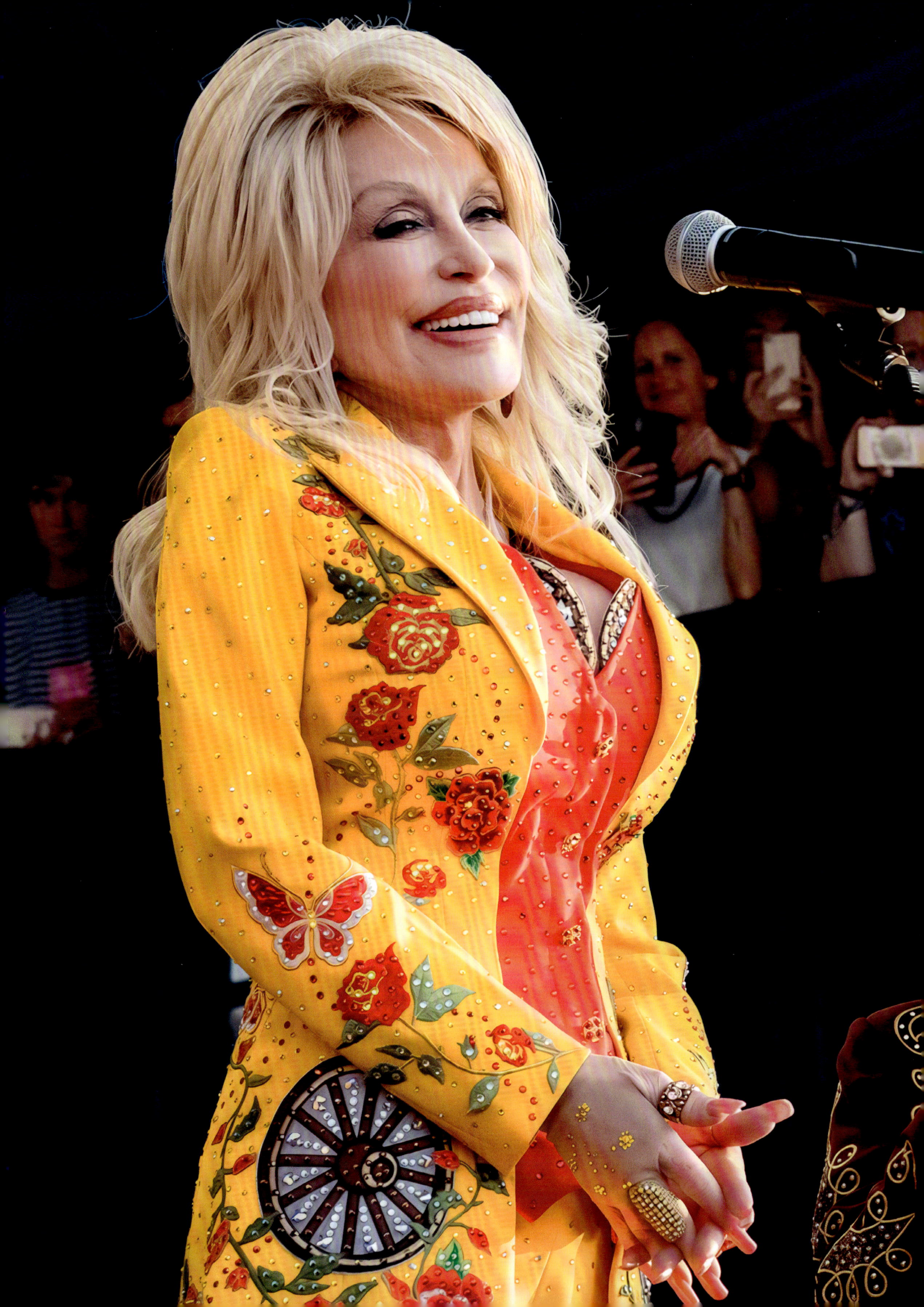

them, "Girl in the Movies," picked up Grammy and Golden Globe nominations! And speaking of the Grammys, in 2019, I loved sharing the stage with Katy Perry, Kacey Musgraves, Miley Cyrus, Maren Morris, and Little Big Town, as we sang a medley of my songs—it was a real honor.

I got another chance to lend my name to fundraising when the Recording Academy came calling. Their MusiCares program, which offers counseling and financial support to people in the music industry with health issues, named me their Person of the Year for 2019, hosting a big banquet and concert where I got to hear a lot of my fellow artists cover my songs. It was kind of like the Kennedy Center Honors but in the Los Angeles creative community instead of the Washington, D.C., setting. Garth Brooks and Trisha Yearwood sang "Old Flames Can't Hold a Candle to You," P!nk covered "Jolene," Yolanda Adams put a gospel touch on "I Will Always Love You," and I closed the night with Linda Perry on "Coat of Many Colors." In what was the most moving part of the evening—and the biggest surprise—Emmylou Harris and Linda Ronstadt, who's had progressive supranuclear palsy for a number of years, presented me with the trophy. Goofy me, I dropped the award on Linda's foot! The award broke, and the academy offered to replace it. But it was such a sentimental night that I insisted on keeping it as is so I would always remember it.

A few months later, I made a surprise appearance of my own at the Newport Folk Festival. I wore a bright yellow outfit with rhinestone roses and wagon wheels—a nod to Porter and the Wagonmasters—and I got to be one of the girls, singing with The Highwomen: Maren Morris, Amanda Shires, Natalie Hemby, and Brandi Carlile. It's really hard to keep a secret, but they did a great job. The crowd had no idea I was coming. I'm sure that some of the artists and some of the people backstage knew, but only a few. They snuck me in from the back. I arrived in a car with darkened windows, and then I quickly went into this little room to change clothes. So when they introduced me, people were genuinely surprised—all I heard was just a big, big roar. Those are the moments you never forget.

The Highwomen created some fierce harmonies for "Eagle When She Flies," and we led the whole crowd in a romp on "Jolene." Brandi and I locked arms for the final verse of "I Will Always Love You."

A few months later, I celebrated my fiftieth anniversary with the Grand Ole Opry, shooting an NBC special that included some great moments. Emmylou Harris sang "To Daddy," Lady A performed "Islands in the Stream," Margo Price did "The Seeker," and Toby Keith covered my song "Kentucky Gambler," the one that Merle Haggard made famous. Buck Trent, who was one of the Wagonmasters, backed me up when I did Porter's song "The Carroll County Accident." And I kept a few songs to do myself.

When the Opry came to me and said, "Okay, you're coming up on fifty years on the Grand Ole Opry, so we need to do a big celebration," I was surprised. I don't even feel like I'm fifty years old most days, let alone like I've spent fifty years as an Opry member! But then I do feel real proud that I've lasted that long and that I'm still around to do it, because many of

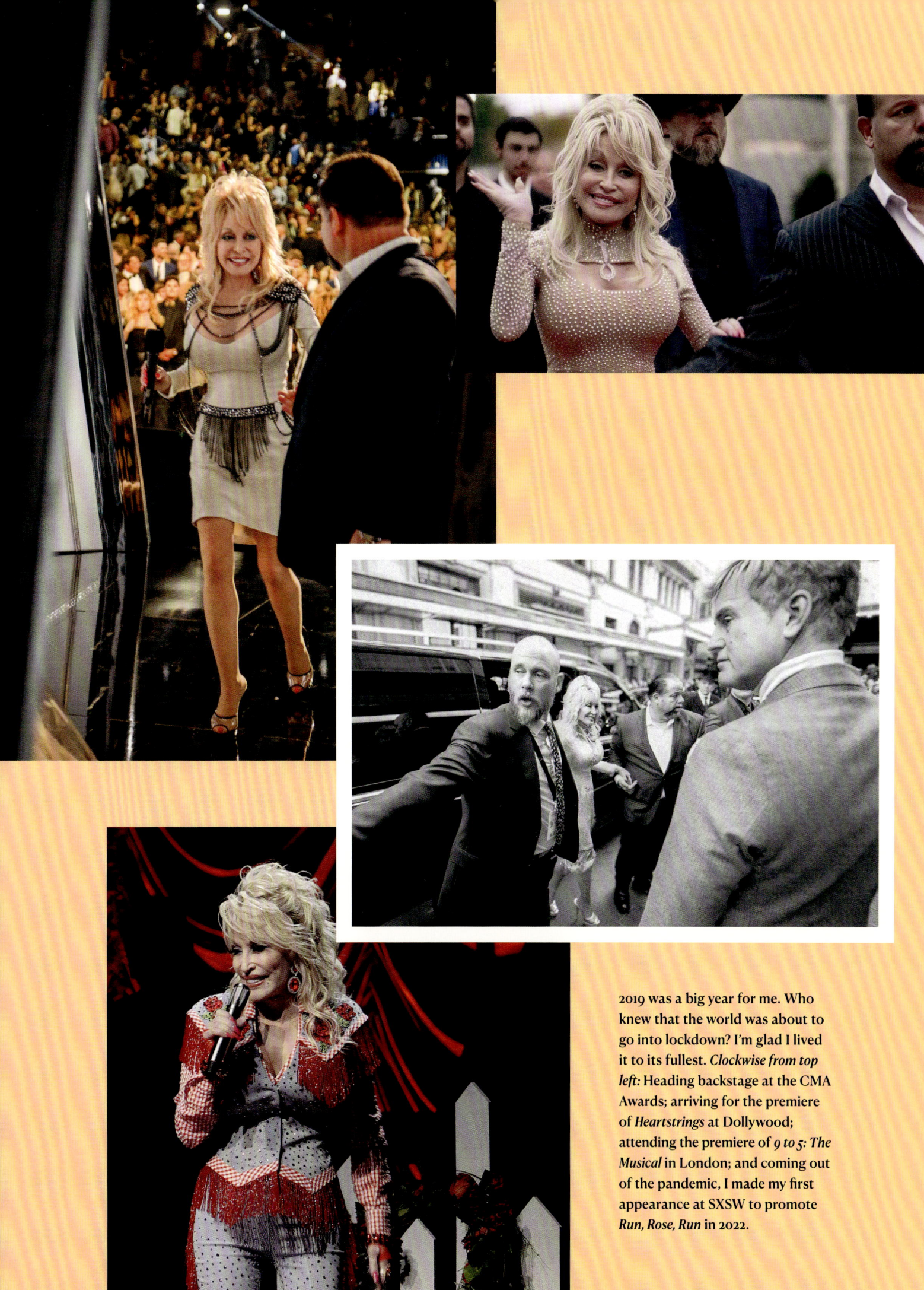

2019 was a big year for me. Who knew that the world was about to go into lockdown? I'm glad I lived it to its fullest. *Clockwise from top left:* Heading backstage at the CMA Awards; arriving for the premiere of *Heartstrings* at Dollywood; attending the premiere of *9 to 5: The Musical* in London; and coming out of the pandemic, I made my first appearance at SXSW to promote *Run, Rose, Run* in 2022.

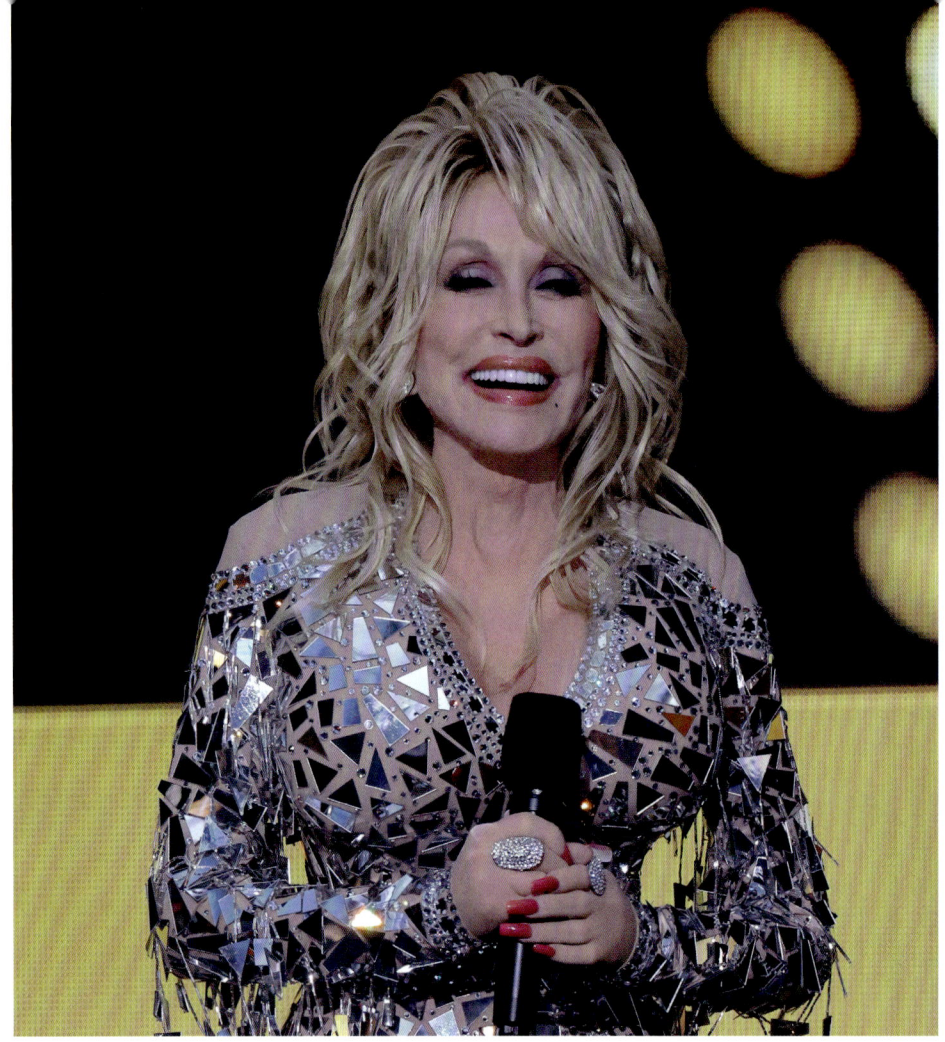

Mirror, mirror . . . who's the shiniest of them all?
That's the outfit I wore to open the show when
I hosted the Academy of Country Music Awards
in 2022. I do love to shine in the spotlight!

my friends that were on the Grand Ole Opry when I became a member are long gone. At this point, I've outlived so many people—not to mention so many plastic surgeons!

And so has my music. The same month that the Opry presented its special, Netflix introduced a series called *Dolly Parton's Heartstrings*, with each of the eight episodes presenting a storyline around one of my songs.

The global pandemic hit in 2020, and when I donated to Vanderbilt's vaccine research, I was able to turn that into a little performance, too, by singing "Jolene" as "Vaccine, vaccine, vaccine." I did the same thing a few years later with one of the hurricanes: "Helene, Helene, Helene." I sang that when I went home to make a donation for my folks in East Tennessee who'd been hard hit by Helene's winds and flooding rainwater.

Thanks to Danny Nozell's foresight, I kept making TV appearances throughout the COVID lockdown. He had built some sound stages in the Nashville area, and they make it possible to shoot TV appearances and interviews and videos without running all over the

Star of the Show

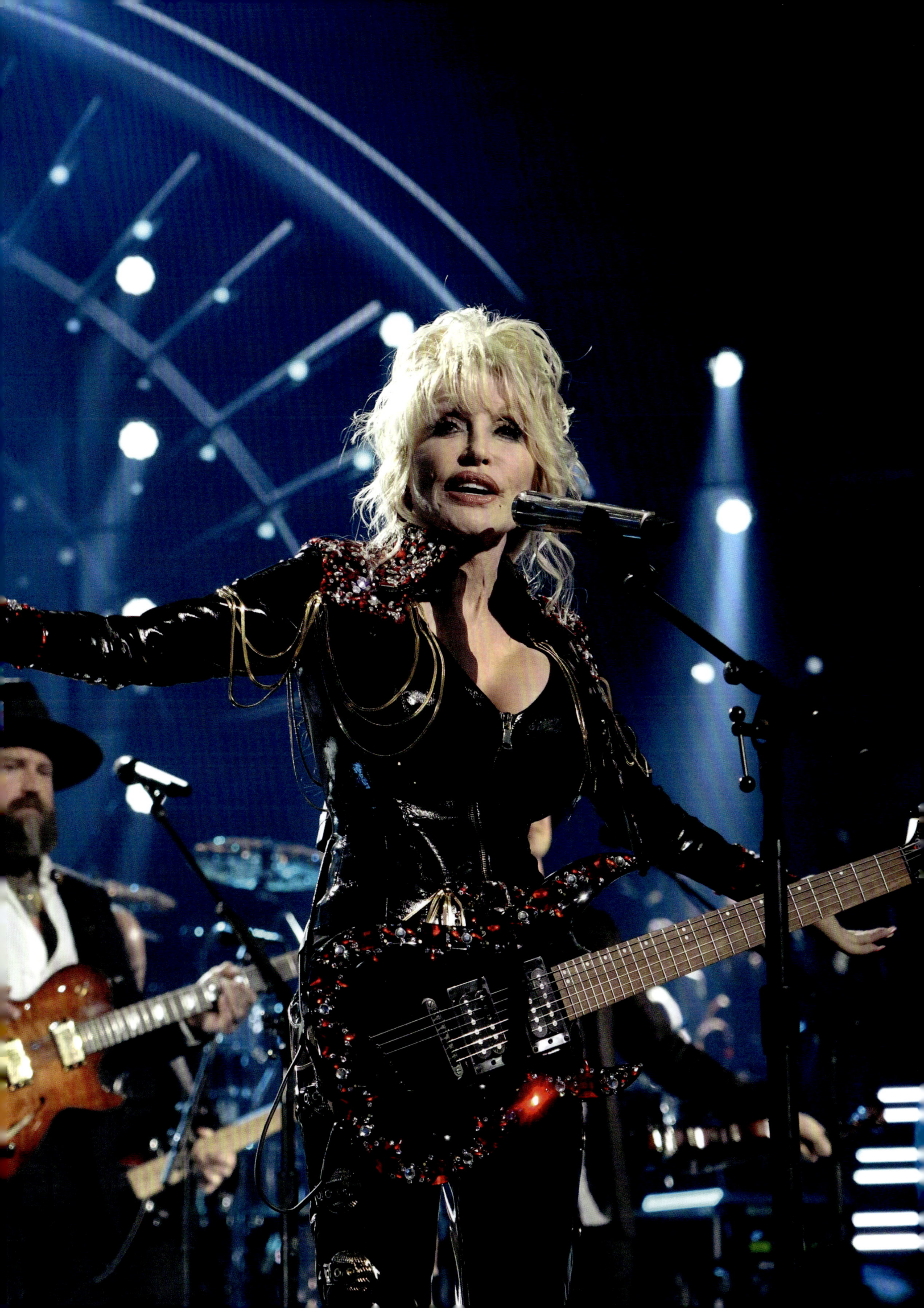

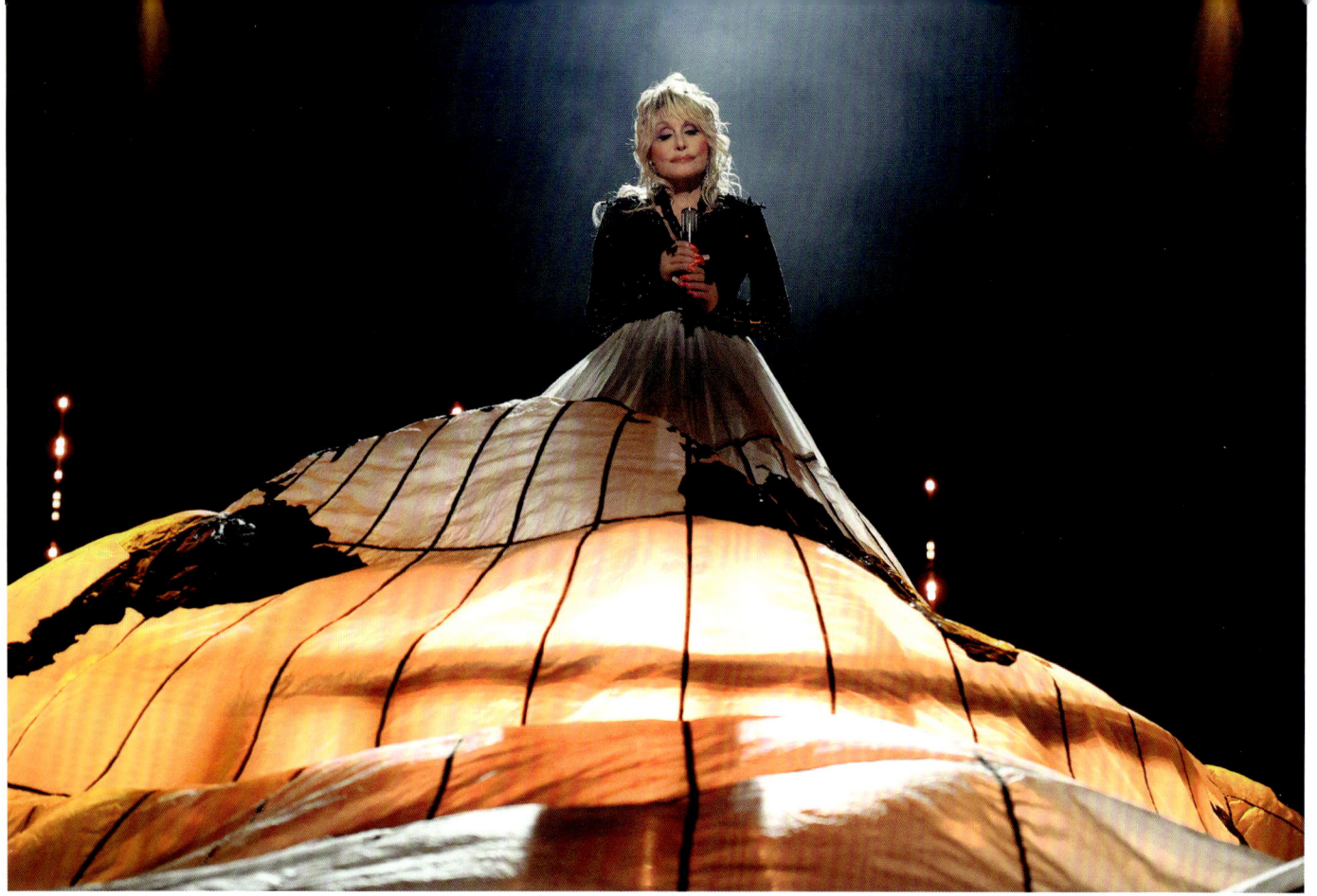

My "World on Fire" performance at the 2023 ACMs was so meaningful to me. I sang the lyrics "Still got time to turn it all around," and I still believe that today.

country. So even when we were all isolated, I was still able to put together the *Holly Dolly Christmas* TV special, make virtual appearances in the Macy's Thanksgiving Day Parade and *Christmas in Rockefeller Center,* and do a guest appearance on the Netflix series *Grace and Frankie,* starring my *9 to 5* buddies Jane Fonda and Lily Tomlin . . . and I did it while following all the safety rules.

I felt like I needed to do something to help people get through the pandemic, and the thing I could do best was entertain families that were at home, so I started reading children's books, through the Imagination Library, from my house. I'd put on my pajamas and sit in bed, and we put the *Goodnight with Dolly* video series up on YouTube for about three months.

After the COVID crisis subsided, I looked for special moments where I could get out in front of an audience again because I still wanted to travel. I can't fathom doing those long tours anymore though. It takes six months to put them together, and you have to stay out for at least a month. But I still do plenty of special appearances and events because we have Danny's studios where we can work up a show.

So I keep my band pretty much intact. They have all found other things to do since we're not touring anymore, but they're always on call if I want to do something. It's easy to work up a show if we get an offer to work a Friday or Saturday night. It's like having Dolly in

Star of the Show

a drawer or Dolly in a box—we have a basic show that we can pull out and tailor to the moment. I don't need to have the whole shebang, like the pyrotechnics and big show numbers we did in the Las Vegas casinos. I can go out and be entertaining by just telling stories and singing the songs, although if we want to work up bigger things, we still can. I realize now, even with all those bells and whistles, all I've ever done on stage is be myself. And I can do that anytime I want just by walking out there!

One of the offers I got coming out of COVID was to perform at the South by Southwest Conference. It was live-streamed around the world from Austin—we called it "Welcome to the Dollyverse"—and in addition to performing music, I had a little chat with James Patterson about our book, *Run, Rose, Run*.

I was asked that spring to host the ACM Awards, which was a nice honor. It marked the first time that the country music industry gathered en masse after the worst of the pandemic. I started the show off in total party spirit, dressed in a shiny outfit that looked like it came straight off a disco ball. Kelsea Ballerini joined me for "Big Dreams and Faded Jeans," a song from the *Run, Rose, Run* companion album, and Kelly Clarkson turned in an epic rendition of "I Will Always Love You." I was extremely flattered, to say the least.

Then in November, I was inducted into the Rock & Roll Hall of Fame. That honor is still probably the most surprising award I've received in my life. I felt that I hadn't done enough in rock to merit it. There are people who have spent their whole life in the rock world who still aren't in the Rock & Roll Hall of Fame, and I felt bad about that. I mean, I'll take anything anyone wants to give me in country or gospel or bluegrass. I feel like maybe I've earned that. But I couldn't think of that much I had ever done to impact rock 'n' roll, except doing some covers of pop and rock songs I liked. None of that felt like it added up enough to be worthy of that kind of award.

They insisted I belonged on the ballot, though, since I've walked my own path in life—that's a rock-star attitude, I guess, even if my music is country! I didn't want to continue making a big deal of it because I hate controversy, especially if I'm the center of it. So I said I would accept it if I could write the song that I was going to sing. I was influenced in my life by so many rock greats, like Jerry Lee Lewis and Elvis Presley and Little Richard and Chuck Berry, and I put all that in the song, "Rockin' It."

The Zac Brown Band backed me up, and I also did a version of "Jolene" where I shared the stage with P!nk, Annie Lennox, Brandi Carlile, Sheryl Crow, Pat Benatar, Judas Priest's Rob Halford, and Duran Duran's Simon Le Bon.

I brought together a different crew around that same time for *Dolly Parton's Mountain Magic Christmas,* which can be thought of as a *Christmas at Dollywood* musical. We shot it in August, so the weather wasn't exactly right for the holiday, but we did dress the park in Christmas decorations to get in the spirit—we just kept them up all the way into the holidays! Willie Nelson and I sang his song "Pretty Paper," and Billy Ray Cyrus, Miley Cyrus, Jimmie Allen, and Jimmy Fallon all stopped by, too, working with the Mighty Fine Band.

STAGE LOOKS
Through the Years

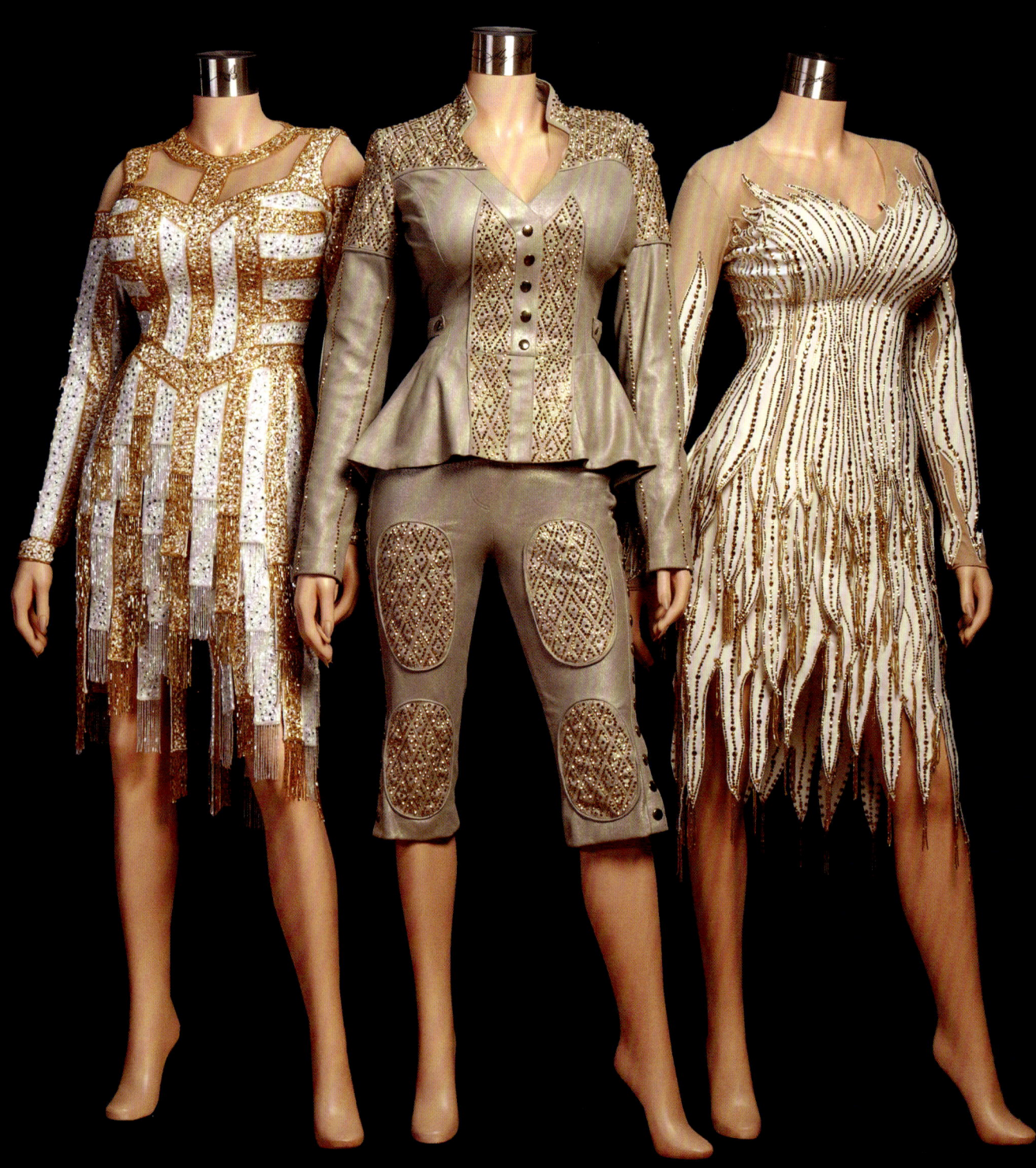

I opened my Pure & Simple Tour in this Robért Behar ensemble.... But there was nothin' simple about it!

I became an Opry member wearing gold, and I wanted to celebrate my fiftieth anniversary with the Opry in gold again.

To celebrate all our golden moments on stage, I wore this Steve Summers look to perform with Kenny Rogers at his farewell concert.

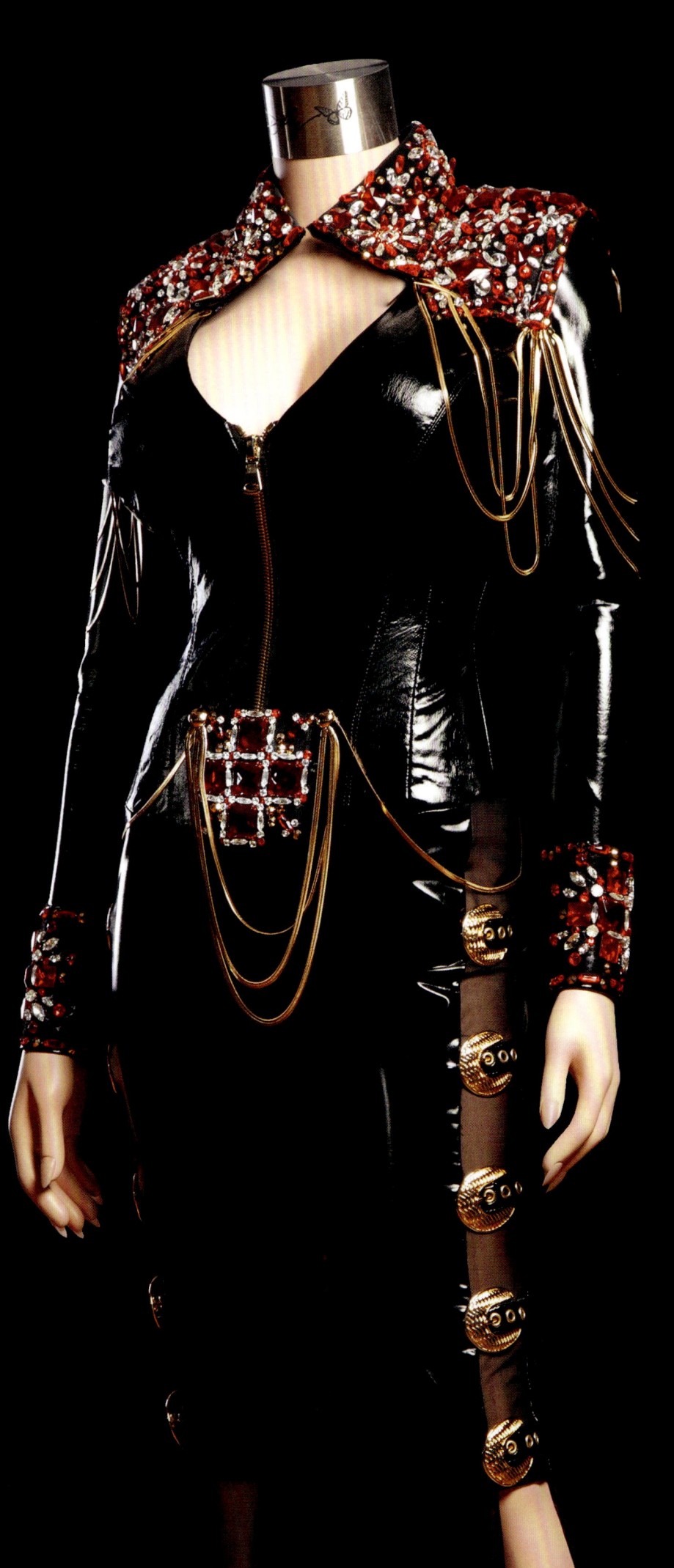

I dreamed about Elvis when we dreamed up this look for my Rock Hall induction ceremony performance!

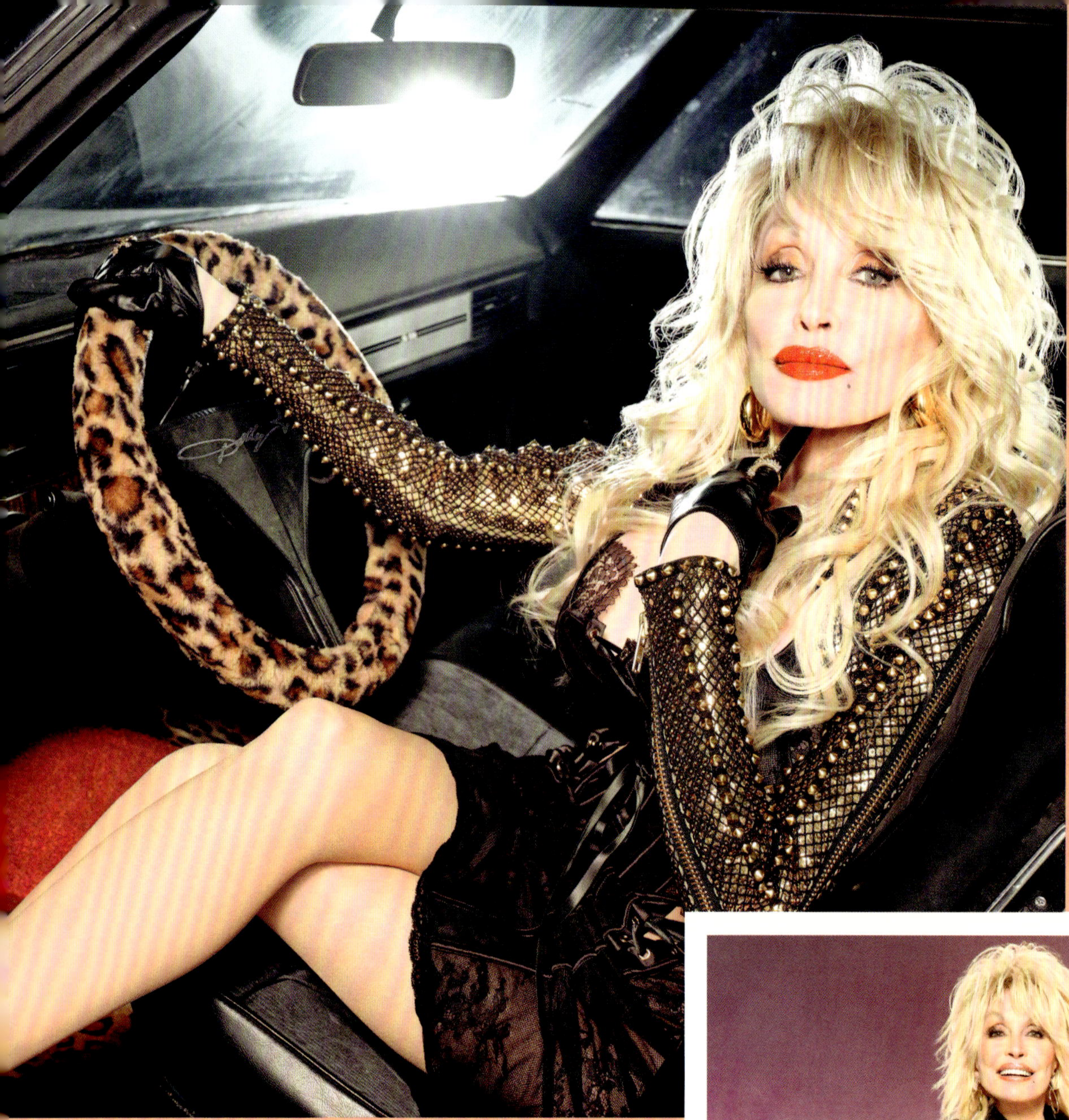

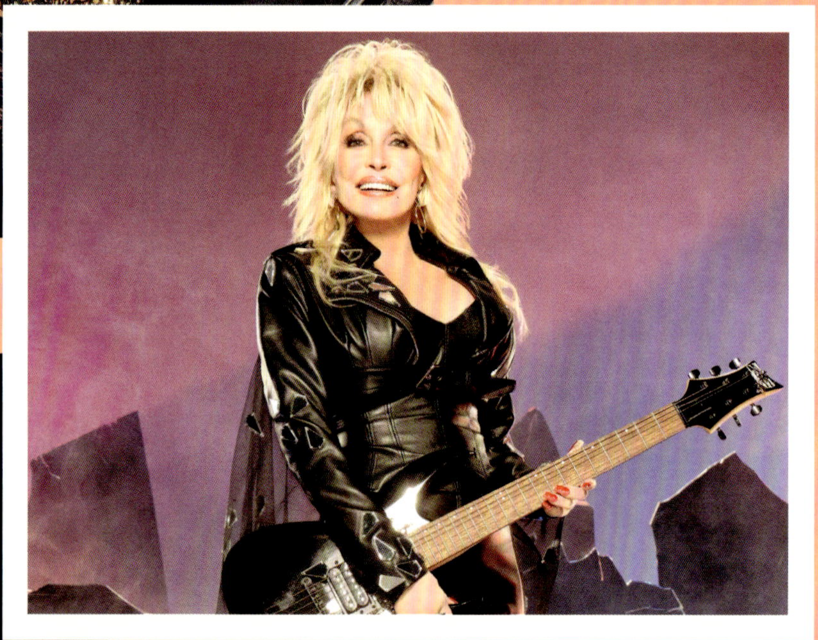

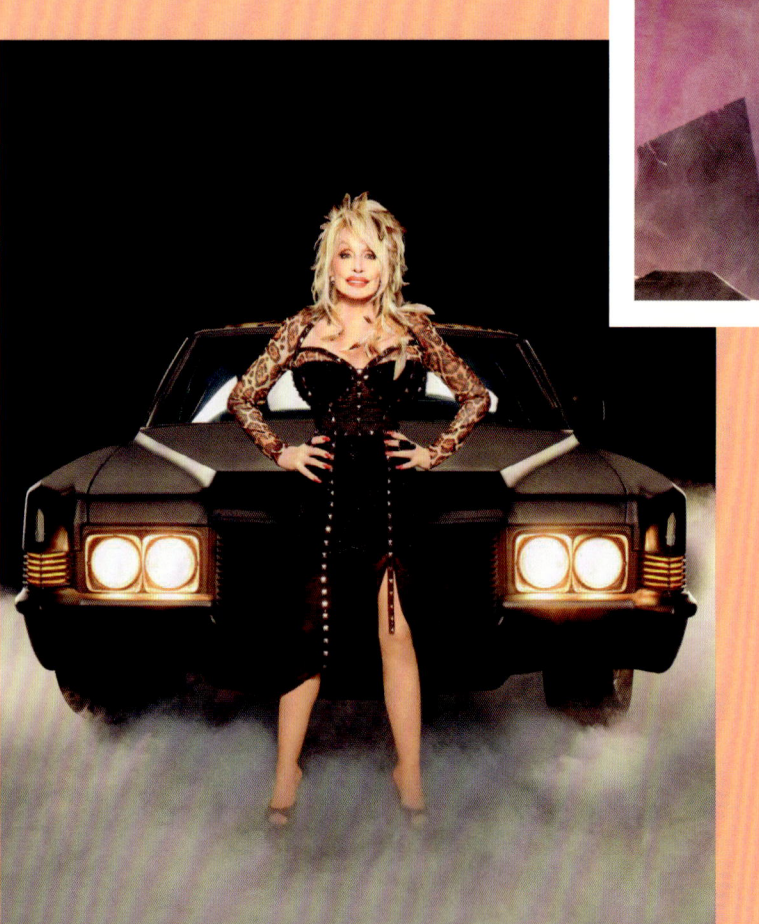

After I was inducted into the Rock & Roll Hall of Fame, I decided to create an album that showed my appreciation. *Rockstar* featured a long list of special guests, including two Beatles, Stevie Nicks, Steven Tyler, Peter Frampton, and many others. Do I look like a rock star . . . sort of?

A few weeks later, I cohosted *Miley's New Year's Eve Party,* ringing in 2023 from Miami on NBC. I had already started work on what became the *Rockstar* album, and you can see it in that show. Miley and I covered Joan Jett's "I Love Rock 'n' Roll" to kick off the night. Joan, in fact, joined me on the album for "I Hate Myself for Loving You." Miley and I also did "Wrecking Ball," and since it has the line "I will always want you," it was easy to turn that into "I Will Always Love You," so we created a little medley out of the songs for the special. We blended them again on the *Rockstar* album.

A ton of people participated in that album, including Paul McCartney, Ringo Starr, Steven Tyler, Peter Frampton, Stevie Nicks, Sting, and Elton John.

When I was singing all those rock 'n' roll songs, I felt like I needed to be true to the melody and true to the rock sound—there's a reason so many people love those songs. And yet I still had to be me—I didn't need to try to sound like anybody else.

I had already started making the *Rockstar* album by the next spring, when I cohosted the ACM Awards in Texas again, this time with Garth Brooks. That seemed like a good place to tease the album, and I debuted an original song, "World On Fire," calling out some of the issues we're facing these days—things that humanity needs to bring people together to address. For that ACM performance, I wore a huge skirt that practically covered the stage with a symbolic map of the globe. Steve Summers came up with that idea—the skirt broke away a minute or so into the song, and then I had just a regular outfit on to finish it, but it was effective. I think it helped me make a powerful statement that I wanted people to hear.

When the *Rockstar* album came out in November 2023, we looked for some big events that could attract attention. After all, it was the most ambitious album I'd ever made, so I wanted to do something ambitious to promote it! I sang "Rocky Top" in front of more than one hundred thousand people at Neyland Stadium in Knoxville at a Tennessee Volunteers football game. Former University of Tennessee quarterback Peyton Manning—a rock star in his own right on the football field—walked me onto the stage.

In what turned out to be an even bigger moment, I put on a Dallas Cowboys cheerleader outfit and performed during halftime for the Salvation Army's annual Red Kettle kickoff at the team's traditional Thanksgiving Day game that's always shown on national TV. Carl always loved the Dallas Cowboys, so there was more than one reason to put on that getup! And it was real, a true Cowboys cheerleader ensemble—we just Dollyized it with some extra sparkles and bling. I thought that if I could pull it off, it would be a cool thing to do. And if I didn't pull it off, people would look past it, saying, "Oh, you know her!"

Nobody in my band knew that I was going to be wearing short-shorts and a button-up top with a tie waist—nobody except Steve Summers and the very few people who were putting the outfit together. I surprised everybody—even my manager—when I took to the stage in the blue-and-white outfit with the Cowboys' signature stars all over it.

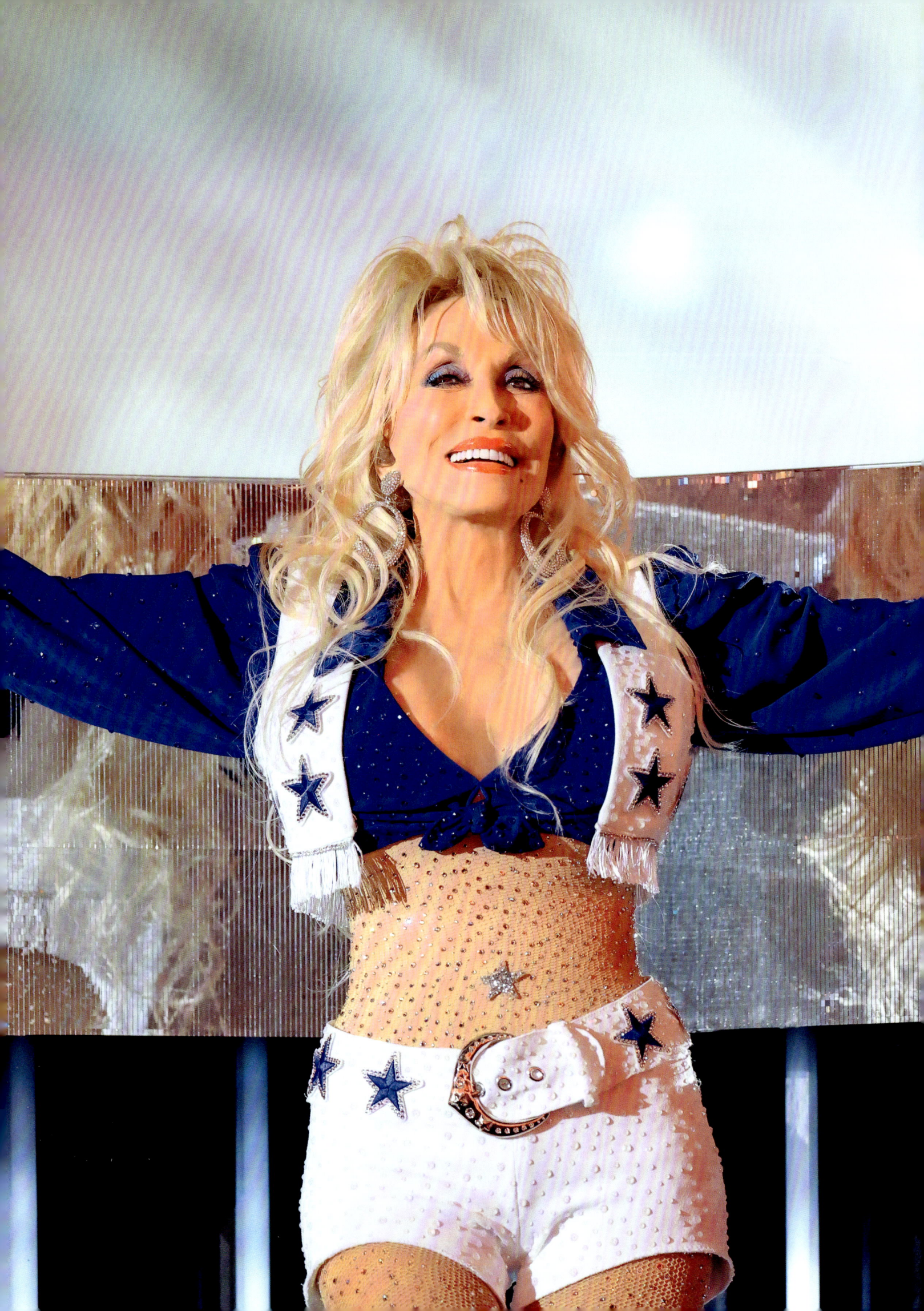

The set included "We Are the Champions" / "We Will Rock You," an appropriate medley for a football game, especially since it was on my just-released *Rockstar* album. That halftime performance is a big deal—it's a national holiday, families eat turkey and pumpkin pie with the game on, and it's one of the biggest TV events of the year. Outside of the Super Bowl or the College Football Playoff National Championship, there may not be another game that's guaranteed to get that much attention.

A million dollars or more was spent on a big stage that was shaped like the Dallas Cowboys star, and we had practiced for days in Nashville. Then when we got to Texas, we rehearsed it again. I would get on this little platform, and they had some hydraulics that were supposed to lift me up, and I was to come out of the top of the star. In my mind, shooting out of the top of the star—that's what made me think about that outfit. But when halftime came, the machinery didn't work.

They said they'd fix it. But Danny Nozell and Bryan Seaver, my security guard, said, "No, you won't." They didn't want to take any chances and end up with me caught in the lift and unable to get out of it. We didn't have time to mess with it, so Danny and Bryan got me out of there, took me around to the front, and we looked for a place where I could sing. The Cowboys cheerleaders were down on the field, so I couldn't go there. You talk about a panic attack! All those millions of people were watching, and my appearance had been hyped in advance. The show had to go on. Somehow. And the clock was ticking.

Finally, they took me around to a little platform at the base of the big star. That's where the staff had all the monitors and all kinds of wires. There was no place for me to really move around and work the stage, just this little space about three feet wide. It was tilted a little forward, and I was stepping between all these wires in my high heels with bright lights in my eyes. There was a lot going on, but when they hit the number, I went into show mode, and we pulled it off. Nobody knew the difference, and I thank the Lord that I had the outfit! We had to overcome a whole lot of stuff, but everybody got a kick out of that cheerleader costume.

There have been other stages and platforms too. I launched a baking goods line with Duncan Hines and a frozen foods line with Conagra around that time; introduced an orchestral program, *Dolly Parton's Threads: My Songs in Symphony;* and developed a musical of my life story, set for a 2026 Broadway debut.

The whole frozen foods thing is a direct result of my life on stage. I have dreams all the time, and many of them have come from having a lot of quiet time between shows and just leaving myself open. But years and years ago, I had a vision that frozen foods would be a great venture for me. It came at a time when I was on the road. Country artists have to eat at truck stops and fast-food joints all the time. To be clear, I'm not putting them down; there've been plenty of times that I had my bus driver pull off at an exit and run in for a hamburger. I love a good burger! But when you're touring hot and heavy, especially if the bus is rolling in the middle of the night, there aren't always a lot of food options available to you.

Having the ability to stock a bus refrigerator with quality food that you can heat up quickly seemed like a good business. I'm sure that lots of regular families have the same need, even though they're not out on tour. We started getting all these offers, and I thought, "Well, maybe this is the right time." We have frozen pies and homestyle macaroni and cheese in the freezer section of the grocery store, and mixes for buttermilk pancakes, biscuits, cornbread, and cakes in the baking aisle. It's just one of those things that I had a calling for, so to speak. I love to cook. And I admit, I love food!

I come up with a lot of ideas. I am a creative person. I know I can't get them all done, but in my mind, I have a filing cabinet with a lot of little drawers, and I put all these thoughts in those little compartments. Then every once in a while something will happen in my daily life and it makes me remember one of those ideas, so I go into that filing cabinet, pull out that idea, and often go, *Well, there it is. It was just waiting its turn!*

One of those ideas that took a long time to develop was *Dolly: An Original Musical,* which premiered at the Fisher Center in Nashville in 2025. I had always wanted to do my life story as a musical or a movie—and a film version might still come along.

Of course, I'd been involved in a theatrical production before, writing the music for *9 to 5: The Musical.* Before that, I didn't know what a Broadway production required. The *9 to 5* project was really what I needed to do to prepare for the autobiographical one.

With my life story, I knew exactly what I wanted to say and how I needed to say it, but I still had fun challenging myself with the new experience of bringing it to life. Of course, we used a lot of songs people know—they find their way in throughout the story. But I also wrote a lot of original music that kind of carries the story from my childhood. I had to write all the songs for Porter too. I got a big kick out of doing that!

I've always believed that one should do everything one can. If you feel like you've been blessed with a gift, a talent, or even the ability to make a change, to make things happen, you need to keep going as long as you can and just do it! It's like that old saying about making hay while the sun shines. Well, the sun's still shining, and the hay's still out there. I planted the seeds, so I'm going to have to do the harvest. Every dream that you dream creates a whole set of new dreams, and I've often joked that I've dreamed myself into a corner! Maybe I have! But that's never stopped me from dreaming big before.

You get all these great offers, all these great opportunities, just based on who you are and what you've done. Some of them you have to turn down. Some of them you cannot. You just feel like it's your duty. If you've got an opportunity to do something great, you should do it, and I'm going to keep doing it as long as I can.

I'm still able to do a lot of things, I have the freedom to do them, and I have the desire. As I've often said, I never know what God's going to call me to do. I pray every day and leave myself wide open to see if I'm supposed to hear a certain thing that I should be doing. I just feel like I have so much more to do, and I'm going to be ready and willing . . . and listening for that call.

Star of the Show

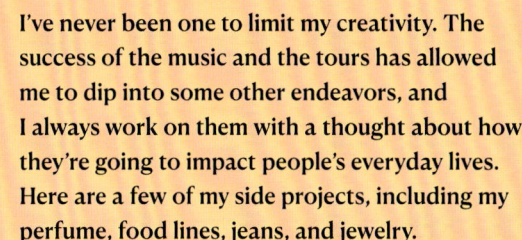

I've never been one to limit my creativity. The success of the music and the tours has allowed me to dip into some other endeavors, and I always work on them with a thought about how they're going to impact people's everyday lives. Here are a few of my side projects, including my perfume, food lines, jeans, and jewelry.

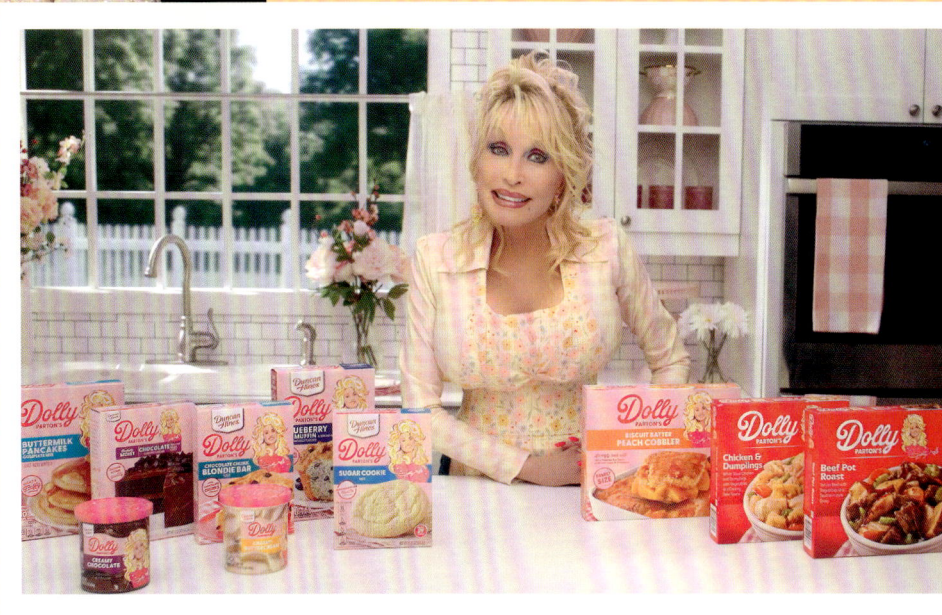

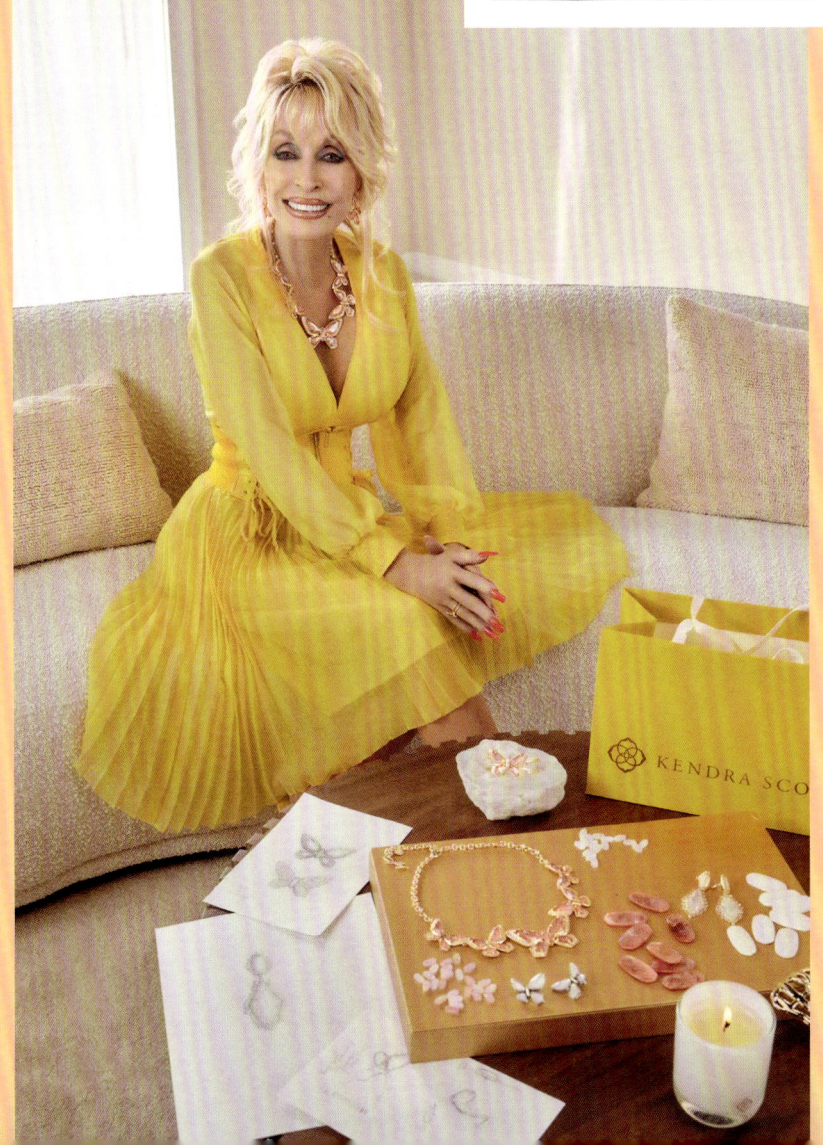

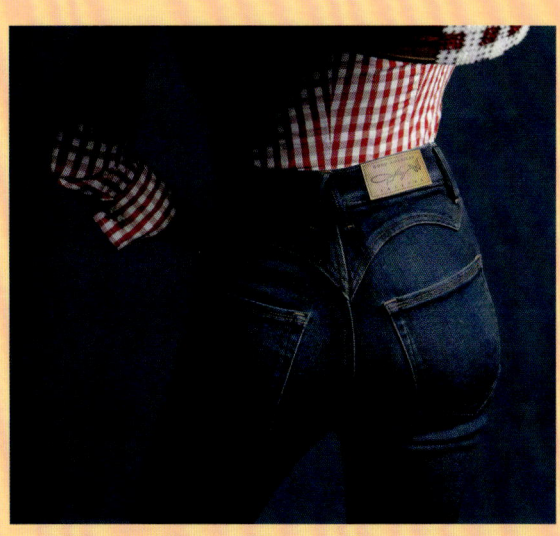

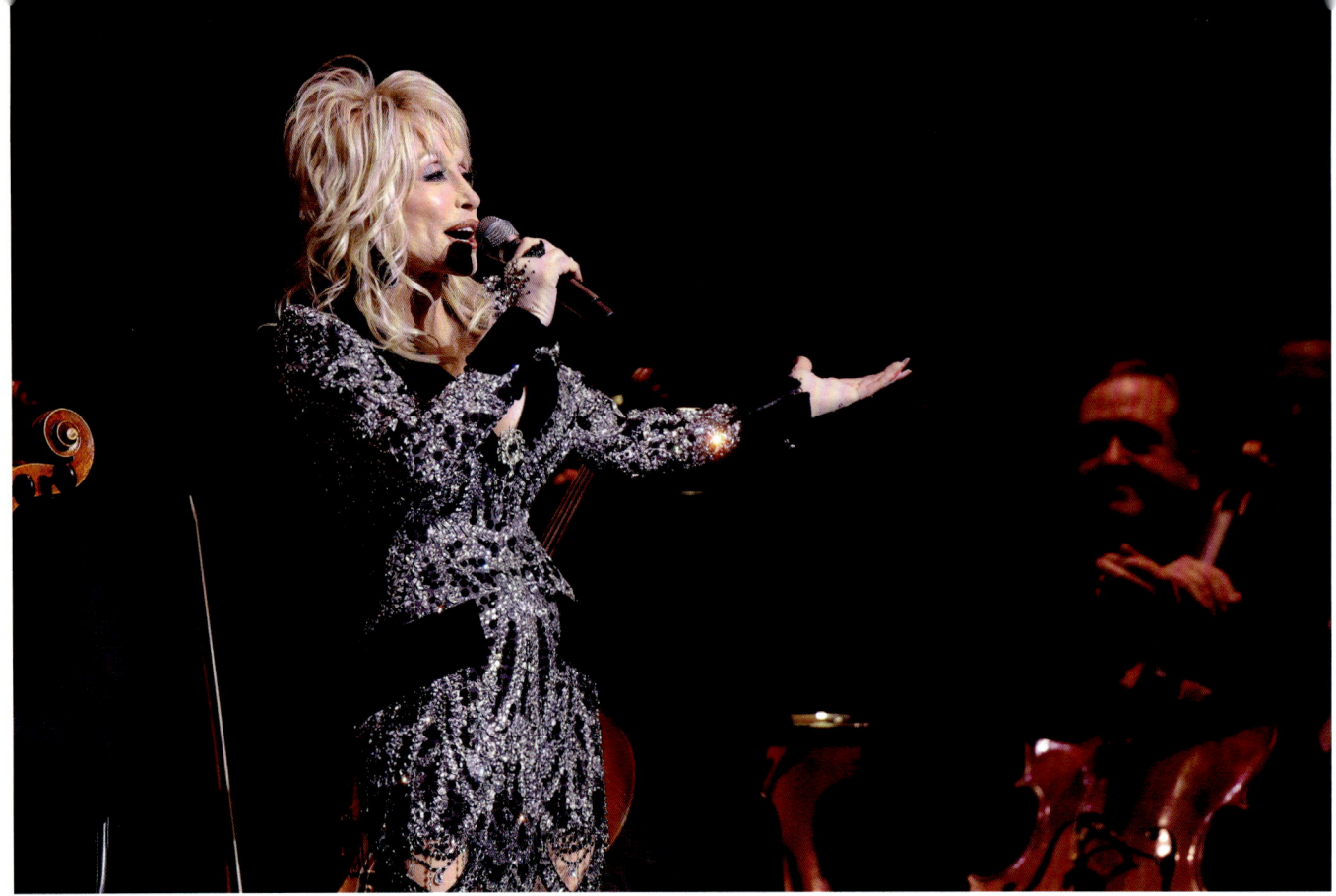

I've had strings on some of my recordings, but this took it to a new level—here I am addressing the crowd during the 2025 premiere of *Threads: My Songs in Symphony* at the Schermerhorn Symphony Center in Nashville.

I live by my gut, so to speak. The God gut is what I call it. I just seem to know what I should and shouldn't do because I pray about things like that. Different people get their answers in different places, but the gut is where the answer usually appears for me.

I'm not a religious fanatic. I don't go to church like many folks do—I believe my church is in my heart. But I also believe in a higher wisdom and a higher power. That's the thing that motivates me. I mean, it's so real to me that I could never deny it. So I just listen for it. It's more of a feeling than anything else, and if it feels right in my gut, that is the voice that I need to hear.

The way that I've been led, I believe I'll finish everything I'm supposed to do while I'm here. I think Mother Teresa once said: "When I'm called before God, when that time comes, I want to be able to say, 'God, I used everything you gave me.'" And that is exactly how I feel. I want to use everything God decides to give me, and then when I'm done, I can rest in peace knowing I've done my best.

When the leaves start falling from the family tree, you know that you're going to fall one day too. And I deal with all those feelings that come with knowing that. But my family tree has deep roots, lots of branches, and lots of leaves, and we'll still be growing. There'll be

Star of the Show

people after me, and hopefully they can use what I've left behind. That feeling doesn't apply only to my family though. I feel the same way about the country music community, and about people all around the world. I hope that when my time comes I'll leave something behind that others can use to lift themselves up.

When I look back at all the concert dates and the TV performances, I know that I've been blessed—*very* blessed. I always wanted to be a star. Not everyone ends up getting to do what they dream of, and that's especially true in entertainment. So many people want to be part of this world, but the number who actually break through is rather small. Out of those who succeed, the number of people who get to make an impact across seven decades is definitely only a tiny fraction of that.

Of course, nobody forces fans to buy a ticket. To keep playing concerts successfully for decades, you have to be offering something in return. And while I've had a good laugh about having two big reasons to come see me, the fact is that people want to be entertained. They want to hear songs they love and, hopefully, can sing along with and relate to. I've often said they come to see me be *them,* and I've tried to do that every time I've stepped on a stage or gone in front of the cameras.

I always wanted to bring some of my Tennessee mountain home with me when I traveled from town to town, but I also wanted to lift people up, make them laugh, and maybe remind them that there's something greater than all of us—especially when we're all together. That's why the sense of community at a concert is so important. Everybody comes to a show with someone or in a group—or maybe they come alone—but they end up being just one member of a larger crowd, everyone together in a shared moment that's the same yet different for each of them. Everyone in the audience brings their own personal history and outlook to the music, whether it's to the working-class story of "9 to 5," the fragile hope of "Love Is Like a Butterfly," the competition and heartbreak in "Jolene," or the spirituality behind "The Seeker."

Being the star of the show has allowed me to live out the dreams I had when I was singing on that little front porch in the Smoky Mountains.

I hope that if you've ever bought a concert ticket, tuned in to watch me on television, or sat through one of my movies, you felt like you got something of value: joy or healing or pure and simple entertainment. I know I got something from you: a chance to share my world and my Tennessee heritage on all sorts of stages around the globe. What a way to make a living! I can never thank you enough.

Being the star of the show has allowed me to live out the dreams I had when I was singing on the porch in the Smoky Mountains.

I hope if you bought a concert ticket or tuned in to watch me on television, or have seen one of my movies, that you felt like you got something of value: joy or healing or pure and simple entertainment. I know I got something from you: a chance to share my world and my Tennessee heritage on all sorts of stages around the globe. What a way to make a living! I can never thank you enough.

DOLLY'S ALBUMS

This discography includes all official studio albums. It does not include hits packages, collections, compilations, EPs, or reissues.

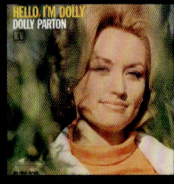
HELLO, I'M DOLLY
Released by: Monument Records
Release date: September 18, 1967
Recorded: 1964–1967
Producer: Fred Foster

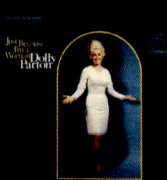
JUST BETWEEN YOU AND ME WITH PORTER WAGONER
Released by: RCA Records
Release date: January 15, 1968
Recorded: October 1967
Producer: Bob Ferguson

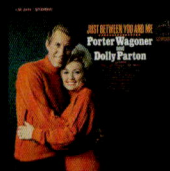
JUST BECAUSE I'M A WOMAN
Released by: RCA Records
Release date: April 15, 1968
Recorded: December 1967
Producer: Bob Ferguson

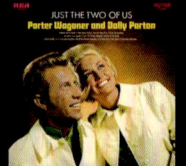
JUST THE TWO OF US WITH PORTER WAGONER
Released by: RCA (Sony)
Release date: September 9, 1968
Recorded: January–May 1968
Producer: Bob Ferguson

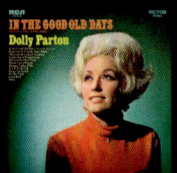
IN THE GOOD OLD DAYS (WHEN TIMES WERE BAD)
Released by: RCA (Sony)
Release date: February 3, 1969
Recorded: September–October 1968
Producer: Bob Ferguson

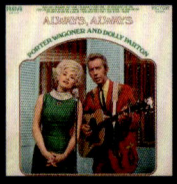
ALWAYS, ALWAYS WITH PORTER WAGONER
Released by: RCA (Sony)
Release date: June 30, 1969
Recorded: December 1968–April 1969
Producer: Bob Ferguson

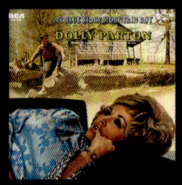
MY BLUE RIDGE MOUNTAIN BOY
Released by: RCA (Sony)
Release date: September 8, 1969
Recorded: September 1968–June 1969
Producer: Bob Ferguson

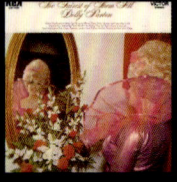
THE FAIREST OF THEM ALL
Released by: RCA (Sony)
Release date: February 2, 1970
Recorded: September 1968–October 1969
Producer: Bob Ferguson

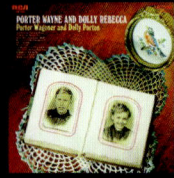
PORTER WAYNE & DOLLY REBECCA WITH PORTER WAGONER
Released by: RCA (Sony)
Release date: March 9, 1970
Recorded: April–December 1969
Producer: Bob Ferguson

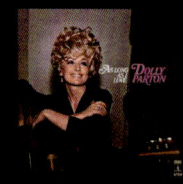
AS LONG AS I LOVE
Released by: Monument
Release date: June 8, 1970
Recorded: 1964–67
Producer: Fred Foster

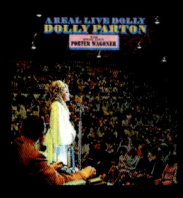
A REAL LIVE DOLLY
Released by: RCA (Sony)
Release date: June 29, 1970
Recorded: April 15, 1970
Producer: Bob Ferguson

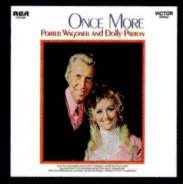
ONCE MORE WITH PORTER WAGONER
Released by: RCA (Sony)
Release date: August 3, 1970
Recorded: April–May 1970
Producer: Bob Ferguson

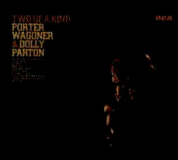
TWO OF A KIND WITH PORTER WAGONER
Released by: RCA (Sony)
Release date: February 8, 1971
Recorded: May–December 1970
Producer: Bob Ferguson

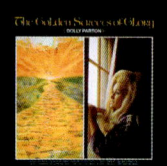
THE GOLDEN STREETS OF GLORY
Released by: RCA (Sony)
Release date: February 15, 1971
Recorded: May 1970
Producer: Bob Ferguson

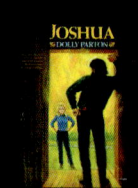
JOSHUA
Released by: RCA (Sony)
Release date: April 12, 1971
Recorded: October 1969–February 1971
Producer: Bob Ferguson

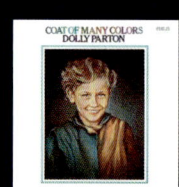
COAT OF MANY COLORS
Released by: RCA (Sony)
Release date: October 4, 1971
Recorded: October 1969–April 1971
Producer: Bob Ferguson

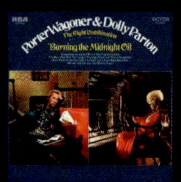
THE RIGHT COMBINATION– BURNING THE MIDNIGHT OIL WITH PORTER WAGONER
Released by: RCA (Sony)
Release date: January 3, 1972
Recorded: December 1970–September 1971
Producer: Bob Ferguson

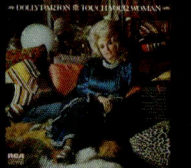
TOUCH YOUR WOMAN
Released by: RCA (Sony)
Release date: March 6, 1972
Recorded: October 1969–January 1972
Producer: Bob Ferguson

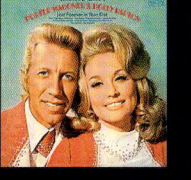
TOGETHER ALWAYS WITH PORTER WAGONER
Released by: RCA (Sony)
Release date: September 11, 1972
Recorded: April 1971–May 1972
Producer: Bob Ferguson

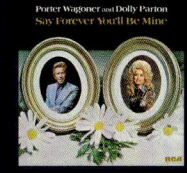
SAY FOREVER YOU'LL BE MINE WITH PORTER WAGONER
Released by: RCA (Sony)
Release date: August 18, 1975
Recorded: May 1972–April 1975
Producers: Porter Wagoner, Bob Ferguson

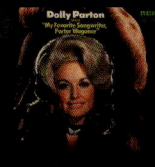
SINGS MY FAVORITE SONGWRITER, PORTER WAGONER
Released by: RCA (Sony)
Release date: October 2, 1972
Recorded: January–June 1972
Producer: Bob Ferguson

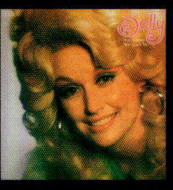
DOLLY: THE SEEKER– WE USED TO
Released by: RCA (Sony)
Release date: September 15, 1975
Recorded: May 1972–December 1974
Producers: Porter Wagoner, Bob Ferguson

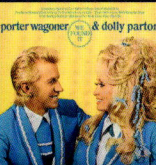
WE FOUND IT WITH PORTER WAGONER
Released by: RCA (Sony)
Release date: February 12, 1973
Recorded: April 1971–November 1972
Producer: Bob Ferguson

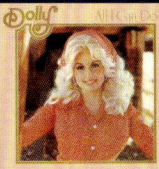
ALL I CAN DO
Released by: RCA (Sony)
Release date: August 16, 1976
Recorded: December 1974–February 1976
Producers: Porter Wagoner, Dolly Parton

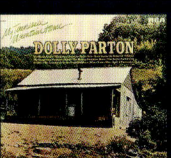
MY TENNESSEE MOUNTAIN HOME
Released by: RCA (Sony)
Release date: April 2, 1973
Recorded: September–October 1972
Producer: Bob Ferguson

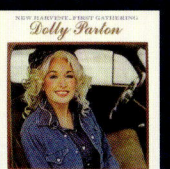
NEW HARVEST... FIRST GATHERING
Released by: RCA (Sony)
Release date: February 14, 1977
Recorded: August–December 1976
Producers: Dolly Parton, Gregg Perry

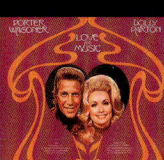
LOVE AND MUSIC WITH PORTER WAGONER
Released by: RCA (Sony)
Release date: July 2, 1973
Recorded: November 1972–April 1973
Producer: Bob Ferguson

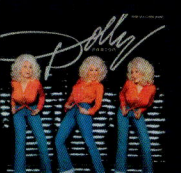
HERE YOU COME AGAIN
Released by: RCA (Sony)
Release date: October 3, 1977
Recorded: June–August 1977
Producers: Gary Klein, Charles Koppelman

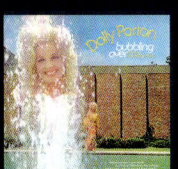
BUBBLING OVER
Released by: RCA (Sony)
Release date: September 10, 1973
Recorded: January 1971–May 1973
Producer: Bob Ferguson

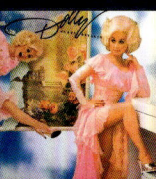
HEARTBREAKER
Released by: RCA (Sony)
Release date: July 17, 1978
Recorded: March 1978
Producers: Gary Klein, Dolly Parton, Charles Koppelman

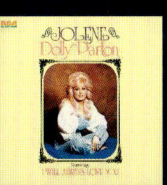
JOLENE
Released by: RCA (Sony)
Release date: February 4, 1974
Recorded: July 1972–December 1973
Producers: Porter Wagoner, Bob Ferguson

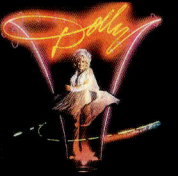
GREAT BALLS OF FIRE
Released by: RCA (Sony)
Release date: May 28, 1979
Recorded: December 1978
Producers: Dean Parks, Gregg Perry, Dolly Parton, Charles Koppelman

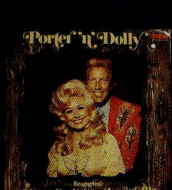
PORTER 'N' DOLLY WITH PORTER WAGONER
Released by: RCA (Sony)
Release date: August 19, 1974
Recorded: September 1971–May 197
Producer: Bob Ferguson

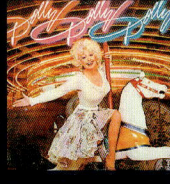
DOLLY, DOLLY, DOLLY
Released by: RCA (Sony)
Release date: April 14, 1980
Recorded: December 1979
Producers: Gary Klein, Charles Koppelman

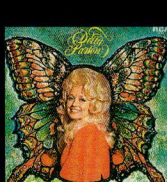
LOVE IS LIKE A BUTTERFLY
Released by: RCA (Sony)
Release date: September 16, 1974
Recorded: September 1972–July 1974
Producer: Bob Ferguson

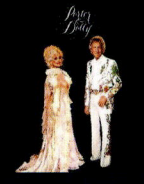
PORTER & DOLLY WITH PORTER WAGONER
Released by: RCA (Sony)
Release date: August 4, 1980
Recorded: May 1968–December 1979
Producer: Porter Wagoner

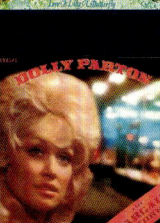
THE BARGAIN STORE
Released by: RCA (Sony)
Release date: February 17, 1975
Recorded: May 1973–December 1974
Producers: Bob Ferguson, Porter Wagoner

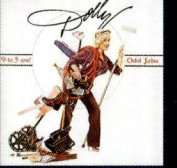
9 TO 5 AND ODD JOBS
Released by: RCA (Sony)
Release date: November 17, 1980
Recorded: April–July 1980
Producers: Mike Post, Gregg Perry

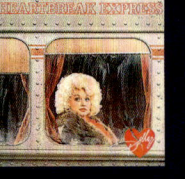
HEARTBREAK EXPRESS
Released by: RCA (Sony)
Release date: March 29, 1982
Recorded: December 1981–January 1982
Producers: Dolly Parton, Gregg Perry

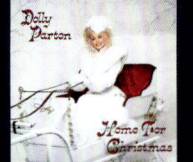
HOME FOR CHRISTMAS
Released by: Columbia (Sony)
Release date: September 11, 1990
Recorded: July 1990
Producers: Gary Smith, Dolly Parton

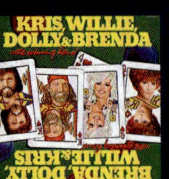
THE WINNING HAND WITH WILLIE NELSON, KRIS KRISTOFFERSON, BRENDA LEE
Released by: Monument Records
Release date: November 1, 1982
Recorded: 1964–1982
Producer: Fred Foster

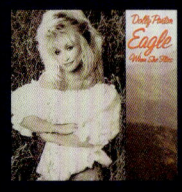
EAGLE WHEN SHE FLIES
Released by: Columbia (Sony)
Release date: March 7, 1991
Recorded: November 1990–February 1991
Producers: Steve Buckingham, Gary Smith, Dolly Parton

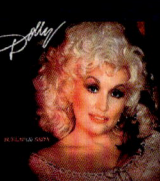
BURLAP & SATIN
Released by: RCA (Sony)
Release date: May 2, 1983
Recorded: March 1983
Producers: Dolly Parton, Gregg Perry

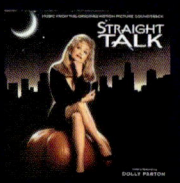
STRAIGHT TALK: ORIGINAL MOTION PICTURE SOUNDTRACK
Released by: Hollywood (UMG)
Release date: March 31, 1992
Recorded: December 1991
Producers: Greg Ladanyi, Dolly Parton

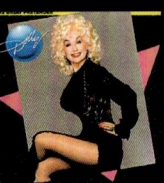
THE GREAT PRETENDER
Released by: RCA (Sony)
Release date: January 23, 1984
Recorded: October–December 1983
Producer: Val Garay

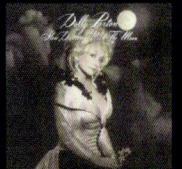
SLOW DANCING WITH THE MOON
Released by: Columbia (Sony)
Release date: February 23, 1993
Recorded: October 1992
Producers: Steve Buckingham, Dolly Parton

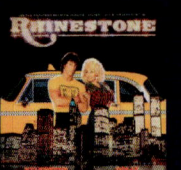
RHINESTONE: ORIGINAL MOTION PICTURE SOUNDTRACK
Released by: RCA Records
Release date: June 18, 1984
Recorded: August 1983–January 1984
Producers: Mike Post, Dolly Parton

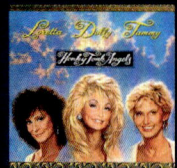
HONKY TONK ANGELS WITH LORETTA LYNN & TAMMY WYNETTE
Released by: Columbia (Sony)
Release date: November 2, 1993
Recorded: February 1993
Producers: Steve Buckingham, Dolly Parton

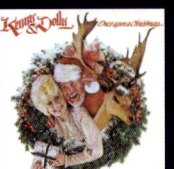
ONCE UPON A CHRISTMAS WITH KENNY ROGERS
Released by: RCA (Sony)
Release date: October 29, 1984
Recorded: August 1984
Producers: David Foster, Kenny Rogers

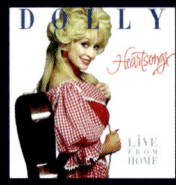
HEARTSONGS: LIVE FROM HOME
Released by: Columbia/Blue Eye Records
Release date: September 27, 1994
Recorded: April 1994
Producers: Steve Buckingham, Dolly Parton

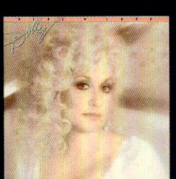
REAL LOVE
Released by: RCA (Sony)
Release date: January 21, 1985
Recorded: November–December 1984
Producer: David Malloy

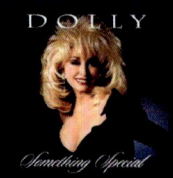
SOMETHING SPECIAL
Released by: Columbia/Blue Eye Records
Release date: August 22, 1995
Recorded: Spring 1995
Producers: Steve Buckingham, Dolly Parton

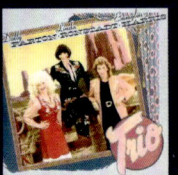
TRIO WITH LINDA RONSTADT & EMMYLOU HARRIS
Released by: Warner Bros.
Release date: March 2, 1987
Recorded: January–November 1986
Producer: George Massenburg

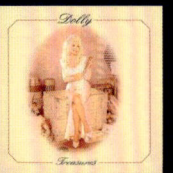
TREASURES
Released by: Rising Tide/Blue Eye Records
Release date: September 24, 1996
Recorded: June 1996
Producer: Steve Buckingham

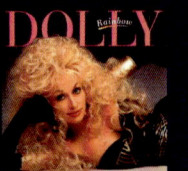
RAINBOW
Released by: Columbia (Sony)
Release date: November 23, 1987
Recorded: July 1987
Producer: Steve Goldstein

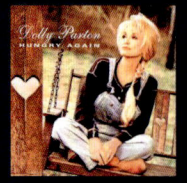
HUNGRY AGAIN
Released by: Decca/Blue Eye Records
Release date: August 25, 1998
Recorded: February 1998
Producers: Richie Owens, Dolly Parton

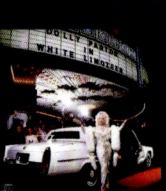
WHITE LIMOZEEN
Released by: Columbia (Sony)
Release date: May 30, 1989
Recorded: February 1989
Producer: Ricky Skaggs

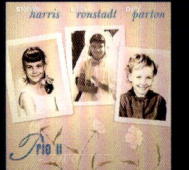
TRIO II WITH LINDA RONSTADT & EMMYLOU HARRIS
Released by: Asylum
Release date: February 9, 1999
Recorded: 1994
Producer: George Massenburg

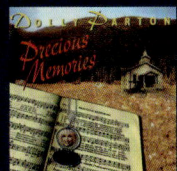
PRECIOUS MEMORIES
Released by: Blue Eye Records
Release date: April 17, 1999
Recorded: Fall 1998
Producers: Richie Owens, Dolly Parton

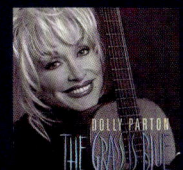
THE GRASS IS BLUE
Released by: Sugar Hill/Blue Eye Records
Release date: October 26, 1999
Recorded: August 1999
Producer: Steve Buckingham

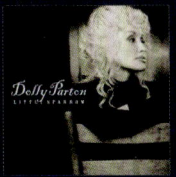
LITTLE SPARROW
Released by: Sugar Hill/Blue Eye Records
Release date: January 23, 2001
Recorded: Summer 2000
Producer: Steve Buckingham

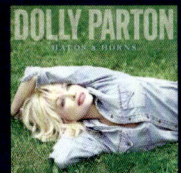
HALOS & HORNS
Released by: Sugar Hill/Blue Eye Records
Release date: July 9, 2002
Recorded: February 2002
Producer: Dolly Parton

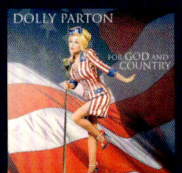
FOR GOD AND COUNTRY
Released by: Welk Music/Blue Eye Records
Release date: November 11, 2003
Recorded: Spring 2003
Producers: Dolly Parton, Kent Wells, Tony Smith

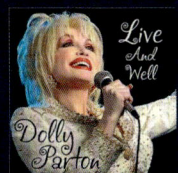
LIVE AND WELL
Released by: Sugar Hill/Blue Eye Records
Release date: September 14, 2004
Recorded: December 2002
Producers: Dolly Parton, Gary Davis

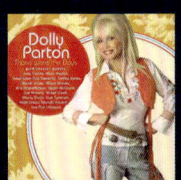
THOSE WERE THE DAYS
Released by: Sugar Hill/Blue Eye Records
Release date: October 11, 2005
Recorded: July 2005
Producer: Dolly Parton

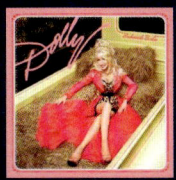
BACKWOODS BARBIE
Released by: Dolly Records
Release date: February 26, 2008
Recorded: 2006–2007
Producers: Kent Wells, Dolly Parton

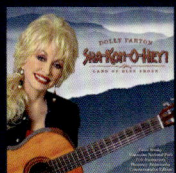
SHA-KON-O-HEY!: LAND OF BLUE SMOKE
Released by: Dolly Records
Release date: February 1, 2009
Recorded: 2008
Producers: Dolly Parton, Tony Smith

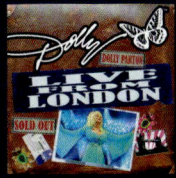
LIVE FROM LONDON
Released by: Dolly Records
Release date: November 10, 2009
Recorded: July 5–6, 2008
Producers: Danny Nozell, Dolly Parton

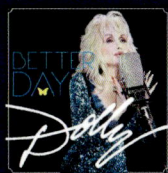
BETTER DAY
Released by: Warner Bros./Dolly Records
Release date: June 28, 2011
Recorded: 2010–2011
Producers: Dolly Parton, Kent Wells

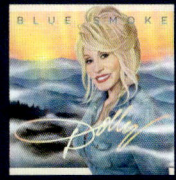
BLUE SMOKE
Released by: Sony Masterworks/Dolly Records
Release date: May 13, 2014
Recorded: 2013
Producers: Kent Wells, Dolly Parton

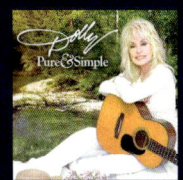
PURE & SIMPLE
Released by: RCA Nashville/Dolly Records
Release date: August 19, 2016
Recorded: 2015–2016
Producers: Dolly Parton, Richard Dennison, Tom Rutledge

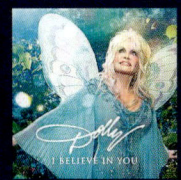
I BELIEVE IN YOU
Released by: RCA Nashville/Dolly Records
Release date: September 29, 2017
Recorded: 2010–2016
Producers: Tom McBryde, Richard Dennison, Tom Rutledge

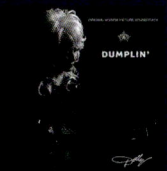
DUMPLIN' ORIGINAL MOTION PICTURE SOUNDTRACK
Released by: RCA Nashville/Dolly Records
Release date: November 30, 2018
Recorded: January–March 2018
Producers: Linda Perry, Dolly Parton

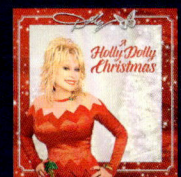
A HOLLY DOLLY CHRISTMAS
Released by: 12 Tone Music/Butterfly Records
Release date: October 2, 2020
Recorded: Spring–Summer 2020
Producers: Kent Wells, Dolly Parton

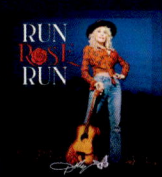
RUN, ROSE, RUN
Released by: Virgin Music/Butterfly Records
Release date: March 4, 2022
Recorded: Spring 2021
Producers: Dolly Parton, Richard Dennison, Tom Rutledge

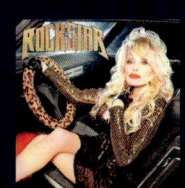
ROCKSTAR
Released by: Big Machine/Butterfly Records
Release date: November 17, 2023
Recorded: 2022–2023
Producers: Kent Wells, Dolly Parton

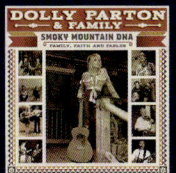
SMOKY MOUNTAIN DNA: FAMILY, FAITH AND FABLES
Released by: Virgin Music/Owepar Records
Release date: November 15, 2024
Recorded: 2011–2024
Producers: Richie Owens, Dolly Parton

DOLLY'S VIDEOS

This music video discography includes all official music videos. It does not include non-directed studio footage clips, social or short-form song content, or live performance music video clips.

"POTENTIAL NEW BOYFRIEND"
Year: 1983
Director: Steve Barron

"REAL LOVE"
(with Kenny Rogers)
Year: 1985
Director: Doug Dowdel

"THE RIVER UNBROKEN"
Year: 1987
Director: Brian Grant

"TO KNOW HIM IS TO LOVE HIM"
(with Emmylou Harris and Linda Ronstadt)
Year: 1987
Director: George Lucas

"THOSE MEMORIES OF YOU"
(with Emmylou Harris and Linda Ronstadt)
Year: 1987
Director: White Copeman

"I KNOW YOU BY HEART"
(with Smokey Robinson)
Year: 1988
Director: Gary Weis

"WHY'D YOU COME IN HERE LOOKIN' LIKE THAT"
Year: 1989
Director: Jack Cole

"LOVE IS STRANGE"
(with Kenny Rogers)
Year: 1990
Director: Gerry Wenner

"ROCKIN' YEARS"
(with Ricky Van Shelton)
Year: 1991
Director: Michael Salomon

"SILVER AND GOLD"
Year: 1991
Directors: Robert Deaton, George Flanigen

"EAGLE WHEN SHE FLIES"
Year: 1991
Director: Mary Lambert

"STRAIGHT TALK"
Year: 1992
Director: Dominic Orlando

"LIGHT OF A CLEAR BLUE MORNING"
Year: 1992
Director: Mary Lambert

"ROMEO"
(with Billy Ray Cyrus, Mary Chapin Carptenter, Pam Tills, Kathy Mattea, and Tanya Tucker)
Year: 1993
Director: Randee St. Nicholas

"MORE WHERE THAT CAME FROM"
Year: 1993
Director: Randee St. Nicholas

"SILVER THREADS AND GOLDEN NEEDLES"
(with Loretta Lynn and Tammy Wynette)
Year: 1993
Directors: Robert Deaton, George Flanigen

"THE DAY I FALL IN LOVE"
(with James Ingram)
Year: 1994
Director: Jim Yukich

"WHEN YOU TELL ME THAT YOU LOVE ME"
(with Julio Iglesias)
Year: 1994
Director: John Hopgood

"JUST WHEN I NEEDED YOU MOST"
Year: 1996
Director: John Lloyd Miller

"PEACE TRAIN" (REMIX)
Year: 1997
Director: Christopher Ciccone

"KNOCKIN' ON HEAVEN'S DOOR"
(with Ladysmith Black Mambazo)
Year: 1997
Director: Joseph Shabalala

"HONKY TONK SONGS"
Year: 1998
Director: Thom Oliphant

"THE SALT IN MY TEARS"
Year: 1998
Director: Guy Guillet

"AFTER THE GOLD RUSH"
(with Emmylou Harris and Linda Ronstadt)
Year: 1999
Director: Jim Shea

"SHINE"
Year: 2001
Director: Brent Hedgecock

"DAGGER THROUGH THE HEART"
Year: 2002
Director: Brent Hedgecock

"STAND BY THE RIVER"
(with Dottie Rambo)
Year: 2002
Director: Stephen Yates

"JOLENE"
(with Mindy Smith)
Year: 2003
Director: Trey Fanjoy

"I'M GONE"
Year: 2003
Director: Sophie Muller

"STEADY AS THE RAIN"
(with The Larkins)
Year: 2003
Director: Unknown

"COLOR ME AMERICA"
Year: 2003
Director: Patrick Isbey

"WELCOME HOME"
Year: 2004
Director: Trey Fanjoy

"THE BLUES MAN"
(with George Jones)
Year: 2005
Director: Joe Thomas

"WHEN I GET WHERE I'M GOING"
(with Brad Paisley)
Year: 2005
Director: Jim Shea

"IMAGINE"
(with David Foster)
Year: 2005
Director: Paula Walker

"TRAVELIN' THRU"
Year: 2006
Director: Duncan Tucker

"HEARTBREAKER'S ALIBI"
(with Rhonda Vincent)
Year: 2006
Director: Trey Fanjoy

"BETTER GET TO LIVIN'"
Year: 2007
Director: Steve Lippman

"JESUS & GRAVITY"
Year: 2008
Director: Steve Lippman

"BACKWOODS BARBIE"
Year: 2009
Director: Trey Fanjoy

"CHANGE IT"
(ft. the cast of *9 to 5: The Musical*)
Year: 2009
Directors: Mike Hagler, Steve Summers

"I AM STRONG"
(with The Grascals)
Year: 2011
Director: David Corlew

"TOGETHER YOU AND I"
Year: 2011
Director: Trey Fanjoy

"YOU CAN'T MAKE OLD FRIENDS"
(with Kenny Rogers)
Year: 2013
Director: Trey Fanjoy

"HOME"
Year: 2014
Director: Justine Feldt

"WHEN I STOP DREAMING"
(with Don Henley)
Year: 2015
Director: Daniel Pearl

"FOREVER COUNTRY"
(with Artists of Then, Now & Forever)
Year: 2016
Director: Joseph Kahn

"HERE I AM"
(with Sia)
Year: 2018
Director: Anne Fletcher

"GIRL IN THE MOVIES"
Year: 2018
Director: Robert Hoffman

"GOD ONLY KNOWS"
(with For King & Country)
Year: 2019
Director: Ben Smallbone

"FAITH"
(with Galantis ft. Mr. Probz)
Year: 2019
Director: Dano Cerny

"THERE WAS JESUS"
(with Zach Williams)
Year: 2020
Director: Matthew Singleton

"WHEN LIFE IS GOOD AGAIN"
Year: 2020
Director: Steve Summers

"WORDS"
(with Barry Gibb)
Year: 2021
Director: Dave Cobb

"DOES HE LOVE YOU"
(with Reba McEntire)
Year: 2021
Director: Dano Cerny

"SOMEDAY IT'LL ALL MAKE SENSE"
(with Bill Anderson)
Year: 2022
Director: Trey Fanjoy

"JOLENE"
(with Olivia Newton-John)
Year: 2023
Director: Andrew Seger

"SEASONS"
(with Bebe Rexha)
Year: 2023
Director: Natalie Simmons

"PEACE LIKE A RIVER"
(with Dionne Warwick)
Year: 2023
Directors: Damon Elliot, Nick Pres

"WE ARE THE CHAMPIONS/WE WILL ROCK YOU"
Year: 2023
Director: Steve Summers

"WHAT'S UP"
(with Linda Perry)
Year: 2023
Director: Steve Summers

"LOOKIN' FOR YOU"
(with Zach Williams)
Year: 2024
Director: Natalie Simmons

"SOUTHERN ACCENTS"
Year: 2024
Director: Trey Fanjoy

"MIDNIGHT BLUE"
(with Melissa Manchester)
Year: 2024
Director: Paul Gervasi

"SOMEBODY'S CHILD"
(with Blessing Offor)
Year: 2024
Director: Steve Summers

"PLEASE, PLEASE, PLEASE"
(with Sabrina Carpenter)
Year: 2025
Directors: Sabrina Carpenter, Sean Price Williams

In Memory

I was so fortunate to have great managers like Don Warden (left) and Sandy Gallin (right) by my side during my career. They each believed I could become the star of the show that I knew I had in me, and they helped me to reach new heights in so many ways. I miss them, and I can't thank them enough.

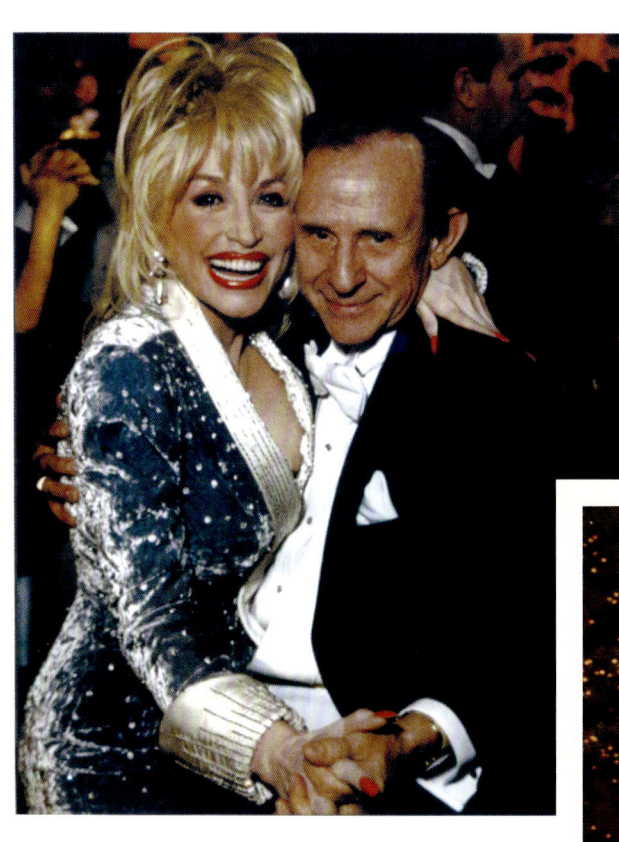

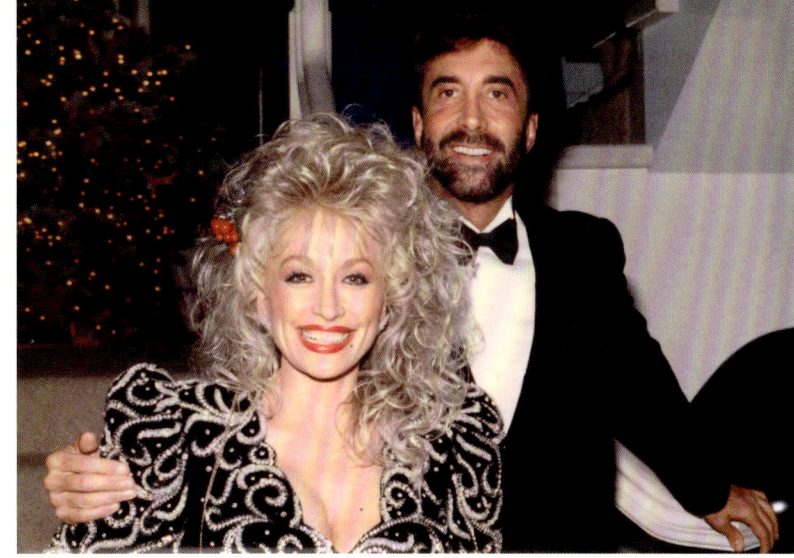

Acknowledgments

From Dolly Parton: I want to sincerely thank my creative team, my sister Rachel Parton George, my niece Rebecca Seaver, Steve Summers, John Zarling, and Devon Larson for their creative input. Your love, time, and devotion has made this book so special to me and I couldn't have done it without all of you.

Tom Roland, I owe you more than thanks for your time, talent, and effort. You have done a wonderful job making my life on the road and on the stage something that I will always be very proud of.

I'd also like to extend a sincere and heartfelt thank-you to: Danny Nozell, Kyle McClain, Peter Laird, Christian Ferguson, J. B. Rowland, Merisa Torneo, Steve Ross, Kelly Ridgway, Marcel Pariseau, Frashier Baudry, Dawson Simmons, Aden Henke, Matt Inman, Emma Campion, Annie Marino, Fariza Hawke, Brianne Sperber, Allison Renzulli, Jana Branson, Dan Zitt, Leah Jackson, Jeff Kleinman, Steve Troha, Allison Gardner, Beth Abernathy, Mason Caviness, Josie Brown, Jeremiah Scott, Ash Summerford, Rolff Zwiep, Mike Simmons, Cordy Witzler, Richard Dennison, Tom Rutledge, Maurice Miner, and Doug Smith.

And, as always, to my Mom, Dad, brothers, and sisters for being my best and first audience.

From Tom Roland: Working with Dolly Parton is a beyond-the-bucket-list moment. Dolly, I will forever be grateful to you for trusting me to help you unlock the heartbeat—and heartbreak—that accompanies life as the *Star of the Show*. To Danny Nozell and John Zarling, thanks for bringing me into the opportunity of a lifetime; and to Ten Speed Press editor Matt Inman, thanks for your endless positivity and admirable adaptability. Appreciation to Team Dolly—Rachel Parton George, Devon Larson, Steve Summers, and Rebecca Seaver—for steering the ship; and to Dolly's band and crew members—Bryan Seaver, Cheryl Riddle, Gregg Perry, Jennifer O'Brien, Jimmy Mattingly, Kent Wells, Michael Davis, Richard Dennison, Richie Owens, Tom Rutledge, and Vicki Hampton—whose insights and memories brought extra dimensions to the project. Thanks to Team Ten Speed—Emma Campion, Annie Marino, Fariza Hawke, Sharon Silva, Terry Deal, and Dan Zitt—for making the job easier than it should be; to Results Global ace, Dawson Simmons, for your ingenuity and organization; and to Doug Smith and the late Don Warden, whose enthusiastic cataloging of Dolly's career were key to this book's existence. Much appreciation to Jeff Kleinman, Steve Troha, and Maurice Miner for timely pats on the back. An additional thanks to my attorney, Lynn Morrow, for your unwavering support. Finally, thanks to Danny Brewington for twenty-five years of partnership and for pushing me forward even when there was no more gas in the tank.

Photography Credits

FRONT COVER
Stacie Huckeba

BACK COVER
Photograph by Vijat Mohindra/Courtesy of Dolly Parton

FRONT MATTER
Page 1: Courtesy of ABC Photo Archives/Getty Images
Page 2: Photograph by Jeremy Westby/Courtesy of Dolly Parton
Pages 4–5: Photograph by Pete Still/Redferns/Getty Images
Page 6: Courtesy of *The News Tribune*
Page 8: Photograph by Kent Gavin
Page 10: Photograph by Hope Powell/Courtesy of Sun Records
Page 11: Courtesy of ABC Photo Archives/Getty Images

INTRODUCTION
Page 12: Photograph by Harry Benson
Page 14–15: Photograph by Jeremy Westby/Courtesy of Dolly Parton

CHAPTER 1
START OF THE SHOW
Page 16: Courtesy of Dolly Parton
Pages 18–20: Courtesy of Dolly Parton
Pages 22–23: Courtesy of Dolly Parton
Page 24: (top left, top right, and middle) Courtesy of Dolly Parton
Page 24: (bottom right) Photograph by Jeremiah Scott
Pages 25–26: Courtesy of Dolly Parton
Page 29: (top, bottom) Photograph by Jeremiah Scott
Page 29: (middle) Photograph by Jeremy Westby/Courtesy of Dolly Parton
Pages 30–31: Courtesy of Dolly Parton
Pages 32–33: Photographs by Jeremiah Scott
Page 34: Courtesy of Dolly Parton
Page 37: Michael Ochs Archives/Getty Images
Page 38: (left, middle) Courtesy of Sony Music
Page 38: (right) Courtesy of Mercury Records/Universal Music Group
Page 39: Courtesy of Dolly Parton

CHAPTER 2
THE PORTER YEARS
Page 40: Photograph by Frank Empson/USA TODAY NETWORK via Imagn Images
Page 42: (clockwise from left) Michael Ochs Archives/Getty Images; Courtesy of Sony Music; Courtesy of Sony Music; Courtesy of Sony Music
Page 43: (clockwise from top left) Photograph by Les Leverett/Opry Archives; Photograph by Fred Foster/Courtesy of Sony Music; Photograph by Les Leverett/Opry Archives; Photograph by Hope Powell; Courtesy of Sun Records; Courtesy of Dolly Parton; Photograph by Bill Preston/USA TODAY NETWORK via Imagn Images
Page 44: Courtesy of Dolly Parton
Page 46: Photograph by Frank Empson/USA TODAY NETWORK via Imagn Images
Page 47: Photograph by Les Leverett/Courtesy of Opry Archives
Page 48: Courtesy of Sony Music
Page 49: Courtesy of Sony Music
Page 50: Courtesy of *Cash Box*
Page 51: Photograph by Les Leverett/Courtesy of Opry Archives
Pages 52–55: Courtesy of Dolly Parton
Page 56: Michael Ochs Archives/Getty Images
Page 57: Courtesy of Dolly Parton
Page 59: (top) Photograph by Les Leverett/Courtesy of Opry Archives
Page 59: (middle) Jack Corn/Courtesy of USA TODAY NETWORK via Imagn Images
Page 59: (bottom) Courtesy of Opry Archives
Page 60: Courtesy of Opry Archives
Page 61: Courtesy of Dolly Parton
Page 63: (top) Photograph by JD Crowder
Page 63: (middle right) Photograph by Joe Rudis/Courtesy of USA TODAY NETWORK via Imagn Images
Page 63: (middle left) Courtesy of The Doug Smith Collection
Page 63: (bottom) Courtesy of Dolly Parton
Page 64: Courtesy of The Everett Collection
Page 65: Courtesy of The Doug Smith Collection
Page 67: (top) Courtesy of Opry Archives
Page 67: (middle and bottom) Courtesy of The Doug Smith Collection
Page 69: Photograph by Jim Herrington
Page 70: Courtesy of The Doug Smith Collection
Page 72: Photographs by Jeremiah Scott
Pages 74–75: Photograph by Frank Empson/Courtesy of USA TODAY NETWORK via Imagn Images
Page 76: Courtesy of Dolly Parton
Page 78: Photograph by Michael Ochs/Getty Images
Page 79: Photograph by Jerry Bailey/Courtesy of USA TODAY NETWORK via Imagn Images

CHAPTER 3
LIGHT OF A BRAND-NEW DAY
Page 80: Photograph by Andrew Putler/Getty Images
Page 82: (clockwise from left) Courtesy of Sony Music; Courtesy of The Doug Smith Collection; Photograph by George Walker IV; Courtesy of USA TODAY NETWORK via Imagn Images; Courtesy of Sony Music
Page 83: (clockwise from top left) Courtesy of Country Music Association; Photograph by Hope Powell/Courtesy of Sun Records; Photograph by Bettmann/Getty Images; Courtesy of The Doug Smith Collection; Courtesy of Sony Music; Courtesy of Sony Music
Page 84: Photograph by Jack Manning/Courtesy of *The New York Times*/Redux
Page 86: Courtesy of Gregg Perry
Pages 87–91: Courtesy of The Doug Smith Collection
Page 92: (top left and bottom) Courtesy of The Doug Smith Collection
Page 92: (top right) Courtesy of Dolly Parton
Page 92: (middle) Courtesy of Gregg Perry
Page 93: Courtesy of *The Tennessean*–USA TODAY NETWORK via Imagn Images
Page 94: (top) Photograph by Keystone Press/Alamy Stock Photo
Page 94: (middle) Photograph by Andrew Putler/Getty Images

Page 94: (bottom left) Courtesy of The Doug Smith Collection
Page 94: (bottom right) Photograph by Chalkie Davies/Getty Images
Pages 96–97: Photograph by Hope Powell/Courtesy of Sun Records
Pages 98–99: Courtesy of Dolly Parton
Page 99: Slick Lawson Archives
Page 100: Photograph by Gerald Holly/Courtesy of USA TODAY NETWORK via Imagn Images
Page 101: Photograph by Slick Lawson
Page 103: Photograph by Rick Diamond/Getty Images
Pages 104–105: Courtesy of Dolly Parton
Pages 106–107: NBCU Photo Bank/NBCUniversal/Getty Images
Page 108: *The Tennessean*
Page 109: Courtesy of Getty Images
Page 110: Courtesy of The Doug Smith Collection
Page 111: Bettmann Archives
Page 112: (top) Courtesy of The Doug Smith Collection
Page 112: (middle) *The Tennessean*
Page 112: (bottom) Mirrorpix/Getty Images
Pages 114: NBCU Photo Bank/NBCUniversal/Getty Images
Pages 115: Courtesy of The Doug Smith Collection
Page 116: Courtesy of Dolly Parton
Page 118: Photograph by Richard McCaffrey/Michael Ochs Archives/Getty Images
Page 119: Photograph by Chris Walter/WireImage
Pages 120–121: Courtesy of Gregg Perry
Pages 122–125: Wardrobe photographs by Jeremiah Scott
Page 125: (top) Courtesy of Dolly Parton
Page 125: (middle) Courtesy of The Doug Smith Collection
Page 125: (bottom) Courtesy of Dolly Parton
Page 126: Courtesy of Dolly Parton
Page 127: Calendar entries by Don Warden/Courtesy of Dolly Parton
Page 130: Photograph by Richard E. Aaron/Redferns
Page 131: Courtesy of Gregg Perry
Page 132: Courtesy of CBS Photo Archives/Getty Images
Page 134–135: Photograph by Jim Garrett/*City News*
Page 137: (top left) Photograph by Bruce Glikas/FilmMagic
Page 137: (top right and bottom) Courtesy of The Doug Smith Collection
Page 138: Courtesy of the Jimmy Carter Presidential Library
Page 139: (top left and bottom) Courtesy of Dolly Parton
Page 139: (top right) Courtesy of Sony Music

Pages 140–141: Courtesy of Dolly Parton and The Doug Smith Collection

CHAPTER 4
SUPERSTAR OF THE SHOW

Page 142: Courtesy of The Doug Smith Collection
Page 144: (clockwise from left) Courtesy of The Doug Smith Collection; Courtesy of Alamy; Courtesy of Alamy; Courtesy of Bei/Shutterstock
Page 145: (clockwise from top left) Courtesy of 20th Century Fox/Disney; Courtesy of Opry Archives; Courtesy of HBO; Courtesy of Dolly Parton; Courtesy of Getty Images; Courtesy of The Everett Collection
Page 146: Courtesy of Dolly Parton
Page 149: (top left) 20th Century-Fox
Page 149: (top right) Courtesy of Dolly Parton
Page 149: (middle) Photograph by Ron Galella/Ron Galella Collection via Getty Images
Page 149: (bottom) 20th Century-Fox
Pages 150–151: Universal Pictures/Alamy Stock Photos
Page 152: Courtesy of The Doug Smith Collection
Page 154: (top) Courtesy of Alamy Stock Image/Universal Pictures
Page 154: (middle) Universal Pictures/Alamy Stock Photo
Page 154: (bottom) Courtesy of Dolly Parton
Pages 156–157: Photograph by Harry Benson
Page 159: ABC Photo Archives/Disney General Entertainment Content via Getty Images
Page 161: Calendar entries by Don Warden/Courtesy of Dolly Parton
Page 162: Courtesy of Dolly Parton
Page 163: (top left and bottom) Courtesy of Dolly Parton
Page 163: (top right) Courtesy of HBO
Page 163: (middle) *The Tennessean*
Page 164: Courtesy of Alamy
Page 165: (left) Wardrobe photographs by Jeremiah Scott
Page 165: (right) Courtesy of The Doug Smith Collection
Page 166: Photograph by Pete Still/Redferns/Getty Images
Page 167: Courtesy of The Doug Smith Collection
Page 169: (top left and top right) Courtesy of Doug Smith Collection
Page 169: (middle and bottom) Courtesy of Dolly Parton
Pages 170–172: Courtesy of Dolly Parton
Page 173: Bettman Archives/Getty Images

Pages 174–175: Courtesy of Dolly Parton and The Doug Smith Collection

CHAPTER 5
FROM HOLLYWOOD TO DOLLYWOOD

Page 176: Courtesy of ABC Photo Archives
Page 178: (clockwise from left) Courtesy of Warner Music; Courtesy of ABC Photo Archives; Photograph by Jim Smeal/Ron Galella Collection via Getty Images; Courtesy of Sony Music
Page 179: (clockwise from top left) Courtesy of Dollywood; Courtesy of Dolly Parton; Courtesy of Sony Music; Courtesy of Universal Music Group; Courtesy of Dolly Parton's Imagination Library; Courtesy of Sony Music
Page 180: Courtesy of ABC Photo Archives
Page 183: Courtesy of Dolly Parton and Dollywood
Page 184: (top left, top right, and middle) Courtesy of Larry Ferguson
Page 184: (bottom) Courtesy of The Doug Smith Collection
Pages 185–186: ABC Photo Archives
Page 187: Courtesy of Dolly Parton and Dollywood
Page 189: Photograph by Robert Blakeman
Page 190: (top) Photograph by Hope Powell/Courtesy of Sun Records
Page 190: (middle) Courtesy of Dolly Parton
Page 190: (bottom) Photograph by Robert Blakeman
Page 191: Courtesy of Dolly Parton
Page 192: Photograph by Robin Platzer/Getty Images
Page 193: Courtesy of The Doug Smith Collection
Pages 194–195: Courtesy of Dolly Parton
Pages 196–197: Wardrobe photographs by Jeremiah Scott
Pages 199–203: Courtesy of ABC Photo Archives
Page 204: Courtesy of Dolly Parton
Page 205: (top right) Courtesy of The Doug Smith Collection
Page 205: (top left) Courtesy of Tri-Star Pictures/The Everett Collection
Page 205: (mid) Courtesy of Dolly Parton
Page 205: (bottom) Courtesy of Tri-Star Pictures/The Everett Collection
Page 206: (top and middle) Courtesy of Dolly Parton
Page 206: (bottom) Courtesy of Larry Ferguson
Page 208: Courtesy of Sony Music
Page 209: NBCU Photo Bank/NBCUniversal via Getty Images
Page 210: Courtesy of The Doug Smith Collection

Photography Credits

Pages 214–215: Photographs by Jeremiah Scott
Page 216: Courtesy of Dolly Parton
Page 217: Courtesy of The Doug Smith Collection
Page 219: Courtesy of ABC Photo Archives
Page 220–221: Courtesy of Dolly Parton and The Doug Smith Collection

CHAPTER 6
RETURNING TO MY ROOTS

Page 222: Photograph by Brian Rasic/Getty Images
Page 224: (clockwise from left) Courtesy of Country Music Association; Courtesy of Dolly Parton; Courtesy of Dolly Parton; Photograph by K. Mazur/WireImage
Page 225: (clockwise from top left) Courtesy of Universal Music Group; Courtesy of Warner Music; Courtesy of Larry Ferguson; Photograph by Steve Jennings; Photograph by Dennis Carney/Courtesy of Dolly Parton; Courtesy of Dolly Parton
Page 226: Photograph by Nicky J. Sims/Redferns/Getty Images
Page 229: Courtesy of Opry Archives
Page 230: Photograph by Kevin Winer/Getty Images
Page 231: Photograph by Kevin Winter/Hulton Archive/Getty Images
Page 232: Courtesy of Dolly Parton
Page 233: (left) Wardrobe photographs by Jeremiah Scott
Page 233: (right) Photograph by Larry Ferguson
Page 235: Courtesy of Dolly Parton
Page 236: (top) Photograph by Paul Drinkwater/NBC/Getty Images
Page 236: (middle) Photograph by Robert Mora/Getty Images
Page 236: (bottom) Courtesy of Alamy Stock Photo
Page 238: Courtesy of Country Music Association
Page 239: Photograph by George Walker/Courtesy of USA TODAY NETWORK via Imagn Images
Page 240: (top and middle) Courtesy of The Doug Smith Collection
Page 240: (bottom) Photograph by Dennis Carney
Page 241: Photograph by Nancy Barr Brandon
Page 242: (top left) Courtesy of Dolly Parton
Page 242: (top right) Courtesy of The Doug Smith Collection
Page 242: (middle and bottom) Courtesy of Dolly Parton
Pages 244–245: Courtesy of Dolly Parton
Page 246: Photograph by Michael Loccisano/FilmMagic for Country Music Association/Getty Images
Page 247: Photographs by Philip Liborio Gandi

Pages 248–249: Courtesy of Danny Nozell
Pages 250–251: Courtesy of Dolly Parton, CTK Enterprises, and The Doug Smith Collection

CHAPTER 7
BETTER DAYS, PURE & SIMPLE

Page 252: Photograph by Fran Strine
Page 254: (clockwise from left) Courtesy of Dolly Parton; Photograph by Bruce Glikas/FilmMagic; Photograph by Jeremy Westby/Courtesy of Dolly Parton; Courtesy of Dolly Parton
Page 255: (clockwise from top left) Photograph by Nancy Barr Brandon/Courtesy of Dolly Parton; Photograph by Steve Jennings; Courtesy of Getty Images; Courtesy of Getty Images; Courtesy of Sandollar Television/Magnolia Hill Productions/NBC; Photograph by Jay Blakesberg; Retro Photo Archive
Page 256: Photograph by Cheryl Riddle/Courtesy of Dolly Parton
Page 257: Photograph by Kevin Winter/Getty Images Entertainment/Getty Images
Page 258: Eric Draper/Courtesy of the George W. Bush Presidential Library
Page 259: Courtesy of *The Tennessean*/USA TODAY NETWORK via Imagn Images
Page 261: Photograph by Mike Coppola/Getty Images
Pages 262–263: Courtesy of Danny Nozell
Page 267: (top left and middle) Courtesy of The Doug Smith Collection
Page 267: (top right) Photographs by David Gahr/Getty Images
Page 267: (bottom) Courtesy of Dolly Parton/Dollywood
Page 268: Photographs by Jeremy Westby/Courtesy of The Doug Smith Collection
Pages 270–271: Photographs by Jeremiah Scott
Pages 272–273: Courtesy of Dolly Parton
Page 275: Courtesy of Dolly Parton
Page 276: Photograph by Jim Dyson/Getty Images Entertainment/Getty Images
Pages 277–278: Courtesy of Dolly Parton
Page 279: (top and middle) Courtesy of Dolly Parton
Page 279: (bottom) Photograph by Tabitha Fireman/Redferns/Getty Images
Pages 280–281: Courtesy of Dolly Parton
Page 282: Courtesy of Zuma Press/Alamy Stock Photo
Pages 283–286: Photographs by Jeremy Westby/Courtesy of Dolly Parton
Page 287: Courtesy of Danny Nozell
Pages 288–289: Courtesy of Dolly Parton
Page 291: Courtesy of Dolly Parton
Pages 292–293: Photograph by Jeremy Westby/Courtesy of Dolly Parton

Pages 294–295: Courtesy of Dolly Parton and CTK Enterprises
Page 297: Courtesy of Dolly Parton

CHAPTER 8
NEW STAGES

Page 298: Photograph by Vijat Mohindra/Courtesy of Dolly Parton
Page 300: (clockwise from left) Courtesy of Chronicle Books; Courtesy of Netflix; Photograph by Ron Jenkins/Getty Images; Courtesy of Ten Speed Press
Page 301: (clockwise from top left) Photograph by Lester Cohen/Getty Images for The Recording Academy; Courtesy of Netflix; Photograph by Vijat Mohindra; Courtesy of Dolly Parton; Courtesy of Owepar Entertainment; Courtesy of Ten Speed Press; Courtesy of Little Brown & Company/Hachette
Page 302: Photograph by Joshua Timmermans/Courtesy of Noble Visions
Page 304: Photograph by Joshua Timmermans/Courtesy of Noble Visions
Page 305: Courtesy of Dolly Parton
Pages 306–307: Photographs by JB Rowland/Courtesy of Dolly Parton
Page 309: (left, right, and middle) Courtesy of Danny Nozell
Page 309: (bottom) Photograph by Michael Loccisano/Getty Images for SXSW
Page 310: Courtesy of Dolly Parton
Page 311: Photograph by Kevin Mazur/Getty Images Entertainment via Getty Images
Page 312: Photograph by Christopher Polk/Penske Media via Getty Images
Pages 314–315: Wardrobe photographs by Jeremiah Scott
Page 316: Photographs by Vijat Mohindra/Courtesy of Dolly Parton
Page 318: Photograph by Ron Jenkins/Getty Images
Page 321: (clockwise from top left) Photograph by Stacie Huckeba/Courtesy of Dolly Parton and Scent Beauty; Photograph by JB Rowland/Courtesy of ConAgra Foods; Photograph by Inez & Vinoodh/Courtesy of Dolly Parton and Good American; Photograph by Trever Hoehne/Courtesy of Dolly Parton and Kendra Scott

BACK MATTER

Page 322: Photograph by Jason Kempin/Getty Images
Pages 324–325: Photograph by Jeremy Westby/Courtesy of Dolly Parton
Pages 326–330: Cover images courtesy of Sony Music, Warner Music, Universal Music Group; Dolly Records, Butterfly Records
Page 331: Courtesy of Dolly Parton

Photography Credits

EBURY PRESS

UK | USA | Canada | Ireland | Australia
India | New Zealand | South Africa

Ebury Press is part of the Penguin Random House group of companies whose addresses can be found at global.penguinrandomhouse.com

Penguin Random House UK
One Embassy Gardens, 8 Viaduct Gardens, London SW11 7BW

penguin.co.uk
global.penguinrandomhouse.com

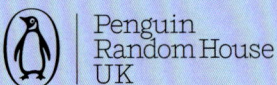

First published by Ten Speed Press in 2025
This edition published by Ebury Press in 2025
1

Copyright © Dolly Parton 2025

The moral right of the author has been asserted.

Penguin Random House values and supports copyright. Copyright fuels creativity, encourages diverse voices, promotes freedom of expression and supports a vibrant culture. Thank you for purchasing an authorised edition of this book and for respecting intellectual property laws by not reproducing, scanning or distributing any part of it by any means without permission. You are supporting authors and enabling Penguin Random House to continue to publish books for everyone. No part of this book may be used or reproduced in any manner for the purpose of training artificial intelligence technologies or systems. In accordance with Article 4(3) of the DSM Directive 2019/790, Penguin Random House expressly reserves this work from the text and data mining exception.

Typefaces: Commercial Type's Canela, E-phemera Fonts' Landry Gothic, and Jessica Hische's Tilda

Editor: Matt Inman | Production editor: Terry Deal | Assistant editor: Fariza Hawke
Designer: Annie Marino | Art director: Emma Campion
Illustrator: Bailey Sullivan
Production designers: Claudia Sanchez and Mari Gill
Production: Jane Chinn
Photo retoucher: Jeremy Blum
Copy editor: Sharon Silva | Proofreaders: Taylor McGowan, Rachel Markowitz, JoAnna Kremer, Alissa Fitzgerald
Publicist: Jane Branson | Marketer: Brianne Sperber

Colour origination by Altaimage Ltd
Printed and bound in China by C&C Offset Printing Company Ltd.

The authorised representative in the EEA is Penguin Random House Ireland, Morrison Chambers, 32 Nassau Street, Dublin D02 YH68.

A CIP catalogue record for this book is available from the British Library

ISBN 9781529958904

 Penguin Random House is committed to a sustainable future for our business, our readers and our planet. This book is made from Forest Stewardship Council® certified paper.

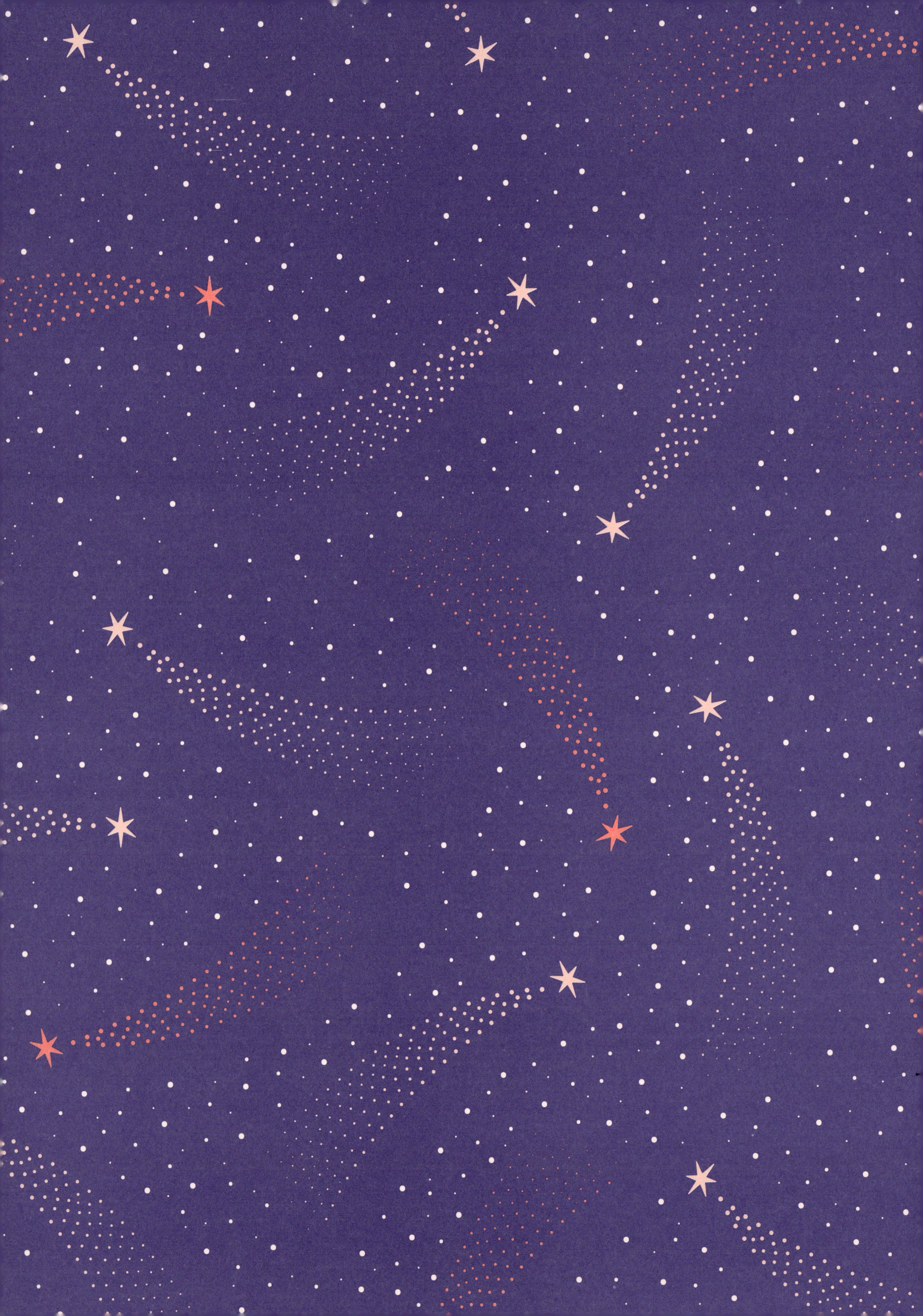